The
American History
Sourcebook

The American History Sourcebook

Joel Makower, Editor

Linda Zaleskie, Associate Editor

A Tilden Press Book

Prentice Hall Press
New York London Toronto Sydney Tokyo

Prentice Hall Press
Gulf+Western Building
One Gulf+Western Plaza
New York, New York 10023

Copyright 1988 by Tilden Press Inc.

PRENTICE HALL PRESS and colophon are registered
trademarks of Simon & Schuster, Inc.

Library of Congress Cataloging-in-Publication Data

The American history sourcebook / edited by Joel Makower. -- 1st ed.
        p.   cm.
    Includes index.
    ISBN 0-13-027491-7 : $40.00. ISBN 0-13-027483-6 (pbk.) : $22.95
    1.   United States--History--Archival resources--Directories.
2.United States--History--Library resources--Directories.
3. Historical museums--United States--Directories. 4.Historic
sites--United States--Directories.   5. United States--History-
-Societies, etc.--Directories.   I. Makower, Joel, 1952-   .
Z1236.A5144 1988
[E173]
973'.025'73--dc19   88-22575
                                                    CIP

Cover designed by Virginia Pope
Manufactured in the United States of America

10 9 8 7 6 5 4 3 2 1

First Edition

Contents

Appendixes

Indexes

Introduction

The search for information about America's rich and varied history can be foreboding, even for seasoned researchers and credentialed historians. We hope we've made the search easier in the pages that follow.

The more than 3,000 organizations and collections cited in this volume were themselves derived from a myriad of resources, many of which are cited in the bibliography in the appendix. All were contacted directly to obtain accurate and up-to-date information about collections, hours, and access. It was necessary, of course, to condense and edit the volume of information we received, making it difficult at times to adequately describe some organizations' vast holdings and resources within the format constraints of this book. You will note that some organizations do not specify days of operation. In such cases, the organization is open daily during the given hours. Other organizations declined to provide a phone number or hours of operation, preferring to be contacted in writing. Many of these, although by no means all, are small organizations with limited staff, but they are no less valuable in the information they can provide. In any case, you are encouraged to contact any organization before visiting to ensure not only that it will be open, but that you can get the assistance you need.

We welcome your comments and suggestions for additional organizations and collections to be included in future editions of this book. Please direct correspondence to Editor, The American History Sourcebook, c/o Tilden Press Inc., 1001 Connecticut Avenue NW, Washington, D.C. 20036.

The editors would like to thank the following individuals for their contributions, suggestions, and assistance: Paul Aron of Prentice Hall Press, Robert Harding and Barbara Humphrys of the Smithsonian Institution's American History Archives Center, Geraldine Jones, Marilyn P. Fenichel, Laura Bergheim, Shelia Stoneham, and Doug Williams.

Organization Listings

Alabama

Alabama Archives and History Library
624 Washington Ave., Montgomery, AL 36130; (205) 261-4361. Collects and preserves AL documents of historic interest. Holdings include census records from 1820, vital statistics from 1935, DAR index to AL wills from 1808-70, newspapers from 1800, military records, and indices to county records. Some genealogical materials. Accepts phone inquiries. Hours: M-F 8-5, Sa 9-5.

Alabama Historical Commission
725 Monroe St., Montgomery, AL 36130; (205) 261-3184. Promotes, preserves, and registers historical, architectural, and archaeological assets of AL. Owns and operates 14 historic properties, including John Tyler Morgan house, Confederate Soldiers' home, boyhood home of Spanish-American War hero Richmond Pearson Hobson, and Ft Morgan. Library has small library on AL history, manuscripts, maps, photos, videotapes on Lurleen Wallace and history of state capitol. Special collection includes survey records, AL Register, and National Register of Historic Places. Materials for in-house use only. Accepts phone inquiries. No fee. Hours: M-F 8-5.

Alabama Space and Rocket Center
1 Tranquility Base, Huntsville, AL 35807; (800) 633-7280. Most complete museum of American Space Program history with rocket exhibits ranging from V-2 through STS-System, with special Wernher von Braun collection of archives, manuscripts, and personal papers. Teacher resource center offers printed and media materials. Accepts phone inquiries. No fee. Hours: Sept-May 9-5, June-Aug 8-6.

Alexander City State Junior College
Thomas D. Russell Library, P.O. Box 699, 908 Cherokee, Alexander City, AL 35010; (205) 234-6346. Serves educational needs of community and has small collection of books by and on AL and AL authors. Accepts phone inquiries. No fee. Hours: M-Th 7:45-9, F 7:45-4.

Army Aviation Museum
P.O. Box 610, Building 6007, Fort Rucker, AL 36362; (205) 255-4584. Collects, restores, preserves, and exhibits operating aircraft, and documents technological and scientific advancements of Army aviation. Museum covers Army aviation from its start in 1942; library holds technical aircraft manuals; photo collection features aircraft research and development; and film/video collection houses materials on Army and limited use aircraft. Accepts phone inquiries. No fee. Hours: research by appt only, M-F 9-4.

Auburn University
Documents Dept., Ralph Brown Draughon Library, Microforms & Documents Dept., Mell St., Auburn, AL 36849; (205) 826-4500. Academic research library with collections of fed documents, archival University materials, papers of Congressmen, USGS and DMA maps, regional photos, film/videotape programs on sporting events, and special collections of AL history, and Dobbins and Petrie papers. Accepts phone inquiries. No fee. Hours: Su 1-midnight, M-Th 7:45-midnight, F 7:45-10, Sa 9-6.

Birmingham-Southern College Library
Documents Dept., 800 Eighth Ave., West, Birmingham, AL 35254; (205) 262-4750. Academic research facility with strong collections on history of AL, Biblical studies, Methodist Conference, and religions. Accepts phone inquiries. No fee. Hours: 8-10.

Black Heritage Council
Alabama Historical Commission, 725 Monroe St., Montgomery, AL 36130; (205) 261-3184. Promotes awareness of AL's historic bldgs reflecting history of black Alabamians. Holdings include National Register nominations and inventories relating to AL cultural resources, and some contemporary photos. Materials for in-house use only. Accepts phone inquiries. No fee. Hours: M-F 8-5.

Constitution Hall Park
301 Madison St., Franklin St. at Gates Ave., Huntsville, AL 35801; (205) 532-7551. Provides representation of 1819 Constitutional Convention in AL, and portrays southern life

during Federal period. Museum consists of reconstructed 19th c bldgs with period furnishings, fiber arts collection, and 19th c printing shop. Library holds materials on 19th c decorative arts and southern history. Accepts phone inquiries. Fee. Hours: M-Sa 9-4.

Fine Arts Museum of the South at Mobile

P.O. Box 8426, Mobile, AL 36608; (205) 343-2667. Dedicated to collecting, preserving, and exhibiting collections. Holdings include southern furniture, 19th and 20th c paintings, decorative arts, and contemporary American crafts. Library holds some reference materials. Accepts phone inquiries. No fee. Hours: Tu-Su 10-5.

First White House of the Confederacy

Box 1861, 644 Washington at Union St., Montgomery, AL 36103; (205) 261-4624. Preserves home of Jefferson Davis and family of spring of 1861. Museum exhibits possessions and decorative arts of Davis family. Holdings in library and archives include manuscripts, maps, photos, films/videotapes, recordings, and genealogical materials relating to Jefferson Davis and family. Accepts phone inquiries. Donations accepted. Archives, library not open to public. Museum hours: M-Sa 8-4:30, Su 9-4:30.

Fort Morgan Museum

Rte. 1, Box 3540, Gulf Shores, AL 36542; (205) 540-7125. Preserves, protects, and interprets Ft Morgan and Mobile Pt history through collections in museum and archives. Holdings include materials on Indians, War of 1812, Civil War, WWI, WWII, 19th c lighthouse lenses, limited letters written from Ft, and photos. Accepts phone inquiries. Fee. Hours: museum 9-5; fort 9-sunset.

Gadsden Public Library

Document Dept., 254 College St., Gadsden, AL 35999; (205) 547-1611. Public library with special collection on AL history. Holdings include maps, photos, census records, Confederate military records, Revolutionary pension files, Index to War of 1812, Mexican War records, and Indian Removal Military records. Seibert collection contains materials from this director of Panama Canal construction. Local history pre-

served in Beggs', Rains', and Martins' collections. Also has newspapers and periodicals from 1867. Accepts phone inquiries. No fee. Hours: M-Th 9-8, F 9-6, Sa 9-5, Su 1-5.

Horseshoe Bend National Military Park

Rte. 1, Box 103, Daviston, AL 36256; (205) 234-7111. Interprets Battle of Horseshoe Bend, and protects battlefield site. Museum exhibits Creek Indian culture from early 1800s, Creek War of 1812, and Horseshoe Bend Battle of 1814; library holds materials on southeast Indian culture, AL history, War of 1812, and Creek War; Creek War and Battle of Horseshoe Bend maps; and films/videotapes on AL history. Accepts phone inquiries. No fee. Hours: 8-4:30.

Huntsville Museum of Art

700 Monroe St., SW, Huntsville, AL 35801; (205) 535-4350. Collects American art from 1700 with concentration in contemporary American graphics. Accepts phone inquiries. No fee. Hours: Tu-F 10-5, Sa 9-5, Su 1-5.

Iron & Steel Museum of Alabama

Tannehill Historical State Park, Rte. 1, Box 124, McCalla, AL 35111; (205) 477-5711. Collects and exhibits artifacts relating to history of technology in early 19th c. Holdings in museum, library, and archives concentrate on iron making and mining. Special emphasis on Tannehill Iron Furnaces. Accepts phone inquiries. Fee. Hours: M-F 8:30-4, Sa-Su 10-5.

Ivy Green: Birthplace of Helen Keller

300 W. North Commons, Tuscumbia, AL 35674; (205) 383-4066. Preserves memory and childhood home of Helen Keller. Museum exhibits main house, outbuildings, celebrated water pump, and grounds. Collections include photos of Keller and family, Anne Sullivan, and Polly Thompson, as well as Keller family artifacts. Accepts phone inquiries. Fee. Hours: M-Sa 8:30-4:30, Su 1-4:30.

Jacksonville State University

Documents Dept., Houston Cole Library, Pelham Rd., Jacksonville, AL 36265; (205) 231-5781. Academic research facility with collections of presidential papers, treaties from 1950, and foreign relations materials since 1899; USGS and DMA maps; and genealogical records from 1790-1910. Also houses special collections of AL, Jacksonville, and Calhoun county history. Accepts phone inquiries. No fee. Hours: M-Th 7:30-10:30, F 7:30-4:30, Sa 10-3, Su 3-9.

Louisiana Books/Documents Collection Colonial Louisiana
520 S. 22nd Ave., Birmingham, AL 35205; (205) 328-5367. Spreads knowledge on southeast US history from 1513-1821 through holdings in museum, archives, and special collections. Library holds Spanish, Mexican, and US manuscripts, maps and archives. Special collection includes church records. Accepts phone inquiries. Consulting fee. Hours: call.

Military Police Corps Regimental Museum
Bldg. 3182, Fort McClellan, AL 36205; (205) 238-3522. Collects historical materials on military Police Corps, and encourages educational programs. Museum exhibits Corps history from Revolutionary War though Grenada with uniform, weapon, combat art, and POW artifact displays; library strong in military history; archives hold maps of conflict sites, photos of Corps functions from WWI, training films and tapes, recordings of Tet Offensive and VIP speeches, and some genealogical records. Accepts phone inquiries. No fee. Hours: M-F 8-4, other times by appt.

Pike Pioneer Museum
248 US Hwy 231 North, Troy, AL 36081; (205) 566-3597. Museum provides historical info from 1800-1900. Holdings include local maps, photos, Civil War records, and genealogical materials. Accepts phone inquiries. Fee. Hours: M-F 8-5, Su 1-5.

Reynolds Library Associates
Reynolds Historical Library, University of Alabama at Birmingham, 1900 University Blvd., Birmingham, AL 35294; (205) 934-4775. Health science rare book and manuscript collection dating from 14th c. Museum exhibits displays on health care in AL; library specializes in rare books and manuscripts in health sciences; archives hold materials on AL health care practi-

Helen Keller, from Ivy Green: Birthplace of Helen Keller.

tioners and institutions. Accepts phone inquiries. No fee. Hours: M-F 8-noon, 1-5.

Scottsboro-Jackson Heritage Center
P.O. Box 53, Scottsboro, AL 35768; (205) 259-2122. Preserves history of northeast AL through museum collections on Cherokee Indians, pioneers of mid-19th c, and Depression era. Accepts phone inquiries. Fee. Hours: Tu-Sa 10-4.

Sloss Furnaces National Historic Landmark
P.O. Box 11781, 20 32nd St North, Birmingham, AL 35202; (205) 324-1911. Preserves and interprets history of Sloss furnaces. Museum exhibits these restored 1927 blast furnaces. Films/videotapes detail history of Birmingham. Accepts phone inquiries. No fee. Hours: Tu-Sa 10-4, Su noon-4.

Southern Museum of Flight
Birmingham Aero Club, 4343 N. 73rd St. North, Birmingham, AL 35206; (205) 833-8226. Dis-

Booker T. Washington and his wife Margaret, from Tuskegee Institute National Historical Site

plays aviation historical artifacts, memorabilia, and aircraft in museum and library holdings. Collections include many books, magazines, photos, and films/videotapes on aviation. Special collection of AL Aviation Hall of Fame. Accepts phone inquiries. Fee. Hours: Tu-Sa 9:30-5, Su 1-5.

Southern Women's Archives
Birmingham Public Library, 2020 Park Place, Birmingham, AL 35203. Documents and preserves materials relating to women's issues. Holdings include AL and US legislative reports on abortion, domestic violence, child support, and related issues; materials from AL Women's Commission correspondence from 1975-79; transcripts of public hearings in AL on women's issues from 1974-80, discussing ERA, pay equity, and women's educational opportunities.

Troy State University Library
Troy, AL 36081; (205) 566-2682. Academic research library has collection of Civil War-era records from regional plantation owner John Dent. Holdings include manuscripts, farming journals, diaries, letters, and memorabilia. Also

holds clippings from 1867-92 newspapers. Accepts phone inquiries. No fee. Hours: call.

Tuskegee Institute National Historic Site

P.O. Drawer 10, Tuskegee, AL 36088; (205) 727-6390. Commemorates lives of Booker Washington and George Carver and their educational and scientific contributions. Museum allows for self-guided tour of Carver's works, lab equip, and by-products, and describes Tuskegee University from its beginnings. Library holds reference materials on Carver and Washington, maps, photos of Washington and Carver, films/videotapes, recording of Carver's last public speech, and Washington's family genealogical records. Accepts phone inquiries. No fee. Hours: 9-5.

University of Alabama Library

Documents Dept., Box S, Capstone Dr., Tuscaloosa, AL 35487; (205) 348-6046. Academic research library serving community with collection of govt documents, including complete Congressional Serial set. Accepts phone inquiries. No fee. Hours: M-Th 8-10, F 8-5, Su 2-10.

University of North Alabama

Document Dept., Collier Library, Morrison Avenue, Florence, AL 35632; (205) 760-4100. Academic support library with archival materials on University history, AL history, maps of AL and US, and special collection of state and university materials now out of print. Accepts phone inquiries (205-760-4469). No fee. Hours: M-Th 8-10, F 8-5, Sa 1-5, Su 2-10.

W.S. Hoole Special Collection

University of Alabama Library, P.O. Box S, Capstone Drive, Tuscaloosa, AL 35487; (205) 348-5512. Academic research library maintains collection of materials on AL history. Library contains books on LA and New Orleans history, AL collection from 1820, extensive materials on AL residents, state documents, and AL imprints. Archive of American Minority Cultures traces ethnic, folk, minority, and women's history and culture through oral and video history documentation. Manuscripts collections cover AL political leaders, authors, plantation and farm owners, business transactions, and Civil War.

Photos date from 1850. Genealogical materials available on many families. Restrictions on use. Accepts phone inquiries. No fee. Hours: M-F 8-4:45, Th eves 6-10.

Alaska

Alaska Pacific University

Consortium Library, 3211 Providence Drive, Anchorage, AK 99508; (907) 786-1848. Academic library maintains selective collection of govt documents, general, reference and historical materials relevant to needs of the school and students. Holdings include Alaskana Collection of historical materials, including archives, maps and photos; Library of American Civilization; CIS Serial Set, 1789-1969. Accepts phone inquiries. No fee. Hours: M-Th 7:30-11, F 7:30-6, Sa 10-6, Su 1-8.

Alaska State Archives

Dept. of Administration, Pouch C, State Office Bldg., Juneau, AK 99811; (907) 465-2275. Collects and preserves documents and materials from AK govt agencies. Accepts phone inquiries. Hours: call.

Alaska State Library

Department of Education, P.O. Box G, 333 Willoughby Ave., Juneau, AK 99811; (907) 465-2925. Serves as state reference and research collection for AK. Holdings include large library, manuscript collections from Alaska Packers Association and many others, maps, many photos, selected genealogical records, and special Russian-American collection. Materials non-circulating. Accepts phone inquiries. No fee. Hours: M-F 9-5.

Alaska State Museum

395 Whittier St, Juneau, AK 99801; (907) 465-2901. Preserves and interprets Alaskan natural and cultural history in form of artifacts and exhibits; reference library; and oral history videotapes. Accepts phone inquiries. Fee. Hours: winter, Tu-Sa 10-4; summer, Tu-Sa 9-7.

Anchorage Historic Properties

524 W. 4th Ave., Suite 202, Anchorage, AK

99501; (907) 274-3600. Corporation administers the Historic Preservation Fund, advises on historic preservation efforts, and promotes interest in preservation work through publications and special events. Accepts phone inquiries. Membership fee. Hours: 8-5.

Anchorage Municipal Libraries

Z.J. Loussac Public Library, 3600 Denali St., Anchorage, AK 99503; (907) 261-4481. Collects info and materials relating to Alaska and adjacent regions. Archives hold Anchorage municipal records, papers of Sen Ted Stevens, and manuscripts from assorted Alaskan notables. No fee. Hours: M-Th 12-9, F-Sa 10-6, Su noon-6.

Anchorage Museum of History and Art

Municipality of Anchorage, 121 W. Seventh Ave, Anchorage, AK 99501; (907) 264-4326. Preserves history of Native Alaskan cultures and art. Museum and library hold materials on regional archaeology and art, Russian-Americans, American art, Alaska history; small collection of diaries from Upper Inlet; Alaskan maps; extensive photo collection on Alaskan Railroad, Nome, Anchorage, Valdez; negative files of Ward Wells; some files on Alaskan artists. Materials noncirculating. Accepts phone inquiries. Fee for museum; no fee for library. Hours: museum Tu-Sa 10-6, Su 1-5; library Tu-F 10-noon, afternoons by appt.

Cook Inlet Historical Society

121 W. Seventh Ave., Anchorage, AK 99501; (907) 264-4326. Preserves regional and Alaskan history through photo, manuscript, and map holdings in library and archives. No fee. Hours: Tu-Su 10-5.

Klondike Gold Rush National Historic Park

P.O. Box 517, Second Ave at Broadway, Skagway, AK 99840; (907) 271-2656. Preserves historic site and structures relating to the Klondike Gold Rush of 1898. Holdings include Visitor Center with exhibits on Klondike Gold Rush and local trails; reference library. Use of library by appt only. Accepts phone inquiries. No fee. Hours: Visitors Center: late May and Sept, 8-6; June-Aug, 8-8; office: M-F 8-5.

Museum of Alaskan Transportation and Industry

P.O. Box 909, Palmer, AK 99645; (907) 745-4493. Maintains, recovers, restores, and preserves transportation and industry contributions to AK history and development. Museum displays transportation and industry artifacts, as well as materials on contributors to industry. Also houses manuscripts, maps, and photos related to AK history as territory and state. Accepts phone inquiries. Donations accepted. Hours: Tu-Sa 8-4.

Samuel K. Fox Museum

P.O. Box 273, Dillingham, AK 99576; (907) 842-2322. Preserves history and art of Bristol Bay area and perpetuates traditional cultures. Museum and photo collection focus on southwest Alaskan Eskimo ethnography and Bristol Bay salmon fishing industry. Material use restricted. Accepts phone inquiries. No fee. Hours: 12:30-5.

Sheldon Museum and Cultural Center

P.O. Box 623, Haines, AK 99827; (907) 766-2366. Collects, preserves, and exhibits history of Indian and pioneer cultures in Upper Lynn Canal region, emphasizing Haines and Chilkat Valley. Museum focuses on Tlingit Indian art and culture, industrial development, and pioneer artifacts of area; research library holds Alaskan fiction and reference works; archive collections of ship logs, early tax and school records, newspapers, and AK military post reports; sizeable photo collection; and small oral history collection. Material for in-house use only. Accepts phone inquiries. Fee. Hours: winter Su, M, W 1-4; summer 1-5 with additional hours to be announced.

Sitka National Historical Park

P.O. Box 738, 106 Metlakatla St., Sitka, AK 99835; (907) 747-6281. Interprets and preserves fort site, history of Battle of Sitka, materials on Tlingit culture, and some info on Russian America. Museum exhibits materials on Russo-American history, totem art, and Battle of 1804; archives and library hold documentary materials. Collections include maps, and extensive photo

The Potlatch of 1904, hosted in Sitka by the Kaagwaantaan Clan of the Tlingit Indians, from Sitka National Historical Park.

files. Films/videotapes on Alaskan history and native culture. Special collections include Old Sitka Archaeological collection, Sheldon Jackson Russian American collection, and E. W. Merrill photo collection. Accepts phone inquiries. No fee. Hours: by appt only; Oct-May, M-F 8-5; June-Sept, 8-5.

Tanana-Yukon Historical Society

P.O. Box 1336, Fairbanks, AK 99707; (907) 457-7834. Preserves small house museum that belonged to James Wickersham, first judge of AK. House furnished with authentic pieces, and displays photos and other exhibits that capture early Fairbanks history. Some local history materials. Accepts phone inquiries. Donations accepted. Hours: summer, May-Sept 11-9.

Tongass Historical Museum

629 Dock St., Ketchikan, AK 99901; (907) 225-5600. Preserves history of southest AK through holdings of museum and library. Holdings include local business records from 1880-1982; mining maps and journals; and large photo collection of local sites, Native villages, and totems. May be restrictions on use. Accepts phone inquiries. Fee. Hours: winter, W-Su 1-5; summer 8:30-5.

University of Alaska

Elmer E. Rasmuson Library, 310 Tanana Drive, Fairbanks, AK 99775; (907) 474-7624. Academic library maintains selective collection of govt documents, general, reference, and historical materials relevant to needs of the school and students. Holdings include federal documents with emphasis on Alaska and the Polar region, including materials relating to wildlife management and environmental issues, and USGS mining, oil/gas records and maps. Some restrictions. Accepts phone inquiries. No fee. Hours: M-F 8-5.

Arizona

Amerind Foundation

P.O. Box 248, Triangle T Rd., Dragoon, AZ 85609; (602) 583-3666. Museum and research facility preserves and promotes Native American history and culture through exhibits, library, and archival collections. Holdings include collec-

tions of ethnographic and archeological artifacts; library collection of publications, manuscripts, and other resource materials on Native Americans, with emphasis on Greater Southwest; El Archivo de Hidalgo del Parral, 1631-1821; facsimile editions of major Mesoamerican codices; records of the Colonial period of New Spain; archeological site files of southern AZ and northern Mexico. Use of library by appt only. Fee. Hours: 10-4.

Arizona Historical Foundation

Hayden Library, Arizona State University, Tempe, AZ 85287; (602) 966-8331. Promotes research into significant areas of AZ history. Library has small collection on AZ and Southwest history from 19th c. Archives holds organizational records of AZ Cattlegrowers Assn; congressional papers of Senators Barry Goldwater and Paul Fannin, records of significant local individuals and businessmen, Japanese Relocation records, manuscripts relating to water issues, maps, large photo collection on AZ and Native Americans, films/videotapes and recordings of Barry Goldwater's political career, oral history interviews, and genealogical records. Some restrictions. Accepts phone inquiries. Fee. Hours: M-F 9-6.

Arizona Historical Society

Southern Arizona Division, 949 E. 2nd. St., Tucson, AZ 85719; (602) 628-5774. Collects, preserves, and promotes history of AZ region through museum, library, and archival collections. Holdings include displays of historic transportation pieces, Mexican cultural artifacts, historic costumes, period rooms, and a life-size mining hall; library has extensive collection of publications and other materials on Western US and AZ history; archives, manuscripts, maps, genealogical materials, and oral history collections; extensive collection of historical photos; educational audiovisual materials. Accepts phone inquiries. No fee. Hours: M-Sa 10-4, Su noon-4.

Arizona Historical Society Library

1242 N. Central, Phoenix, AZ 85005; (602) 255-4470. Collects, preserves, and interprets AZ history through collections in museum, library, and archives. Holdings include manuscripts, maps, photos, films/videotapes, and oral history recordings. Materials non-circulating. Accepts phone inquiries. Hours: call.

Arizona State Capitol Museum

1700 W. Washington, Pheonix, AZ 85007; (602) 255-4675. Interprets AZ territorial and state govt history. Museum housed in restored 1900 Capitol bldg. Library holds large collection on AZ history and biography from 1860, including newpapers, clippings, and periodicals. Archival materials consist of AZ state, county, and local records from 1863 documenting political, economic, and social history. Large road and railroad map collection. Many photos on AZ subjects, scenes, and pioneers. Collection on American genealogy from 1620-1910. Materials for in-house use only. Accepts phone inquiries. No fee. Hours: M-F 8-5.

Arizona State Historic Preservation Office

800 W. Washington, Suite 415, Phoenix, AZ 85007; (602) 255-4009. Preserves and promotes historical and archeological resources of AZ, with holdings that include photos, maps, and files of Natl Register and State Inventory historic properties. Archeological site data restricted. Accepts phone inquiries. No fee. Hours: 8-5.

Arizona State University

Tempe, AZ 85287; (602) 965-3387. Collection of local and AZ govt documents from 1912. Univ library also has holdings that include a museum, archives, special collections, manuscripts, maps, photos, and recordings. Some materials non-circulating. Accepts phone inquiries (602-965-3390). No fee. Hours: M-Th 8-10, F 8-5, Sa 10-5, Su 1-4.

Bisbee Mining and Historical Museum

P.O. Box 14, 5 Copper Queen Plaza, Bisbee, AZ 85603; (602) 432-7071. Collects, preserves and interprets mining and social history of Bisbee, AZ and residents with exhibits on mining, and ethnic and cultural artifacts. Holdings include Phelps Dodge Hospital records; library, large collections of manuscripts, maps, and architectural drawings; photos of Bisbee, Cochise County, Northern Sonora, and Mexican areas and resi-

dents; biographic files, oral history tapes; small 1930s Bisbee film collection. Restrictions on use of some collections. Accepts phone inquiries. No fee. Hours: M-Sa 10-4, Sun 1-4.

Center for Creative Photography

University of Arizona, 843 E. University Blvd., Tucson, AZ 85721; (602) 621-7968. Contains photos of poverty-stricken and victimized regional residents from 1940-70. Holdings portray Hopi, Navajo, and Papajo Indians on reservation, in urban settings, and at acculturation centers. Accepts phone inquiries. Hours: call.

Century House Museum

Arizona Historical Society, 240 S. Madison Ave., Yuma, AZ 85364; (602) 782-1841. Historic 1870s building houses exhibits, collections on history of lower Colorado River region (includes AZ, parts of CA and Mexico). Holdings include photos, archives, maps; films/videotapes of Yuma County and AZ history and residents; Yuma County family histories; drawings of early Ft Yuma; reproductions of Mexican paintings of martyrdom of Spanish priests. Accepts phone inquiries. No fee. Hours: Oct-Apr, Tu-Sa 10-4, Su noon-4; May-Sept, Tu-Sa 10-4.

Colorado River Indian Tribes Museum, Library, and Archives

Rte. 1, Box 23-B, 2nd Ave. and Mohave Rd., Parker, AZ 85344; (602) 669-9211, ext 213. Preserves cultural artifacts of area and reservation's four Tribes (Mohave, Chemehuevi, Navajo, and Hopi). Holdings include library, photos, films/videotapes, recordings; archives with historical, ethnological, and anthropological research work; and relevant govt documents. Accepts phone inquiries. No fee. Hours: M-F 8-5.

Desert Caballeros Western Museum

P.O. Box 1446, 20 North Frontier St., Wickenburg, AZ 85358; (602) 684-2272. Preserves and displays local and state history and art. Holdings include Western Art Gallery; turn-of-century street scene; furnished period rooms; mineral collection, Indian artifacts, mining equipment; cactus garden; library. Maps, photos shown by appt only; Films/videotapes shown according to set schedule. Accepts phone inquiries. Fee. Hours: M-Sa 10-4; Su 1-4.

Fort Bowie National Historic Site

Dos Cabezas Star Rte., Box 6500, Wilcox, AZ 85643; (602) 847-2500. Preserves and interprets Ft ruins and history of Butterfield stage coach. Small reference library and archival collection holds documents, artifacts, and photos from fort. Some maps and items from Ft Bowie/Chiricuahua Indian period. Accepts phone inquiries. No fee. Hours: 8-5.

Fort Huachuca Museum

ASH-PTS-PM, Fort Huachuca, AZ 85613; (602) 538-3638. Preserves and interprets history of Ft Huachuca and surrounding region in form of artifacts, travelling exhibits, photos, small library, and archives. Accepts phone inquiries. No fee. Hours: M-F 9-4, Sa-Su 1-4.

Hubbell Trading Post National Historic Site

Box 150, Rte. 264, Ganado, AZ 86505; (602) 755-3475. Stresses and describes importance of Indian trader from 1870s-1900s, with emphasis on J. L. Hubbell family. Library and archives contains archival and reference material on traders and interaction with Navajo; photos of Hubbell family and activities at post; and genealogical records of Hubbell family. Accepts phone inquiries. No fee. Hours: winter, 8-5; summer, 8-6.

John Wesley Powell Memorial Museum

Box 547, #6 Lake Powell Blvd., Page, AZ 86040; (602) 645-9496. Promotes and preserves history of Maj John Wesley Powell and Colorado River Exploration; City of Page and its residents; and Colorado Plateau Native American culture from 1869. Holdings include library materials on Maj Powell 1869-1902, construction of the Grand Canyon Dam, history of Lake Powell from 1937; historical photos from 1869; films/videotapes; artifacts relating to Powell's life, City of Page and residents, Colorado River rafting, and Native Americans. Accepts phone inquiries. Donations accepted. Hours: May-Sept 8-8; Oct-Nov and Feb-Apr, M-F 9-5.

Mesa Room

Mesa Public Library, 64 East 1st St., Mesa, AZ 85201; (602) 834-2207. Public library with history room of materials on local, AZ, and Native American histories. Collections include oral histories, Sanborn maps for Mesa, city histories and documents, and regional environmental studies. Some restrictions. Accepts phone inquiries. No fee. Hours: M-Th 9:30-9, F-Sa 9:30-5:30; Sept-May Su 1:30-5:30.

Mission San Xavier Del Bac

Rte. 11, Box 645, San Xavier Rd., Tucson, AZ 85746; (602) 294-2624. Interpretive museum, located at the original San Xavier Mission (a 1783 Spanish colonial Indian mission) preserves history of the mission and its residents in form of artifacts, restored rooms and records. Accepts phone inquiries. Fee. Hours: 9-6.

Mohave Museum of History and Arts

400 W. Beale St., Kingman, AZ 86401; (602) 753-3195. Preserves and documents the history of Mohave County and Northwest AZ in form of museum exhibits, library, and archival collections. Holdings include historical artifacts and displays, including items relating to transportation, mining and ranching, and local Native American cultures; special collections of local turquoise, US Presidential portraits, and materials on Andy Devine's life and times; library; archives; mining and ranching manuscripts; mining maps; photos, films/videotapes, oral history recordings, and genealogical records; collection of local newspapers from 1881. Accepts phone inquiries. Donations accepted. Hours: M-F 10-5, Sa-Su 1-5.

Naaltsoos Ba' Hoogan Library

Navajo Community College, Tsaile, AZ 86556; (602) 724-3311 ext. 132. Preserves collection of materials on Navajo history and other tribes of Southwest. Holdings cover geology, geography, sociology, archaeology, and anthropology of Four Corners region. Accepts phone inquiries. Hours: call.

National Historic Fire Foundation

6101 E. Van Buren, Phoenix, AZ 85008; (602) 275-3473. Collects, preserves and displays history of firefighting from 18th c. Holdings include artifacts, library, photos of historic fires and firefighters. Accepts phone inquiries. Fee. Hours: M-Sa 9-5.

photos. Access and use subject to staff availability. Accepts phone inquiries. No fee. Hours: M-F 8-5.

Northern Arizona University Library

Documents Division and Special Collections, Box 6022, Flagstaff, AZ 86011; (602) 523-2171. Maintains selective collection of US govt documents including records of Forest Service from 1900, USGS from 1878, and Bureau of Census from 1790. Special collections hold materials from 1917 Bisbee Deportation during WWI, papers of WWII correspondent and UPI asst gen mgr Robert Eunson, materials on Pacific and European theatres, Gens MacArthur and Eisenhower, and AP news articles from Korean War era. Also holds materials on Navajo, Harasupai, Acoma, and Laguna Indian reservations from 1922-27. Accepts phone inquiries (602-523-6812). No fee. Hours: M-Th 7:30-11, F 7-6, Sa 10-6, Su noon-11.

Phoenix Public Library

Documents Division, 12 East McDowell Rd., Phoenix, AZ 85004; (602) 262-6451. Public library maintains selective collection of US govt documents, and Arizona History Collection. Accepts phone inquiries (602-261-8667). No fee. Hours: M-Th 9-9, F-Sa 9-6, Su 1-5.

Pima Air Museum

6000 E. Valencia Rd., Tucson, AZ 85706; (602) 574-0462. Museum preserves and displays aviation history in form of restored aircraft, aviation artifacts, photos, maps, and film/videotapes. Proposed library for future. Accepts limited phone inquiries. Fee. Hours: 9-5, with no admittance after 4.

Pioneer Arizona Museum

Box 1677, Black Canyon Stage, Phoenix, AZ 85029; (602) 993-0212. Museum complex collects, preserves, and promotes domestic history of AZ, from 1800 to 1902, in form of restored craft workshops, industrial, and residential buildings furnished with period items and equipment; demonstrations of blacksmithing, tin and gunsmithing, cooking, quilting, weaving, farming, and printing; small library available for research. Accepts phone inquiries. Fee. Hours: W-Su 9-4.

Pioneer Museum

Arizona Historical Society, Rte. 4, Box 705, N. Ft. Valley Rd., Flagstaff, AZ 86001; (602) 774-6272. Collects, preserves, and promotes history of Flagstaff and Coconino County, AZ and notable residents from region in form of exhibits, photographic displays, and archival collections. Historical society holdings include area artifacts, historical displays; George Hochderffer Collection of photos; archives (location: Northern AZ Univ Special Collections Library) with manuscripts, maps, Tony Richardson Collection, and AZ Lumber and Timber records. Archival material non-circulating. Accepts phone inquiries. Donations accepted. Hours: M-Sa 9-5, Su 1:30-5.

Pioneers' Cemetery Association

P.O. Box 63342, Phoenix, AZ 85082; (602) 275-2734. Assn researches and restores pioneer cemeteries to aid in genealogical studies, with holdings that include cemetery maps and photos, and genealogical records. Accepts phone inquiries. No fee. Hours: W-Su 10-4.

Sharlot Hall Museum

415 W. Gurley St., Prescott, AZ 86301; (602) 445-3122. Collects, preserves, and displays history of Yavapai County, AZ and the Southwest US in form of historic buildings, museum, library, and archival collections. Holdings include first Governor's mansion (1864) and two Victorian-style homes; log structures and school house replicas; library; archives with maps, manuscripts, newspapers, diaries, ephemera, and photos, 1850-1940; collection of oral history recordings, cowboy folklore, poetry, and music; Western Indian baskets; Sharlot M. Hall (writer and collector) Archives. Materials are non-circulating. Accepts phone inquiries. Donations accepted. Hours: Summer, Tu-Sa 9-5, Su 1-5; winter, Tu-Sa 10-4, Su 1-5.

Sons of Sherman's March to the Sea

1725 S. Farmer Ave., Tempe, AZ 85281; (602) 967-5405. Org devoted to preserving history and legends of Gen Sherman and his Civil War exploits. Holdings include small library of Sherman-related books and publications. Accepts phone inquiries. Fee for membership. Hours: call.

University Art Museum

Arizona State University, Matthews Center, Tempe, AZ 85287; (602) 965-2874. Museum preserves and exhibits historic and contemporary art works, with holdings that include American arts and crafts; contemporary American ceramics; American crockery; contemporary and historic American and European prints; Latin American art and folk art. Accepts phone inquiries. No fee. Hours: M-F 8-5, Su 1-5.

University of Arizona Library

Documents Division, University of Arizona, Tucson, AZ 85721; (602) 621-4871. Supports research needs of University and local community with large collection of US govt documents and microfiche from 1870s; extensive National Archives microfilm collection of Southwestern Army post records and dispatches from US consuls in Latin America; records of Arizona census schedules from late 19th c. Materials circulate to AZ residents only. Accepts phone inquiries. No fee. Hours: M-Th 8-9, F 8-5, Sa 10-6, Su 1-5.

Yavapai College Library

1100 East Sheldon St., Prescott, AZ 86301; (602) 776-2260. College library maintains selective collection of US govt documents and reference materials relevant to needs of students and area residents. Holdings include AZ state, county, and local documents and maps. Documents and periodicals are non-circulating. Accepts phone inquiries. No fee. Hours: M-Th 7-10, F 7-6, Su 1-9.

Arkansas

Arkansas History Commission

1 Capitol Mall, Little Rock, AR 72201; (501) 682-6900. Collects, preserves, and makes available source materials on AR history. Library and archives hold manuscript, maps, photos, films/videotapes, recordings, and genealogical records on AR history and govt from 1541. Materials non-circulating. No fee. Hours: M-Sa 8-4:30.

Arkansas Oil and Brine Museum

P.O. Box 77, (Rte. 1, Box 116), Smackover, AR 71762; (501) 725-2877. Interest in Arkansas oil and brine technology. Museum includes exhibits

depicting industry from 1920. Holdings include library, archives, maps, photos, films, and oral histories. Answers phone inquiries. No fee. Hours: M-F 9-5; Su 1-5.

Arkansas Post National Memorial

Rt. 1, Box 16, Gillett, AR 72055; (501) 548-2432. Interest in settlement of Lower Mississippi Valley. Museum includes artifacts of fur trade, river transport, Civil War, settlement, and local government. Answers phone inquiries. Admission fee. Hours: M-Su 8-5, except Christmas.

Arkansas Supreme Court Library

Documents Division, Justice Building, Little Rock, AR 72201; (501) 682-2147. Law library has collection of law treatises and primary materials from 1850 with special collection of AR documents. Materials non-circulating. Accepts phone inquiries. No fee. Hours: M-F 8-5.

Arkansas Territorial Restoration

3rd & Scott, Little Rock, AR 72201; (501) 371-2348. Interprets frontier experience in AR and researches material culture. Museum exhibits artifacts from mid-19th c. Library holds materials on museology, decorative arts, and material culture. Collection of research data on early artists and artisans of AR. Fee. Hours: M-Sa 9-5, Su 1-5.

Civil War Round Table Associates

P.O. Box 7281 (9 Lefever Lane), Little Rock, AR 72217; (501) 225-3996. Historical org devoted to study of Civil War history and contemporary events relevant to Civil War history. Holds annual meetings and sponsors tours. Accepts phone inquiries. No fee. Hours: M-F 9-5.

Confederate Historical Institute

P.O. Box 7388, (9 Lefever Lane), Little Rock, AR 72217; (501) 225-3996. Devoted to study of history of Confederate States of America. Preserves historic sites, publishes quarterly journal, and maintains library. Answers phone inquiries. No fee. Hours: M-F 9-5.

Drew County Historical Museum

404 S. Main, Monticello, AR 71655. Preserves history of Monticello and Drew county. Mu-

seum housed in turn-of-century home with period furnishings. Archives contains local and state history, Civil War letters, family histories, local and state maps, photos, tapes of local programs, and genealogical records. Materials for in-house use only. No fee. Hours: museum, Tu-F 1-5, Sa-Su 2-5; archives, 1-4.

Fort Smith National Historic Site

P.O. Box 1406, (corner of 2nd Street and Rogers Avenue), Fort Smith, AR 72902; (501) 783-3961. Interprets over 80 years of American government policy toward Native Americans. Museum features artifacts from military (1817-71) and judicial (1872-96) occupations of fort. Library holdings include books, archives, manuscripts, maps, photos, and film/videotapes. Accepts phone inquiries. Admission fee; over 62 and under 12 free. Hours: 9-5, except Christmas.

Frisco Depot Railroad Museum

P.O. Box 652, 813 Main St., Van Buren, AR 72956; (501) 474-2761. Preserves and exhibits artifacts of passenger train era. Museum is reconstructed train depot and displays telegraph machinery, conductor uniforms, train schedules, and office furnishings. Also holds state maps. Accepts phone inquiries. No fee. Hours: M-F 9-5.

Harding University

Documents Division, Beaumont Memorial Library, Station A, Box 928 (900 E. Center St.), Searcy, AR 72143; (501) 268-6161. Holdings include GPO Arkansas maps. Borrowing limited to authorized users. Accepts phone inquiries. No fee. Hours: M-F 8-5.

Lum 'n' Abner Museum and Jot 'Em Down Store

P.O. Box 38, Pine Ridge, AR 71966; (501) 326-4442. Displays history of Ouachita Mt area, Pine Ridge town history, and Lum & Abner radio history. Museum displays history of Lum & Abner from 1931-50s, and local history from 1900-40. Holdings include manuscripts; maps; Lum & Abner movies, photos, and programs; and county genealogical records. Accepts phone inquiries. Fee. Hours: Mar-Nov 15, Tu-Sa 9-5, Su noon-5; winter, M-Sa 10-2.

Melting Pot Genealogical Society

400 Winans, Hot Springs, AR 71901; (501) 262-4975. Focus on genealogical research. Holdings include library, manuscripts, maps, and photographs. Answers phone inquiries. Use restricted to fee-paying members. Hours: M-F 10-10.

Museum of Automobiles

Rte. 3, Petit Jean Mountain, Morrilton, AR 72110; (501) 727-5427. Displays automobiles that led to evolution of car style and construction. Exhibits change, but date from turn-of-the-century to modern models. Accepts phone inquiries. Fee. Hours: 10-5.

Old State House

300 West Markham St., Little Rock, AR 72201; (501) 371-1749. Museum of AR state history focuses on Victorian period and decorative arts. Library holds reference materials and collection of Charles Thompson architectural drawings. Other holdings include wallpaper collection and paper lab, maps, American cut glass of Brilliant period, and collection of 19th c flags. Accepts phone inquiries. Donations accepted. Hours: M-Sa 9-5, Su 1-5.

Old Washington Historic State Park

Box 98, Washington, AR 71862; (501) 983-2684. Collects, preserves, and interprets artifacts related to history of Washington, AR 1824-74. Holdings include modest library, Southwest Arkansas Regional Archives, some maps and photos. Accepts phone inquiries. Fee for guided tour. Hours: M, W-Sa 9-4; Su 1-5.

Olin C. Bailey Library

Hendrix College, Front and Washington Sts., Conway, AR 72032; (501) 450-1288. Academic research facility affiliated with United Methodist Church. Archives has limited collection of AR Methodist Church materials, and small collection of AR history books from late 19th and early 20th c. Accepts phone inquiries. No fee. Hours: M-Th 8-noon, F 8-5.

Order of the Indian Wars

P.O. Box 7401 (#9 Lefever Lane), Little Rock, AR 72217; (501) 225-3996. Historical org devoted to study of Indian Wars history. Publishes scholarly articles and sponsors tours. Accepts phone inquiries. No fee. Hours: M-F 9-5.

Ouachita Baptist University

Special Collections, Arkadelphia, AR 71923; (501) 246-4531. Houses Arkansas Baptists' State Convention materials, including materials on Baptist missionaries and missions, and rare materials from Baptist history; American culture series of pre-1874 American materials; Black History Collection; Collection of Theology and Church History in North America; microcard collection of early writings on music from Eastman School of Music; Sen John McClellan collection of files and public service; and local history records. Accepts phone inquiries. No fee. Hours: M-Th 8-10, F 8-5, Sa 10-4.

Ozark Folk Center

Hwy. 382, Moutain View, AR 72560; (501) 269-3851. Records, preserves, and interprets folklife of Ozark mountain region. Museum displays craft items pre-1940. Library holds books on southern mountain regional culture and folklore. Archives collect folklore and oral history recordings, manuscripts, maps, photos, films/ videotapes on Ozark music and crafts, and genealogical records on AR families. Materials for in-house use only. Accepts phone inquiries. Fee. Hours: May-Oct 8-5; Nov-Apr, 8-4:30.

Patent Model Museum

400 North 8th St., Fort Smith, AR 72901; (501) 782-9014. Repository of authentic models of Early American Inventions from 1835-80s. Also has pictures/drawing of inventions destroyed in 1836 Patent Office fire. Accepts phone inquiries. No fee. Hours: M-F 9-4.

Pea Ridge National Military Park

Pea Ridge, AR 72751; (501) 451-8122. Commemorates Civil War battle that saved Missouri for the Union. Holdings include museum, library, maps, slide show, and genealogical records of soldiers who fought in battle. Accepts phone inquiries. Fee. Hours: M-Su 8-5, except Thanksgiving, Christmas, and New Year's.

Prairie Grove Battlefield State Park

P.O. Box 306, (U.S. Hwy 62 East), Prarie Grove, AR 72753; (501) 846-2990. Civil War battle-field. Museum includes artifacts of Battle of Prairie Grove. Accepts phone inquiries. No fee. Hours: M-Su 8-5.

Siloam Springs Museum

P.O. Box 1164, (112 N. Maxwell St.), Siloam Springs, AR 72761; (501) 524-4011. Local history museum and archives. Holdings include exhibits, archives, photographs, and manuscripts. Answers phone inquiries. No fee. Hours: W-Sa noon-5; June-Aug., Tu-F 10-5; Sa noon-5.

Southwest Arkansas Regional Archives

P.O. Box 134, Washington, AR 71862; (501) 983-2633. Collects and preserves primary and secondary source materials on southwest AR history. Archives hold letters, diaries, familiy histories, scrapbooks, sheet music collection, early AR maps from 1800, historic photos, limited films/videotapes, genealogical records. Special Trammell Trace, Claud Garner, and Carrigan collections. Materials non-circulating. Accepts phone inquiries. No fee. Hours: M, W, Th, F 9-4; Su 1-5.

Stuttgart Agricultural Museum

921 E. 4th St., Stuttgart, AR 72160; (501) 673-7001. Collects, preserves, and interprets history of rice, soybean, fish, and waterfowling industry on Grand Prairie of AR. Exhibits include farm equipment, farm home memorabilia, Indian duck effigy pots, decoys, and guns. Library holds info on tractor histories, farms, waterfowling; maps on local area; extensive photo file; oral and visual histories of early day farmers from region; and duck recordings from Cornell University ornithology lab. Accepts phone inquiries. Donations accepted. Hours: Tu-Sa 10-noon, 1-4, Su 1:30-4:30.

University of Arkansas

Documents Division, Mullins Library, Fayetteville, AR 72701; (501) 575-5516. Holdings include extensive government map collection and NASA space photos. Accepts phone inquiries. No fee. Hours: M-F 8-5, Sa 12-4, Su 1-5.

University of Arkansas at Little Rock Library

Documents Division, 2801 S. University Ave.,

Little Rock, AR 72204; (501) 569-3120. Academic research library with large collection of historic AR manuscripts, maps, and photos of residents and scenes. Accepts phone inquiries. No fee. Hours: M-Th 8-11, F 8-5, Sa-Su 1-5.

California

Air Force Audio/Video Center

Department of Defense Motion Media Records Center, 1352d Audio/Visual Squadron/Records Ctr/DOSR, Norton AFB, CA 92409; (714) 382-3826. Provides video and motion picture stock footage to military and non-military users. Holds 67 million 16mm films, 54 million 35mm films, and 177 thousand videos pertaining to Air Force, Navy, Marines, and Army. Use subject to Services Public Info Office approval. Accepts phone inquiries. Fee for research. Hours: M-F 7:15-4:15.

Allen Knight Maritime Museum

Monterey History and Art Association, P.O. Box 805, 550 Calle Principal, Monterey, CA 93942; (408) 375-2553. Preserves artifacts from fishing and whaling industries during Monterey sailing ship era through museum exhibits. Small library provides reference for maritime and Navy research; archives include voyage logs and Lloyd's registers; large photo collection of sailing ships of early 20th c. Accepts phone inquiries. No fee. Hours: summer, Tu-F 10-4, Sa-Su 2-4; nonsummer, Tu-F 1-4, Sa-Su 2-4.

American Carousel Museum

655 Beach St., Suite 400, San Francisco, CA 94109; (415) 928-0550. Preserves, restores, and exhibits American Carousel Animals. Museum holds changing exhibits of approx 75 carousel animals dating from 1885-1927, with emphasis on American carvings. Some German, French, English, and Mexican figures included. Library provides reference books, photo albums, and historic cards based on carousels. Archives has photos and newspaper articles on carousels no longer in use. Videotape on restoration and museum available. Accepts phone inquiries. Fee. Hours: Nov-Mar 10-5, Apr-Oct 10-6.

American Historical Association

Pacific Coast Branch, c/o Secty/Treas, Dept. of History, Loyola Marymount University, Los Angeles, CA 90045; (213) 642-2806. Promotes study of history and represents interests of historian from Rockies to Pacific Coast. Accepts phone inquiries. No fee. Hours: M-F 8-5.

American Indian Historical Society

1493 Masonic Avenue, San Francisco, CA 94117. Publishes literature documenting Indian life, culture, and mistreatment under auspices of Indian Historical Press.

American Indian Resource Center

6518 Miles Ave., Huntington Park, CA 90255; (213) 583-1461. Preserves cultural aspects of Native American population in Los Angeles, and makes info available on this group. Major focus on Indians of Southwest, but all tribes north of Mexico represented. Holdings include books, magazines, newspapers, tribal newsletter, govt publications, college catalogs, audio recordings, 16mm films, Indian Census Rolls, and clipping and pamphlet file. Center also provides referral services for locating agencies serving Native American population. Accepts phone inquiries. No fee. Hours: call.

American Museum of Quilts and Textiles

766 S. 2nd St., San Jose, CA 95112; (408) 971-0323. Preserves, collects, and displays quilts and textiles from 1850 with emphasis on early 20th c. Accepts phone inquiries. No fee. Hours: Tu-Sa 10-4.

American Society of Military History

Patriotic Hall, 1816 S. Figueroa St., Los Angeles, CA 90015; (213) 746-1776. Collects, restores, and exhibits military materials and equip. Museum houses largest collection of inter-service military equip on exhibit in west. Other holdings include limited maps, and photos from WWI-WWII. Accepts phone inquiries. Fee. Hours: M-F 9-4:30.

American Victorian Museum

P.O. Box 328, 325 Spring St, Nevada City, CA 95959; (916) 265-5804. Preserves and displays 19th c art, artifacts, crafts, and industry in form of museum and special collections. Holdings include machinery, graphics, decorative art works, and other Victorian era items; 19th c photo collection of local subjects; special collections of Pre-Raphaelite art, 19th c inventions, and Staffordshire pottery. Accepts phone inquiries. No fee. Hours: March-Jan, 10-4; Feb, by appt.

Anne Kent California Room

Marin County Free Library, Civic Center Administration Bldg., San Rafael, CA 94903; (415) 499-6058. Collects materials on histories of CA, San Francisco Bay area and Marin Cty. Library and archives focus on documentation of local history, with collections of maps, manuscripts, photos, and films/videotapes; small oral history collection; some genealogical records; and limited collection of Frank Lloyd Wright materials. Materials non-circulating. Accepts phone inquiries (415-499-7419). No fee. Hours: M, W, Th, F 10-6, Tu 10-8:30.

Antelope Valley Indian Museum

15701 East Ave M, Lancaster, CA 93535; (805) 942-0662. (Mailing address: c/o CA Dept of Parks and Recreation, High Desert District, 4555 West Ave G, Lancaster, CA 93536) Preserves, displays, and interprets history and culture of the CA and Southwest Indians. Accepts phone inquiries. Fee. Hours: Oct-June, second weekend of each month, 11-4; group tours, Tu, Th by appt.

Arcadia Public Library

20 West Duarte Road, Arcadia, CA 91006; (818) 446-7112. Public library maintains collection of local historical materials, including photos, directories, maps, newspapers, and other archival materials. Most historical items are non-circulating. Accepts phone inquiries (818-446-6589). No fee. Hours: M-Th 10-9, F-Sa 10-6.

Archive of Performing Arts

Doheny Memorial Library, University of California, University Park, Los Angeles, CA 90089; (213) 743-2311. Collects and preserves materials from movie studios, publicity depts, story depts, actors, producers, directors, and writers from film industry. Holdings include Warner Bros films from 1920-68, Universal Pictures office records and screenplays, MGM screenplays from 1919-58, 20th Century Fox screenplays from 1916-67, David Wolper videotapes,

and historical collections of posters, photos, soundtracks, oral histories, picture cameras, projectors, and other equip. Accepts phone inquiries. Hours: call.

Asian Pacific Resource Center

1550 West Beverly Blvd., Montebello, CA 90604; (213) 722-7292. Serves info needs of Asian Pacific peoples and makes info on these groups available to public. Holdings concentrate on history, accomplishments, and cultural heritage of peoples from China, Japan, Korea, the Philippines, and Vietnam. Collections include books, magazines, dissertations, pamphlets, 16mm films, slides, and audio and video tapes. Info services offered for locating agencies serving Asian Pacific community. Accepts phone inquiries. No fee. Hours: call.

Association for Northern California Records and Research

P.O. Box 3024, Chico, CA 95927. Collects public records of northeast CA from 19th and early 20th c. Holdings include manuscripts, maps, genealogical materials, and many photos of the region. No fee.

Bancroft Library

University of California, Berkeley, CA 94720; (415) 642-3781. Documents history of western North America, with emphasis on western plains states, CA, and Mexico. Holdings include Mark Twain project of author's notebooks, corrrespondence, manuscripts, and special materials. Regional oral history office has interviews with people involved in agriculture, arts, conservation, printing, labor, politics, winemaking, and University of CA history. Pictorial collection includes paintings, drawings, photos, and documentations of CA and western US history. Restrictions on use. Accepts phone inquiries. No fee. Hours: M-F 9-5, Sa 1-5.

Barbie Doll Hall of Fame

Doll Studio, 325 Hamilton Ave., Palo Alto, CA 94301; (415) 326-5841. Museum preserves Barbie dolls, outfits, accessories, and other dolls from 1959. Holdings include first Barbies, variety of Ken dolls, Barbie's female counterparts, and displays on evolution of Barbie doll. Accepts phone inquiries. Fee. Hours: Tu-Sa 10:30-4.

Barlow Society for the History of Medicine

634 S. Westlake Ave., Los Angeles, CA 90057; (213) 483-4555. Promotes art and science of medicine through museum collection of surgical instruments, artifacts, and medical art. Library provides medical reference materials, and photos of physicians and medical institutions. Special collections include materials on CA medicine, Osleriana, George Dock, Theodore Curphey, and William Molony. Some restrictions. Accepts phone inquiries. No fee. Hours: M-F 8:30-5.

Berkeley Historical Society

P.O. Box 1190, 1325 Grant St., Berkeley, CA 94701. Collects, preserves and promotes history of Berkeley and residents in form of library, archives, manuscripts, maps, photos, and oral history collection. Materials non-circulating. Accepts phone inquiries. No fee. Hours: M-F 9-noon.

Black Resource Center

150 E. El Segundo Blvd., Los Angeles, CA 90061; (213) 538-3350. Supports research into social, historical, musical, and cultural aspects unique to black experience. Library has scholarly books, dissertations, diaries, letters, govt publications, 16mm films, videotapes, recordings, black periodicals and newspapers, and posters. Special black musical artists collection. Materials non-circulating. Accepts phone inquiries. No fee. Hours: M-Th 10-8, F-Sa 10-5.

Burbank Public Library

110 N. Glenoaks Blvd., Burbank, CA 91502; (818) 953-9737. Library maintains Warner collection for film industry production needs. Covers costumes, military, crime and criminals, transportation, license plates, and Sears catalogs. Accepts phone inquiries. No fee. Hours: call.

Cabot's Old Indian Pueblo Museum

P.O. Box 1267, 67616 E. Desert View Ave., Desert Hot Springs, CA 92240; (619) 329-7610. Museum was home of trader; now houses photos and exhibits on N. CA Indians and culture. History of Desert Hot Springs from 1913 in photos. Some restrictions on use. Accepts phone inquiries. Fee. Hours: W-Su 9:30-4.

California Genealogical Society

P.O. Box 77105, 300 Brannan St., Ste. 409, San Francisco, CA 94107; (415) 777-9936. Promotes research of family histories by gathering and preserving vital records. Holdings include large library of genealogical records, federal census records from 1850, and periodicals. Materials non-circulating. Accepts phone inquiries. Fee. Hours: T-Th 9-4, Sa 10-3.

California Historical Society

Southern California Branch, 4201 Wilshire Blvd., Los Angeles, CA 90010; (213) 937-1848. Collects, studies, and promotes CA history. Museum displays photomurals of early Los Angeles scenes. Library has materials on CA and western frontier history. Archives holds Dominguez family papers, publications and records of LA Area Chamber of Commerce, letters and papers of other LA families, maps, large collection of photos from southern CA and the western states, and collection of oral history recordings. Accepts phone inquiries. Donations accepted. Hours: Tu-F 1-4.

California Museum of Photography

University of California, Riverside, CA 92521; (714) 787-4787. Collects, exhibits, and provides interpretation of photography as cultural history. Museum houses images and apparatus from 1840s; library has some reference materials. Special Keystone-Mast collection of original stereoscopic prints and negatives on American subjects from 1890s-1930s. Accepts phone inquiries. No admission fee. Hours: galleries W-Su, noon-5; collections by appt.

California State Archives

1020 "O" St., Rm. 130, Sacramento, CA 95814; (916) 445-4293. Collects and preserves CA govt records of historic value in museum, library, and archives. Holdings date from 1849 and include assorted railway and railroad maps; Department of Transportation and other state agency projects; prison, census, and military records; papers of Earl Warren from 1924-53; and papers of Robert Kennedy assassination investigation from 1968-75. May be some restrictions on use of materials. Accepts phone inquiries. No fee. Hours: M-F 8-5.

California State Capitol Museum

State Capitol, Room 124, Sacramento, CA 95814; (916) 324-0333. Provides tours and interpretive programs on state history and Capitol restoration. Museum houses original executive offices from 1900-10 and exhibits on Capitol history. Collection of photos and films documents Capitol's history and restoration. Accepts phone inquiries. No fee. Hours: 9-5.

California State University, Fresno

Special Collections, Henry Madden Library, Shaw & Maple Aves., Fresno, CA 93740; (209) 488-3195. Academic research library holds materials on WWII rationing in US and Germany. Accepts phone inquiries. No fee. Hours: call.

California State University, Fullerton

Library, Special Collections, P.O. Box 4150, Fullerton, CA 92634; (714) 773-3449. Academic research library holds materials relating to WWII. Collection of archival materials on Holocaust, oral history interviews detailing Japanese relocation to internment camps in US, and nearly complete materials from the League of Nation available. Accepts phone inquiries. No fee. Hours: call.

California State University, Fullerton

Oral History Program, University Library, 431, 800 N. State College Blvd., Fullerton, CA 92634; (714) 773-3580. Holds audio and archival records of many Southwestern Americans' participation in historic events. Interviews on Pres and Mrs Nixon; members of Asian American, Native American, Afro-American, Jewish, Hispanic American, and Scandinavian communities; southeastern Utah residents recalling frontier experiences; family and personal histories during World Wars, Depression, pioneering era, and Mormon colonization in Mexico; environmental studies; prominent CA, Philippine, NOW, and law enforcement officials; and workers in uranium, early automobile, coal mining, astronomy industries. Accepts phone inquiries. No fee. Hours: M-Th 10-4 and by appt.

California State University, Hayward

Library, Documents Division, Hayward, CA 94542; (415) 881-3765. Selective depository serves educational and research needs of community with large collections of US, CA, and UN publications. Also holds extensive collection of CA, AZ, and NV topographic maps. Accepts phone inquiries. No fee. Hours: M-Th 8-9, F 8-5, Sa 10-5, Su 12-6.

California State University at Northridge

Special Collections, Oviatt Library, 18111 Nordhoff St., Northridge, CA 91330; (818) 885-2285. Academic research library holds collection of migrant camp records maintained by US Govt between 1935-39. Accepts phone inquiries. Hours: call.

California State University at Sacramento

Library, 2000 Jed Smith Dr., Sacramento, CA 95819; (916) 454-6643. Library maintains special collection on dissent and social change materials. Contains left- and right-wing political and alternative lifestyle materials, some dating to 1890. Holdings include books, pamphlets, periodicals, newsletters, and newspapers. Accepts phone inquiries. Hours: call.

Carpinteria Valley Historical Society and Museum

956 Maple Ave., Carpinteria, CA 93013; (805) 684-3112. Collects, preserves, and exhibits history of Carpinteria Valley and its residents. Museum and library focus on Chumash Indian culture from Spanish-Mexican period, American pioneer life and customs, and regional oil industry development; map collection of local, county, and land-grant planning from 1880s; oral history collection; and genealogical records for many early pioneer families. Some restrictions on use of materials. Accepts phone inquiries. No fee. Hours: Su, Tu-F 1:30-4, Sa 11-4.

Cecil Green Library

Manuscript Collections, Stanford University Libraries, Stanford, CA 94305; (415) 723-9108. Academic research library has materials on western Americana covering mining, regional authors, railroads, American Civil War, and early American statesmen. Holdings include papers of New Almaden quicksilver mines, business and legal records of Goodwin Knight, farm labor materials, and correspondence and literary manuscripts of John Steinbeck, Jack London, Bruce Bliven, John Galsworthy, Janet Lewis, Somerset Maugham, and DH Lawrence. Early American history and govt materials, and correspondence of early American statesmen included in Elmer Robinson collection. Accepts phone inquiries. No fee. Hours: call.

Charles W. Bowers Memorial Museum

2002 N. Main St., Santa Ana, CA 92706; (714) 972-1900. Preserves, promotes, and displays art, culture, and history of the peoples of the Pacific Rim, Orange County, CA, and Southern CA. Holdings include extensive collection of cultural, historical, and art objects and artifacts; library with publications and archival materials; photo archives; extensive stereopticon history collection. Accepts phone inquiries. Donations accepted. Hours: Tu-Sa 10-5, Su noon-5.

Cherokee Heritage and Museum Association

4226 Cherokee Rd., Oroville, CA 95965; (916) 533-1849. Preserves memorabila relating to residents and the history of Cherokee. Museum and archives include collections of manuscripts, maps, photos, and genealogical records. Accepts phone inquiries. Donation accepted. Hours: call.

Chicano Resource Center

4801 East 3rd St., Los Angeles, CA 90022; (213) 264-0155. Provides in-depth coverage of Chicano experience in US, including politics, folklore, customs, education, art, language, health, and history of Mexico. Holdings include books, magazines, pamphlets, films, records, video and audio tapes, filmstrips, dissertations, newspapers, artifacts, and prints. Also offers info and referral services for locating agencies serving Chicano community. Accepts phone inquiries. No fee. Hours: call.

Chinese Historical Society of America

17 Adler Place, San Francisco, CA 94133; (415) 391-1188. Society runs museum, which preserves Chinese-American history from 1785 through exhibits, archival material, manuscripts,

photo collection, and uncataloged oral history tapes. Also coordinates speakers and publications. Donations accepted. Hours: Tu-Sa 1-5.

Civil Engineer Corps/Seabee Museum

Naval Construction Battalion Center, Code 22M CBC, Port Hueneme, CA 93043; (805) 982-5163. Provides historical context for Corps activities and recruits, by collecting cultural and military artifacts from Seabee overseas projects. Archival materials include deployment cruise books from WWII to Vietnam; official unit histories and manuals from 1860; photos, slides and movies; and outstanding officer papers and memorabilia. Materials for in-house use only. Accepts phone inquiries. No fee. Hours: M-F 8-4:30, Sa 9-4:30, Su 12:30-4:30.

Claremont Colleges

Ella Strong Denison Library, Scripps College, Claremont, CA 91711; (714) 621-8150 ext. 3941. Academic research library provides historical materials for contemporary women's movement. Holds women's history materials on Ida Rust Macpherson collection covering humanistic accomplishments of women, suffrage and emancipation, domestic economy, and women in Westward migration. Accepts phone inquiries. No fee. Hours: call.

Clarke Memorial Museum

240 E. St., Eureka, CA 95501; (707) 443-1947. Preserves regional history with emphasis on Native American cultures of northwestern CA, and subsequent settlements from 1850-1950. Museum displays major collections on Hoopa, Karuk, and Yurok Indians, with some exhibits on Humboldt county history, firearms, Victorian textiles, and decorative arts. Archives hold large collection of country photos from 1850-1950. Accepts phone inquiries. No fee. Hours: by appt, Tu-Sa noon-4.

Colton Hall Museum

City Museum, Civic Center, Pacific St. between Madison and Jefferson, Monterey, CA 93940; (408) 375-9944. Dedicated to preserving Monterey history, emphasizing city's CA Constitutional Convention in 1849. Archival materials on Monterey from 1770; maps of city from 1849; photos from 1880s; and genealogical records of 1849 Convention delegates. Special Oliver collection of photos from 1900. Accepts phone inquiries. No fee. Hours: Nov-Mar, 10-4, Mar-Nov 10-5.

Contra Costa County Library

Documents Division, 1750 Oak Park Blvd., Pleasant Hill, CA 94523; (415) 646-6434. Public library houses Californiana collection, with emphasis on history of northern CA, San Francisco Bay Area, and Contra Costa county. Holdings include maps and clipping files from local papers. Materials for in-house use only. Accepts phone inquiries. No fee. Hours: M-Th 10-9, F-Sa 10-6.

Cultural Heritage Foundation of Southern California

3800 Homer St., Los Angeles, CA 90032; (818) 449-0193. Foundation preserves and promotes history of Victorian architecture and culture in form of Heritage Square Museum complex, library, and archival collections. Holdings include restored, furnished Victorian buildings in village setting, 1865-1914, housing historical ephemera and artifacts; small library, archives, and photo collection. Library, archives and photo collection closed to public. Does not accept phone inquiries. Fee. Hours: Sa-Su and holidays, noon-4.

Death Valley House

National Park Service, Death Valley National Monument, Death Valley, CA 92328; (619) 786-2331. Provides information on cultural and natural history of Death Valley National Monument through holdings in museum, library, and archives. Extensive photo collection and small oral history tape library. Some restrictions on use of archival and museum materials. Accepts phone inquiries. Fee. Hours: Tu-Sa 8-5.

Directors Guild of America

7950 Sunset Blvd., Los Angeles, CA 90046; (213) 656-1220. Active labor union represents directors and collects materials on union and industry history. Library holdings include DGA publications and archival oral history info; archive of historical film and TV labor movement materials; manuscripts on specific directors; films/videotapes of director tributes and colloquia.

Accepts phone inquiries. No fee. Hours: M-F 9-5:30.

East Bay Negro Historical Society

5606 San Pablo Ave., Oakland, CA 94608; (415) 658-3158. Relates history of blacks in CA and West through museum holdings of local artifacts from 1850 and library and archival holdings. Collections include manumission papers issued by slave masters in 1850s; early CA maps, extensive family photos, films on early CA black pioneers, Oakland, East Bay early black settlers. Special local history records, and materials from men's and women's orgs, athletes, musicians, churches, and politicians. Materials for in-house use only; use of archival materials requires prior staff approval. Accepts phone inquiries. No fee. Hours: Tu 12:30-7, W-F 12:30-5.

Eastern California Museum

Box 206, 155 N. Grant St., Independence, CA 93526; (619) 878-2411 ext. 2259. Preserves and studies historic and prehistoric natural and cultural development of eastern CA in form of museum exhibits, library, and archival collections. Holdings include artifacts of local Native Americans, early pioneers, and the Manzanar Relocation camp; mineral specimens; library with CA literature, and materials on regional geology, anthropology, flora, and fauna; archives with local family history files; county assessor maps; collection of local historical photos; collection of local Paiute and Panamint Shoshone basketry. Accepts phone inquiries. Donations accepted. Hours: Su-M, Th-F noon-4, Sa 10-4.

El Pueblo De Los Angeles State Historic Park

City of Los Angeles, 845 N. Alameda St., Los Angeles, CA 90012; (213) 680-2525. One of 27 buildings at heart of Los Angeles birthplace; studies and preserves materials on city's early history and development. Holdings include those in house museums, library, archives, manuscripts, and map, photo, and oral history collections. Hours: call.

Electronics Museum and De Forest Archive

Foothill College, 12345 El Monte Rd., Los Altos Hills, CA 94022; (415) 960-4383. Preserves history of electronics with emphasis on Lee De Forest, early radio era, and Silicon Valley. Museum displays Douglas Perham collection of early electronics, first radio broadcast station, KQW, and Farnsworth TV tubes. Library has materials on early electronics in form of monographs, texts, and manuals. Archives holds Lee De Forest (Father of Radio) papers and photos of northern CA electronics industry. Accepts phone inquiries. No fee. Hours: archive by appt, Th-F 9:30-4:30, Su 1-4.

Emigrant Trail Museum

P.O. Box 9210, 12593 Donner Pass Rd., Truckee, CA 95737; (916) 587-3841. Documents westward movement along California Trail and history of Donner party from 1840-70. Museum and library collections center on pioneers, railroad, logging, and Gold Rush; archival material on Donner Party includes artifacts and photos; some manuscripts and maps. Accepts phone inquiries. Fee. Hours: 10-noon, 1-4.

Eugene O'Neill National Historic Site

1000 Kuss Rd., Danville, CA 94526; (415) 838-0249. Preserved home of playwrite Eugene O'Neill memorializes his life and work in form of displays of his personal and family items and furnishings, and through performing arts park and educational programs. Guided tours required, by appt. Accepts phone inquiries. Donations accepted. Reservations required. Hours: Tours: 10 and 1:30; office: 8-4:30.

Film/Television Archive

University of California, Los Angeles, CA 90024; (213) 206-8013 film, or 8014 TV. Collects and preserves over 7000 films from 20th Century Fox, Paramount, and Republic Studios films. Special film collections from Preston Sturges and Joseph von Sternberg. Accepts phone inquiries. Hours: call.

First Interstate Bank Athletic Foundation

2141 W. Adams, Los Angeles, CA 90018; (213) 614-4111. Maintains collection of documentary materials on sports and Olympic tournaments. Holdings include newspaper sports sections; college and university materials; souvenir publications from amateur, college, and pro events; ledgers of sports halls of fame; and assorted memorabilia. Accepts phone inquiries. Hours: call.

Fitz Hugh Ludlow Memorial Library

P.O. Box 99346, San Francisco, CA 94109. Library collections focus on drug culture of 1950s-70s, and corresponding literature, music, and art of the period. Holdings include writings of Beat poets, memoirs, materials on hippies, drug-related pornography, drug cuisine, underground newspapers, newspaper clippings, and regional artifacts. Accepts important mail inquiries only.

Fort Crook Historical Museum

Box 397, Fall River Mills, CA 96028; (916) 336-5110. Preserves and promotes pioneer history of eastern Shasta County, CA in form of artifacts and exhibits relating to pioneers and Native Americans; library, archives, manuscripts, maps, photos, recordings, genealogical records, and turn-of-the-century home replica. Use of research collections by permission only. Accepts phone inquiries. Donations accepted. Hours: May-Oct, noon-4.

Fort Point and Army Museum Association

P.O. Box 29163, Bldg. T-3, Funston Ave & Presidio Blvd, Presidio of San Francisco, CA 94129; (415) 921-8193. Supports curation of Civil War fort and Army museum with focus on military history in Presidio area. Substantial library resources; small archival and manuscript collections; extensive map holdings from Army map service; photos of military operations; and limited Army training films. Accepts phone inquiries. No fee. Hours: M-F 8:30-4:30.

Frances Howard Goldwyn Hollywood Regional Library

L.A. Public Library, 1623 Ivar Ave., Los Angeles, CA 90028; (213) 467-1821. Collects, preserves, and interprets motion picture, radio, and TV industry historical materials. Holdings include large number of scripts, biographical collections, films from 1920s, posters, lobby cards, scrapbooks, vertical file materials, publicity stills, and correspondence. Accepts phone inquiries. Hours: call.

Francis Bacon Library

655 N. Dartmouth Ave., Claremont, CA 91711; (714) 621-8045. Maintains collection of correspondence between American literary figures in 1920s-50s, including Clifford Odets, William Carlos Williams, Helen Keller, Henry Miller, Lewis Mumford, Catherine Drinker Bowen, Irving Stone, and others. Accepts phone inquiries. Hours: call.

Fresno County Free Library

2420 Mariposa St., Fresno, CA 93721; (209) 488-3195. Serves as depository for US documents from 1920. Special holdings include Californiana regional history collection; William Saroyan Collection; and oral history collection from 1975, emphasizing the Japanese-American experience. Some circulation restrictions. Accepts phone inquiries. No fee. Hours: M-W 9-9, Th 12-9, F 9-6, Sa 1-5.

Fullerton Museum Center

301 N. Pomona Ave., Fullerton, CA 92632; (714) 738-6545. Exhibits permanent collection of historic costumes and textiles, as well as major travelling collections. Holdings are international and regionally significant pieces. Accepts phone inquiries. Fee. Hours: Tu-W 11-4, Th-F 11-9, Sa-Su 11-4.

Gardena Public Library

Los Angeles Public Library, 1731 West Gardena Blvd., Gardena, CA 90247; (213) 323-6363. Public library maintains general and historical materials relevant to needs of community. Holdings cover history and culture of Japanese-Americans, including dissertations on their treatment during WWII, and books and microforms of newspapers published in the internment camps of WWII. Accepts phone inquiries. No fee. Hours: M-Th 10-9, F 10-6, Sa 10-5.

Gene Autry Western Heritage Museum

P.O. Box 710, Los Angeles, CA 90078; (818) 841-7656. Acquires, preserves, and interprets info and artifacts documenting history and peoples of American West. Museum displays Western artifacts from 16th c, including firearms, horse equip, clothing, and vehicles. Library holds materials on fictional West, as well as Western material culture. Archives contain primary sources on career of Gene Autry, letters and documents on 19th c American West, scripts from TV and motion pictures on West, movie stills, small collection of Western film, recordings from Autry's career, and oral history interviews. Accepts phone inquiries. No fee. Hours: call.

Geological Survey Library

Department of Interior, 345 Middlefield Road MS 955, Menlo Park, CA 94025; (415) 329-5090. Performs geological investigations and cartography for US. Holdings include large library on earth and related sciences; geological and topographic maps of western US; and aerial photos and colored slides of CA and San Francisco Bay area. Material for in-house use only; ILL available. Accepts phone inquiries (415-329-5027). No fee. Hours: M-F 7:45-4:15.

Graduate Theological Union Library

Public Services and Research Collections, 2400 Ridge Rd., Berkeley, CA 94709; (415) 649-2400. Collection focuses on new religious movement in US since 1960, including Hinduism, Buddhism, Sikhism, Sufism, occultism, neopaganism, and feminist spirituality. Holdings cover issues in deprogramming, separation of church and state, and responses of mainstream religions and concerned citizens groups. Library is also depository for Unification Church in America, Church of Scientology, and International Society for Krishna Consciousness in America. Hours: call.

Harrison Memorial Library

Ocean and Lincoln Sts., Carmel, CA 93921; (408) 624-4629. Preserves small collection of original Edward Weston photos. Materials for in-house use only, and with staff supervision. Accepts phone inquiries. Hours: call.

Held-Poage Memorial Home and Research Library

Mendocino County Historical Society, 603 W. Perkins St., Ukiah, CA 95482; (707) 462-6969. Collects and preserves materials on history of Mendocino county, CA, and Native Americans from 1700. Photo collection documents regional CA history; maps include Mendocino county, Indian lands; microfilm available of county census and newspapers; Estle Beard and Edith Van Allen Murphey manuscript collections. Materials for in-house use only; ILL available. Accepts phone inquiries. No fee. Hours: Tu, Th, Sa 2-4, and by appt.

Historical Society of Long Beach

P.O. Box 1869, Senior Center, 1150 E. 4th St., Long Beach, CA 90801; (213) 435-7511. Preserves historic materials for Long Beach residents and researchers, with special collection from local movie studio. Archives hold large collection of pamphlets, scrapbooks, legal files, and records of Chamber of Commerce and civic clubs; real estate plat maps; large collection of photos, postcards, and albums; oral history interviews; genealogical records; and rare collection of memorabilia from Balboa Movie Studio. Materials non-circulating. Accepts phone inquiries. No fee. Hours: Tu-Th 10-3, and by appt.

Historical Society of Southern California

200 East Ave. 43, Los Angeles, CA 90031; (213) 222-0546. Collects and preserves all materials relating to history of Pacific Coast and southern CA. Sponsors regular meetings for members and general public, and participates in educational projects. Holdings include photos from 1890-1920 and set of Southern CA Quarterly from 1884, but public availability still in question. Accepts phone inquiries. Donations accepted. Hours: W-Su 1-4.

Holt-Atherton Pacific Center for Western Studies

University Library, University of the Pacific, Stockton, CA 95211; (209) 946-2404. Research center maintains collection of historical materials relating to the univ and regional development. Holdings include extensive collection of publications, serials, and newspapers related to Western US and CA settlement and development; univ archives; manuscripts and other materials on Western Americana, with emphasis on CA and San Joaquin County and Valley, and Mother Lode; extensive photo collection of local subjects; Lawton Harris' Folk Dance Collection of recorded music; Fry Library of Methodist History. Some restrictions. Accepts phone inquiries. No fee. Hours: M-F 9-5.

Honnold Library Special Collections

Claremont Colleges, Ninth & Dartmouth, Claremont, CA 91711; (714) 621-8150. Preserves materials relating to WWII and WWI. Holdings include materials on German propaganda and medals; US recruitment effort; War Bond and Liberty Bond posters; Howard Mills collection on War Bonds; soldiers' handbooks and scrapbooks; photos; maps; and recordings. Accepts phone inquiries. No fee. Hours: call.

Hoover Institution on War, Revolution, and Peace

Stanford University, Stanford, CA 94305; (415) 723-2058. Holdings cover Pacifism and peace movement and materials from WWI. Pacifism collection has Alice Park papers from 1883-1957; materials on Ford Peace Ship Expedition of 1915-1916, child labor legislation, labor movement, feminism, socialism, civil liberties, and women's reform movements. WWI materials include records of 1914-24 Commission for Relief in Belgium, American William Drayton WWI experiences in Serbian army, European role in WWI, and Paris Peace Treaty. WWII materials include papers of Adm Cooke, Gen Richardson, Brig Gen Boyd, and Haydon Boatner. Some film industry MPRC papers from 1927-41. Accepts phone inquiries. No fee. Hours: M-F 8-5, Sa 9-1.

Jack London State Historic Park

2400 London Ranch Rd., Glen Ellen, CA 95442; (707) 938-5216. Preserves and interprets the history of life and writing of Jack London in form of his home, 1876-1955, with his belongings, including South Seas souvenirs, photos, and books and journalistic works. Accepts phone inquiries. Park entrance fee. Hours: home: 10-5; grounds: 8-sunset.

James S. Copley Library

Copley Newspapers, P.O. Box 1530, 1134 Kline St., La Jolla, CA 92038; (619) 454-0411, ext. 341. Preserves and makes available historical resources on American Revolution, Southwest, John C. Fremont, Jessie B. Fremont, Robinson Jeffers, Benito Juarez, Abraham Lincoln, Samuel Clemens, and assorted Presidential correspondence. Museum displays art and memorabilia. Library contains large collection of books, documents, and letters on American history, literature, and arts. Other holdings include limited maps, and films/videotapes. Materials available for use by scholars by application. Accepts phone inquiries. No fee. Hours: M-F 10-noon, 1-3.

Jesse Peter Memorial Museum

Santa Rosa Junior College, 1501 Mendocino Ave., Santa Rosa, CA 95401; (707) 527-4479. Native American art museum exhibits CA, Southwest, Plains and Plateau Indian, Eskimo, and Northwest coast arts from 19th and 20th c. Small collection of reference materials. Photo murals depicting Native American life from past to present also exhibited. Accepts phone inquiries. No fee. Hours: M-F noon-4.

John Muir National Historic Site

National Park Service, 4202 Alhambra Ave., Martinez, CA 94553; (415) 228-8860. Acquaints public with Muir and his ecological concerns by maintaining small oral history collection, museum, and collection of Muir papers. Most papers at Univ of Pacific, Stockton. Hours: call.

Kern County Museum

3801 Chester Ave., Bakersfield, CA 93301; (805) 861-2132. Collects and preserves materials documenting history of Kern County from 1870. Museum and library concentrate on local and western history; archives holds large Chinese collection; considerable collection of historic local and CA maps; and large photo archive of area residents and scenes. Accepts phone inquiries. Fee. Hours: museum, M-F 8-5, Sa-Su 10-5; research by appt only.

La Purisma Mission
State Historic Park

California Dept. of Parks & Recreation, RFD Box 102, Purisima & Mission Gates Rds., Lompoc, CA 93436; (805) 733-3713. Preserves history of restored Franciscan mission from 1769-1835, and documents Chumash Indian culture. Also materials and photos of mission restoration 1934-42. Accepts phone inquiries. Fee. Hours: photo archives by appt; museum 9-4:30.

Labor Archives and Research Center

San Francisco State University, 480 Winston Dr., San Francisco, CA 94132; (415) 564-4010.

Collects, organizes, and preserves materials of N. CA labor movement, concentrating on history of workers' lives and unions. Museum and library cover CA, San Francisco, and western labor history; archives house records of Bay area unions and San Francisco Labor Council; photo collection includes People's World newspaper files and some Dorothea Lange prints; recordings of Labor Radio News Project, Labor Archives Programs, and Golden Gate Bridgeworkers oral histories. Hours: call.

Lancaster Library

1150 West Ave. J, Lancaster, CA 93534; (805) 948-5020. Preserves local history of CA's Antelope Valley, and serves as regional resource for Los Angeles county residents. Archival holdings include first editions of books on region, collection of handwritten journals, maps from USGS and county board of supervisors, many photos, film on Valley history, and collection of local newspapers. Holdings document construction of first railroads from 1870-75; Los Angeles Aqueduct; 1928 San Francisco Dam Disaster; and Colorado Aqueduct construction from 1928-35. Materials for in-house use only. Accepts phone inquiries. No fee. Hours: M-Th 10-9, F-Sa 10-6, Su 1-5.

Lane Medical Library

Stanford University, Medical Center, Stanford, CA 94305; (415) 723-6831. Holds archival materials of Lane Hospital School of Nursing and Stanford University School of Nursing. Also has reports of experiences of nurses captured on Bataan, Philippine Islands, during WWII. Hours: call.

Laws Railroad Museum
and Historical Site

P.O. Box 363, Silver Canyon Rd., Bishop, CA 93514; (619) 873-5950. Preserves natural, civic, literary, and ecclesiastical history of area with collections ranging from railroad history to pioneers. Museum erected on site of historic Carson & Colorado Railroad Station. Library holds old books, musical instruments, art work, old maps, rather extensive collection of local photos, genealogical records of Valley pioneers, and Indian and pioneer artifacts. Accepts phone inquiries. Donations accepted. Hours: 10-4.

Abraham Lincoln, from the Lincoln Shrine's archives at the Smiley Public Library.

Lincoln Memorial Shrine

Smiley Public Library, 125 W. Vine St., Redlands, CA 92373; (714) 798-7636. Collects materials on Lincoln and his times, including broadsides, letters, prints, campaign materials, and pamphlets. Also holds philatelic collection from Civil War era. Accepts phone inquiries. No fee. Hours: call.

Long Beach Museum of Art

Film Division, 2300 East Ocean Blvd., Long Beach, CA 90803; (213) 439-2119. Media arts program of this art museum houses largest video art collection on west coast. Works date from 1968. Materials for in-house use only. Accepts phone inquiries (213-439-07510). Fee. Hours: M-Sa 9-5.

Long Beach Public Library

Documents Division, 101 Pacific Ave., Long Beach, CA 90802; (213) 590-6944. Stores records of CA and federal govt, and disseminates their info. Holdings include selected US documents from 1933 and CA documents from 1946; USGS topographic maps of CA, AZ, HI, and NV; nautical charts; and service records of Army, Navy, and Air Force in War of Rebellion. Materials circulate to members only or on ILL. Accepts phone inquiries. No fee. Hours: M 10-8, Tu-Sa 10-5:30, Su 12-5.

Los Angeles Art Association Galleries

825 N. La Cienega Blvd., Los Angeles, CA 90069; (213) 652-8272. Exhibition space devoted to displaying works of regional artists; maintains archives with materials on Southern CA artists, and membership files from 1924. Accepts phone inquiries. Hours: Tu-F noon-5, Sa 11-5.

Los Angeles Herald Examiner Library

Box 2146 Terminal Annex, Los Angeles, CA 90015; (213) 744-8417. Library provides information services to newspaper staff in form of back issues and clippings from 1930s, and news photos from 1920s. Collections primarily for in-house use; public use for verification purposes only. Accepts phone inquiries (213-744-8419; photos: 744-8396). Research/labor fee. Hours: 1-4.

Los Angeles Public Library

630 W. Fifth St., Los Angeles, CA 90071; (213) 612-3200. Social sciences dept. has special collection on women's role in society with focus on suffrage and liberation movements, and black studies collection on slavery, abolition, civil rights, and black experience in US. Holdings include clippings, pamphlets, periodicals, govt publications, and popular and scholarly works. History dept. has WWII personal papers and memoirs, diplomatic histories, peace treaties, official reports and archives of US and other countries, materials from LA Times correspondent Tom Treanor, and unit histories. Accepts phone inquiries. Hours: call.

Louis B. Mayer Library

American Film Institute, 2021 Northwestern Ave., Los Angeles, CA 90027; (213) 856-7655. Collects, preserves, and encourages scholarship relating to film and film industry. Holdings include large collection of film and TV scripts, oral history interviews, stills from Columbia studios films, and research collections on lives of writer Stewart Stern, Buster Keaton, director Henry Hathaway, Harry Horner, and George Byron Stage. Also include clipping files on all aspects of movie industry. Accepts phone inquiries. Hours: call.

Malki Museum

Morongo Indian Reservation, 11-795 Fields Rd., Banning, CA 92220; (714) 849-7289. Preserves cultural heritage of Cahuilla Indians and other Southern CA tribal groups. Museum displays artifacts, baskets, pottery, granaries, and bows and arrows. Library has small reference collection of Native Americans, with emphasis on CA Indians. Archives holds photos, letters from CA Indian agents, and John Peabody Harrington ethnographic field notes. Also publishes scholarly books. Accepts phone inquiries. No fee. Hours: Th-Su 10-5.

March Field Museum

22 AREFW-PACM, March Air Force Base, CA 92518; (714) 655-3725. Depicts history and heritage of March Field, and its involvement with Strategic Air Command. Museum documents history of March Field from 1918, and

displays 39 vintage aircraft. Library contains military reference materials and several films/videotapes. Accepts phone inquiries. No fee. Hours: M-F 10-4, Sa-Su noon-4.

Margart Herrick Library and Film Archive

Academy of Motion Picture Arts & Sciences, 8949 Wilshire Rd., Beverly Hills, CA 90211; (213) 278-4313. Fosters arts and sciences of motion pictures. Library houses materials on all facets of motion picture history and development from 1881. Holdings include books, periodicals, clipping files, photos, screenplays, posters, and lobby cards. Manuscript collection contains Paramount scripts, MPAA Production Code files, Lux Radio Theatre scripts, and materials from Huston, Cukor, Hitchcock, Peckinpah, Sennett, Pickford, Head, Hopper, Parsons, and many others. Photos from MGM, Paramount, RKO, DeMille, and Ince. Over 8000 films from early silent era. Recordings from personalities and soundtracks. Accepts phone inquiries. No fee. Hours: by appt; M, Tu, Th, F 9-5.

Marin Museum of the American Indian

P.O. Box 864, 2200 Novato Blvd, Novato, CA 94948; (415) 897-4067. Preserves, interprets, and displays history and culture of Native Americans, with emphasis on CA regional tribes. Holdings include artifacts and permanent and changing exhibits on the Coast Miwok Indians and other native cultures; reference library; Native Plant Garden; archaeological site in adjacent park. Accepts phone inquiries. No fee. Hours: Tu-Sa 10-4, Su noon-4.

Mariposa Museum and History Center

P.O. Box 606, 5119 Jessie St., Mariposa, CA 95338; (209) 966-2924. Preserves materials and records from "49er" era to 1890. Library holds info on Yosemite, John C. Fremont, and gold miners; manuscripts on Chief Tenaya and regional Chinese settlers; area mining maps; and photos of area mines and residents. Some genealogical records on early settlers. Materials for in-house use only. Accepts phone inquiries. No fee. Hours: M-Th 10-4.

Marshall Gold Discovery State Historic Park

P.O. Box 265, 310 Back St, Coloma, CA 95613; (916) 622-3470. Preserves and interprets site of the discovery of gold at Sutter's Sawmill that spawned the CA gold rush, in form of museum, library, and archival collections. Holdings include regional artifacts and exhibits relating to James Marshall, the gold discovery, and the gold rush; library with materials on regional history, 1820-1930; diaries and letters from the gold rush era; copies of historical maps; photos of local subjects from 1850; films/videotapes on local subjects; genealogical file on early Coloma residents. Accepts phone inquiries. Fee. Hours: 8-5.

Max Factor Museum

1666 N. Highland Ave., Los Angeles, CA 90028; (213) 463-6668. Museum preserves Factor's studio, including collections of old advertisements, studio portraits from stars, wig blocks and hair pieces from Hollywood notables, makeup and accessories used by Factor, machines used to manufacture creams, and first makeup used for TV. Accepts phone inquiries. No fee. Hours: M-Sa 9-5.

McGeorge School of Law Library

University of the Pacific, 3282 Fifth Ave., Sacramento, CA 95817; (916) 739-7131. Supports student and legal community research with federal, CA, and NV govt documents. Also holdings in international law, UN, and EEC. International materials for legal community only. Accepts phone inquiries. No fee. Hours: Su-Th 8-12, F-Sa 8-11.

Millikan Memorial Library Archives

California Insitute of Technology, 1201 E. California Blvd., Pasadena, CA 91125; (818) 356-6419. Academic research library documents 19th and 20th c advances in science and technology. Holdings include papers of Caltech scientists and administrative officers; manuscript collections on American political, social, and intellectual history; materials on development of aeronautics, physical sciences, seismology, and molecular biology; political conditions in Europe between WWI and WWII; and family letters on

American life during Civil War. Maps, photos, slides, recordings, and videotapes/films available. Accepts phone inquiries. No fee. Hours: call.

Mills College Library

5000 McArthur Blvd., Oakland, CA 94613; (415) 430-2116. Holdings include books and other materials on women's suffrage, etiquette, and education in 19th c. Accepts phone inquiries. No fee. Hours: call.

Mingei International Museum of World Folk Art

P.O. Box 553, La Jolla, CA 92038; (619) 453-5300. Dedicated to furthering understanding of world folk arts through museum exhibitions, reference library, and films/videotapes of arts and demonstrations. Accepts phone inquiries. Fee. Hours: Tu-Th, Sa 11-5, F 11-9, Su 2-5.

Model Colony History Room

Ontario City Library, 215 East C St., Ontario, CA 91764; (714) 988-8481. Maintains collection of research materials relating to history and development of Ontario, CA. Holdings include archives with records of Ontario social/cultural orgs and businesses, including Ontario Land & Improvement Co, Armstrong Nurseries, and General Electric Flatiron plant; diaries and manuscripts of early local settlers; maps of colony lands from 1883, and Sanborn Fire Insurance maps; photos of local subjects and businesses from 1883; US Census for San Bernardino County, CA 1860-1910; biography and obituary files; local oral histories. Collection is non-circulating. Accepts phone inquiries. No fee. Hours: Tu-Sa 1-5.

Monterey History and Art Association

P.O. Box 805, 550 Calle Principal, Monterey, CA 93942; (408) 372-2608. Curates Casa Serrano house museum, Mayor Hayes O'Donnel library of local and CA history, and historic Joseph Boston general store. Special collection of costumes dating from 1880-1940. Accepts phone inquiries. No fee. Hours: M-F 9-4.

Museum of Modern Mythology

693 Mission, Ninth Fl., San Francisco, CA 94105; (415) 546-0202. Preserves and documents characters created for US advertising. Exhibits cover Mr. Bubble, Poppin' Fresh, Campbell Soup Kids, Jolly Green Giant, Michelin Man, Ronald McDonald, Chiquita Banana, Cap'n Crunch, Mr Peanut, California Raisins, Uncle Sam, Post Office Eagle, and some stars from TV shows who endorsed products. Accepts phone inquiries. Fee. Hours: Th-Sa noon-5.

National Archives—Los Angeles Branch

2400 Avila Rd., Laguna Niguel, CA 92677; (714) 643-4221. Branch of the National Archives preserves and maintains collection of US govt historical materials. Holdings include library with genealogical research materials; archives with regional records, 1851-1966, including materials from AZ, southern CA, and Clark County, NV, and naturalization records from Los Angeles and San Diego Superior Courts; extensive collections of maps, and photos; US Census and Revolutionary War records, 1790-1910; pre-Presidential records of Richard Nixon, 1948-1965; Sirhan trial exhibits, 1968-1975. Researcher ID card required. Accepts phone inquiries. No fee. Hours: M-F, first Sa of each month 8-4:30.

National Archives—San Francisco Branch

1000 Commodore Dr., San Bruno, CA 94066; (415) 876-9009. Preserves and makes available US govt research records on N. CA, HI, NV, and Pacific Trust territories. Collections include archival materials of 83 federal agencies from 1850; maps of National Park Service, Bureau of Land Management and Army Corps of Engineers; photos of local mining, Chinese immigration, and irrigation projects; recordings of Tokyo Rose zero hour tapes; microfilm of all US census records from 1790-1910; some naturalization records; and building plans for ships and area architecture. In-house use only. Accepts phone inquiries. No fee. Hours: M, Tu, Th, F 8-4:30, W 8-8:30.

National Center for Film and Video Preservation

American Film Institute, Box 27999, 2021 North Western Ave., Los Angeles, CA 90027; (213)

856-7637. National center serves to coordinate moving image preservation activities of US archives and film and TV industry. Provides filmographic resource information on archives and media arts centers. Also developing central listing for TV and film archival holdings and programs called National Moving Image Database. Hours: call.

National Maritime Museum

Golden Gate National Recreation Area, Fort Mason, Foot of Polk and Hyde Sts., San Francisco, CA 94123; (415) 556-3002. Preserves and interprets Pacific Coast maritime history, with emphasis on shipbuilding, through holdings in large library, museum and archives. Collections include extensive photo and archival material on Pacific maritime in 19th and 20th c; many voyage logbooks; large collection of charts and maps; historic unedited film footage; thousands of sea chantey recordings; and limited collection of marine paintings and artwork. Accepts phone inquiries (library 556-9870; archives 556-9876; collections 556-3797). Fee for museum; no fee for library, archives or collections. Hours: library, Th-F 1-5, Sa 10-5; collections by appt only.

Native Daughters of the Golden West

Reina del Mar Parlor 126, P.O. Box 404, Santa Barbara, CA 93102. Women's organization documents history of CA women active in CA history, conservation and social welfare. Collections include scrapbooks of activities and minutes, and photographs of Old Spanish Days Fiesta and other civic events in Santa Barbara since 1926. Materials can be used when accompanied by member.

Newport Harbor Art Museum

850 San Clemente Dr., Newport Beach, CA 92660; (714) 759-1122. Preserves, exhibits, and interprets modern and contemporary art, with emphasis on post-1945 works. Collection houses more than 2,000 works of sculpture, paintings, photos, and works on paper. Library provides reference materials, manuscripts on museum exhibitions and holdings, and slides of contemporary art. Fee. Hours: Tu-F 10-5, Sa 10-6, Su noon-6.

Norman F. Sprague Memorial Library

Claremont Colleges, 12th & Dartmouth, Claremont, CA 91711; (714) 621-8150. Holds materials concentrating on early aviation, history of ballooning, WWI and WWII military aviation, pioneer flights and pilots, and women in aviation. Collection includes cartoons, songs, diaries, journals, Liberty Bond posters, clippings, photos, and pamphlets. Accepts phone inquiries. No fee. Hours: call.

Oakland History Room

Oakland Public Library, 125 Fourteenth St., Oakland, CA 94612; (415) 273-3222. Devoted to study of CA history and development of East Bay. Special collection of Jack London novels, letters, and research files. Holdings also include manuscripts from Joaquin Miller, Ina Coolbrith, maps from 1892, clipping file of state and local events from 1920s, books on all aspects of state and local history, photos from 1869, city directories from 1869-1943, and Alameda county voting registers from 1867-1944. Accepts phone inquiries. No fee. Hours: Tu, Th noon-8:30; W, F 10-5:30; Sa 1-5:30.

Oakland Museum

1000 Oak St., Oakland, CA 94607; (415) 273-3842. Collects, preserves, and interprets artifacts relating to history, art, and natural sciences of CA. Museum collects costumes and textiles, tools and technology, decorative arts, 19th-20th c; large collection of photos of Bay Area events, industry, transportation, and popular culture; special Boardman collection of survey maps and documents from 1850-1900. May be some restrictions. Accepts phone inquiries. No fee. Hours: M-F 8:30-noon, 1-5.

Occidental College Library

1600 Campus Rd., Los Angeles, CA 90041; (213) 259-2810. Academic library and selective US document depository with archival Occidental materials. Special collections of detective fiction, and works of Robinson Jeffers and Risdon Lincoln. Materials non-circulating. Accepts phone inquiries. No fee. Hours: 8-5.

Old Mint Museum

5th & Mission Sts., San Francisco, CA 94103;

(415) 974-0788. Documents federal govt's role in historical, cultural, and economic development of CA and West through museum and library holdings. Special collections include pioneer collections of gold coins, mint coins, and gold bars. Accepts phone inquiries. No fee. Hours: 10-4.

Old Monterey Jail

Dutra St., Civic Center, Monterey, CA 93940; (408) 375-9944. Museum of jail operating from 1854-1956, with exhibits on its construction, history, and inmates. Accepts phone inquiries. No fee. Hours: Nov-Mar 10-4, March-Nov 10-5.

Orange County Law Library

Govt Documents Depository, 515 N. Flower St., Santa Ana, CA 92703; (714) 834-3397. Public library supporting general public as well as legal community with focus on CA legislative history. Holdings include extensive patent records; working papers of US Congress since 1970; and Sumner collection of CA Constitutional Revision Commission papers and ballot pamphlets from 1912-70. Accepts phone inquiries. No fee. Hours: M-Th 8-10, F 8-6, Sa 9-6.

Pacifica Radio Archive

5316 Venice Blvd., Los Angeles, CA 90019; (213) 931-1625. Preserves and makes available radio programs of Pacifica stations, and programs of interest from other stations. Programs from 1949 preserved, with good coverage of various social movement, peace movement, certain schools of psychology, and poetry and music. Most programs are interviews, documentaries, and speeches. May be restrictions. Accepts phone inquiries. Fee for staff research. Hours: 9-5; other hours by appt.

Palm Springs Public Library

300 South Sunrise Way, Palm Springs, CA 92262; (619) 323-8294. Public library maintains selective collection of govt documents, general and historical materials relevant to needs of community. Holdings include local history vertical file material; local newspaper collection from 1934; extensive collection of maps, with emphasis on USGS topographic maps; collection of publications relating to history of the surrounding des-

ert area. Accepts phone inquiries. No fee. Hours: M-Th 9-8, F 10-5:30, Sa 9-5:30.

Pepperdine University

Special Collections, Payson Library, 24255 Pacific Coast Highway, Malibu, CA 90265; (213) 456-4243. Holds archival material for University and Church of Christ. Special collections include Edward Metcalf Collection of Lawrence of Arabia titles, and rare 1816 edition of Magna Carta. Materials circulate within University community. Phone inquiries accepted (213-456-4238). No fee. Hours: M-Th 8-11, F 8-5, Sa 10-5, Su noon-11.

Plaza De La Raza

3540 N. Mission Rd., Los Angeles, CA 90031; (212) 223-2475. Hispanic cultural and educational art center maintains gallery and collection of Mexican Folk Art. Some restrictions. Accepts phone inquiries. No fee. Hours: 8:30-6.

Portuguese Historical and Cultural Society

P.O. Box 161990, Sacramento, CA 95831; (916) 392-1048. Preserves and promotes Portuguese culture and history in Northern CA region in form of library and archival collections. Holdings include library with materials on Azorean history, culture, and customs from 1600; small collection of historical manuscripts; photos and genealogical records of Portuguese families in Sacramento, CA area. Accepts phone inquiries. No fee. Hours: call.

Presidio Army Museum

Bldg. 2, Presidio of San Francisco, San Francisco, CA 94129; (415) 561-4115. Preserves Presidio of San Francisco history from Spanish era to Vietnam War. Museum housed in former Old Station hospital. Holdings include library, archives, maps; photo collection spans Army movement to western frontier, Spanish American War, Philippine Insurrection, fire and earthquake of 1906, and more recent San Francisco events; extensive oral history collection. Accepts phone inquiries. No fee. Hours: Tu-Sa 10-4.

Railway and Locomotics Historical Society

Pacific Coast Chapter, c/o McMorris M. Dow,

430 Melrose St., San Francisco, CA 94127; (415) 587-5163. Studies and compiles railroad history and equip, and operates Cable Car museum. Museum exhibits include 3 historic cable cars, tools, grips, braking mechanisms, paintings, photos, video, and records. Accepts phone inquiries. Membership fee. Hours: call.

Ralph Milliken Museum Society

P.O. Box 868, Los Banos, CA 93635; (209) 826-4079. Preserves Ralph Milliken's manuscripts, and Pioneer-era historical items in form of museum, library, and archival collections. Holdings include Ralph Milliken Museum; small library with local and American history publications; archives of Indian artifacts, 19th-20th c; manuscripts relating to Pioneer families, Miller and Lux files, and agricultural development; local and military historical maps and surveys; photos and posters of local historical events; small collections of oral history recordings; military posters; phonographs, records of 1920s. Does not accept phone inquiries. Donations accepted. Hours: Th 9-3, Sa-Su 11-3.

Ramona Pioneer Historical Society

Guy B. Woodward Museum, P.O. Box 625, 645 Main St., Ramona, CA 92065; (619) 789-7644. Collects and preserves materials relating to history of CA, San Diego county, and Ramona. Holdings include small collection of Ramona govt, school, and cemetery records; regional maps; photos of Ramona residents from early 20th c; oral histories from residents who served in Civil War; and memorabilia relating to Ramona settlers. Accepts phone inquiries. Fee. Hours: Th-Su 1-4.

Rancho Los Alamitos
Historic Site and Gardens

6400 Bixby Hill Rd., Long Beach, CA 90815; (213) 431-3541. Preserves the home and grounds of this historic S. CA ranch, its grounds, and its residents. Some archival material and film footage of ranch operation and social events from early 20th c. Materials non-circulating. Accepts phone inquiries. No fee. Hours: W-Su 1-5.

Rancho Los Cerritos

City of Long Beach, 4600 Virginia Rd., Long Beach, CA 90807; (213) 424-9423. Preserves

and interprets history of 19th c adobe structure and the lifestyle and economy in rural California of the time. Museum, archives, photos relating to home emphasize lives of regional sheep ranchers in 1870s; research library of CA and S. CA history; oral histories from Long Beach residents; Sarah Bixby Smith manuscript collection. Accepts phone inquiries. No fee. Hours: W-Su 1-5.

Redwood City Public Library

881 Jefferson Ave., Redwood City, CA 94063; (415) 369-3738. Public library and selective US govt depository. Archives hold materials, maps, and photos on Redwood City and CA history. Accepts phone inquiries. No fee. Hours: M-Th 10-9, F-Sa 10-5, Su 1-4.

Robert Louis Stevenson House

California Dept. of Parks & Recreation, 525 Polk St., Monterey, CA 93940; (408) 649-7118. Restored house in which Robert Louis Stevenson stayed while in Monterey. Several rooms devoted to Stevenson memorabilia. Accepts phone inquiries. Fee. Hours: Mar-Oct, 10-5; Nov-Apr, 10-4.

Rosemead Library

8800 Valley Blvd., Rosemead, CA 91770; (818) 573-5220. Provides reference resources on CA and Southern CA. Library contains large collection on CA culture with emphasis on Gold Rush period. Other holdings include CA census materials from 1850-1910 and LA city directories from 1887-1942. Materials non-circulating. Accepts phone inquiries. No fee, Hours: M-Th 10-9, F-Sa 10-6, Su 1-5.

Roy Rogers and Dale Evans Museum

15650 Seneca Rd., Victorville, CA 92392; (619) 243-4547. Preserves artifacts from lives of Rogers and Evans, including collection of costumes, saddles, trophies, awards, honors, guns, and religious books and records. Accepts phone inquiries. Fee. Hours: 9-5.

Sacramento History Center

Museum & History Division, Dept. of Parks & Community Services, 1930 J St., Sacramento, CA 95814; (916) 449-2057. Preserves Sacramento area history with holdings in museum and archives. Museum exhibits chronicle city's development through Native Age, Age of Colonization, and Gold Rush through Age of Modernization; details region's agricultural developments; and displays artifacts, newspapers, cartography, printing, and theatre memorabilia from Gold Rush period. Archives hold city and county records, business records, private manuscripts from 1850s, various maps, historic photos, KCRA daily news film from 1950s-70, and local genealogy materials. Accepts phone inquiries. Fee. Hours: museum, 10-5; archives, M-F 8:30-noon.

Sacramento Public Library

Central Library, 828 I St., Sacramento, CA 95814; (916) 449-5203. General public library collecting US depository documents since 1880; holds some CA documents; comprehensive Sacramento city and county documents. Accepts phone inquiries. No fee. Hours: M, W 9-6, Tu, Th 9-9, F 1-5, Sa 9-5.

Saint Mary's College Library

Moraga, CA 94575. Academic research library holds collection of materials on history of US West, including small library, clipping files, and correspondence.

Salvation Army
Western Territorial Museum

30840 Hawthorne Blvd., Rancho Palos Verdes, CA 90274; (213) 541-4721. Preserves and displays archival material of Salvation Army work in western states. Primary holdings include an extensive photo collection, and audio recordings of Salvation Army speeches, bands, and songs. Accepts phone inquiries. No fee. Hours: M-F 8:15-4:15.

San Clemente Historical Society

Conference of California Historical Societies, P.O. Box 283, 2501 S. El Camino Real, Unit 312, San Clemente, CA 92672; (714) 492-3142. Preserves and collects early San Clemente historic artifacts, including memorabilia of Richard Nixon's 11-year residency. Museum holdings include newspapers, maps, aerial and historic photos, film on San Clemente from 1925-30, and oral history interviews with regional settlers. Accepts phone inquiries. No fee. Hours: 9-4.

San Diego Aerospace Museum

2001 Pan American Plaza, Balboa Park, San Diego, CA 92101; (619) 234-8291. Promotes study of aviation and space history with museum exhibits and research library. Holdings include approx 60 aircraft, archive of aerospace history and technical material, manuscripts by CA aviation personalities, aeronautical charts, films and videos, and oral history recordings. Special Ryan aeronautical library; aviation history in China and Mexico; info on Air Mail pioneers; and military aircraft development and operations. Accepts phone inquiries. Fee. Hours: 10-4.

San Diego County Law Library

Documents Division, 1105 Front St., San Diego, CA 92101; (619) 531-3900. Provides legal info and services to San Diego legal community. Library holdings focus on CA law and courts, and US Supreme Court arguments. In-house use only. Accepts phone inquiries. Fee. Hours: M-Th 8-9, F 8-5, Sa 10-5.

San Diego Historical Society
Research Archives

Box 81825, 1649 El Prado, Balboa Park, San Diego, CA 92101; (619) 232-6203. Collects and interprets objects, documents, photos, and literary and artistic works illustrating San Diego history. Photo collection contains over one million images photographed by professional photographers from 1869 of San Diego, Baja CA, and Southwest Indians. Other holdings include newspaper negatives, and photos of Native Americans. Also has limited films/videotapes. Fee for non-members. Hours: W-Sa 10-4.

San Diego Maritime Museum

1306 N. Harbor Drive, San Diego, CA 92101; (619) 234-9153. Museum housed aboard three 19th c ships that exhibit maritime history. Substantial research library covers subjects from Revolutionary War era and holds large photo collection; archival ship and boat plans; MacMullen and Brown manuscripts; maps; and collection of Kingsbury Passenger Liner brochures. Accepts phone inquiries. Fee. Hours: museum, 9-8; library, M-Th 9-4; research by appt.

San Diego Public Library

820 E St., San Diego, CA 92101; (619) 236-

5800. Public library maintains selective collection of govt documents, historical materials, and special collections. Holdings include USGS topographic maps of Western US, and US city and state maps; regional photos, including Edward S. Curtis folios of North American Indians; oral history tapes; genealogical materials, including CA Census records, biography files, and Kelly family papers; local records, directories, postcards, and ephemera; San Diego newspaper files; collections relating to dime novels, CA minorities, mining, and shipping, and the World Wars. Some restrictions. Accepts phone inquiries. No fee. Hours: M-Th 10-9, F-Sa 9:30-5:30.

San Diego State University

Malcolm Love Library, San Diego, CA 92182; (619) 265-5832. Academic research library has collection of Civil War memorabilia. Holdings include documents, letters, maps, drawings, pictures, soldiers' scrapbooks, Confederate money, newspapers, and sheet music from 1811-69. Desi Arnaz collection of film and TV production materials includes films, videotapes, outtakes, scripts, and correspondence. Library also maintains collections of sheet music from 1817 and silent film sheet music. Materials non-circulating. Accepts phone inquiries. No fee. Hours: call.

San Fernando Historical Mission

Archival Center, 15151 San Fernando Mission Blvd., Mission Hills, CA 91345; (818) 365-1501. Collects and preserves CA Catholic heritage by maintaining archive and library. Holdings include documents, diaries, manuscripts, brochures, small photo collection, and books on CA and American Catholics. Use restricted to qualified researchers. Accepts phone inquiries. No fee. Hours: 8:30-4:40.

San Francisco Academy of Comic Art

Library, 2850 Ulloa, San Francisco, CA 94116; (415) 681-1737. Maintains large collection of pulp magazines, major US newspapers, and Hearst papers. Holdings include films/videotapes, books, magazines, posters, 19th-20th children's books, extensive collection of comic strips, many comic books, mystery books, and science fiction books and pulp magazines. Accepts phone inquiries. Hours: call.

San Francisco African American Historical Society

Fort Mason Center, Bldg. C165, San Francisco, CA 94123; (415) 441-0640. Provides museum, art and library on history and culture of black Californians with focus on Bay Area and northern CA. Museum exhibits African and Afro-American artifacts from early 1800s. Library has research materials on contemporary Black Californians and Africans and Afro-Americans from other parts of world. Archives contains works of Sargent Johnson and blacks of West, manuscripts, maps, photos, films/videotapes, and recordings. Special collection of materials from Mary Ellen Pleasant. Accepts phone inquiries. Donations accepted. Hours: Tu-Sa noon-5.

San Francisco Architectural Heritage Foundation

2007 Franklin St., San Francisco, CA 94109; (415) 441-3000. Protects and preserves San Francisco architecture and history through holdings in museum, library, and archives. Haas-Lilienthal House museum reflects family residence from 1886-1972; library concentrates on area architectural and historic preservation; archival material of building-by-building downtown San Francisco architectural survey; some Sanborn Fire Insurance maps dating from 1880s. Material use restricted. Accepts phone inquiries. Fee. Hours: 9-5.

San Francisco Chronicle

901 Mission St., San Francisco, CA 94119; (415) 777-1111. Houses paper's clipping files from 1906-84. Library not open to public. Accepts phone inquiries. Hours: W-F 10-1, 2-5.

San Francisco Fire Department Museum

St. Francis Hook and Ladder Society, 260 Golden Gate Ave., Presidio Ave between Pine & Bush Sts., San Francisco, CA 94102; (415) 861-8000, ext. 365. Collects apparatus, artifacts, and memorabilia of San Francisco Fire Dept from 1849. Holds some photos and genealogical records. Accepts phone inquiries. No fee. Hours: by appt for photo and genealogy use; Th-Su 1-4.

San Joaquin County Historical Museum

P.O. Box 21, 11793 N. Micke Grove Rd., Lodi, CA 95241; (209) 334-6561. Preserves and interprets local history, with emphasis on agriculture. Museum and library house items of local interest; archives hold records of agriculture, county govt, and education from 19th c; maps of Delta Reclamation in 20th c; regional photo collection; county oral history collection; registry of county marriages from 19th c; special collection of tractor manuals and exhibits. Accepts phone inquiries. Parking fee. Hours: W-Su 1-5.

San Jose Historical Museum

San Jose Parks & Recreation Dept., 635 Phelan Ave., San Jose, CA 95112; (408) 287-2290. Documents history of San Jose and Santa Clara valley with archival materials, manuscripts, maps, photos, collection of Bulmore materials from Almaden Quicksilver mines, newspapers from 1880s-1940s, and other ephemera. Materials for in-house use only. Accepts phone inquiries. Fee. Hours: W 1-4; Sa 1-4; or by appt.

San Jose Museum of Art

110 S. Market St., San Jose, CA 95113; (408) 294-2787. Collects, presents, and interprets visual arts, with focus on 20th c American arts. Museum exhibits reflect mission statement; library holdings include periodicals and slides. Accepts phone inquiries. No fee. Hours: Tu-F 10-6, Sa 10-4, Su 10-4, Su noon-4.

San Luis Obispo County Historical Museum

San Luis Obispo County Historical Society, Box 1391, 696 Monterey St., San Luis Obispo, CA 93406; (805) 543-0638. Collects, preserves, and exhibits local history. Holdings of museum, library, and archives document govt, school, and business activity. Accepts phone inquiries. No fee. Hours: by appt only, W-Su 10-4.

Santa Barbara Historical Society

P.O. Box 578, Santa Barbara, CA 93102; (805) 966-1601. (Street address: 136 E. De la Guerra St., Santa Barbara, CA 93101) Preserves and documents Santa Barbara history through mu-seum and library holdings. Collections dating from 1782 are paintings, costumes, and ranching memorabilia; extensive photos of Santa Barbara area and surrounding cities; oral histories of Santa Barbara residents; and collection of family records from 1850-1954. Materials non-circulating. Accepts phone inquiries. No fee. Hours: museum; Tu-F 12-5, Sa-Su 1-5; library; Tu-F 12-4.

Santa Barbara Trust for Historic Preservation

P.O. Box 388, 123 E. Canon Perdido St., Santa Barbara, CA 93102; (805) 966-9719. Reconstructed and restored Spanish colonial fortress and home of city of Santa Barbara. Library and archives house materials exploring Spanish colonial and Mexican history in Southwest. Collections include maps and photos depicting early Santa Barbara, and reconstruction of Presidio. Accepts phone inquiries. No fee. Hours: M-F 9-4:30, Sa-Su noon-4.

Santa Clara University

Govt. Documents, Orradre Library, Santa Clara, CA 95053; (408) 554-5436. Depository library collecting federal documents from 1964 and CA documents from 1952. Restrictions on use. Accepts phone inquiries. Hours: M-F 8-5, Th 6-10.

Schonberg Hall Music Library

University of California, Los Angeles, CA 90024; (213) 825-4881. Holds special collection of popular music collections. Works by George Antheil, Hugo Davise, Walter Lantz, Harry Lubin, Henry Mancini, Alex North, Eugene Zador, Ed Powell, Andre Previn, and Mortimer Wilson represented. Other collections include Roth Library of American Theater Music, Meredith Wilson Library of Popular Sheet Music, and Library of American Motion Picture Music. Accepts phone inquiries. No fee. Hours: call.

Seaver Center for Western History Research

Natural History Museum of Los Angeles County, 900 Exposition Blvd., Los Angeles, CA 90007; (213) 744-3359. Preserves history of S. CA through museum and library collections. Holdings include several thousand maps relating west coast history, large photo collection on S. CA and Southwest from 1880-1940, and limited manuscript materials. Accepts phone inquiries. No fee. Hours: Tu-F 1-4.

Sierra Historic Sites Association

P.O. Box 451, 497777 Road 427, Oakhurst, CA 93644; (209) 683-6570. Collects, preserves, and promotes history of Eastern Madera County, CA, with emphasis on the Fresno Flats area and residents in form of museum, library, and archival collections. Holdings include artifacts from Fresno Flats, 1860-1830; research library with local historical materials; archives with books, newspapers, court records, and other local historical materials; journals of an early settler, 1861-1901, with info on weather, crops, and other settlers; local maps; photos and genealogical records of early families; oral history recordings. Accepts phone inquiries. Fee. Hours: Tu-Sa 1-3, Su 1-4.

Silverado Museum

Box 409, 1490 Library Lane, St. Helena, CA 94574; (707) 963-3757. Preserves works and memorabilia of Robert Louis Stevenson through large collection of manuscripts, letters, photographs, paintings, sculptures, and first and variant editions of the author's works. Materials non-circulating. Accepts phone inquiries. No fee. Hours: Tu-Su 12-4.

Social Sciences Collection

University of California, University Research Library, 405 Hilgard Ave., Los Angeles, CA 90024; (213) 825-6414. Describes and preserves materials on history of women and literature by women from 1920, and materials on Japanese Americans. Japanese American Research project collection made up of oral histories, personal papers of families, war relocation and camp internment, and materials on Japanese social, cultural, and economic orgs. Women's literature project has pamphlets, periodicals, manuscripts, and photos. Accepts phone inquiries. No fee. Hours: call.

Society of California Pioneers

456 McAllister St., San Francisco, CA 94102; (415) 861-5278. Preserves and promotes 19th c

history and culture of CA in form of art gallery, library, and children's CA history gallery. Holdings include collections and displays of 19th c CA paintings and artifacts; research and reference library; archives, manuscripts, maps, and photos, pre-1850-1880; films/videotapes of early CA history, including construction of the Golden Gate Bridge. No fee. Hours: M-F 10-4.

Sonoma County Library

Third & E Sts., Santa Rosa, CA 95404; (707) 545-0831. Public library collects material documenting history of Sonoma County and Santa Rosa from 1850. Holdings include maps, photos, and genealogical records for area. Special collections on wine and Luther Burbank. Hours: call.

Southern California Library
for Social Studies & Research

6120 South Vermont Ave., Los Angeles, CA 90044; (213) 759-6063. Documents labor history, particularly activities of social movements, minorities and leftist groups, in S. CA. Large library on political and social activism history; records of Bridges Deportation case, Civil Rights Congress, American Committee for Protection of Foreign Born; small photo collection of Los Angeles black community history, anti-Vietnam War demonstrations, and labor demonstrations; documentary labor films from 1930-70; large labor rally recording collection from 1950, with speeches by Martin Luther King, Jr., and Cesar Chavez. Materials non-circulating. Accepts phone inquiries. No fee. Hours: Tu-Sa 10-4.

Southwest Museum

Box 128, 234 Museum Dr., Los Angeles, CA 90042; (213) 221-2163. Collects and preserves materials relating CA, Native American, Hispanic, and American West history. Museum holds art and artifacts; extensive library and archival materials support historical and anthropological research of West; maps, photos, and audio recordings provide historical documentation. Accepts phone inquiries (213-221-2164). Fee. Hours: by appt; Tu-Sa 11-5, Su 1-5.

Southwestern University

Document Depository, School of Law Library, 675 South Westmoreland Ave., Los Angeles, CA

Howard Hughes in the cockpit of the Spruce Goose before its first and only flight, from the Spruce Goose-Howard Hughes Flying Boat, Wrather Port Properties.

90005; (213) 738-6725. Provides materials for academic study and research at Southwestern by housing US Govt document collection since 1975. Accepts phone inquiries. No fee. Hours: M-F 9-5, and irregular additional hours on eves and Sa-Su.

Spruce Goose—Howard Hughes Flying Boat

Wrather Port Properties, Ltd., P.O. Box 8, Long Beach, CA 90801; (213) 435-3511. Center facilitates aviation research, emphasizing Spruce Goose and other Hughes aircraft and advances.

Museum exhibits Spruce Goose, and Howard Hughes' aviation, motion picture and personal history; small library; archives of Hughes memorabilia; large collection of photos from Summa Corporation archives; videotapes; and several oral histories from Hughes Aircraft employees. Approval of some material use through Summa Corp. Accepts phone inquiries. Fee. Hours: attractions, winter 10-6, summer 9-9; exhibits, M-Sa 9-5.

Stagecoach Inn Museum

Conejo Valley Historical Society, P.O. Box 1692,

Thousand Oaks, CA 91360; (213) 590-6944. (mailing address: 51 S. Ventu Pk. Rd., Newbury Park, CA 91320). Preserves 20th c stagecoaches, and pioneer and Chumash Indian memorabilia. Collections include photo documentation of local Chumash Indian pictographs and Conejo pioneer oral history tapes. Accepts phone inquiries. Fee. Hours: library by appt; museum, W, Th, F, Su 1-4.

Supreme Court of California Library

State Building Annex, Room 4241, 455 Golden Gate Ave., San Francisco, CA 94102; (415) 557-1922. Collections provide legal research material for CA Supreme Court and staffs. Hours: 9-5.

Surveyors' Historical Society

P.O. Box 160502, Sacramento, CA 95816; (916) 445-5086. Preserves survey notes, instruments, records, and artifacts. Hours: call.

Telephone Museum

1145 Larkin St., San Francisco, CA 94109; (415) 441-3918. Preserves and exhibits telephone industry artifacts and archival materials in museum, library, and archival collections. Museum exhibits include telephones, cable switchboards, and mechanical and solid state switching equip; library holds books, pamphlets, trade journals, and telephone books; archives house Pacific Telephone presidents' files, and annual reports of AT&T, Pacific Telephone and Telegraph, and new Baby Bells. Some manuscripts, maps, and films/videotapes. Large photo collection with emphasis on CA, OR, WA, NV. Accepts brief phone inquiries. No fee. Hours: M-Th 9-3:30.

Theatre Arts Library

University of California, Los Angeles, CA 90024; (213) 825-4880. Maintains collections of reference materials on film, radio, and TV industries. Contains many photos and clippings from 1930-60; early film posters, programs, and ad campaign materials from 1915; large collection of scripts from Fox, 20th Century Fox, and MGM; extensive oral history collection; donations from Tony Barret, Walt Disney, Preston Sturges, and Haskell Wexler; film festival collection; art direction collection; music cue sheets from early silent

films; and extensive file of film subjects from 1920 to present. Accepts phone inquiries. No fee. Hours: call.

Theatre Historical Society of America

P.O. Box 767, San Francisco, CA 94101; (415) 983-8688. Records popular culture history of movie, vaudeville, and opera theaters through preservation of theater design and architectural heritage. Collections donated by Loew's Theatre, Ben Hall, Terry Helgesen, Bill Peterson, Bill Clifford, and Chicago Architectural Photographing Company. Holdings include photos, memorabilia, scrapbooks, sketches, blueprints, and negatives of theaters and their decoration and function. Hours: call.

Treasure Island Museum

Building No. 1, Treasure Island, San Francisco, CA 94130; (415) 765-6182. Preserves and interprets history of Navy, Marine Corps, and Coast Guard in Pacific, as well as history of Treasure Island. Holdings include exhibits, photos and films/videotapes on China Clipper flying boats, and military services in Pacific from 1813; small library on Treasure Island history; memorabilia, blueprints and photos from 1939-40 Golden Gate International Exposition. Accepts phone inquiries. No fee. Hours: museum, 10-3:30; library, Tu-Sa, 10-3:30.

University Art Museum

University of California, 2625 Durant Ave, Berkeley, CA 94720; (415) 642-1207. Museum maintains and exhibits extensive collection of art, with strengths in post-WWII contemporary works. Holdings include the Pacific Film Archives, an extensive collection of film prints for use by students, scholars, and filmmakers. Accepts phone inquiries. Fee. Hours: W-Su 11-5.

University of California, Davis

Special Collections, Shields Library, Davis, CA 95616; (916) 752-1624. Academic research library has special Contemporary Issues Collection with materials on political and social reform movements from 1960s. Materials cover African Peoples Socialist Party, Ku Klux Klan, Oystershell Alliance, B'nai Brith, and others. Accepts phone inquiries. No fee. Hours: call.

University of California, Los Angeles

Special Collections Dept., University Research Library, 405 Hilgard Ave., Los Angeles, CA 90024; (213) 825-6414. Preserves morgue of "Los Angeles Daily News" complete with clippings, research files, negatives, and prints; large photo morgue from "Los Angeles Times;" special collections on Lionel Barrymore, Tony Curtis, Jack Benny, Eddie Cantor, John Houseman, Ernie Kovacs, Stanley Kramer, Charles Laughton, Rod Serling, and King Vidor; early animated pictures; Johnson Negro film collection; and materials on Hollywood Studio Strike. Accepts phone inquiries. Hours: call.

University of California, Riverside

P.O. Box 5900, 4045 Canyon Crest Dr., Riverside, CA 92517; (714) 787-3714. Academic research library maintains collection of science fiction materials dating from 16th-17th c to present. Holdings include many pulp magazines, Gothic fiction, science fiction films/videotapes, shooting scripts, and author collections from Jules Verne, HG Wells, Edgar Rice Burroughs, and Philip Dick. Hours: call.

University of California, Santa Barbara

Arts Library, Music Library, Santa Barbara, CA 93106; (805) 961-3261. Music library holds extensive collection of works by Bernard Herrmann, including scores from Hitchcock films and operatic works. Accepts phone inquiries. No fee. Hours: call.

University of California, Santa Barbara

Dept. of Special Collections, Library, Santa Barbara, CA 93106; (805) 961-2477. Academic research library has collection of materials on US Civil War, Abraham Lincoln, slavery, abolition, and movement Westward. Accepts phone inquiries. No fee. Hours: call.

University of California, Santa Barbara

Map and Imagery Division, Library, Santa Barbara, CA 93106; (805) 961-2477. Academic research library holds large collection of maps, relief models, and atlases for period 1975-80. Holdings include Landsat images, aerial photos, and large collection of reference materials. Accepts phone inquiries. No fee. Hours: call.

Urban Archives Center

California State University, Northridge, South Library, Rm. 205, Northridge, CA 91330; (818) 885-2487. Collects and preserves the papers of Los Angeles County, CA voluntary assns and personalities. Holdings include archival materials from area Chambers of Commerce; Education, Ethnic, Labor, Political, and Women's History collections of materials from county's activist groups and voluntary assns from 1900; Los Angeles City Historical Society Photographic Collection, and other local photos; records of local Motion Picture Screen Cartoonists Guild, LA Typographical Union, and others; special collections on the Watts riots, and other local historical events. Some restrictions. Accepts phone inquiries. No fee. Hours: M-F 9-4:30, W 9-9, Sa 9-4.

Walt Disney Archives

The Walt Disney Company, 500 S. Buena Vista, Burbank, CA 91521; (818) 840-5424. Collects and preserves Disney archival material, with emphasis on Walt Disney, Disney films, Disneyland, and Disney World. Accepts phone inquiries. No fee. Hours: by appt only; M-F 8-5.

Weaverville Joss House State Historic Park

California State Park System, Drawer 217, Corner of Oregon & Main Sts., Weaverville, CA 96093; (916) 623-5284. Protects, maintains, and interprets the only active Chinese temple built during the CA Gold Rush. Accepts phone inquiries. Fee. Hours: 10-5; Nov, Th-M 10-5.

West Covina Regional Library

1601 W. Covina Pkwy., West Covina, CA 91790; (818) 962-3541. Public library maintains selective collection of govt documents, general and historical materials relevant to needs of community. Holdings include volumes of Presidential papers, public laws, federal and CA bills and laws; current maps and historical atlases; US govt posters; immigration passenger lists, 1870-1910; census materials. Accepts brief phone inquiries.

No fee. Hours: M-Th 10-9, F-Sa 9-5, Su 1-5.

Western America Skisport Museum

P.O. Box 38, Soda Springs, CA 95728; (916) 426-3313. Preserves history of skiing in region. Museum displays early skis produced during Gold Rush era, costumes, trophies, memorabilia from western skiing greats, and videotapes of skiing events. Accepts phone inquiries. No fee. Hours: winter, Tu-F noon-4, Sa-Su 11-5; summer, same but closed Tu.

Western Jewish History Center

Judah L. Magnes Museum, 2911 Russell St., Berkeley, CA 94705; (415) 849-2710. Collects, preserves, and maintains collections of research materials on Jewish people and their culture and contributions in the Western US in form of library, and archival collections. Holdings include library collection of publications and theses from 1849; extensive archival collections of maps, manuscripts, and papers from 1849, with emphasis on CA area; collections of photos and oral history materials; genealogical records; archives of Judah L. Magnes, David Lubin, Rosalie Meyer Stern, and San Francisco area Jewish orgs and synagogues. Materials are non-circulating. Accepts phone inquiries. Some research fees. Hours: M-Th, noon-4.

Western Railway Museum

P.O. Box 3694, 5848 State Hwy. No. 12, San Francisco, CA 94119; (415) 534-0071. Preserves historic railroad info and memorabilia. Holdings include library; archival material in form of reports, correspondence, blueprints of CA railroads; and photo and negative files of railroad photos. Restrictions on use. Accepts phone inquiries. No fee. Hours: by appt.

Whittier College

Special Collections, Wardman Library, 13406 E. Philadelphia St., Whittier, CA 90608; (213) 693-0771. Academic research library holds special collection of aerial CA photos from 1927-63. Photos were from some of earliest flights over Los Angeles and CA area. Accepts phone inquiries. No fee. Hours: call.

William S. Hart Park and Museum

24151 N. San Fernando Rd., Newhall, CA 91321

(805) 254-4585. Park and museum preserves history of life and times of silent film star William S. Hart in the form of his retirement home and estate grounds. Holdings include Hart's home, furnished with his personal belongings, including Indian beadwork, Navajo rugs, and western paintings; archival collections, including manuscripts, personal papers, scripts, and photos (location: Seaver Center for Western History Research, Los Angeles County Museum of Natural History, 900 Exposition Blvd, Los Angeles, CA 90007; 213-744-3359). Research by appt only. Accepts phone inquiries. No fee. Museum hours: winter, W-F 10-1, Sa-Su 11-4; summer, W-Su 11-4.

Women's Heritage Museum

1509 Portola Ave., Palo Alto, CA 94306; (415) 321-5260. Promotes public education in women's history with occasional tours of Spanish-Mexican early CA house. Borrows state exhibits periodically. Accepts phone inquiries. House open only sporadically. Hours: call.

Women's History Research Center

2325 Oak St., Berkeley, CA 94708. Holds informational materials on issues related to women, including changing sex roles, biology, mental and physical health, women and life cycles, birth and population control, sex and sexuality, and the experience of black and Third World women. All materials on microfilm. Hours: write for permission and availability.

Workman and Temple Family Homestead Museum

15415 E. Don Julian Rd., City of Industry, CA 91744; (818) 968-8492. Studies, preserves, interprets social history and material culture of southern CA during 1840s, 1870s, and 1920s. Site composed of mid-19th c Workman house and 1920s Temple residence. Library collects materials on regional life and architecture. Archives hold research materials on family histories and periods covered in museum, photos documenting Workman and Temple families, and preserving history of site restoration. Oral history interview collection. Some restrictions. Accepts phone inquiries. No fee. Hours: M-F 9-5.

Colorado

Air Force Academy

Academy Library, DFSEL-D, Colorado Springs, CO 80840; (303) 472-4774. Academy library maintains selective collection of US govt documents and other references relevant to Academy curriculum and needs of students and researchers. Holdings include archives of Academy history and operations from 1954; large collections of manuscripts; Col R. Gimbel Aeronautics History Collection of artifacts and materials dating back to 2700 BC. On-site use for non-Academy researchers. Accepts phone inquiries. No fee. Hours: M-Th 7:15-11, F 7:15-5, Su 2-11.

Aurora History Museum

City of Aurora, 1633 Florence St., Aurora, CO 80010; (303) 360-8545. Collects, preserves, and interprets artifact and documentary collections concerning Aurora from 19th c. Library and archives hold Aurora newspapers and photos, political papers, local planning maps, and city files; photos of landmarks, local figures; papers of Paul Beck, Hilbert Meyer, and William Smith; and Drapela Aviation collection. Materials non-circulating. Accepts phone inquiries. No fee. Hours: Tu-F 9-4, Sa by appt.

Buffalo Bill Memorial Museum

Rte. 5, Box 950, 987 Lookout Mountain Rd., Golden, CO 80401; (303) 526-0744 or 0747. Presents history of Buffalo Bill Cody, West, and Wild West Cody Exhibition through art and artifacts. Museum, library, and archives contain manuscripts, maps, photos, films/videotapes, and extensive collection of posters. Fee. Hours: Nov-Apr, 9-4; May-Oct, 9-5.

Clear Creek Historic Mining and Milling Museum

P.O. Box 1498, Idaho Springs, CO 80452; (303) 567-2421 (winter: 567-2354). Preserves history of local mine and mill industries from 1800 in the form of machinery and equipment, mining and regional maps, and photos of CO mines. Accepts phone inquiries. Fee. Hours: 9-4.

Colorado College

Tutt Library, 1021 North Cascade Ave., Colorado Springs, CO 80903; (303) 473-2233. College library maintains selective collection of US govt documents and literature of American West and Southwest relevant to needs of students and community. Holdings include Congressional publications from 1789 and Smithsonian Institution publications from 1846. Accepts phone inquiries (ext 2662). No fee. Hours: 9-5.

Colorado Division of State Archives and Public Records

1313 Sherman St., Rm 1B-20, Denver, CO 80203; (303) 866-2055. Office stores permanent historical public records of CO. Holdings include public records from 1859; photos; selected marriage and divorce records. Does not accept phone inquiries. Some repro and search fees. Hours: 8-4:45.

Colorado Genealogical Society

P.O. Box 9671, Denver, CO 80209. Provides genealogical info and support materials, holds regular meeting and sponsors activities, and publishes regularly. All materials housed at Denver Public Library Genealogy Division. Fee for membership; meetings free.

Colorado Historical Society

1300 Broadway, Denver, CO 80203; (303) 866-2305. Preserves and interprets historical documents and material concerning CO history, and makes them available to public. Museum documents CO heritage, including Indian culture, Gold Rush era, mining, and railroads. Library focuses on CO and Western history, and holds large collection of manuscripts from well known Coloradoans Gov John Evans, H.A.W. Tabor, and Charles Boettcher; many maps of CO and West; extremely large collection of photos, all west of MI River; extensive newsfilm relating to historic state events; strong oral history collection; and special collections on cattle industry. Accepts phone inquiries. No fee. Hours: Tu-Sa 10-4:30.

Colorado Railroad Museum

P.O. Box 10, Golden, CO 80402; (303) 279-4591. Preserves and displays history of CO railroad development and industry in form of museum exhibits, library, and archival collections.

Soldiers of Tenth Mountain Infantry Division, from the Colorado Ski Museum exhibit on skiing soldiers.

Holdings include CO railroad artifacts and equipment, primarily of former narrow gauge lines; restored/preserved locomotives, cars, and trolleys; reference library and archives with publications, railroad co-operating papers, and ephemera; extensive collections of railroad maps and photos; films/videotapes; recordings of railroad sounds; collection of day-to-day operating records of Rio Grande Southern Railroad, 1890-1951. Materials are non-circulating. Accepts phone inquiries. Fee for museum. Hours: 9-5.

Colorado School of Mines

Library, 14th & Illinois, Golden, CO 80401; (303) 273-3697. School library maintains museum, library, and archival collections relating to study and history of mines and mining work and technology. Holdings include exhibits with emphasis on mineral and fossil specimens; library collection of materials on engineering and geology; archives with collections on history of school, school publications, and photos; historical manuscripts relating to mining and mineral resources in the Western US, late 1800s-early 1900s; extensive collection of geologic and topographic maps; films/videotapes of school events; paintings by Arthur Lake. Some restrictions. Accepts phone inquiries. No fee. Hours: M-F 7:30-5.

Colorado Ski Museum

Ski Hall of Fame, P.O. Box 1976, 15 Vail Rd., Vail, CO 81658; (303) 476-1876. Preserves and interprets history of skiing in CO in the form of Hall of Fame and displays. Holdings include historic equipment, presidential artifacts, ski fashions; 10th Mountain Division artifact collection; library, photos, films/videotapes; audio ski histories. Accepts phone inquiries. No fee. Tu-Sun noon-5. Hours: call.

Colorado Springs
Fine Arts Center Library

30 W. Dale St., Colorado Springs, CO 80903; (303) 634-5581. Museum reference library with holdings on American visual arts from 1800s; collections on art and anthropology of Indians of the Southwest and Mexico; folk art of Mexico and Central America; museum archives of The Broadmoor Art Academy 1919-1935 and Colorado Springs Fine Arts Center from 1936. Circulation to members, local univ students and faculty only. Accepts phone inquiries (ext 327). Fee for museum only for non-members. Hours: Tu-Sa 9-5.

Colorado State University

Library, Fort Collins, CO 80523; (303) 491-1881. Academic library maintains selective collection of govt documents, general, reference, and historical materials relevant to needs of the school and students. Holdings include university archives; literary manuscripts of L. Niel Smith, William Ehrhart, and local history manuscripts; geologic, topographic, national park and forest maps; Rare Books Collection; Germans from Russia Collection; Imaginary Wars Collection; Vietnam War Literature Collection. Accepts phone inquiries. No fee. Hours: 8-10 .

Colorado Supreme Court Library

B-112 State Judicial Bldg., 2 E. 14th Ave., Denver, CO 80203; (303) 861-1111. State law library maintains large collection of state and federal legal reports, treatises, and all US state and federal statutes. Accepts phone inquiries (ext 172). No fee. Hours: M-F 8-5:30.

Engineering and Research Center

US Bureau of Reclamation, Denver Federal Center, D-823, P.O. Box 25007, Denver, CO 80225; (303) 236-6963. Houses current and archival materials on US water resources, hydrology, dam construction and safety, reclamation project histories and specifications from 1910, and Dolores archaeological project. Accepts phone inquiries. No fee. Hours: 7:30-4.

Fort Vasquez Visitor Center

P.O. Box 728, 13412 Hwy 85, Platteville, CO 80651; (303) 785-2832. Fur trade museum preserves reconstructed remains of fort. Some genealogical records. Accepts phone inquiries. Fee. Hours: winter, 9-3; summer, 10-5.

Four Mile Historic Park

715 South Forest St., Denver, CO 80222; (303) 399-1859. Oldest house and working farm in Denver commemorates history as tavern and stagecoach, and houses small library on history of Denver. Restrictions on use. Accepts phone inquiries. Fee. Hours: Tu-Su 11-5.

Frontier Historical Society
and Museum

1001 Colorado Ave., Glenwood Springs, CO 81601; (303) 945-4448. Preserves history of Glenwood Springs and Garfield county area. Museum displays cover Ute Indians, Victorian Health Spa, polo, and coal mining. Archival holdings include maps, photos, films/videotapes, oral history recordings, and genealogical records. Accepts phone inquiries. Fee. Hours: winter, Tu-Sa noon-4:30; Summer, M-Sa noon-4:30.

Golden Library

923 Tenth St., Golden, CO 80401; (303) 279-4585. Preserves and documents history of Jefferson county region and state of CO through holdings in library and archives. Collections include civic records, maps, photos from early 20th c, census records, newpapers, law records, and genealogical materials. Accepts phone inquiries. No fee. Hours: M-Th 10-9, F-Sa 10-5, Su noon-5.

Kit Carson Museum
and Historical Society

425 Carson, Las Animas, CO 81054; (303) 456-0899. Preserves and displays history of eastern CO in form of artifacts and museum exhibits, library, manuscripts, photos, and special collections. Accepts phone inquiries. No fee. Donations requested. Hours: call.

Koshare Indian Museum

P.O. Box 580, 115 West 18th St., La Junta, CO 81050; (303) 384-4801. Presents Native Americans as artists or as subjects of art. Museum exhibits Indian art and artifacts, Taos founders, and rugs, baskets, katcina dolls, and pottery. Library has reference info on American Indians, large photo collection, and limited films/videotapes. Materials for in-house use only. Accepts phone inquiries. No fee. Hours: Su-F noon-5, Sa 10-5.

Lafayette Miners Museum

P.O. Box 186, 108 E. Simpson, Lafayette, CO 80026; (303) 665-7030. Collects, preserves, and displays history of Lafayette county and coal mining from 1887. Holdings include tools, costumes; photos, library, archives, manuscripts; coal mine location maps; films/videotapes, oral histories. Accepts phone inquiries (303-666-6686). No fee. Hours: Tu 2-4; and by appt.

Leslie J. Savage Library

Western State College, Gunnison, CO 81230; (303) 943-2103. Academic research library with selective federal and state depository materials and Western CO collection, including historical newspapers. Accepts phone inquiries. No fee. Hours: M-Th 7:45-11, F 7:45-4:30, Sa 10-6, Su 3-11.

McAllister House Museum

National Society of Colonial Dames, CO, 423 N. Cascade Ave., Colorado Springs, CO 80903; (719) 635-7925. Restored home serves as museum for family and local history. Holdings include photos, documents, and ephemera related to Maj Henry Mac Allister family. Materials for in-house use only. Accepts phone inquiries. No fee. Hours: Sept-Apr, Th-Sa 10-4; May-Aug, W-Sa 10-4, Su noon-4.

Museum of the American Numismatic Association

818 N. Cascade, Colorado Springs, CO 80903; (303) 632-2646. Assn museum promotes education, awareness, and appreciation of numismatics through exhibits and research materials. Holdings include coins, paper money, tokens, medals froom 600 B.C.; research library, archives, photos, films/videotapes and slides; Arthur Braddan Coole Library on Oriental Numismatics. Accepts phone inquiries. No fee. Hours: Tu-Sa 8:30-4.

Museum of Western Art

1727 Tremont Pl., Denver, CO 80202; (303) 296-1880. Collects, preserves, interprets, and exhibits art of the Western US with emphasis on Civil War-era-WWII. Holdings include collections of masterworks by Bierstadt, Moran, Farny, Russel, Remington, Blumenschein, O'Keefe, and others. Accepts phone inquiries. Fee. Hours: Tu-Sa 10-4:30.

Museum of Western Colorado

P.O. Box 20000-5020, 4th and Ute, Grand Junction, CO 81502; (303) 242-0971. Collects, preserves, interprets, and displays social and natural history of western CO in form of history museums, Dinosaur Valley Exhibit (location: 4th and Main) and Cross Orchards Living History Farm (location: 3073 F Rd). Holdings include historic, and archeologic/ethnographic artifacts; paleologic/geologic specimens; library; museum archives from 1965; photos from 1880s; historic and USGS maps; film/videotapes; recordings from Mesa County Oral History Collection; historic firearms collection; Corn Collection of historic road construction equipment; Whiskey Creek Trestle and cars from Uintah Railway. Accepts phone inquiries. Fee. Hours: Su-Sa 10-4:45.

National Archives—Denver Branch

P.O. Box 25307, Bldg. 48, Denver Federal Center, Denver, CO 80225; (303) 236-0817. Archives preserves historically valuable records created by numerous federal agencies in CO, UT, WY, ND, SD, MT, NM 1850-1960. Holdings include large collections of records from Bureau of Land Management, US District Courts, Bureau of Indian Affairs, and Bureau of Reclamation; photos, mainly from Bureau of Reclamation 1900-1960; microfilms of federal census schedules 1790-1910 for all states, Revolutionary War service records and pension applications; homestead, court, and Indian census records. Accepts phone inquiries. No fee. Hours: M-F 7:30-4.

1920 Pikes Peak or Bust Rodeo, from the Pro Rodeo Hall of Champions and Museum of the American Cowboy.

Pioneer Museum

P.O. Box 472, 300 E. Main, Trinidad, CO 81082; (719) 846-7217. Preserves and interprets history of Trinidad, CO area and residents in form of artifacts and relics of pioneers 1860-early 1900s; restored homes; small library, archives, photo and genealogical/biographical record collections. Accepts phone inquiries. Fee. Hours: 8-5.

Pioneers' Museum

215 S. Tejon, Colorado Springs, CO 80903; (303) 578-6650. Collects, preserves and interprets history of Pikes Peak region and residents. Holdings include Native American and pioneer artifacts, minerals, medical paraphernalia, and crafts collections relating to history of city of Colorado Springs from 1850; library, museum and city archives, and small film/videotape collection; diaries and manuscripts from 1859; photos from 1860. Accepts phone inquiries (303-578-6929). No fee. Hours: M-F 10-5.

Pro Rodeo Hall of Champions and Museum of American Cowboy

101 Pro Rodeo Drive, Colorado Springs, CO 80919; (303) 593-8840. Preserves and displays history of the rodeo and the cowboy. Holdings include exhibits on history and development of rodeo; library; archives with records of Cowboy Turtles Assn, Rodeo Cowboys Assn, Professional Rodeo Cowboys Assn; large photo and slide collection from 1900; films/videotapes of all Natl Finale Rodeos and others, early Wild

West shows; Everett Bowman collection. Accepts phone inquiries. Fee. Hours: summer, 9-5; winter, Tu-Sa 9-4:30, Su noon-4:30.

Rocky Mountain News

400 W. Colfax, Denver, CO 80204; (303) 892-5000. CO's oldest daily newspaper (est 1859) preserves past articles and photos in on-site library. Accepts phone inquiries. No fee. Hours: 9-5.

University of Colorado

Documents Division, Boulder, CO 80309; (303) 492-8834. Maintains selective collection of govt documents, general, reference, and historical materials relevant to needs of the school and students. Holdings include collections of intl documents, including depository materials from UN, OAS, and various European communities; foreign and state documents; extensive collection of technical reports. Some restrictions. Accepts phone inquiries. No fee. Hours: M-Th 8-9, F 8-5, Sa 10-5, Su 1-9.

University of Southern Colorado Library

2200 N. Bonforte Blvd., Pueblo, CO 81001; (303) 549-2333. Academic library maintains selective collection of govt documents, general, reference, and historical materials relevant to needs of the school and students. Holdings include school archives; rare book room with records of local residents; Federal depository materials of CO and surrounding states; films/videotapes and recordings; Slavic Heritage Collection. Accepts phone inquiries. No fee. Hours: M-Th 7-10, F 7-5, Sa 9-5:30, Su 1-10.

Ute Pass Historical Society and Museum

P.O. Box 2, Cascade, CO 80809; (303) 684-2204. Collects and preserves history of the Ute Pass area and residents. Holdings include artifacts and exhibits on Ute Pass area pioneers, Ute Indians, CO Midland Railroad, Pikes Peak Hwy, and Pikes Peak Hillclimb Auto Race; archives with materials from CO Midland Railroad, Midland Terminal Railway, and Ute Pass area from 1880s; maps, photos, and oral history interviews. Accepts phone inquiries (303-684-2201). Fee. Hours: museum, Memorial Day-Labor Day, 10-5; office, M-F 8-noon.

Western Historical Collection

University of Colorado, Library, Boulder, CO 80309; (303) 492-8834. Academic research library preserves history of western American activities and individuals. Women's suffrage collection has materials on activities and social reforms. Collection contains 19th-20th c minutes, reports, pamphlets, and publications on WCTU activities in prison reform, day care, care for unwed mothers, and prohibition. Also preserves correspondence and reports of Women's International League for Peace and Freedom, founded in 1915. Campion collection has materials on mining in Leadville from 1887-1922. Also holds National Farmer's Union records from 1902-66. Accepts phone inquiries. No fee. Hours: call.

Western History Department

Denver Public Library, 1357 Broadway, Denver, CO 80203; (303) 571-2009. Public library maintains large collection of research materials on America west of the Rocky Mountains. Holdings include manuscripts, business records, scrapbooks and diaries, maps, photos, films/videotapes, architectural drawings and clippings files; mining records and reports; trade catalogs; records and memorabilia of Buffalo Bill's Wild West shows and other frontier theatre programs. Extensive collection of Western US newspapers and photos. Collection is non-circulating. Accepts phone inquiries. No fee. Hours: M-W 10-9. Th-Sa 10-5:30, Su 1-5.

Western Museum of Mining & Industry

1025 North Gate Rd., Colorado Springs, CO 80921; (303) 598-8850. Preserves, promotes, and displays history of American West's mining heritage and culture through special events, museum exhibits, artifacts, and library. Holdings include mining relics and reconstructions of a ten-stamp ore mill, hoist house, and mine blacksmith shop. Accepts phone inquiries. Fee. Hours: 9-4.

Western Research Room

Pueblo Library District, 100 E. Abriendo Ave., Pueblo, CO 81004; (303) 549-9601. Maintains collection of research materials on history of

American West, with emphasis on CO, Rocky Mountains West, northern NM, Pueblo CO, and the Arkansas River Valley. Holdings include Territorial Archives of NM; large historical map collection including Sanborn Insurance maps of Pueblo and nearby communities; large photo collection, including series of Penitente photos; films/videotapes, census indexes, family genealogies, oral history interviews, and Pueblo newspaper archives. Collection is non-circulating. Accepts phone inquiries. No fee. Hours: Tu noon-4, 7-9, W 1-5, Th noon-4:30, F 9-noon, 2-6.

Connecticut

American Clock and Watch Museum

100 Maple St., Bristol, CT 06010; (203) 583-6070. Preserves artifacts, history, and records of American clock and watch industry and makers. Museum displays horological items. Library has reference materials on horology from 1500. Archives holds trade catalogs from 1852, accounting records, files of clock and watchmakers, and photos. Fee. Hours: M-F 11-5.

American Indian Archaeological Institute

P.O. Box 260, Rte. 199, Curtis Rd., Washington, CT 06793; (203) 868-0518. Preserves history of American Indian life in Northeast from Ice Age through museum exhibits and library materials. Special collections of Algonquin basketry and archaeological artifacts. Accepts phone inquiries. Donations accepted. Hours: library by appt; institute M-Sa 10-5, Su noon-5.

American Political Life Museum

University of Hartford, 200 Bloomfield Ave., West Hartford, CT 06117. Museum documents presidential politics, heritage, and campaigns from George Washington to Ronald Reagan. Sub-collections cover George Washington, Abraham Lincoln, black history, Confederacy, CT politics from Federalist era to present, reform movements, abolition, women's suffrage, and temperance. Major parties, platform issues, and political music also exhibited. Scheduled to open fall 1988.

American Radio Relay League

Museum of Amateur Radio, 225 Main St., Newington, CT 06111; (203) 666-1541. Displays and records data on amateur/ham radio. Exhibits include tubes, tuners, transmitters and artifacts from amateur radio operators. Accepts phone inquiries. No fee. Hours: M-F 9-4.

Bridgeport Public Library, Historical Collections

925 Broad St., Bridgeport, CT 06604; (203) 576-7417. Preserves materials on Bridgeport and regional history, with emphasis on govt, labor, and orgs. Library houses collections on CT and local history. Archives retains personal and organizational records, as well as cultural and labor history from 1700s; maps of Bridgeport region; extensive photos of area residents, activities, and architecture; and extensive genealogical collection for New England area. Special collection of circus materials, with focus on P.T. Barnum and associates. Collection contains personal letters, photos, circus ephemera, and posters. Accepts phone inquiries. Hours: M-F 9-5, and Labor Day-April, Sa 9-5.

Burndy Library

Electra Square, Norwalk, CT 06856; (203) 838-4444. Library holds Louis Pasteur's copies of his own writings, publications, manuscripts, and photos. Accepts phone inquiries. Hours: call.

Coast Guard Museum

U.S. Coast Guard Academy, New London, CT 06320; (203) 444-8512. Preserves history of Coast Guard, US Life Saving, and US Lighthouse Service through holdings in museum, library, and archives. Accepts phone inquiries. No fee. Hours: M-F 8-5.

Connecticut Firemen's Historical Society, Inc.

230 Pine St., Manchester, CT 06040; (203) 694-8436. Preserves history of fire service, with emphasis on CT. Museum displays fire service memorabilia from 18th-20th c. Library provides limited reference with emphasis on first half of 20th c. Some photos available. Accepts phone inquiries. Donations accepted. Hours: mid April-mid Nov F-Sa 9-5, Su noon-5.

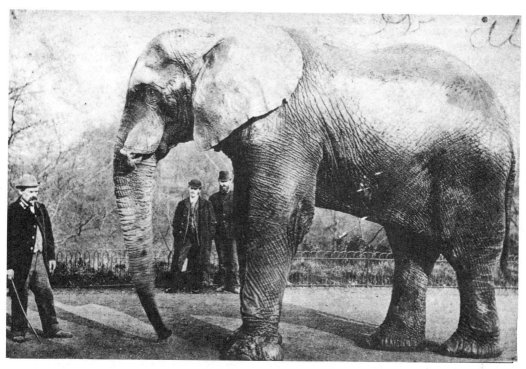

Jumbo the Elephant and trainer Matthew Scott, from the Bridgeport Public Library Historical Collections.

Connecticut Historical Society Library and Museum

1 Elizabeth St., Hartford, CT 06105; (203) 236-5621. Preserves early US, New England, and CT history up to 1900. Holdings in museum include furniture, costumes, and early Americana. Library contains maps, atlases, CT imprints, sermons, trade catalogs, and almanacs from 17th c. Manuscript collection contains extensive collection of personal correspondence, diaries, town records, military papers, and business and club records. Extensive photo collection dates from 1850. Genealogical records include vital statistics, published family histories, periodicals, and regional guides. Special collection of literature for children. Accepts phone inquiries. Hours: library, Tu-Sa 9-5; museum, Tu-Su 9-5.

Connecticut Society of Genealogists

P.O. Box 435, 2906 Main St., Glastonbury, CT 06033; (203) 633-4203. Membership org specializes in CT genealogy. Publishes quarterly and bi-monthly newsletter, performs genealogical searches, provides ancestry service, offers genealogical supplies, and provides sources of info and references. Services for members only. Fee for membership. Hours: M-F 8:30-4.

French-Canadian Genealogical Society of Connecticut

P.O. Box 45, Tolland, CT 06084; (203) 872-0138. Furthers the preservation of Franco-American heritage. Genealogy library contains thousands of listings for US citizens, maps covering all Acadia, videotaped lectures on French-Canadian genealogy, and Herbert collection of

Acadian genealogy. After first visit, patrons required to become members. Accepts phone inquiries. No fee. Hours: M-W 4-8:30, Sa 9-5, Su 1-4.

Glebe House

Box 245, Hollow Rd., Woodbury, CT 06798; (203) 263-2855. Interprets life and times of loyalist Anglican clergyman and family during Revolution, with emphasis on genesis of American Episcopal Church. Museum exhibits regional and local 18th c furnishings and Episcopal church memorabilia. Library holds some local and historical files, reference materials, and books belonging to 18th-19th c clergy. Archives contains early sermons and manuscripts, photos, and limited genealogical materials. Accepts phone inquiries. Donations accepted. Hours: Apr-Oct, Sa-W 1-5; Nov, Sa-W 1-4; other times by appt.

Goshen Historical Society

Old Middle Rd., Goshen, CT 06756; (203) 491-9610. Provides research materials on lives and occupations within community. Museum exhibits display art, archaeology, and natural history. Library contains materials on local history, maps, photos, oral history interviews, and genealogical materials. Materials non-circulating. Accepts phone inquiries. No fee. Hours: 9-4.

Hartford Public Library

Hartford Collection, 500 Main St., Hartford, CT 06103; (203) 525-9121. Collects and organizes materials relating to history of Hartford. Collection includes records of city civic orgs; Noah Webster collection of 18th and 19th c political and religious pamphlets; music scores by Dudley Buck and John Spencer Camp; papers and pictures by Herbert Stoeckel of Hartford Courant; Horace Wells collection, Gwen Reed collection on black history; and Bulkeley collection of children's books printed in Hartford. Other holdings include large collection of maps, many photos, and manuscripts. Accepts phone inquiries. No fee. Hours: M-Th 9-9, Sa 9-5, and Oct-May, Su 1-5.

Historical Museum of Medicine and Dentistry

230 Scarborough St., Hartford, CT 06105; (203) 236-5613. Collects and preserves medical and dental instruments of CT practitioners that were made between 1775-1930. Museum displays special room on Horace Well (father of anesthesiology). Library holds medical journals and texts from 1846. Archives hold records of Hartford Medical and Dental Societies, as well as Lemuel Hopkins Medical Assn and Litchfield County Medical Assn. Manuscripts include materials from Gershom Bulkeley and Horace Wells. Photos document military anaesthesia equip from WWII. Accepts phone inquiries. No fee. Hours: M-F 9-4:30.

Historical Museum of Gunn Memorial Library

Wykeham Rd., Washington, CT 06793; (203) 868-7756. Preserves period house furnished with Washington artifacts. Archives collect manuscripts, maps, photos, and genealogical materials. Accepts phone inquiries. No fee. Hours: Tu and Th 1-4, Sa noon-3.

Historical Society of the Town of Greenwich

39 Strickland Rd., Cos Cob, CT 06807; (203) 869-6899. Collects and preserves history of Greenwich, encourages historical research, and makes available historical info. Museum exhibits cover 300 years of local history, and include 18th c American furniture. Library has reference materials on CT and Greenwich history, covering local fine arts, history, architecture, and furniture. Archives holds Society's records; letters, deeds, and wills from 17th-20th c; oral history interviews; maps of 18th-20th Greenwich, Sanborn maps, and Beers atlases; small collection of photos; and special collection on 1913 Armory Show. Restrictions on use. Accepts phone inquiries. Fee. Hours: Tu, Th 10-2.

Indian and Colonial Research Center

Main St., Old Mystic, CT 06372; (203) 536-9771. Small library and museum on Indian history. Museum houses collection of Woodland Indian artifacts. Library documents Colonial American and Indian history and anthropology. Holdings include 18th-19th c papers of southeastern CT, maps, photos, and genealogical records. Restrictions on photos and manuscripts.

Accepts phone inquiries. No fee. Hours: Mar 15-Nov Tu, Th, Sa 2-4; or by appt.

Knights of Columbus Headquarters Museum

1 Columbus Plaza, New Haven, CT 06507; (203) 772-2130. Chronicles history, formation, and activities of Knights of Columbus as both an insurance and fraternal org. Museum collection includes fine and decorative arts on org activities from 1882, exhibits on founder Michael McGivney, WWI Relief work, and Catholic Church and Vatican. Library contains strong collection on Christopher Columbus, Catholic Church, and ethnic history. Archives contains manuscripts, photos, films/videotapes, and genealogical materials on org history, church, and secular history. Special collections on Irish history in US, CT, and New Haven, and 1893 World Columbian Expo in Chicago. Accepts phone inquiries. No fee. Hours: 8-4:30.

Lock Museum of America

P.O. Box 104, 130 Main St., Terryville, CT 06786; (203) 589-6539. Preserves history of locks through exhibits of mail locks, padlocks, colonial locks, safe locks, doorknob locks, and Yale locks. Accepts phone inquiries. Hours: May-Oct, 1:30-5; other times by appt.

Lyman Allyn Museum

625 Williams St., New London, CT 06320; (203) 443-2545. General art museum is strong in decorative arts, paintings, sculpture, dolls, dollhouses, and furniture. Library has reference materials. Photo collection concentrates on 19th c New London. Materials non-circulating. Accepts phone inquiries. No fee. Hours: Tu-Sa 11-5, Su 1-5.

Mark Twain Memorial

351 Farmington Ave., Hartford, CT 06105; (203) 247-0998. Home of Twain from 1874-91. House is furnished with original pieces and decorative arts of Louis Comfort Tiffany and Associated Artists. Accepts phone inquiries. Fee. Hours: Jun-Oct, Dec 9:30-4; Nov, Jan-May, Tu-Sa 9:30-4, Su 1-4.

Museum of Art, Science, and Industry

4450 Park Ave., Bridgeport, CT 06604; (203) 372-3521. Art and science museum with collection of American and decorative art, as well as P.T. Barnum collection. Accepts phone inquiries. Fee. Hours: Tu-F 11-5, Sa-Su noon-5.

Musical Instrument Collection

Yale University, P.O. Box 2117, 15 Hillhouse Ave., New Haven, CT 06520; (203) 432-0822. Dedicated to documentation and exposition of history of music through historical instruments. Museum holds over 800 musical instruments from 1550-1900, with emphasis on European and American stringed and wind instruments, and keyboard instruments. Library has reference materials on musical instruments, and archives hold info on collection holdings. Accepts phone inquiries. Hours: Sept-May, Tu-Th 1-4, Su 2-4; June-July, Tu-Th 1-4.

National Art Museum of Sport

University of New Haven, West Haven, CT 06516; (203) 932-7197. Collects and exhibits artists' representations of athletes and sports history in form of original paintings, sculpture, and lithographs. Images depict hockey players, jockeys, downhill racers, divers, boxers, Olympics, auto racing, and noted sports personalities. Accepts phone inquiries. No fee. Hours: library, 9-5; gallery by appt only.

Nautilus Memorial/Submarine Force Library and Museum

Box 571, Naval Submarine Base, New London, Groton, CT 06349; (203) 449-3174. Preserves history of submarining. Museum preserves midget submarines from Japan, Italy, Germany, and US. Features include first nuclear powered sub, Nautilus, working periscopes, authentic submarine control room, and displays on evolution of US Submarine Force. Library and archives have research materials. Holdings include photos and films/videotapes. Accepts phone inquiries. No fee. Hours: archives by appt; Apr 15- Oct 14, W-M 9-5; Oct 15-Apr 14, W-M 9-3:30.

New England Air Museum

Aeronautical Historical Association, Bradley International Airport, Windsor Locks, CT 06096; (203) 623-3305. Preserves materials on New England aviation, and particular records of interest in general aviation. Museum documents aviation from beginnings through exhibits of aircraft engines and materials. 140 aircraft in collection. Library houses aviation books, periodicals, art work, and prints. Archives contain materials on New England aviation, Vincent Burnelli, Witteman, photo, and oral histories, films/videotapes, and manuscripts. Accepts phone inquiries. Fee. Hours: by appt only, 10-5.

New Haven Colony Historical Society

114 Whitney Ave., New Haven, CT 06510; (203) 562-4183. Research library provides materials and assistance for study of New Haven. Library holds many printed items, manuscripts, maps and atlases, broadsides, architectural drawings, rare books, family and local histories, sermons, and biographies. Archives contain materials from Bassett Co, women's diaries, and mayors Celentano, Twining, and Stiles. Selected files on Roger Sherman, Eli Whitney, Benedict Arnold, and others. Special collection is Dana scrapbook collection complemented by clipping file. Materials non-circulating. Accepts phone inquiries. Fee for library; donation accepted for museum. Hours: museum & library, Tu-F 10-4:45, museum also Sa-Su 2-5.

P.T. Barnum Museum

820 Main St., Bridgeport, CT 06604; (203) 576-7320. Preserves life of P.T. Barnum and Tom Thumb. Museum exhibits include carriage Thumb and wife Lavinia traveled in, their bed, and their wedding outfits. Other holdings include circus wagons, posters, portraits of Barnum family, and Jenny Lind display. Accepts phone inquiries. Hours: Tu-Sa noon-5; other times by appt.

Prudence Crandall Museum

P.O. Box 47, Junction of Rtes 14 and 169, Canterbury, CT 06331; (203) 546-9916. Preserves and disseminates info on Prudence Crandall, blacks in CT pre-Civil War, and local history. Museum houses changing exhibits on Prudence Crandall's first academy for black women in New England. Library retains materials on blacks, women's studies, history, local history, and education. Materials for in-house use only. Accepts phone inquiries. Fee. Hours: W-Su 10-4:30.

Raymond E. Baldwin Museum of Connecticut History

Connecticut State Library, 231 Capitol Ave., Hartford, CT 06106; (203) 566-3056. Collects, preserves, and exhibits CT history through museum collections on state politics, military, industry, and numismatics. Museum exhibits portraits of all governors, clocks, carriages, historic collection of guns produced by Colt Co, and Selden automobile. Accepts phone inquiries. No fee. Hours: M-F 9-4:45, Sa 9-12:45.

Salmon Brook Historical Society

16 Hummingbird Lane, 208 Salmon Brook St., Granby, CT 06035; (203) 653-3965. Preserves, collects, studies, teaches, and publishes Granby history. Museum in 1753 Abijah Rowe house with period furnishings. Library holds materials on local, state, and American history, with focus on Granby and regional history from 1786. Archives retain personal and business documents from 18th and 19th c, photos relating to Granby, and extensive genealogical research materials on Granby residents. Special collections include Granby WWI militia records, Granby carriage manufacturer records, and Loomis Bros. Materials non-circulating. General store records from 1856-1920. Accepts phone inquiries. No fee. Hours: May-Oct, Su 2-4, or by appt.

Shore Line Trolley Museum

17 River St., East Haven, CT 06512; (203) 467-6927. Preserves, restores, and operates trolley cars over historic Branford Electric Railway. Museum exhibits in trolley main station bldg include cars and related equipment. Library provides reference materials, manuscripts, maps, and photos. Accepts phone inquiries. Fee. Hours: spring & fall, Sa-Su 11-5; summer, 11-5.

Southern Connecticut State University

Hilton C. Buley Library, 501 Crescent St., New Haven, CT 06515; (203) 397-4370. Academic research library with special Carolyn Sherwin collection of historical children's literature. Accepts phone inquiries. No fee. Hours: M-F 8-10, Sa 1-5, Su 1-9.

Stamford Historical Society, Inc.

1508 High Ridge Rd., Stamford, CT 06903;

(203) 329-1183. Collects artifacts of material culture of Stamford and region. Museum exhibits 18th and 19th c American decorative arts. Library has materials on genealogy and local history, Stamford ephemera, and photos of 19th-20th c Stamford. Archives holds some Stamford city records, materials of past mayors and city officials, and maps. Accepts phone inquiries. Donations accepted. Hours: Tu-Su noon-4.

Stowe-Day Foundation
77 Forest St., Hartford, CT 06105; (203) 522-9258. Preserves history of Stowe, Beecher, Hooker, Gillett, Warner, and Twain families. Museum displays 19th c decorative arts with emphasis on Harriet Beecher Stowe. Library documents 19th c authors and Americana, especially Harriet Beecher Stowe, Lyman Beecher family, Mark Twain, woman's suffrage, black history, and architecture. Manuscripts from Stowe, Twain, Katharine Day, William Gillette, suffragist Isabella Hooker, and Twain in-laws, Langdon family. Foreign editions of Uncle Tom's Cabin, advertising broadsides, programs, and sheet music available. Materials non-circulating. Accepts phone inquiries. Fee for museum, no fee for library. Hours: M-F 9-4:30.

Tobacco Museum
96 West Putnam Ave., Greenwich, CT 06830; (203) 869-5531. Preserves tobacco-related art, artifacts, and historical materials. Accepts phone inquiries. No fee. Hours: by appt.

Trinity College Library
300 Summit St., Hartford, CT 06106; (203) 527-3151. Academic research library holds extensive collection of materials on Curtis family of CT and NY, including US Congressman William E. Curtis, Chief Justic William Curtis, Mary Ann Scovill Curtis, and Asst Sec of Treas William E. Curtis Jr. Also holds materials on McLanahan and Muhlenberg families of PA, US Congressman Andrew Gregg, and PA Gov Joseph Heister. Accepts phone inquiries. No fee. Hours: call.

University of Bridgeport
Wahlstrom Library, 7th Floor, 126 Park Ave., Bridgeport, CT 06601; (203) 797-4076. Academic research library has collections of Age of Discovery, Lincoln, Socialism, and McKew Parr

materials. Accepts phone inquiries. No fee. Hours: M-Th 8:30-11, F 8:30-6, Su 1-11.

University of Connecticut
Special Collections, Homer Babbidge Library, 369 Fairfield Rd., Storrs, CT 06268; (203) 486-2513. Alternative press collection contains periodicals and newspapers from 1960 of alternative or underground nature, representing left- and right-wing viewpoints. Also holds archives of First Casualty Press, which documented Vietnam veterans' experiences in Vietnam. Accepts phone inquiries. No fee. Hours: call.

Wadsworth Atheneum
600 Main St., Hartford, CT 06103; (203) 278-2670. Oldest public art museum in US collects colonial American and 19th c French and British art, as well as collections of Samuel Colt's own antique firearms and Wallace Nutting's colonial American furniture from 1630. Accepts phone inquiries. Hours: Tu-Su 11-5.

Wesleyan Film Archives
Omnibus-Saudek Collection, Wesleyan University, Center for the Arts, 301 Washington Terrace, Middletown, CT 06457; (203) 347-9411, ext. 2259. Acquires and preserves important film/theatre/TV materials on Ingrid Bergman, Frank Capra, Kay Francis, Elia Kazan, Raoul Walsh, Omnibus series, and American movie posters from 1925. Bergman collection consists of scrapbooks, letters, photos, scripts, diaries, diaries, and memorabilia from 1933-82; Capra collection has marked scripts, stills, posters, scrapbooks, production info, and personal notes; Francis collection has scrapbooks and diaries from 1930s; Kazan collection has scripts, notes, journals, photos, and letters; Walsh collection has scripts, scrapbooks and stills. Restrictions vary. Accepts phone inquiries. May be fee. Hours: by appt M-F 9-5.

Yale University Drama Library
Box 1903A, Yale Station, 222 York St., New Haven, CT 06520; (203) 432-1555. Collection pertains to dramatic arts and performance, covering all aspects of theatre, film, opera, and dance. Include audiotapes of Yale Drama School and Repertory Theatre productions, plays, and readings, as well as materials on dramatic design.

Accepts phone inquiries. No fee. Hours: call.

Delaware

Barratt's Chapel and Museum

RD 2, Box 25, Frederica, DE 19946; (302) 335-5544. Serves as shrine for United Methodist community. Museum houses collection of UM memorabilia, library for reference info, and archives of peninsula conference. May be restriction. Accepts phone inquiries. No fee. Hours: Sa-Su 1:30-4:30.

Delaware Agricultural Museum

866 N. Dupont Hwy, Dover, DE 19901; (302) 734-1618. Collects, preserves, and promotes agricultural history of DE through exhibits, library and archival collections, educational programs, and publications. Holdings include agricultural artifacts from early settlements through 1945; preserved 19th c farming community buildings and furnishings; library and archives with large collection of publications and other materials relating to region's agriculture and settlement; small collection of DE maps; photos of the museum, collections, and historic subjects; Blacksmith Conference videotapes; oral history tapes. Accepts phone inquiries. Fee for museum. Hours: M-F 10-4.

Delaware Art Museum

2301 Kentmere Pkwy, Wilmington, DE 19806; (302) 571-9590. Museum displays American and European art, with emphasis on the works of Howard Pyle and the Brandywine School, American Illustrators, and English Pre-Raphaelite painters. Holdings include reference library with materials on American art and illustrators after 1850; Howard Pyle Archives and Library; Brandywine School Archives; John Sloan Archives; Samuel Bancroft Archives; rare manuscripts; photo archives of John Sloan, Bertha Corson Day, Elizabeth Shippen Green, Frank Schoonover, and Everett Shinn; and N. C. Wyeth Collection. Some restrictions. Accepts phone inquiries (library: ext 29). No fee. Hours: library, M-F 9-4.

Delaware Bureau of Museums and Historic Sites

Division of History and Cultural Affairs, P.O. Box 1401, 102 S. State St., Dover, DE 19903; (302) 736-5316. Oversees preservation and management of eleven museums and historic sites located throughout the state of DE, including Island Field Museum (South Bowers), The John Dickinson Plantation (Dover), State House (Dover), New Castle Court House (New Castle), Zwaaendael Museum (Lewes), Allee House (Smyrna), Octagonal School House (Dover), Prince George's Chapel (Dagsboro), and the State Museum Complex (Dover). Restrictions and fees vary by site. Visitors Center (Federal and Court Streets, Dover, DE; 302-736-4266) accepts phone inquiries about all sites. Hours: visitor center: M-Sa 8:30-4:30, Su 1:30-4:30; hours of sites vary.

Delaware Society for Preservation of Antiquities

606 Stanton-Christiana Rd., Newark, DE 19803; (302) 998-3792. Preserves historic Hale Byrnes house, which was important Revolutionary War site. Archives contains history of house and reproductions of papers and maps on its Revolutionary role. No fee. Hours: by appt only.

Delaware Technical and Community College Library

Rte. 18, P.O. Box 610, Georgetown, DE 19947; (302) 856-9033. Academic library maintains selective collection of govt documents, technical, reference, and historical materials relevant to needs of the school and students. Holdings include DE census tapes; Delmarva collection. Accepts phone inquiries. No fee. Hours: M-Th 8-10:30, F 8-4:30, Sa 8:30-1.

Hagley Museum and Library

Eleutherian Mills-Hagley Foundation, P.O. Box 3630, Wilmington, DE 19807; (302) 658-2400. Museum and research center preserves and promotes history of American industry, technology, and economic growth through educational programs, exhibits and artifacts, and library/archival collections. Holdings include artifacts and displays on 19th c life and industry; research library with manuscripts, photos, publications and other materials on history of American business and technology from the 18th c; archival materials on entrepreneurs and other prominent business figures; large collection of maps, mainly of mid-Atlantic region. Library/archival collection non-circulating. Accepts phone inquiries. No fee. Hours: M-F 8:30-4:30; 2nd Sa of month 9-4:30.

Historical Society of Delaware

505 Market St., Wilmington, DE 19801; (302) 655-7161. Preserves and promotes DE history in form of museums, library, and archival collections. Holdings include Old Town Hall (Wilmington), with changing historical exhibits; George Read II House (New Castle), restored Federal house, 1797-1804; library with publications, newspapers, ephemera, and other DE historical materials from 17th c; collection of manuscripts and records from DE businesses, orgs, military units, politicians, and private citizens; DE maps from 1450; extensive photo collection; films/videotapes; genealogical records. Library materials non-circulating. Accepts phone inquiries. No fee. Hours: library M 1-9, T-F 9-5; museum: call.

Nanticoke Indian Association

Rte. 4, Box 107A, Millsboro, DE 19966; (302) 945-7022. Preserves history of Nanticoke and other Indian tribes. Museum exhibits local artifacts, regalia, crafts, and tools. Library holds materials on history of DE, Nanticoke Indian, and other tribes; photos of pow wows and special occasions; and videotapes on Nanticokes. Accepts phone inquiries. Fee. Hours: W 9-4, Sa noon-4.

University of Delaware

Hugh Morris Library, S. College Ave., Newark, DE 19717; (302) 451-2238. Academic research library holds assorted papers of DE Senator Willard Saulsbury, including telegrams from Woodrow Wilson relating to work of Democratic National Committee and party politics. Accepts phone inquiries. No fee. Hours: call.

Winterthur Library

Henry Francis Du Pont Winterthur Museum Inc., Winterthur, DE 19735; (302) 656-8591. Museum library preserves and maintains collection of materials on history of fine and decorative arts of the US before 1914. Holdings include extensive collection of art history publications and periodicals; archive of Du Pont family, early

corporate, and Winterthur farm records; extensive collection of documents relating to American arts, artists, and craftsmen prior to 1900; American maps, 18th-19th c; extensive photo collection of American painting, sculpture, and decorative arts; E.D. Andrews Memorial Shaker Collection; Waldron Collection of paper dolls, toys, and children's books. Accepts phone inquiries. No fee. Hours: M-F 8:30-4:30.

District of Columbia

AAUW Educational Foundation Library

American Association of University Women, 2401 Virginia Ave., NW, Washington, DC 20037; (202) 785-7763. Holdings include books and vertical file materials on forerunner of AAUW, AAUW archives, publications since 1920, collections on women's suffrage and equal rights, and materials on adult, continuing, and higher education for women. Hours: by appt only; M-Tu, Th-F 8-4.

AFL-CIO Library

815 16th St., NW, Room 102, Washington, DC 20006; (202) 637-5297. Library emphasis on theory, practice, and history of labor movement in US. Holdings include large library; materials on convention proceedings, union journals, and state federation publications; and vertical files on labor history and current related issues. Materials non-circulating. Hours: M-F 9-4:30.

Afro-American Communities Project

National Museum of American History, Smithsonian Institution, Room C-340, Washington, DC 20560; (202) 357-3182. Performs analysis of social, political, and economic structure of free black communities from Revolutionary period to Civil War. Regions examined are Boston, Buffalo, Chicago, Cincinnati, Detroit, New York, Oberlin, Philadelphia, Pittsburgh, and San Francisco. Project has compiled most extensive data base on free blacks in antebellum North from 1850 and 1860 censuses, military description books of Veteran's Administration for Civil War, and materials on black abolitionist leaders. Retains marginal archive and manuscript collection of military records, probate records, and census data. Accepts mail inquiries. No fee. Hours: M-F 8-5.

Afro-American Life and History Study Association

1407 14th St., NW, Washington, DC 20005; (202) 667-2822. Promotes study of Afro-American life and history, and publishes literature on subject. Library in planning stage. No fee. Hours: 9-5.

Air Force Association Research Library

1750 Pennsylvania Ave., Washington, DC 20006; (202) 637-3300. Small library of materials on military aviation history and military budget. Open to qualified researchers only. Hours: M-F 9-5:30.

Albert Ruger Collection

Geography and Map Division, Library of Congress, Madison Bldg., Rm. B01, Washington, DC 20540; (202) 287-6277. Map collection contains detailed "bird's eye view" of cities and towns in more than 20 states on eastern seabord. Most date from 1860s-70s. Materials non-circulating. No fee. Hours: M-F 8:30-5, Sa 8:30-12:30.

Alexander Graham Bell Family Collection

Manuscript Division, Library of Congress, Madison Bldg., Rm. 102, Washington, DC 20540; (202) 287-5383. Contains large collection of materials on Bell's personal and professional life. Holdings include diaries, correspondence, financial and legal records, lab notebooks from 1865-1922, and documentation of early patent disputes and marketing of telephone. Materials non-circulating. Photo collection in Prints and Photograph Division. No fee. Hours: M-Sa 8:30-5.

Alfred Whital Stern Collection of Lincolniana

Rare Books and Special Collections Division, Library of Congress, Jefferson Bldg., Rm. 204, Washington, DC 20540; (202) 287-5434. Documents life, speeches, and political career of President Lincoln. Holdings include Lincoln's scrapbook on his campaign against Stephen Douglas, copy of first edition of Lincoln and Douglas debates, campaign biographies, materials on Lincoln's assassination and funeral, life mask, and manuscript dispatching Joseph Hooker as commander of Army of Potomac. Materials non-circulating. Accepts phone inquiries. No fee. Hours: M-F 8:30-4:45.

Alternative Press Collection

Serial and Government Publications Divisions, Library of Congress, Madison Bldg., Rm. 135, Washington, DC 20540; (202) 287-5647. Retains American underground newspapers from mid-1960s to present. Over 300 titles from 26 states are represented. Hours: M-F 8:30-9, Sa 8:30-9, Su 1-5.

Amateur Hour Collection

Motion Picture, Broadcasting, and Recorded Sound Division, Library of Congress, Madison Bldg, Rms. 338 and 115, Washington, DC 20540; (202) 287-5840 and 7833. Documents history of "Amateur Hour" 20-year radio and TV history with collection of broadcast recordings, films, applications for appearance, and correspondence. Some early performances by Sinatra, Sills, Kaye, Boone, and others. Recordings found in this division; papers and applications in Music Division. Materials non-circulating. No fee. Hours: M-F 8:30-5.

American Almanac Collection

Rare Books and Special Collections Division, Library of Congress, Jefferson Bldg., Rm. 204, Washington, DC 20540; (202) 287-5434. Contains large collection of American almanacs from 17th-19th c from most states. Holds all editions of "Poor Richard's Almanack." Materials non-circulating. No fee. Hours: M-F 8:30-4:45.

American Catholic Historic Association

Catholic University of America, Mullen Library, Suite 318, Washington, DC 20064; (202) 635-5079. Promotes scholarly study of Catholic Church history, and assists researchers. Holds no collections other than own archives. Accepts phone inquiries. No fee. Hours: M-F 9-5.

American Civil Liberties Union Library

122 Maryland Ave, NE, Washington, DC 20002; (202) 544-1681. Legislative library specializes in civil liberty and govt info issues. Holdings include books, materials on hearings, and congressional reports. Hours: by appt only, M-F 9-5.

American Colonization Society Collection

Manuscript Division, Library of Congress, Madison Bldg., Rm. 102, Washington, DC 20540; (202) 287-5383. Preserves records, letters, reports, and business materials of group formed to relocate black Americans to Liberia. Most materials date from 1823-1912 and document colonization of Liberia and state of slaves and freedmen in antebellum US. Materials non-circulating. No fee. Hours: M-Sa 8:30-5.

American Film Institute Collection

Motion Picture, Broadcasting, and Recorded Sound Division, Library of Congress, Madison Bldg., Rms. 338 and 115, Washington, DC 20540; (202) 287-5840 and 7833. Preserves large collection of movies acquired by AFI. Holdings include many silent films produced in early 1900s by independent companies; large assortment of films produced in 1920s-40s; short films of operas, minstrel shows, vaudeville acts, and speeches; and some US and Polish Yiddish language films. Materials non-circulating. No fee. Hours: M-F 8:30-5.

American Historical Association

400 A St., SE, Washington, DC 20003; (202) 544-2422. Membership org promotes historical studies, collects and preserves historical manuscripts, and disseminates historical research works. Accepts phone inquiries. Hours: call.

American History Archives Center

National Museum of American History, Smithsonian Institution, Constitution Ave. and 12th & 14th Sts., Washington, DC 20560; (202) 357-3270. Manuscripts complement museum's emphasis on technology, cultural history, and sociology. George Clark Radioana collection of photos and biographies relate radio's effect on American life. Leo Baekeland papers show inventor's journals, patents, notebooks, and photos. Allen Du Mont collection holds personal files on cathode-ray invention and manufacture in 1930s. Julian Black's Joe Louis scrapbooks are manager's clippings on career of boxer, 1935-44. William Hammer collection documents engineer's part in Edison projects. Duke Ellington collection holds musician's personal scores and orchestrations, memorabilia from overseas and local tours, scrapbooks, tape recordings, and photos. Faris and Yamna Naff Arab American collection relates Mid-Eastern assimilation process. Accepts phone inquiries. No fee. Hours: M-F, 10-5.

American Institute of Aeronautics and Astronautics Archives

Manuscript Division, Library of Congress, Madison Bldg, Rm. 102, Washington, DC 20540; (202) 287-5383. Collection documents history of aeronautics, development of air force, and biographies of astronauts. Holdings include research files, clippings, articles, questionnaires, and original manuscripts on each astronaut. Materials date from 1939-62. Materials non-circulating. Prints and photos division holds related drawings, posters, and printed ephemera. No fee. Hours: M-Sa 8:30-5.

American Map Collection

Geography and Map Division, Library of Congress, Madison Bldg., Rm. B01, Washington, DC 20540; (202) 287-6277. Preserves large collection of North American maps and charts from 1750-90. Holdings include rare VA, NY, SC, GA, PA, and Philadelphia maps. Materials non-circulating. No fee. Hours: M-F 8:30-5, Sa 8:30-12:30.

American Military Institute

3309 Chestnut St., NW, Washington, DC 20015; (202) 767-5201. Natl military professional assn seeking to stimulate and advance study of military history and encourage acquisition and preservation of manuscripts, publications, relics, and other materials. Members are civilian and uniformed professional and amateur historians in national defense and military affairs. Accepts phone inquiries. Hours: call.

American Newspaper Publishers Association Library

P.O. Box 17407, Dulles Airport, (11600 Sunrise Valley Dr., Reston, VA 22091), Washington, DC 20041; (703) 648-1090. Focuses on history of journalism and related news issues. Library oldings include periodicals and clipping files on histories of newspapers, freedom of press, reporting techniques, and newspaper publishings. Materials for in-house use only. Hours: M-F 9-4:45.

American Psychiatric Association Library

1400 K St, NW, Washington, DC 20005; (202) 682-6080. Library's holdings concentrate on history of American psychiatry, psychoanalysis, community and social psychiatry, and child and adolescent psychiatry. Hours: by appt only, M-F 9-5.

Anacostia Museum

1901 Fort Place, SE, Washington, DC 20020; (202) 287-3380. Mounts exhibits, conducts research, holds photo and archival materials, and answers public inquiries on Afro-American history and culture. Accepts phone inquiries. Materials non-circulating. No fee. Hours: museum, 10-5; library, by appt, M-F 10-5.

Anarchism Collection

Rare Books and Special Collections Division, Library of Congress, Jefferson Bldg., Rm.204, Washington, DC 20540; (202) 287-5434. Preserves history and philosophy of anarchism through collection of writing by major figures and materials on their lives. Holdings include books, pamphlets, serials, and ephemera printed for French, German, Italian, Russian, Spanish, and Yiddish communities between 1850s and 1970s. Materials non-circulating. Materials donated by Antony's family found in Manuscript Division. No fee. Hours: M-F 8:30-4:45.

Anderson House, Headquarters, and Museum

Society of Cincinnati, 2118 Massachusetts Ave., NW, Washington, DC 20008; (202) 785-2040. Serves as museum and library on American Revolution period from 1760-1820, with emphasis on French contribution to American independence. Museum exhibits cover Revolution, weapons, portraits, and fine arts of Europe and Asia. Library concentrates on Revolution. Archives holds Society of Cincinnati records from 1783, with manuscript collection on American Revolution figures, maps, and photos. Special George Rogers Clark collection of books and maps relating to history of Old Northwest. Materials for in-house use only. Accepts phone inquiries. No fee. Hours: library, M-F 10-4; museum, Tu-Sa 1-4.

Andrew Jackson Collection

Manuscript Division, Library of Congress, Madison Bldg., Rm. 102, Washington, DC 20540; (202) 287-5383. Collection of materials from Andrew Jackson. Holdings include papers and maps, correspondence, transcripts, speeches, and written orders—all on microfilm. Materials non-circulating. No fee. Hours: M-Sa 8:30-5.

Angelo Rizzuto Collection

Prints and Photograph Division, Library of Congress, 101 Independence Ave., SE, Washington, DC 20540; (202) 287-6394. Contains large collection of New York City photos from 1950s-60s. Holdings depict Manhattan scenes and people. Materials non-circulating. No fee. Hours: M-F 8:30-5.

Architect of the Capitol

U.S. Capitol, Washington, DC 20515; (202) 225-1222. Holds records on construction of US Capitol and related bldgs, and history of art collection. Museum displays paintings, murals, sculpture, and decorative arts from early 19th c. Library provides reference materials on Capitol, artists of collection works, and history of DC. Archives contains historic manuscripts and records on Capitol construction, correspondence from Capitol architects, large collection of architectural drawings, many photos and slides, film/videotape footage of recent Capitol construction projects, recordings of some important ceremonies, and genealogical records of artists and architects. Accepts phone inquiries. No fee. Hours: M-F 9-4:30.

Architecture and Planning Library

Howard University, 2366 6th St., NW, Washington, DC 20059; (202) 636-7773 or 7774.

Resource center for School of Architecture and Planning holds collection of materials on architecture, bldg construction and technology, art history, decorative art, urban design, community development, and stereophotogrammetric maps of DC. Materials for in-house use only. Hours: M-Th 8:30-8, F 8:30-5, Sa 1-5.

Archive of Folk Culture

Library of Congress, Jefferson Bldg., Rm. G-152, Washington, DC 20540; (202) 287-5510. General repository preserves and presents American folklife through extensive collection of folk music and lore. Holdings include large collection of field recordings, folk tales, oral histories, tapes of folklore, fieldnotes, manuscripts, and other raw materials from all states and regions of US. Many transcripts of recordings available. Accepts phone inquiries. No fee. Hours: M-F 8:30-5.

Archives of American Art

Smithsonian Institution, American Art and Portrait Gallery, 8th & F Sts, NW, Balcony 33h, Washington, DC 20560; (202) 357-4251. Archives hold large collection of documentary material on American visual arts from 18th c. Holdings include business and personal papers of artists, dealers, critics, museums, art orgs, and auction and exhibition catalogs; over 3,000 oral history interviews; large photo collection; records of 1913 Armory Show; personal papers of artists such as Thomas Cole, Ben Shahn, David Smith, and Jackson Pollock. Accepts phone inquiries. No fee. Hours: open to qualified researchers by appt, M-F 10-5.

Armed Forces Medical Museum

Armed Forces Institute of Pathology, Building #54. AFIP-WRAMC, Georgia Ave. & Butternut St., NW, Washington, DC 20306; (202) 576-2348. Provides historical, social, cultural, and technological context for health issues by presenting major medical trends since 1862. Holdings include research records for yellow and typhoid fevers, Armed Forces VD education films, Lincoln and Garfield autopsy materials, extensive collection of pathological specimens, Civil War medical arts materials, historic medical teaching aids, and diagnostic and postmortem examination tools. Otis archives hold records

from museum curators, papers on military and civilian researchers and practioners, archives of electron microscopy, and large photo collection. Accepts phone inquiries. Donations accepted. Hours: M-F 9:30-4:30.

Armed Forces Radio and Television Service Collection

Motion Picture, Broadcasting, and Recorded Sound Division, Library of Congress, Madison Bldg., Rms. 338 and 115, Washington, DC 20540; (202) 287-5840 and 7833. Incomplete collection of educational, musical, and dramatic recordings supplied to military stations overseas and on ships in 1940s. Materials non-circulating. No fee. Hours: M-F 8:30-5.

Armed Services Editions Collection

Rare Books and Special Collections Division, Library of Congress, Jefferson Bldg., Rm.204, Washington, DC 20540; (202) 287-5434. Preserves collection of paperbacks published for US armed forces from 1943-47 during WWII. Includes everything from poetry to bestsellers. Materials non-circulating. No fee. Hours: M-F 8:30-4:45.

Armenian Assembly of America

122 C St., NW, Suite 350, Washington, DC 20001; (202) 393-3434. Promotes interest and concerns of Armenian Americans. Library contains books on Armenian, Turkish, and Greek history, culture, and current events; materials on Holocaust and genocide; and complete collection of US Armenian newpapers. Archives hold clippings on topics concerning Middle East, Turkey, Greece, Soviet Armenia, and human and minority rights. Photo archive of prominent Armenian Americans and Armenian communities in US; films/videotapes on Armenian history and culture; and oral history interviews with Armenian genocide survivors. Accepts phone inquiries. No fee. Hours: M-F 9-5.

Army Audiovisual Center

Visual Media Library, Pentagon 5A470, Washington, DC 20310; (202) 697-0715. Selects still photo/video footage for Visual Info Documentation Program for Dept of Defense and Army. Holdings document Army units, equipment, events, and training exercises. Serves official clients only. Accepts phone inquiries. Fee. Hours: M-F 8-4:30.

Army Pentagon Library

ANRAL, Room 1A518, Pentagon, Washington, DC 20310; (202) 697-4301. Library documents military art and science, political and social science, foreign affairs, govt, Army studies, and military unit histories. Large collection of materials include documents, periodicals, and reference materials. Restricted to those with Pentagon clearance; ILL available. Hours: M-F 9-4.

Associated Publishers, Inc.

1407 14th St., NW, Washington, DC 20005; (202) 265-1441. Oldest Afro-American publishing firm in US supports study of African history by supplying educational materials to schools, colleges, churches, and individuals. Publications cover history kits in black American issues, tracing family history, and African traditions and culture. Also has photos available. Fee for research. Hours: M-F 9-5.

Association of American Railroads

50 F St., NW, Room 5800, Washington, DC 20001; (202) 639-2334. Library holds materials on American railroad history and transportation economics. Holdings include 19th c stockholder reports, railroad statistical data, and rail industry periodicals. Some materials for in-house use only. Hours: by appt only, M-F 9-4.

Association of American Railroads

Information Letter and Photographic Services, 1920 L St., NW, Washington, DC 20036; (202) 639-2100. Retains photo collection of over 250 years of railroad trains, tracks, trips, and trials. Accepts phone inquiries. No fee. Hours: call.

B'nai B'rith Klutznick Museum

1640 Rhode Island Ave., NW, Washington, DC 20036; (202) 857-6583. Collects and displays both modern and ancient Judaica. Museum exhibits cover Jewish life cycle, holidays, synagogue, Sabbath, and time line. Some films/videotapes of Hanukkah. Accepts phone inquiries. No fee. Hours: Su-F 10-5.

Ben Franklin Collection

Manuscript Division, Library of Congress, Madison Bldg., Rm. 102, Washington, DC 20540; (202) 287-5383. Microfilmed collection of materials written by Franklin from 1770s-80s. Includes personal papers, correspondence, journals, records, articles, and documents of Franklin's diplomatic service in France. Materials non-circulating. No fee. Hours: M-Sa 8:30-5.

Bethune Museum and Archives

1318 Vermont Ave., NW, Washington, DC 20005; (202) 332-1233. Promotes awareness of black women's history through large collection on contributions in civil rights, employment, education, health, housing, and intl relations. Holdings include reports of National Council on Negro Women, National Committee on Household Employment, National Alliance of Black Feminists, National Association of Fashion and Accessory Designers; papers of Jeanetta Welch Brown, Polly Cowan, Jeanne Dago, Jennie Austin Fletcher, etc; photos of prominent black women; vertical files; recordings of 1963 March on Washington and Mary McLeod Bethune interview with Eleanor Roosevelt. Accepts phone inquiries. No fee. Hours: Tu-F 10-4, Su 12:30-4.

Black Catholic History Project

Office of Black Catholics, P.O. Box 29260, 5001 Eastern Ave., Washington, DC 20017; (301) 853-4579. Responds to needs and concerns of black Catholics and black community, and provides education, leadership development, and training in black culture and heritage. Museum holdings cover black Catholics in southern MD from 1634-1800. Library concentrates on black Catholic history from 19th c with biographies of black Americans and women, black history, religion, liturgy, theology, and literature. Archives holds org's records, manuscripts, maps of MD and DC, photos from 1800s, films/videotapes, and oral history recordings of black Catholics. Materials can be used when accompanied by org member. Accepts phone inquiries (301-853-3800). No fee. Hours: call.

Brady-Handy Collection

Prints and Photograph Division, Library of Congress, 101 Independence Ave., SE, Washington, DC 20540; (202) 287-6394. Large collection of historic photos and views of Washington, DC, from 19th and early 20th c. Some images include photos of Civil War scenes, and portraits of congressmen, govt leaders, and celebrities. Materials non-circulating. No fee. Hours: M-F 8:30-5.

Broadcast Pioneers Library

1771 N St., NW, Washington, DC 20036; (202) 223-0088. Library/archive concentrates on preserving history of TV and radio. Holdings include broadcasters' papers, scrapbooks, large collection of oral history interviews, extensive photo collection, recordings of speeches and interviews, and periodicals. Hours: by appt only; M-F 9-5.

Bureau of Alcohol, Tobacco, and Firearms

Reference Library, 1200 Pennsylvania Ave., NW, Washington, DC 20226; (202) 566-7557. Preserves regulatory history of Bureau and its control over alcohol, tobacco, firearms, and explosives industries. Special collection of records from hearings on repeal of Prohibition. Open to public with written permission from Disclosure or Division chief. Hours: M-F 7-3:30.

Business and Professional Women's Foundation

Marguerite Rawalt Resource Center, 2012 Massachusetts Ave., NW, Washington, DC 20036; (202) 293-1200. Documents experience of working women, including economic issues, education, motherhood, and sex roles. Holdings include extensive vertical file collection of newspaper clippings, documents, periodical articles, and studies, and oral history collection of over 200 interviews. Hours: call.

Cabinet of American Illustration

Prints and Photograph Division, Library of Congress, 101 Independence Ave., SE, Washington, DC 20540; (202) 287-6394. Collection of cartoons, cover designs, sketches for posters, and illustrations for children's books, novels, and magazines from late 19th-early 20th c US illustrators. Drawings arranged by artist. Materials non-circulating. No fee. Hours: M-F 8:30-5.

Capitol Historical Society

200 Maryland Ave., NE, Washington, DC 20002;

(202) 543-8919. Encourages interest in architectural history of Capitol Bldg. Conducts tours, publishes irregularly, and sponsors research. Accepts phone inquiries. No fee. Hours: M-F 8:30-4:30.

Carnegie Survey of Southern Architecture

Prints and Photograph Division, Library of Congress, 101 Independence Ave., SE, Washington, DC 20540; (202) 287-6394. Collection of architectural photos from South between 1933-40. Concentration on MD, VA, SC, NC, GA, LA, AL, FL, and MO. Materials non-circulating. No fee. Hours: M-F 8:30-5.

Cartographic and Architectural Branch

National Archives, Pennsylvania Ave. & 8th St., NW, (street address: 841 Pickett St., Alexandria, VA) Washington, DC 20408; (703) 756-6700. Maintains and preserves 11 million maps/charts, aerial photos, and architectural/engineering drawings and plans. Archives has exploration and scientific surveys dating from Lewis & Clark to John Wesley Powell; public land surveys/settlement records from OH, IN, IL, IA, KS, MO, AL, MS, and WI; Bureau of Indian Affairs maps; nautical/coastline charts; USGS maps from 1879; census maps from 1840; urban development maps from 1890; maps of US neighbors and Europe; military maps from Queen Anne's War through Vietnam; design drawings of national monuments and parks; and 1935-45 aerial photos. Holds agency records of US Weather Bureau, Census Bureau, Customs Service, Public Bldgs and Parks of Natl Capitol, Bureau of Land Management, Interior Dept, Bureau of Mines, Office of Chief of Engineers, Forest Service, Soil Conservation Service, American Expeditionary Forces, Tenn Valley Authority, Defense Intelligence Agency, and others. Accepts phone inquiries. Researcher's card required. No fee. Hours: M-F 8-4:30.

Catholic University

John Mullen of Denver Memorial Library, 620 Michigan Ave., NE, Washington, DC 20064; (202) 635-5070. Academic research library holds collections on architecture; papers of 19th and 20th c labor leaders Terence Powderly, John

Mitchell, John Brophy, and Philip Murray; O'Donovan Rossa Papers on Fenian Brotherhood in America; 17th and 18th c Clementine literature and church history; drama; Semitics; and collection on theology and Catholic materials. Accepts phone inquiries. Hours: call.

Channing Pollock Theatre Collection

Howard University, 500 Howard Place, NW, Washington, DC 20059; (202) 636-7259. Collection documents 19th and 20th c English and American drama and theatre with holdings including books, manuscripts, photos, playbills, posters, broadsides, and memorabilia from performing arts. Materials for in-house use only. Accepts phone inquiries. Hours: M-F 8:30-5.

Charles Louis Seeger Collection

Music Division, Library of Congress, Madison Bldg., Rm. 112, Washington, DC 20540; (202) 287-5504. Holds collection of materials from 1930s Workers' Music League. Group provided musical protest materials, marches, and undertook musical support of workers. Collection includes music, songbooks, concert programs, periodicals, news clippings, notes, and sheet music from USSR, UK, and US. Materials non-circulating. No fee. Hours: M-Sa 8:30-5.

Charles Todd and
Robert Sonkin Collection

Archive of Folk Culture, Library of Congress, Jefferson Bldg., Rm. G-152, Washington, DC 20540; (202) 287-5510. Collection of recordings made in CA migratory labor camps from 1940-41. Interviews, songs, and ballads on tape from OK, AR, MO, and TX migrants who settled in Fresno, Tulare, and Kern counties. Holdings include field notes. Materials non-circulating. No fee. Hours: M-F 8:30-5.

Civil Rights Commission

National Clearinghouse Library, 1121 Vermont Ave., NW, Washington, DC 20005; (202) 376-8177. Maintains library collection of civil rights publications from 1957-date. Accepts phone inquiries. Hours: call.

Civil Rights Library

Dept. of Justice, 10th St. & Pennsylvania Ave., NW, Rm. 7618, Washington, DC 20530; (202)

633-4098. Holds extensive collection of books, periodicals and other materials on civil rights, civil liberties, constitutional law, and demographics. Hours: by appt M-F 9-5.

Civil War Drawing Collection

Prints and Photograph Division, Library of Congress, 101 Independence Ave., SE, Washington, DC 20540; (202) 287-6394. Contains eyewitness drawings of War events by Civil War newspapermen. Holdings include records of camp life, marches, and important war events, most drawn for "Harper's Weekly," "Frank Leslie's Illustrated Newspaper," and "Illustrated News." Arranged by subject and chronology. Materials non-circulating. No fee. Hours: M-F 8:30-5.

Civil War Photograph Collection

Prints and Photograph Division, Library of Congress, 101 Independence Ave., SE, Washington, DC 20540; (202) 287-6394. Maintains large collection of photos taken by Brady studios and others on Civil War. Photos detail camp life, artillery, fortifications, railroads, ships, bridges, towns, battlefields, and officers and soldiers. Materials non-circulating. No fee. Hours: M-F 8:30-5.

Collection of Advertising History

National Museum of American History, Smithsonian Institution, East Wing, 3rd Fl, Constitution between 12th & 14th Sts., NW, Washington, DC 20560; (202) 357-3270. Collects and preserves US advertising and marketing materials from late 1800s. Pepsi-Cola collection has company oral histories; TV, print, and outdoor ads; and ad campaign materials. Warshaw collection holds 19th & 20th c trade cards, pamphlets, catalogs, posters, letters, and invoices. NW Ayer advertising agency records collect ad campaign tearsheets and posters from 1889-1970. Modern advertising collection documents Marlboro, Alka Seltzer and other ad campaigns since WWII with oral histories and print, radio, and TV ads. Norcross 20th c greeting cards, Zippo, and Famous Amos collections included. Accepts phone inquiries. No fee. Hours: M-F 10-5.

Columbia Historical Society

1307 New Hampshire Ave., NW, Washington,

DC 20036; (202) 785-2068. Collects, teaches, and preserves history of DC. Museum housed in Christian Heurich Mansion. Library preserves Washington history from 1790, archives of historical society, manuscripts from 1698-1986, maps of Washington, and large collection of photos from 1850. Publishes newsletter. Accepts phone inquiries. No fee. Hours: W, F, Sa 10-4.

Comic Book Collection

Serial and Government Publications Divisions, Library of Congress, Madison Bldg., Rm. 135, Washington, DC 20540; (202) 287-5647. Retains large collection of comic books and titles, spanning all subject matter. Some issues from 1930s, but most from 1950s. Materials non-circulating. No fee. Hours: M-Sa 8:30-9, Su 1-5.

Confederate States of America Collection

Rare Books and Special Collections Division, Library of Congress, Jefferson Bldg., Rm. 204, Washington, DC 20540; (202) 287-5434. Documents many publications issued in South during Civil War. Holdings include materials from state govts, congresses, depts, and offices of Confederate States of America, as well as Confederate almanacs, sermons, literature, materials on military sciences and politics, and production surveys. Materials non-circulating. No fee. Hours: M-F 8:30-4:45.

Congressional Publications Collections

Law Library, Library of Congress, Madison Bldg., Rm. 240, Washington, DC 20540; (202) 287-5065. Large collection of publications includes bills and resolutions in various stages of completion, reports and documents, and debates and proceedings. Materials non-circulating. No fee. Hours: M-F 8:30-9:30, Sa 8:30-5, Su 1-5.

Congressional Speech Collection

Rare Books and Special Collections Division, Library of Congress, Jefferson Bldg., Rm. 204, Washington, DC 20540; (202) 287-5435. Contains copies of many speeches given by members of Congress from 1825-1940. Speeches cataloged by speaker. Materials non-circulating.

No fee. Hours: M-F 8:30-4:45.

Corcoran Gallery of Art Archives

17th St. & New York Ave., NW, Washington, DC 20006; (202) 638-3211. Archives for Gallery and School of Art specializes in info on American artists and their work from 1869. Most material in vertical files, accumulated through Corcoran's collecting, exhibiting, and educational programs. Hours: by appt only.

Criminal Library

Dept. of Justice, 10th St. and Pennsylvania Ave., NW, Rm. 100 FTRI, Washington, DC 20530; (202) 724-6934. Holdings focus on criminal law, evidence, business crime, organized crime, espionage, and terrorism. Hours: by appt M-F 9-5.

Customs Service Library and Information Center

U.S. Customs Service, 1301 Constitution Ave., NW, Rm 3340, Washington, DC 20229; (202) 566-5642. Concentrates on Customs info and regulations. Materials cover some history of customs duties and tariffs from 1789. Primary focus on Customs legal, business and economic, scientific and technical operations in tariff and trade, cargo, shipping and navigation, drugs, and law enforcement. Hours: M-F 10-4.

Daughters of the American Revolution Museum

1776 D St., NW, Washington, DC 20006; (202) 879-3242. Preserves US history, genealogy, and decorative arts. Exhibits include memorabilia from first DAR president general in 1890, Caroline Scott Harrison; collection of silver, glass, textiles, handcrafts, and needlework predating Industrial Revolution; 33 period rooms depicting 33 different states; extensive library on American family history and genealogy, with collection of state and local records; research collection on history and people of American Revolution; and assorted other materials since 1607. Accepts phone inquiries. Hours: M-F 9-4, Su 1-5.

Defense Department Still Media Depository

Code LGP-R, Washington, DC 20374; (202)

433-2166. Specializes in photos of all Defense Dept. services, with over 2 million negatives and slides. Hours: by appt, M-F 8:30-4:30.

Democratic National Committee Research/Issues Library

430 South Capitol St., SE, Washington, DC 20003; (202) 863-8072. Collects materials on Congress, politics, national and international news, legislation, personalities, agriculture, elections, and issues related to Democratic party. Vertical file materials on National Committee also available. Hours: by appt only M-F 9-6.

Department of Interior Museum

Department of Interior, Office of the Secretary, 18th & C Sts., NW, Washington, DC 20240; (202) 343-2743. Interprets and presents history and purpose of bureaus in Dept. of Interior. Museum displays North American Indian arts and crafts, feather headdresses, and dioramas on Indian life and relationship to whites; displays on mining and Hoover Dam; Eskimo exhibits of decorative clothing; and collection of artifacts depicting Dept. history. Library holds Dept of Interior archives, large collection of dissertations, and rare book collection. Accepts phone inquiries. No fee. Hours: M-F 8-4.

Department of Justice Main Library

Tenth St. & Constitution Ave., NW, Rm. 5400, Washington, DC 20530; (202) 633-3775. Large collection of materials on history of Justice Dept, federal and state laws, political science, public administration, American history, business, and taxation. Hours: by appt only M-F 9-5.

Department of Labor Library

200 Constitution Ave., NW, Washington, DC 20210; (202) 523-6992. Library houses one of most extensive collections on labor and economics in country. Holdings include American labor union proceedings, constitutions, and reports; American labor newspapers; International Labor Org documents, publications, and foreign labor union materials. Materials for in-house use only. Hours: M-F 8:15-4:45.

Department of State Diplomatic Reception Rooms

2201 C St., NW, Washington, DC 20520; (202) 647-1990. Official US govt entertaining rooms. Contain American decorative arts from 1725-1830. Some photos of collection objects available. Accepts phone inquiries. No fee. Hours: by appt only, M-F 8:30-5.

Department of State Library

2201 C St., NW, Washington, DC 20520; (202) 647-1062. Serves as main info source for Dept's activities in foreign areas of world. Holdings document economic, cultural, social, political, diplomatic, domestic, and foreign legal issues, as well as other subjects related to work of Dept. of State. Closed to public except when material is unavailable elsewhere in DC. Hours: M-F 8:15-5.

Department of Transportation Main Library

400 Seventh St., SW, Washington, DC 20590; (202) 366-2565. Holds materials on federal govt's administration of transportation programs. Collections include secondary source materials on roads, railroads, and maritime-related subjects from early 20th c; railroad accident investigation reports from 1911-66; shipping records from Coast Guard and American Bureau of Shipping; reports of US Lifesaving Service and US Ice Patrol; history of Transportation Dept. development; and large subject card index for transportation periodical literature from 1921-82. Materials for in-house use only. Accepts phone inquiries. No fee. Hours: 9-4.

Dime Novel Collection

Rare Books and Special Collections Division, Library of Congress, Jefferson Bldg., Rm. 204, Washington, DC 20540; (202) 287-5434. Preserves large collection of popular paperback fiction from 19th c. Most books deal with fictional Indian and pioneer tales, detectives, society romances, and rags-to-riches tales, and were printed in serial format. Materials non-circulating. No fee. Hours: M-F 8:30-4:45.

Dimock Gallery

George Washington University, 730 21st St., NW, Washington, DC 20052; (202) 994-1525. Professional showcase for art and University teaching gallery collects and displays American art, fine arts, and art history. Museum displays

19th and 20th c works with emphasis on Washington art and local history, materials related to George Washington, and historic portraiture. Library holds research materials. Archives has vertical files on artists in collection; maps and plans of DC; and contemporary photo works and slide shows. Special collections include materials on US Grant III, Washingtoniana, Lloyd Wright, pre-Columbian and tribal art, and MFA theses. Accepts phone inquiries. No fee. Hours: Tu-F 10-5, Sa noon-5.

Diplomatic Branch

National Archives, Pennsylvania Ave. & 8th St., NW, Washington, DC 20408; (202) 523-3218. Retains records from Dept of State foreign and domestic posts, House of Representatives sound recordings, photos from Philippine War Damage Commission, Displaced Persons Commission, US Information Agency, Constitutional Convention of Continental and Confederate Congresses, and Arms Control and Disarmament Agency. Accepts phone inquiries. Researcher's card required. No fee. Hours: M-F 8:45-5.

District of Columbia Housing and Community Development

1133 North Capitol St., NE, Rm. 203, Washington, DC 20002; (202) 535-1004. Collects materials focusing on DC urban renewal activities from 1951 to present. Holdings include newspaper clippings, photos, and archival records. Materials non-circulating. Hours: M-F 8:15-4:45.

District of Columbia Preservation League

1116 F St., N.W., Fourth Floor, Washington, DC 20004; (202) 737-1519. Org dedicated to preserving historic architecture of downtown region of District of Columbia and promoting architectural heritage of future construction. Library has research materials and files on bldgs and structures dating to 19th c. Accepts phone inquiries. No fee. Hours: M-F 9-7.

District of Columbia Public Library

Documents Division, 901 G St., NW, Washington, DC 20001; (202) 727-1261. Public library provides largest collection of Washington, DC local history through archival holdings, maps of region, photos, film collection, genealogical records, and special collection of Washington Star newspaper photos and clippings, and black studies documentation. Accepts phone inquiries (202-727-1111). No fee. Hours: M-Th 9-9, F-Sa 9-5:30, Su 1-5.

Division of Agriculture and Natural Resources

National Museum of American History, Smithsonian Institution, Constitution Ave. between 12th & 14th, Washington, DC 20560; (202) 357-2095. Preserves materials on US agriculture, food technology, forestry, and fisheries. Collections include agricultural history photographs, patents from 1839, farming periodicals from 1869-1963, photos on food technology, trade catalogs from 19th c, industry records from textile mills and mining operations, records of mining machinery makers from Goodman Company, patent documents from cotton picking industry, collections on coal mining, Joy Manufacturing Co collection from 1919-60, Lehigh Valley Coal Co records, Philadelphia & Reading Coal Co records, and Pittsburgh Consolidation Coal Co records. Accepts phone inquiries. No fee. Hours: M-F 9-5.

Division of Armed Forces History

National Museum of American History, Smithsonian Institution, Constitution Ave. between 12th & 14th, NW, Washington, DC 20560; (202) 357-1883 and 1781. Preserves materials relative to history of US armed forces. Museum collections include uniforms, accoutrements, field equipment, flags and colors, medals and honors, ship models, manuscripts, and ordnances. Special collections include National Firearms collection of armed forces firearms and edged weapons; Gondola "Philadelphia" from Revolutionary War; War of 1812 Star Spangled Banner from Ft McHenry; George Washington's uniform, battle sword, and marquee; military posters from 1860s; weapon dealer catalogs, and Charles Post articles from Spanish-American War. Accepts phone inquiries. No fee. Hours: by appt.

Division of Ceramics and Glass

National Museum of American History, Smithsonian Institution, Constitution Ave. between 12th & 14th, NW, Washington, DC 20560;

(202) 357-1786. Preserves and displays glass and ceramic objects. Holdings include Washington Cathedral collection of stained glass formulas and samples. Mueller Machine Co Library has reference materials used for identification of ceramics and glass housed in division. Photos available from reference files. Some materials may be located in American History Archives Center (357-3270). Accepts phone inquiries. No fee. Hours: 8:45-5:15.

Division of Community Life

National Museum of American History, Smithsonian Institution, Constitution Ave. between 12th & 14th, NW, Washington, DC 20560; (202) 357-2385. Maintains collection on American popular culture, eduction, religion, and ethnicity. Holdings include artifacts from sports, entertainment, and music; manuscripts; photo collection; and limited recordings. Collection of East European folk costumes also housed here. Faris and Yamna Naff Arab American collection contains over 300 oral history interviews, materials from Arab-American press, historical materials documenting Arab adjustment to US, photos of Arab American life, and personal papers and documents. Accepts phone inquiries. No fee. Hours: M-F 8:45-5:15.

Division of Computers, Information, and Society

National Museum of American History, Smithsonian Institution, Constitution Ave. between 12th & 14th, NW, Washington, DC 20560; (202) 357-2392. Preserves history of mathematical calculation and instruments, including sundials, calculating devices, slide rules, calculators, and computers. Holdings include photos and paintings, films/videotapes, biographical materials on significant figures in computer and mathematical history, records of computer societies and orgs from 1953-70, computer history materials from 1943, oral histories documenting computer development from 1967, materials on history of psychology, and clippings from Data Processing Digest from 1956-70. Some materials may be in Archives Center. Accepts phone inquiries. No fee. Hours: call.

Division of Costume

National Museum of American History, Smithsonian Institution, Constitution Ave. between 12th & 14th, NW, Washington, DC 20560; (202) 357-3185. Documents appearance of Americans from 17th c through museum collection of clothing and accessories of men, women, and children. Also displays on manufacturing and sale of clothing. Library and archives hold costume-related materials, clothing manufacturers' records, photos of limited items in collections, Hart Schaffner and Marx men's clothing co records, published fashion photo plates from 1790-1895, Jantzen Knitting Mills collection of materials from 1925-73, J.B. Simpson records from 1888-1955, and Dorothy Shaver papers from Lord & Taylor, 1926-1959. Restrictions on some materials. Accepts phone inquiries. No fee. Hours: M-F 9-5.

Division of Domestic Life

National Museum of American History, Smithsonian Institution, Constitution Ave. between 12th & 14th, NW, Washington, DC 20560; (202) 357-2308. Preserves and maintains collection of material culture comprising domestic life and daily activity. Library contains reference materials on furniture, architecture, metalware, and childhood and household artifacts. Holdings include scrapbooks, broadsides, greeting cards, advertising, theater programs, valentines, tickets, published illustrations, and advertisements demonstrating American culture. Photos of everyday life in US, Van Alstyne Folk Art collection, 19th c Harry Peters prints, and postcard collection. Personal papers from Allan Herschel, Conwell family, Ludwig papers on New England stonecarving, and others. Accepts phone inquiries. No fee. Hours: call.

Division of Electricity and Modern Physics

National Museum of American History, Smithsonian Institution, Constitution Ave. between 12th & 14th, NW, Washington, DC 20560; (202) 357-2820. Maintains collection of materials on development of electrical communication, lighting, radio, transformers, telegraph, radar, and electron tubes. Library contains materials on particle accelerators, atomic frequency standards, and physics during Weimar period. Archive contains biographical materials on inventors and scientists, photos, films/videotapes,

William Terrell papers on FCC from 1911-65, Western Union collection on development of telegraphy from 1840-1961, Saul Dushman collection on GE history, and many other personal collections. Some materials may be in American History Archives. Accepts phone inquiries. No fee. Hours: call.

Division of Engineering and Industry

National Museum of American History, Smithsonian Institution, Constitution Ave. between 12th & 14th, NW, Washington, DC 20560; (202) 357-2058. Maintains collection of materials on civil and mechanical engineering. Library has small collection of civil engineering reference materials. Archive holds engineering drawings and records of major machine builders and works; photos of production engineering, timekeeping mechanisms, office work pieces, robots, automation, and locks and keys; and manuscripts on biographical materials, bridge specifications from 1874-1922, historical preservation and industrial archaeology collection from 1964, New York bridges records, Alaskan Railroad and Bridge materials, Baltimore & Ohio Railroad records, and others. Accepts phone inquiries. No fee. Hours: call.

Division of Graphic Arts

National Museum of American History, Smithsonian Institution, Constitution Ave. between 12th & 14th, NW, Washington, DC 20560; (202) 357-2877. Maintains collection of materials related to printing, typesetting, papermaking, and bookbinding in US. Holdings include info files on equipment, techniques, and persons involved in printing industry; photos; trade literature from 18th c; Fairfax Herald records from 1906-66; Ben Franklin's press; and first linotype machines. Accepts phone inquiries. No fee. Hours: call.

Division of Medical Sciences

National Museum of American History, Smithsonian Institution, Constitution Ave. between 12th & 14th, NW, Rm. 5000, Washington, DC 20560; (202) 357-2145. Collects, documents, and interprets history of health sciences in US. Museum has extensive collection of artifacts on medicine, pharmacy, dentistry, and public health

from late 18th-20th c. Library has reference materials and large trade catalog collection. Manuscript archive has historical collection of patent medicine ads, WWI venereal disease posters, and news clippings; personal papers from Union Army dentist Black, inventor of chloroform Guthrie, first ether anesthetist Long, medical history materials from 1740-1955, and others; large photo collection; and 20th c medical films/tapes. Accepts phone inquiries. No fee. Hours: by appt, 8:45-5:15.

Division of Musical History

National Museum of American History, Smithsonian Institution, Constitution Ave. between 12th & 14th, NW, Washington, DC 20560; (202) 357-1707. Preserves American music history through collection of musical instruments, recordings, photos of keyboard instruments, and trade and reference books. Holdings include organ design info files and recordings of traditional music from VT, VA, NC, and Mexico. Iconography file includes images of musical instruments available in painting and sculpture. Accepts phone inquiries. No fee. Hours: call.

Division of Photographic History

National Museum of American History, Smithsonian Institution, Constitution Ave. between 12th & 14th, NW, Rm. 5715, Washington, DC 20560; (202) 357-2059. Documents history of photography with collection of cameras, images, and pre-motion picture apparatus from 1839. Large photo collection includes daguerreotypes, tintypes, stereo photos, and images from Underwood & Underwood. Library has materials on history of photography and photographers, photo equipment patents, press releases and clippings on photo developments, posters, and limited correspondence from inventors and photographers. Library for researchers only. Accepts phone inquiries. No fee. Hours: M-F 9-5.

Division of Physical Sciences

National Museum of American History, Smithsonian Institution, Constitution Ave. between 12th & 14th, NW, Washington, DC 20560; (202) 357-2482. Preserves history of scientific instruments, particularly those used in US. Holdings date from 18th c, and include instruments used in surveying, navigation, chemistry, and physics. Maintains collection of Natl Weather Service figures and notes on barometers from 1888-1905; graphic representations of scientific apparatus, instruments, scientists, and charts; copies of patents, trade literature, and old prints dealing with chemistry; Edward Acheson papers on graphite; American Optical Co records and photos from 1914-24; Celluloid Co records from 1890-93; and others. Some materials may be in American Archives. Accepts phone inquiries. No fee. Hours: M-F 9-5.

Division of Political History

National Museum of American History, Smithsonian Institution, Constitution Ave. between 12th & 14th, NW, Washington, DC 20560; (202) 357-2008. Collects and preserves materials on presidents, First Ladies, labor, black history, and women's suffrage. Library has reference collection of books and journals, moderate collection of photos, some film/video campaign spots from 1980, and recordings. Manuscript collections include John Adams correpondence from 1775-1865, John Halderman papers from 1850-99, sculptress and feminist Adelaide Johnson papers from 1878-1946, correspondence and documents from feminist and attorney Belva Ann Lockwood, Natl Woman's Party materials from 1914-17, and Nat Wilcox papers from 1834-74. Accepts phone inquiries. No fee. Hours: call.

Division of Textiles

National Museum of American History, Smithsonian Institution, Constitution Ave. between 12th & 14th, NW, Washington, DC 20560; (202) 357-1889. Preserves textile machinery, implements, and fabrics used or produced in US since 17th c. Small part of collection exhibited in Museum of American History. Holdings include important historical machines such as the original Eli Whitney cotton gin model, Elias Howe sewing machine patent model, and Slater spinning frame and carding machine; large collection of full-sized sewing machines; collection of hand sewing implements, including spinning wheels, treadle looms, and hand shuttles; and large collection of raw fibers, yarns, fabrics, and hand sewn accessories in form of quilts, samplers, lace, and tapestries. Accepts phone inquiries. No fee.

Hours: by appt only, M-F 9-4:30.

Division of Transportation

National Museum of American History, Smithsonian Institution, Constitution Ave. between 12th & 14th, NW, Washington, DC 20560; (202) 357-2025. Division provides resources on road, rail, and marine transportation history. Holdings include exhibits in Museum of American History and reference library and archival materials. Large collection of ship, locomotive, and auto photos available, as well as ship plans. Other collections include marine transportation photo and history collections from 19th c, railroad and firefighting equip photo and history collections, road vehicles history and photo collections, Baldwin locomotive registers from 1831-1956, Merchant Marine Survey Records, and Pullman Co photos. Accepts phone inquiries. No fee. Hours: by appt.

Documents of First Fourteen Congresses

Rare Books and Special Collections Division, Library of Congress, Jefferson Bldg., Rm. 204, Washington, DC 20540; (202) 287-5434. Preserves Congressional documents from 1789-1817, includes presidential messages to Congress, legislative journals, and materials on secret proceedings and from executive journals. Materials non-circulating. No fee. Hours: M-F 8:30-4:45.

Drug Enforcement Administration Library

1405 I St., NW, Washington, DC 20537; (202) 633-1369. Collects and preserves materials on history, study, and control of narcotics and dangerous drugs. Holdings include books, vertical file materials, and journals. Hours: M-F 9-5:30.

Dumbarton House

2715 Q St., NW, Washington, DC 20007; (202) 337-2288. Historic house museum presenting early 19th c architecture and decorative arts. House furnished with English and American decorative arts from Federal period. Library has small genealogical collection. Manuscript holdings include historic letters written by Thomas Jefferson, George Washington, James Madison, and other early patriots. House retains number of collection pieces handed down through George Washington family. Accepts phone inquiries. No fee. Hours: library by appt; museum, M-Sa 9-12:30.

Early Copyright Records Collection

Rare Books and Special Collections Division, Library of Congress, Jefferson Bldg., Rm. 204, Washington, DC 20540; (202) 287-5434. Holds collection of US Copyright records and accession reports from 1790-1870. Also has large collection of title pages from authors who intended to publish their work. Materials non-circulating. No fee. Hours: M-F 8:30-4:45.

Edison Laboratory Collection

Motion Picture, Broadcasting, and Recorded Sound Division, Library of Congress, Madison Bldg., Rms. 338 and 115, Washington, DC 20540; (202) 287-5840 or 7833. Preserves collection of films made by Edison Company for various Edison industries. Films include some of earliest releases, and document early sound experiments and promotional activities. Edison himself in 1920s newsreels. Materials non-circulating. No fee. Hours: M-F 8:30-5.

Edward Curtis Collection

Prints and Photograph Division, Library of Congress, 101 Independence Ave., SE, Washington, DC 20540; (202) 287-6394. Collection of photos of North American Indians from early 20th c. Photos include Indians from the Plains states, northern Pacific coast, northern and central CA, and western desert and central plateau. Materials non-circulating. No fee. Hours: M-F 8:30-5.

Environmental Protection Agency Library

401 M St., SW, Rm 2904, Washington, DC 20460; (202) 382-5921. Holdings focused on environmental and management subjects of EPA interest. Collections cover water pollution and quality, air pollution, hazardous wastes, pesticides, noise pollution, and radiation. Also material on projects related to issues. Materials include technical reports, documents, books, newspapers, and newsletters. Hours: M-F 8-5:30.

Equal Employment Opportunity Commission Library

Documents Division, Room 242, 2401 E St., NW, Washington, DC 20507; (202) 634-6990. Enforces prohibition of employment discrimination as detailed in Title VII of 1964 Civil Rights Act. Library consists of mostly legal and social science materials. Archives contains EEOC publications. Materials for in-house use only. Accepts phone inquiries. No fee. Hours: M-F 9-5:30.

Ex-Slave Narrative Collection

Rare Books and Special Collections Division, Library of Congress, Jefferson Bldg., Rm. 204, Washington, DC 20540; (202) 287-5434. Collection of transcribed interviews with former slaves and related WPA paperwork and documentation. Most interviews date to 1930s. Materials non-circulating. No fee. Hours: M-F 8:30-4:45.

Executive Office of the President Library

New Executive Office Bldg., 726 Jackson Place, NW, Room G12, Washington, DC 20503; (202) 395-3654. Provides support info to Executive Office of President agencies, covers federal govt policies, and supports operations. Special collections include historical materials on reorganization of federal govt, past presidents, and presidency. Hours: by appt only, M-F 9-5:30.

Explorers Hall

National Geographic Society, 1145 17th St., NW, Washington, DC 20036; (202) 857-7000. Increases and diffuses geographic knowledge. Museum exhibits explain human development through time; life of mysterious cliffdwellers in southwest CO; Robert Peary's North Pole expedition and Richard Byrd's 1929 flights over the poles; and Jacques-Yves Cousteau's work and development of Aqua-Lung and Diving Saucer. Library holdings include maps, films/videotapes, and recordings. "National Geographic" publications available. Accepts phone inquiries. No fee. Hours: M-Sa 9-5, Su 10-5.

Farm Security Administration Collection

Prints and Photograph Division, Library of

Congress, 101 Independence Ave., SE, Washington, DC 20540; (202) 287-6394. Documents rural life and conditions, as well as life in urban communities and domestic impact of war effort. Covers conditions of sharecroppers and migrant workers. Includes documenting paperwork from photographers. Cataloged by geographic region. Materials non-circulating. No fee. Hours: M-F 8:30-5.

Federal Election Commission Law Library

999 E St., NW, Rm. 801, Washington, DC 20463; (202) 376-5312. Federal Law library maintaining campaign finance materials from 1971 to present. Materials for in-house use; ILL available. Accepts phone inquiries. No fee. Hours: M-F 9-5.

Federal Mine Safety and Health Review

Commission Library, 1730 K St., NW, Washington, DC 20006; (202) 653-5458. Designated depository library reviews complaints and claims based on mine safety and health matters. Small collection on coal mines and safety. Accepts phone inquiries. No fee. Hours: 8-4:30.

Feinberg-Whitman Collection

Manuscript Divisional Collections Division, Library of Congress, Madison Bldg., Rm. 102, Washington, DC 20540; (202) 287-5383. Documents life and work of Walt Whitman. Collection includes papers, photos, early editions of Whitman's work, personal letters written and received, manuscripts from 1876-1889, proofs of most of his publications, and secondary research materials. Materials non-circulating. No fee. Hours: M-Sa 8:30-5

Folklife Archive and Folkways Records Archive

Office of Folklife Programs, Smithsonian Institution, 955 L'Enfant Plaza, SW, Rm. 2600, Washington, DC 20560; (202) 287-3251. Preserves materials generated in research for Festival of American Folklife, Smithsonian Folklife Studies Monograph/Film Series, and exhibitions and programs. Extensive documentation of folk traditions in U.S. and other countries available, with emphasis on occupation, family, musical traditions, Afro-American culture, Native American culture, and other ethnic groups. Moses and Frances Asch collection contains recordings of music, spoken word from significant Americans, historic events, and sounds of technology and nature. Accepts phone inquiries. No fee. Hours: by appt, 9-5.

Founders Graduate Library

Howard University, 500 Howard Place, NW, Washington, DC 20059; (202) 636-7252. Major research library with special collection of anti-slavery materials and urban documents. Also retains collection of films and videotapes on blacks in US and Third World, including biographies of Malcom X, Martin Luther King, Jr., Muhammed Ali, Frederick Douglass, Jesse Owens. Materials for in-house use only. Hours: M-Th 8-10, F 8-9, Sa 9-6, Su 1-10.

Frederick Douglass Home

1411 W St., SE, Washington, DC 20020; (202) 426-5960. Preserves Douglass's memory and personal artifacts in restored historic house. Library has books owned by Douglass. Library not open to general public. Accepts phone inquiries. No fee. Hours: Oct-Apr 9-4, Apr-Oct 9-5.

Freedom of Information Act Reading Room

Federal Bureau of Investigation, 9th St. & Pennsylvania Ave., NW, Washington, DC 20535; (202) 324-3762. Makes available preprocessed FBI case files on American Indian Movement, Ma Barker family, Black Panthers, Al Capone, Chappaquiddick, Cointelpro, John Dillinger, Albert Einstein, El Salvador Churchwomen Killings, Pretty Boy Floyd, Errol Flynn, Patty Hearst kidnapping, Ernest Hemingway, Lindberg baby kidnapping, John Hinckley, Alger Hiss, Howard Hughes, Hubert Humphrey, JFK, Martin Luther King, Huey Long, National Negro Congress, Robert Oppenheimer, Oswald family, Elvis Presley, Jack Ruby, UFOs, Watergate, SNCC, Weatherman Underground, and others. Others through Freedom of Info application. Accepts phone inquiries. Hours: call.

Freer Gallery of Art

Smithsonian Institution, Jefferson Dr. at 12th St., SW, Washington, DC 20560; (202) 357-

2104. Dedicated to research and exhibition in fields of Asian and late 19th and early 20th c American art. Museum exhibits include major collection of works by James McNeill Whistler. Library has large collection of reference materials. Archives holds Whistler's correspondence, papers of Charles Lang Freer, and materials relating to Asian art. Photos also available. Accepts phone inquiries. No fee. Hours: museum to close in summer of 1988 for 3-yr reconstruction project; office open M-F 9-5.

Friends Meeting of Washington Library

2111 Florida Ave., NW, Washington, DC 20008; (202) 483-3310. Collects materials on Society of Friends (Quakers) and related general religious topics. Hours: by appt only, Su 11-2.

Gallaudet College Library

800 Florida Ave., NW, Washington, DC 20002; (202) 651-5582. Academic research library holds special collection of materials on deaf people and deafness, with Baker Collection of books from 1526 to Civil War. Permission required for use of collection. Hours: M-Th 8-midnight, F 8-10, Sa 9-10, Su 1-midnight.

General Foods Corporation Collection

Motion Picture, Broadcasting, and Recorded Sound Division, Library of Congress, Madison Bldg., Rms. 338 and 115, Washington, DC 20540; (202) 287-5840 or 7833. Contains broadcast recordings and scripts from 1930-40s radio shows sponsored by General Foods. Holdings include materials from "Adventures of the Thin Man," "Fanny Brice Show," "Jack Benny Show," "Lum and Abner," and others. Materials non-circulating. No fee. Hours: M-F 8:30-5.

General Services Administration Library

CFL, Room 1033, 18th & F Sts., NW, Washington, DC 20405; (202) 535-7788. Provides library services for GSA, and acts as repository for GSA publications. Library holds basic materials on American history, including 19th c reports of Supervisory Architect of US Treasury, and histories of public buildings and American architecture. Map collection holds real estate survey

maps of Washington area. Special collections from Federal Acquisition Institute on govt procurement, and Karel Yasko on history of public bldgs and structures. Accepts phone inquiries. No fee. Hours: M-F 8-4:30.

George and Ira Gershwin Collection

Music Division, Library of Congress, Madison Bldg., Rm. 112, Washington, DC 20540; (202) 287-5504. Contains large collection of materials on lives and work of Gershwins. Holdings include music, manuscripts, papers, photos, and book and record collection. Materials non-circulating. No fee. Hours: M-Sa 8:30-5.

George Grantham Bain Collection

Prints and Photograph Division, Library of Congress, 101 Independence Ave., SE, Washington, DC 20540; (202) 287-6394. Preserves extremely large collection of New York City news photos from early 20th c. Bain was one of NYC's earliest news picture agencies. Most document NYC, but some eastern US as well. Materials non-circulating. No fee. Hours: M-F 8:30-5.

Georgetown University

Special Collections, P.O. Box 37445, 37th and O Sts., NW, Washington, DC 20057; (202) 625-4173. Academic research library holds special collection of materials on Dickens; Parsons Collection of works by US Catholic authors pre-1831; Shea Collection of materials on early Americana, American Indians, and American Catholic history; Civil War correspondence and papers; Robert F. Wagner papers; McCarthy Historical Project Archive; WWII materials on psychological warfare, papers of Amb Martin Herz, and Cold War and US foreign policy; American Political Science Assn archives; and photos from publisher of "Motion Picture Herald" and "Motion Picture Daily." Accepts phone inquiries. No fee. Hours: M-Th 8:30-midnight, F 8:30-10, Sa 10-10, Su 11-midnight.

Harry Houdini Collection

Rare Books and Special Collections Division, Library of Congress, Jefferson Bldg., Rm. 102, Washington, DC 20540; (202) 287-5434. Contains extensive collection of materials on life of Houdini, magic, spiritualism, and witchcraft.

Holdings include photos, playbills, periodicals, pamphlets, scrapbooks of memorabilia, and ephemera on Houdini. Materials non-circulating. No fee. Hours: M-F 8:30-4:45.

Henry James Collection

Rare Books and Special Collections Division, Library of Congress, Jefferson Bldg., Rm. 102, Washington, DC 20540; (202) 287-5434. Contains early editions of works by James, including first English and American editions of James's writings and other contributions. Materials non-circulating. No fee. Hours: M-F 8:30-4:45.

Heywood Broun Memorial Library

Newspaper Guild, 1125 15th St., NW, Washington, DC 20005; (202) 296-2990. Library preserves books and periodicals documenting labor movement, labor relations, and newspaper and magazine industry. Materials non-circulating. Hours: non-members admitted with permission of librarian; M-F 9-5.

Hirshhorn Museum and Sculpture Garden Archive

Smithsonian Institution, 8th St. and Independence Ave., SW, Washington, DC 20560; (202) 357-3230. Museum's modern art collection is complimented by Joseph Hirshhorn's Art Collection papers from 1948-66, Samuel Murray Papers from 1869-1941 on Thomas Eakins, and MacRae papers 1857-1955 from Assn of American Painter and Sculpture from 1912-15. Accepts phone inquiries. No fee. Hours: by appt, 10-5.

Historic American Building Survey

Prints and Photograph Division, Library of Congress, 101 Independence Ave., SE, Washington, DC 20540; (202) 287-6394. Collection contains documentation of American architecture and bldgs since 1933. Provides detailed record of structures slated for destruction, including photos, drawings, and historical and architectural materials. Materials non-circulating. No fee. Hours: M-F 8:30-5.

Historic American Buildings Survey

National Park Service, P.O. Box 37127, 1100 L St., NW, Rm. 6101, Washington, DC 20013;

(202) 343-9599. Documents and collects records on historic and vernacular bldgs across US. Documentation materials include photos and drawings, and are deposited with Library of Congress. Accepts phone inquiries (202-343-9625). No fee. Hours: call.

Historic American Engineering Board

Prints and Photograph Division, Library of Congress, 101 Independence Ave., SE, Washington, DC 20540; (202) 287-6394. Documents important examples of American engineering, including monuments, threatened with destruction. Holdings include drawings, photos, and historical and technical info. Materials non-circulating. No fee. Hours: M-F 8:30-5.

Historic American Engineering Record

National Park Service, P.O. Box 37127, Washington, DC 20013; (202) 343-9625. Prepares archival documentation of important structures and industrial processes through US and territories, both to encourage their preservation and ensure their records in case of demolition or loss. Documentation includes photos, maps, drawings, flow charts, and films. Materials are deposited in Prints and Photos division of Library of Congress. Accepts phone inquiries (202-343-6399). No fee. Hours: call.

Historical Photograph Collections

National Museum of American History, Smithsonian Institution, Constitution Ave. at 12th and 14th Sts., NW, Washington, DC 20560; (202) 357-3270. Collects and preserves photos and photographer's materials relating to American history. Donald Sultner-Welles collection is large source of documentary images in color slide and photo form. Underwood & Underwood collection, 1895-1921, relates to Keystone-Mast collection at CA Museum of Photography. Ira Hill collection of studio portraits dates from 1920-38. Accepts phone inquiries. No fee. Hours: M-F, 10-4:30.

House of Representatives Library

Cannon Bldg, Rm B-18, Washington, DC 20515; (202) 225-0462. Library preserves legislative documents and records dating to Contintental Congress. Holdings include House and Senate reports, documents, Congressional Records, Globe, Annals, and Directories, House bills and debates since 6th Congress, House Committee hearings, and Supreme Court reports. Materials for public reference only. Hours: by appt, M-F 9-5:30.

Human Studies Film Archive

Museum of Natural History, Smithsonian Institution, Room E307, Washington, DC 20560; (202)357-3349. Collects, preserves, and makes available anthropological film and video records for research use. Holdings focus on these historic and contemporary films, shot by both professionals and amateurs, dating to 1908. Collection also includes photos, filmmaker logs, notes, journals, and translations; and original audiotape recordings of sync and non-sync sound from films and videotapes. May be some restrictions. Accepts phone inquiries. No fee. Hours: 9-5

International Brotherhood of Teamsters

25 Louisiana Ave., NW, Washington, DC 20001; (202) 624-6978. Library holds materials on labor relations, companies, and other unions, as well as documentation of industrial relations, labor history, law business, and transportation. Not open to public; ILL available. Hours: M-F 9-5.

J. Robert Oppenheimer Collection

Manuscript Division, Library of Congress, Madison Bldg., Rm. 102, Washington, DC 20540; (202) 287-5383. Documents life and work of this physicist who worked on development of atomic bomb. Collection includes papers, voice recordings, books, printed lectures, scientific notes, memoranda, photos, and clippings from 1947-67. Much on his involvement with atomic bomb and role of atomic energy in international affairs. Materials non-circulating. No fee. Hours: M-Sa 8:30-5.

Jedediah Hotchkiss Collection

Geography and Map Division, Library of Congress, Madison Bldg., Rm. B01, Washington, DC 20540; (202) 287-8530. Contains papers of Major Hotchkiss pertaining to Civil War. Includes maps used by Gens. Lee and Jackson, sketchbooks, and manuscripts. Materials non-circulating. Hotchkiss correspondence, diaries, notebooks, and related materials found in Manuscript Division. No fee. Hours: M-F 8:30-5, Sa 8:30-12:30.

Jelly Roll Morton Collection

Archive of Folk Culture, Library of Congress, Jefferson Bldg., Rm. G-152, Washington, DC 20540; (202) 287-5510. Collection includes recordings from jazz musician Jelly Roll Morton. Materials non-circulating. No fee. Hours: M-F 8:30-5.

Jewish Historical Society of Greater Washington

701 3rd St., NW, Washington, DC 20001; (202) 789-0900. Preserves local Jewish community history in this first DC synagogue. Holdings include exhibits and photos. Videotape and oral history of local Jewish community available. Accepts phone inquiries (301-881-0100). No fee. Hours: Su 11-3; during week by appt.

Joint Library of Surgeons

Pentagon, DASG-AAFJML-P, Rm. 1B473, Washington, DC 20310; (202) 695-5752. Library specializes in medicine, hospital administration, nursing, public health, and aerospace and aviation medicine. Special collections on US Army Surgeon General's reports from 1817, military medicine, and military medical manuals from 1860s. Not open to public; ILL available. Hours: M-F 7:30-4.

Joseph Allen Collection

Prints and Photos Division, Library of Congress, 101 Independence Ave., SE, Washington, DC 20540; (202) 287-6394. Collection of photos of churches, colleges, govt bldgs, residential structures, and historic monuments from eastern and midwestern states from 1945-67. Comprehensive regional survey materials for Washington, DC. Cataloged geographically. Hours: M-F 8:30-5.

Joseph Henry Papers Collection

Smithsonian Institution, Arts and Industries Bldg., 2188, 900 Jefferson Drive, SW, Washington, DC 20560; (202) 357-2787. Collection encourages research on life of first secretary of Smithsonian Institution, early Smithsonian heritage, and development of science in mid-19th c America. Other holdings include Bell-Henry library of Alexander Graham Bell papers on scientific experiments. Appts must be made to visit collection 24 hrs in advance. Accepts phone inquiries. No fee. Hours: by appt only, 9-5.

Joseph Meredith Toner Collection

Rare Books and Special Collections Division, Library of Congress, Jefferson Bldg., Rm. 102, Washington, DC 20540; (202) 287-5434. Collection documents history of American medicine from 18th and 19th c. Holdings include publications, papers, early American imprints, large collection of books, scrapbooks, maps, newspaper clippings, and manuscripts. Materials non-circulating. No fee. Hours: M-F 8:30-4:45.

Judicial, Fiscal, and Social Branch

National Archives, Pennsylvania Ave. & 8th St., NW, Washington, DC 20408; (202) 523-3218. Preserves records and materials from US District Courts, Coast Guard, Postal Service, Federal Housing Administration, Customs Service, Social Service Administration, Dept of Justice, FBI, Immigration and Naturalization Service, Food and Drug Administration, Public Health Service, Bureau of Prisons, US Attorneys and Marshalls, War Finance Corp, Public Housing Administration, War Relocation Authority, Warren Commission on JFK assassination, Supreme Court, Office of Censorship, American Revolution Bicentennial Administration, Watergate Prosecution Force, Commission on Civil Rights, Confederate and Civil War Records of US Treasury Dept, Secret Service, and National Security Council. Accepts phone inquiries. Researcher's card required. No fee. Hours: M-F 8:45-5.

L'Enfant Trust

1425 21st St., NW, Washington, DC 20036; (202) 347-1814. Preserves qualified bldgs through facade easements, and collects info on architecture and neighborhood history. Accepts phone inquiries. No fee. Hours: F-W 9:30-3.

Lewis & Clark Collection

Geography and Map Division, Library of Congress, Madison Bldg., Rm. B01, Washington, DC 20540; (202) 287-6277. Collection in-

cludes maps thought to have belonged to Clark, as well as maps of region used during Clark's involvement with Bureau of Indian Affairs. Materials non-circulating. No fee. Hours: M-F 8:30-5, Sa 8:30-12:30.

Library and Printed Archives Branch

National Archives, Pennsylvania Ave. & 8th St., NW, Washington, DC 20408; (202) 523-3049. Preserves large collection of materials from Govt Printing Office, Dept of Navy from 1798-1947, and Adjutant General's Office. Accepts phone inquiries. Researcher's card required. No fee. Hours: M-F 8:45-5.

Lincoln Museum

Ford's Theatre, 511 10th St., NW, Washington, DC 20004; (202) 426-6924. Relates story of Lincoln assassination and its importance in American history, and distributes info to encourage research. Museum houses exhibits on John Wilkes Booth, his conspirators, and Lincoln. Small on-site library holds slides, cassette tapes, movies and books on assassination and Washington. Storage vault in Greenbelt, MD holds rare volumes on Lincoln. Archives hold research files on assassination, Lincoln, Ford's Theatre, and Civil War. Maps belonging to Booth also available. Accepts phone inquiries. Fee. Hours: 9-5, closed for performances.

Look Magazine Collection

Prints and Photograph Division, Library of Congress, 101 Independence Ave., SE, Washington, DC 20540; (202) 287-6394. Contains huge collection of photos taken for "Look" publication from 1940s-71. Includes photos on many areas of American culture, including entertainment industry. Materials non-circulating. No fee. Hours: by appt only; M-F 8:30-5.

Machine Readable Branch, National Archives

Pennsylvania Ave. & 8th St., NW, Washington, DC 20408; (202) 523-3218. Preserves and maintains collection of materials from Office of Education, Social Security Administration, Joint Chiefs of Staff, Securities and Exchange Commission, National Science Foundation, Sec of Defense, Employment and Training Commission, Natl Oceanic and Atmospheric Administration, Dept of Transportation, Executive Office of the President, Natl Institutes of Health, and Commission on Civil Rights. Accepts phone inquiries. Researcher's card required. No fee. Hours: M-F 8:45-5.

Marine Corps Historical Center and Museum

Marine Corps Headquarters, Code HDS4, Washington Naval Yard, Building 58, Washington, DC 20380; (202) 433-3447 or 4253. Documents military and naval history with emphasis on Marine Corp and amphibious warfare. Holdings include large library, documents, and unit histories. Historians available for indepth consultation on Marine Corps history. Accepts phone inquiries. No fee. Hours: M-F 8-4:30.

Mary Pickford Collection

Motion Picture, Broadcasting, and Recorded Sound Division, Library of Congress, Madison Bldg., Rms. 338 and 115, Washington, DC 20540; (202) 287-5840 or 7833. Collection of 100 of actress Pickford's films. Materials non-circulating. No fee. Hours: M-F 8:30-5.

McGuffey Reader Collection

Rare Books and Special Collections Division, Library of Congress, Jefferson Bldg., Rm. 102, Washington, DC 20540; (202) 287-5434. Holds collection of these texts, which were used to standardize instruction of language skills in US elementary schools. Materials non-circulating. No fee. Hours: M-F 8:30-4:45.

Meet the Press Collection

Motion Picture, Broadcasting, and Recorded Sound Division, Library of Congress, Madison Bldg., Rms. 338 and 115, Washington, DC 20540; (202) 287-5840 or 7833. Collection documents materials from CBS series from 1945. Holdings include papers of show's producer, letters, autographs, transcripts, scrapbooks, news clippings, and audio and video tapes of shows. Some materials in Manuscript Division. Materials non-circulating. No fee. Hours: M-F 8:30-5.

Military Court of Appeals Law

450 E St., NW, Washington, DC 20442; (202) 272-1466. Library concentrates on military crimi-

nal law. Holdings include Supreme Court decisions, US Court of Military Appeals records, court-martial reports, military justice materials, and some armed service regulations. Restricted to staff and members of Court bar; special permission for others from librarian. Hours: M-F 8:30-5.

Modern Military Branch

National Archives, Pennsylvania Ave. & 8th St., NW, Washington, DC 20408; (202) 523-3218. Preserves records and materials of Veterans Administration, Army Air Forces, Bureau of Naval Personnel, Office of Quartermaster General, Office of the Surgeon General, American Battle Monuments Commission, Marine Corps, Selective Service System, National Guard Bureau, War Dept Claims Board, War Ballot Commission, WWII Occupation Headquarters, Army Staff, Sec of Defense, WWII Theaters of War, Army Commands from 1942, Air Force Headquarters and Commands, Defense Logistics Agency, Adjutant General's Office, and Paymaster General. Accepts phone inquiries. No fee. Researcher's card required. Hours: M-F 8:45-5.

Modern Military Headquarters Branch

National Archives, Pennsylvania Ave. & 8th St., NW, Washington, DC 20408; (202) 523-3218. Holds materials and documents from Army Air Forces, War Dept General and Special Staffs, War Production Board, Joint Chiefs of Staff, War Crime Records from WWII, collection of Foreign Records seized since 1941, Strategic Bombing Survey, Office of Chief of Chaplains, CIA, Army Staff, Sec of Defense, Allied Operational and Occupation Headquarters during WWII, Intl Military Agencies, Army Commands, Air Force Headquarters, Joint Commands, Defense Nuclear Agency, Office of Provost Marshal General, Adjutant General's Office, and Natl Security Agency. Accepts phone inquiries. Researcher's card required. No fee. Hours: M-F 8:45-5.

Moorland-Spingarn Research Center

Howard University, 500 Howard Place, NW, Washington, DC 20059; (202) 636-7239. One of most comprehensive collections on black experience in US. Holdings include oral histories, prints and photos, manuscripts, maps, recordings, and film/videotapes. Accepts phone inquiries. No fee. Hours: M-Th 9-7:30, F-Sa 9-4:30.

Motion Picture, Sound, and Video Branch

National Archives, Pennsylvania Ave. & 8th St., NW, Stack Office 18E, Washington, DC 20408; (202) 786-0041. Preserves and makes available audiovisual documentation of various topics, incl farming, labor, environment, urban affairs, military, civil defense, nuclear power, aviation, space exploration, and intl relations. Contributions from Air Force (incl footage of bombing damage to Hiroshima and Nagasaki), Army Signal Corps, Navy, Office of War Information, Peace Corps, Supreme Court, NASA, Sec of Agriculture from 1928-55, Marine Corps, Bureau of Naval Personnel (with films of US leaders and loan drives), Coast Guard, Post Office from 1921-34 (footage of FDR, Hoover, and Earhart), Dept of State from 1911-56, WPA from 1931-39, Bureau of Indian Affairs from 1908-21, Office of Chief Signal Officer (FDR inaugurations, Lindbergh flight, Hindenburg disaster), ABC, Fox-Movietone News, League of Nations, March of Time Stock Film Library, Milo Ryan Phono Archive, Mutual Radio News, NPR, News of the Day, Paramount and Universal Newsreels, and much more. Also has stock footage dept. Accepts phone inquiries. No fee. Hours: M-F 8:45-5.

NAACP Collection

Manuscript Division, Library of Congress, Madison Bldg., Rm. 102, Washington, DC 20540; (202) 287-5383. Contains collection of non-current materials from National Association for the Advancement of Colored People (NAACP) from 1909-70. Holdings include correspondence, records, clippings, legal briefs, trial transcripts, speeches, and assorted documentation of growth and activities after 1919. Materials non-circulating. Some pictorial info housed in Prints and Photography Division. No fee. Hours: M-Sa 8:30-5.

NASA Audio/Visual Branch

(Code FP) Public Information Division, 400 Maryland Ave., SW, Washington, DC 20546; (202) 453-8383. Preserves collection of photos documenting space exploration. No fee. Hours: M-F 8-4:30.

NASA History Office

NASA Headquarters, Washington, DC 20546; (202) 453-8300. (street address: Reporters Bldg, 300 7th St., SW) Holdings document history of US space program, including presidential materials from Hoover to Reagan; Congressional documents from 1918; materials on USSR space activities; papers of NASA administrators; NASA headquarters materials from 1958; materials on all NASA space centers from 1958; unmanned programs from 1945; earth orbiting satellites; documents on all manned space flights from 1953; materials on space science from 1851; biographies of US and foreign space personnel from 1800s; space-related cartoons; and materials on impact of space activities. Accepts phone inquiries. No fee. Hours: M-F 8-4:30.

National Air and Space Museum

Information Management Division, Smithsonian Institution, 7th St. and Independence Ave., SW, Washington, DC 20560; (202) 287-3480. Public research facility contains photos, pamphlets, clippings, reports, manuscripts, technical manuals, drawings, and articals on all aspects of aviation and space science history. Other holdings include Air Force pre-1954 photo collection on videodisc and NASA photos. Media resource unit holds more than 4,000 aerospace films (357-4721). Archival Support Center holds more than 2 million aircraft engineering drawings from 1890s-1970s; technical manuals; scrapbooks, photos, and personal papers of those who have contributed to aerospace field; and corporate archives. Accepts phone inquiries. No fee. Hours: by appt, vary by division.

National Air and Space Museum

Smithsonian Institution, Sixth St., and Independence Ave., SW, Washington, DC 20560; (202) 357-3133. Supports specialized research, exhibition, and public programs on air and space history. Library documents history of aviation and space, flight technology, aerospace industry, biographies, history and technology of lighter-than-air craft, rocketry, earth and planetary sciences, and astronomy. Archives contains extensive vertical file collection of photos, drawings, and documents. Some films/videotapes available. Special Admiral DeWitt Clinton Ramsey Room has rare and scarce aeronautica and astronautica of museum library. For use by qualified researchers only. Accepts phone inquiries. No fee. Hours: by appt, M-F 10-4.

National Anthropological Archives

National Museum of Natural History, Smithsonian Institution, 10th St. and Constitution Ave., NW, Washington, DC 20560; (202) 357-1986. Collection of materials from archives of Bureau of American Ethnology from 1879, which housed research materials on Native Americans. Holdings include historical manuscripts on linguistics, ethnology, archaeology, physical anthropology, and history of Native Americans. Other holdings include records of national and regional anthropological orgs, as well as art, drawings, and paintings by American Indians and western explorers. Extensive collection of photos of American Indians available. Accepts phone inquiries. No fee. Hours: 9-5.

National Association of Broadcasters

Library and Info Center, 1771 N St., NW, Washington, DC 20036; (202) 429-5490. Collects info on radio and TV broadcasting industry, including books, periodicals, vertical file materials, and NAB publications. Accepts phone inquiries. Hours: public by appt; Tu-F noon-5.

National Broadcasting Company Radio Collection

Motion Picture, Broadcasting, and Recorded Sound Division, Library of Congress, Madison Bldg., Rms. 338 and 115, Washington, DC 20540; (202) 287-5840 or 7833. Collection of NBC radio broadcasts from 1933-70. Includes large amount of materials from WWII-era. Collection composed of news, speeches by presidents and national figures, entertainment, broadcasts on 1939 World's Fair, Olympic Games, and United Nations. Materials non-circulating. No fee. Hours: M-F 8:30-5.

National Building Museum

440 G St, NW, Judiciary Square, NW, Washington, DC 20001; (202) 272-2448. Celebrates building arts through programs, exhibitions, and publications. Museum displays cover prominent architects, building trades and craftsmen, historic preservation, and building materials. Offers educational programs for children and adults. Restrictions on use. Accepts phone inquiries. No fee. Hours: M-F 10-4, Sa-Su noon-4.

National Child Labor Committee Collection

Manuscript Division, Library of Congress, Madison Bldg., Rm. 102, Washington, DC 20540; (202) 287-5383. Documents child labor history and working conditions from 1904-35. Collection includes official records, correspondence, speeches, reports, press releases, field notes, unpublished studies, minutes from meetings, and scrapbooks. Materials non-circulating. No fee. Hours: M-Sa 8:30-5.

National Civil Rights Library

1121 Vermont Ave., Rm. 709, Washington, DC 20425; (202) 376-8114. Collects materials on civil and women's rights. Also holds materials on minorities, age, handicapping conditions, education, sociology, employment, housing, population, and legal issues. Hours: M-F 8:45-5:30.

National Endowment for the Arts Library

Old Post Office Bldg, Rm. 213, 12th St. & Pennsylvania Ave., NW, Washington, DC 20506; (202) 682-5485. Documents all aspects of 20th c American arts, including development, financing, management, preservation, and promotion. Holdings include publications, agency documents, research reports, and vertical file materials. Accepts phone inquiries. Hours: by appt only, M-F 9-5:30.

National Endowment for the Humanities Library

Old Post Office Bldg., Rm. 216, 1100 Pennsylvania Ave., NW, Washington, DC 20506; (202) 786-0245. Provides reference materials for those applying for grants and researching subjects for application. Holdings include major biographical and bibliographic material aids in all areas of social sciences and humanities. Hours: by appt only, M-F 8:30-1:30, 2:20-5.

National Firearms Museum

National Rifle Association, 1600 Rhode Island Ave., NW, Washington, DC 20036; (202) 828-6198. Illustrates firearm development and role in country's history. Museum displays many firearms from earliest examples through modern. Library reference materials cover firearm topics. Accepts phone inquiries (202-828-6194). No fee. Hours: library by appt only; museum, 10-4.

National Gallery of Art

4th & Constitution Ave., NW, Washington, DC 20565; (202) 737-4215 M-F/842-6188 Sa-Su. Preserves Western man's achievements in paintings, sculpture, and graphic arts from Middle Ages, and includes large collection of 20th c art. Library and archives hold photos, slides, films/videotapes, and special collections. Accepts phone inquiries. No fee. Hours: M-Sa 10-5, Su noon-9.

National Labor Relations Board Library

1717 Pennsylvania Ave., NW, Room 900, Washington, DC 20570; (202) 254-9056. Serves as national resource for materials on US primary labor relations law, labor history, economics, and political science. Holdings include all NLRB publications, and materials on NLRB and National Labor Relations Act. Accepts phone inquiries. No fee. Hours: M-F 8:30-5.

National Museum of American Art

Office of Research Support, Smithsonian Institution, Corner of 9th and G Sts., NW, Washington, DC 20560; (202) 357-1626. Maintains research materials, art data records, and large collection of photo images on American art and artists. Museum provides art info through several databases: Inventory of American Paintings before 1914, Inventory of American Sculpture, pre-1877 Art Exhibit Catalog Index, Smithsonian Art Index (list of all Smithsonian drawings, prints, paintings, and sculptures in scientific, technical, and historical collections), Smithsonian Permanent Collection Database, Peter Juley and Son Collection of American art and artist photos from 1896-1975, and slide and photos archives. Accepts phone inquiries. No

fee. Hours: by appt only, M-F 9-5.

National Museum of American Art

Smithsonian Institution, 8th & G Sts., NW, Washington, DC 20560; (202) 357-2700. Collects and exhibits 250 years of American art, including paintings, sculptures, graphics, folk art, and photographs. Museum houses more than 34,000 works. Large library holds research materials, clipping files, and other documentation on American art; art photos for research in Peter Juley & son collection; collections of miniature paintings; and Herbert Waide Hemphill, Jr. collection of American folk art. Also retains Smithsonian art index, inventories of American paintings pre-1914 and sculpture, and pre-1877 art exhibition catalogue project. Accepts phone inquiries. No fee. Hours: 10-5:30.

National Museum of American History Library

Smithsonian Institution, Rm 5016, 12th & Constitution Ave., NW, Washington, DC 20560; (202) 357-2414. Supports research, exhibition, and public programs of Smithsonian, as well as public interest in American history and history of science and technology. Library houses materials on engineering, military history, transportation, science, applied science, decorative arts, domestic and community life, American history, and history of science and technology. Special collections include US Patent Specifications early records; large collection of trade literature from 19th and 20th c; and materials on or by world fairs from 1851. Materials circulate to Smithsonian staff only; ILL available. Accepts phone inquiries. No fee. Hours: by appt, M-F 10-5:15.

National Numismatics Collection

National Museum of American History, Smithsonian Institution, Constitution Ave. between 12th & 14th, NW, Washington, DC 20560; (202) 357-1798. Maintains collection of materials on historical and modern currency. Library holds rare books, materials, and photos. Information files of historic interest available, as well as Brotter papers on monetary policy from 1930-46, International Monetary Conferences, silver and gold question, and inflation. Special collections include US Mint materials from Treasury Department, Chase Manhattan, and Lilly Company. Accepts phone inquiries. No fee. Hours: call.

National Parks Service, Curatorial Services

P.O. Box 37127, 1100 L St., NW, Washington, DC 20013; (202) 343-8142. Oversees and establishes policies and procedures for National Park Service collections. Holds central catalog records for all units of Park Service. Also acts as clearinghouse of excess objects available for exchange and loan. Accepts phone inquiries. No fee. Hours: 7:45-4:15.

National Philatelic Collection

National Museum of American History, Smithsonian Institution, Constitution Ave. between 12th & 14th, NW, Washington, DC 20560; (202) 357-1796. Collects and preserves philatelic and postal history items from US and world for public research. Library has large collection of reference materials from various countries covering wide range of subjects. Archives have Post Office press releases and clipping files, Railway Mail Service and Air Mail Service files, and US and Canal Zone Postal Service stamp production files. Other holdings include maps of postal routes, Pony Express, and Airmail and Railway routes; photos of mail handling, transportation, Post Offices and stamps; and audiotapes of philatelist interviews. May be restrictions. Accepts phone inquiries. No fee. Hours: M-F 10-noon, 1:30-4.

National Photo Company Collection

Prints and Photograph Division, Library of Congress, 101 Independence Ave., SE, Washington, DC 20540; (202) 287-6394. Collection of news photos of Washington, DC events from 1910-30. Holdings describe events during administrations of Wilson, Harding, Coolidge, and Hoover. Arranged chronologically. Materials non-circulating. No fee. Hours: M-F 8:30-5.

National Portrait Gallery

Smithsonian Institution, F St. at 8th., NW, Washington, DC 20560; (202) 357-2390. Exhibits and studies portraiture of men and women who have made significant contributions

to US history, development, and culture. Museum displays paintings, sculpture, graphics, and photos. Library shared with Museum of American Art has materials on American art and biography including clipping and pamphlet file on artists and art institutions. Catalog of American Portraits provides documentation of over 80,000 likenesses of important Americans. Other holdings include Peale family papers, Time cover artworks, Civil War collection, and Living Portrait Artists File for reaching current artists. Accepts phone inquiries. No fee. Hours: 10-5:30.

National Public Radio Collection

Motion Picture, Broadcasting, and Recorded Sound Division, Library of Congress, Madison Bldg., Rms. 338 and 115, Washington, DC 20540; (202) 287-5840 or 7833. Collection of broadcast recordings of NPR cultural programs. Includes some news and public affairs programs. Materials non-circulating. No fee. Hours: M-F 8:30-5.

National Security Archive

1755 Massachusetts Ave., NW, Ste 500, Washington, DC 20036; (202) 797-0882. Provides access to internal federal govt unclassified and declassified documents on matters of foreign, intelligence, defense, and intl economic policy. Holdings composed of govt reports, oral histories, congressional reports and testimonies, official court records, materials from presidential libraries, and materials released under Freedom of Information Act. Sample materials include State Dept communications on fall of Shah of Iran, cargo logs from Southern Air Transport's Iran-contra supply flights, cables on US military bases in Phillipines, and daily logs from cabinet member meetings. Accepts phone inquiries. Donations accepted. Hours: M-F 9-6.

National Trust for Historic Preservation

1785 Massachusetts Ave., NW, Washington, DC 20036; (202) 673-4000. Encourages public participation in preserving sites, districts, and objects significant in American history and culture. Library housed at School of Architecture, University of MD, College Park, MD. Holdings include photos of 17 historic properties, and films/videotapes on historic preservation activities and properties. Accepts phone inquiries. Fee to visit museum properties. Hours: M-F 9-5.

Naval Historical Center

Washington Navy Yard, Building 44, 9th & M Sts., SE, Washington, DC 20374; (202) 433-4131. Serves Navy, govt agencies, and research needs. Museum covers Revolution through Vietnam War emphasizing heroes, battles, diplomacy, and exploration with displays of artifacts, ship models, and art. Library covers US and foreign navies and naval sciences. Operation Archives hold records of historic value from WWII. Curator branch has photos, art, uniforms, and flags. Early history branch collects US naval history from around world. Contemporary history branch covers WWII to present. Ships' Histories Branch holds files on Navy ships. Naval aviation branch has documents and photos. Materials non-circulating. Accepts phone inquiries. No fee. Hours: M-F 9-4.

Naval Historical Foundation

Washington Navy Yard, Building 57, Washington, DC 20374; (202) 433-2005. Collects and preserves unofficial papers and artifacts relating to US Navy, Marin Corps, Coast Guard, and Merchant Marine. Most materials on deposit at Manuscript Division of Library of Archives. Onsite repository of naval artifacts and memorabilia open to public. Fee for membership. Hours: 8-4:30.

Naval Historical Foundation Collection

Manuscript Division, Library of Congress, Madison Bldg., Rm. 102, Washington, DC 20540; (202) 287-5383. Contains collection of materials on Naval history in America from Revolutionary War to WWII. Holdings include over 250 separate personal collections. Materials non-circulating. No fee. Hours: M-Sa 8:30-5.

Naval Observatory Library

34th St. and Massachusetts Ave., NW, Washington, DC 20390; (202) 653-1499. Collects materials on astronomy, mathematics, physics, and geophysics. Holdings include publications from observatories all over world from 19th c, rare books on astronomy from 1500-1800, star

charts and maps, and periodicals. Hours: open to qualified researchers by permission of librarian; M-F 8-4:30.

Naval Photographic Center

Film Depository Division, U.S. Naval Station (near Bolling AFB), Washington, DC 20374; (202) 433-2115. Collects and preserves film footage on Naval history from 1956. Over 45 million ft of 16mm film and 18 million ft of 35mm film available. Subject matter includes Navy personnel, installations, and munitions; Vietnam War; Washington sites; and significant figures. Restrictions on use. Accepts phone inquiries. Fee for staff research. Hours: by appt; M-F 7:15-3:45.

Navy and Old Army Branch

National Archives, Pennsylvania Ave. & 8th St., NW, Washington, DC 20408; (202) 523-3218. Preserves extensive collection of materials from Army Air Forces, Bureau of Ships, Bureau of Naval Personnel, Office of Chief of Naval Operations, Bureau of Medicine and Surgery, Bureau of Aeronautics, Dept of Navy, Naval Observatory, Office of Quartermaster General, War Dept collection of Revolutionary War Records, Office of Sec of War, War Dept collection of Confederate Records, American Expeditionary Forces, Marine Corps, Office of Chief of Ordnance, Chiefs of Arms, Soldiers' Home, Commissary General of Prisoners, Office of Naval Research, Army Mobile Units, Continental Army Commands, Army Overseas Operations and Commands, Military Academy, Naval Academy, and Adjutant General's Office. Accepts phone inquiries. Researcher's card required. No fee. Hours: M-F 8:45-5.

Navy Memorial Museum

Washington Navy Yard, Building 76, Washington, DC 20374; (202) 433-4882. Collects, preserves, and displays naval artifacts and artwork depicting Navy history from Revolution. Large museum collection exhibits ships, airplanes, weapons, uniforms, historic displays on Revolutionary, Civil, Spanish-American, and World Wars; library documents naval history with large collection; archives hold operational records of WWII, and large collection of historic photos. Accepts phone inquiries (202-433-

2651). No fee. Hours: winter, M-F 9-4; summer, M-F 9-5; Sa-Su 10-5.

New York World-Telegram and Sun Collection
Prints and Photograph Division, Library of Congress, 101 Independence Ave., SE, Washington, DC 20540; (202) 287-6394. Collection of over 1 million photos of New York culture and history from 1920s-60s. Holdings cover politics, transportation, labor, housing, entertainment, and cultural developments. Materials non-circulating. No fee. Hours: M-F 8:30-5.

New Yorker Collection
Prints and Photograph Division, Library of Congress, 101 Independence Ave., SE, Washington, DC 20540; (202) 287-6394. Collection of drawings from "New Yorker" magazine from 1960. Organized by artist. Materials non-circulating. No fee. Hours: M-F 8:30-5.

Nixon Presidential Materials Project
National Archives—Main Branch, Pennsylvania Ave. & 8th St., NW, (Street address: 845 S. Pickett, Alexandria, VA 22304), Washington, DC 20408; (202) 756-6498. Curates Nixon administration historical materials, including files of Charles Colson, John Dean, John Ehrlichman, John Haldeman, Alexander Haig, Ron Zeigler, and other admin figures; White House subject files on govt agencies, branches, and special interests; photos taken by or given to official White House photographers during Nixon administration; audio tapes of Nixon and wife, Spiro Agnew, and Gerald Ford, including China trip advance telecommunications; motion picture films of Nixon diplomatic activities; and 2-inch videotapes of PBS and public affairs programs taped off-air. Accepts phone inquiries. No fee. Hours: M-F 8-4:30.

Octagon Museum
American Institute of Architects Foundation, 1799 New York Ave., NW, Washington, DC 20006; (202) 638-3221. Preserves and interprets this federal period house museum, and promotes architectural and allied arts awareness. Museum houses 2 galleries with exhibitions on architecture and allied arts. Archives hold prints and drawing collection of American Architec-

Spiro Agnew and Richard Nixon at the 1968 Republican National Convention, from the Nixon Presidential Materials Project of the National Archives.

tural Foundations, including archives and library of Richard Morris Hint and other architects. Accepts phone inquiries. Fee. Hours: Tu-F 10-4, Sa-Su noon-4.

Office of Printing and Photographic Services
Smithsonian Institution, Washington, DC 20560; (202) 357-1933. Maintains library of nearly 1 million negatives from Smithsonian photographers from late 1800s. Holdings include Pullman and Chaney collections on rail transportation, National Anthropolocial Archives collection and documentation of Smithsonian exhibits and artifacts. Offices in American History, Natural History, Air and Space Museum, Museum Support Center, and Smithsonian Tropical Research Institute. Accepts phone inquiries. Fee. Hours: M-F 9-5.

Oliver Wendell Holmes Library
Rare Books and Special Collections Division, Library of Congress, Jefferson Bldg., Rm. 102, Washington, DC 20540; (202) 287-5434. Contains Holmes family collection of works on jurisprudence, constitutional law, philosophy,

history, etc. Materials non-circulating. No fee. Hours: M-F 8:30-4:45.

Oscar Hammerstein II Collection

Music Division, Library of Congress, Madison Building, Rm. 112, Washington, DC 20540; (202) 287-5504. Collection of papers, works, and music of Hammerstein. Holdings include scripts, notes, librettos, correspondence, photos, printed music, playbills, press notices, awards, and extensive materials on "South Pacific," "Flower Drum Song," and "Sound of Music." Materials non-circulating. No fee. Hours: M-Sa 8:30-5.

Panama Canal Commission Library

2000 L St., NW, Ste. 550, Washington, DC 20036; (202) 634-6441. Library holds materials on history of Panama Canal construction, ratification of 1977 Canal Treaty, general info on Canal and Canal zone, and annual reports of Canal Commission and Canal zone govt. Accepts phone inquiries. Hours: M-F 8-4:30.

Paper Print Collection

Motion Picture, Broadcasting, and Recorded Sound Division, Library of Congress, Madison Bldg., Rms. 338 and 115, Washington, DC 20540; (202) 287-5840 or 7833. Collection of paper contact prints of films registered for copyright from 1894-1915 that were later retored to projectible film stock. Prints include everything from first few frames to entire film. Includes films by Edison Co., Biograph Co., American Mutoscope, D.W. Griffith, and George Melies. Materials non-circulating. No fee. Hours: M-F 8:30-5.

Peabody Museum Collection

Archive of Folk Culture, Library of Congress, Jefferson Bldg., Rm. G-152, Washington, DC 20540; (202) 287-5510. Contains recordings of speech and songs of Native Americans from 1890s-1910s. Documentation covers Passamaquoddy Indians of ME, Zuni and Hopi Indians of AZ, Nez Perce, Navaho, and other CA Indians. Materials non-circulating. No fee. Hours: M-F 8:30-5.

Peace Corps Information Services

806 Connecticut Ave., NW, Washington, DC

20562; (202) 254-6886. Maintains collection of materials on social, political, economic, and health issues related to Peace Corps volunteer work from 1961. Accepts phone inquiries. Hours: call.

Peale Family Papers

National Portrait Gallery, Smithsonian Institution, 8th and F Sts., NW, Washington, DC 20560; (202) 357-2565. Maintains collection of Peale family papers ranging from 1735-1885, and covering work and lives of Peales in MD and Philadelphia. Holdings include documents, correspondence, diaries, manuscripts, and secondary literature; some photos on work of Charles Willson Peale's work; materials on Philadelphia Academy of Fine Arts, Academy of Natural Sciences in Philadelphia, Long and Wilkes Expeditions, US Mint, and early history of photography. Accepts phone inquiries. No fee. Hours: by appt only, M-F 10-5.

Phillips Collection

1600 21st St., NW, Washington, DC 20009; (202) 387-2151. Museum of modern art and art sources. Holdings include 19th-20th c American and European paintings and sculpture. Library has monographs on Phillips Collection artists, and books on 19th-20th c art. Accepts phone inquiries. Donations accepted. Hours: Tu-Sa 10-5, Su 2-7.

Pictorial Archives of Early American Architecture

Prints and Photograph Division, Library of Congress, 101 Independence Ave., SE, Washington, DC 20540; (202) 287-6394. Collection of photos of American architecture dating from 17th, 18th, and 19th c. Photos arranged by location. Materials non-circulating. No fee. Hours: M-F 8:30-5.

Postal Service Library

475 L'Enfant Plaza, SW, Washington, DC 20260; (202) 268-2904 or 2905. Collects and preserves materials on postal history, law, technology, and social sciences. Holdings include Congressional serial set, reports, photos, postal histories and materials, periodicals of postal employee organizations, and Universal Postal Union studies. Accepts phone inquiries. No fee. Hours: M-F 9-5.

Presidential Papers Collection

Manuscript Division, Library of Congress, Madison Bldg., Rm. 102, Washington, DC 20540; (202) 287-5383. Contains collection of papers from 23 of the US Presidents. Holdings include writings, notes, correspondence, speeches, and financial records of Presidents Washington, Jefferson, Madison, Monroe, Jackson, Van Buren, William Harrison, Tyler, Polk, Taylor, Pierce, Lincoln, Johnson, Grant, Garfield, Arthur, Cleveland, Benjamin Harrison, McKinley, Roosevelt, Taft, Wilson, and Coolidge. Materials non-circulating. No fee. Hours: M-Sa 8:30-5.

Renwick Gallery of National Museum of American Art

Smithsonian Institution, Pennsylvania Ave. at 17th St., NW, Washington, DC 20560; (202) 357-2531. Collects and exhibits American crafts. Library provides reference materials on crafts and their design. Archives hold vertical file material on artists and galleries in following media: glass, ceramics, baskets, metal, wood, jewelry, fiber, and handmade paper. Photo collection includes slides of collections and from individual artists, as well as photos of bldg. Film collection on specific areas of craftmaking and design. Accepts phone inquiries. No fee. Hours: 10-5:30.

Republican National Committee Library

310 First St., SE, Washington, DC 20003; (202) 863-8626. Provides library and reference services for Republican Party political, historical, and economic interests. Holdings emphasize current political issues, foreign affairs, economics, political science, agriculture, and energy; large collection of materials on history and activities of Republican party; and election statistics for state and national races. Hours: by appt only, M-F 9-5:30.

Richard Rogers Collection

Music Division, Library of Congress, Madison Bldg., Rm. 112, Washington, DC 20540; (202) 287-5504. Contains collection of manuscripts, scores, and works for musicals and films created by Richard Rogers, some in partnership with Oscar Hammerstein II. Materials cover all periods of Rogers' career. Materials non-circulating. No fee. Hours: M-Sa 8:30-5.

Sanborn Fire Insurance Map Collection

Geography and Map Division, Library of Congress, Madison Bldg., Rm. B01, Washington, DC 20540; (202) 287-6277. Map collection contains important cartographic record of growth and development in over 12,000 US cities and towns. Sanborn Insurance maps, used to estimate fire risk to urban structure, describe construction materials, height, function, and location of lot lines. Most maps fall between 1876 and 1961. Materials non-circulating. No fee. Hours: M-F 8:30-5, Sa 8:30-12:30.

Scientific, Economic, and National Resources Branch

National Archives, Pennsylvania Ave. & 8th St., NW, Washington, DC 20408; (202) 523-3218. Preserves records of Natl Recovery Administration, Sec of Agriculture, Fish and Wildlife Service, National Labor Relations Board, Coast Guard, Weather Bureau, Census Bureau, Civilian Conservation Corps, Office of Sec of Interior, Land Management Bureau, Govt of Virgin Islands, Works Project Administration, Fine Arts Commission, Bureau of Indian Affairs, Natl Park Service, Women's Bureau, Farmers Home Administration, Soil Conservation Service, Bureau of Reclamation, Federal Trade Commission, DC Rent Commission, Rural Electrification Administration, Bureau of Employment Security, Reconstruction Finance Corporation, War Mobilization and Reconversion Office, Export-Import Bank, Indian Claims Commission, Natl Federation of Arts and Humanities, Natl Science Foundation, DC Govt, Atomic Energy Commission, Equal Employment Opportunity Commission, Enviromental Protection Agency, and Natl Highway Traffic Safety Administration. Accepts phone inquiries. No fee. Researcher's card required. Hours: M-F 8:45-5.

Scottish Rite Supreme Council Library

1733 16th St., NW, Washington, DC 20009; (202) 232-3579. Masonic library preserves materials on org's history, philosophy, religion, philology, and antiquities, with emphasis on American history and biography. Collections include autograph letter collections of Masonic and Freemasonry interest; materials on Freemasonry around world; William Smith collection of Burnsiana; Carman collection of Lincolniana; and collection of works on soldier and scholar, Albert Pike. Accepts phone inquiries. Hours: M-F 8-4.

Senate Library

Capitol Building, Rm. S-332, Washington, DC 20510; (202) 224-7106. Preserves legislative history of US Senate. Holdings include Senate and House bills and resolutions from 15th Congress to present; American history materials and government biographies; official proceedings and records of Congress, and writings of noted Senate members. Restricted to Senators and Senate organizationss, with exceptions when in the best interest of Congress. Hours: M-F 9-5:30.

Sewall-Belmont House

144 Constitution Ave., NE, Washington, DC 20002; (202) 456-3989. Museum and art gallery concentrating on suffrage movement and commemorating Alice Paul's fight for women's rights. Library closed for restoration at present. Some photos and videotape on right to vote. Accepts phone inquiries. No fee. Hours: Tu-F 10-3, Sa-Su noon-4.

Smithsonian Archives

Smithsonian Institution, Arts & Industries Building #2135, 900 Jefferson Dr., SW, Washington, DC 20560; (202) 357-1420. Preserves and maintains official records of Smithsonian, to promote study of 19th c American science. Library collects small number of Smithsonian reports, publications, monographs, and archival publications; archives hold official Smithsonian records from 1846-1983; manuscript collection includes papers of Smithsonian secretaries, curators, scientific staff, and certain professional societies; large photo collection of Smithsonian personnel and buildings; video history program documents science and technology developments; and few oral history recordings from Smithsonian figures. Accepts phone inquiries. No fee. Hours: M-F 9-5.

Smithsonian Institution Bibliographic Information System

Archives Center (and other Smithsonian Museums), 12th and Constitution Ave., NW, Washington, DC 20560; (202) 357-3270. SIBIS is automated on-line database that provides a comprehensive listing of Smithsonian Institution archival collections and holdings, records, photos, films, manuscripts, books, and other informational sources. Database provides access by titles, subjects, forms of material, or key words. Terminals available to public can be found in the Human Studies Film Archives, the Air & Space Museum Records Management Division, the Smithsonian Anthropological Archives, the American History Archives Center, the Office of Folklife Programs, the Smithsonian Archives, and the Archives Photograph Survey Project. Accepts phone inquiries. No fee. Hours: vary by division.

Smithsonian Densmore Collection

Archive of Folk Culture, Library of Congress, Jefferson Building, Room G-152, Washington, DC 20540; (202) 287-5510. Documents music and ethnology of North American Indians through large collection of audio recordings made by Smithsonian Instituion ethnology researchers from 1900-30. Collection includes papers and photos from Frances Densmore, scrapbooks, drafts for her academic lectures and reviews, and a chronology of her career in this field. Materials non-circulating. No fee. Hours: M-F 8:30-5.

Society for Industrial Archaeology

National Museum of American History, Smithsonian Institution, Constitution Ave. between 12th & 14th, NW, Rm 5020, Washington, DC 20560; (202) 357-2228. International org promotes study and preservation of physical survival of technical and industrial past. Sponsors field investigations, research, recording, and dissemination of info on all aspects of industrial archaeology through publications, meetings, and field trips. Accepts phone inquiries. Membership fee. Hours: M-F 9-5.

Still Pictures Branch

National Archives, Pennsylvania Ave. & 8th St., NW, Washington, DC 20408; (202) 523-3236.

President Dwight Eisenhower and Soviet Premier Nikita Krushchev meeting in 1959, from the National Archives Still Photo Division.

Holds several million photos and graphics of US social, cultural, economic, environmental, technological, and political history. Images include American Indians, homes, and activities, 1833-1941; American West expeditions, military life, pioneer towns, transportation, and mining, 1848-1912; Civil War civilian and military activities, personnel, equipment, and battlefield scenes; Revolutionary War, Declaration of Independence, military campaigns, and Colonial and British leaders; US Navy ships from 1775-1941; black American art, outstanding blacks, and art exhibits, 1928-67; 19th c American cities and events; and many others. Accepts phone inquiries. Researcher's card required. No fee. Hours: M-F 8:45-5.

Supreme Court Library

1 First St., NE, Washington, DC 20543; (202)479-3170. Serves research needs of Justices, law clerks, and members of Supreme Court Bar. Collection strong in American legislative history and materials about Court and its justices. Only Records and Briefs Collection and Transcripts of Oral Argument Collection open to public. Hours: M-F 9-4:15.

Susan B. Anthony Collection

Rare Books and Special Collections Division, Library of Congress, Jefferson Bldg, Rm 204, Washington, DC 20540; (202) 287-5434. Contains collection of papers and library materials from Anthony; official reports of national suffrage conventions; and addresses made to Congress after 1869. Holdings include Anthony's scrapbooks. Materials non-circulating. No fee. Hours: M-Sa 8:30-5.

Technical Report Collection
Science and Technology Division, Library of Congress, Adams Bldg., Fifth Floor, Science Reading Room, Washington, DC 20540; (202) 287-5639. Contains largest collection of scientific and technical reports from 1940s to date. Materials originate from Dept of Education, Dept of Defense, NASA, Office of Education, and agencies preceding them. Hours: M-F 8:30-9, Sa 8:30-5, Su 1-5.

Television News Study Service
George Washington University, University Library, 2130 H St., NW, Washington, DC 20052; (202) 676-7218. Serves as reference and research center for analysis of TV news in U.S. Holds most network newcasts and specials from 1968 and Democratic and Republican conventions of 1968, 1972, and 1976. Sponsors seminars, conferences, and workshops. Open to scholars and researchers. Accepts phone inquiries. No fee. Hours: M-F 8:30-10, Sa 10-6, Su noon-10.

Temple Sinai Library
3100 Military Rd., NW, Washington, DC 20015; (202) 363-6394. Library holds materials on Judaica, with concentrations on comparative religion, Holocaust, Jewish history and philosophy, and American Judaism. Holdings include small reference library and vertical/clipping file. Hours: M-F 9-5, Su 9-noon.

Theodore Roosevelt Association Collection
Motion Picture, Broadcasting, and Recorded Sound Division, Library of Congress, Madison Bldg., Rms. 338 and 115, Washington, DC 20540; (202) 287-5840 or 7833. Collection of early news films on Roosevelt's career and later life, covering his Rough Rider days and focusing on 1909-19. Collection also includes footage of his funeral and various tributes to him. Materials non-circulating. No fee. Hours: M-F 8:30-5.

Tobacco Institute Library
1875 Eye St., NW, Suite 800, Washington, DC

20006; (202) 457-4880. Private library concentrates on smoking and health controversy, with some publications on tobacco economics available. Open to members; ILL available. Hours: M-F 9-5.

Treasury Exhibit Hall
Fifteenth St. & Pennsylvania Ave., NW, Washington, DC 20220; (202) 566-5221. Preserves history of Customs Dept and Treasury activities. Displays include exotic drug paraphernalia and smuggling devices; various containers sent to Bureau of Alcohol, Tobacco, and Firearms by distillers; counterfeiting exhibits and photos from Secret Service. Accepts phone inquiries. Hours: M-F 9:30-3:30.

United Artists Collection
Motion Picture, Broadcasting, and Recorded Sound Division, Library of Congress, Madison Bldg., Rms. 338 and 115, Washington, DC 20540; (202) 287-5840 or 7833. Collection of silent and sound films, shorts, and cartoons produced by United Artists from 1913-48. Holdings include sound features released by Monogram Pictures Corp, "Popeye" cartoons, and Technicolor camera negatives. Materials non-circulating. No fee. Hours: M-F 8:30-5.

United Nations Recordings Collection
Motion Picture, Broadcasting, and Recorded Sound Division, Library of Congress, Madison Bldg., Rms. 338 and 115, Washington, DC 20540; (202) 287-5840 or 7833. Contains collection of recordings from United Nations proceedings from 1946-63. Holdings include unedited transcriptions of UN proceedings in original languages. Materials non-circulating. No fee. Hours: M-F 8:30-5.

University of the District of Columbia Library
4200 Connecticut Ave., NW, Bldg. 39, Washington, DC 20008; (202) 282-3901. Academic research library has special collections on black American history. Holdings include Atlanta University Black Culture collection and Slave Narrative and Source Materials Collection. Materials circulate within University community only. No fee. Hours: M-Th 8am-9pm, F 8-6, Sa 9-1.

Vance Randolph Collection

Archive of Folk Culture, Library of Congress, Jefferson Bldg., Rm. G-152, Washington, DC 20540; (202) 287-5510. Collection of Ozark folk music, field recordings, and accompanying ethnological papers and photographs. Most materials from southern MO and northeaster AR region include fiddle tunes and banjo pieces. Randolph's research notes, clippings, photos, and correspondence cover period from 1930s-60s. Materials non-circulating. Music Division holds Randolph's collection of "unprintable" Ozark music, lyrics, rhymes, and sayings. No fee. Hours: M-F 8:30-5.

Veterans' Administration

Central Office Library, 810 Vermont Ave., NW, Room 976, Washington, DC 20420; (202) 389-3085. Library provides info on VA and military history, and materials on aging, health care, herbicides, and public admin. Hours: M-F 8-4:30.

Voice of America Collection

Motion Picture, Broadcasting, and Recorded Sound Division, Library of Congress, Madison Bldg., Rms. 338 and 115, Washington, DC 20540; (202) 287-5840 or 7833. Collection of recordings of Voice of America music from 1945, including orchestral, jazz, and vocal numbers. Materials non-circulating. No fee. Hours: M-F 8:30-5.

Washington Dolls' House Museum

5236 44th St., NW, Washington, DC 20015; (202) 244-0024. Studies and preserves dolls' houses and toys of interest to collectors in terms of architecture, decorative arts in miniature, and the study of social history. Museum displays depict Baltimore row houses, NJ seaside hotel, Capitol and White House, and other Americana. Accepts phone inquiries. Fee. Hours: Tu-Sa 10-5, Su noon-5.

Washington Post Library

1150 15th St., NW, Washington, DC 20071; (202) 334-6966. Preserves substantial reference sources, clipping files, background files, and photogrphic library for Washington Post staffers. Privileges extended to other members of the press. Accepts special requests by mail, addressed to Director of Information Services. Hours: call.

Washington Press Photo Bureau Collection

Prints and Photograph Division, Library of Congress, 101 Independence Ave., SE, Washington, DC 20540; (202) 287-6394. Photo collection of prominent Washingtonians from late 1930s-40s. Large collection is indexed by portrait sitter's name, occupation, and date. Materials non-circulating. No fee. Hours: M-F 8:30-5.

White House Historical Association

740 Jackson Place, NW, Washington, DC 20503; (202) 737-8292. Enhances understanding and appreciation of White House in nation's history. Publishes books and produces slide programs on White House and its occupants. Accepts phone inquiries. Hours: 9-4:30.

Wilbur and Orville Wright Collection

Manuscript Division, Library of Congress, Madison Bldg., Rm. 102, Washington, DC 20540; (202) 287-5383. Contains materials from lives, experiments, and work of Wright brothers. Collection includes diaries, notebooks, family papers, correspondence, scrapbooks, legal and business documents, and diaries and notebooks from flights. Materials non-circulating. No fee. Hours: M-Sa 8:30-5

Willard Rhodes Collection

Archive of Folk Culture, Library of Congress, Jefferson Bldg., Rm. G-152, Washington, DC 20540; (202) 287-5510. Collection of field recordings of Native American music from 1940s-52. Recordings include 50 tribes primarily from western US. Materials non-circulating. No fee. Hours: M-F 8:30-5.

William Faden Collection

Geography and Map Division, Library of Congress, Madison Bldg., Rm. B01, Washington, DC 20540; (202) 287-6277. Collection of maps from French & Indian and Revolutionary Wars, drawn by British military engineers. Materials non-circulating. No fee. Hours: M-F 8:30-5, Sa 8:30-12:30.

William Tecumseh Sherman Collection

Manuscript Division, Library of Congress, Madison Bldg., Rm. 102, Washington, DC 20540; (202) 287-5383. Collection of General Sherman's correspondence, military documents, photos, memorabilia, and assorted personal papers. Over half of collection details his post-Civil War career. Manuscript of Sherman's "Memoirs," and journal from Mexican War included. Materials non-circulating. Collection of Sherman's maps held in Geography and Map Division. No fee. Hours: M-Sa 8:30-5.

Woodbury Lowery Collection

Geography and Map Division, Library of Congress, Madison Bldg., Rm. B01, Washington, DC 20540; (202) 287-6277. Materials in collection relate to Spanish colonies in North America from 1750-90. Covers regions in FL, NM, CA, TX, and LA. Materials non-circulating. No fee. Hours: M-F 8:30-5, Sa 8:30-12:30.

Woodrow Wilson House Museum

2340 S St., N.W., Washington, DC 20008; (202) 673-5517. Historic house museum preserving life and presidential history of Wilson. Archives contain papers and documents related to Wilson, diary of Wilson's nurse, photos of Wilson family and Paris Peace Conference, films/videotapes on Wilson, and recording of Wilson's 1923 radio address. Accepts phone inquiries. Fee. Hours: Tu-Su 10-4.

Woodrow Wilson Library

Rare Books and Special Collections Division, Library of Congress, Jefferson Bldg., Rm. 102, Washington, DC 20540; (202) 287-5434. Holds materials from Wilson's personal library, including his mementos, works, and literature. Some medals and personal awards in collection. Materials non-circulating. No fee. Hours: M-F 8:30-4:45.

Woody Guthrie Collection

Archive of Folk Culture, Library of Congress, Jefferson Bldg., Rm. G-152, Washington, DC 20540; (202) 287-5510. Contains recordings and papers of singer Woody Guthrie. Materials non-circulating. No fee. Hours: M-F 8:30-5.

Works Project Administration Poster Collection

Prints and Photograph Division, Library of Congress, 101 Independence Ave., SE, Washington, DC 20540; (202) 287-6394. Collection of WPA-produced posters from 1930s, created to publicize exhibits, community activities, theater productions, and health and education programs in 20 states. Materials non-circulating. No fee. Hours: M-F 8:30-5.

Works Projection Administration Folklore Collection

Archive of Folk Culture, Library of Congress, Jefferson Bldg., Rm. G-152, Washington, DC 20540; (202) 287-5510. Collection of WPA materials on American folklore from 1936. Holdings include research files on NY and New England, folklore, socioethnic studies, black studies, and CA field studies of ethnic and migrant communities. Materials non-circulating. No fee. Hours: M-F 8:30-5.

Florida

Air Force Armament Museum

Elgin Air Force Base, Rte. 85 N, Fort Walton Beach, FL 32542; (904) 882-4062. Portrays Air Force armaments including guns, missiles, rockets, guns, maps, photo collection, and small collection of training films. Accepts phone inquiries. No fee. Hours: 9:30-4:30.

American Nudist Research Library

4425 S. Pleasant Hill Rd., Kissimmee, FL 32741; (305) 933-2866. Preserves historic nudist materials. Library has magazines and books on nudism dating to 1947. Archives contain court materials from cases concerning nudity and assorted legal documents; theses on nudism; maps of nudist resorts in US and Europe; resort photos and photo albums; videotapes on difference clubs and TV programs concerning nudism; and recordings from various club owners and individuals responsible for early acceptance of nudism. Accepts phone inquiries. No fee. Hours: 1-4.

Bay County Public Library

Documents Dept., 25 W. Government St., Panama City, FL 32401; (904) 785-3457. Serves general public with collections of local and nautical maps, local history special collection and photos, and genealogical records. Accepts phone inquiries. No fee. Hours: M-W 10-8, Th-F 10-5, Sa 10-3.

Broward County Historical Commission

100-B Southeast New River Drive, Fort Lauderdale, FL 33301; (305) 765-5872. Researches history of county and southern FL. Museum, library, and archives hold resource materials on marine, archaeological, and historical subjects; some maps from 1500, photographs of Broward county; oral history interviews with county pioneers; genealogical materials; and vertical files on current events. Materials non-circulating. Accepts phone inquiries. No fee. Hours: M-F 8-4:30.

Collier County Museum

Collier County Government Center, 3301 Tamiami Trail East, Naples, FL 33962; (813) 774-8476. Preserves and interprets Collier county history with museum exhibits, research library, local manuscripts, small map collection, extensive collection of photos, oral history recordings, and newspaper archives. Accepts phone inquiries. No fee. Hours: research facilities by appt; museum, M-F 8-5.

Coral Gables Historic Preservation Division

Planning Division, P.O. Drawer 141549, 405 Biltmore Way, Coral Gables, FL 33134; (305) 442-6443. Protects city's historic architecture, and holds photo, newspapers, and promotional publications documenting Coral Gables' development and boom in 1920s. Materials non-circulating. Accepts phone inquiries. No fee. Hours: 8-5.

Dade Heritage Trust

190 S.E. 12th Terrace, Miami, FL 33131; (305) 358-9572. Preserves and promotes interest in county history through holdings in museum, library, and archives. Museum has 1910 doctor's office display; library and archives hold photos, films/videotapes, and recordings on history and people of county. Accepts phone inquiries. No fee. Hours: 9-5.

Decorative and Propoganda Arts Collection

Miami-Dade Community College, 300 NE Second Ave., Bldg. One, Third Floor, Miami, FL 33132; (305) 347-3429. Wolfson collection of decorative arts contains large collection of European and US design artifacts dating from 1855-1945. Holdings include furniture, blueprints, WPA posters, souvenirs from World Fairs, and exhibits on development of artist's programs during Depression. Accepts phone inquiries. No fee. Hours: M-F 10-5.

Don Garlits Museum of Drag Racing

13700 S.W. 16th Ave., I-75, Exit #67, Ocala, FL 32676; (904) 245-8661. Preserves and displays rich and varied history of America's largest motorsport. Museum displays 75 racing and vintage cars dating from 1908. Archives contain literature, articles, and memorabilia from 1940s. Photos and vintage film/videotape footage chronicle milestones in drag racing from 1950s. Accepts phone inquiries. Fee. Hours: 10-5.

Ernest Hemingway Home and Museum

P.O. Box 1519, 907 Whitehead, Key West, FL 33040; (305) 294-1575. Works to inform public on life and work of Hemingway. Accepts phone inquiries. Fee. Hours: 9-5.

Florida Aviation Historical Society

Heritage Park Museum, P.O. Box 127, Indian Rocks Beach, FL 34635; (813) 595-2772. Preserves FL aviation history and machinery through museum, library, and archives housed at Heritage Park Museum, Largo, FL. Museum exhibits world's first airliner, 1914 Benoist Airboat, and artifacts. Library and archives contain manuscripts, photos, films/videotapes, and recordings. Accepts phone inquiries. No fee. Hours: call.

Florida Folklife Bureau

P.O. Box 265, US Route 41 and State Rd. 136, White Springs, FL 32096; (904) 397-2192. Documents and preserves FL folklife through collections of manuscripts, photos, films/videotapes, and recordings. May be restrictions. Accepts phone inquiries. No fee. Hours: M-F 8-5.

Florida International University Library

Documents Section, University Park Campus, 8th St, Southwest and 107th Avenue, Miami, FL 33174; (305) 554-2470. Library contains collection of materials on Caribbean region and politics, Latin American history, local history, and North American Indian history. Map collection includes USGS, topographic, and CIA maps. Other special collections include NEROT collection of Jewish materials and Levi Marrero collection of record on India's political deals with Cuba. Accepts phone inquiries. No fee. Hours: M-Th 8-midnight, F 8-8, Sa 9-8, Su 1-11.

Florida State Museum

University of Florida, Museum Rd. & Newell Dr., Gainesville, FL 32611; (904) 392-1721. Promotes research and education in natural history and anthropology of Southeast and Caribbean region. Museum focuses on history, anthropology, and archaeology; library concentrates on paleontology. Holdings include some films/videotapes and recordings. Accepts phone inquiries. No fee. Hours: M-Sa 8-5, Su 1-5.

Florida State University

Special Collections, Strozier Library, Tallahassee, FL 32306; (904) 644-3271. Collects materials dealing with FL, including rare books, vertical files, and pamphlets. Library resources document travel and exploration of FL and early colonies. Archives hold materials and photos of University from 1857-1970s; manuscripts from FL and Southeast business, politics, plantations, and authors; rare FL maps; Jackson Ice Civil Rights Tapes and transcripts; and McGregor collection of early Americana. Materials non-circulating. Accepts phone inquiries. No fee. Hours: M-F 9-6.

Florida Supreme Court Library

Supreme Court Building, Tallahassee, FL 32399; (904) 488-8919. Library provides legal reference materials. Holdings include papers of former Justices, photos and portraits of court personnel and Supreme Court Justices, oral history interviews, and archives of state Supreme Court Historical Society. Materials non-circulating, and

cannot be copied. Fee for reproduction services. Hours: M-F 8-5.

Fort Caroline National Memorial

12713 Ft. Caroline Rd., Jacksonville, FL 32225; (904) 641-7155. Preserves historic French 1564-65 colony of Ft Caroline. Museum exhibits artifacts from Ft, as well as artifacts of aboriginal and European cultures. Library houses reference materials. Accepts phone inquiries. No fee. Hours: 9-5.

Fort Lauderdale Historical Society

P.O. Box 14043, 219 SW 2nd Ave., Fort Lauderdale, FL 33302; (305) 463-4431. Collects, preserves, and interprets history of Ft Lauderdale and south FL. Museum holds changing exhibits covering period 1830-1950. Library houses materials on local and state history. Archive has extensive Broward and surrounding county historical materials dating from 20th c, pioneer family manuscripts, maps from 1500s, large collection of photos from 1890s, and collection of oral history interviews. Restrictions on use. Accepts phone inquiries. No fee. Hours: M-F 10-4.

Haydon Burns Public Library

Document Dept., 122 N. Ocean St., Jacksonville, FL 32202; (904) 630-2665. Academic support library with collections of FL and GA topographical maps and special FL collection. Some materials non-circulating. Accepts phone inquiries. No fee. Hours: M-Th 10-9, F-Sa 10-6, Su 1-5.

Henry Morrison Flagler Museum

Whitehall Historic House Museum, P.O. Box 969, Palm Beach, FL 33480; (305) 655-2833. Preserves Flagler mansion and preserves history of FL East Coast (FEC) Development. Museum housed in restored mansion. Archives contains materials from Flagler family and FEC Development; manuscripts; railroad and construction maps; photos of Flaglers, FEC railroad and hotels, and Key West Extension; and film on Flagler's part in developing FL east coast. Some materials available to professional researchers only. Accepts phone inquiries. Fee. Hours: Tu-Sa 10-5, Su noon-5.

Heritage Park/Pinellas County Historical Museum

11909 125th St. N., Largo, FL 34644; (813) 462-3474. Museum comprises 20 bldgs, library, and archives. Museum exhibits local history materials from pre-Columbian period. Library documents FL and Pinellas county history. Archive holds photos, manuscripts, newspapers, maps, large collection of videotapes on county and state history, genealogical records, and Javnus collection of papers and photos. Accepts phone inquiries. No fee. Hours: Tu-Sa 10-4.

Hialeah John F. Kennedy Library

190 W. 49th St., Hialeah, FL 33012; (305) 821-2700. Public library has special collection on FL history and genealogies. Accepts phone inquiries. No fee. Hours: M-Th 10-9, F-Sa 9:30-5.

Hillsborough County Historical Commission Museum

County Court House, Room 250, Tampa, FL 33602; (813) 272-5919. Collects and preserves local history during Spanish-American War. Holdings include some Indian artifacts, guns from Spanish-American War, swords from Civil War; library materials on southern genealogy and Indians; historic maps of FL and Tampa; photos of Spanish-American War soldiers; and genealogical and census records from 19th c. Materials non-circulating. Accepts phone inquiries. No fee. Hours: M-F 10-4.

Historic Florida Militia

42 Spanish St., St. Augustine, FL 32084; (904) 829-9792. Educational living history association recreates military units and their history. Accepts phone inquiries. Fee for membership. Hours: call.

Historic Saint Augustine Preservation Board

P.O. Box 1987, 48 King St., St. Augustine, FL 32084; (904) 824-3355. Preserves, documents, and interprets historic sites and buildings in St. Augustine and St. Johns county. Outdoor museum details Spanish settlers' impact on region through living history presentation; library holds manuscripts, maps, photos, and sources on Hispanic studies; manuscript collections provide archaeological field notes on historical research; collection of Sanborn maps and colonial surveys; photos of architecture, museum, and archaeological documentation of St. Augustine; recordings of Spanish music and oral histories; and genealogical records. Accepts phone inquiries. Fee. Hours: library by appointment only; museum 9-5.

Historical Museum of Southern Florida

101 W. Flagler St., Miami, FL 33130; (305) 375-1492. Preserves history of region with museum, library, and archival holdings. Library holds archives of Miami Chamber of Commerce, personal papers, memoirs, diaries, developers' materials, maps of Florida and Caribbean from 1500s, large photograph collection from 1883, small film and videotape collection, oral history interviews from 1950s, and archaeological objects. Special collection of Woodrow Wilkings regional architectural records. Accepts phone inquiries. Fee. Hours: M-Sa 10-5, Th 10-9, Su 12-5.

Historical Society and Avon Park Museum

P.O. Box 483, Avon Park, FL 33825; (813) 452-0850. Collects and preserves history of Avon Park and region through holdings in museum, library, and archives. Collections include regional artifacts, pictures, publications, newspapers, maps, and genealogical records from 1880s. Accepts phone inquiries. Donations accepted. Hours: M-F 10-4, Su 2-4.

Historical Society Museum

Historical Society of Okaloosa and Walton counties, Inc., P.O. Box 488, 115 Westview Ave., Valparaiso, FL 32580; (904) 678-2615. Collects, preserves, and displays history and development of Okaloosa and Walton counties. Museum exhibits artifacts and sponsors tours and heritage craft classes. Library holds complete set of Official Records of War of Rebellion, as well as materials on local and FL history. Archive holds official Okaloosa county records, local maps and photos, oral history interviews, and some genealogical materials. Accepts phone inquiries. No fee. Hours: Tu-Sa 11-4.

International Swimming Hall of Fame

One Hall of Fame Dr., Fort Lauderdale, FL 33316; (305) 462-6536. Honors athletes in swimming, diving, synchronized swimming, water polo, and water safety, and provides resource materials on sports. Museum displays memorabilia on aquatic sports and athletes from 1700. Library documents all aquatic sports. Archives hold rare books and scrapbooks, thousands of aquatic athlete and event photos, films/videotapes of events and athletes, recordings of clinics and speeches, Daumier prints, and Weissmueller medal collection. Accepts phone inquiries. Fee. Hours: M-Sa 10-5, Su 11-4.

Jacksonville Historic Landmarks Commission

Mayor's Office, City Hall, 220 E. Bay St., Jacksonville, FL 32202; (904) 630-1776. Advises city officials and agencies on historic and cultural preservation matters. Holdings include site files of 800 bldgs, sites, and objects of historic interest, photos of same, and small collection of local history items. Accepts phone inquiries. No fee. Hours: M-F 8-5.

Kennedy Space Center

Library Historical Documents Collection, NWSI-E, Room 1533, Kennedy Space Center, FL 32899; (305) 867-2407. Collections document significant parts of history of Skylab, Apollo-Soyuz, and Space Shuttle programs. Holdings include photos of visits by Pres Kennedy, Johnson, Nixon, and Carter; Apollo-era documents; Apollo 204 accident papers and documentation; Wernher von Braun rocketry and biographical materials; official records of Deputy Director from 1963; Gemini records from 1962-66; records of Mercury program from 1959-65; monographs and chronologies of Marshall Space Flight Center; archival photo collection; press kits from 1963-75; Space Shuttle materials; and mission histories from Saturn/Apollo launches. Accepts phone inquiries. No fee. Hours: M-F 7:30-4.

Lake Wales Museum and Cultural Center

325 S. Scenic Hwy., Lake Wales, FL 33853; (813) 676-5443. Collects, conserves, exhibits, and studies materials on Lake Wales history. Museum exhibits focus on local citrus, cattle, and phosphate industries from 1852; library holds research materials on local, county, and state history; archives collect printed materials, local maps and photos, oral history interviews with pioneers, railroad memorabilia, and a textile collection. Accepts phone inquiries. Donations accepted. Hours: call.

Lakeland Public Library

Documents Dept., 100 Lake Morton Dr., Lakeland, FL 33801; (813) 686-2168. General library serves as federal depository for FL. Also retains special collection on local history on Lakeland and Polk counties. Accepts phone inquiries. No fee. Hours: M-Th 9-9, F and Sa 9-6, Su 1:30-5.

Lightner Museum

P.O. Box 334, 75 King St., St. Augustine, FL 32084; (904) 824-2874. Displays 19th c antiques and artifacts with emphasis on decorative arts. Maintains library with research materials on museum collections. Accepts phone inquiries. Fee. Hours: 9-5.

Louis Wolfson II Media History Center

Miami-Dade Public Library, 101 W. Flagler St., Miami, FL 33130; (305) 375-4527. Only film/TV archive in FL collecting materials representing 40 years of FL history. Holdings include over 3000 hrs. of film/videotape, small photo collection on FL film/TV personalities, and daily news scripts from WTUJ-TV in Miami, from 1950s-70s. Accepts phone inquiries. Fee. Hours: by appt, 9-5.

Loxahatchee Historical Society

P.O. Box 1506, 805 North W.S. One, Jupiter, FL 33458; (305) 747-6639. Preserves local history with emphasis on Loxahatchee River life and Jupiter Lighthouse. Museum houses exhibits on Indian artifacts, Spanish shipwrecks, Seminole Indian wars, and German U-Boats from World War II; some films/videotapes on local pioneers and historic places; and a few genealogical records. Accepts phone inquiries. No fee. Hours: 9-5.

Manatee County Public Library

Eaton Room, 1301 Barcarrota Blvd., West, Bradenton, FL 34205; (813) 748-5555. Collects FL and local history materials. Library holds collections on Manatee county and state. Archive contains large collection of local history photos, oral history transcripts, local historical society speeches, FL maps from 1830s-1980s, and county maps from 1850-1980s. Some genealogical materials also available. Materials non-circulating. Accepts phone inquiries. No fee. Hours: M-Sa 10-5.

Museum of Florida History

500 S. Bronough St., R.A. Gray Bldg., Tallahassee, FL 32399; (904) 488-1484. Collects, preserves, exhibits, and interprets FL cultural history, and promotes appreciation of state history. Museum houses 18th c artifact collection including clothing, furnishings, and decorative items; holds materials on capitol history and restoration, political heritage, mission period, and Indian/Spanish interaction. Special collections include labels from FL products such as citrus, cigars, vegetables; and FL political items ranging from cartoons to campaign materials. Accepts phone inquiries. No fee. Hours: M-F 9-4:30, Sa 10-4:30, Su noon-4:30.

Naval Aviation Museum

U.S. Naval Air Station, Bldg. 3465, Pensacola, FL 32508; (904) 452-3604. Selects, collects, preserves, and exhibits memorabilia on development and history of US Naval aviation from 1911 to Space Age. Museum holds 160 aircraft with 60 on display; library concentrates on naval history with manuscript and photo collections. Accepts phone inquiries. No fee. Hours: 9-5.

Northern Map Company

9288 S.W. 182nd Terrace, Dunnellon, FL 32630. Mail order company offers large collection of US and Canadian maps detailing railroads, canals, cities, and townships from all 50 states. Most materials date from 19th c to present. Write for catalog.

Norton Gallery and School of Art

1451 S. Olive Ave., West Palm Beach, FL 33401; (305) 832-5194. Museum holds collections of 19th and 20th c art including Oriental art. Library provides some reference materials. Library materials circulate only to members. Donations accepted. Hours: library, M-F 10-5.

Orange County Historical Society

812 E. Rollins Ave., Orlando, FL 32803; (305) 898-8320. Preserves and researches Orange county heritage and generates interest in local history. Museum holds records and exhibits on local central FL history. Library collects maps, photos, and pamphlets on topics of regional history interest. Accepts phone inquiries. No fee. Hours: Tu-F 10-4, Sa-Su 1-5.

Otto G. Richter Library

University of Florida, P.O. Box 248214, Memorial Dr., Coral Gables, FL 33124; (305) 284-3155. Academic support facility collecting federal documents, Congressional materials, and southeastern US maps from 1939. Some historical maps. Material circulation limited. Accepts phone inquiries. No fee. Hours: M-Th 8-9, F 8-5, Sa 9-5, Su 1-9.

P.K. Yonge Library of Florida History

University of Florida, 404 Library, W., Gainesville, FL 32611; (904) 392-0319. Academic research library promoting scholarship in FL history through collections of 20th c political manuscripts, FL and Caribbean maps, small photo collection, and largest collection of FL newspapers in US. Special collection of colonial British and Spanish Florida documents. Accepts phone inquiries. No fee. Hours: M-F 8-noon, 1-4:45.

Palm Beach Landmarks Preservation Commission

P.O. Box 2029, 45 Coconut Row, Palm Beach, FL 33480; (305) 838-5430. Coordinates activities of preservation committee and works with community orgs. Library and archives retain architectural drawings, building plans, land-use maps, and photos of structures nominated for Federal Register of Historic Places. Accepts phone inquiries. No fee. Hours: M-F 8:30-5.

Pensacola Historical Society

Pensacola Historical Museum, 405 S. Adams St.,

Pensacola, FL 32501; (904) 433-1559. Collects, preserves, and interprets historical Pensacola and Escambia county materials. Museum has geological and archaeological artifacts from 18th & 19th c Spanish and British occupations; library concentrates on Pensacola and Escambia manuscripts, maps, genealogical materials, newspapers, and ephemera; map collection includes plans, architectural drawings, and land grants from Spanish, British, and French occupation, and Colonial period; large photo collection from 1860s; city promotional films from 1950s; records and tapes of Pensacola music from 1907; letters of Stephen Mallory, Secretary of Confederate Navy. Materials non-circulating. No fee. Hours: M-Sa 9-4:30.

Pioneer Florida Museum

P.O. Box 335, Dade City, FL 34297; (904) 567-0262. Houses collections depicting pioneer family life in FL. Museum consists of train depot, church, and school house dating to early 20th c. Library holdings not cataloged, but include manuscripts, maps, photos, and genealogical records. Accepts phone inquiries. Fee. Hours: Tu-Sa 1-5, Su 2-5.

Putnam County Archives and History Commission

P.O. Box 1976, 512 St. Johns Ave., Palatka, FL 32078; (904) 329-0330. Collects and preserves Putnam county history with govt, photo, local history, and manuscript materials. Museum houses primarily Putnam county artifacts, small manuscript collection from 1880s, county maps and photos, oral history interviews, genealogical records, and business records of Wilson Cypress Company. Accepts phone inquiries. Fee. Hours: M-F 8:30-5.

Riverside Avondale Preservation

2624 Riverside Ave., Jacksonville, FL 32204; (904) 389-2449. Preserves structures and character of Riverside and Avondale. Archival holdings include site files and photos on houses and bldgs in neighborhood and FL. Accepts phone inquiries. No fee. Hours: M-F 9-5.

Saint Augustine Historical Society

271 Charlotte St., St. Augustine, FL 32084;

(904) 824-2872. Collects early FL and St. Augustine materials in museum, library and archives. Holdings include business and govt records, early Spanish documents from 1600, regional maps, extensive collection of photos from 1882, oral history interviews, and genealogical records from early families. Materials non-circulating. Accepts phone inquiries. No fee. Hours: M-F 9-noon, 1-5.

Saint Petersburg Public Library

Documents Dept., Reference Dept., 3745 Ninth Ave. North, Saint Petersburg, FL 33713; (813) 893-7928. Local reference library with federal document, local history, and genealogical holdings. Map collection consists of FL, Dept of Interior, and CIA maps; photo collection consists of many postcards of early FL scenes; and newspaper archive with indexes from 1920s. Materials non-circulating. No fee. Hours: M-Th 9-9, F-Sa 9-5:30.

Stephen Foster State Folk Culture Center

P.O. Drawer G, U.S. 41 N, White Springs, FL 32096; (904) 397-2733. Highlights FL folk culture and commemorates life of Foster. Museum displays scenes from Foster's music from 1800s, copies of Foster's Lilliana collection, and FL folk culture exhibits. Accepts phone inquiries. Fee. Hours: 9-5.

Tallahassee Historical Society

P.O. Box 5123, Tallahassee, FL 32314. Provides forum for local history research, holds monthly meetings, and publishes journal of local history irregularly. No fee.

Tampa-Hillsborough County Public Library System

Special Collections, 900 N. Ashley St., Tampa, FL 33602; (813) 223-8865. Provides services in genealogy, state history, Tampa history, and collection of state, local, and federal documents. Holdings include early maps of FL from 1770-1875, photos of Tampa from 1885-1955, and genealogical reference books on region from PA to TX, including New England and 13 colonies. Must have valid card for ILL use. Accepts phone inquiries. No fee. Hours: M-Th 9-9, F 9-6, Sa 9-5.

Thomas Edison Winter Home and Museum

2350 McGregor Blvd., Fort Meyers, FL 33901; (813) 334-3614. Educational and historic shrine to Edison and his accomplishments. Large museum exhibits inventions and memorabilia of Edison; photo collection details his work in FL and NJ; and genealogy records provide insight into Edison family. Accepts phone inquiries. Fee. Hours: M-Sa 9-4, Su 12:30-4.

Thomas G. Carpenter Library

University of North Florida, 4567 St. John's Bluff Rd., Jacksonville, FL 32216; (904) 646-2617. Academic research library serving northeast FL and southern GA region. Holdings include University archives, USGS and DMA maps, photo collection on Jacksonville social activist Eartha White, papers of state Senator Jack Mathews, and papers of Jacksonville city planner Arthur Solee. Materials circulate within University community. Accepts phone inquiries. No fee. Hours: M-Th 9-9, F 9-5, Sa 11-4, Su 2-6.

University of Florida Libraries

Special Collections, W. University Ave., Gainesville, FL 32611; (904) 392-0637. Academic research library has manuscript collection dealing with Haiti, revolutionary period, and later era. Collection includes large group of notaries' papers on early slave trade. Accepts phone inquiries. No fee. Hours: call.

University of West Florida

Special Collections, 11000 University Parkway, Pensacola, FL 32514; (904) 474-2213. Acquires, preserves, and disseminates info on west FL history from settlement era. Library collections include rare books, family diaries, and manuscripts from region, maps of southeastern US states from 1690s, west FL photos from 1863, civic and religious records from 1720, and genealogical research files. Accepts phone inquiries. No fee. Hours: M-F 8-4:30, Sa 8-noon.

Georgia

Agnes Scott Library

E. College Ave., Decatur, GA 30030; (404) 371-6339. Academic reference library has collection of materials on slavery's effect on Old South Frontier before 1860. Hours: call.

Albany Museum of Art

311 Meadowlark Dr., Albany, GA 31702; (912) 439-8400. Provides access to 19th and 20th c American and European art, and traditional African art through collections, programs, and activities. Museum collections include American decorative arts, paintings, drawings, and prints; African objects, and small ancient collection. Library holds reference materials on African art and general art topics. Photo collection includes work of some contemporary regional photographers. Accepts phone inquiries. Fee. Hours: Tu-F noon-5.

Andersonville National Historic Site

Hwy. 49, Box 85, Andersonville, GA 31711; (912) 924-0343. Promotes understanding of prisoner of war experience during Civil War through holdings in museum, library, and archives. Museum and library preserve materials on POW history; archives hold letters and diaries of POWs, Civil War manuscripts, maps, and small photo collection. Also offers programs on Civil War education. Some restrictions on use. Accepts phone inquiries. No fee. Hours: 8-5.

Atlanta Historical Society

3101 Andrews Dr., N.W., Atlanta, GA 30305; (404) 261-1837. Preserves and displays archival materials and artifacts relating to history of Atlanta. Museum holds 19th c artifacts, Civil War exhibits focusing on Atlanta campaign and resurgents; library emphasizes Atlanta, GA, Civil War, and South; archival materials on local businesses, govt, architectural firms, Atlanta, and Academy Theatre; collection of Atlanta Sanborn Fire Insurance maps, and GA maps from 19th c; large photo archive on Atlanta and residents from mid-19th c; small film/video archive; genealogical records; and Atlanta architectural library and manuscript collection. Accepts phone inquiries. Fee. Hours: M-Sa 9-5:30, Su noon-5.

Atlanta-Fulton Public Library

Documents Division, 1 Margaret Mitchell Square, Atlanta, GA 30303; (404) 688-4636. Library provides govt documents from 1880 in depository collection, with emphasis on Executive and

Legislative branches, Agriculture Department, Atlanta, and Fulton county. Materials circulate only to Fulton county residents. Accepts phone inquiries. No fee. Hours: M-F 9-6, Tu-Th 9-8, Sa 10-6, Su 2-6.

Augusta College
Document Dept., Reese Library, 2500 Walton Way, Augusta, GA 30910; (404) 737-1748. Academic support library with collections on local history and genealogy of Southeast. Materials for in-house use only. Accepts phone inquiries. No fee. Hours: M-Th 7:45-10:30, F 7:45-5, Sa 9-5, Su 1:30-9:30.

Augusta Richmond County Museum
540 Telfair St., Augusta, GA 30901; (404) 722-8454. Collects and exhibits artifacts of historic and scientific interest in museum. Library and archive holdings include manuscripts, maps, photos, films/videotapes, recordings, and genealogical records. Library and archive open to researchers only. Fee. Hours: Tu-Sa 10-5, Su 2-5.

Berry College Memorial Library
Document Department, Mount Berry Station, Rome, GA 30149; (404) 232-5374. Academic research library with holdings documenting college's history as well as a special collection of Martha Berry papers. Some restrictions. Accepts phone inquiries (404-236-2221). No fee. Hours: call.

Big Shanty Museum
P.O. Box 418, 2829 Cherokee St., Kennesaw, GA 30144; (404) 427-2117. Preserves history of Civil War and trains through museum exhibits. Accepts phone inquiries. Fee. Hours: M-Sa 9:30-5:30, Su noon-5:30.

Bryan Lang
Historical Library
P.O. Box 725, Woodbine, GA 31569; (912) 576-5601. Preserves and disseminates Camden county and surrounding area history. Collections include 19th c records of port of St. Mary's, genealogical records, and Lang and Coastal Highway collections on local history. Materials non-circulating. Accepts phone inquiries. No fee. Hours: M-F 8-5.

Cable News Network Library
One CNN Center, Atlanta, GA 30348; (404) 827-1335. Sells and licenses video from CNN news archives from June of 1980. No public access to library; do not rent or lend video. Accepts phone inquiries. No fee. Hours: 10-6.

Chattahoochee Valley
Art Association
P.O. Box 291, 112 Hines St., La Grange, GA 30241; (404) 882-3267. Art museum for west GA and east AL region holds small collection of works by American artists and craftspersons, with files kept on each artist. Prior arrangements must be made to use collections. Accepts phone inquiries. No fee. Hours: Tu-F 9-5, Sa 9-4, Su 1-5.

Chickamauga-Chattanooga
National Military Park
P.O. Box 2128, US Hwy 27, Fort Oglethorpe, GA 30742; (404) 866-9241. Provides materials for research and instruction through library and museum holdings. Museum collection includes Fuller guns, Civil War artifacts, and cannon monuments; library focuses on Civil War and military history; other collections of Civil War maps, photos, and some films and tapes. Accepts phone inquiries. No fee. Hours: library by appt, 8-4:45.

Chief John Ross House
P.O. Box 863, Rossville, GA 30741; (404) 861-3954. Home is furnished with period antiques, and has collections of photos, genealogical records, and some Cherokee artifacts. Accepts phone inquiries. No fee. Hours: 9:30-5:30; May-Sept, Th-Tu 1-5.

Chieftains Museum
501 Riverside Pkwy., Rome, GA 30161; (404) 291-9494. Preserves heritage of local community and Ridge House. Museum exhibits cover life of Maj Ridge and early Cherokee Indians from 1790s. Library documents Cherokee and Rome history from 1883; archive contains some business materials from local merchants; map and photo collections trace county from 1860s. Special collections include hats from 1920-60, Coca-Cola memorabilia from Barron collection, and artifacts from 1830s trading post run by

Ridge. Accepts phone inquiries. Donations accepted. Hours: Tu-F 11-4, Su 2-5.

Coastal Georgia Historical Society

Museum of Coastal History, P.O. Box 1136, 101 12th St., St. Simons Island, GA 31522; (912) 638-4666. Collects, preserves, interprets, and disseminates history and culture of coastal GA region. Museum of local history exhibits dating from mid-18th c; library on local and regional history, museum administration, lighthouses, and arts and crafts; collections of local manuscripts, photos, and films/videotapes. Special collection of Couper family papers. Accepts phone inquiries. Fee. Hours: by appt only, Memorial Day-Labor Day, Tu-Sa 10-5, Su 1:30-5; Labor Day-Memorial Day, Tu-Sa 1-4, Su 1:30-4.

Coca-Cola Company Archives

P.O. Drawer 1734, Atlanta, GA 30301; (404) 676-3491. Preserves materials relating to history, marketing, and advertising of Coca-Cola around world from 1886. Museum, library, and archives contain photos, films/videotapes, and recording. Accepts phone inquiries. Hours: by appt only, M-F 9-5.

Columbus College

Simon Schwob Memorial Library, Columbus, GA 31993; (404) 568-2042. Academic library holds govt publications and special collection on Chattahoochee Valley history. Accepts phone inquiries. No fee. Hours: M-F 8-11, Sa 9-6, Su 2-10.

Columbus Museum

P.O. Box 1617, 1202 Front Ave., Columbus, GA 31902; (404) 322-0400. Studies, preserves, and exhibits Deep South history and culture. Museum collections include southeastern fine arts, historical and folklife materials, and Native American holdings. Archival materials include regional folk music recordings, oral history interviews, and maps and photos from 19th c. Some restrictions. No fee for admission. Hours: Tu-F 10-5, Sa-Su 1-5.

Confederate Naval Museum

Box 1022, 202 4th St., Columbus, GA 31902; (404) 327-9798. Interprets history of Confederate States Navy, Jackson and Chattahoochee gunboats, and naval operations on Apalachicola-Chattahoochee River system. Museum displays salvaged remains of gunboats and naval history artifacts and ship models; small reference library and archive on Civil War naval history; manuscript collection on Confederate naval operations and history; photos and films/videotapes on salvage of Jackson and Chattahoochee gun boats; and special James Warner collection on Naval Iron Works, 1862-66. Accepts phone inquiries. Donations requested. Hours: Tu-F 10-5, Sa-Su 10-1.

Crawford W. Long Medical Museum

College St., Jefferson, GA 30549; (404) 367-5307. Preserves and promotes history of Dr. Long's career in medicine and the complementary history of anesthesia, as well as Jackson County history from 18th c. Library and archives document Long's life and role in medicine; maps and photo collection provide background on Jackson county and its residents. Accepts phone inquiries. Donations accepted. Hours: Tu-Sa 10-1, 2-5.

Dahlonega Courthouse Gold Museum

P.O. Box 2042, Dahlonega, GA 30533; (404) 864-2257. Educates and interprets GA's gold rush history. Museum displays artifacts and exhibits on Rush. Library has resource materials on Gold Rush, geology, Dahlonega gold coins, and Cherokee Indians. Archives holds county census records, newspapers, and correspondence with US Mint; 1832 land grant and gold maps; photos of Gold Rush era; and small genealogical collection. Some restrictions. Accepts phone inquiries. Fee. Hours: Tu-Sa 9-5, Su 2-5:30.

Dalton College Library

Documents Dept., 213 N. College Dr., Dalton, GA 30720; (404) 272-4575. Serves Whitfield county residents with general collection of govt depository materials; CIA, congressional, and district maps; and special GA/Dalton collection. Accepts phone inquiries. No fee. Hours: M-Th 8-10, F 8-5, Sa 2-5.

DeKalb Historical Society

Old Courthouse on the Square, Decatur, GA

30030; (404) 373-1088. Collects and preserves historic DeKalb county materials. Museum exhibits cover Civil War artifacts and photos, and other county materials from 1822-1922. Library houses small collection on local history and genealogy. Archives have special DAR collection, maps, photos, oral history project interviews, and old newspapers. Materials non-circulating. Due to small staff, accepts only very brief phone inquiries. Donations accepted. Hours: by appt; museum, M-F 9-4; archives, 8:30-4:15.

Dublin-Laurens Museum

P.O. Box 1461, Academy & Bellevue at Church, Dublin, GA 31040; (912) 272-9242. Preserves artifacts, clothing, arts, crafts, and documents of county and state historic value. Holds some maps, photos, and manuscripts. Special collection of Lila Moore Keen paintings. Accepts phone inquiries. No fee. Hours: Tu-Sa 1-4:30.

Eatonton-Putnam County Historical Society

P.O. Box 331, 114 North Madison Ave., Eatonton, GA 31024; (404) 485-6442. Conserves and encourages education on local history and architecture. Society maintains 1840s Greek Revival Bronson House and Tavern Inn. Archives hold local history materials, photos, and genealogical materials. Restrictions. Accepts phone inquiries. Fee for Bronson House museum. Hours: by appt only, W-Su 1-5.

Elijah Clark State Park Museum

P.O. Box 293, Rte. 4, Lincolnton, GA 30817; (404) 359-3458. Recognizes Revolutionary War Gen Elijah Clark, and interprets Colonial living. Museum consists of two log cabins furnished with replica artifacts of period. Accepts phone inquiries. No fee. Hours: 8-5.

Emory University

Special Collections, Robert Woodruff Library, Atlanta, GA 30322; (404) 727-6868. Preserves collection of materials on "Atlanta Constitution" journalists, including Henry Grady, Corra Harris, Joel Chandler Harris, Ralph McGill, Claude Sitton, and others. No fee. Hours: call.

Fayette County Historical Society

P.O. Box 421, Fayetteville, GA 30214; (404) 487-2000. Perpetuates history of Fayette county through holdings in library and archives. Collections document Civil War activities and invovement, local business and organization records, genealogy of local residents, and photographic history from 1880s. Accepts phone inquiries. No fee. Hours: call.

Fort King George Historic Site

P.O. Box 711, Darien, GA 31305; (912) 437-4770. Interprets coastal state history with emphasis on residents and Ft King George. Museum covers history of aboriginal inhabitants during and before Spanish, British, Scottish, and Sawmiller occupation; library and archive document heritage of Ft and surrounding area; manuscript and map collections detail Ft's surroundings; photos describe local sawmill, lumber, and dairy industries; and genealogical records available on Scots of McIntosh and Ft officers. Accepts phone inquiries. Fee. Hours: Tu-Sa 9-5, Su 2-5:30.

Fort Pulaski National Monument

P.O. Box 98, Tybee Island, GA 31328; (912) 786-5787. Preserves and interprets site and history of American seacoast fortification from 1750-1870. Exhibits include drawbridges, dikes, and demilunes; archives hold documentation of Ft Pulaski restoration from 1925-44; and library retains photos on Civil War activities and historic preservation. Accepts phone inquiries. Fee. Hours: 9-4.

Georgia Agrirama Development Authority

State Museum of Agriculture, P.O. Box Q, Tifton, GA 31794; (912) 386-3344. Preserves and demonstrates GA's agricultural heritage. Outdoor living history museum portrays rural GA life from 1800-1900; research library focuses on southern agriculture and heritage; archives hold business and rural living documentation materials; unpublished reports on Wiregrass, Georgia history; Sanborn fire insurance maps of some GA towns; agricultural photos and portraits; film on turpentine industry; and genealogical collection. Some restrictions. Accepts phone inquiries. Fee. Hours: Labor Day-May 9-5, June-Labor Day 9-6.

Georgia Department of Archives and History

330 Capitol Ave., SE, Atlanta, GA 30334; (404) 656-2350. Promotes, maintains, and protects state and local govt records, and makes them accessible to public. Holdings include official state and local records; personal, business, and genealogical records from 19th c; state and county maps; and photo documentation of GA's economic, social, cultural, and political history from mid 19th c. Some restrictions. Accepts phone inquiries. No fee. Hours: M-F 8-4:30, Sa 9:30-3:30.

Georgia Historical Society

501 Whitaker St., Savannah, GA 31499; (912) 651-2128. Collects, preserves, and disseminates info on GA history with holdings in library and archives. Collections include 19th & 20th c manuscripts, maps, photos, genealogical records, and Central GA Railway records. Some restrictions. Accepts phone inquiries. No fee. Hours: M-F 10-5. Sa 9-1.

Georgia Historical Society

Hart County Branch, 2073 McLendon Ave., NE, Atlanta, GA 30307; (404) 377-5612. Records and preserves history of pioneer settlers, homes, sites, and families of county. Library holds extensive family records and research materials, census records, newspapers, and estate records; county landowner maps from 1890; small photo collection on settlers; oral history interviews; genealogical records; and special collections from DAR library of Hart county. Accepts mail inquiries with SASE. No fee. Hours: call.

Georgia Humanities Resource Center

Henderson Library, Georgia Southern College, Statesboro, GA 30460; (912) 681-5482. Promotes and circulates media programs produced with funding from GA Endowment for Humanities. Holdings include films, videotapes, and recordings relating GA and southeastern history and culture, as well as other humanities topics. Some restrictions. Accepts phone inquiries. Fee. Hours: M-F 8-5.

Georgia State Library

40 Capitol Square, 301 Judicial Building, Atlanta, GA 30334; (404) 656-3468. Research library with focus on law and govt history. Other materials include early GA and county maps, GA history collection, and slave diary. Materials non-circulating. No fee. Hours: M-F 8:30-5.

Georgia Trust for Historic Preservation

1516 Peachtree St., NW, Atlanta, GA 30309; (404) 881-9980. Preserves GA's cultural heritage with emphasis on architecture. Curates 2 museums: Rhodes Hall in Atlanta, and Hay house in Macon. Provides technical assistance resources for historic preservationists. Some restrictions. Accepts phone inquiries. Fee. Hours: M-F 9-5.

Historical Society of Alma-Bacon County

P.O. Box 2026, 405A West 11th St., Alma, GA 31510; (912) 632-8450. Preserves history and genealogy of county through holdings in Bacon county public library and Heritage Center. Museum holds inactive county records and early 20th c artifacts, archival materials, manuscripts, photos, recordings, and films/videotapes; library collections include genealogical materials and local history collection. Accepts phone inquiries. No fee. Hours: call.

Indian Museum State Park

P.O. Box 3969, Jackson, GA 30233; (404) 775-7241. Describes history of Indian Springs through holdings in museum and archives. Museum exhibits cover Creek Indians, Hotel Era, and Indian Spring history. Archives retains doctor's tools from 19th c; manuscript of 1821 and 1825 Treaty of Indian Springs; maps of Indian tribes of southeast and Creek Nations of 1800; and photos of Menewa, Opothleyoholo, William McIntosh, hotels from 1823, dummy train, and town of Jackson. Accepts phone inquiries. No fee. Hours: Su-Sa 7am-10pm.

Jarrell Plantation, Georgia State Historic Site

Jarrell Plantation Rd., Rte. 1, Box 220, Juliette, GA 31046; (912) 986-5172. Promotes, preserves, and protects history of this 15 bldg farm complex, and maintains collection of family artifacts, tools, machinery, and clothing. Library holds reference materials on farm life, Civil War, local history, and crafts; archive holds photos and papers of Jarrell family, aerial and topographic maps of plantation, oral history interviews with Jarrell family, and some genealogical records. Accepts phone inquiries. Fee. Hours: Tu-Sa 9-5, Su 2-5.

Jimmy Carter Presidential Library and Museum

1 Copenhill Ave., Atlanta, GA 30307; (404) 331-3942. Collects, preserves, and promotes research and educational use of President Carter's career record and issues of time. Museum displays items related to Carter's career, including many gifts given to First Family; library holds books on careers of President and Mrs. Carter and his administration, federal records related to administration, materials of major figures and Carter family, extensive collection of photos, and film/videotape library. Must prove need for library use and be over 16. Accepts phone inquiries. Fee. Hours: research, M-F 9-4:45; museum, M-Sa 9-4:45, Su noon-4:45.

Juliette Gordon Low Girl Scout National Center

142 Bull St., Savannah, GA 31401; (912) 233-4501. Period home commemorates early Girl Scouting, 18th c decorative arts, and life of Juliette Low. Museum holds Low's artwork from 1860-1927, decorative arts, and Girl Scout artifacts and memorabilia; archival Gordon family and early Girl Scout documents; Low's letters from 1870-1920s; photos of Gordon family, Girl Scout memorabilia; genealogical info relative to Low; silent film on Scouts from 1918; and special collection on founding of Girl Scouts in 1912. Accepts phone inquiries. Fee. Hours: M-Tu, Th-Sa 10-4, and Feb-Nov, Su 12:30-4:30.

Kennesaw Mountain National Battlefield Park

P.O. Box 1167, Marietta, GA 30061; (404) 427-4686. Preserves national battlefield park through museum and library holdings. Accepts phone inquiries. No fee. Hours: research by appt; museum, 8:30-5.

Little White House Historic Site

Georgia Dept. of Natural Resources, Box 68, Georgia Hwy 85 West, Warm Springs, GA 31830; (404) 655-3511. Preserves and presents GA residence of Franklin D. Roosevelt. Museum displays items owned by FDR and donated in his honor; library holds books owned by FDR, and books about him and his presidency; photo collection on FDR, his family, and his friends in Warm Springs region; and film/video library on FDR and his presidency, polio research, and general social themes of 1930s. Materials for in-house use only. Accepts phone inquiries. Fee. Hours: 9-4:30.

Martin Luther King Center for Nonviolent Social Change

Library and Archives, 449 Auburn Ave., Northeast, Atlanta, GA 30312; (404) 524-1956. Preserves Rev. King's philosophy on civil rights and history of his movement and activities. Holdings include obscure info and memorabilia, oral history interviews, and manuscripts from various civil rights orgs from 1950s-60s. Materials noncirculating. Accepts phone inquiries. Hours: 9-5:30.

Medical College of Georgia Library

Laney Walker Blvd., Augusta, GA 30902; (404) 721-3441. Library maintains small special collection of late 18th and early 19th c midwifery and women's medicine materials. Accepts phone inquiries. Hours: call.

Mercer University

Stetson Memorial Library, Macon, GA 31207; (912) 744-2968. Preserves Baptist history through archival materials of GA Baptist Convention and GA Baptist Historical Society. Holdings include some diaries, genealogical materials, and church records. Some GA and Mercer University history also available. Accepts phone inquiries. No fee. Hours: M-F 9-noon, 1-5.

Middle Georgia College

Roberts Memorial Library, Sarah St., Cochran, GA 31014; (912) 934-7882. Academic research library with special collection on GA history and genealogy. Holdings include county materials, some rare books on GA, and facsimiles. Accepts phone inquiries. No fee. Hours: M-Th 8-10, F 8-5, Su 6-10.

Middle Georgia Historical Society

935 High St., Macon, GA 31201; (912) 743-3851. Preserves historic, architectural, and esthetic heritage of Macon and middle GA. Restored 1840 museum house of poet Sidney Lanier houses his memorabilia; library holds reference materials on local history and Lanier, photos of historic Macon bldgs, and film on Lanier's life. Accepts phone inquiries. Fee. Hours: M-F 9-1, 2-4; Sa 9:30-12:30.

Museum and Archives of Georgia Education

C.P.O. 95, 131 S. Clark St., Milledgeville, GA 31061; (912) 453-4391. Collects and preserves researched written and oral documents on GA education history. Museum contains artifacts pertaining to education history; library holds old textbooks; archives hold some collections of GA educators; photo collection of GA schoolhouses and educational topics; oral history interviews; and yearbook and memorabilia collections. Accepts phone inquiries. No fee. Hours: M-F noon-5, Sa-Su 1-5.

National Infantry Museum

U.S. Army Infantry Center, Fort Benning, GA 31905; (404) 545-2958. Honors infantrymen and two centuries of service through holdings in museum, library, and archives. Museum displays US and foreign infantry weapons, US and German WWII uniforms, and equipment from 1750. Library holds large collection of books and huge collection of photos, some detailing history of Ft Benning. Archives holds presidential items, maps of WWII battlefields, Army manuals from late 19th and early 20th c, posters from WWI and WWII, limited films/videotapes, and limited recordings. Restrictions on library use. Accepts phone inquiries. No fee. Hours: Tu-F 10-4:30, Sa-Su 12:30-4:30.

Navy Supply Corps Museum

Navy Supply Corps School, Prince Ave & Oglethorpe St., Athens, GA 30606; (404) 354-7349. Documents development and growth of Navy Supply Corps, the division's functions, and some of its noteworthy participants. Museum exhibits display Navy and Corps history from 1795 with uniforms, navigational equipment, galley gear, paintings, and personal memorabilia; library on general navy history; archival Supply Corps materials including photos, records, manuals, cruise books, newsletters, and directories; and oral history interviews with former Supply Corps Chiefs. Accepts phone inquiries. No fee. Hours: M-F 8-4:30.

New Echota

1211 Chatsworth Hwy., Calhoun, GA 30701; (404) 629-8151. Former capital of Cherokee Indian nation from 1825-38 now preserves history of southeast Indian and Cherokee cultures from early 19th c through holdings in museum and library. Holdings include Cherokee Indian census of 1835, some genealogical materials, and Cherokee newspaper archives from 1828-34. Accepts phone inquiries. Fee. Hours: Tu-Sa 9-5, Su 2-5:30.

Northeast Georgia Area Planning and Development Commission

305 Research Drive, Athens, GA 30610; (404) 548-3141. Coordinates historical preservation activities in Athens region. Library concentration on state and local architectural history; archives hold collection of field surveys of historical architecture, maps, and small photo file. Accepts phone inquiries. No fee. Hours: M-F 8:30-5.

Ocmulgee National Monument

1207 Emery Hwy, Macon, GA 31201; (912) 752-8257. Preserves artifacts and history of region from Paleo-Indian period through historic Creek Indian period. Museum exhibits and interprets artifacts; library houses southeastern Native American history materials; archives hold maps, photos, and films/videotapes on site's history and monument development. Materials for in-house use only. Accepts phone inquiries. Fee. Hours: 9-5.

Old Fort Jackson

1 Old Fort Jackson Rd., Savannah, GA 31401; (912) 232-3945. Provides programs on heritage of coastal region with small museum and library holdings on local military and maritime activities. Accepts phone inquiries. Fee. Hours: library, by appt; museum, Tu-Su 9-5.

Roselawn Museum

P.O. Box 128, 224 W. Cherokee Ave., Cartersville, GA 30120; (404) 386-3410. House museum of evangelist Samuel Porter Jones exhibits furniture, paintings, and documents of Rebecca Latimer Felton, documents of United Daughters of Confederation, and religious writing and publications by Jones. Other holdings include limited pre-Civil War maps, materials on local history, small collection of photos, and works of art by Hal Morrison, late 1800s. Accepts phone inquiries. Donations accepted. Hours: M-F 10-5.

Ships of the Sea Museum

503 River St., Savannah, GA 31401; (912) 232-1511. Preserves maritime artifacts and history in museum and library with collections of ship models, artifacts, artwork, and reference materials from 1600s. Accepts phone inquiries. Fee. Hours: 10-5.

Southeastern Railway Museum

P.O. Box 1010, 3966 Buford Hwy, Duluth, GA 30136; (404) 476-2013. Preserves operation of historical railroad equipment, locomotives, and rolling stock. Museum houses over 40 railroad cars; library holds blueprints, newspaper clippings, maps, and photos. Accepts phone inquiries. Fee. Hours: Sa 9-5.

Sunbury Historic Site

Rte. 1, Box 236, Midway, GA 31320; (912) 884-5999. Preserves and protects remains of earthwork of Ft Defiance, and interprets history of Sunbury. Museum revives history of "dead" town of Sunbury, with emphasis on Revolutionary War activities and battles. Archives hold land-grant records, wills, church records, and court proceedings. Most date to 19th c. Materials for in-house use only. Accepts phone inquiries. Fee. Hours: M-F 9-5.

Temple Mickve Israel

Archives Museum, 20 E. Gordon St., Savannah, GA 31401; (912) 233-1547. Synagogue holds small collection of artifacts on Savannah Judaica from Colonial and Victorian eras to present. Holdings in library and museum include congregational records and uncataloged manuscripts.

Accepts phone inquiries. No fee. Hours: archives by appt; museum, 9-5.

Thomas County Historical Society

P.O. Box 1922, 725 N. Dawson St., Thomasville, GA 31799; (912) 226-7664. Interprets life and thought of Thomas county's past by collecting and preserving its history in museum, library, and archives. Museum houses Victorian bowling alley, 1870s frame house, and historic vehicles; archival materials from county and city govts; manuscript collection includes personal papers, local school and church records, Sanborn maps from 1889-1928, large photo collection and some film footage of local events, oral history recordings, and special collection of plantation owners' business records from 1857-72. Accepts phone inquiries. Fee. Hours: Sa-Th 2-5; other hours by appt.

Troup County Historical Society

P.O. Box 1051, 136 Main St., La Grange, GA 30241; (404) 884-1828. Preserves, protects, and makes available materials on county and resident history. Museum concentrates on county artifacts from 1828 and collection of local textile magnate Fuller Callaway items; library holds local history and genealogical materials for GA, AL, VA, SC, NC, and materials on Indians and immigration; archives hold civic and government records for region, manuscript collection, Sanborn maps, extensive photo collection, and films/videotapes on local visits by Griffin Bell, Jimmy Carter, and John F. Kennedy. Accepts phone inquiries. No fee. Hours: M-F 9-5, Sa 9-1.

University of Georgia

Main Library, Athens, GA 30602; (404) 542-3256. Academic research library holds large collection of materials on GA history, including maps, pictures, and considerable sheet music collection. Large collection of papers from US Congressmen John Davis, Maston O'Neal, Robert Stephens, Jr, John Pilcher, Dudley Hughes, and Govs Carl Sanders, Lester Maddox, and Hoke Smith. Also has collection of Arbitron TV and radio program ratings from 1949-present. Accepts phone inquiries. No fee. Hours: call.

Washington-Wilkes Historical Museum

308 E. Robert Tommbs Ave., Washington, GA 30673; (404) 678-2105. Preserves Washington-Wilkes memorabilia in house museum. Holdings include some Civil War period letters, maps of GA and Wilkes county, local photos, Civil War memorabilia including Jefferson Davis camp chest and guns, and Indian artifacts. Restrictions on use. Accepts phone inquiries. Fee. Hours: Tu-Sa 10-5, Su 2-5.

West Georgia College

Annie Belle Weaver Special Collections, Irvine Sullivan Ingram Library, Reference Dept., Carrollton, GA 30118; (404) 836-6495. Academic research library with college archival holdings from 1906, old maps, photos, genealogical records, and special collections on local history and sacred harp music. Some restrictions. Accepts phone inquiries. No fee. Hours: M-Th 8-10, F 8-5, Sa 10-5, Su 3-10.

White County Historical Society

Box 487, Cleveland, GA 30528; (404) 865-2767 p.m./865-4679 a.m.. Restores and preserves landmarks and collects local history. Museum and library hold limited collections of maps, photos, films/videotapes, recordings, and genealogical records. Restrictions on use. No fee. Hours: call.

Wormsloe Historic Site

7601 Skidaway Rd., Savannah, GA 31406; (912) 352-2548. Museum preserves home of GA settler Noble Jones with archaeological exhibits, archives, and photos. Accepts phone inquiries. Fee. Hours: Tu-Sa 9-5, Su 2-5:30.

Wren's Nest

Joel Chandler Harris Assn, 1050 Gordon St., S.W., Atlanta, GA 30310; (404) 753-7735. Interprets life and writings of Joel Chandler Harris, world-famous author of Uncle Remus stories. Museum is author's home from 1881-1908, and contains family furnishings and memorabilia. Library of first edition books, late 19th c family photos, and recordings of Uncle Remus stories available. Accepts phone inquiries. Fee. Hours: Tu-Sa 10-5, Su 2-5.

Hawaii

Army Museum of Hawaii

P.O. Box 8064, Honolulu, HI 96830; (808) 543-2639. Explains Hawaii's military history and impact on national defense; exhibits role of US Army in region. Accepts phone inquiries. Donation accepted. Hours: Tu-Su 10-4:30.

Bishop Museum Library

1525 Bernice St., P.O. Box 1900A, Honolulu, HI 96817; (808) 848-4147. Collects and preserves materials relating to natural and cultural history of Hawaii and Pacific region with books, journals, archives, manuscripts, maps, and reference files. Photos, films/videotapes housed in Dept of Visual Collections. Some restrictions on material use. Accepts phone inquiries. No fee. Hours: Tu-F 10-3, Sa 9-noon.

Center for Oral History

University of Hawaii, 2424 Maile Way, Porteus Hall 724, Honolulu, HI 96822; (808) 948-6259. Gathers, preserves, and promotes oral histories of Hawaii's people through recording projects, publications, videotapes, and resource/research center. Holdings include oral history transcripts from 1900, videotapes and audiovisual presentations on Hawaiian history from 1900, oral history tape recordings from 1900. Appt requested for consultation. Accepts phone inquiries. No fee. Hours: M-F 8-4:30.

Hawaii Chinese History Center

111 N. King St., Room 410, Honolulu, Oahu, HI 96817; (808) 521-5948. Preserves and promotes history of Chinese in Hawaii through publications, library, and archival collections. Holdings include publications and reference materials; maps of Hawaii and China; photos; oral history tapes of elderly Chinese; genealogical records. Materials are non-circulating. Accepts phone inquiries. No fee. Hours: M, Th-F 10-noon.

Hawaii State Library

Hawaii and Pacific Division, 478 S. King St., Honolulu, HI 96813; (808) 548-2344. Collects, preserves, and maintains collection of historical research materials relating to Hawaii and the Pacific region. Holdings include extensive collections of reference publications and materials; maps; genealogical materials, including 1900, 1910 Census records, ship manifests, and family group sheets; James Tice Phillips Collection; Admiral Thomas Papers. Some restrictions. Accepts phone inquiries (808-548-2346). No fee. Hours: M, W, F-Sa 9-5; Tu,Th 9-8.

Hawaiian Historical Society

560 Kawaiahao St., Honolulu, HI 96813; (808) 537-6271. Maintains large research library on Hawaii history with focus on 19th c. Holdings include many letters, journals, unpublished papers, notes, and biographical materials; maps of Hawaii and Pacific; photos of Hawaiian people, buildings, and scenery; Hawaiian language book and newspaper collection; records of early Hawaii and Pacific voyages; and 19th c Hawaiian newspapers. Society also presents lecture series and publications. Materials non-circulating. Accepts phone inquiries and mail inquiries. Fee for research. Hours: M-F 10-4.

Joseph Smith Library

Brigham Young University, Hawaii Campus, 55-220 Kulanui St., Laie, HI 96762; (808) 293-3850. Academic library maintains selective collection of govt documents, general, reference and historical materials relevant to needs of the school and students. Holdings include archives with univ and local historical materials and artifacts from Pacific Rim Basin; local historical photos; special collections on Mormonism, Hawaii, and the Pacific Rim Basin. Accepts phone inquiries (808-293-3878). No fee. Hours: M-Th 7-11, F 7-9, Sa 9-5.

Kauai Museum Association

P.O. Box 248, Lihue, Kauai, HI 96766. Relates history of Kauai through museum exhibits and photos collection. Accepts phone inquiries. Fee. Hours: M-F 9-4:30.

Lihue Public Library

4344 Hardy St., Lihue, HI 96766; (808) 245-3617. Public library maintains selective collection of govt documents, general and historical materials relevant to needs of community. Holdings include state and local maps; videotapes of local events and people; genealogical research

materials, including ships' passengers lists, 1843-1900, Census records, 1900, 1910; local newspaper indexes from 1929; Wilcox Collection of rare books on Hawaii and the Pacific; local historical materials on Kauai and Niihau. Some restrictions. Accepts phone inquiries. No fee. Hours: M-W 8-8, Th-F 8-4:30, Sa 8-noon.

Lyman House Memorial Museum

Hawaii Museums Association, 276 Haili St., Hilo, HI 96720; (808) 935-5021. Preserves history of Hawaii Islands and people. Holdings include archival materials on missionaries in Hilo; large photo collection on island history; Hawaiian volcano exhibit; small oral history collection. Accepts phone inquiries. Fee. Hours: M-Sa 9-4.

Mission Houses Museum

Hawaiian Mission Children's Society, 553 S. King St., Honolulu, HI 96813; (808) 531-0481. Historic house museums and site preserve early 19th c American missionary way of life. Holdings include two Mission furnished family homes, from 1821 and 1831; working 1841 printing office; library with missionary records, Hawaiian church records, manuscripts, publications, and art-on-paper, 1820-1900; archives of Congregational Church in Hawaii and Pacific, 1853-1947; manuscripts, letters, journals, and mission reports, 1820-1900; Hawaiian and Pacific maps; photos, photo albums, daguerreotypes, and ambrotypes; educational films/videotapes; missionary genealogies. Accepts phone inquiries. Fee. Hours: museum: 9-4; library: M-F 10-4.

Pacific Submarine Museum

Naval Submarine Base, Pearl Harbor, HI 96860; (808) 471-0632. Preserves history of WWII naval activities, with emphasis on underwater maneuvers. Museum exhibits missiles and torpedoes, submarine models, materials on deep-sea diving and salvaging, and Arctic exploration during WWII. Accepts phone inquiries. Hours: call.

Pu'uhonua National Historical Park

P.O. Box 129, Honaunau, HI 96726; (808) 328-2326. Preserves and interprets history and culture of regional Hawaiians, up until 1819. Holdings include small library; approx 40 reports from local archaelogical digs and corresponding base map; photos and negatives; and videotapes of parks cultural festival. Accepts phone inquiries. Fee. Hours: 7:30-5:30.

Supreme Court Law Library

Judiciary Bldg., 417 S. King St., Honolulu, HI 96813; (808) 548-7434. Provides legal resource and research materials. Holdings circulate only to courts and bar members. Accepts phone inquiries (808-548-7432). No fee. Hours: M-F 7:45-4:15.

University of Hawaii at Hilo

Documents Division, Edwin H. Mookini Library, 523 W. Lanikaula St., Hilo, HI 96720; (808) 961-9525. Supports University's research and educational needs with library, archival University materials, collection of geological survey maps, films/videotapes, and Hawaii County documents. Materials circulate only to card holders. Accepts phone inquiries (808-961-9346). No fee. Hours: M-Th 7:45-10:30, F 7:45-4, Su 1-10:30.

USS Arizona Memorial

National Park Service, 1 Arizona Memorial Dr., Honolulu, HI 96818; (808) 422-2771. Preserves and illustrates the attack on Pearl Harbor through museum exhibits and artifacts, research library, and archival USS Arizona materials. Holdings include maps, photo archive, and videotapes of dive surveys, oral histories, and WWII events. Library and videos for research use only. Accepts phone inquiries (808-422-0561). No fee. Hours: call.

Idaho

Boise Public Library

715 Capitol Blvd., Boise, ID 83702; (208) 384-4076. Community center for info, education, and recreation has special Northwest room on ID and regional state histories. Holdings include large collection of books, govt documents, out-of-print materials, USGS maps, Boise genealogical records from 1905, ID history pamphlet/clipping files, Peter Cohn philatelic collection, and selective index to ID publications from 1864-1940s. Northwest room materials for in-house use only. Accepts phone inquiries. No fee. Hours: Tu-Th 10-9, F 10-6, Sa-Su 1-5.

Canyon County Historical Society

P.O. Box 595, Nampa, ID 83651; (208) 476-7611. Collects, preserves and promotes history of Canyon County, ID and residents in form of museum with artifacts and exhibits; small library; local historical manuscripts; railroad maps; photos, films/videotapes, and genealogical records; special collection of materials on Edison. Accepts phone inquiries. Donations accepted. Hours: Tu-Sa 1-5.

Castle Museum

P.O. Box 454, Juliaetta, ID 83535; (208) 276-3081. Preserves and displays history of Juliaetta, ID area. Holdings include glasswares; clothing; furniture; photo archives of local residents and places circa 1900. Accepts phone inquiries. Donations accepted. Hours: 9-5.

Coeur d'Alene Mining District Museum

P.O. Box 1167, 509 Bank St, Wallace, ID 83873; (208) 753-7151. Preserves and interprets history of mining and life in region from 1884. Holdings include maps of mining locations 1890-1926; photos of mines 1884-1940s; videotapes of mining work; genealogical records of local pioneers. Accepts phone inquiries. Fee. Hours: winter, M-F 9-5; summer, 8:30-6.

Custer Museum

P.O. Box 136, Clayton, ID 83227; (208) 838-2201. Museum preserves mining history of region in form of artifacts and photos of mining activities, area and residents during period from 1900-1911. Accepts phone inquiries. Donations accepted. Hours: Jul-Labor Day, 9:30-6:30.

Daughters of Utah Pioneers Relic Hall

Old Mill Rd., 420 Clay St., Montpelier, ID 83254; (208) 847-1069. Exhibits photos and artifacts of early Bear Lake Valley settlers. Museum houses antique chairs, hand pumping organ, tools, dishes, clothing, spinning wheel, and photographs. Materials for in-house use only. Accepts phone inquiries. No fee. Hours: daytime only.

Elmore County Historical Foundation

P.O. Box 204, Mountain Home, ID 83647. Collects, preserves and promotes history of Elmore County, ID and residents in form of museum, library, archives, manuscripts, maps, photos, recordings, genealogical records, and special collections. Does not accept phone inquiries. Donations accepted. Hours: F-Sa 1:30-4:30, or by appt.

Idaho State Library

325 W. State St., Boise, ID 83702; (208) 334-2150. Preserves and maintains archival collections of ID state documents and records. Accepts phone inquiries. No fee. Hours: M-F 9-5.

Idaho State University

Eli Oboler Library, Box 8089, Pocatello, ID 83209; (208) 236-3249. Academic research library has collection on Intermountain West history, focusing on ID and region. Manuscript collection include Fred Dubois papers from 1886-1921, Lemhi Indian agency records from 1892-1907, and Minnie Howard papers from 1890-1965. Materials for in-house use only. Accepts phone inquiries. No fee. Hours: M-Th 8-4, 6:30-10:30; F 8-4; Su 2-10:30.

Latah County Historical Society

110 S. Adams St., Moscow, ID 83843; (208) 882-1004. Preserves and interprets history of Latah County area and residents in form of artifacts, library, archives, manuscripts, maps, photos from late 1800s, and oral history transcripts. Accepts phone inquiries. Donations accepted. Hours: T-F 10-4:30.

Museum of North Idaho

P.O. Box 812, 115 N.W. Blvd., Coeur D'Alene, ID 83814; (208) 664-3448. Collects, preserves, displays and interprets history of Kootenai County area until 1950. Holdings include exhibits on geology, Native Americans, early settlers, logging, mining; small library and archives; photos 1880-1950; oral history tapes on labor movement in local timber industry. Accepts phone inquiries. No fee. Hours: T-Sa 11-5.

Nez Perce County Historical Society and Luna House Museum

3rd and C Sts., Lewiston, ID 83501; (208) 743-2535. Collects and exhibits items of historic value to Nez Perce county. Museum and library documents county history from 1804. Archives hold hotel registers, fire dept records, hospital records, county maps, some photos of area Nez Perce Indians, and oral history tapes from local pioneers. Also holds paintings of Nez Perce Chief Joseph. Accepts phone inquiries. No fee. Hours: Tu-Sa 9-5.

Nez Perce National Historical Park

P.O. Box 93, Hwy. 95, Spalding, ID 83551; (208) 843-2261. National park commemorates legends and history of Nez Perce Indians and other early residents of region, in form of preserved historic sites, museum, library and special collections. Holdings include artifacts from Nez Perce culture; contact with Lewis and Clark expedition; Spalding Mission site; photos. Accepts phone inquiries. No fee. Hours: 8-4:30.

Northwest Nazarene College

Documents Division, John E. Riley Library, Nampa, ID 83651; (208) 467-8606. College library maintains selective collection of US govt documents and other materials relevant to college needs. Holdings include collections on the history of the college and the Church of the Nazarene. Borrowing restricted to local citizens and students; ILL available. No fee. Hours: M-Th 8-11, F 8-5, Sa 9-5:30, 7-10.

Regional History Department

P.O. Box 2168, 415 Spruce Ave. North, Ketchum, ID 83340; (208) 726-5544. Dept serves as depository and research center for materials relating to history of region, in form of oral history tapes, manuscripts, diaries, journals, maps, photos, films, and court and tax records from mid-19th c. Collection is non-circulating, and some restrictions apply on use of rare items. Accepts phone inquiries. No fee. Hours: M, W 9-5, Tu,Th noon-5, Sa 1-5 or by appt.

University of Idaho Library

Special Collections, Moscow, ID 83843; (208) 885-6344. Dept houses special collections of Univ library, with emphasis on ID and Northwest territory materials. Holdings include Day-Northwest History Collection; ID state documents; Basque history collections; Sir Walter

Scott collection; Ezra Pound collection; Bernard-Stockbridge photo collection of historic ID subjects; old athletic department films; small genealogical records collection; archives of personal and business papers of people and companies involved in hardrock mining, regional history and Psychiana religion. No ILL; materials may not leave room. Accepts phone inquiries (885-7951). No fee. Hours: M-F 8-5.

Upper Snake River Valley Historical Society

P.O. Box 244, Rexburg, ID 83440; (208) 356-9101. Society preserves history of eastern ID and Teton Flood in form of museum exhibits, library, manuscripts, records, maps, photos, films/videotapes, and recordings of local people and events. Accepts phone inquiries. No fee. Hours: summer, M-Sa 10-5; winter, M-F 10-4.

Illinois

Abraham Lincoln Association

Old State Capitol, Springfield, IL 62701; (212) 782-45836. Preserves and makes accessible landmarks associated with Lincoln's life, encourages and promotes collection and dissemination of info on Lincoln's life and careers, and observes each anniversary of Lincoln's birth. Accepts phone inquiries. No fee. Hours: call.

Airchive Association

521 S. Glenwood, Springfield, IL 62704; (217) 789-9754. Provides info about non-technical aspects of aviation for public. Museum collections include many model aircraft and kits; large photo and slide collection; many magazines; clipping files on aircraft, airlines, combat groups, model aircraft history; small collection of silk maps used by fliers in Pacific in WWII; small oral history collection; and small local aviation history clipping file. Accepts phone inquiries. No fee. Hours: by appt only.

Alton Area Historical Society and Research Library

P.O. Box 971, 415 E. 12th St., Alton, IL 62002; (618) 462-0595. Collects materials on local and regional history. Museum exhibits range from Lewis & Clarke expedition to rivers and industry of area. Library holds scrapbooks and printed materials on local life from 1910. Special Robert Wadlow collection. Materials non-circulating. Accepts phone inquiries. No fee. Hours: Th-Sa 1-4.

American Indian History Center

Newberry Library, 60 W. Walton St., Chicago, IL 60610; (312) 943-9090. Preserves materials on American Indians and Midwest. Research library holds Americana collection, manuscripts on history of book, extensive collection on history of cartography, photos of Plains Indians and Midwest, and extensive genealogical materials. Special collections on modern writers and early music. Stacks are closed. Accepts phone inquiries. Donations accepted. Hours: 9-5.

American Medical Association

Library and Archival Services, 535 N. Dearborn St., Chicago, IL 60610; (312) 645-4818 lib, 4999 archives. Maintains comprehensive collection on sociology and economics of medicine from 1964. Holdings cover history of AMA and constituent societies, including resource file on American physicians. Photos, poster, prints, and drawings of AMA presidents, officers, buildings, and offices available. Also has material on medical fraud, quackery, and memorabilia from 1902. Closed to public. Accepts phone and mail inquiries. Hours: 8:30-4:45.

Anthropology Museum

Stephens Bldg., Northern Illinois University, DeKalb, IL 60115; (815) 753-0230. Preserves artifacts and materials on Southwest and Plains Indians from 1850, as well as New Guinea. Library houses small collection on anthropology of N. American Indians. Large photo collection on all areas of anthropology. Accepts phone inquiries. No fee. Hours: M-F 9-5, Sa 10-4.

Argonne National Laboratory

Reactor Science/Engineering Branch Library, 9700 S. Cass Ave., Argonne, IL 60439; (312) 972-2000. Maintains thorough collection of scientific and technical reports on atomic science and nuclear energy. Holdings include materials from AEC, ERDA, DOE, and NRC. May be restrictions. Accepts phone inquiries. Hours: by appt.

Augustana College Library

Special Collections, Augustana College, 35th St. & 7th Ave., Rock Island, IL 61201; (309) 794-7317. Collects and preserves items relating to College, local, and Upper MI Valley region history. Archives contain College records, manuscript collections, and faculty and alumni publications; maps; photos; and collection of rare books on Upper MI Valley, Indians, and local history. Materials non-circulating. Accepts phone inquiries. No fee. Hours: M-F 8:30-noon, 1-4:30.

Billy Graham Center Museum

Wheaton College, 500 E. College Ave., Wheaton, IL 60187; (312) 260-5157. Collects and preserves history of evangelism and missions from 18th c in museum, library, and archival holdings. Exhibits include film footage of Billy Sunday, memorabilia from famous evangelists, artifacts from Salvation Army and YMCA, and great deal of Graham memorabilia. Accepts phone inquiries. Donations accepted. Hours: M-Sa 9:30-5:30, Su 1-5.

Bishop Hill Heritage Association

P.O. Box 1853, Bishop Hill, IL 61419; (309) 927-3899. Interprets Bishop Hill's Swedish Communal Society and its relationship to Utopian movement and Swedish immigration in 19th c. Museum traces history of Swedes in Bishop Hill from 1846-1917; archives hold colony's records; photo collection features regional scenes and residents from 1855-1920; genealogical research services available; oral history interviews and Philip Stoneberg papers; and historical film/video programs for rent. Accepts phone inquiries. No fee. Hours: museum, Apr-Dec 9-5; archives open year round.

Blackburn College

Documents Division, Lumpkin Library, Carlinville, IL 62626; (217) 854-3231. Academic research library with archives of college history and genealogical records of Blackburn family. Accepts phone inquiries. No fee. Hours: M-F 8-11, Sa 10-5, Su 1-11.

Bryant Cottage State Historic Site

146 E. Wilson St., Bement, IL 61813; (217) 678-8184. Preserves materials on construction and occupancy of home and life of F.E. Bryant from 1856-1880. Accepts phone inquiries. No fee. Hours: 9-5.

Canal Archives and Regional History Collection

Lewis University, Rte. 53, Romeoville, IL 60441; (815) 838-0500. Collects material on US canals, concentrating on IL & MI Canal, its corridor, and IL canals in general. Archives include maps, documents, newspaper, photographs, and prints; manuscripts relate to canal business and correspondence; small map collection on canal in general; photo collection on IL & MI Canal; films/videotapes and recordings on Canal corridor. Accepts phone inquiries. No fee. Hours: by appt, M-F 9-4.

Chicago Architecture Foundation

1800 S. Prairie, Chicago, IL 60616; (312) 326-1393. Seeks to further public appreciation of Chicago architecture and its social history by maintaining 2 museums and offering over 50 architectural tours of Chicago structures. One museum of Chicago's oldest surviving bldg, Henry Clarke House; other is John Glesser House, designed by Henry Hobson Richardson and furnished with original pieces. Accepts phone inquiries (312-782-1776). Fee. Hours: call.

Chicago Genealogical Society

P.O. Box 1160, Chicago, IL 60690. Collects and preserves records of ancestors, and publishes and circulates relative literature.

Chicago Historical and Architectural Landmark Commission

320 N. Clark St., Room 516, Chicago, IL 60610; (312) 744-3200. Makes recommendations for landmark designations and alterations. Library holds materials on history and architecture of Chicago and some info on American architecture, maps and data from Historic Building Survey, and photos of potential landmarks and significant buildings in region. Accepts phone inquiries. No fee. Hours: 8:30-4:30.

Chicago Historical Society

Clark St. at North Ave., Chicago, IL 60614;

(312) 642-4600. Preserves personal papers and archives of orgs active in Chicago area from 17th c. Materials cover early history of IL, Old Northwest, Lincoln, American Revolution, and Civil War. Large collection of materials on regional women's orgs, including Chicago Women's Club, Chicago Women's Liberation Union, Hyde Park Travel Club, National Council of Jewish Women-Chicago Section, National Woman Suffrage Assn, City Club of Chicago, Chicago Cubs, Chicago fire of 1871, 1886 Haymarket Riot, lake and river disasters from 1679-47, assassin Charles Guiteau, inventor Charles Pullman, and Chicago Expo of 1893. Hours: call.

Chicago Jewish Historical Society

618 S. Michigan Ave., Chicago, IL 60605; (312) 663-5634. Collects and preserves Chicago Jewish history through holdings in museum, library, and archives. Holdings in different institutions, and include manuscripts, maps, photos, films/videotapes, and recordings. Accepts phone inquiries. No fee. Hours: call.

Chicago Maritime Society

Newberry Library, 60 West Walton Place, Chicago, IL 60637; (312) 943-9090. Collects, interprets, and disseminates info on Chicago and northeastern IL maritime history. Museum, library, and archives contain photos of 19th c port of Chicago and Great Lakes maritime; films/videotapes on maritime development; recordings of 19th c maritime laborers music; and collection of 19th c maritime crafts. Materials for in-house use only. Accepts phone inquiries. No fee. Hours: by appt, M-F 9-5.

Chicago Public Library

Special Collections, Cultural Division, 78 E. Washington St., Chicago, IL 60611; (312) 269-2800. Public library preserves large collection of promotions and publicity publications from 1893 Chicago Columbian Expo, materials from Expo Board of Directors member James Wellsworth. Also holds extensive collection of materials on Civil War and American History. Holdings include slavery pamphlets; letters and papers of soldiers and officers; photos of battlefields and individuals; military accessories; manuscripts from Grant, Sherman, and Breckinridge; Reconstruction materials; and Confederate battle plans.

Accepts phone inquiries. No fee. Hours: call.

Chicago State University

Paul and Emily Douglas Library, 95th St. at King Dr., Chicago, IL 60628; (312) 995-2284. Academic research library with collections of govt documents on education from 1870. Materials for in-house use only. Accepts phone inquiries. No fee. Hours: M-F 8-8:30, Sa 11-5, and Su 1-5.

Des Plaines Historical Museum

789 Pearson St., Des Plaines, IL 60017; (312) 391-5399. Preserves historical records of Des Plaines in historical house museum. Library has local reference materials, archives, manuscripts, maps of local and Chicago area, extensive photo collection, oral histories, and extensive genealogical resources. Accepts phone inquiries. No fee. Hours: M-F 9-5.

Downers Grove Historical Society

831 Maple Ave., Downers Grove, IL 60515; (312) 963-1309. Collects historical material on region and residents. Museum is housed in Victorian home; small library holds records of 1840-60 censuses, cemeteries, govt, schools, obituaries, and births; some local pictures, maps, and newspapers. Accepts phone inquiries. No fee. Hours: 8:30-4:30.

Earl Hayter Regional History Center

Northern Illinois University, Swen Parson Hall, Rm. 155, DeKalb, IL 60115; (815) 753-1779. Acquires, preserves, and makes available historical records for northern IL region. Regional collection documents agriculture, politics, ethnic heritage, commerce and industry, role of women, and urban expansion in IL's 18 northern counties. University archives documents institution's development. Local govt records include tax records, circuit court cases, probate records, school board minutes, planning commission documents, naturalization papers, and militia roll records. Materials non-circulating. Accepts phone inquiries. No fee. Hours: M-F 8-4:30.

Early American Museum and Gardens

P.O. Box 669, Mahomet, IL 61853; (217) 586-2612. Collects and preserves materials on east central IL before 1950, with emphasis on Grand Prarie. Museum highlights material and regional culture, and migration, settlement, and daily life of residents. Also materials on trades, education, govt, tools, and lighting. Accepts phone inquiries. Fee. Hours: May and Sept, Sa-Su 10-5; June-Sept, M-F.

Eastern Illinois University

Document Division, Booth Library, Charleston, IL 61920; (217) 581-6092. Academic support library specializing in IL regional govt documents, maps, and regional folk art. Archival holdings of University and community; topographical, CIA, Army, and USGS maps; depository holdings of official IL govt agency records; and Tarble Arts Center museum of East Central Illinois folk arts and crafts. Accepts phone inquiries. No fee. Hours: M-Th 8-11:45, Sa 9-5, Su 1:30-11:45.

Elmhurst Historical Museum

120 Park Ave., Elmhurst, IL 60126; (312) 833-1457. Collects and preserves local history through extensive museum and archival collections from 19th c. Museum holdings include artifacts, archives, manuscripts, newspapers, maps, photos, movies, sound recordings, and special genealogy library; archival materials include many family, civic, and business records, as well as federal and state census records, Sanborn Fire Insurance maps, and local newspapers; large collection of photos, movies, maps, blueprints, architectural drawings, and posters. Accepts phone inquiries. No fee. Hours: M-F 9-5, Sa 10-5.

Everett McKinley Dirksen Congressional Leadership Research

Broadway and 4th St., Pekin, IL 61554; (309) 347-7113. Fosters understanding of Congress and leadership through museum exhibits and archival materials. Holdings include Senate Minority Leader Everett Dirksen and Congressman Harold Veble's papers and memorabilia; photos, films/videotapes, and recordings from Dirksen collection. Accepts phone inquiries. No fee. Hours: exhibit hall, M-F 9-5, Sa 9-5; reference, M-F 9-5.

Fort Massac Historic Site

P.O. Box 708, Metropolis, IL 62960; (618) 524-9321. Small museum displays artifacts and articles found on site, dating to 18th and 19th c. Some archival materials available. Accepts phone inquiries. No fee. Hours: W-Su 10-4:30.

Frank Lloyd Wright Home and Studio Foundation

951 Chicago Ave., Oak Park, IL 60302; (312) 848-1976. Preserves and operates first home and studio of Wright from 1909. Library includes family's collections, and rare books written and signed by Wright. Archives contain drawings used in and slides from bldg restoration. Manuscript collection includes 2 of son's books. Photos of history and restoration. Some videotapes on Wright, Prairie School of Architecture, and foundation lectures. Genealogical materials. Materials non-circulating. Accepts phone inquiries. No fee. Hours: W-Sa 1-4.

Frankfort Area Historical Society and Museum

2000 E. St. Louis St., West Frankfort, IL 62896; (618) 932-6159. Researches and preserves history of area through museum exhibits on mining and minerals, one-room school, kitchen, parlor, and tea room. Library has small collection of local newspapers dating to 1919, maps, photos, and genealogical materials. Other holdings include limited Civil War, WWI, and WWII uniforms and memorabilia. Accepts phone inquiries. No fee. Hours: W-Th 9-4, Su 1:30-4.

Galena-Jo Daviess County Historical Society

211 S. Bench St., Galena, IL 61036; (815) 777-9129. Collects, preserves, and interprets history of Galena and Federal Lead Mine District. Museum exhibits lead mining, steam boat, and early settlement history from 1820s-40s; govt, business, and genealogical records; and art works by Thomas Nast and John Mix Stanley. Accepts phone inquiries (815-777-0200). Fee. Hours: museum 9-5; library M-F 3-5.

Galesburg Public Library

Special Collections, 40 E. Simmons St., Galesburg, IL 61401; (309) 343-6118. Holds govt documents, extensive collection of IL histories, atlases, photos, and manuscripts from 1850. Also census, cemetery, and genealogical records. Bulk of holdings document IL state and local history, Civil War, Lincoln, and Carl Sandburg. Accepts phone inquiries. No fee. Hours: M-Th 9-9, F-Sa 9-5.

Gardner Museum of Architecture and Design
332 Maine St., Quincy, IL 62301; (217) 224-6873. Encourages preservation of Quincy's architectural heritage through collection of architectural ornamentation, historic photos, and special design exhibits. Library has small library on architecture, architects, restoration manuals, and design themes; collection of Sanborn Fire Insurance Maps; and small collection of photos of Quincy architecture. Accepts phone inquiries. Fee. Hours: Apr-June and Oct-Dec, Sa-Su 1-5.

Garfield Farm and Tavern Museum
P.O. Box 403, 3N016 Garfield Rd., La Fox, IL 60147; (312) 584-8485. Provides living history through farm and museum. Library holds materials on 19th c farming, museum science, and historic preservation. Collections include manuscripts, maps, photos, and genealogical materials for Garfield and Mighell families. Accepts phone inquiries. Fee. Hours: June-Sept, W-Su 1-4; or by appt.

Grove National Historic Landmark
Glenview Park District, 1421 Milwaukee Ave., Glenview, IL 60025; (312) 299-6096. Interprets history of this family home of Kennicott's from 1856-66 with museum, archival, and photographic holdings. Accepts phone inquiries. No fee. Hours: M-F 8-4:30, Sa-Su 9-5.

Hancock County Historical Society
P.O. Box 68, Carthage, IL 62321. Collects and preserves history of county and residents through library of newspapers, scrapbooks, personal histories, and plat books. Most materials date to 1850s. Materials for in-house use only. Accepts mail inquiries but charges fee for research. No fee for admission. Hours: winter, M,W,F 9-3; summer, M-F 9-3.

Hartung's Automotive Museum
3623 W. Lake St., Glenview, IL 60025; (312) 724-4354. Displays large collection of early 20th c autos, trucks, tractors, motorcycles, license plates, bicycles, and various tools. Motorcycles range from Indians to Harley Davidsons, with many early makes represented; car makes include Hertz, Studebaker, Crosley, and Ford. Accepts phone inquiries. Donation accepted. Hours: call.

Hauberg Indian Museum
Black Hawk State Historic Site, 1510 46th Ave., Rock Island, IL 61201; (309) 788-9536. Interprets daily life and seasonal activities of Sauk and Fox Indians from 1800. Museum displays material culture of both tribes. Library provides reference materials, Indian trade journals, and photos of tribe members from 1910-40. Accepts phone inquiries. No fee. Hours: Dec-Mar, W-Su 8:30-noon, 1-4; Apr-Nov, 8:30-noon, 1-4.

Hebrew Theological College
Saul Silber Memorial Library, 7135 N. Carpenter Rd., Skokie, IL 60077; (312) 674-7750. Academic research library has special collection on Holocaust. Accepts phone inquiries. No fee. Hours: call.

Historical Museum of Addison
131 W. Lake St., Addison, IL 60101; (312) 628-1433. Displays artifacts, documents, and photos pertaining to Addison history from 1833. House museum contains artifacts from 1865-1920. Archive holds old maps of village, photos of early residents and bldgs, and genealogical records. Accepts phone inquiries. No fee. Hours: Sa 10-2, and by appt.

Historical Pictures Service
601 W. Randolf St., Chicago, IL 60606; (312) 346-0599. Commercial org lends historical photos, engravings, drawings, paintings, and maps for fee. Accepts phone inquiries. Fee. Hours: call.

Illinois Historic Preservation Agency
Old State Capitol, Springfield, IL 62701; (217) 782-4836. Research library specializing in IL history, Lincolniana, and Civil War history. Library holds published and unpublished national, state, and local histories dating from 19th c.; maps, plat books, and atlases of IL counties, state, and region; photos of Civil War, politics, business, industry, and families; large collection of films relating IL political events; extensive

tape holdings on IL Constitutional Convention of 1970; genealogical and city records from early 19th c; extensive collection of IL newspaper titles from 1814. Special collection on Lincoln. Materials non-circulating. Accepts phone inquiries. No fee. Hours: M-F 8:30-5.

Illinois Historical Survey

University of Illinois, Library 346, 1408 W. Gregory Dr., Urbana, IL 61801; (217) 333-1777. Collects, preserves, and makes available published and manuscript sources relating to local, state, and regional history. Accepts phone inquiries. No fee. Hours: M-F 9-6.

Illinois Labor History Society

28 E. Jackson Blvd., Chicago, IL 60604; (312) 663-4107. Promotes public interest in labor history in IL, and produces learning resources. Focus of materials on Meat Packing Union materials from 1940-68. Small library and limited photos available. Accepts phone inquiries. No fee. Hours: by appt.

Illinois State Archives

Archives Bldg., Springfield, IL 62756; (217) 782-4682. Repository of state and local govt records of legal, historic, and other value. Collection of state legislature, judiciary, and agencies from 1809; local records from 1737; federal land survey maps, airports, IL and MI Canal construction, counties, legislative reapportionment, and abandoned mines; photos of state institutions, buildings, employees, officials, projects, and penal institution inmates; and records of census, military service, and county registers. Accepts phone inquiries. No fee. Hours: M-F 8-4:30, Sa 8-3:30.

Illinois State Historical Library

Illinois Historic Preservation Agency, Old State Capitol, Springfield, IL 62701; (217) 785-7948. Collects and preserves materials on IL history. Library has materials on Lincoln, Civil War, Mormons, western travel, and 19th and 20th c genealogy. Lincoln collection contains biographies, his speeches, and correspondence. Manuscripts describe family, political, and social activities and maps cover IL and Midwest. Photos, films/videotapes, and recordings also available. Materials non-circulating. Accepts phone inquiries. No fee. Hours: M-F 8:30-5.

Illinois State Museum

Spring and Edwards Sts., Springfield, IL 62706; (217) 782-7386. Preserves materials on natural history, anthropology, and art of IL. Library holds maps and photos. Materials for in-house use. Accepts phone inquiries (217-782-6623). No fee. Hours: M-F 8:30-5.

Illinois State University

Special Collections, Milner Library, School & College Sts., Normal, IL 61761; (309) 438-7442. Academic research library has large collection of materials on Abraham Lincoln and the Civil War period. Holdings cover speeches, biographical materials, books on slavery and religion, newspaper clippings, pamphlets, and ephemera. Accepts phone inquiries. No fee. Hours: call.

Illinois Valley Community College

Documents Division, Jacobs Memorial Library, RR No. 1, Oglesby, IL 61348; (815) 224-2720. Supports academic research needs of college community depository of federal, state, and nuclear regulatory materials. Holdings also include small map collection. Accepts phone inquiries. No fee. Hours: M-Th 7:30-9:30, F 7:30-4:30.

Illinois Wesleyan University Sheean Library

Documents Division, P.O. Box 2899, Park & University Sts., Bloomington, IL 61702; (309) 556-3175. Academic support library with University archival holdings from 1850. Also houses Gernin collection of 20th c English language mystery novels. Materials circulate only to area residents. Accepts phone inquiries. No fee. Hours: M-F 8-12, 1-4.

Institute of Labor and Industrial Relations Library

University of Illinois, 504 E. Armory, Champaign, IL 61820; (217) 333-2380. Preserves labor union history and memorabilia. Holds extensive vertical file of materials. Accepts phone inquiries. Hours: call.

International Historic Films

Box 29035, Chicago, IL 60629; (312) 436-8051. Commercial mail order co offers extensive collection of narrative and documentary films from WWII, McCarthy era, and Vietnam. Films cover German history, training, fighting and atrocities; Battle of Midway, Iwo Jima, and Aleutians; Frank Capra's "Why We Fight" series; wartime productivity and transportation; FDR speeches; US and British training films; black soldiers; Japanese relocation; assorted govt-produced WWII films; aviation films; interviews with Joe McCarthy; Communist-scare; Korean War; Cuban missile crisis; and Navy, Army, and Marines in Vietnam. Accepts phone inquiries. Fee. Hours: call.

International Museum of Surgery and Hall of Fame

1524 N. Lake Shore Dr., Chicago, IL 60610; (312) 642-3555. Promotes science and artistry of surgery by preserving written materials on development of surgery throughout world. Accepts phone inquiries. Accepts donations. Hours: Tu-Sa 10-4, Su 11-5.

Italian Cultural Center

1621 N. 39th Ave., Stone Park, IL 60165; (312) 345-3842. Promotes Italian culture and preservation of Italian heritage. Museum exhibits sculptures, paintings, materials on Italians in Chicago, and replica of St. Peter's Basilica. Library holds research materials in Italian and English. Archives contains oral history interviews, photos, and recordings in Italian. Accepts phone inquiries. Fee. Hours: M-F 8:30-4:30, Sa 10-4.

Jane Addams' Hull-House

University of Illinois at Chicago, P.O. Box 4348, 800 Halstead St., Chicago, IL 60680; (312) 413-5353. Preserves and interprets history of social welfare pioneer Jane Addams, Hull-House settlement, and surrounding neighborhood. Museum comprised of two original Hull-House buildings with restored rooms and rotating exhibits. Photos and film/videotapes available for viewing at museum. Accepts phone inquiries. No fee. Hours: M-F 10-4; in summer, Su 1-4.

Jewish Genealogical Society of Illinois

P.O. Box 481022, North Shore Congregation Israel Library, Niles, IL 60648; (312) 564-1025. Promotes and assists in genealogical research for any person with Jewish ancestors or interest in Jewish family research. Library collection holds research materials. Archives hold publications on Jewish genealogy, with emphasis on holocaust materials; maps of Europe; and collection of genealogical materials. Materials for in-house use only. Accepts phone inquiries. Membership fee. Hours: by appt.

John Brown Historical Association of Illinois

5933 S. Aberdeen St., Chicago, IL 60621; (312) 436-6731. Maintains collective library, archival materials, photos, and other materials on John Brown; and encourages and promotes research, art and creative interpretations of John Brown story. Library houses materials on abolition and US history from 1800-60. Archives hold some letters and research materials related to Brown. Some films/videotapes also available. Accepts phone inquiries. No fee. Hours: by appt.

Kankakee County Historical Society Museum

8th Ave. and Water St., Kankakee, IL 60901; (815) 932-5279. Concentrates on preservation of Kankakee County and IL history. Museum houses Indian exhibits and restorations of Dr. Small home and one-room schoolhouse; maps of region; many photos of region and residents; some genealogical records and films/videotapes available. Accepts phone inquiries. No fee. Hours: M-F 10-3, Sa-Su 1-4.

Lake Forest College

Donnelley Library, College & Sheridan Rds., Lake Forest, IL 60045; (312) 234-3100. Academic research library holds wealth of info on railroad history and travel. Holdings include mid-20th c books and periodicals on Western railroads and mountain narrow gauge, world narrow gauge, and short lines, and steam railroads. Munson-Paddock collection includes train illustrations, maps, and timetables from 1850-1950, with some narrations on travelling by rail in West. Accepts phone inquiries. No fee. Hours: call.

Landmarks Preservation Council of Illinois

53 W. Jackson Blvd., Suite 752, Chicago, IL 60604; (312) 922-1742. State-wide preserva-

tion org with small collection of reference materials and photos. Technical assistance and brochures available. Accepts phone inquiries. No fee. Hours: 9-5.

Lincoln Log Cabin State Historic Site

RR 1, Box 175, Lerna, IL 62440; (217) 345-6489. Maintains farm of Thomas and Sarah Bush Lincoln, and maintains collection of local and mid-19th c antiques. May be some restrictions. Accepts phone inquiries. No fee. Hours: 8:30-dusk.

Long Grove Historical Society

RFD, Box 3110, Long Grove, IL 60047; (312) 634-9440. Preserves one-room schoolhouse, schoolbooks, and materials relating to Long Grove history. Collections include some maps, photos, and manuscripts; also oral history recordings and genealogical records. Accepts mail inquiries. No fee. Hours: by appt.

Loyola University of Chicago

E.M. Cudahy Memorial Library, 6525 N. Sheridan Rd., Chicago, IL 60626; (312) 508-2646. Holds large collection of substantiating materials on World War I period political and economic activities in region. Documents cover Child Labor Bill, Labor Marches from 1902-32, Railroad Strike from 1916-20, WWI, War Industries Commission, Air Board of Chicago, Allied Debts to United States, and Bolshevism and Communism from 1924-27. Accepts phone inquiries. No fee. Hours: call.

Madison County Historical Society

715 N. Main St., Edwardsville, IL 62025; (618) 656-7562. Collects, preserves, and promotes history of county and its residents through exhibits in restored 19th c home, museum, library, and archives. Holdings include Native American and pioneer artifacts, newspapers, civic and government records, early pioneer manuscripts, county and township maps from 1861 and 1926, photos of area houses and residents, and genealogical records from 1820-60. Special collections of Indian artifacts, costumes, N.O. Nelson/Leclaire papers, and Gillham family papers. Accepts phone inquiries. No fee. Hours: W-F 9-4, Sa 1-4.

McLean County Historical Society

201 E. Grove St., Bloomington, IL 60701; (309) 827-0428. Museum houses large collection of American Indian, textile, and military artifacts relating to McLean County and its residents. Holdings include materials on 33rd and 94th regiments during Civil War. Library collects historical materials on Illinois and Old Northwest Territory. Some county maps and photos of residents. Restrictions on use. Accepts phone inquiries. No fee. Hours: M-F 9-5, Sa-Su 1-5.

Mennonite Heritage Center

P.O. Box 819, Metamora, IL 61550; (309) 367-2551. Preserves, collects, and maintains historical materials relating to Mennonites. Museum, library, and archival holdings include manuscripts, maps, photos, and genealogical records. Accepts phone inquiries. No fee. Hours: May-Oct 10-4.

Millikin University

Staley Library, 1184 W. Main St., Decatur, IL 62522; (217) 424-6211. Academic research library holds collection of materials on Stephen Decatur, hero of War of 1812. Materials for in-house use only. Accepts phone inquiries. No fee. Hours: call.

Modern Woodmen of America

Mississippi River at 17th St., Rock Island, IL 61201; (309) 786-6481. Preserves and makes available history of group and its members for family genealogists, historians, and others. Museum, archives, photos, and genealogy records document woodmen's activity from 1882; some magazines, camp registers, and consolidation records from 1883-1946. Not open for public research; all inquiries handled by society's historian. Accepts phone inquiries. No fee. Hours: M-F 8-4:30.

Museum of Broadcast Communications

800 S. Wells St., Chicago, IL 60607; (312) 987-1500. Provides public with access to radio and TV heritage, principally from Midwest and Chicago. Museum displays Edgar Bergen memorabilia and puppets and vintage radio and TV sets. Archives holds collection of jazz performances;

German U-505 submarine captured by US naval task force during World War II, from the Museum of Science and Industry.

Kukla, Fran, and Ollie Shows, large collection of local, regional, and national radio programs; local newscast collction; Kraft Music Hall and Theatre productions; and other locally and nationally produced programs from 1920s-40s. Materials for in-house use only. Accepts phone inquiries. Donations accepted. Hours: W-F noon-5, Sa 10-5, Su noon-5.

Museum of Science and Industry

University of Chicago Library, 57th St. & Lake Shore Drive, Chicago, IL 60637; (312) 684-1414. Furthers understanding of science and technology by explaining their principles, applications, and implications. Preserves exhibits on development of marine transportation, Indianapolis racing cars, antique automobiles, German U-505 submarine captured during WWII, historic trains, and historic fire-fighting equipment.

Also displays of Apollo 8, Aurora 7 Mercury, and astronaut training equip. Accepts phone inquiries. Fee. Hours: M-F 9:30-4, Sa-Su 9:30-5:30.

Music Library

Northwestern University, 1937 Sheridan Rd., Evanston, IL 60201; (312) 491-3434. Preserves and documents 20th c music through collections of manuscripts, books, recordings, part of Moldenhauer archive, and collection of John Cage notations. Hours: call.

Naperville Heritage Society—Naper Settlement

201 W. Porter Ave., Naperville, IL 60540; (312) 430-6010. Preserves and interprets Naperville's 19th c history. Museum composed of number of working shops, businesses, and residents; library collects local letters, journals, business records;

some county and regional maps; sizeable photo collection; oral history interviews and files on local families. Accepts phone inquiries. No fee for research; fee for museum. Hours: research, M-F 9-4.

National Archives—Chicago Branch
National Archives & Records Administration, 7358 S. Pulaski Rd., Chicago, IL 60629; (312) 581-7816. Repository of permanent records of federal agencies in Great Lakes area. Holdings include records of IL, IN, MI, MN, OH, and WI courts from 1800s-1960s; federal agency field office records of Army Corps of Engineers, Bureau of Indian Affairs, War Manpower Commission, Housing Authority, Bureau of Marine Inspection and Navigation from 1850s-1960s; naturalization records; census records from 1790-1910; Revolutionary War pension and military records; NY passenger arrival lists; some 19th century IRS records. Accepts phone inquiries. No fee. Hours: M-F 8-4:15.

National Trust for Historic Preservation
Midwest Regional Office, 53 W. Jackson, Suite 1135, Chicago, IL 60604; (312) 939-5547. Clearinghouse for info on historic preservation in OH, MN, MI, IN, IL, WI, MO, and IA. Library contains materials and makes referrals on preservation law, funding, and local community organization. Accepts phone inquiries. No fee. Hours: 9-5.

Nauvoo Restoration
Box 215, Young & Main Sts., Nauvoo, IL 62354; (217) 453-2237. Includes 14 restored homes from 1840s, furnished with period antiques. Some genealogy materials. Accepts phone inquiries. No fee. Hours: 8-6.

Newberry Library
60 W. Walton St., Chicago, IL 60610; (312) 943-9090. Library collects materials documentings Western American experience. Holdings include Edward Ayer and Everett Graff collections on overland travel, local documents, and biographies and autobiographies. Special Elmo Scott clipping collection holds materials on Indians, frontiersmen, correspondence, and US Army, which once appeared in syndicated newspaper columns. Accepts phone inquiries. Hours: call.

Northern Illinois University
Documents Division, Founders' Memorial Library, De Kalb, IL 60115; (815) 753-1932. Academic research library with holdings of legislative materials on federal govt from 1700s. Accepts phone inquiries. No fee. Hours: M-Th 11-8, F 1-5, Sa 1-5.

Northwestern Memorial Hospital Archives
516 W. 36th St., Chicago, IL 60609; (312) 908-3090. Collects and makes available records of hospital and preceding institutions. Museum holds items relating to childbirth and home-births in Chicago from 1880s, as well as surgical instruments; library specializes in Chicago health care from 1849; archival administrative and medical records from area hospitals; manuscripts of William, James, and Charles Deering, Norman Dwight Harris, and other prominent Chicagoans; map, photo, and genealogical collections; physician training films; and some oral history interviews with hospital personnel. Collections open to qualified researchers. Accepts phone inquiries. No fee. Hours: M-F 8:30-5.

Northwestern University Library
Documents Division, Evanston, IL 60208; (312) 491-3130. Serves library community with collection of US govt documents from 1776, and collection of IL documents from 1971. Materials non-circulating. Accepts phone inquiries. No fee. Hours: M-Th 8-5, 7-10; F-Sa 8:30-5.

Northwestern University Library
Special Collections, 1937 Sheridan Rd., Evanston, IL 60201; (312) 491-3635. Preserves materials from those involved in Woman's Liberation Movement from early 1960s, publications from black and student movements, and other left-wing materials. Holdings include small literary press books; feminist, gay, and lesbian materials; newsletters; newspapers; pamphlets; posters; and ephemera. Accepts phone inquiries. No fee. Hours: call.

Oliver P. Parks Telephone Museum
529 S. 7th St., Springfield, IL 62721; (217) 753-

8463. Preserves history of telephone equipment and industry. Museum displays Alexander Graham Bell replica, background info on telephone, and extensive collection of phones, including Picture-Phone sets. Accepts phone inquiries. No fee. Hours: May-Sept, 9-4:30; Apr-Oct, M-Sa 9-4:30; Nov-Mar, M-F 9-4:30.

Peace Museum
430 W. Erie St., Chicago, IL 60610; (312) 440-1860. Preserves memorabilia and work of peace activists. Holdings include art and artifacts of antiwar and peace movements, displays on peace protests, writings and teachings of noted nonviolence leaders, and folk art. Accepts phone inquiries. Fee. Hours: Tu-Su noon-5, Th noon-8.

Pearson Museum
Southern Illinois University School of Medicine, P.O. Box 19230, 801 North Rutledge, Springfield, IL 62794; (217) 785-2128. Preserves history of health care delivery in Upper MI River Basin Area, and Midwest US in general. Museum exhibit early medical artifacts. Library holds reference materials on medicine. Archives retain materials on early physicians and medical practice, manuscripts on regional medicine, early maps of area as related to medicine, photos of early doctors and dentists and their instruments, genealogical materials, and rare books on venereal diseases and disinfected mail. Accepts phone inquiries. Donations accepted. Hours: M-F 8:30-4:30, appts suggested.

Peoria Historical Society Library
Bradley University Library, Special Collections Center, Peoria, IL 61625; (309) 677-2822 or 2823. Preserves history of Central IL Valley. Library holds local history materials including WPA photo collection, WPA newspaper index for 1834-62, atlases, works by Peoria authors, large photo collection, and vertical file of pamphlets, clippings, and manuscripts. Manuscript collection includes East collection on Peoria and French settlement; David McCulloch collection of early Peoria documents; George May collection. Some maps of Peoria from 1852. Materials non-circulating. Accepts phone inquiries. No fee for library; fee for regional museum. Hours: M-F 1-5, and by appt.

Peoria Public Library
Documents Division, 107 Northeast Monroe St., Peoria, IL 61602; (309) 672-8844. Provides info and educational resources to general public with special holdings of govt documents, local historical materials, and Peoria genealogy. Holdings include some diaries, ledgers, maps, photos, and rare books. Accepts phone inquiries. No fee. Hours: M-Th 9-9, F-Sa 9-6.

Poplar Creek Public Library
Documents Division, 1405 S. Park Blvd., Streamwood, IL 60103; (312) 837-6800. Public library serving public with collection of depository documents, historical regional records, and map holdings. Special collection of offical War of Rebellion records and Pacific Railroad Survey, 1850s-60s; USGS topographical and IL maps. Also houses IL State Library's large children's book collection. Restrictions on some materials. Accepts phone inquiries. No fee. Hours: M-Th 9-9:30, F-Sa 9-5, Su 12-5.

Principia College
Documents Division, Marshall Brooks Library, Elsah, IL 62028; (618) 374-2131. Academic support library acting as govt document depository. Materials for in-house use only. Accepts phone inquiries. No fee. Hours: call.

Printers Row Printing Museum
715 S. Dearborn, Chicago, IL 60605; (312) 987-1059. Maintains working 19th c print shop and exhibits on printing trade. Library holds books and periodicals from 1890-1930. Archive collects posters, broadsides, and newspapers of 18th and 19th c and some photos of equipment. Accepts phone inquiries. No fee. Hours: Sa 9-5, Su 10-3.

Public Works Historical Society
1313 East 60th St., Chicago, IL 60637; (312) 667-2200. Works to document and recognize achievement of those involved in public works profession by promoting programs providing historical perspective. Also building oral history collection. Accepts phone inquiries. No fee. Hours: call.

Saint Clair County Historical Society
701 E. Washington St., Belleville, IL 62220;

(618) 234-0600. Preserves and maintains local historic structures and sites. Museum reconstructs Victorian home and living; small library provides some local history; small photo collection of early residents and scenes; and genealogical records on local families. Accepts phone inquiries. Fee. Hours: M-W, F-Sa 12-3, Su 2-4.

Sangamon State University

Oral History Office, Sheperd Rd., Springfield, IL 62708; (217) 786-6521. Collects, processes, and promotes American oral history memoirs. Holdings specialize in transcripts of oral histories from many aspects of modern history. Key holdings in IL politics, labor, agriculture, and social history; also WWII, race and ethnicity, women, and local history. Some restrictions on use. Accepts phone inquiries. No fee. Hours: M-F 9-4.

Sangamon Valley Collection

Lincoln Library, 326 South 7th St., Springfield, IL 62701; (217) 753-4910. Collects current and historic IL manuscripts, maps, photos, genealogical records, and newspaper clippings. Photo collection is extensive, and maps include Sanborn Fire Insurance editions. Materials non-circulating. Accepts phone inquiries. No fee. Hours: M-Th 9-9, F 9-6, Sa 9-5.

Southern Illinois University, Carbondale

Special Collections, Delyte W. Morris Library, Carbondale, IL 62901. Academic research library holds materials on southern IL history, theatre and political theatre, expatriate authors, and Irish literature.

Swedish Historical Society of Rockford

404 S. 3rd St., Rockford, IL 61104; (815) 963-5559. Perpetuates memory of Swedish immigrants in Winnebago County. Museum housed in home of John Erlander, one of earliest Swedes in Rockford. Library holds many old Swedish books. Materials for in-house use only. Accepts phone inquiries. Fee. Hours: Feb-Dec, Su 2-4.

Swenson Swedish Immigration Research Center

Augustana College, Box 175, 3520 7th Ave.,

Rock Island, IL 61201; (309) 794-7204. Archive and major research center preserves and interprets Swedish immigration to North America from 1638. Library and archives have extensive materials on Swedish genealogy, immigrant societies, cultural life, orgs, literature/publishings, fine arts, travel and exploration in US, biography, churches and religious life, and literature. Other holdings include papers on Bishop Hill Utopian Colony, Swedish Midwest settlement, topographical farm maps, photos of Swedish immigrant experience, music, and extensive Swede-related church records. Materials do not circulate. Accepts phone inquiries. No fee. Hours: Sept-May 8:30-noon, 1-5; summer, closes 4:30.

Theatre Historical Society of America

2215 W. North Ave., Chicago, IL 60647; (312) 252-7200. Records popular history of theatre world through collections on architectural history. Archive holds extensive collection of photos, clippings, programs, books, and blue prints of some 7000 theatres. Accepts phone inquiries. Research fee. Hours: Tu 9-4, and by appt.

Time Was Village Museum

1325 Burlington St., Mendota, IL 61342; (815) 539-6042. Collects many objects dating from early 20th century, including cars, furnishings, coaches, toys, and glassware. Fee. Hours: May-Nov, 10-5.

Ukrainian National Museum

2453 W. Chicago Ave., Chicago, IL 60622; (312) 276-6565. Collects, classifies, and displays samples of Ukrainian cultural heritage. Museum exhibits of costumes, embroidery, and crafts: large library on East European and Ukrainian topics; archives of church and civic leaders, poets, and writers; uncataloged map and photo collections; and some recordings. Accepts phone inquiries. Fee. Hours: 8-1.

Ulysses S. Grant's Home State Historic Site

908 3rd St., Galena, IL 61036; (815) 777-0248. Former home of Ulysses Grant before the Civil War, this house serves as IL historic site. Accept phone inquiries (815-777-3310). No fee. Hours: 9-5.

Chicago's Randolph Street Theatre District in the 1920s, from the Theatre Historical Society Archives.

University Museum

Southern Illinois University, Carbondale, IL 62901; (618) 453-4388. Houses collection of European and American paintings and drawings with emphasis on 19th and 20th c; 19th and 20th c photos; 20th c sculpture; musical instruments; archaeology; costumes; decorative arts; Southern history; and American Indian artifacts. No fee. Hours: M-F 9-3, Su 1:30-4:30.

University of Chicago Library

Dept. of Special Collections, 1100 E. 57th St., Chicago, IL 60637; (312) 702-8705. Academic research library contains research materials on early American history, including constitutional history, black history, Lincolniana, history of Ohio Valley and Midwest, and technological history. Special collections include Barton collection on Lincoln, Durrett collection on KY and OH Valley history, and ethnohistory collection on contact between whites and Native Americans in MI Valley. Also maintains collection of materials dealing with construction of Argonne National Laboratory and Manhattan Project research at Univ of Chicago. May be some restrictions on use. Accepts phone inquiries. May be fee. Hours: by appt, M-F 8:30-5, Sa 9-5.

University of Illinois

Archives, Rm. 19, 1408 W. Gregory Dr., Urbana, IL 61801; (217) 333-1056. Provides archival and manuscript resources for administrative, teaching, and research purposes. Holdings include official University records and faculty, staff, and student papers; large collection of maps; large collection of photos; collection of films/videotapes, with emphasis on athletic events; and collection of broadcast and oral history recordings. Accepts phone inquiries. No fee. Hours: M-F 8-noon, 1-5.

University of Illinois at Chicago Library

Special Collections, P.O. Box 8198, 801 S. Morgan, Chicago, IL 60607; (312) 996-2742. Academic research library holds materials documenting Chicago citizens, orgs, and activities. Collections include Chicago Board of Trade archives; large collection of materials from Century of Progress World's Fair; Ben Rietman/

Emma Goldman letters; Women in Communications materials; Women for Peace records; Container Co Archives; Chicago Urban League archives; Immigrants Protective League papers; and printing design collections. Materials noncirculating. Accepts phone inquiries. No fee. Hours: M-F 8:30-4:45.

Video Data Bank

School of the Art Institute, 280 South Columbus Dr., Chicago, IL 60603; (312) 443-3793. Major cultural institution provides a broad-based collection of tapes on and by artists that is accessible to students historians, researchers, educators, and artists. Holdings include the archives of Castelli-Sonneband Tapes and Film Collection and a large collection of films/videotapes: On Arts & Artists series, Avalanche Video Pioneer Series, CAT Fund, Art Park documents and interviews, Artist TV Network programs, individual artist tapes, and Video Data Bank series. Materials copyrighted. Accepts phone inquiries. Fee. Hours: M-F 9-5.

West Chicago Historical Museum

132 Main St., West Chicago, IL 60185; (312) 231-3376. Collects, preserves, and exhibits local history materials with emphasis on railroad development, records, and archival holdings. Museum focuses on settlement and growth of West Chicago from 1830-1910 with emphasis on railroad influence; library collects history and statistics of railroads and John Gates biographical materials; archival materials of many local and regional railroad companies; maps and photos relative to area rail activity; and some genealogy and obituary materials. Accepts phone inquiries. No fee. Hours: Archival materials by appt only; May-Dec, Th-F 1-4, Sa 11-3; other times by appt.

Western Museum

Western Illinois University, Sherman Hall, 3rd Floor, Macomb, IL 61455; (309) 298-1727. Regional historic museum with exhibits of Civil War artifacts; trapping paraphernalia; farming equipment; turn-of-century Dr's office, dentist's office, and drug store; barbed wire, radios, Indian artifacts, and University history. Other holdings include a special Carl Sandburg collec-

President Ulysses S. Grant, from the Ulysses Grant Home State Historic Site.

tion. Museum holdings include manuscripts, maps, photos, and recordings. Accepts phone inquiries. No fee. Hours: M-F 1-4.

Wings and Things Museum

RR 2, Box 19, Delavan, IL 61734; (309) 244-7389. Preserves examples of model and full size aircraft through museum exhibits on plane construction and archival aviation materials. Holdings include maps of Viet Nam and other air charts; many photos and models of aircraft. Accepts phone inquiries after 6:30 p.m. Donations accepted. Hours: by appt.

World Heritage Museum

484 Lincoln Hall, 702 S. Wright St., Urbana, IL 61801; (217) 333-2360. Collects, preserves, and interprets artifacts from cultures of North America, ancient Near East, Egypt, Greece, Rome, Medieval Renaissance, Northern Europe, Africa, and Orient. Small library relating to collections, manuscripts on Egypt and Medieval history, maps of world, and photos. Accepts phone inquiries. No fee. Hours: M-F 9-4, Su 2-5.

Indiana

Allen County Public Library

Documents Dept., 900 Webster St., Box 2270, Fort Wayne, IN 46801; (219) 424-7241. Maintains large collection of US govt documents and general and historical reference materials. Holdings include US govt documents from 1896 (currently recieves 97% of available materials); large collection of Allen County genealogical records, including census, tax, court, church, military, immigration and municipal records; deeds, wills, diaries, journals, and letters; adoption, marriage, divorce and death certificates; photos, charts and other family records. Accepts phone inquiries. No fee. Hours: M-Th 9-9, F-Sa 9-6, Su (except summers), 1-6.

Allen County
Fort Wayne Historical Society

302 E. Berry St., Fort Wayne, IN 46802; (219) 426-2882. Preserves, interprets, and displays history of Allen County and Fort Wayne, IN in form of museum, archives, and reproduction of original fort (Location: 107 S. Barr St). Holdings include artifacts from 1819, and early jail; pioneer and Civil War-era manuscripts, letters and books; local police, theatre and business records; local maps from 1820s; large photo collection of local subjects; small reference library; films/videotapes and genealogical records. Some restrictions. Accepts phone inquiries. Fee. Hours: museum: Tu-F 9-5, Sa-Su noon-5; fort: Apr-Oct, Tu-Su, 9-5; office: M-F 9-5.

Anderson Public Library

Document Dept., 111 E. 12th St., Anderson, IN 46016; (317) 641-2456. Public library maintains selective collection of local, state, and US records, as well as general and historical references, and special collections. Holdings include Madison County, IN records from 1843; local, town, city, county, and town records; CIA and USGS maps; genealogical records; and Wendell Hood Sheet Music Collection, 1930-1960s. Some restrictions. Accepts phone inquiries. No fee. Hours: M-Th 9-9, F-Sa 9-5:30, Su 1-5.

Army Finance Corps Museum

MG Emmett J. Bean Center, Indianapolis, IN 46249; (317) 542-2169. Illustrates history of Finance Corps branch of US Army. Museum holdings include Army items and military and non-military money from ancient times to present. Library holds small collection on general military and Finance Corps history. Accepts phone inquiries. No fee. Hours: M-F 8-4:30.

Auburn-Cord-Duesenberg Museum

P.O. Box 271, 1600 S. Wayne St., Auburn, IN 46706; (219) 925-1444. Educates public on significant history of Auburn-Cord-Duesenberg classic automobiles. Museum displays over 150 autos, other autos from Auburn and state of IN, and assorted foreign and domestic cars. Archives contains collection of literature and blueprints on Auburns, Cords, and Dusenbergs, as well as others; photos; videotapes on museum and Auburn automobile company from 1927-36; oral history recordings from company employees and officers; and extensive design drawings from Alan Leamy and Gordon Buehrig. Materials non-circulating. Accepts phone inquiries. Fee. Hours: Oct-Apr 10-5, May-Sept 8-6, by appt only.

Benjamin Harrison Memorial Home

1230 N. Delaware St., Indianapolis, IN 46202; (317) 631-1898. Preserves, promotes, and displays home, belongings, and accomplishments of President Benjamin Harrison. Holdings include preserved 1875 house with original furnishings, campaign memorabilia, and other personal artifacts of President Harrison; Harrison's personal library, and related works on his life and times; personal papers of the Harrison family; political and family photos and portraits. Use of library by appt only. Accepts phone inquiries. Fee house tour: Hours: home: M-Sa 10-4, Su 12:30-4; office: M-F 9-5.

Butler University

Irwin Library Rare Book Room, 4600 Sunset Ave., Indianapolis, IN 46208; (317) 283-9236. Library has special Lincoln collection, consisting of books and pamphlets on Civil War, newspaper clippings, manuscripts, and memorabilia. Accepts phone inquiries. No fee. Hours: call.

Byron R. Lewis Historical Library

Vincennes University, 1002 N. First St., Vincennes, IN 47591; (812) 885-4330. Library maintains collection of reference materials on history of Vincennes, IN region and residents. Holdings include small museum; historical reference collection; archives, manuscripts, maps, photos, films/videotapes; extensive collection of regional genealogical records; oral history recordings; Regional History Collection. Collections are non-circulating. Does not accept phone inquiries. No fee. Hours: M-F 8-4:30, 7-10.

Calumet Regional Archives

3400 Broadway, Gary, IN 46408; (219) 980-6628. Collects and preserves records and documents on northwest IN and residents with emphasis on 20th c urban history. Holdings include historical reference materials, manuscripts, maps, photos, and recordings relating to region's minorities and ethnic groups, churchs, community and health orgs, labor, industry, politics, and environmentalists. Some restrictions. Accepts phone inquiries. No fee. Hours: M-F 8-4:30.

Conner Prairie

13400 Allisonville Rd., Noblesville, IN 46060;

(317) 776-6000. Museum and historic area preserves and displays history and lifestyles of first generation IN settlers. Holdings include living history village, circa 1836; William Conner home, circa 1823; a Pioneer Adventure area relating to 1836-1855 era; library, archives, and maps relating to 19th c IN. Research facilities used by special arrangement only. Accepts phone inquiries. Fee. Hours: museum: Tu-Sa 10-5, Su noon-5; office: M-F 8:30-5.

Culbertson Mansion
State Historic Site

914 E. Main St., New Albany, IN 47150; (812) 944-9600. Collects, preserves, and interprets history of affluent Culbertson family's life and times in form of restored French Second Empire Mansion (circa 1867-1869) and period pieces. Holdings include interpretive displays of Victorian era artifacts; archive of letters and documents on family and mansion history; small photo collection. Some restrictions. Accepts phone inquiries. No fee. Hours: Tu-Sa 9-5, Su 1-5.

DePauw University and Indiana
United Methodism Archives

Special Collections of DePauw & United Methodist Church, DePauw University, Roy O. West Library, Greencastle, IN 46135; (317) 658-4500. Preserves and displays history of univ and United Methodist Church in IN in form of displays, library, and archives. Holdings include artifacts, manuscripts, maps and records of univ and church from 19th c; photos and slides from 1850; films/videotapes from 1935; recordings of univ functions from 1950; genealogical records of local, church, and univ-connected families; Putnam County Historical Society local history records, 1850-1980; Society of Professional Journalists/Sigma Delta Chi records, 1920-1980. Some restrictions. Accepts phone inquiries. Genealogical research fees. Hours: summer, M-F 8-4; winter M-F, 8-5 and Tu eves 6-9:30.

Drake's Midwest
Phonograph Museum

2245 State Rd 252, Martinsville, IN 46151; (219) 342-7666. Preserves history of recorded sound and shows development and innovations in phonographs. Museum displays authentic and working spring-wound, hand-driven, and weight-driven phonographs from 1858-1920. Library contains resource materials on machines and their histories. Recording library contains over 50 thousand discs and 5 thousand cylinders. Accepts phone inquiries. Fee. Hours: call.

Eugene V. Debs Foundation

P.O. Box 843, Terre Haute, IN 47808; (812) 237-3443. Preserves and maintains Eugene V. Debs Home (location: 451 N 8th) as a museum of early American labor, socialist and radical political history. Museum collection (at Debs Home) contains memorabilia from Debs' personal life and work as labor leader and socialist party Presidential candidate, including personal and campaign photos, posters, awards, union plaques, and some of the home's original furniture. Accepts phone inquiries. No fee. Hours: W-Su 1-4:30 or by appt.

Grouseland Home of William Henry Harrison

Francis Vigo Chapter of DAR, 3 W. Scott St., Vincennes, IN 47591; (812) 882-2096. Museum is restored home of William Henry Harrison, first Gov of Indiana Territory and 9th Pres of US. Archives and library contain genealogical materials. Accepts phone inquiries. Fee. Hours: Jan-Feb, 11-4; Mar-Dec 9-5.

Henry Blommel Historic Automotive Data Collection

Rte. 5, Connersville, IN 47331; (317) 825-9259. Personal collection preserves and maintains history of the auto industry in form of library and archival collections. Holdings include records and reference materials on Cord Corp. and other manufacturers; industry accounting journals and other business documents; manuscripts, maps, and photos; some genealogical records of IN families. Accepts phone inquiries. No fee. Hours: call.

Historic Landmarks Foundation of Indiana

3402 Boulevard Place, Indianapolis, IN 46208; (317) 926-2301. Foundation promotes, oversees historic preservation of important IN sites and landmarks through operation of two historic

house museums, educational programs, lectures, tours, special events, library, photos, films/videotapes and recordings. The Morris Butler House (1204 N. Park Ave, Indianapolis, IN 46202; 317-636-5409) built in 1865, houses collection of 19th c decorative arts; The Huddleston Farmhouse Inn Museum (U.S. 40, Cambridge City, IN; 317-478-3172) has 1840-1855 period furnishings, restored barn, springhouse and smokehouse. Foundation and sites accept phone inquiries. Donations accepted. Hours: office: M-F 9-5; sites: call for hours.

Historic New Harmony

344 W. Church St., New Harmony, IN 47631; (812) 682-4488. Org promotes and preserves history of New Harmony, IN, with emphasis on Harmonist and Owen attempts at communal living in early 18th c through community tours, museum and archival holdings. Holdings include archives, manuscripts, maps, photos, films/videotapes, recordings, and genealogical records of area residents. Accepts phone inquiries. Fee. Hours: summer, 9-4; winter, call for hours.

Hobart Historical Society

P.O. Box 24, 706 E. Fourth St., Hobart, IN 46342; (219) 942-2724. Society preserves and promotes history of Hobart, IN and residents in form of museum, library, and archival collections. Holdings include clothing, furniture, tools, and other artifacts from 1840s; newspapers, periodicals and other references related to area history; archives of Hobart civic, cultural and social orgs; Hobart Township census and other records; local and area maps and photos; obituary records of Hobart families from 1890. Collections are non-circulating. Accepts phone inquiries. No fee. Hours: Sa 10-3 or by appt.

Indiana Historical Society

315 W. Ohio St., Indianapolis, IN 46202; (317) 232-1882. Collects, preserves, and promotes IN's history through programs, exhibits, publications, and extensive research library. Library contains rare books, manuscripts, photos, maps, and pictures relating to history of IN and Old Northwest. Manuscripts include papers of Civil War soldiers, records of settlement of Northwest and IN territories, and late 19th and early 20th c social history. Other holdings include maps,

photos of IN and some towns, and genealogical records. Library has collections on blacks, medicine, military, women, and ethnicity. Accepts phone inquiries. No fee. Hours: Sept-May M-F 8-4:30, Sa 8:30-4; closed Sa June-Aug.

Indiana Jewish Historical Society

203 W. Wayne St., Fort Wayne, IN 46802; (219) 422-3862. Collects, preserves and publishes historical material about the 200 yrs of Jewish life in IN. Holdings include archival histories of communities and families; records of orgs and cemeteries; photos of temples and businesses; genealogical charts of families. Accepts phone inquiries. No fee. Hours: 9-2.

Indiana State Library

140 N. Senate Ave., Indianapolis, IN 46204; (317) 232-3734. Library has collection of Indiana-related materials on historical, contemporary, lifestyle, religious, and scientific topics. Holdings include papers of citizens, companies, and orgs; maps; photos; recordings; and Indiana county histories and state documents. Accepts phone inquiries. No fee. Hours: M-F 8-4:30.

Indiana State Museum and Memorials

202 N. Alabama St., Indianapolis, IN 46204; (317) 232-1637. Collects, preserves, and interprets cultural and natural history of IN in form of museum, reference library, and special collections. Holdings include displays of rare maps, photos, and artworks; textile and costumes; natural history specimens; research materials and publications. Library open to public by appt only. Accepts phone inqiries. No fee. Hours: M-Sa 9-4:45, Su noon-4:45.

Indiana Supreme Court

Law Library, State House Rm. 316, Indianapolis, IN 46204; (317) 232-2557. Legal library maintains collection of IN and other law-related reference materials. Holdings include IN Supreme Court Briefs from 1854; IN legislative journals from 1857; collection of early IN legal treatises. Collection is non-circulating. Accepts phone inquiries. No fee. Hours: M-F 8:30-4:30.

Indiana University

Lilly Library, Seventh St., Bloomington, IN 47405; (812) 335-0100. Academic library holds special collection of Lincoln materials, including papers and correspondence with family and members of his family. Library also has papers of film directors John Ford and Orson Welles, including materials on Welles' involvement with Federal Theatre Project, Mercury Theatre, RKO Studios, and film and radio industries. Accepts phone inquiries. Hours: call.

Indiana University/Purdue University at Fort Wayne

Documents Dept., Helmke Library, 2101 E. Coliseum Blvd., Fort Wayne, IN 46805; (219) 481-6505. Univ library maintains selective collection of local, state, and US govt documents, general and historical reference materials, and school archives. Holdings include 80% of US Serial Set and most congressional publications from 1970; univ archives include correspondence, brochures, programs, oral histories, and large photo collection, from 1919; USGS and Defense Mapping Agency maps. Accepts phone inquiries. No fee. Hours: M-Th 8-midnight, F 8-5, Sa 9-6, Su noon-midnight.

Indiana War Memorial

431 N. Meridian St., Indianapolis, IN 46204; (317) 635-1964. Memorial to IN veterans of war and museum for military memorabilia. Museum displays memorabilia of IN soldiers from Battle of Tippecanoe through present. Large collection of photos of soldiers and maps available. Accepts phone inquiries. No fee. Hours: 8-4:30.

Indianapolis Motor Speedway Hall of Fame Museum

4790 W. 16th St., Indianapolis, IN 46222; (317) 248-6747. Preserves and displays automotive history of Indianapolis and the Motor Speedway through restored vehicles, hall of fame and museum exhibits, library, and special collections. Holdings include 32 race cars that won the Indy 500 race; trophies and artifacts; racing paintings and drawings; research materials and publications; official AAA competition records, 1909-1955; extensive collection of racing-related photo negatives from 1909; Indy 500 Video Collection and racing films; audio tapes of racing programs and interviews; Rudolf Caracci-

Ray Harroun, winner of the first Indianapolis 500 in 1911, from the Indianapolis Motor Speedway Hall of Fame Museum.

ola Trophy Collection. Accepts phone inquiries. Fee. Hours: 9-5.

Indianapolis/Marion County Public Library

P.O. Box 211, 40 E. St. Clair St., Indianapolis, IN 46206; (317) 269-1733. Provides collection of historical materials on IN and US history. Library has large collection concentrating on IN, Civil War, WWII, and Vietnam War. Other holdings include maps, recordings, and IN county histories. Materials circulate to county residents only; ILL available. Accepts phone inquiries. No fee. Hours: M-F 9-9, Sa 9-5, Su 1-5.

Institute for Sex Research Library

Indiana University, 416 Morrison Hall, Bloomington, IN 47401; (812) 335-7686. Preserves large collection of materials on sexual activity, including behavioral and social aspects; erotic literature and sexual ephemera; research materi-

als of Kinsey Studies; semitraditional erotic poetry and song of 17th and 18th c England; and collections of bawdy limericks, double-entendre, puns, slang, graffiti, slang, special dictionaries, proverbs, and sayings. Some restrictions. Hours: call.

John Dillinger Museum

P.O. Box 869, State Rd 46, Nashville, IN 47448; (812) 988-7172. Preserves artifacts and events of John Dillinger's life. Museum exhibits include displays on Dillinger's childhood, crimes, slaying, clothing, tombstone, and deathmask. Other holdings include accounts of his death, photos, and materials on other notorious gangsters. Accepts phone inquiries. Fee. Hours: Mar-Nov, 10-6; Dec-Feb, 1-5.

Johnson County Historical Museum and Society

150 W. Madison St., Franklin, IN 46131; (317)

736-4655. Collects and preserves history of Johnson County, IN and residents in form of museum and archival collections. Holdings include geological specimens, Indian, pioneer and other artifacts from 1820; journals and diaries from Civil War; local atlases and fire maps; photos of local subjects; genealogical records from 1820. Accepts phone inquiries, but prefers written inquiries. Donations accepted. Hours: Tu-F 10-noon, 1-4, Sa 10-3, and by appt.

La Porte County Historical Society

La Porte County Complex, La Porte, IN 46350; (219) 326-6808. Promotes historical preservation of county. Museum consists of furnished pioneer log cabin, Victorian parlor and music room, 1920s kitchen, and 1900 doctor's and dentist's offices. Displays include Indian artifacts and antique firearms. Library has small reference collection. Archive holds town's original land charter of 1832; church and individual histories; maps from 1874; photos; and genealogical records. Accepts phone inquiries. No fee. Hours: M-F 10-4:30.

Michael Horan Parachuting Resources Library

115 N 13 St., Richmond, IN 47374; (317) 962-4379. Collects and preserves largest collection of historical and rare materials on parachuting in US. Includes materials on skydiving. Hours: call.

Michigan City Historical Society

P.O. Box 512, Heisman Harbor Rd., Washington Park, Michigan City, IN 46360; (219) 872-6133. Preserves and promotes the history of Michigan City and Lake Michigan Lighthouse Service in form of Old Lighthouse Museum, library, and archival collections. Holdings include artifacts and exhibits on local and maritime history, and lighthouse service from 1830; reference library and archives with research materials, genealogical records, and photos of local families, events, lighthouse service, shipwrecks, and other maritime items; local and area maps from 1800; Indian artifacts; exhibit on launching of first Great Lakes submarine. Research by appt. Accepts phone inquiries. Fee. Hours: Tu-Su 1-4.

Morrison-Reeves Library

Document Dept., 80 N. Sixth St., Richmond,

IN 47374; (317) 966-8291. Public library maintains selective collection of local, state and US govt documents, general reference, local historical materials, and special collections. Holdings include local genealogical records, county histories, Richmond City directories, cemetery and census records for Wayne and surrounding counties; abstracts of Quaker records; Brown Room Civil War and Lincoln collections; Richmond City Collection; Wayne County Collection. Accepts phone inquiries. No fee. Hours: Sept-May, M-Th 9-9, F-Sa 9-5:30; June-Aug M-Th 9-7, F-Sa 9-5:30.

New Harmony Workingmen's Institute

P.O. Box 368, 407 Tavern St., New Harmony, IN 47631; (812) 682-4806. Preserves history and materials of intellectual activity surrounding Robert Owen's utopian experiment at New Harmony from 1825-27. Museum displays 19th c art and artifacts from era of Harmonists Owen and Maclure, with emphasis on early scientists. Library contains manuscripts and publications relating to history of the town and region. Archive documents Owen-Maclure community and history of New Harmony through collections of maps, photos, genealogical records, and manuscripts. Accepts phone inquiries. Hours: qualified researchers by appt; Tu-Sa 10-4:30.

Northern Indiana Historical Society

112 S. LaFayette Blvd., South Bend, IN 46601; (219) 284-9664. Society preserves and promotes history of St Joseph River Valley Region and residents in form of museum, library, and archival collections. Holdings include costumes, indian artifacts, antique toys and mechanical banks, industrial historical items, holiday decorations, and other artifacts; library with fur trading references, court documents 1830s-1920s, local and state histories; archives with diaries, personal papers, civic org records, govt documents, large photo collection; manuscripts and maps from early 19th c; films/videotapes, recordings and genealogical records. Research by appt. Accepts phone inquiries. No fee. Hours: M-F 9-5, Su 1-4.

Organization of American Historians

112 N. Bryan St., Bloomington, IN 47401;

(812) 335-7311. Promotes study and research of history by sponsoring publications on topics such as women's history, public history, and teaching of history on secondary level. Accepts phone inquiries. Hours: M-F 8-5.

Purdue University Libraries

Special Collections, West Lafayette, IN 47907; (317) 494-2831. Holds collection on Amelia Earhart, including charts, maps, medals, certificates, letters, telegrams, and other memorabilia; and papers of Earl Butz, Sec of Agriculture under Pres Nixon and Ford. Accepts phone inquiries. No fee. Hours: call.

Richlyn Library

Documents Dept., 2303 College Ave., Huntington, IN 46750; (219) 356-6000. Christian Liberal Arts Institution library maintains selected collection of govt documents, and historical materials relevant to college and church needs and history. Holdings include museum with artifacts from the United Brethren Church and the college, and archives with related materials. Does not accept phone inquiries. No fee. Hours: M-Th 7:30-11, F 7:30-4, Sa 2-5, Su 8:30-11.

Studebaker National Museum

120 S. St. Joseph, (2nd museum at 520 Lafayette Blvd.), South Bend, IN 46601; (219) 284-9714. Preserves and displays Studebaker heritage and collection. Museum presents timeline history of Studebaker Corp. from 1865-1966, and materials on other South Bend industrial history. Over 75 vehicles displayed. Archives contains Studebaker promotional literature, catalogs, and sales and financial records; photos of Studebaker products and advertising; promotional, historical, and training films from Studebaker; and local Industrial products. Accepts phone inquiries. No fee. Hours: Tu-F 10-4:30, Sa 10-4, Su noon-4.

Tippecanoe Battlefield Museum

P.O. Box 225, Railroad St., Battle Ground, IN 47920; (317) 567-2147. National Historic Landmark museum preserves and displays history or region and of Tippecanoe Battle of 1811 that led to War of 1812. Holdings include local historical, cultural and military artifacts from prehistoric Indians through election of President William Henry Harrison; maps of Harrison's troops encampments; historical film on events of 1811 that led to battle; special collections. Accepts phone inquiries. Fee. Hours: Feb-Dec, M-Sa 10-5, Su 1-5.

Tippecanoe County Historical Association

909 South St., LaFayette, IN 47901; (319) 742-8411. Collects, preserves and researches history of Tippecanoe County, IN and residents in form of special events, museum, library and historical resource center. Holdings include Moses Fowler House Museum, which exhibits Karling Hill miniature collection, pioneer artifacts, and mid-19th c furnishings; Alameda McCollough Library at Wetherhill Historial Resource Center (1001 South St.) with reference publications and archives of manuscripts and records on local history. Use of archives by previously arranged appt only. Accepts phone inquiries. No fee. Hours: museum: Feb-Dec, Tu-Su 1-5; library: Feb-Dec, Tu-F 1-5.

Tri-State Genealogical Society

c/o Willard Library, 21 First Ave., Evansville, IN 47710; (812) 425-4309 (Willard Library). Society preserves and interprets history of southern IN, southeastern IL, and western KY in form of special events and reference and archival collections housed at Willard Library. Holdings include rare books; city directories from 1855; genealogical research materials on Tri-State families; local histories, manuscripts, newspapers (in German and English); materials on river history; archives with manuscripts, court, church, cemetery and census records; photos of early Evansville area; Thrall Art Book Collection. Collections are non-circulating. Library accepts phone inquiries. No fee. Library hours: Tu-Sa 9-5, Su 1-5.

University of Southern Indiana, Evansville

Library, 8600 University Blvd., Evansville, IN 47712; (812) 464-1824. Collects and preserves materials on communal societies from past and present. Holdings cover historic communes, correspondence with contemporary communes, and brochures and newsletters. Accepts phone inquiries. Hours: call.

Washington County Historical Society

307 E. Market St., Salem, IN 47167; (812) 883-6495. Society preserves and promotes study of genealogical and cultural history of Washington County, IN and residents. Holdings include museum with displays of artifacts from county families; library of genealogical research material, including family files, church records, scrap books, obituaries and other records (not limited to local area); early land entries and plat maps of Washington County. Library collection is non-circulating. Accepts phone inquiries. Fee. Hours: Tu-Su 1-5.

Wesleyan Church Archives and Historical Library

P.O. Box 50434, 8050 Castleway Drive, Indianapolis, IN 46250; (317) 576-1315. Archives serves as official repository for historical documents of the Wesleyan Church. Holdings include small museum with church artifacts from late 19th c; large library with research materials on American Methodism, anti-slavery movement, and American Holiness Movement; archives with church documents, periodicals, and minutes from 1830s; manuscripts of sermons and other church-related compositions; photos from church-related conferences, events and institutions from late 19th c; recordings of church business and sermons from 1950s; genealogical records. Some restrictions. Accepts phone inquiries. No fee. Hours: M-F 8-4:30.

William Howard Mathers Museum

Indiana University, 416 N. Indiana Ave., Bloomington, IN 47405; (812) 335-7224. (Mailing address: 601 E. Eighth St, Bloomington, IN 47405) Museum preserves and promotes study of anthropology, history, and folklore. Holdings include intl collection of artifacts, photos and exhibits; large reference library; archives of extended collection documentation; small collection of local history manuscripts and photos; small film collection; Wanamaker Collection of American Indian photos, 1908-1921; Boulton Musical Instruments collection; Ellison Plains Indian collection; Greist Eskimo collection. Some restrictions. Accepts phone inquiries. No fee. Hours: Tu-F 9-4:30, Sa-Su 1-4:30.

Iowa

Amana Heritage Society

P.O. Box 81, Amana, IA 52203; (319) 622-3567. Collects, preserves, and interprets paper, documents, materials, and artifacts relating to Amana communal society. Museum specializes in preserving material culture and fine and folk arts of 19th and early 20th c; library on Amana, communal societies, and Pietism from 1700; archives of Amana Society from 1700; collections of letters, diaries, account books, maps, photos, song and hymn recordings, genealogies, and oral history interviews. Accepts phone inquiries. Fee. Hours: museum, Apr-Nov 10-5; library, M-F by appt.

American Archives of the Factual Film

Iowa State University, Iowa State University Library, Ames, IA 50011; (515) 294-6672. Preserves and studies business, industrial, scientific, and educational films. Holds over 10,000 non-theatrical films, and papers of organizations and individuals active in producing them. Accepts phone inquiries. No fee. Hours: M-F 8-11:50, 1-5.

Antique Airplace Association

Rte 2, Box 172, Ottumwa, IA 52501; (515) 938-2773. Helps find, restore, and fly antique and classic airplanes, and provides medium of exchange for info between members. Museum, library, and archives hold manuscripts, maps, photos, films/videotapes, and recordings. Special collection of Rearwin Aircraft and Engine files. Accepts phone inquiries. Fee for membership. Hours: 9-5.

Archives of American Agriculture

Special Collections Dept., Iowa State University, Library, Ames, IA 50011; (515) 294-6672. Collects unpublished materials on agriculture from individuals, businesses, and orgs. Archives hold many University papers on agriculture and other manuscripts, including those of conservationist Margaret Black, farmer protest groups, George Washington Carver, National Association of Farm Broadcasters, and many other individuals and orgs. Film collection holds large collection of films concentrating on machinery, conservation, and production. May be some restrictions. Accepts phone inquiries. No fee. Hours: M-F, 8-11:50, 1-5.

Archives of American Veterinary Medicine

Special Collections Dept., Iowa State University Library, Ames, IA 50011; (515) 294-6672. Collects unpublished materials on veterinary medicine from individuals, businesses, and orgs. Holdings include materials from faculty, alumni, administrative units, and other groups. Small film/videotape collection on aspects of field. May be some restrictions. Accepts phone inquiries. No fee. Hours: M-F 8-11:50, 1-5.

Boone County Historical Society

P.O. Box 1, Boone, IA 50036; (515) 432-1931. Promotes interest in state and local history by collecting and preserving historical memorabilia, and reprinting books, documents, and maps. Museums on railroad, rural schooling, and county history sponsored by society. Holdings include railroad union and Boone records; some letters and documents; maps; local photos; and genealogies. Accepts phone inquiries. Donations accepted. Hours: by appt; summer, Su.

Boone Railroad Historical Society

P.O. Box 603, Boone, IA 50036; (515) 432-4249. Preserves history of railroads in IA. Accepts phone inquiries. No fee. Hours: 9-4.

Buffalo Bill Museum of Le Claire

P.O. Box 284, 200 N. River Dr., Le Claire, IA 52753; (319) 289-5580. Preserves River, Indian, and local history. Museum collection includes steamboat "Lone Star," Indian artifacts, and local history artifacts dating to mid-19th c. Archives displays first flight recorder (black box) and other invention of area resident James Ryan; Civil War musical instruments; photos of Riverboats, Buffalo Bill Cody Show, and early Le-Claire families; genealogical records of river pilots, early settlers, and Buffalo Bill. Accepts phone inquiries. Fee. Hours: May 15-Oct 15, 9-5; winter, Sa-Su 9-5.

Carnegie-Stout Public Library

Documents Dept., 11th & Bluff Sts., Dubuque,

IA 52001; (319) 589-4225. General public library with collections of IA, IL, and WI USGS maps, local history items from IL and WI, genealogical records, and local newspapers from 1837. Accepts phone inquiries. No fee. Hours: Labor Day-Memorial Day, M-Th 10-8, Sa 9-5, Su 1-5; Memorial Day-Labor Day, M, W 10-8, Tu, Th, F 10-6, Sa 10-5.

Cedar Falls Historical Society

303 Franklin St., 303 Clay St., Cedar Falls, IA 50613; (319) 266-5149. Preserves Black Hawk county history through holdings in museum, library and archives. Collections include maps, photos, recordings, genealogical records, and films/videotapes. Accepts phone inquiries. No fee. Hours: W-Su 2-4.

Davenport Public Library

Special Collections, 321 Main St., Davenport, IA 52801; (319) 326-7902. Resource for history, genealogy, and politics of Davenport, Scott county, and IA. Library and archives have court, burial, and tax records; Davenport photos from 1900-50; genealogical records; and newspapers. Accepts phone inquiries. No fee. Hours: M-Tu 10-8:30; W-Sa 10-5:30.

Drake University

Documents Division, Cowles Library, 28th St. & University Ave., Des Moines, IA 50311; (515) 271-2814. Supports University's research needs with collection of US govt documents, some dating from 1791. Holdings also include USGS topographical maps of IA, and a special collection of J.N. Darling cartoon proof sheets from 1914-48. Hours: call.

Dubuque History Center

Loras College, Wahlert Memorial Library, P.O. Box 178, Dubuque, IA 52001; (319) 588-7125. Collects and preserves local history materials and publishes studies of local interest. Library contains large collection of state and federal documents. Archives contains original manuscripts, photos, census materials, newspapers, vertical files, maps, county and city records, genealogical records, and entire Center for Dubuque History archives history collection. Materials non-circulating. Accepts phone inquiries. Fee for research. Hours: call.

Effigy Mounds National Monument

RR 1, Box 25A, Harpers Ferry, IA 52146; (319) 873-3491. Preserves historical burial grounds. Museum provides orientation to history of upper MI; library and archives hold manuscripts, maps, and photos on regional archaeology. Library and archive access limited to archaeology. Fee. Hours: 8-5.

Fayette County Helpers Club and Historical Society

100 N. Walnut St., West Union, IA 52175; (319) 422-5797. Collects county history, records, and memorabilia in museum, library, and archives. Holdings include manuscripts, maps, photos, recordings, and genealogical records. Accepts phone inquiries. Donations accepted. Hours: M-F 8-noon, 1-4:30.

Fort Dodge Historical Foundation—Fort Museum

P.O. Box 1798, US 20 & Museum Rd., Fort Dodge, IA 50501; (515) 573-4231. Preserves and exhibits items on IA and Ft Dodge history. Museum consists of recreated military frontier fort and village; library houses small local history collection; photo collection; genealogical records, and special Karl King memorabilia. Accepts phone inquiries. Fee. Hours: appt required for use of library, photos, and genealogical collections; museum, May-Oct, M-Sa 9-5, Su noon-5.

George Wyth House and Viking Pump Museum

303 Franklin St., Cedar Falls, IA 50613; (319) 277-8817. Art Deco museum in home setting with period furnishings and interior. Archives focus on history of Viking Pump and local area. Accepts phone inquiries. No fee. Hours: call.

Graceland College

DuRose Room, Frederick Madison Smith Library, Lamoni, IA 50140; (515) 784-5362. Researches and preserves history of Reorganized Church of Latter Day Saints (RLDS church), local area, and Graceland College. Library has reference materials on RLDS, archival materials on Restoration history from 1830, manuscripts, photos, and genealogical records. Special collections include materials on Lamonia, IA, and

Decatur county history. Accepts phone inquiries. No fee. Hours: M, W, F 10-noon, Tu 1-3, Th 1-3, 7-9, Su 7-9.

Herbert Hoover National Historic Site

P.O. Box 607, Parkside Dr., West Branch, IA 52358; (319) 643-2541. Preserves and interprets historically significant properties associated with Herbert Hoover. Museum houses exhibits on Hoover's career and presidency; library holds collection of his presidential papers; archive maintains collection of furnishings, maps, photos, recordings, genealogical records, and films/videotapes relating to Hoover. Also some local history items. Library open to researchers only. Accepts phone inquiries. Fee. Hours: 8-5.

Herbert Hoover Presidential Library

National Archives & Records Administration, P.O. Box 488, Parkside Dr., West Branch, IA 52358; (319) 643-5301. Preserves and displays Hoover's life, times and contributions to society. Museum exhibits art objects, graphics, textiles, and other artifacts owned by Hoovers. Library focuses on 20th c American history. Archive has Hoover's papers from 1921-64 and maps from early 20th c China and WWI Europe; large photo collection covering Hoover family, WWI famine relief, 1927 MI floods, presidency, and Hoover Dam construction; professional and home film footage of Hoover from 1920s; recordings of Hoover addresses, and oral history interviews. Apply to director for access to historical collection. Accepts phone inquiries. No fee. Hours: M-F 8:45-noon, 12:30-4:45, Sa 9-noon.

Historic General Dodge House

621 Third St., 605 Third St., Council Bluffs, IA 51503; (712) 322-2406. Fully restored house museum presents lifestyle, history, and cultural aspirations of Gen Grenville Dodge. Library focuses on Dodge, his family papers, photos, and some genealogical records on immediate descendants. Also collection of local history artifacts ranging from Christmas tree ornaments to pressed glass from early 1900s. Accepts phone inquiries. Fee. Hours: Feb-Dec, Tu-Sa 10-5, Su 1-5.

Herbert and Lou Henry Hoover, from the Herbert Hoover Presidential Library.

Iowa State Education Association, Salisbury House

4025 Tonawanda Dr., Des Moines, IA 50312; (515) 279-9711. Preserves and exhibits collection on IA education; first, rare, and limited editions of works by D.H. Lawrence and James Joyce; and manuscripts by authors, artists, and statesmen. Supervised use only. No fee. Hours: M-F 8-4:30.

Iowa State Historical Society

Capitol Complex, Des Moines, IA 50319; (515) 281-6200. Collects, preserves, and makes available materials relating to IA history. Museum displays North American Indian archaeology, geology, natural history, Civil War, farm equipment, transportation, and IA history. Library has large collection on IA, US, and IA newspapers. Archives holds records of state govt agencies; manuscripts of IA politics, Civil War, womens' groups, and agriculture history; maps; large collection of photos; genealogical records; and Aldrich collection of 3-4 thousand autographs of famous people. Materials for in-house use only. Accepts phone inquiries. No fee. Hours: Tu-Sa 9-4:30.

Iowa State University Library

Documents Division, Ames, IA 50011; (515) 294-3642. Academic research library with emphasis on agriculture and applied sciences. Collects government documents and geological, Forest Service, and CIA maps. Accepts phone inquiries. No fee. Hours: M-Th 8-10, F 8-5, Sa-Su 1-5.

Iowa State University Library

Special Collections, Ames, IA 50011; (515) 294-6672. Maintains archives of University, American Archives of Factual Film, Archives of American Culture, Archives of American Veterinary Medicine, Statistics Archive, Evolution/Creation Archive, Little Blue Books Archive, and Underground Comics Archive. University Archive holds records of staff and administration, papers of faculty, and large photograph collection. Other holdings include Austin Adams family papers, with correspondence from Ralph Waldo Emerson and A. Bronson Alcott. Accepts phone inquiries. No fee. Hours: M-F 8-11:50, 1-5.

Iowa Western Community College

Document Dept., Library, 2700 College Rd., Box 4-C, Council Bluffs, IA 51502; (712) 325-3247. Provides educational research support. Holds college archives. No fee. Hours: M-Th 8-9, F 8-4:30, Sa 10-2.

Jasper County Historical Society

P.O. Box 834, 1700 S. 15th Ave. West, Newton, IA 50208; (515) 792-9118. Preserves county history through holdings in museum and library, including maps, photos, films/videotapes, and recordings. Special Maytag Co exhibit on all models of Maytags, from first to latest machines. Accepts phone inquiries. Fee. Hours: May-Oct 1-5, and by appt.

La Porte City FFA Agricultural Museum

413 Chestnut, La Porte City, IA 50651; (319) 342-2640. Exhibits feature agriculture and home economics, as well as doctor's office, dentist's office, and barber shop. Military, religious, and school items on display as well. Collection strong in agricultural tools and machinery. Donations accepted. Hours: call.

Laura Ingalls Wilder Park and Museum

P.O. Box 354, Burr Oak, IA 52101; (319) 735-5916. Preserves hotel Ingalls once worked in, and provides info on Ingalls' travels. Hotel museum is furnished in 19th c period fashion; library holds some history on Burr Oak area; maps of Ingalls travels; and photos and genealogical records of Ingalls family. Fee. Hours: by appt.

Liberty Hall Historic Center

1300 W. Main St., Lamoni, IA 50140; (515) 784-6133. Educates public on Midwestern Victorian culture in small-town America. Museum housed in home from 1881-1906 period. Manuscript collection contains materials from Fredrick Madison Smith library and Graceland College. Other holdings include maps, photos, and genealogical collections. Accepts phone inquiries. No fee. Hours: M-F 10-4, Sa 10-noon.

Mamie Doud Eisenhower Birthplace

P.O. Box 55, 709 Carroll St., Boone, IA 50036; (515) 432-1896. Mamie Doud Eisenhower's restored birthplace with museum and library holdings. Museum exhibits chronology of her life, two gowns, and some Frank Miller cartoons. Library holds many materials on Eisenhowers, their families, and local history. Manuscript collection of genealogical materials, clipping, and periodicals. Map collection includes fire insurance and plat book maps from early 20th c. Many photos and slides. Some videotapes of home restoration, TV programs, and David Eisenhower. Recordings of Eisenhower interviews. Some restrictions. Accepts phone inquiries. Fee for museum; no fee for library. Hours: Apr-May, Tu-Su 1-5; June-Oct, 12:30-5.

Mennonite Historical Society of Iowa

P.O. Box 576, 411 Ninth St., Kalona, IA 52247; (319) 656-3271. Preserves and symbolizes Mennonite life and faith through art, artifacts, literature, and documents. Museum contains local artifacts. Library has books by and about Amish/Mennonites dating to 1553. Other materials include German books, Mennonite bibliography, diaries, personal collections, local history manuscripts, map locating Jesse James cabin, photos, oral history recordings, and genealogical records. Accepts phone inquiries. Fee. Hours: Apr 15-Oct 15, 10-4.

Midwest Old Settlers and Threshers Association

RR 1, Threshers Rd., Rte. 1, Mt. Pleasant, IA 52641; (319) 385-8937. Association dedicated to preserving agricultural heritage by maintaining museum, library, and archives. Museum holds exhibits on agricultural machinery powered by horse, steam, and gas from 1860-1935, and American Tent and Repertoire Theatre from 1860. Library contains research materials on agriculture, and theatre props, manuscripts, and memorabilia. Archive collections in advertising and theatre; photo collection; film/videotape holdings; and oral history recordings. Accepts phone inquiries. Fee. Hours: M-F 8-4; Memorial Day-Labor Day, open M-Su.

Midwest Riverboat Buffs

P.O. Box 1225, Keokuk, IA 52632; (319) 524-3286. Society interested in history of steamboats and other Mississippi River traffic. Holds few photos and publishes semi-annual newsletter. Accepts phone inquiries. No fee. Hours: 9-11.

National Balloon Museum

P.O. Box 149, 711 N. E St., Indianola, IA 50125; (515) 961-8415. Preserves history and artifacts of ballooning from 1800. Holdings include baskets, balloons, uniforms, and flight logs; balloon race records; and artifacts from military ballooning applications. Accepts phone inquiries. Donations accepted. Hours: M-F 9-4.

Northern Iowa Area Community College Library

Documents Division, 500 College Dr., Mason City, IA 50401; (515) 421-4326. Provides material for academic research for college and local community with govt document holdings; small photo collection; some films and videotapes. Accepts phone inquiries. No fee. Hours: M-Th 7:30-9, F 7:30-4:30.

Office of State Archaeologist

University of Iowa, Eastlawn Bldg., Iowa City,

IA 52242; (319) 335-2389. Performs research and educational role in IA archaeology. Small museum features prehistoric and historic artifacts from archaeological sites; library contains reports and unpublished archaeology students' manuscripts since 1920s, maps, and photos of sites. Some restrictions. Accepts phone inquiries. Hours: M-F 8-4:30.

Pioneer Museum and Historical Society of North Iowa

P.O. Box 421, 286 Willowbrook Dr., Mason City, IA 50401; (515) 423-9431. Preserves local history through exhibits of 19th c loom, Regina music box, telephone equipment, steam engines, blacksmith shop and operation, early flash powder cameras, and display on movie "Music Man." Accepts phone inquiries. Fee. Hours: W-F, Su noon-6.

Public Library of Des Moines

Document Dept., 100 Locust St., Des Moines, IA 50308; (515) 283-4259. Provides access to local history materials on Des Moines, Polk County, and IA. Holdings include newspapers, pamphlets, periodicals, and clipping files; maps and atlases; photos and postcards; oral history interviews; genealogical records; IA govt records; IA authors collection; and biographical scrapbooks. Materials non-circulating. Accepts phone inquiries (515-283-4152). No fee. Hours: M-Th 9-9, F 9-6, Sa 9-5.

Scottish Heritage Society of Iowa

P.O. Box 155, Des Moines, IA 50311. Preserves Scottish-American culture, music, dance, and lore in Iowa, as well as info on settlement area of numerous Scot descendents. Maintains small collection of genealogical records, but no permanent headquarters.

Sioux City and Iowa Heritage Center

Sioux City Public Library, 705 Sixth St., Sioux City, IA 51105; (712) 279-6179. General library serving community needs, with special collections of federal census info, genealogical materials, DAR, WPA Historical Records Survey publications on Sioux City history, area newspaper collections, and assorted manuscripts, maps, and photos. Materials for in-house use only.

Accepts phone inquiries. No fee. Hours: M-Th 9-9, F-Sa 9-5; Sept-May, also Su 1-5.

Sioux City Public Museum and Historical Association

2901 Jackson St., Sioux City, IA 51104; (712) 279-6174. Collects, preserves, and displays items of historical, anthropological, and scientific value to Sioux City. Archives store papers, documents, and diaries; map collection relating to Sioux City from 1880-1960; extensive photo collection; and large collection of TV news file film from 1960s-1980s. Accepts phone inquiries. No fee. Hours: museum and archives, M-F 9-5; archives, Sa 9-5, Su 2-5.

State Historical Society of Iowa

Iowa Dept. of Cultural Affairs, 402 Iowa Ave., Iowa City, IA 52240; (319) 335-3916. Records, collects, and preserves state, national, and local histories, biographies, and govt documents; personal papers, business and civic records, and materials on labor, women's history, Civil War, education, lumber trade, and civil engineering; thousands of IA and upper Midwest maps from 19th c; many photos of IA towns, people, railroads, steamboats, entertainment, military, Amana Colony and Mesquakie Indians; extensive oral history collection, with emphasis on labor and IA folk artists; thousands of KCRG-TV newscasts; many genealogical materials; and architectural plans and broadsides. May be restrictions. Accepts phone inquiries. Hours: Tu-Sa 9-4:30.

Tama County Historical Society

200 N. Broadway, Toledo, IA 52342; (515) 484-6767. Preserves county heritage through museum displays of pioneer, military, and Indian artifacts; library holdings of newspapers, land and court records, 19th c maps, photos, and genealogical records; and oral history interviews with older county residents. Accepts phone inquiries. No fee. Hours: W-Sa 1-4.

University of Iowa Libraries

Special Collections, Iowa City, IA 52242; (319) 335-5921. Collects and preserves materials on 19th-20th c US history. Manuscript collection has materials on agriculture, labor, US Vice Pres Henry Wallace, journalism, railroads, women's

activities, pop culture, Progressive Party, and Civil War. Map collection includes sheet maps, Sanborn fire insurance maps for IA, plat books, and aerial photos of IA. Photo collection strong on railroads, tent Chautauqua, and Univ history. Videotape collection has original videos from Artists' TV Network from 1970s-80s. Special holdings on western Americana, Lincoln, Poe, left- and right-wing material, and typography. Accepts phone inquiries. No fee. Hours: M-F 9-noon, 1-5.

Upper Iowa University

Special Collections, Henderson-Wilder Library, Fayette, IA 52142; (319) 425-5270. Academic support library with special collection of NASA memorabilia, including photos, stamps, letters, banners, buttons, and cassette tapes from 1960s. Accepts phone inquiries. No fee. Hours: M-Th 7:30-5, 7-11; F 7:30-5, Sa-Su 2-5.

Vesterheim-Norwegian-American Museum

502 W. Water St., Decorah, IA 52101; (319) 382-9681. Preserves, interprets, and studies materials relating to life and culture of Norwegian-Americans. Museum holdings documents immigration experience with large collection of items; remainings archival and library holdings range from manuscripts and maps to photos and films/videotapes, but are not cataloged. Accepts phone inquiries. Fee. Hours: May-Oct 8-5, Nov-Apr 10-4.

Kansas

Air Force Historical Foundation

Kansas State University, Dept. of History, Eisenhower Hall, Manhattan, KS 66506; (913) 532-6733. Publishes aviation quarterly covering WWI through Vietnam. Accepts phone inquiries. No fee. Hours: 8-5.

Army Combat Studies Institute

US Army Command and General Staff College, ATTN: ATZL-SWI, Fort Leavenworth, KS 66027. Publishes research publications on US military combat, as well as military operations of Japan, Germany, Russia, and China. Official users may use materials on request; others may obtain from Govt Printing Office. Accepts mail inquiries.

Augusta Historical Museum
P.O. Box 545, 305 State St., Augusta, KS 67010; (316) 775-5655. Preserves history of Augusta, Butler county, and KS. Museum and library hold maps and photos from 19th c. Accepts phone inquiries. Donations accepted. Hours: M-F 11-3, Sa-Su 2-4.

Baker University
Collins Library, Baldwin City, KS 66006; (913) 594-6451 ext. 414. Academic research library with archival materials of East Kansas Methodist Conference and University. Museum collects rare Bibles, and covers their printing and writing history. May be some restrictions. Accepts phone inquiries. No fee. Hours: M-F 8-5 and M-Th 6:30pm-11pm, Sa 1-4, Su 1-5 and 7pm-11pm.

Benedictine College Library
Documents Division, North Campus, Second & Division Sts., Atchison, KS 66002; (913) 367-5340. Academic support library with collections on local and KS history. Special collection on Lewis & Clark. Some materials for in-house use only. Accepts phone inquiries. No fee. Hours: M-F, Sa-Su 1-5.

Boot Hill Museum
Front St., Dodge City, KS 67801; (316) 227-8188. Preserves and interprets history of Dodge City and southwest KS, with interest in social, govt and business records. Museum is reconstructed area of 1876 downtown businesses. Collections date from mid 19th c, and include maps, photos, journals, newspapers, and family papers. Restrictions on use. Accepts phone inquiries. Fee. Hours: summer 8-8, winter 9-5.

Cavalry Museum
P.O. Box 2160, Bldg. 205, Fort Riley, KS 66442; (913) 239-2737. Traces history and traditions of US Horse Cavalry from 1775-1950 through museum, library and archival holdings. Library holds materials on military and cavalry history, field manuals and journals; several diaries, maps of Ft Riley; thousands of photos of Cavalry; and complete set of 1940s Cavalry training films.

Materials for in-house use only. Accepts phone inquiries (913-239-2743). No fee. Hours: 9-4:30.

Chisholm Trail Museum Corporation
502 N. Washington, Wellington, KS 67152; (316) 326-2174. Commemorates pioneers of Wellington and Sumner counties through museum collection of artifacts, small library, and considerable genealogical collection. Materials for in-house use only. Accepts phone inquiries. Donation accepted. Hours: winter, Sa-Su 1-4; summer, Tu-Th, Sa-Su 1-4.

Cloud County Historical Society and Museum
635 Broadway, Concordia, KS 66901; (913) 243-2866. Collects, preserves, exhibits, and encourages study in Cloud County and KS historical items and records. Museum exhibits materials on military, medical, and household items from 1868-1950. Library holds collections on Concordia and local area; atlases of county; US maps from 1853; some photos from 1860s with emphasis on people, industries, sports, and social organizations in area; some materials on German Prisoner of War Camp WWII; and genealogical records. Materials for in-house use only. Accepts phone inquiries. No fee. Hours: M-Sa 1-5.

Colby Community College
Document Division, H.F. Davis Memorial Library, 1255 South Range, Colby, KS 67701; (913) 462-3984. Academic research library serving student body and northwest KS with selective collection of federal documents and holdings on KS history. Accepts phone inquiries. No fee. Hours: M-W 8am-9pm, Th 8-6, F 8-5.

Decatur County Historical Society
Last Indian Raid in Kansas Museum, 258 S. Penn Ave., Oberlin, KS 67749; (913) 475-2712. Preserves history of county and its people with extensive county records from 19th c. Holdings include birth, marriage, contagious disease, land, Civil War veterans, and school records; 25 personal memoirs on last Indian raid of 1878; newspapers from 1880-1980; family films; and genealogical collections. Info on old post offices

and ghost towns of Decatur county. Accepts phone inquiries. Fee. Hours: winter, Tu-F 10-4, summer, Tu-Su 10-4.

Dickinson County Historical Museum

412 S. Campbell, Abilene, KS 67410; (913) 263-2861. Preserves and promotes county history with govt and civic records, maps, photos, and genealogical records. Most date from late 19th c. Extensive photo collection, and special C.W. Parker photo & business materials. Accepts phone inquiries. Fee. Hours: Apr-Sept, M-F 10-4:30, Su 1-5.

Elizabeth Watkins Community Museum

1047 Massachusetts St., Lawrence, KS 66044; (913) 841-4109. Preserves, documents, and interprets history of Lawrence, Douglas, and KS from 1819. Museum, library, and archives contain subject files, manuscripts, maps, photos, genealogical records, and assorted local history items. Materials primarily for in-house use. Accepts phone inquiries. No fee. Hours: Tu-Sa 10-4, Su 1:30-4.

Emmett Kelly Museum

202 E. Main St., Sedan, KS 67361; (316) 725-3470. Preserves collection of artifacts from life and career of Emmett Kelley and his son Emmett Kelly Jr. Holdings include clown makeup, costumes, props, photos, and other memorabilia. Accepts phone inquiries. Donations accepted. Hours: Late May-Labor Day, 1-5; and by appt.

Emporia State University

Special Collections, William Allen White Library, Emporia, KS 66801; (316) 343-1200, ext. 5037. Academic research library concentrates on children's literature and its authors. Collection includes manuscripts, illustrations, papers, and photos from William Allen White, Mary White, May Massee, Louis Lenskie, Elizabeth Yates, and Ruth Garver Gagliardo. Other holdings include Normaliana collection, children's literature collection, rare book collection, W.A. White children's book award collection and archives, and historical children's literature collection. Special collections are non-circulating. No fee. Hours: M-F 8-5, or by appt.

Emmett Kelly, Sr., from the Emmett Kelly Museum

Fort Hays State University Archives

Folklore and Oral History Collection, Forsyth Library, 600 Park St., Hays, KS 67601; (913) 628-4431. Academic research library preserves experiences of KS residents through collections on Western culture, Eastern European immigrants, and oral history interviews. Special Collections include Ethnic Heritage Studies Collection on Russian, Czech, German, and Bohemian cultures and immigration; Western Collection materials on KS history and Great Plains cattle industry; Oral History Collection documents regional experience in Dust Bowl era, Depression, wars, and folklore and superstitions. Transcriptions available. Accepts phone inquiries. Some restrictions. Accepts phone inquiries. No fee. Hours: M-Th 8-10:30, F 8-5, Sa 9-5, Su 2-10.

Fort Larned National Historic Site

Rte. 3, Larned, KS 67550; (316) 285-6911. Interprets role of Ft Larned on Sante Fe Trail and its role in westward expansion through holdings in museum, library, and archives. Some material on Indian Wars on southern plains. Materials for in-house use only. Accepts phone inquiries. Fee. Hours: summer, 8-5; winter, 9-5.

Fort Scott National Historic Site
Old Fort Blvd., Fort Scott, KS 66701; (316) 223-0310. Commemorates Ft role in westward expansion, Civil War, and subsequent skirmishes. Restored buildings represent Ft and its furnishings from 1842-53. Holdings include some period uniforms and weapons. Small reference library on Indian frontier, westward expansion, Bleeding Kansas, and Civil War; some maps; small historic and comtemporary photo collection. Accepts phone inquiries. Fee. Hours: June-Labor Day, 8-6; Labor Day-June 8-5.

Frontier Army Museum
Fort Leavenworth, ATTN: ATZK-GOP-MU, Reynolds and Gibbon, Fort Leavenworth, KS 66027; (913) 684-3191. Preserves comprehensive history of Frontier army and Ft Leavenworth, the oldest continuously occupied post west of MI River. Museum exhibits horse-drawn vehicles, frontier army weapons and uniforms, Indian artifacts, and replica pioneer cabin. Library has research materials related to museum, including maps and photos. Accepts phone inquiries. No fee. Hours: M-Sa 10-4, Su noon-4.

Frontier Historical Park
Rte. 2, Box 338, Hays, KS 67601; (913) 625-6812. Preserves history of Ft Hays and its operations from 1865-90. Museum consists of restored Ft buildings, two with period furnishings. Library holds small collection on Indian War era military operations, and old post records. Accepts phone inquiries. No fee. Hours: Memorial Day-Labor Day, Tu-Sa 9-6, Su-M 1-5; Labor Day-Memorial Day Tu-Sa 9-5, Su-M 1-5.

Galena Mining and Historical Museum Association
P.O. Box 367, 300 W. 7th St., Galena, KS 66739; (316) 783-1371. Preserves local mining artifacts, mineral displays, photos, and antiques from 1850. Donations accepted. Hours: call.

Historic Wichita-Sedgwick County
Old Cowtown Museum, 1871 Sim Park Dr., Wichita, KS 67203; (316) 264-0671. Historic village museum recreation of Wichita and Sedgwick counties from 1865-1880. Holdings include archives and photos of region. Restrictions on material use. Accepts phone inquiries. Fee. Hours: 10-5.

Kansas Collection
University of Kansas, Spencer Research Library, Lawrence, KS 66045; (913) 864-4272. Academic research facility has materials on KS history from 19th-20th c. Manuscripts include records of orgs, businesses, and churches, covering social, political, and cultural history of blacks and women in KS and region. Holdings include personal papers of first accredited woman war correspondent Peggy Hull Deuell and art therapist Mary Huntoon, org records of KS League of Women Voters, MO State Assn of Parliamentarians, and women's literary and service clubs; maps from 1920; photos of celebrations, families, minorities, and architectural styles; and films/videotapes of KS and regional history. Accepts phone inquiries. No fee. Hours: M-F 8-5, Sa 9-1, Su 9-1.

Kansas Museum of History
Kansas State Historical Society, 6425 W. 6th St., Topeka, KS 66615; (913) 272-8681. Collects, preserves, and interprets materials on Kansas history and people. Museum holdings include ethnological and archaelogical material, costumes, decorative arts, furniture, textiles, military machinery, agricultural tools, and drawings and paintings from 19th and 20th c.; small library devoted to material culture of Kansas and western US. Accepts phone inquiries. No fee. Hours: M-Sa 9-4:30, Su 12:30-4:30.

Kansas State Historical Society
120 W. 10th St., Topeka, KS 66612; (913) 296-3251. Collects, preserves, and disseminates info on history of KS. Museum documents American West from 1854, with some materials on general Ammerican history and Colonial period. Library and archives contain manuscripts, maps, photos, films/videotapes, recordings, and genealogical records. Special collections of Santa Fe Railroad archives, and materials from historic sites and regional archaeology. Accepts phone inquiries. No fee. Hours: research center, M-F 8-5, Sa 8-noon; museum, M-Sa 9-4:30, Su 1-4:30.

Kansas State University

Special Collections and Archives, Farrell Library, Manhattan, KS 66506; (913) 532-6516. Academic research library holds papers and letters of Dan Casement, son of Union Pacific RR builder Jack Casement. Holdings cover Dan's opposition to New Deal and attempts to publicize. Accepts phone inquiries. No fee. Hours: call.

Kansas Supreme Court
Law Library

Kansas Judicial Center, 301 W. 10th St., Topeka, KS 66612; (913) 296-3257. Provides law library services to judicial, legislative, and executive branches of state government, as well as bar members. Holdings include appellate level court reports and statutes for all states from territorial days; many legal periodicals and treatises; and briefs of KS appellate level court cases. Materials circulate only to attorneys and state employees. Accepts phone inquiries. No fee. Hours: M-F 8-5.

Kansas Wesleyan University

Documents Division, Memorial Library, 100 E. Claflin, Salina, KS 67401; (913) 827-5541. Academic support library acting as federal govt document depository for general public and University community. Also collects some Kansas Wesleyan archival materials. Accepts phone inquiries. No fee. Hours: 12:30-5.

Laird Wilcox Collection of
Contemporary Political Movement

University of Kansas, Kenneth Spencer Research Library, Lawrence, KS 66044; (913) 864-4274. Holdings emphasize far-right and left political materials from 1950. Libertarians, white supremacists, National Socialist Party, and conservatives represented on right; left-wing movements represented through student movements from 1960-72. Holdings include correspondence, oral history interviews, audio recordings of political debates and speeches, and archives of Kansas Free Press. Accepts phone inquiries. Hours: call.

Lyon County Historical
Society and Museum

118 E. 6th Ave., Emporia, KS 66801; (316) 342-0933. Collects and preserves county arti-facts and archival materials. Museum houses artifacts from 1850; library holds family histories, scrapbooks, papers, and birth and death records; maps, photos, and some oral histories. Materials for in-house use only. Accepts phone inquiries. No fee. Hours: Tu-Sa 9-5, Su 2-5.

Mennonite Immigrant
Historical Foundation

P.O. Box 231, Goessel, KS 67053; (316) 367-8200. Preserves history of immigration of Russian Mennonites to Goessel region in 1874 through museum collections of household, farm, school, and church artifacts. Some materials from first Mennonite hospital in US, and limited collection of maps, photos, and genealogical materials. Accepts phone inquiries. Fee. Hours: May-Sept, Tu-Sa 10-5, Su 1-5; Oct-Dec and Mar-Apr, Tu-Su 1-4.

Mennonite Library and Archives

Bethel College, 300 E. 27th St., North Newton, KS 67117; (316) 283-2500. Promotes study of Anabaptist and Mennonite history, life, and thought. Library concentration on pacifism and conscientious objection; archives on General Conference Mennonite Church, Bethel College, and other organizations; manuscripts and large number of photos of Mennonite leaders and families; maps of early Mennonite settlements; Schowalter oral history collection on WWI and WWII conscientious objectors; and genealogical records of Mennonite families and churches. Accepts phone inquiries. No fee. Hours: M-F 8-12, 1-5.

Midwest Historical
and Genealogical Society

P.O. Box 1121, 1203 North Main, Wichita, KS 67201; (316) 264-3611. Collects and preserves genealogical and historical book collection covering most of US and some foreign countries. Other holdings include maps of KS counties and other states, family histories in book form, and KS cemetery records. Materials circulate to members only. Accepts phone inquiries. Fee. Hours: Tu-Sa 9-4.

Museum of
Independent Telephone

412 S. Campbell, Abilene, KS 67410; (913)

263-2681. Collects historic telephony materials in forms of maps, photos, bulletins, catalogs, manuscripts, and historic recordings. Accepts phone inquiries. Fee. Hours: M-F 9-4:30.

Old Castle Museum Complex

Baker University, 515 5th, Baldwin City, KS 66006; (913) 594-6809. Preserves KS pioneer artifacts relating to early religious, educational, and social life. Museum holdings include Southwest and Plains Indians artifacts; pioneer housewares, tools, and furniture; dental and medical items; 19th c printing shop wares, linotype, and Allen hand press; old Bibles and religious materials; walking cane collection; antique camera collection; Civil War muskets, bayonets, powder flasks, and bullet molds; and a small US coin collection. Hours: call.

Pioneer Adobe House Museum

Ash and D Sts., Hillsboro, KS 67063; (316) 947-3775. Conserves and interprets immigrant Dutch-German Mennonite culture in Central Kansas from 1874. Museum depicts life and furnishings of pioneer Mennonite farmers. Holdings include maps of KS and S. Russia; small collection of early photos of Hillsboro; limited genealogical records. Local archives held in Tabor College Library in Hillsboro, KS. Accepts phone inquiries. Hours: Mar-Dec, Tu-Sa 9-12, 1:30-4:30.

Pittsburg State University

Leonard H. Axe Library, Pittsburg, KS 66762; (316) 231-7000. Academic support library with extensive manuscript holdings, special collections, and archives of regional archival materials. Collections include University archives from 1903; early 20th c manuscripts of JA Wayland, E. Haldeman-Julius, Eva Jessye, and southeast KS; limited map, recording, and genealogical collections; and special Albert Bigelow Paine, Joe Skubitz, and Spiritualist collections. Accepts phone inquries. No fee. Hours: M-Th 7:45-11, F 7:45-5, Sa 9-5, Su 2-11.

Pony Express Museum

c/o Curator, 605 N. 11th St., Marysville, KS 66508; (913) 562-3052. Original Pony Express home station restored as museum. Collections include local history items and photos. Accepts phone inquiries. Fee. Hours: 10-5.

Rooks County Historical Society

517 S. 2nd St., Stockton, KS 67669; (913) 425-7217. Preserves history of Rooks county, KS, and local families through holdings in museum, library, and archives. Materials include cemetery, naturalization, and govt records; some newspapers and genealogies; photos, maps, and recordings of historical programs. Accepts phone inquiries. No fee. Hours: M-W 9-4.

Sante Fe Trail Center

Rte. 3, Larned, KS 67550; (316) 285-2054. Preserves history of geographic known as Santa Fe Trail, with interests in KS history, War of the Rebellion, and Civil War. Museum and library cover Trail history; archives holds research materials, maps, photos, oral history interviews, and genealogical records of Trail traders and local residents. Accepts phone inquiries. Fee for museum; no fee for library. Hours: 9-5.

Sante Fe Trail Historical Society

1115 10th St., Box 668, Baldwin City, KS 66006; (913) 594-6862. Preserves history of Santa Fe Trail sites in Douglas City area and collects maps and photos of area. Publications on area history available. Accepts phone inquiries. No fee. Hours: 9-5, and by appt.

Smokey Valley Genealogical Society

211 W. Iron, Ste. 205, Salina, KS 67401; (913) 825-7573. Preserves materials for members researching family roots, and gathers genealogical records for Saline county. Holdings include archival county and family records, photos, and library of genealogical materials. Also some materials genealogical on other states. Materials circulate only to members. Accepts phone inquiries. No fee. Hours: M-Th noon-4, Th 6-8, Sa noon-4.

Stafford County Historical and Genealogical Society

100 S. Main, Stafford, KS 67578; (316) 234-5664. Museum exhibits 14 rooms of furniture, clothing, paintings, and memorabilia from Stafford county. Library has large collection of reference materials. Archives holds genealogical materials and local history records, maps from early 20th c, family and county-interest photos,

tapes of interviews with early pioneers. Accepts phone inquiries. No fee for museum, fee for research. Hours: Tu, W, Th 10-3.

Trading Post Historical Museum

Rte. 2, Box 145-A, Trading Post, KS 66075; (913) 352-6441. Preserves history and artifacts of region through holdings in museum, archives, and photo and map collections. Museum exhibits articles from area settlers, Native Americans, territorial and Civil Wars, WWI, WWII; archives preserve many business and govt records, as well as special John Brown collection of photos, family, and family history; manuscripts on coal mining history in Linn County; maps of trading posts, Indian lands, WWII; and a large photo collection on pioneers, Winnebago Indians of NB, and area land marks. Materials for in-house use only. Accepts phone inquiries. Donations accepted. Hours: T-Sa 9-5, with Su 1-5 from Mar-Nov.

United Methodist Historical Library

Baker University, Baldwin City, KS 66006; (913) 594-6451. Collects materials on Methodist, KS, and University history through holdings in museum, library, and holdings. Some manuscripts, maps, photos, and genealogical records. Some materials non-circulating. Accepts phone inquiries. Fee for employee research services. Hours: M-W, F 9-noon, and by appt.

University of Kansas Medical Center

Clendening History of Medicine Library, Rainbow Blvd. at 39th, Kansas City, KS 66103; (913) 588-7040. Preserves medical history with collections of papers from Jakob Henie and Howard Atwood Kelly and correspondence from Joseph Lister, Florence Nightingale, and Samuel Jay Crumbine. Accepts phone inquiries. Hours: call.

Wichita State University

Ablah Library, Box 68, Wichita, KS 67208; (316) 689-3591. Academic research facility with strengths in KS history, American Indians, and Civil War. Also retains University archives. Manuscript collection includes American anti-slavery movement collection, William Lloyd Garrison papers collection, KS and Great Plains history, and papers of members of Congress from KS and 7 other states. Special collection has

historic KS maps. Other holdings include Sedgwick county court dockets, Thurlow Lieurance music collection, and editorial cartoon collection. Accepts phone inquiries. No fee. Hours: M-F 8-5.

Kentucky

Appalachian Museum of Berea College

P.O. Box 2298, Jackson St., Berea, KY 40404; (606) 986-9341, ext. 6078. Depicts lifestyles and values of Appalachian people before industry came to region. Museum exhibits demonstrate regional farming, cooking, hunting, weaving, and crafts. Collection of slide/tape presentations available on mining, log structures, craftsmen, dulcimer making, blacksmithing, sawmill industry, quilting, and other facets of Appalachian life. Accepts phone inquiries. Fee. Hours: M-Sa 9-6, Su 1-6.

Appalachian Oral History Project

Alice Lloyd College, Pippa Passes, KY 41844; (606) 368-2101. Project serves as educational resource to inform college students and prepare them for life in the Appalachian region, especially southeastern KY. Holdings include large collection of photos and oral history tapes relating to Appalachian residents; collection of books by Appalachian authors, and about region. Accepts phone inquiries. No fee. Hours: M-Th 8-10, F 8-4, Su 5-10.

Behringer-Crawford Museum

P.O. Box 67, 1600 Montague Rd., Devon Park, Covington, KY 41012; (606) 491-4003. Preserves and displays natural and cultural history of northern KY and residents from prehistoric times. Holdings include regional paleontological items from Ordovician and Pleistocene times; relics of regional prehistoric human cultures; historical and industrial artifacts from 19th c KY life; regional fine arts collections; reference library; archives with historic letters, and Greeneline Steamers Corp documents; maps; and photos of regional political figures and steamboats. Access to research collections by written request only. Accepts phone inquiries. Fee. Hours: Tu-Sa 10-5, Su 1-5.

Blue Grass Trust for Historic Preservation

Hunt Morgan House, 201 N. Mill St., Lexington, KY 40508; (606) 253-0362. Trust runs historic 1814 Federal Style House museum that preserves history of Lexington's Hunt and Hunt Morgan families. Holdings include period furnishings, 1814-1840, and artifacts relating to John W. Hunt (builder of the house and first KY millionaire), John Hunt Morgan (Confederate General) and Thomas Hunt Morgan (winner of Nobel Prize for Genetic Research). Accepts phone inquiries. Fee. Hours: museum: March-Dec, Tu-Sa 10-4, Su 2-5; office: M-F 9-5.

Centre College

Grace Doherty Library, Danville, KY 40422; (606) 236-5211, ext. 292. Academic research library holds archives of college, rare book collection, selective US govt documents, and LeComte Davis collection. Accepts phone inquiries. No fee. Hours: M-F 8-11, Sa 9-6, Su 1-11.

Eastern Kentucky University

Eastern Kentucky University Archives, Cammack Bldg., Rm. 26, Richmond, KY 40475; (606) 624-2760. Archives preserves documents and other historical materials of univ and region. Holdings include historical records of Eastern Kentucky Univ from 1906, including papers of Presidents H.L. Sonovan and Robert R. Martin; large collection of manuscripts, including paper of KY Gov Keene Johnson and letters of Cassius M. Clay; 20th c photos of univ and local subjects, and America Correction Assn Photo Collection, 1900-1960; University athletic game films from 1938 and Kentucky High School Athletic Association championship game films from 1955; university Oral History Center tape collection. Some restrictions on use. Accepts phone inquiries. No fee. Hours: M-F 8-4:30 during academic year.

Filson Club

1310 S. Third St., Louisville, KY 40208; (502) 635-5083. Collects, preserves and publishes historical material, with emphasis on Louisville and KY topics. Holdings include museum with paintings, weapons, textiles, tools and other artifacts, Pioneer times-early 20th c; library with historical KY books, music, maps, broadsides, and ephemera; archives contain personal and family papers, late 18th c through early 20th c; large collection of photos, daguerreotypes, tintypes, and other historic photographic images; collections of historical materials on Southern US states, Lewis and Clark expeditions, flags, and signers of Declaration of Independence. Accepts phone inquiries. No fee. Hours: M-F 9-5, Sa 9-noon.

Frymire Weather Service and Museum

P.O. Box 33, 314 N. Chestnut St., Irvington, KY 40146; (502) 547-3951. Preserves and promotes history of the Weather Tree and folklore remedies and inventions. Collection includes cockfight artifacts, including Gaffs used in great Louisville, KY cockfight of 1892; Dick Frymire (Treeologist)'s Folkology and Home Remedies Book; photos; medicinal devices such as Madstone used to treat rabies 1830-1950, anti-smoking device, Back Pain Zapper, and Gut Zapper; other folklore contraptions, including Mosquito Zapper, Fry-Hut Relaxer, and Fish Finder and Attractor. Accepts phone inquiries. Donations accepted. Hours: 9-5.

Historic Homes of Louisville Foundation

414 Baxter Ave., London House, Louisville, KY 40204; (502) 568-6397. Foundation preserves and maintains history and cultural heritage of Louisville, KY area and residents in form of two historic homes. The Farmington Historical Home (3033 Bardstown Rd, Louisville, KY, 40205; 502-452-9920) was built by John and Lucy Speed in 1810 from plans by Thomas Jefferson; the Locust Grove Historical Home (561 Blankenbaker La, Louisville, KY 40207; 502-896-2433), built in 1790, was home to Gen George Rogers Clark. Holdings include period KY furnishings and family belongings and artifacts. Each house accepts phone inquiries. Fee. Hours: M-Sa 10-4:30, Su 1:30-4:45.

Historic Landmarks and Preservation Districts Commission

727 W. Main St., Louisville, KY 40202; (502) 587-3501. Promotes and oversees preservation of historic sites in Louisville, KY through creation of preservation guidelines, research proj-

ects, and educational programs. Holdings include small reference library with materials on art and architecture (mostly American Victorian); maps of Louisville and Jefferson County, KY; photos of preservation projects. Accepts phone inquiries. No fee. Hours: 8:30-5.

Historic Preservation Commission

Lexington-Fayette Urban County Govt, 200 E. Main St., Lexington, KY 40507; (606) 258-3000. Commission encourages preservation of Lexington, KY area's historic buildings and sites through publications, and library with resource materials on older home renovation. Accepts phone inquiries. No fee. Hours: 8-5.

Homeplace—1850

Land Between the Lakes, Golden Pond, KY 42231; (615) 232-6457. Living history farm depicts mid-19th c upland southern culture of west KY and TN. Library holdings relate to period and region. No fee. Hours: Mar-Nov 9-5.

International Museum of the Horse

Kentucky Horse Park, 4089 Iron Works Pike, Lexington, KY 40511; (606) 233-4303, ext 231. Museum preserves and displays history and importance of the horse and its relationship with man. Holdings include exhibits on all breeds and equestrian activities from Eohippus (first horse) to modern horses; large reference library with publications and research materials. Accepts phone inquiries. Hours: call.

Jackson Purchase Historical Society

RFD 1, Box 94, Hardin, KY 42048; (502) 527-8347. Membership org that fosters interest in history of eight western KY counties. Archives are kept at Murray State University's Pogue Library. Holdings include papers of author Jesse Stuart, Govs Ned Breathill and Harry Lee Waterfield, Congressman Carroll Hubbard, and others. Other collections include maps of Jackson Purchase areas of TN, KY, MS and Ft Jefferson and Murray region; small photo collection; large oral history collection; recordings of Vice-Pres Alben Barkley; genealogical records; and John Waters collection of local history items. Materi-

als non-circulating. Accepts phone inquiries. No fee. Hours: 7-3:30.

Jefferson County Office of Historic Preservation

Suite 204, Louisville Gardens, 525 W. Muhammad Ali Blvd., Louisville, KY 40202; (502) 625-5761. Maintains public county govt records and maintains county historic properties. Museum collects artifacts and documents relating to county-operated children's home from 1920-80. Library has reference materials on state and local history and culture. Archives have county govt records from 1780, including tax, estate, and legal records; pioneer-era correspondence; local and state political, geological, historical and other maps; photos of properties in Jefferson county; videotapes from children's home; oral history collections; and genealogical materials. Research with staff supervision only. Accepts phone inquiries. No fee. Hours: 8-5.

Kentucky Department for Libraries and Archives

Library and Archives Dept., 300 Coffee Tree Rd., P.O. Box 537, Frankfort, KY 40602; (502) 875-7000, ext 108. Preserves and maintains collection of KY local, county and state public records and documents. Holdings include collection of the KY Genealogical Society (county, local and family histories); state and local govt documents, military and census and other records; topographic, Sanborn Fire, and state agency maps; photos; filmed records of the KY General Assembly, Dept of Transportation, and Office of the Governor. Also shares facilities with KY Oral History Comission, which holds records from state oral history program. Some restrictions. Accepts phone inquiries. No fee. Hours: M-Sa 8-4:15.

Kentucky Genealogical Society

P.O. Box 153, Frankfort, KY 40602; (502) 564-7496 day; 875-4452 eve. Collects, preserves, and publishes materials of genealogical interest and provides educational programs. Library has limited genealogies, family histories, and KY maps. Publishes quarterly, holds seminars, and provides genealogical assistance. Accepts phone inquiries. Membership fee. Hours: M-Sa 8-4:15.

World War II Stuart Light Tank, from the Patton Museum of Cavalry and Armor

Kentucky Historical Society

P.O. Box H, Frankfort, KY 40602; (502) 564-3016. Collects, preserves and promotes history of KY through special programs, museum, library, and archival collections. Holdings include historical exhibits and artifacts from pre-statehood times; reference library with materials on KY history and genealogy; collection of pre-20th c KY manuscripts; KY maps from 1750s; photos (mosty of central KY, 1890-1940); genealogical documents and records. Accepts phone inquiries. No fee. Hours: office: M-F 8-4:30; museum and library: 8-4:30.

Kentucky Museum and Library

Western Kentucky University, Bowling Green, KY 42101; (502) 745-2592. Univ museum and library preserve and promote KY history. Holdings include artifacts of KY culture; extensive library with reference materials, newspapers and ephemera; Folklife Archives (FA); maps from 1792; 19th c sheet music; postcards from 1890s; photos of KY subjects and Ewing Galloway photo collection (national subjects); archives, manuscripts, films/videos, recordings; genealogical and census records; South Union, KY Shaker records, 1805-1920. Some restrictions. Accepts phone inquiries (502-745-4878). No fee. Hours: museum: Tu-Sa 9:30-4, Su 1-4; library: M-F 8-4:30, Sa 9-4:30; archive: M-F 8-4:30.

Kentucky State University

Documents Dept., Blazer Library, Frankfort, KY 40601; (502) 227-6857. Univ library maintains general reference materials and selective collection of govt documents and materials on history of the school. Holdings include Univ records, photos, and student newspapers from 1929; special collections on black American and African history, and on black higher education in KY. Accepts phone inquiries (502-227-6858). No fee. Hours: M-Th 8-10:30, F 8-6, Sa 10-4, Su 1:30-9.

Lincoln Homestead State Park

Rte. 1, Springfield, KY 40069; (606) 336-7461. State park marks beginning of the Lincoln Trail, and preserves the history and early homes of President Abraham Lincoln's parents, Thomas Lincoln and Nancy Hanks. Holdings include a replica of the log cabin childhood homestead of Thomas Lincoln; the original Francis Berry cabin, home to Nancy Hanks during her courtship with Thomas Lincoln; a replica of a period carpenter/blacksmith shop; period artifacts, furnishings and tools. Accepts phone inquiries. Fee. Hours: May-Sept, 8-6.

Louisville Historical League, Inc.

The Peterson-Dumesnil House, 301 S. Peterson Ave., Louisville, KY 40206; (502) 895-4745.

League preserves and promotes history of Louisville area in form of special events and topical slide presentations. Holdings include manuscripts, maps, photos, films/videotapes, and recordings used in production of slide presentations, which cover the history of Louisville, Louisville railroads and trolleys, architectural treasures, the history of Crescent Hill, the 1937 flood, and the history of Louisville-area amusement parks (including Fontaine Ferry Park). Restrictions on use of slide presentations. Accepts phone inquiries until 9. Membership fees. Hours: call.

Luscher's Farm Relics of Yesterday
Rte. 9, Manly-Leestown Rd., Box 630-A, Frankfort, KY 40601; (502) 875-2755. Preserves and displays history of farm life and work of farmer, in form of relics, equipment, tools, and machinery used in early days of American farming. Holdings include treadmills, power sweeps, reapers, threshers, wagons, buggies, tractors, a steam engine, and household items and implements. Accepts phone inquiries. Fee. Hours: summer, M-Sa 10-4, Su 1-4.

Murray State University
Special Collections, Waterfield Library, 15th & Olive Sts., Murray, KY 42071; (502) 762-2053. Regional academic library with special collections on regional KY history, Boy Scouts, and culture and people of western KY and neighboring states. Wrather West KY museum highlights social, cultural, and economic development. National Scouting Museum exhibits collection of Norman Rockwell paintings, and displays on scouting ethics and history. Forrest Pogue special collections library holds materials on Civil War; regional railroads, religion, and pioneer music; Tennessee Valley Authority records; archives of KY poet laureate Jesse Stuart; memorabilia of actress Alney Norell; and papers of C.L. Timberlake. Accepts phone inquiries. No fee. Hours: call.

Museum of Anthropology
Room 200, Landrum Academic Center, Northern Kentucky University, Highland Heights, KY 41076; (606) 572-5259. Univ museum preserves and displays prehistory of northern KY, maintains collection of Native American Indian arts and ethnographic/folk arts of other world regions, and provides learning and laboratory facilities for archeology students. Holdings include artifact and changing exhibits; small research library with materials on archaeology in northern KY, the Ohio Valley, and contiguous areas; archeological reports and manuscripts; photos related to archeological work. Accepts phone inquiries. No fee. Hours: M-F 9-3:30 while school is in session; other times by appt.

Northern Kentucky Historical Society
P.O. Box 151, Fort Thomas, KY 41075; (606) 441-7000. Preserves and promotes history of northern Kentucky and residents in form of library, archives, and photos. For use by members only. Does not accept phone inquiries. Membership fee. Hours: by appt only.

Northern Kentucky University
W. Frank Steely Library, Highland Heights, KY 41076; (606) 572-5683. Univ library has collection of general reference and microfilm. American and KY history materials relevant to needs to the students and curriculum. Historical collections include the Library of American Civilization, HERSTORY, Western Americana, Confederate Imprints, The Tuskegee Institute Clippings File, The KY Thousand: A Basic Library of Kentuckiana. Accepts phone inquiries. No fee. Hours: M-Th 8-9, F 8-4:30, Sa 11-5, Su 4-9.

Office of Historic Properties
Berry Hill Mansion, Louisville Rd., Frankfort, KY 40601; (502) 564-3000. Advises on, manages, and cares for state-owned historic properties and furnishings. Holdings include resource center with guidelines, reports, and other info to assist historical societies, museums, preservationists, etc; regional and state maps; photo inventory of state-owned historic properties; videotaped tours of historic sites; museum educational tapes; taped oral histories of prominent KY citizens; state, local, and county histories; research collections on KY archicture, and the Civil War; conservation laboratory. Accepts phone inquiries. No fee. Hours: M-F 8-5.

Office of Vital Statistics
Dept for Health Services, 275 E. Main St.,

Frankfort, KY 40621; (502) 564-4212. Collects, preserves, and issues certified copies of birth and death records from 1911 and marriage and divorce records from 1958. Accepts phone inquiries. Statutory fee for certified copies. Hours: M-F 7:30-5.

Oral History Association

University of Kentucky, P.O. Box 926, University Station, Lexington, KY 40506; (606) 257-1688. Scholarly assn concerned with collection, preservation, and dissemination of oral history info. Provides advice, guidance, and research aid for individual involved in oral documentation; publishes directory, newsletter, and review; and holds annual meetings. Accepts phone inquiries. No fee. Hours: M-F 8-4:30.

Patton Museum of Cavalry and Armor

4554 Fayette Ave., P.O. Box 208, Fort Knox, KY 40121; (502) 624-6350. U.S. Army museum preserves and displays history of cavalry and armor weapons from Revolutionary War times. Holdings include displays on weaponry development, uniforms, tanks and other armored vehicles; exhibit on early Ft Knox; collection of Gen George Patton artifacts; reference library; Col Robert J. Icks Collection of photos on historical development of armored vehicles around the world. Use of library by appt. Accepts phone inquiries. No fee. Hours: M-F 9-4:30; May-Sept, Sa-Su 10-6; Oct-Apr, Sa-Su 10-4:30.

Portland Museum

2308 Portland Ave., Louisville, KY 40212; (502) 776-7678. Collects, exhibits, and interprets artifacts relating to history and culture of Portland and its relationship with Ohio River. Museum exhibits cover regional Native Americans and Portland Canal and Wharf. Archives contains Portland women's archive, historic local photos, archive of home movies, and limited genealogical records. Accepts phone inquiries. Fee. Hours: M-F 10-4:30.

Preservation Alliance of Louisville and Jefferson County

716 W. Main St., Louisville, KY 40202; (502) 583-8622. Preserves and maintains historic, cultural, and architectural resources of Louisville and Jefferson County, KY through preservation projects, reference library and archival collections. Holdings include reference publications on area architecture, history, and preservation theory and technique; archives with photos, slides, architectural embellishments; slide presentations on local history and architecture; 19th c US maps; special collections on local history. Accepts phone inquiries. Fee. Hours: M-F 9-5.

Red River Historical Society

P.O. Box 195, 512 Main St., Clay City, KY 40312; (606) 663-2555. Collects and preserves materials on history of Red River. Museum and archives contain manuscripts, maps, photos, and genealogical materials of local interest. Accepts phone inquiries. No fee, Hours: by appt.

Riverview, the Historic Hobson House

1100 W. Main St., Bowling Green, KY 42101; (502) 843-5565. Restored Civil War House was home of youngest Union army colonel and only throughbred horse farm in area during Civil War period. Museum contains period furniture. Holdings include Riverview manuscripts, photos pertinent to Hobsons, genealogcal records, and some historic artifacts relative to Civil War. Accepts phone inquiries. Fee. Hours: Tu-Sa 10-noon, 1-5, Su 1-5.

Schmidt Coca-Cola Museum

Coca-Cola Bottling Company of Elizabethtown, 1201 N. Dixie Ave., Elizabethtown, KY 42701; (502) 737-4000. Preserves large collection of Coca-Cola Co. memorabilia from 1886. Holdings include advertising trays, soda fountain signs and artifacts, playing cards, and assorted advertising paraphernalia. Accepts phone inquiries. Fee. Hours: M-F 9-4.

Sons of the American Revolution

1000 S. 4th St., Louisville, KY 40203; (502) 589-1776. Chapter of the National Society of the Sons of the American Revolution (SAR) preserves and promotes history of the Revolutionary War. Holdings include museum with artifacts and exhibits, large historical and genealogical library with references on colonial times and the Revolutionar War; archives with society and membership records; genealogical records of all SAR members, and Colonial records 1630-1800. Collection is non-circulating, and the archive closed to the public. Accepts phone inquiries. Fee for non-members. Hours: 1-4:30.

University of Kentucky Libraries

Maps and Documents Division, Lexington, KY 40506; (606) 257-3139. Academic research library and depository for US, UN, and KY publications and documents. Map dept holds wide variety of KY street maps from different periods in history, Sanborn insurance maps of many cities and towns from 1880s-1930s, topographic maps, army defense maps from all over world, and charts, atlases, and gazetteers. Depository materials include KY state documents, materials from Ohio Valley and Appalachian region govts, UN documents, and some publications from European communities. Accepts phone inquiries. No fee. Hours: M-Th 8-10, F 8-4:30, Sa 10-4, Su 2-10.

University of Louisville

Documents Dept., Ekstrom Library, Belknap Campus, Louisville, KY 40292; (502) 588-6759. Univ library maintains selective collection of US govt documents, Smithsonian Institution reports (including annual reports of the American Historical Assn), CIA country maps, NASA photos, and War Dept collection of selected Civil War records. Accepts phone inquiries. No fee. Hours: M-Th 8-11, F 8-6.

University of Louisville Archives

University of Louisville, Louisville, KY 40292; (502) 588-6674. Univ archives preserves documents, records, manuscripts and other materials relative to the history of the school, area, state, and educational needs of the students. Holdings include library with materials on local history and archival management; archives of univ, and related educational, cultural, and business institutions; Oral History Center collections; manuscripts relating to Louisville area history, with emphasis on post-Civil War era; photos of univ subjects. Some restrictions. Accepts phone inquiries. No fee. Hours: M-F 8-4:30, or by appt.

University of Louisville Photographic Archives

Ekstrom Library, Louisville, KY 40292. Pre-serves works of outstanding photographers in relation to developments in art and technology of photography and pictorial record of sociological and historical aspect of area. Holdings include photos of actresses and actors of Louisville's Macauley Theatre; Standard Oil of NJ's effect on region in 20th c; Farm Security Administration's series on rural life from 1935-42; commercial photos from 1934-72; photos of KY mountain folkways; and Jones and Laughlin Steel Corp Picture library.

West-Central Kentucky Family Research Association

P.O. Box 1932, 5215 Veach Rd., Owensboro, KY 42301; (502) 684-4150. Genealogical society covers 19-county area, and preserves, collects, and makes available info on family history within that area. Library has reference materials, private genealogical collections, limited maps and photos, federal census and KY tax lists, and surname index for nearly 2000 residents. Accepts phone inquiries. Fee for membership. Hours: M-F 9-9, Sa 9-6, Su 2-5.

Louisiana

Amistad Research Center

Tulane University, Tilton Hall, 6823 St. Charles Ave., New Orleans, LA 70118; (504) 865-5535. Collects and preserves primary source materials on history of America's ethnic minorities, with emphasis on Afro-Americans, American Indians, and immigrant groups. Holdings include records of American Missionary Assn, Race Relations Dept of Anti-Defamation League, Catholic Committee of South, National Association of Human Rights Workers; papers of Harlem poet Countee Cullen, educator and civil right leader Mary McLeod Bethune, 20th c civil rights lawyer Alexander Tureaud, 19th c black attny and judge George Ruffin, and Operation Crossroads Africa director James Robinson. Materials non-circulating. Accepts phone inquiries. No fee. Hours: M-Sa 8:30-5.

Cammie G. Henry Research Center

Northwestern State University of Louisiana, Watson Library, Natchitoches, LA 71497; (318)

357-4585. Academic research library holds materials on history of northwest LA, LA, and regional residents. Holdings include papers of University presidents from 1884; manuscripts on LA history, literature, biography, and botany; maps from 1650; photos; and special collections from Melrose, Egan family, Elizabeth Lawrence, Caroline Dormon, Federal Writers Project, James Aswell, and Speedy Long. Restrictions on use. No fee. Hours: M-F 8-5.

Center for History of Louisiana Education

Northwestern State University, Teacher Education Center, Natchitoches, LA 71497; (318) 357-4396. Preserves early educational progress in LA from 1714 to present. Holdings include artifacts pertaining to education in state, school board minutes, notebooks and monographs on education, and genealogical records. Accepts phone inquiries. No fee. Hours: 8-4.

Fort Polk Military Museum

P.O. Drawer R, Bldgs 916 & 917, S. Carolina Ave., Fort Polk, LA 71459; (318) 535-7905 or 4840. Collects, preserves, studies, and exhibits objects illustrating story of US Army at Ft Polk. Museum display uniforms, weapons, and memorabilia from Civil War to present. Outdoor displays of tanks, missiles, and helicopters. Library provides reference on military history from Civil War, with emphasis on WWII. Archives has histories of units, post commanders, and recipients of Medal of Honor; maps; and large photo collection on Ft, training, dignitaries, equip, and ceremonies. Accepts phone inquiries. No fee. Hours: M-F 8-4:30, Sa-Su 8-5.

Historic New Orleans Collection

533 Royal St., New Orleans, LA 70130; 504-523-4662. Collects, preserves, and makes available items related to Louisiana's history and culture. Holdings include extensive library and collections of maps, drawings, prints, architectural drawings, photos, and paintings; large manuscript and microfilm collection; extensive genealogocial records; and materials on Louisiana Purchase, Battle of New Orleans, Civil War, Mississippi River life, French Quarter, and Mardi Gras. Accepts phone inquiries. No fee; charge for house and gallery tour. Hours: 10-4:45.

Lasalle Museum Association

P.O. Box 1019, Jena, LA 71342; 318-992-6210. Collects and preserves local history items. Library holdings include books, maps, photos, films/videotapes, recordings, and genealogical records. Accepts phone inquiries. No fee. Hours: W-Th 1-4.

Law Library of Louisiana

Supreme Court Building, 301 Loyola Ave., New Orleans, LA 70112; (504) 568-5705. Provides legal research assistance to LA judiciary, bar, and general public. Library covers all area of American and Commonwealth law. Has extensive collection of case reports, legislative acts, and revised statutes from all states from colonial and territorial periods to present. Also holds some rare LA materials and primary sources in American and Commonwealth law. Materials noncirculating. Accepts phone inquiries. No fee. Hours: M-Th 9-9, F-Sa 9-5.

Le Comite des Archives de la Louisiane

P.O. Box 44370, Baton Rouge, LA 70804; 504-355-9906. Preserves an interest in genealogical and historical preservation and provides general assistance to the Louisiana state archives. Holdings include parish and census records, books, and Civil War records. Answers phone inquiries. Annual membership fee. Hours: M-F 6am-9pm.

Leonard Washington Memorial Library

Southern University in New Orleans, 6400 Press Dr., New Orleans, LA 70126; (504) 282-4401. Academic research library preserves collection of Afro-French literature and cultural materials, and University photos. Materials circulate to academic community only. Accepts phone inquiries. No fee. Hours: M-Th 8-11, F 8-11, Sa 9-5, Su 2-6.

Longfellow Evangeline State Commemorative Area

1200 N. Main St., St. Martinville, LA 70582; (318) 394-3754. Focus on Cajun culture and early French settlers of Louisiana. Facilities include museum with artifacts of 18th and 19th c. Answers phone inquiries. Admission fee. Hours: M-Su 9-5.

Louisiana Purchase Transfer of 1903 as depicted in "Raising of the Flag," from the Louisiana State Museum.

Louisiana and Lower Mississippi Valley Collections

Louisiana State University, Hill Memorial Libraries, Baton Rouge, LA 70803; (504) 388-6568. Covers history, economy, politics, and culture of region with emphasis on French & Spanish colonial periods; early English and ethnic settlements, ante- and post-bellum life and culture; river navigation; Southern agriculture; Southern writers; Southern families; 20th c political leaders of LA; pre-20th c regional political leaders and orgs; slavery; black life and culture; and lumber, sugar, fur, seafood, railroad, and steamboat industries. Holdings include manuscripts, maps, photos, pamphlets, documents, audiovisual materials, and prints. Materials non-circulating. No fee. Hours: M-F 9-5, Sa 9-1.

Louisiana Historical Association Confederate Museum

929 Camp St., New Orleans, LA 70130; 504-523-4522. Preserves artifacts and memorabilia of Civil War. Archives, manuscripts, maps, and photos housed at Tulane University, Howard-Tilton Memorial Library. Accepts phone inquiries. Museum admission fee. Hours: M-Sa 10-4.

Louisiana State Museum

751 Chartres St., 400 Esplanade Ave., New Orleans, LA 70116; (504) 568-6968. Holds extensive documentary materials on LA political activity, Civil War history, Mardi Gras, Native Americans, costumes & textiles, jazz, maps, furniture, and art. Gallery shows 18th-19th c regional landscapes and portraits; decorative arts displays furniture, glass, and ceramics; costume & textiles show 18th c fabrics, dress, and accessories; technology & commercial collection houses Civil War Pioneer submarine; extensive photo holdings; jazz collection of instruments, music, photos, and film of greats; Historic Center holds manuscripts from Spanish colonial, Civil War, and LA Purchase. No research in Historic Center. Accepts phone inquiries. Fee. Hours: W-F 10-4:45.

Loyola University

Special Collections and Archives, 6363 St. Charles Ave., New Orleans, LA 70118; (504) 865-3186. Collections reflect influence of Loyola University and Catholic Church on New Orleans and South. Library covers Catholic Church history with emphasis on LA and Jesuits. Also has books on LA from 17th c. Archives holds University records. Manuscript collections has papers of orgs and individuals related to Loyola, such as Fr Louis Twomey and former Mayor Moon Landrieu. May be restrictions on use. Accepts phone inquiries. No fee. Hours: M-F 8:30-4:45.

New Orleans Public Library

Louisiana Division, 219 Loyola Ave., New Orleans, LA 70140; (504) 596-2610. Collects and preserves records of New Orleans government, and materials relating to history of New Orleans and Louisiana. Holdings include New Orleans city archives from 1769; manuscripts; maps, plans, and surveys; extensive photo collection; films/videotapes produced by city agencies and WVUE-TV news films 1968-80; wire and disc recordings of city council meetings, 1950s-60s; genealogical records; Mardi Gras collection from 1850s; early sheet music collection. Restrictions on special collections. Accepts phone inquiries. No fee. Hours: M-Th 10-6; F-Sa 10-5.

New Orleans Voodoo Museum

724 Dumaine St., New Orleans, LA 70116; (504) 523-7685. Preserves and explains history of voodoo and its practices in LA. Museum exhibits voodoo dolls, Gris-Gris bag, ritual candles, potions, amulets, zombie-making, tarot card reading, and history of voodoo practitioners. Tours available. Accepts phone inquiries. Fee. Hours: 10-dusk.

Our Lady of Holy Cross College Library

Learning Resource Center, 4123 Woodland Dr., New Orleans, LA 70131; (504) 394-7744, ext. 101. Academic research library has special collection on LA history, and collects federal depository materials. Other holdings include manuscripts, maps, photos, films/videotapes, and recordings. Accepts phone inquiries. No fee. Hours: M-Th 7-9, F 8:30-3, Sa 9-4.

Pioneer Heritage Center

Louisiana State University, 8515 Youree Dr.,

Shreveport, LA 71115; (318)797-5332. Interest in history of northwest Louisiana during settlement and early development (1830-60). Holdings include museum and artifacts, including slide/tape presentations. Answers phone inquiries. Donation requested. Hours: M-F 1:30-4:30.

Preservation Resource Center of New Orleans

604 Julia St., New Orleans, LA 70130; (504) 581-7032. Promotes preservation of New Orleans historic architecture. Library documents architecture and history of New Orleans' neighborhoods and historic districts. Some maps available. Accepts phone inquiries. No fee. Hours: 9-5.

Rudolph Matas Medical Library

Tulane University, 1430 Tulane Ave., New Orleans, LA 70012. Holds special Elizabeth Bass collection of personalized materials on women doctors. Hours: call.

Tulane University

Special Collections Division, Howard-Tilton Library, 7001 Freret St., New Orleans, LA 70118; (504) 865-5685. Materials relate to 18th-20th c New Orleans, south LA, and south MO history. Special William Ransom Hogan Jazz Archive contains archival jazz music and materials on musicians, including scores, serials, and catalogs. Special political ephemera collection has pamphlets, newletters, and periodicals from left and right, gay and lesbian, civil rights and white supremacist orgs. Some materials on Brown vs. Board of Education. Hours: M-F 8:30-5, Sa 9-1.

University of Southwestern Louisiana Library

Archives and Special Collections, 302 East St. Mary Blvd., Lafayette, LA 70503; (318) 231-6031. Preserves institutional archives and southwestern LA materials. Library houses printed materials and state documents relating to LA. Archives contain University records. Southwestern LA manuscripts on agriculture, architecture, horticulture, and politics. Maps from 18th c. Other collections include photos, archival films from E.W. Willis and Fred Packard collections, and local news videotapes from network news. Strong genealogical materials on Acadiana and

southwest LA. Acadian and Creole folklore collection and records from LA Colonial Records Project available. Materials non-circulating. Accepts phone inquiries. No fee. Hours: M, Tu 7:30-9; W-F 7:30-4:30, Sa 9-1.

West Baton Rouge Historical Association

845 N. Jefferson, Port Allen, LA 70767; (504) 383-2392. Promotes interest in history of West Baton Rouge Parish. Archives include letters from Confederate soldiers, oral histories of residents, Mississippi River navigation charts 1881-85, and genealogical records. No fee. Hours: Tu-Sa 10-4:30, Su 2-5, M by appt.

Maine

Bangor Historical Society

159 Union St., Bangor, ME 04401; (207) 942-5766. Preserves history of Penobscot Valley region. Museum housed in restored Greek revival home of 1834. Exhibits include 19th c paintings and furnishings. Photo collection includes 19th and 20th c Bangor scenes, and 1930s houses in Bangor. Accepts phone inquiries. No fee. Hours: Tu-F, Su noon-4.

Bar Harbor Historical Society

34 Mt. Desert St., Bar Harbor, ME 04609; (207) 288-3838. Preserves town's historic past through materials in museum, library, and archives. Museum exhibits include hotel registers, artifacts, newspapers, and business records from 1870s. Library contains books written by summer residents, some on Bar Harbor. Archives document incorporation of town of Eden. Other holdings include maps, photos, films, recordings, scrapbook on fire of 1947, and papers of George B. Dorr, founder of Acadia National Park. Accepts phone inquiries. No fee. Hours: mid-June-mid-Sept, M-Sa 1-4.

Bates College

Document Dept., George & Helen Ladd Library, Lewiston, ME 04240; (207) 786-6271. Academic research library and selective govt publications depository. Library has materials on American and New England history. Documents do not circulate. Accepts phone inquiries (207-786-6263). No fee. Hours: Su-Th 8-10, F 8-5.

Bates College Art Gallery

Olin Arts Center, Lewiston, ME 04240; (207) 786-6158. Museum maintains collection of 19th and 20th c American art with special Marsden Hartley memorial collection. Accepts phone inquiries. No fee. Hours: Tu-Sa 10-4, Su 1-5.

Boothbay Railway Village

P.O. Box 123, Rte. 27, Boothbay, ME 04537; (207) 633-4727. Operates two foot gauge steam railroad and displays on transportation and rural life from 1880 to 1940. Museum exhibits materials on railroad, general store, firehouse, and antique vehicles from 1907-40. Other holdings include photos of railroad history, and films/videotapes of steam railroads in action. Accepts phone inquiries. Fee. Hours: mid-June-mid Oct 9:30-5.

Boothbay Theatre Museum

Corey Lane, Boothbay, ME 04537; (207) 633-4536. Preserves, conserves, and exhibits theatrical memorabilia from 18th c. Museum displays stage jewelry, costumes, potraits, sculptures, playbills, figurines, set designs, set models, and set designs. Library focuses on theatre history and biographies. Large photo collection of actors, actresses, theatres, sets, and theatre structures. Recordings include hundreds of plays, musicals, and interviews with theatre personalities. Special collections on Roland Young, Booth family, "Doc" Rockwell, Lewis and Norton, and Louis Galloway. Accepts phone and mail inquiries. Donations accepted. Hours: June 15-Sept 15; tours by appt.

Bowdoin College Library

Documents Division, Brunswick, ME 04011; (207) 725-8731. Holds Oliver Otis Howard papers, consisting of large collection of materials from his service in Civil War, founding of Freedmen's Bureau, presidency of Howard University, and Supt of US Military Academy at West Point; papers of Gov Chamberlain of ME, who later was Sec of Treasury; papers of Charles Henry Howard and his involvement with American Missionary Association, and service in Civil War; and papers on military history of McArthur

family, in Limington, ME, during Civil War and Reconstruction. Accepts phone inquiries. Hours: call.

Castine Scientific Society

P.O. Box 196, Castine, ME 04421. Museum composed of Wilson Museum, John Perkins House, Blacksmith shop, and Hearse House. Archives hold antique books, diaries, ledgers, maps, photos from 1880s, genealogical records, and materials in Indians of North and South American.

Colby College

Miller Library, Waterville, ME 04901; (207) 872-3308. Academic research library with special collections on ME authors, modern Irish literature, and papers of William James family. Materials circulate to library card holders only. Accepts phone inquiries. No fee. Hours: 8:30-4:30 with additional eve and Sa-Su hours.

Dyer Library and York Institute Museum

371 Main St., Saco, ME 04072; (207) 282-3031 or 283-3861. Preserves materials related to Federal period decorative arts, Saco history, and Civil War. Museum has 1780-1850 fine and decorative arts, industrial textile collection, and folk paintings. Archives has materials on Saco from 1673; records of local families, businesses, and maritime; 18th c maps of York country and ME; oral histories from textile and tanning workers; and genealogical materials. Special collection of John Haley papers and Civil War diaries. Accepts phone inquiries. Donations accepted. Hours: library, M, W, F 10-5, Tu-Th 10-8, Sa 9-noon; museum, Nov-Apr, Tu-W 1-4, Th 1-8, May-Oct, Tu-W, F 1-4, Th 1-8, Sa 9-3.

Fishermen's Museum

Rte. 130, New Harbor, ME 04554; (207) 677-2726. Preserves history of ME fishing industry. Museum displays model fishing boats, fishermen's tools, and old photos and documents on fishing industry. Chart documents all ME lighthouses. Accepts phone inquiries (207-677-2494). Donations accepted. Hours: M-F 10-5, Su 11-5.

Fort Kent Historical Society

P.O. Box 181, Fort Kent, ME 04743; (207)

834-5121. Preserves Ft history with collection of photos from late 1800s and 2 videotapes of photos and films from Ft past. Accepts phone inquiries. No fee. Hours: call.

Freeport Historical Society
P.O. Box 358, 45 Main St., Freeport, ME 04032; (207) 865-3170. Preserves local history through holdings at museum properties and archives. Museum consists of 1830 residence and large saltwater farm. Archives holds materials on saltwater farming in 19th c; manuscripts; local maps; extensive photo collection; films/videotapes from parades; WWII; and shipbuilding; oral history interviews; and genealogical records. Accepts mail inquiries. Donations accepted. Hours: by appt only, M-F 9-5.

Historical Society of Wells and Ogunquit
P.O. Box 801, Rte. 1, Wells, ME 04090; (207) 646-5323 or 7803. Educates, collects, and preserves historical and genealogical materials relating to towns of Wells and Ogunquit. Museum and library house collection of town manuscripts, maps, photos, town records, genealogcal records, and tintypes. Accepts phone inquiries. Donations accepted. Hours: Th 1-4.

Kennebunkport Historical Society
P.O. Box 1173, Kennebunkport, ME 04046; (207) 967-2751. Preserves primary and secondary source materials on town's history. Museum houses paintings, furniture, household items, and clothing owned by local families. Library has materials on town history from mid-1600s, including manuscripts, family records, extensive photo collection, and records of town's families. Accepts phone inquiries. Donations accepted. Hours: June-Oct, Tu, F 1-4; or by appt.

Living Heritage Society
Acadian Village, P.O. Box 165, Rte. 1, Van Buren, ME 04785; (207) 868-2691/ 5042 in winter. Depicts progress and growth of Valley region and Acadian inhabitants. Museum houses artifacts of early 19th-20th c. Hours: call.

Maine Historical Society
485 Congress St., Portland, ME 04101; (207)

774-1822. Collects, preserves, studies, and makes available historical records and other materials related to ME. Museum displays boyhood home of Henry Wadsworth Longfellow. Library and archives contain genealogies, town histories, records, large manuscript collection relating to ME history, maps, photos, films/videotapes, Henry Know papers, Fogg autograph collection, and records of Kennebec proprietors. Accepts phone inquiries. Research fee for non-members. Hours: Tu, W, F 9-5, Th 9-7, and second Sa of month 9-5.

Maine Law and Legislative Reference Library
State House Station 43, Augusta, ME 04333; (207) 289-1600. Public law library for use of legislature, state govt agencies, judiciary, attorneys, and ME citizens. Holdings include ME state and federal documents, and legislative materials including ammendments, debate, roll calls, journals, and calendars. Special collections include newspaper clipping files on political and legislative topics, and biographical files for ME legislators and attorneys. Accepts phone inquiries. No fee. Hours: M-F 8-5.

Maine Maritime Museum
963 Washington St., Bath, ME 04530; (207) 443-1316. Promotes understanding of maritime history with emphasis on ME. Museum exhibits date to 1607. Library has substantial collection of reference materials on coastal ME and maritime. Archive covers history of Bath in 19th and 20th c with collections of manuscripts, maps and sea charts, many photos from 1849, film footage of maritime activities, oral history interviews, card index of ME sea captains, and ship data file. Closed stacks. Accepts phone inquiries. Fee. Hours: by appt.

Maine State Archives
State Capitol, Station 84, Augusta, ME 04333; (207) 289-5790. Preserves and makes available records of ME. Holdings include all govt agency materials from 1820, many maps, photos of Civil War Cartes-de Visite and ME Civil War officers; variety of state and local govt records; materials on Northeastern boundary controversy; and papers of Gov Percival Baxter. Accepts phone inquiries. No fee. Hours: M-F 8:30-4.

Maine State Library

Cultural Building, State House Station #64, Augusta, ME 04333; (207) 289-5600. Preserves and collects materials on state history. Library contains research collection materials; manuscripts from important Maine residents; maps from 1700s; photos on Aroostook and lumbering history; genealogical materials on Maine, New England, Quebec, and Maritimes; and papers of Governor Baxter. Materials circulate to state residents only. Accepts phone inquiries. No fee. Hours: M, Tu, W, F 9-5, Th 9-9, and Sa-Su noon-5.

Maine State Museum

State House, Station 83, Augusta, ME 04333; (207) 289-2301. Furthers cultural and educational interests of state, by presenting and preserving exhibits on environment and culture. Museum displays decorative arts, exhibits on technology, archaeology, and animals. Accepts phone inquiries. No fee. Hours: M-F 9-5, Sa 10-4, Su 1-4.

National Center for the Study of History

Rural Route 1, Box 679, Cornish, ME 04020; (207) 637-2873. Encourages and promotes educational activities in nontraditional areas of historical research through publications, seminars, and counseling. Materials cover info on public history methodology, applications, orgs, and related topics. Restrictions. Accepts phone inquiries. No fee. Hours: 9-5.

New England Electric Railway Historical Society

Seashore Trolley Museum, Drawer A, Log Cabin Rd., Kennebunkport, ME 04046; (207) 967-2712. Preserves streetcars and history of Street Railway Industry. Museum demonstrates restored trolleys, artifacts, photos, and authentic models. Accepts phone inquiries. Fee. Hours: mid-June-Labor Day 10-5, late April-mid-June/Labor Day-Oct Sa-Su noon-5.

Norlands Living History Center

Box 3395, RFD 2, Livermore Falls, ME 04254; (207) 897-2236. Preserves heritage of reknowned Washburn family, and history of region. Museum housed in Washburn family home and is completely furnished with original artifacts. Library contains pre-1899 books on Civil War and portraits by Healy and Skeele. Archives retains Wasburn family letters and documents, with emphasis on political climate during Civil War; Livermore civic records; manuscripts on France during Franco-Prussian War; photos of Washburn family, local activities, and crowned heads of Europe in 1870s; and special collection of WWI books by Stanley Washburn, war correspondent. Accepts phone inquiries. Fee. Hours: July-Aug, Tu-Su 10-4; or by appt.

Northeast Archives of Folklore and Oral History

University of Maine, South Stevens Hall, Orono, ME 04469; (207) 581-1891. Dedicated to preservation of ME folklife heritage and Atlantic provinces of Canada. Museum exhibits logging tools and models of logging operations from 1860. Library has materials on folklore, oral history, and logging industry. Archives contains photos; folkore and local legends; materials on riverdriving; videotapes on local history; large collection of oral histories from loggers, riverdrivers, and farmers; and folk tales and folk songs. Accepts phone inquiries. No fee. Hours: M-F 8:30-4:30.

Northeast Historic Film

Neworld Plaza, Blue Hill Falls, ME 04615; (207) 374-2736. Preserves and makes accessible northern New England moving images, films, and videotapes. Large collection includes original materials and reference copies of industrial, amateur, and dramatic productions, as well as TV news. Restrictions on some materials. Accepts phone inquiries. Fee. Hours: M-F 9-5.

Peary-MacMillan Arctic Museum

Hubbard Hall, Bowdoin College, Brunswick, ME 04011; (207) 725-3416. Dedicated to scholarly research in Arctic topics, ranging from anthropology and history of exploration to ecology and sociology. Museum displays Arctic exploration artifacts, ethnographic collections, and natural history specimens and photos. Library holds special collection of materials on Arctic topics. Archival holdings include personal papers, manuscripts, and photos of Donald B. MacMillan, Robert Bartlett, and other explorers; maps and charts of explorations; large collection of photos; and extensive film footage of MacMillan explorations. Accepts phone inquiries. No fee. Hours: by appt only, Sept-June, Tu-F 10-4, Sa 10-5, Su 2-5; June-Aug, Tu-Sa 10-8.

Penobscot Marine Museum

P.O. Box 498, Church St., Searsport, ME 04974; (207) 548-2529. Interprets maritime history of Penobscot Bay area, including residents and ships. Museum, library, and archives hold manuscripts, maps, photos, films/videotapes, recordings, and genealogical materials. Stacks are closed, and archival materials restricted. Accepts phone inquiries. No fee for library. Hours: Late May-mid-Oct, museum, M-Sa 9-5, Su 1-5, library, M-Sa 9-5; mid-Oct-late May, library M-Sa 10-3.

Penobscot National Historical Society

P.O. Box 313, Old Town, ME 04468; (207) 827-6545. Preserves and promotes Penobscot Indian culture. Museum and library document Penobscot Indian Nation. Archive contains info on historical events, photos, maps on tribes and their regions, films/videotapes on Indian's cultural activities and pageants, recordings of Penobscot legends, dances, and songs, census listings on Penobscot members, and collection of medicine plants. Restrictions on use. Accepts phone inquiries. Fee. Hours: appts in a.m.; open to public noon-4.

Portland Fire Museum

International Fire Buffs Association, P.O. Box 3161, Portland, ME 04104. Fire museum preserves artifacts from Great Fire of July 4, 1866. No fee. Hours: summer, M 7am-9pm, Sa 2-4.

Shaker Museum

RFD 1, Sabbathday Lake, Poland Spring, ME 04274; (207) 926-4597. Preserves history of Shakers from 1700s in England to settlement in ME. Museum exhibits Shaker furnishings, textiles, farm equipment, and artifacts from 1782. Library has material by and on Shakers. Archives holds extensive collection on Shakers in ME. Manuscript collection has Shaker letters, diaries, deeds, religious biographies, and music. Other holdings include maps, many photos, oral histories, large genealogical library, and videotapes of

news coverage on Shakers. Special collection on radical religious sects and communal groups. Accepts phone inquiries. Donations accepted. Hours: Memorial-Columbus Day, M-Sa 10-4:30; library by appt.

University of Maine at Presque Isle

Documents Dept. and Reference, 181 Main St., Presque Isle, ME 04769; (207) 764-0311. Academic research library collects federal and Maine documents, including maps. Other holdings include Aroostook county photos and history materials. Accepts phone inquiries. No fee. Hours: M-Th 7:45-10, F 7:45-5, Sa 9-5, Su 2-10.

Wells Auto Museum

P.O. Box 496, Rte. 1, Wells, ME 04090; (207) 646-9064. Records, preserves, and displays materials on automotive development in US. Museum houses over 65 cars, motorcycles, and bicycles showing progress in design and engineering in first half of 20th c. Other displays include license plates of New England states, photos, tools, and other items. Antique arcade games and nickelodians also on display. Accepts phone inquiries. Fee. Hours: mid-June-mid-Sept, M-F 10-5; Memorial Day weekend-Columbus Day weekend, Sa-Su 10-5.

Westbrook College

Library, 716 Stevens Ave., Portland, ME 04103; (207) 797-7261 Ext. 330. Collects works of ME women writers, including Mrs. Robert Peary, Mary Ellen Chase, Florence Jacobs, Celia Thaxter, and Edna St. Vincent Millay. Holdings include manuscripts, scrapbooks, rare books, and memorabilia. Accepts phone inquiries. No fee. Hours: M-Th 8-9:30, F 8-5, Sa 10-4, Su noon-9:30.

William A. Farnsworth Library and Art Museum

P.O. Box 466, 19 Elm St., Rockland, ME 04841; (207) 596-6457. Victorian-era homestead and art museum preserve collections of 17th-20th c American art, decorative arts, textiles, glass, ceramics, furniture, and sculpture. Artists represented have ties with ME. Library and archives contain reference on Maine artists Louise Nevelson; N.C., Andrew, and Jamie Wyeth; and Robert Indiana. Other collections include maps, pho-

Group of blacksmiths, from the Allegany Community College Appalachian Collection.

tos, films/videotapes on specific artists, genealogical materials, and some local materials. Accepts phone inquiries. Fee. Hours: archives by appt; museum, winter, Tu-Sa 10-5, Su 1-5; summer, M-Sa 10-5, Su 1-5.

Yarmouth Historical Society
Museum of Yarmouth History, P.O. Box 107, Main St., Yarmouth, ME 04906; (207) 846-6259. Promotes history of Yarmouth, ME and Old Yarmouth, MA. Museum contains changing exhibits of artifacts from Yarmouth history. Library has materials for local history research, including manuscripts, photos, oral history re-

cordings, and genealogical materials. Accepts phone inquiries. No fee. Hours: Tu, Th 1-5, W 10-5, 6-8, F 10-5.

Maryland

1840 House
Baltimore City Life Museums, 800 E. Lombard & Front Sts., Baltimore, MD 21202; (301) 396-3279. Simulates life in 1840 Baltimore through living history museum in reconstructed home of wheelwright John Hutchinson. Sponsors par-

ticipatory programs. Accepts phone inquiries. Fee. Hours: Tu-Sa 10-4, Su noon-4.

Albin Kuhn Library and Gallery

University of Maryland, Baltimore Campus, 5401 Wilkens Ave., Baltimore, MD 21228; (301) 455-2346. Academic resource library has Edward Howard collection of 18th-19th c travelogues of visitors to Baltimore and MD. Holdings describe historical and cultural atmosphere and War of 1812. Other holdings include papers belonging to Francis Scott Key and some 20th c materials. Accepts phone inquiries. No fee. Hours: call.

Allegany Community College Library

Documents Division, Willow Brook Rd., Cumberland, MD 21502; (301) 724-7700. Academic research facility serving students and area residents with concentration on Appalachian and western MD history. General library strong in WWII history. Special Appalachian collection holds small collection of rare books covering industrial history to regional manners and social customs; oral history interviews with approx 300 residents; photos collection on local and western MD subjects, genealogical records, and pamphlets and clippings. Accepts phone inquiries. No fee. Hours: M-Th 8-9, F 8-4:30, Su 2-6.

American Studies Association

University of Maryland, 2100 Taliaferro Hall, College Park, MD 20742; (301) 454-2533. Natl org of persons interested in American studies, and institutions sympathetic to assn interests. Sponsors meetings, publications, and activities to support American studies. Does not maintain research collection. Accepts phone inquiries. Fee for membership. Hours: call.

Antietam National Battlefield

P.O. Box 158, Sharpsburg, MD 21782; (301) 432-5124. Preserves, protects, and interprets site of bloodiest one-day battle in Civil War history. Museum displays uniforms, weapons, and equipment. Library concentrates on MD campaign, including regimental histories, memoirs, and unpublished studies. Map collection includes battle sequence maps. Large photo collection holds prints, and slides related to battle. Limited genealogical materials, and video-otape on Lincoln's visit to Antietam. Special collection of Confederate officer Henry Kyd Douglas's personal library. Accepts phone inquiries. Fee. Hours: May 30-Labor Day 8-6; rest of year 8:30-5.

Armed Forces Radiobiology Research Institute Library

Naval Medical Center, Bldg 42, Bethesda, MD 20814; (301) 295-0428. Collects materials on last 20 years on radiobiology, radiation physics, cancer research, and general radiation causes and effects. Special collections of United States Naval Radiological Defense Laboratory and Atomic Bomb Casualty Commission official reports. Materials non-circulating. Accepts phone inquiries. Hours: M-F 7:30-4.

Army Ordnance Museum

Aberdeen Proving Ground, Aberdeen, MD 21005; (301) 278-3602. Museum holds complete collection of weapons used all over world. Exhibits include bombs from 1942, German railway cannons, American M-65 atomic cannon, 1956 Vulcan aircraft gun, and many others. Accepts phone inquiries. Hours: Tu-F noon-4:45, Sa-Su 10-4:45.

B & O Museum

Pratt & Poppleton Sts., Baltimore, MD 21223; (301) 237-2381 and 2387. Museum preserves history of first railroad in US, the Baltimore & Ohio line. Museum exhibits include models of different B&O lines; menus and artifacts from Royal Blue line in 1891; passenger coach seats; station clocks; railroad passes; and drawings and prints. Accepts phone inquiries. Hours: W-Su 10-4.

Babe Ruth Birthplace, Maryland Baseball Hall of Fame

216 Emory St., Baltimore, MD 21230; (301) 727-1539. Preserves history of baseball and players in MD, including exhibits on Earl Weaver, Orioles, Babe Ruth, and James Emory Foxx. Holdings include Ruth's jersey, a home-run ball from 1914, his travelling case, photo album, and life-size bionic model of Ruth; and materials on history of Orioles and their World Series highlights. Accepts phone inquiries. Fee. Hours: Apr-Oct 10-5, Nov-Mar 10-4.

Baltimore Center for Urban Archaeology

Baltimore City Life Museums, 800 East Lombard & Front Streets, Baltimore, MD 21202; (301) 396-3156. Collects, conserves, interprets, and exhibits artifacts from 18th and 19th c Baltimore homes, industries, and shops. Displays include ceramics and glassware, and excavation pit, and a working archaeological library. Accepts phone inquiries. Fee. Hours: Tu-Sa 10-4, Su noon-4.

Baltimore City Archives and Records Center

211 E. Pleasant St., Baltimore, MD 21202; (301) 396-4863. Collects, preserves, and administers city's municipal govt historical records from 1729. Holdings include maps, photos, genealogical records, passenger lists, WPA Historical Records Survey materials, and city directories. Accepts phone inquiries. No fee. Hours: M-F 8:30-4:30, and Sept-May, Sa 8-noon.

Baltimore Museum of Industry

1415 Key Hwy, Baltimore, MD 21230; (301) 727-4808. Interprets Baltimore and MD industrial, social and technological history of Baltimore and MD. Museum recreates work settings and industry of 1750 with vertical files and local history works. Archives hold local business records, 1880-1980. Manuscript collection holds Baltimore labor-lawyer letters, advertisement artwork, and business ephemera. Local maps and photos available, with emphasis on workers and MD Shipbuilding & Drydock Co. Small collection of Baltimore company-related films,1930-60. Bethlehem Steel Co. Baltimore Shipyards ship repair records, 1910-80. Some restrictions. Accepts phone inquiries. Fee. Hours: Sa 10-5, Su noon-5; M-F by appt.

Baltimore Public Works Museum

701 Eastern Ave., Baltimore, MD 21202; (301) 396-5565. Preserves, collects, and exhibits history of public works. Museum houses changing exhibits relating to water, transportation, utilities, and construction in city. Library holds small collection on historical and contemporary urban history and public works. Photo archive holds construction photos dating from 1907-20. Limited films/videotapes available. Requests are reviewed on individual basis. Accepts phone inquiries. Fee. Hours: W-Su 11-5.

Barron's C & O Canal

P.O. Box 356, Snyders Landing Road, Sharpsburg, MD 21782; (301) 432-8726. Provides info on C & O Canal history. Museum holds canal artifacts from 1828-1924; library and archives document company operations with collections of maps, photos, genealogical records, and oral history interviews with boat captains. May be some restrictions. Accepts phone inquiries. No fee. Hours: Sa-Su 9-5.

Calvert County Historical Society

P.O. Box 358, Duke St., Prince Frederick, MD 20678; (301) 535-2452. Collects, preserves, and publishes historical facts for cultural purposes. Small museum emphasizes Colonial period. Library houses genealogical reference sources for county and MD. Archives collect family papers, maps, photos uncataloged as yet, and oral history tapes. Accepts phone inquiries. No fee. Hours: W-F 10-3.

Calvert Marine Museum

P.O. Box 97, SR 2, Solomons, MD 20688; (301) 326-2042. Collects and interprets artifacts, info, and cultural resources relating to history of Patuxent River and adjacent Chesapeake Bay. Museum covers regional natural history. Library has materials on local history pertaining to War of 1812. Archives holds business records on shipbuilding and other local industries; small collection of maps; large collection of photos; films and some historic footage on seafood industry; and genealogical materials. Materials noncirculating. Accepts phone inquiries. May be fee. Hours: M-F 10-4:30.

Carroll Mansion

Baltimore City Life Museums, 800 E. Lombard St., Baltimore, MD 21202; (301) 396-3523. Museum house of Charles Carroll, last-surviving signer of Declaration of Independence. Home illustrates elegant lifestyle of early 19th c Baltimore families. Accepts phone inquiries. Fee. Hours: Tu-Sa 10-4, Su noon-4.

Catoctin Furnace Historical Society

12320 Auburn Rd., 12670 Catoctin Furnace

Rd., Thurmont, MD 21788; (301) 271-2306. Preserves structures, historical records, and economic and cultural history of Catoctin iron works from 1776-1903. Museum center undergoing restoration at present; houses some genealogical and historical materials. Accepts phone inquiries. Hours: 9-5.

Chesapeake Bay Maritime Museum

Navy Point, P.O. Box 636, Mill St., St. Michaels, MD 21663; (301) 745-2916. Preserves Chesapeake Bay's culture and heritage through exhibits on Bay history, boat building, commercial crabbing and oystering, yachting, waterfowling, and navigation. Library houses vertical file and reference materials on maritime history, manuscripts, large photo collection, films/videotapes on regional boatbuilding and fishing industries, and oral history interviews. Special Harry Walsh collection of decoys and waterfowling artifacts, and Howard Chapelle collection of ship plans and personal memorabilia. Accepts phone inquiries. Fee. Hours: Jan-Feb, Sa-Su 10-4; Mar-Apr, 10-4; Apr-Oct, 10-5; May-Sept, Sa 10-7; Oct-Dec, 10-4.

Columbia Union College

Theofield Weis Library, 7600 Flower Ave., Takoma Park, MD 20912; (301) 891-4218. Academic research library holds materials on Seventh-Day Adventist history. Library contains file of Adventist periodicals from 1863-1960. Other materials availably on church history and theology. Hours: open to scholars; M-Th 8-10, F 8-1.

Costume Society of America

P.O. Box 73, 55 Edgewater Dr., Earlville, MD 21919; (301) 275-2329. Membership org for individuals involved in fields related to costume and its history and conservation. Members range from museum, university, and historical society employees to fashion and theater industries. Some members have private libraries and collections. Accepts phone inquiries. Hours: call.

Courtyard Exhibition Center

Baltimore City Life Museums, 800 E. Lombard & Front Sts., Baltimore, MD 21202; (301) 396-9910. Preserves story of how Baltimore residents, neighborhoods, business community, and

govt spawned urban revitalization. Library holds reference materials on city history including news clippings, large photo collection, graphics, motion picture film from 1920s-50s, maps, and memorabilia. Accepts phone inquiries. Fee. Hours: Tu-Sa 10-4, Su noon-4.

Enoch Pratt Free Library

400 Cathedral St., Baltimore, MD 21201; (301) 396-5430. Maintains collection of US, MD, and Baltimore documents, as well as materials from other city and state govts. Also has special Mencken collection. Audio-visual dept holds large collection of films on blacks in US, films by Baltimore-area filmmakers, and silent era films. Accepts phone inquiries. No fee. Hours: M-Th 10-9, F-Sa 9-5, Su 1-5.

Flickinger Foundation for American Studies

300 St. Dustan's Rd., Baltimore, MD 21212; (301) 323-6284. Investigates and promulgates ideas and interrelationships of US people and life from earliest origins. Library holds materials on American Revolution and mid-Atlantic region. Special collection of Gen Daniel Morgan manuscripts. Accepts phone inquiries. Hours: call.

Fort George G. Meade Museum

ATTN: AFZI-PTS-MU, Fort Meade, MD 20755; (301) 677-6966. Collects, preserves, and interprets history of Ft and 1st US Army. Museum exhibits large collection of artifacts from 20th c. Library details 20th c US and European military culture and history. Archival materials include letters, orders, Army publications, maps, and photos. Accepts phone inquiries. No fee. Hours: Tu-Sa 11-4, Su 1-4.

Fort McHenry National Monument and Historic Shrine

E. Fort Ave., Baltimore, MD 21230; (301) 962-4290. Preserves and presents site that was key to defense of Baltimore in War of 1812, and commemorates men whose bravery inspired creation of National Anthem. Museum exhibits artifacts and archaeological items pertaining to ft's history from 1776. Library has materials on War of 1812, Battle of Baltimore, and "Star-Spangled Banner." Archives contain holdings on Bombardment of ft and photos from WWI era. Special collections include Bowie firearms, Holloway papers on writing of National Anthem, and Walter Lord materials from his book "Dawn's Early Light." Materials for in-house use only. Accepts phone inquiries. Fee. Hours: summer, 8-8; rest of year, 8-5.

Friends of the College Park Airport

P.O. Box Y, College Park, MD 20740; (301) 864-5844. Fosters and preserves nation's oldest airport. Museum documents airport history from 1909 and displays aviation artifacts. Library has reference materials, photos, and reproductions of archival film footage. Accepts phone inquiries. No fee. Hours: F-Su noon-4.

Goddard Space Flight Center Library

Mail Code 252, Greenbelt, MD 20771; (301) 344-6244 and 6930. Science and technology research library focuses on astronomy, physics, mathematics, space sciences, communications, and remote sensing. Library holdings include NASA microfiche collection, extensive research materials, and many journals. Accepts phone inquiries. No fee. Hours: M-F 8-6.

H.L. Mencken House

Baltimore City Life Museums, 1524 Hollins St., Baltimore, MD 21223; (301) 396-7997. Preserves home of Henry Louis Mencken and his original furniture and belongings. Accepts phone inquiries. Fee. Hours: Tu-Sa 10-4, Su noon-4.

Hampton National Historic Site

535 Hampton Lane, Towson, MD 21204; (301) 823-7054. Protects and interprets architecture of home and lifestyle of wealthy 18th and 19th c family. Museum displays decorative arts and furnishings of period. Library holds reference materials on period, maps, photos, and genealogical records on Ridgely family. Accepts phone inquiries. No fee. Hours: 9-5.

Harford Community College Library

Documents Division, 401 Thomas Run Rd., Bel Air, MD 21014; (301) 836-4131. Academic research library with collection of federal govt documents from 1967. Accepts phone inquiries. No fee. Hours: M-Th 8:30-10:15, F 8:30-4:30, Sa 10-3.

Health Sciences Library

University of Maryland, Baltimore, 111 S. Green St., Baltimore, MD 21201; (301) 328-7996. Maintains small collection of works by Florence Nightangale, including her notebooks, nursing manuals, and correspondance. Materials noncirculating. No fee. Accepts phone inquiries. Hours: call.

Historic Saint Mary's City

P.O. Box 39, Rte. 5 and Rosecroft Rd., St. Mary's City, MD 20686; (301) 862-0990. Preserves, studies, and interprets site of MD founding in 1634, emphasizing colonial period. Museum displays sailing ship reconstruction, and artifacts from tobacco plantation, Indian longhouse, and archaeological sites. Library preserves colonial history, architecture, and ceramics. Photo collection documents archaeological digs and 19th and 20th c images of St. Mary's county. Films/videotapes of archaeological and living history available. Accepts phone inquiries. Fee. Hours: by appt.

Historic Society of Talbot County

P.O. Box 964, 25 S. Washington St., Easton, MD 21601; (301) 822-0773. Preserves local history with holdings in museum, library, and archives. Holdings include manuscripts, documents, photos, and collection of decorative arts. Accepts phone inquiries. Fee. Hours: Tu-Sa 10-4, Su 1-4.

Historic Star Spangled Flag House and War of 1812 Museum

844 E. Pratt St., Baltimore, MD 21202; (301) 837-1793. Maintains house where Mary Pickersgill created flag that flew over Ft McHenry. Museum collection commemorates War of 1812 and artifacts from Battle of Baltimore. Library and archives contains small reference collection on 1812 era. Accepts phone inquiries. Fee. Hours: M-Sa 10-4, Su 1-4.

Historical and Architectural Preservation Commission

118 N. Howard St., Tower Suite Rm. 606, Baltimore, MD 21201; (301) 396-4866. Designates and administers historic districts and landmarks within Baltimore City and curates Edgar Allen Poe House and Museum. Library contains

materials on historic preservation planning, law, and techniques; resources on MD, Baltimore, and Baltimore neighborhood history; Sanborn and other maps from 1896; photos and slides of city landmarks and districts, significant structures, and various bldgs; inventory and evaluation of all city-owned statues, monuments, and landmarks; and survey vertical file materials. Accepts phone inquiries. No fee. Hours: M-F 8:30-4:30.

Historical Society of Carroll County

210 E. Main St., Westminister, MD 21157; (301) 848-6494. Reflects lifestyles and history of people living in 19th c Carroll County. Historic house museum displays period furnishings, textiles, tools, and memorabilia of Rural Free Delivery system. Holdings also include maps, photos, greeting cards, business advertisements and genealogical records. Some films/videotapes available. May be some restrictions. Accepts phone inquiries. Fee. Hours: Tu-F 9-4, and June-Sept, Sa-Su noon-4.

Historical Society of Cecil County

135 E. Main St., Elkton, MD 21921. Preserves local artifacts and documents, and makes them available to public. Museum reconstructs country store, kitchen, and log house. Library contains records of property rights, pensions, taxes, and census; manuscript collection; maps and photos; genealogical records for MD; and special Gilpin and Fassitt collections. Some restrictions. Fee for non-members. Hours: Th noon-4.

Historical Society of Harford County

33 Courtland West., Bel Air, MD 21014; (301) 838-7691. Preserves and shares historic Harford county and MD materials. Museum contains exhibits on Hays house. Library and archives hold maps, photos, and limited manuscripts and genealogical records. Special collection of books on Booth family in Mahoney collection. Materials non-circulating. Accepts phone inquiries. Fee for membership. Hours: Th 9:30-3:30.

History of Medicine Division

National Library of Medicine, Department of Health and Human Services, 8600 Rockville Pike, Bethesda, MD 20894; (301)496-5405. Provides materials for scholarly research in health science history. Large library holds books, pamphlets, dissertations, and journals from pre-1814 period on health-related topics. Archives holds materials of Natl Library of Medicine and health institutions such as Medical Library Assn. Manuscript collection contains personal papers, institutional records, and some pre-1600 Western and Arabic materials, all related to health issues. Large photo collection. Archive of historical American medical films from 1917, and oral histories relating to American biomedical topics also available. Accepts phone inquiries. No fee. Hours: M-F 8:30-5.

Institute of the History of Medicine

Johns Hopkins University, 1900 E. Monument St., Baltimore, MD 21205; (301) 955-3662. Academic research facility maintains strong collection on US medical history. Accepts phone inquiries. Hours: call.

Jewish Historical Society of Maryland

Jewish Heritage Center, 15 Lloyd St., Baltimore, MD 21202; (301) 732-6400. Collects, preserves, and presents materials related to history of Jewish life in MD. Museum exhibits cover period of 1656-1929, and include photos and artifacts of emigration to MD. Library documents local Jewish history. Archival holdings include individual records and papers relating to local Jewish institutions. Small map collection. Large photo collection, some dating pre-1940s. Film/videotape collection. Recordings of cantorial music from 1915-30, Yiddish music, and oral history interviews. Special collections of Friedenwald family and Benjamin Szold papers. Accepts phone inquiries. Fee. Hours: museum, M, Th 11-2, Su 1:30-4; library by appt.

Johns Hopkins University

Milton Eisenhower Library, 34th & Charles St., Baltimore, MD 21218; (301) 338-8360. Academic research library with large collection of maps, atlases, govt documents, and materials from 1840-44 presidential candidate James Birney. Birney materials include reports, biographies, newspapers from 1790, proslavery works, and rare books. Materials non-circulating. Accepts phone inquiries. No fee. Hours: 8:30-5, M-F.

Londontown Publik House
and Gardens

839 Londontown Rd., Edgewater, MD 21037.
Preserves and interprets history of restored house
and gardens with holdings in library and archives. Materials available include maps, early
photos, and genealogical records. Accepts phone
inquiries. No fee. Hours: Mar-Dec, Tu-Sa 10-4,
Su 1-4.

Lovely Lane Museum

2200 St. Paul St., Baltimore, MD 21218; (301)
889-4458. Preserves and disseminates history
and heritage of Baltimore United Methodist
conference and predecessors. Museum displays
Methodist and Wesleyan artifacts from 1700.
Library concentrates on Methodist and United
Brethren. Archives retain Baltimore Conference
materials, journals and papers of clergy, maps,
photos, genealogical materials, and local church
histories. No genealogical searches except for
clergy ancestors. Accepts phone inquiries. No
fee. Hours: M-F 10-4.

Maryland Historical Society

201 West Monument Street, Baltimore, MD
21201; (301) 685-3750. Collects materials on
MD history. Museum exhibits historical, decorative, and fine arts from pre-Colonial era; children's
history display; early MD paintings and furniture; textiles and costumes; and toys and dolls.
Library holds large 17th-20th c MD state history
collection, including materials on biography, genealogy, arts, and culture. Archives retain Historical Society's records from 1844. Extremely
large collection of family personal and business
papers; maps; photos; genealogical records; the
Star Spangled Banner; 19th c American silver;
Carroll family papers; and largest display of Peale
family paintings. Accepts phone inquiries. Fee.
Hours: Tu-F 11-4:30, Sa 9-4:30, and Oct-Apr,
Su 1-5.

Maryland Historical Trust

1517 Ritchie Hwy., Arnold, MD 21012; (301)
974-2212. Preserves, protects, and enhances
significant sites and structures in MD history.
Holdings include maps, photos, vertical files,
architectural drawing, historic structure reports,
archaeological site reports for MD and other
states, National Register nomination forms, and

selected cultural resource surveys. Genealogical
collection and references. Also collection of visual education materials for free loan. Archaeology materials not for public use. Accepts phone
inquiries. No fee. Hours: 8:30-4:30.

Maryland State Archives,
Hall of Records

350 Rowe Blvd., Annapolis, MD 21401; (301)
974-3914. Preserves and makes available MD
state records. Library devoted to MD and US
history. Archives holds state, county, and local
records. Manuscript collection hold private papers
of individuals and families from 1634. Maps date
from 1634, and photos from 1850. Some genealogical records. Accepts phone inquiries. No fee.
Hours: M-Sa 8:30-4:30.

Maryland State Law Library

Courts of Appeal Bldg., 361 Rowe Blvd., Annapolis, MD 21401; (301) 269-3395. Provides
legal and general info to state's appellate courts
judiciary, executive, and legislative branches as
well as public. Library documents Anglo-American law from 1600, and US, MD, and local
history from 1600. Other holdings include maps
of MD state and county and Chesapeake Bay;
MD genealogical materials; Audubon's elephant
portfolios; MD Women's Hall of fame; and
collection on English legal history. Accepts phone
inquiries. No fee. Hours: M, W, F 8:30-4:30;
Tu, Th 8:30-9; Sa 9-4.

Montgomery County
Historical Society

111 W. Montgomery Ave., Rockville, MD 20850;
(301) 762-1492. Preserves and provides education on Montgomery county history. Museum
composed of two historic 19th c homes. Library
contains published histories and records. Archival holdings include scrapbooks, diaries, maps
and plats, and early newspapers. Photo collection
and genealogical materials also available. Some
artifacts and furnishings from Civil War kept in
storage. Accepts phone inquiries. Fee. Hours:
Tu-Sa noon-4.

Montgomery County
History Collection

Montgomery County Department of Libraries,
99 Maryland Ave., Rockville, MD 20850; (301)

279-1953. Maintains collection of maps, photos, and recordings of county interest in library. Accepts phone inquiries. No fee. Hours: M-Th 9-9, F-Sa 9-5, Su 1-5.

Museum of Dentistry

University of Maryland Dental School, 666 W. Baltimore St., Baltimore, MD 21201; (301) 328-8314. Reference collection of dental artifacts available to professionals and laymen. Museum collects memorabilia of dentistry, concentrating on school's history as first dental school in world. Accepts phone inquiries. No fee. Hours: by appt only, 9-4:30.

National Agriculture Library

Department of Agriculture, Rte. 1, Beltsville, MD 20705; (301) 344-3755. Extensive collection of papers on agriculture, with at least one copy of all substantial publications in field of agriculture. Holdings include technical reports on botany, chemistry, forestry, food and nutrition, and water resources; large collection of rare books; extensive photo collection; many maps; large poster collection; art; oral histories; large seed and trade catalog collection; papers of special asst to Sec of Agriculture, Julian Friant, from 1888-1939; Charles North papers from 1869-1961; American Agriculture College Editors records from 1913; and John Davis papers. Accepts phone inquiries. No fee. Hours: M-F 8-4:30.

National Capital Trolley Museum

P.O. Box 4007, 1313 Bonifant Rd., Silver Spring, MD 20904; (301) 384-6088. Preserves and operates street railway equip. Museum maintains 14 streetcars and exhibits related artifacts. Library holds reference materials, maps, and photos of electric railway equip and railroad. Fee. Hours: library by appt; Sa-Su noon-5.

National Colonial Farm of the Accokeek Foundation

3400 Bryan Pt. Rd., Accokeek, MD 20607; (301) 283-2113. Recreates middle class life on southern Maryland tobacco plantation before the Revolutionary War. Living history museum displays agricultural and domestic life of period. Accepts phone inquiries. Fee. Hours: Tu-Su 10-5.

National Institute of Justice

Box 6000, 1600 Research Blvd., Rockville, MD 20850; (301) 251-5500. Documents all aspects of criminal justice, juvenile justice, crimonology. Holdings include large collection of documents, audio and visual materials, and vertical file materials. Consultation available on topics related to police, crime prevention and security, courts, juvenile justice, corrections, and criminology. Accepts phone inquiries. No fee. Hours: M-F 9-5.

National Ocean Service Map Library

6501 Lafayette Ave., Riverdale, MD 20737; (301) 436-6978. Collections include large collection of maps, charts, and surveys from US Coast and Geodetic Survey; many city plans from all over the country; large collection of Civil War maps; and atlases and reference books. Hours: by appt only, M-F 8:30-4.

Naval Academy

Nimitz Library, Annapolis, MD 21402; (301) 267-2233. Preserves rare and historic works on naval and general maritime history. US Navy materials include Naval Academyclass albums,students' Lucky Bags, and student publications, oral history interviews with US naval officers, ships' logs from 1796-1938, WWII naval action reports, and pictures of officers, foreign ships, WWII naval news photos. Also preserves papers of Navy officers Vice Admiral Wilson Brown, Commander George Bache, Admiral Harry Knapp, Admiral Harry Knapp, Lieutenant Edwin DeHaven, and Admiral David Dixon Porter. Hours: call.

Ocean City Museum Society

P.O. Box 603, South Second St., Ocean City, MD 21842; (301) 289-4991. Preserves both Ocean City, MD and US Life Saving Service history. Museum exhibits cover sport and commercial fishing, bathing suits, shipwrecks, and lifesaving in region. Other holdings include Coast Guard maps, large photo collection, films/videotapes on Coast Guard and commercial fishing history. Special collection of lifesaving artifacts. Accepts phone inquiries. Fee. Hours: research by appt only; museum, summer 11-10, winter noon-4; May and Oct 11-4.

Peale Museum

Baltimore City Life Museums, 225 Holliday St., Baltimore, MD 21202; (301) 396-1149. Oldest original museum bldg in US holds collection of Baltimore photos, prints, and paintings. Many by members of Rembrandt Peale family. Special exhibit on Baltimore rowhouses. Garden area exhibits 20th c relief carvings and sculptures. Accepts phone inquiries. Fee. Hours: Tu-Sa 10-5, Su noon-5.

Prince George's County Memorial Library

Films Division, 6532 Adelphi Rd., Hyattsville, MD 20782; (301) 699-3500. Large historic film collection offers classic US films from D. W. Griffith to present. Notables include early films from Lumiere brothers, Thomas Edison, Melies, Chaplin, Keaton, Langdon, Deren, and others. Some animated and children's classics available. Accepts phone inquiries. No fee. Hours: M-F 9-5.

Prince George's County Memorial Library—Bowie Branch

Selima Room, 15210 Annapolis Rd., Bowie, MD 20715; (301) 262-7000. Holds special collection of books and periodicals on horse breeding and horse racing, with emphasis on horses from MD farms. Accepts phone inquiries. No fee. Hours: M-Th 9-9, F 1-6, Sa 9-5, Su 1-5.

Saint Mary's County Historical Society

P.O. Box 212, 11 Court House Dr., Leonardtown, MD 20650; (301) 475-2467. Collects, preserves, describes, and makes available info, artifacts, and documents related to St. Mary's county history. Society supports old jail museum and farm museum. Library provides reference materials. Archive holds private papers, and records from churches and mortuaries. Small collection of maps and architectural photos. Materials non-circulating. Accepts phone inquiries. No fee. Hours: Tu-Sa 10-4.

Salisbury State College

Blackwell Library, College & Camden Ave., Salisbury, MD 21801; (301) 543-6130. Academic resource library with special MD history

room, and Les Callette room on Civil War history. Borrowing privileges limited. No fee. Hours: M-Th 8-midnight, F 8-10, Sa 10-5, Su noon-midnight.

Sandy Spring Museum

P.O. Box 1484, 2707 Olney-Sandy Spring Rd. (Rt. 108), Sandy Spring, MD 20832; (301) 774-0022. Preserves and presents material culture of Sandy Spring area through museum displays of costumes, farm tools, furnishings, and samplers. Library concentrates on local history, and holds business account books, diaries, maps, photos, and genealogical records. Accepts phone inquiries. Fee. Hours: M, W, Th, Su noon-4.

Seafarer's Harry Lundeberg School of Seamanship

Paul Hall Library and Maritime Museum, Piney Point, MD 20674; (301) 994-0010. Collects and preserves historical maritime artifacts. Holdings include archival materials and cover maritime labor union history. Accepts phone inquiries. Hours: call.

Sojourner Truth Room

Prince George's County Memorial Library-Oxon Hill, 6200 Oxon Hill Rd., Oxon Hill, MD 20745; (301) 839-2400. Public library holds special collection of literature by and about black Americans. Collection covers black women, family, literature, slavery, and military and slave narratives. Holdings include films, recordings, periodicals, US govt publications, and some rare items. Accepts phone inquiries. No fee. Hours: M-Th 9-9, F 1-6, Sa 9-5, Su 1-5.

Steppingstone Museum Association

461 Quaker Bottom Rd., Havre de Grace, MD 21078; (301) 939-2299. Depicts lifestyle of early 20th c Harford county farm. Museum housed in farm house, and contains period furniture, tools, and farm equipment. Accepts phone inquiries. Fee. Hours: 8:30-4:30.

Surratt Society

Mary E. Surratt House and Tavern, P.O. Box 427, 9110 Brandywine Rd., Clinton, MD 20735; (301) 868-1121. Provides materials for ongoing research into Civil War era in MD, with emphasis on assassination of Lincoln. Museum exhibits document period lifestyle in 19th c. Library covers Lincoln assassination, local history, Civil War era, and antiques. Society also offers knowledge and resources of some 700 members, many of whom are experts in Lincoln studies and assassination materials, Civil War, and Victorian life. Accepts phone inquiries. Fee. Hours: Mar-Dec, Th-F 11-3, Sa-Su noon-4.

Towson State University

Fine Arts Building, Room 457, Towson, MD 21204; (301) 321-2462. Academic research facility maintains collection on Thomas Edison and phonograph collection, and John Phillip Sousa and band collection. Accepts mail inquiries addressed to: Edwin L. Gerhardt, 4926 Leeds Ave., Baltimore, MD 21204. Hours: call.

United Methodist Historical Society, Baltimore Conference

2200 St. Paul St., Baltimore, MD 21218; (301) 889-4458 (on M & F only). Preserves and makes available records, books, and artifacts of United Methodist Church with emphasis on Baltimore conference. Museum documents Methodist history from 1730s. Library covers church policy, missions, education, Sunday School, theology, annual conferences, and biography. Archives holds records of Baltimore, Washington, MD, PA, and central PA denominations; manuscripts from Asbury, Wesley, Jones, Goucher, and others; maps of MD; photos of clergy, churches, and church groups; and histories of local churches in Baltimore Conference. Open to church historians and researchers. Accepts phone inquiries. No fee. Hours: M, F 10-4.

University of Baltimore

Special Collections, Langsdale Library, 1420 Maryland Ave., Baltimore, MD 21201; (301) 625-3460. Academic research facility with material collection of Steamship Historical Society & Library, University archives, archives and manuscripts of many Baltimore orgs, large collection of steamship photos, photos of Baltimore area from 1900, Abell newsfilm collection of WMAR-TV from 1947-81. Some restrictions. Accepts phone inquiries. No fee. Hours: M-F 8:30-4.

University of Maryland Libraries

College Park, MD 20742; (301) 454-2853.

College libraries serve as academic research facilities with special collections on Katherine Anne Porter; MD history; maps from US Army Map Service; files of Industrial Union of Marine and Shipbuilding Workers of America; Wallenstein collection of musical scores; International Piano Archives, MD collection; research collections of American Bandmasters Assn, Assn of Wind and Percussion Instructors, and Music Educators National Conference; Thomas Cook collection on political science; Richard Van Mises collection on mathematics and applied sciences; and documents of UN and League of Nations. Accepts phone inquiries. No fee. Hours: call.

Washington College

Document Division, Clifton Miller Library, Washington Ave., Chestertown, MD 21620; (301) 778-2800. Academic research library with holdings of US govt documents, college archival materials, Chesapeake Bay archives, and Revolutionary War source documents. Some materials restricted. Accepts phone inquiries. No fee. Hours: M-Th 8:15-midnight, F 8:15-10, Sa 10-10, Su noon-midnight.

Massachusetts

Adams National Historic Site

P.O. Box 531, 135 Adams St., Quincy, MA 02269; (617) 773-1177. Preserves historic bldgs and memorabilia of Adams family, and provides visitors with interpretation of family lifestyle of 4 generations of Adamses. Site includes three homes: Peacefield/Old House site, John Adams birthplace, and John Quincy Adams birthplace. Library contains extensive materials from each Adams reflecting the diversity of their interests, photos, and genealogical materials. Accepts phone inquiries. Fee. Hours: Apr 19-Nov 10, last tour at 4:15.

Addison Gallery of American Art

Phillips Academy, Chapel Ave., Andover, MA 01810; (617) 475-7515. Preserves American art dating from 16th c, including paintings, sculpture, prints, drawing, and photos. Artists represented include West, Copley, Samuel F.B. Morse, Cole, Durand, Inness, Homer, Remington,

Hassam, Whistler, Cassatt, Sargent, Prendergrast, "the Eight," Dove, Marin, Sheeler, Hartley, Soyer, Hopper, Burchfield, Shahn, Wyeth, Kline, Pollock, Stella, and others. Films and photos also available from 1940s, video from 1970s. Special collection of models show evolution of American shipping from Mayflower to steam. Archives and library provide reference materials. Accepts phone inquiries. No fee. Hours: Sept-July, Tu-Sa 10-5, Su 2:30-5.

Afro-American History Museum
46 Joy St., Boston, MA 02114; (617) 742-1854. Provides historical info on blacks' contributions to MA through museum and library holdings. Accepts phone inquiries. Hours: Tu-F 10-4.

American Antiquarian Society Library
185 Salisbury St., Worcester, MA 01609; (617) 755-5221. Society maintains research library on American history, literature, and culture from 1640-1877, with collection of two-thirds of total pieces known to have been published during that period. Holdings include advertising trade cards, political caricatures, circusiana, graphic arts, maps, currency, printings and related arts, sheet music, state and local histories and documents, US govt documents, transportation, valentines, early religious history and literature, and writings and portraits of Mather family. Library is chief repository of early American newspapers. Open to adult researchers by application. Accepts phone inquiries. No fee. Hours: M-F.

American China Trade Museum
215 Adams St., Milton, MA 02186. Museum collection, archive, and library devoted to preservation history of China Trade with Boston from 1784-1900. Holdings include papers of Capt Robert Bennet Forbes and other China Trade documents.

American Jewish Historical Society
2 Thornton Rd., Waltham, MA 02154; (617) 891-8110. Collects materials pertaining to American Jewish experience. Museum displays artifacts and paintings. Library contains archives of major national Jewish orgs, papers of prominent American Jews, photos, and genealogical

records. Special collections of Yiddish theater posters, sheet music, and American Rabbinica. Accepts phone inquiries. No fee. Hours: M-Th 8:30-5, F 8:30-2, Su 2-5.

American Textile History Museum
800 Massachusetts Ave., North Andover, MA 01845; (617) 686-0191. Collects and preserves technological, manufacturing, labor and design history of American textile industry. Museum displays tools and machines made or used in preparing, spinning, weaving, knitting, and finishing cotton, silk, or flax in US from 1620. Library has materials on textile-related subjects. Archives holds materials on New England textile industry and companies, photos and other images, films/videotapes, and recordings. Special collections include fabrics and pre-industrial and industrial machines. Materials for in-house use only. Accepts phone inquiries. Fee. Hours: museum, M-F 9-5, Sa-Su 1-5; library, Tu-F 9-4.

Amherst College Library
Special Collections and Archives, Marshall Irving Bloom Collection, Amherst, MA 01002; (413) 542-2319. Academic research library holds Bloom collection of materials from Liberation News Service, and Margaret Mead's materials. Accepts phone inquiries. No fee. Hours: call.

Ancient and Honorable Artillery Company
Faneuil Hall, Boston, MA 02109; (617) 227-1638. Museum houses artifacts dating to 1600s. Library contains materials on history of Company, and military records of Civil War, War of 1812, WWI, WWII, manuscripts, maps, photos from wars, and genealogical records on members. Holdings restricted to members unless Mayor of Boston makes special request. Accepts phone inquiries. No fee. Hours: 10-4.

Andover Historical Society
97 Main St., Andover, MA 01810; (617) 475-2236. Collects, preserves, and exhibits historical artifacts of local significance, and provides interesting and educational services for Andover. Museum in home of 1819 home of Amos Blanchard, and interprets Andover's role in 1820-40 period. Library and archives hold manuscripts, maps, photos, oral history tapes, and genealogi-

cal records. Accepts phone inquiries. Fee. Hours: library, M-F 9-5; museum, M-F 1-3.

Ashfield Historical Society

P.O. Box 277, Main St., Ashfield, MA 01330; (413) 628-4541. Preserves and displays all aspects of Ashfield's past. Preserves large collection of photos of MA families at home and work in 1881 Howes Brothers Collection. Also contains special collections of memorabilia from Ashfield residents, including artist Edwin Romanzo Elmer, writers Charles Eliot Norton and George Williams Curtis, and early birth control advocate Dr. Charles Knowlton. Howes Collection closed to public. Accepts phone inquiries, but would prefer mail inquiries. Donations accepted. Hours: Memorial Day-Labor Day, Su 1-4; call for other hours.

Association for Gravestone Studies

46 Plymouth Rd., Needham, MA 02192; (617) 455-8180. Encourages preservation and protection of gravemarkers and gravestones, and emphasizes their importance in our heritage. Archives retain books, manuscripts, unpublished papers and dissertations, field notes, and photo collections on New England gravestones. Accepts phone inquiries. Hours: M-F 9-4.

Attleboro Area Industrial Museum

42 Union St., Attleboro, MA 02703; (617) 222-3918. Central repository for historical data on Attleboro area companies. Museum documents area's industrial past. Library contains some reference books, maps, photos, and recordings of some prominant industrialists. Accepts phone inquiries. No fee. Hours: 9-4.

Baker Library

Harvard University School of Business Administration, Soldiers Field, Boston, MA 02163. Holds many materials on historical aspects of business and economics including original company records, company histories, business records, biographies, and histories of industries. Strong in 19th c history of New England enterprises, textile firms, international trade, China trade, railroad, Northeast merchant families, and small businesses. Holdings include photos, trade cards, money, trade catalogs, and business cartoons.

Basketball Hall of Fame

1150 West Columbus Ave., Springfield, MA 01103; (413) 781-6500. Preserves history of basketball, its great players, and evolution of the game. Exhibits include photos of players, basketballs they used, uniforms, and plaques. Other holdings include recordings of games and players' voices. Accepts phone inquiries. Hours: call.

Blindiana Museum

Perkins School for the Blind, 175 N. Beacon St., Watertown, MA 02172; (617) 924-3434. Preserves history of Perkins School for the Blind, and history of education for blind and deaf persons. Museum displays include Helen Keller speeches, books, and memorabilia; Braille and embossed books; recreational and educational aids; and photos of classes. Accepts phone inquiries. No fee. Hours: M-F 8:30-5.

Boston Art Commission

Environment Department, Room 805, Boston City Hall, Boston, MA 02201; (617) 725-3850. Responsible for aquiring, curating, and interpreting Boston's public art. Collection includes portraits, paintings, and sculpture of people and events from periods in American history. Commission has archival materials dating from 1890, and photos of all exterior art and most interior art in the city. Accepts phone inquiries. Hours: M-F 9-5.

Boston College

Rare Books and Manuscripts, Thomas P. O'Neill Library, 140 Commonwealth Ave., Newton, MA 02167; (617) 552-3221. Academic research library holds materials on Carribean exploration, slave industry, and piracy. Holdings cover British, French, and Spanish settlements, and large collection of Anasi folk tales. Materials non-circulating. Accepts phone inquiries. No fee. Hours: call.

Boston Landmarks Commission

Boston City Hall, Room 805, Boston, MA 02201; (617) 725-3850. Historic preservation agency has archival manuscripts, maps, and photos on Boston architecture and neighborhoods. Collections organized by street addresses and geographical regions. Hours: by appointment only, M-F 9-5.

Boston Marine Society

National Historical Park, Bldg. 32, Charlestown Navy Yard, Boston, MA 02129; (617) 242-0522. Preserves Boston's maritime heritage with museum, library, and archival holdings of manuscripts, maps, membership records from 18th c, and collection of models and paintings. Restrictions on use. Accepts phone inquiries. No fee. Hours: M-F 10-3.

Boston Public Library

Rare Books and Manuscripts, Copley Square, Boston, MA 02117; (617) 536-5400. Holds significant materials on economic and political relationships between New England and Maritime Provinces in 18th c, with some materials on Abolitionists and antislavery movement. Also holds collection of early American caricatures, including some from Thomas Nast. Hours: M-Th 9-9, F-Sa 9-5, Su 2-6.

Boston Tea Party Ship

Congress St. Bridge, Boston, MA 02210; (617) 338-1773. Interprets colonial uprising as well as 18th c merchant sea life. Museum exhibits explain Tea Party's role in Revolution. Library holds reference materials on colonial, nautical, and Tea Party history, including maps, propaganda, list of conspirators, and audio presentations. Full-size model of a tea ship displayed. Accepts phone inquiries. Fee. Hours: 9-dusk.

Boston University

Special Collections, Mugar Memorial Library, 771 Commonwealth Ave., Boston, MA 02215; (617) 353-3736. Academic research library has collection of materials, papers, background files, memoranda, correspondence, and memorabilia from all Presidential Administrations from Pres Coolidge to Pres Nixon. Also holds large collection of papers from mystery and science fiction writers in film, radio, and TV; 14 years of "Little Orphan Annie" art; and personal collection of Arthur Fiedler scores and sound recordings, manuscripts, photos, memorabilia, and test pressings of performances. Accepts phone inquiries. No fee. Hours: call.

Boston University Film Archive

College of Communication, 640 Commonwealth Ave., Boston, MA 02215; (617) 353-3498. Makes film footage available for reproduction and research purposes. Archive retains collection of newsfilm from local TV station from 1958-1969. Subjects include local, national, and international matters. Restrictions on use. Accepts phone inquiries (617-353-3450). No fee. Hours: M, W, F 9-5.

Bostonian Society

Old State House, 206 Washington St., Boston, MA 02109; (617) 242-5610. Promotes study of Boston history and preservation of its antiquities. Museum houses paintings, furniture, clothing, and artifacts pertaining to Boston with emphasis on American Revolution. Library (located at 15 State St, 3rd fl) provides research materials on Boston business, architecture, and social history. Archives holds autopsies from Boston Massacre, Revolutionary War broadsides, large collection of maps, large photo collection, genealogical materials, magazines, blueprints of Boston bldgs, and Boston Maritime holdings. Materials noncirculating; stacks are closed. Accepts phone inquiries. Fee. Hours: library, M-F 9:30-4:30; museum, call.

Brandeis University Collection

Goldfarb Library, 415 South St., Waltham, MA 02254; (617) 647-4670. Academic research library has special Holocaust survivors collection, Jewish resistance collection, and Theresienstadt concentration camp documents. Holdings include oral histories from survivors living in US, daily orders from Nazi command, and materials on role Jewish resistance to Nazis. Other holdings include archives of Abraham Lincoln Brigade, Dibner collection on history of science, collection of radical pamphlets, and dime novel collection. Materials circulate only to members of Boston Library Consortium. Accepts phone inquiries. No fee. Hours: call.

Bunker Hill Monument

Boston National Historical Park, Charlestown Navy Yard, Bldg 5, Boston, MA 02129; (617) 242-5641. Commemorates Revolutionary War battle through museum, library, and archival holdings. Museum displays materials relating to battle. Boston National Historic Park has library and archival holdings, including photos. Contact Park librarian (617-242-5615) or curatorial division (617-242-5615) for lending practices. Accepts phone inquiries. No fee. Hours: monument, 9-4:30; exhibits, 9-5.

Cape Cod Pilgrim Memorial Association

Provincetown Monument and Museum, P.O. Box 1125, Provincetown, MA 02657; (617) 487-1310. Preserves Provincetown and MA history through exhibits of whaling equipment, shipwreck artifacts from British Man-o-war Somerset, Pilgrim and Indian artifacts, Commander Donald B. MacMillan materials, and examples of Provincetown arts and crafts. Accepts phone inquiries. Fee. Hours: winter, 10-4; summer, 10-5.

Cardinal Spellman Philatelic Museum

235 Wellesley St., Weston, MA 02193; (617) 894-6735. Promotes philately through exhibitions and research. Museum displays stamps from medieval letters to new issues from worldwide sources. Library holds large reference collection on philately from 1890s. Special collections include Pres Eisenhower and Gen Ridgeway's stamp collections. Library open only to members. Accepts phone inquiries. No fee. Hours: Tu-Th 9-4, Su 1-5.

Carey Memorial Library

1874 Massachusetts Ave., Lexington, MA 02173; (617) 862-6288. Library holds materials on Battle of Lexington and Concord, and well as historical documents on Lexington. Accepts phone inquiries. Hours: call.

Chesterwood

P.O. Box 248, Off Mohawk Lake Road, Stockbridge, MA 01262; (413) 298-3579. Preserved home and studio contain largest exhibit of sculptor Daniel Chester French's work. Collection include over 800 casts, models, and finished pieces. Studio is equipped with original tools, supplies, and equip. Accepts phone inquiries. Hours: May-Oct, 10-5.

College of Our Lady of the Elms

Special Collections, Alumnae Library, 291 Springfield St., Chicopee, MA 01013; (413) 598-8351. Academic research library with library materials on American history, Civil War and Presidential papers. Special collection on 19th c author and political theorist Edward Bellamy, including letters and photos. Recordings include complete run of recorded anthology of American music. Accepts phone inquiries. No fee. Hours: M-F 8:30-4:30.

Computer Museum

300 Congress St., Museum Wharf, Boston, MA 02210; (617) 426-2800. Preserves and exhibits history of computers in US. Museum exhibits largest computer ever built, hardware and software displays, and audiovisual displays. Accepts phone inquiries. Hours: W, Sa-Su 11-6, Th-F 11-9.

Country Dance and Song Society of America

17 N. South St., Northampton, MA 01060; (413) 584-9913. Non-profit org preserves history, promotes enjoyment, and encourages research into traditional forms of US and English dances, music, and songs. Publishes annually, sponsors dance camps for adults, and markets its own records and books. Library holds reference materials on dance history, but is not in site. Accepts phone inquiries. No fee. Hours: M-F 9:30-5.

Crane Museum

Off Rte. 9, Dalton, MA 01226; (413) 648-2600. Preserves history of Crane Company and manufacture of paper in general. Displays include presidential and first family cards and invitations, counterfeiting exhibits, and models of papermill structures. Hours: June-Sept, M-F 2-5.

Essex Institute

132 Essex St., Salem, MA 01970; (617) 744-3390. Collects, preserves, and interprets Essex county history. Museum consists of 8 historic houses furnished with decorative period arts. Library covers early English and US history and travel; New England history, literature, and art; and 1911 Western travel in China. Manuscript collection has Essex county family papers, business materials, and personal and literary manuscripts from 17th-20th c; New England maps; maps of early Chinese and East Asian explora-

tion; many photos from MA and China; oral history interviews; extensive genealogical materials; and special Nathaniel Hawthorne collection. Accepts phone inquiries. Fee. Hours: Tu-F 9-4:30, and June-Oct, add Mondays.

Fall River Historical Society

451 Rock St., Fall River, MA 02722; (617) 679-1071. Preserves history of Fall River, including town's history as Underground Railroad stop and home of Lizzie Borden. Museum exhibits 16 rooms of memorabilia, including town portraits, period furniture, and household items. Borden artifacts include photos of Borden family, jurors, and displays from crime, as well as newspaper stories and some letters. Accepts phone inquiries. Hours: Mar-Dec, Tu-F 9-4:30 and Apr-Nov, Sa-Su 2-4.

Francis Countway Library of Medicine

Harvard University Medical School, 10 Shattuck St., Boston, MA 02115; (617) 732-2142. Large medical library is strong in serials and all aspects of medical history. Holdings include medical Judaica, Osleriana, papers of Oliver Wendell Holmes and William Rimmer, non-medical and travel books by drs, materials on X-ray history, prints and medical satire, phrenology, witchcraft, gynecology and obstetrics, medical illustration, birth control and sex research, medical numismatics, anatomy, anesthesia, alchemy, dental medicine, psychiatry, plastic surgery, and surgery. Hours: call.

Friends of the Blue Hills Trust

1894 Canton Ave., Milton, MA 02186; (617) 326-0079. Volunteer org protects and preserves resources of Blue Hills and Neponset River Reservations. Library holds materials on reservation, manuscripts, maps, photos, films/videotapes on regional railroad, Indian quarries, and Civilian Conservation Corps. Accepts phone inquiries. No fee. Hours: call.

General Society of Mayflower Descendants

P.O. Box 3297, 4 Winslow St., Plymouth, MA 02361; (617) 746-3188. Historic house museum and library provide genealogical materials for research into Pilgrim ancestry. Museum housed in 1754 home of Edward Winslow. Library contains manuscripts, vital records, and town and county histories on Mayflower families from 1620. Non-members restricted to 2 hours per day in library. Accepts phone inquiries. Fee. Hours: museum, Memorial Day-mid-Sept, 10-5; Library 1:30-3:30.

Hancock Shaker Village

P.O. Box 898, Pittsfield, MA 01202; (413) 443-0188. Preserves and interprets faith and culture of Society of Shakers. Museum displays materials on Shaker history and culture from 1789. Library holds info on Shaker mechanics, agriculture, industry, and comparative religion and communitarian studies. Archives retains manuscripts, photos, maps, and recordings of Shaker music. Materials for in-house use only. Accepts phone inquiries. No fee. Hours: by appt, M-F 10-5.

Harvard University Film Archive

Carpenter Center for the Visual Arts, 24 Quincy St., Cambridge, MA 02138; (617) 495-4700. Collects and preserves materials related to cinema history. Library concentrates on film history, with clipping files on 2000 films and 500 directors. Film collection includes many US-produced 16mm and 35mm films, with emphasis on film as cinematic art. Permission may be required from curator. Accepts phone inquiries. Fee. Hours: 9:30-2.

Henry E. Simonds Memorial Archival Center

15 High St., Winchester, MA 01890; (617) 721-7146. Promotes local history through collection of artifacts, library holdings, and archival records of town orgs, families, and individuals. Other holdings include maps from 1854, photo collection, and genealogical records. Materials non-circulating. Accepts phone inquiries. No fee. Hours: M, W 6-9:30, Sa 10-3.

Heritage Plantation of Sandwich

P.O. Box 566, Sandwich, MA 02563; (617) 888-0340. Conserves town records and makes Sandwich historical materials available to public. Library focuses on genealogical and historical subjects. Archives holds town records from 1651, maps of Sandwich, photos, genealogical records,

First Lady Jackie Kennedy conducting a televised tour of the White House in 1962, from the John F. Kennedy Library.

and microfilm of local newspapers. Special collections include Cape Cod Canal artifacts and Boston Sandwich Glass Co memorabilia. Materials for in-house use only. Accepts phone inquiries. Fee. Hours: M-F 8:30-2:30.

Historic Neighborhoods Foundation

2 Boylston St., Boston, MA 02116; (617) 426-1885. Promotes awareness and appreciation of urban neighborhoods, architecture, and urban design. Library and archives contain maps, extensive slide collection on Boston downtown and neighborhoods, and local history items. Fee for membership and programs. Hours: M-F 9-5.

House of Seven Gables

54 Turner St., Salem, MA 01970; (617) 744-0991. Memorializes life of Nathaniel Hawthorne with museum, library, and archives collections. Historic site consists of three 17th c houses, two 18th c. houses, and two 19th c. structures, all strong in Hawthorne-related materials. Library holds large collection of published works by Hawthorne, including first and foreign editions. Archives hold extensive materials on American Settlement House Movement, with emphasis on Caroline Emmerton, and development of House of Seven Gables. Manuscript collection holds materials on Hawthorne and family, navigational

maps, photos, and oral histories. Accepts phone
inquiries. Fee. Hours: Jul-Aug 9:30-5:30, Sept-
June 10-4:30.

Indian Motorcycle Museum

33 Hendee St., Springfield, MA 01139; (413)
737-2624. Museum collects, preserves, and
exhibits Indian motorcycles of all designs. Holdings include first motorcycle ever, built in 1885;
collapsible Indians used during WWII; miniature motorcycle collection; and special collection on women cyclists. Accepts phone inquiries.
Fee. Hours: M-Su 10-5.

John F. Kennedy Library

National Archives and Records Administration,
Columbia Point, Boston, MA 02125; (617)
929-4534. Preserves and makes available memorabilia of John Kennedy. Museum houses exhibits on President from 1917-68. Library concentrates on mid-20th c US history, govt, and
politics. Archive contains large collection of papers
from John Kennedy, many friends, family, and
associates. Extensive collection of photos on
Kennedy's life and administration. Large collection of films/videotapes and recordings also
available. Special collections include papers of
Ernest Hemingway. Accepts phone inquiries.
Fee. Hours: museum, 9-5; research, M-F 8:30-
4:30.

Kendall Whaling Museum

P.O. Box 297, 27 Everett St., Sharon, MA
02067; (617) 784-5642. Collects, preserves,
interprets, and researches cultural aspects of
whaling throughout history. Museum displays
paintings, prints, tools, and ethnological materials from Dutch, British and European, American, Japanese, Native North American, Polyne-
sian, and Pacific Basin cultures. Library has
materials on decorative and fine arts, cetology,
exploration, voyages, and ethnology. Archive
retains whaling logbooks, journals, and diaries
from 18th-20th c; 16th-20th c European and
American maps; many photos; historic whaling
films; and recordings of sea music and whales.
Member research only. Accepts phone inquiries.
Fee. Hours: Tu-Sa 10-5, research by appt only.

Lynn Historical Society

125 Green St., Lynn, MA 01902; (617) 592-

2465. Collects and preserves artifacts and research materials on Lynn. Museum has 4 period
rooms, with exhibitions on history of firefighting
in Lynn, medicines, and shoe industry. Archives
contain jouranls of shoe manufacturers, newspaper clippings, maps, and genealogical records.
Materials non-circulating. Accepts phone inquiries. Fee. Hours: M-F 9-4, Sa-Su 1-4.

Lynn Public Library

North Common St., Lynn, MA 01902; (617)
595-0567. Public library has vital genealogical
records of MA to 1850, Essex Institute historical
collections, records of Mayflower descendents,
and NY genealogical and biographical records.
Accepts phone inquiries. No fee. Hours: M-W 9-
9, Th 9-6, F-Sa 9-5.

Marblehead Historical Society

P.O. Box 1048, 161 Washington St., Marblehead, MA 01945; (617) 631-1069. Preserves,
collects, and maintains items pertaining to Marblehead and its history. Museum is Georgian
mansion furnished in original paneling and wallpaper, decorative arts, and furniture. Archive
maintains manuscripts, ships' logs, Revolutionary War Registers, photos, genealogical records.
Civil War museum also on site. Accepts phone
inquiries. Fee. Hours: May-Oct, M-Sa 9-4.

Mary Baker Eddy Museum

Longyear Historical Society, 120 Seaver St.,
Brookline, MA 02146; (617) 277-8943. Museum preserves memory and artifacts of this
founder of Christian Science. Holdings include
manuscripts, books, photos, portraits, and
memorabilia of Eddy and her associates. Accepts
phone inquiries. Hours: Tu-Sa, Su pm.

Mashpee Wampanoag
Indian Tribal Council

P.O. Box 1040, Mashpee, MA 02649; (617)
477-0208. Preserves history of Wampanoag tribe
through displays of Indian artifacts, archival town
documents, photos, films/videotapes, and genealogical records. Restrictions on use. Accepts phone inquiries. No fee. Hours: 9-5.

Massachusetts
Archaeological Society

Robbins Museum of Archaeology, 42 Union St.,

Attleboro, MA 02703; (617) 222-5470. Preserves largest collection of Indian artifacts in and from southeast New England. Library and archives contain reference materials and records of society, as well as audiovisual materials. Accepts phone inquiries. Donations accepted. Hours: W 10-3.

Massachusetts Historical Commission

80 Boyleston St., Boston, MA 02116; (617) 727-8470. State agency preserves materials on historic MA structures. Holdings include Inventory of Historic Bldgs and Historic National Register Properties, which consist of detailed files on many properties. Some maps and photos. Accepts phone inquiries. No fee. Hours: M-F 9-5.

Massachusetts Historical Society

1154 Boyleston St., Boston, MA 02215; (617) 536-1608. Holdings include Adams family papers, and materials relating to MA and New England. Accepts phone inquiries. Hours: 9-4:45.

Massachusetts Institute of Technology

Special Collections, Cambridge, MA 02139; (617) 253-5681. Holds materials from Howe, Manning, and Almy, 1913 partnership of women architects. Collection includes blueprints, drawings, research materials, correspondence, financial data, reports, materials from housing projects in OH and New England. Hours: call.

Massachusetts Society of Mayflower Descendents

101 Newbury St., Boston, MA 02116; (617) 266-1624. Promotes genealogical research and education through collections in library and archives. Holdings include family manuscripts and histories. Access limited to members and prospective members. Accepts phone inquiries. No fee. Hours: 9-4.

Massachusetts State Archives

State House, Room 55, 220 Morrissey Blvd., Boston, MA 02125; (617) 727-2816. Preserves and manages records of legislature, Executive Office, and agencies of MA. Extensive military records from Colonial Period Wars, Revolutionary Period including Shays' Rebellion, War of 1812, Civil War, and Spanish-American War. Other records include census schedules from 1790; MA registrations of births, marriages, and deaths from 1841-90; Boston 1848-91 immigration passenger lists; naturalization records from 1885-1931; MA Gov's office archives, land grants, legislature, and mercantile affairs; and papers on ME, Eastern Land, and Plymouth Colony. Some materials require special permission. Accepts phone inquiries. No fee. Hours: M-F 8:45-5, Sa 9-3.

Mayflower Society Museum

4 Winslow, Plymouth, MA 02360; (617) 2590. Preserves genealogical materials and artifacts from Mayflower descendents. Holdings include will of John Winslow, photo of Emerson, and genealogical library. Accepts phone inquiries. Fee. Hours: call.

Melville Room

New Bedford Free Public Library, 613 Pleasant St., New Bedford, MA 02740; (617) 999-6291. One of nation's most extensive collections on American whaling, with large collection of documents used in whaling, logbooks, seamen's card file of men who sailed from New Bedford Custom's District. Hours: call.

Middlesex Canal Association

P.O. Box 333, Billerica, MA 01821. Promotes interest and preservation of Middlesex Canal that ran from Boston to Lowell from 1793-1854. Archival material, maps, and photos housed in Univ of Lowell library special collections.

Milford Historical Commission

2 Nicholas Rd., Milford, MA 01757; (617) 473-3560. Preserves and protects historical assets of Milford through museum collection of Civil War artifacts, library collection of Civil War books and publications, and archival Milford newspapers, directories, and reports. Holdings include Ernest Bragg's "History of Milford," maps, photos, films, recordings, and genealogical records. Accepts phone inquiries. Hours: call.

Nantucket Historical Association

P.O. Box 1016, Nantucket, MA 02554; (617)

228-1655 or 1894. Preserves Nantucket and maritime history. Museum, library, and archives contain manuscripts, maps, photos, films/videotapes, recordings, and genealogical records. Restrictions. Accepts phone inquiries. Fee. Hours: May- Sept, 9-5.

Natick Historical Society

58 Eliot St., South Natick, MA 01760; (617) 235-6015. Preserves history and artifacts of local heritage in museum, archives, and library. Holdings include letters to Caleb Strong from 1745-1819, maps, photos, and genealogical records. Special Henry Wilson vice-president collection, Horatio Alger, Jr collection, and John Eliot and Natick Indians collection. Accepts phone inquiries. No fee. Hours: W 2-4:30, Sa 10-12:30.

National Archives—Boston Branch

380 Trapelo Rd., Waltham, MA 02154; (617) 647-8100. Preserves and makes available records of federal agencies in six New England states. Holdings include materials from US district courts and circuit courts; customs and Coast Guard records for New England ports; Army Corps of Engineers materials; naval district and shore establishment records, including Boston, Portsmouth, and NH naval shipyards; WWII MIT Radiation Laboratory records; census schedules and indexes from 1790-1910; Revolutionary War pension application files and military service records for entire US, and New England naturalization records from 1790-1906. Accepts phone inquiries. No fee. Hours: M-F 8-4:30, and first Sa of month 8-4:30.

National Center for Jewish Film

Brandeis University, Lown #102, Waltham, MA 02254; (617) 899-7044. Film library, archive, repository, and study center preserve pictorial record of Jewish experience. Library and archive preserve large collection of film for study and distribution for educational, cultural, and entertainment purposes. Collections include photos from Yiddish feature films, Rutenberg & Everett Yiddish film library, film materials on European Jewry and Holocaust, materials on Jews in history of American silent film. Films include documentaries, dramas, and Nazi propoganda materials, dating from 1909. Some materials restricted. Accepts phone inquiries. Fee. Hours: M-F 9-5.

National Plastics Museum

Old School House, Rte. 117, Leominster, MA 01453; (617) 537-1751. Museum commemorates plastics industry and its start in Leominster. Accepts phone inquiries. Hours: call.

Naumkeag

P.O. Box 792, Stockbridge, MA 01262; (413) 298-3239. Historic house museum preserves history of Stanford White, the Gilded era, and Fletcher Steele. House is furnished with 17th-19th c pieces. Archives preserves plans of and letters on Naumkeag gardens and photos from Choates family travels to Europe and Egypt in 1890 and 1900. Materials for in-house use only. Accepts phone inquiries. No fee. Hours: M-F 9-4.

New Bedford Free Public Library

Documents Dept., 613 Pleasant St., New Bedford, MA 02740; (617) 999-6291. Provides materials on local community. Library and archives hold sermons of Unitarian minister William Potter, and Black merchant Paul Cuffe. Other holdings include maps, photos, films/videotapes, recordings, and genealogical materials on southeastern MA and French Canada. Special collections on whaling and Quakers. Accepts phone inquiries (617-999-5515). No fee. Hours: M-Th 9-9, F 9-5, Sa 9-5.

New Bedford Glass Society

50 N. 2nd St., New Bedford, MA 02740; (617) 994-0115. Museum and archives of American art glass from 1870-1950. Library has small reference collection. Archives holds materials on glass industry, catalogs, photos, designs and sketches, and advertising materials. Other collections include videotapes of contemporary glass artists, and oral histories of New Bedford workers. Materials non-circulating; glass study only with curatorial supervision. Accepts phone inquiries. Hours: M-F 9-5.

New Bedford Whaling Museum

18 Johnny Cake Hill, New Bedford, MA 02740; (508) 997-0046. Collects, preserves, and interprets American whaling industry and relationship to New Bedford. Museum has paintings, prints, drawings, furniture, decorative arts, folk art, tools, and ship models. Library follows

American whaling history from 1650. Archives has Old Dartmouth Historical Society records from 1903; 19th-20th c maps and charts; many photos on local area, whaling, Eskimos, and Arctic; special Batchelder whaling collection and Boodwin maritime history collection. Intl Maritime collection has whaling, merchant, and exploration voyage logs and journals. Material non-circulating. Accepts phone inquiries. Fee. Hours: museum, M-Sa 9-5, Su 1-5; library M-F 9-5.

New England Historic Genealogical Society

99-101 Newbury St., Boston, MA 02116; (617) 536-5740. Genealogical and local history research center. Museum exhibits include antique Far East furniture imported during China Trade period and oil paintings. Library holds large reference collection. Archives contain Society's records to 1845, manuscripts, maps of Boston and New England, small photo collection, census and church records, and papers of Winifred Lovering Holman, Algernon Aspinwall, John Insley Coddington, John Hutchinson Cooke, and Harold Bowditch. Manuscripts and rare books for members only; research materials don't circulate. Fee. Hours: Tu, F, Sa 9-5, W-Th 9-9; closed Sa before Monday holidays.

New England Methodist Historical Society

Southern New England Conference, 745 Commonwealth Ave., Boston, MA 02215; (617) 353-3034. Documents history of Methodist church in New England from 1784 through collections in library and archival Conference records. Open to qualified users only. No fee. Hours: M-F 9-4.

New England Quaker Research Library

P.O. Box 655, North Amherst, MA 01059. Preserves materials on Quakers and Quaker concerns, pacifism, racism, feminism, poverty, and religion.

Norman Rockwell Museum at Stockbridge

Main St., Stockbridge, MA 01262; (413) 298-3869. Collects, preserves, studies, interprets, and exhibits materials on life and career of Rockwell. Museum holds approx 50 Rockwell originals. Archives retain photos, tearsheets, publications with Rockwell illustrations, and artist's studio artifacts. Films/videotapes, and recordings also available. Accepts phone inquiries. Fee. Hours: 10-5.

Northampton Historical Society

46 Bridge St., Northampton, MA 01060; (413) 584-6011. Collects, preserves, exhibits, and fosters interest in history of Northampton and CT Valley. Museum consists of two 18th c homes, and 19th c home and barn with exhibits on CT valley Indians, signs, and weathervanes. Archives retains records of Pro Brush Corporation, letters and account books of local families and businesses from 18th-20th c, 19th-20th c maps, large photo collection, 1938 film on Northampton, recording of Calvin Coolidge speech, Shepherd family papers, and 19th c sheet music. Accepts phone inquiries. Fee for museum; no fee for researchers. Hours: Tu-F 9-5.

Northeast Document Conservation Center

Abbott Hall, 24 School St., Andover, MA 01810; (508) 470-1010. Performs paper conservation, bookbinding, and preservation microfilming. Also provides consultation, workshops, and preservation assistance. Accepts phone inquiries. Fee. Hours: M-F 8:30-4:30.

Old Colony Historical Society

66 Church Green, Taunton, MA 02780; (617) 822-1622. Museum and library preserve Plymouth Colony history. Exhibits include military artifacts, portraits, furnitures, tools, silver, and household artifacts. Library holds materials on local history, genealogy, Civil War, and American history. Archives holds family papers, church and town records, southern MA maps, and southern MA photos on architecture and people. Special collection of Francis Baylies papers. Materials non-circulating. Fee. Hours: Tu-Sa 10-4.

Old North Church

193 Salem St., Boston, MA 02113; (617) 523-6676. Historic Revolutionary War site that maintains worship services. Museum displays

Norman Rockwell at work on a portrait of Robert F. Kennedy, from the Norman Rockwell Museum at Stockbridge.

church artifacts. Accepts phone inquiries. Donations accepted. Hours: 9-5.

Old South Meeting House

310 Washington St., Boston, MA 02108; (617) 482-6439. Preserves and interprets history of Old South Meeting House, its founding in Puritan Boston, and its role in American Revolution. Documentation covers Boston Tea Party meetings. Some photos available. Archives stored at New England History and Genealogy Society preserve Old South's history from 1872. Accepts phone inquiries. Fee. Hours: call.

Old Sturbridge Village Research Library

Old Sturbridge Village, 1 Old Sturbridge Village Rd., Sturbridge, MA 01566; (508) 347-3662. Outdoor living history museum recreates regional rural life from 1790-1840. Museum has over 500,000 material culture artifacts of New Englanders. Library has reference materials on social and material history of rural New England. Archives contains records, manuscripts, diaries, and broadsides relevant to museum's history; maps of 18-19th c New England; and photos. Special collections cover historical agriculture, Bullord family papers; Merino Dudley Woolen Manufacturing; and Charles Eddy collection. Materials non-circulating. Accepts phone inquiries. No fee. Hours: M-F 8:30-5.

Paul Revere Memorial Association

19 North Square, Boston, MA 02113; (617)

523-2338. Preserves and presents 17th-19th c Boston and colonial history with emphasis on Paul Revere and family. Assn operates Paul Revere house, with its 17th-18th c furnished rooms, exhibits, and grounds; and Pierce/Hickborn House. Library and archives house manuscripts, maps, photos, genealogical materials, and films/ videotapes. Accepts phone inquiries. Fee. Hours: Apr-Oct 9:30-5:15; Nov-Apr 9:30-4:15.

Peabody Institute Library

Danvers Archival Center, 15 Sylvan St., Danvers, MA 01923; (617) 774-0554. Academic research library has papers of abolitionist Parker Pillsbury, consisting of 19th c antislavery tracts and books. Also holds Ellerton Brehaut collection on New England witchcraft trials, 17th-18th c books on subject, and transcripts of all known trial records. Large collection of manuscripts, photos, newspapers, and maps available. Accepts phone inquiries. No fee. Hours: M-Th 9-9, F 1-5, Sa 9-5, Su 1-5.

Phillips Library

Peabody Museum of Salem, East India Square, 161 Essex St., Salem, MA 01970; (508) 745-1876. Museum preserves maritime history, ethnology of Japanese and Native Americans, Asian export art, and natural history of Essex county. Holdings in library and archives include manuscripts, large collection of charts, and extensive photo collection on maritime history. Materials non-circulating. Accepts phone inquiries. Fee. Hours: M-F 10-5.

Pilgrim Society
and Pilgrim Hall Museum

75 Court St., Plymouth, MA 02360; (508) 746-1620. Ensures continuing and expanding appreciation of Pilgrims and their contribution to American heritage. Museum exhibits Pilgrim artifacts, Native American displays, and Plymouth history from 1620. Library has materials on Pilgrim, Plymouth, and New England history, including rare books; local family histories from 1604; personal and business records; earliest MA state documents; 17th c maps; photos of Plymouth scenes, people, and events; limited films/ videotapes; some recordings; and genealogical records. Accepts phone inquiries. Fee. Hours: 9:30-4:30.

Pioneer Valley Planning Commission

26 Central St., West Springfield, MA 01089; (413) 732-2463. Regional planning agency involved in historic preservation. Library holds materials on architecture, community plannings, and historic preservation. Archives retains photos and manuscript research materials on historic sites and structures in Hampden and Hampshire counties, and base and specialized maps for communities in those counties. Library materials for in-house use only. Accepts phone inquiries. Hours: M-F 8-5.

Plymouth Historical Commission

Pilgrim Hall, 75 Court St., Plymouth, MA 02360; (617) 746-1620. Holds materials on preservation of Plymouth history through archival materials and photos. Accepts phone inquiries. No fee. Hours: M-F 9-5.

Plymouth Plantation

P.O. Box 1620, Warren Ave., Plymouth, MA 02360; (617) 746-1622. Covers Plymouth colony history from 1620-92, and provides living history presentations. Museum exhibits include Mayflower II ship, 1627 Village, and Wampanoag Settlement. Library contains materials on all aspects of early modern English culture. Archives holds Mayflower II records and organizational documens. Materials for in-house use only. Accepts phone inquiries. Fee for museum; no fee for library. Hours: appointment suggested for use of library, M-F 9-4; museum, Apr-Nov 9-5.

Plymouth Public Library

North St., Plymouth, MA 02360; (617) 746-1927. Public library holds pre-1800s records, journals, diaries, and laws of Plymouth Colony and town. Accepts phone inquiries. No fee. Hours: call.

Quincy Historical Society

8 Adams St., Adams Academy Building, Quincy, MA 02169; (617) 773-1144. Museum and research library with materials on Quincy and South Shore from prehistory. Library specializes in Adams family and local history. Archives retains town and city records, manuscripts, maps, photos, film records of local businesses, oral history interviews, and genealogical records.

Special collections include Howard Johnson collection, Shipyard collection, Granite Industry collection, first commercial railroad collection, and Grand Army of Republic collection. Accepts phone inquiries. No fee. Hours: M-F 9:30-3:30, Sa 12:30-3:30.

Ropes Memorial

318 Essex St., Salem, MA 01970; (617) 744-0718. Preserves household belongings of 4 generations of Nathaniel Ropes and Joseph Orne families, from 1750-1907. Museum consists of 1727 house with original furnishings and Ropes and Orne family items. Accepts phone inquiries. Fee. Hours: June-Oct Tu-Sa 10-4, Su 1-4:30.

Salem Maritime National Historic Site

Custom House, 174 Derby St., Salem, MA 01970; (617) 744-4323. Studies, preserves, and presents Salem's maritime history and remaining waterfront historic structures and wharves; and interprets role of US Customs Service and cultural resources management. Museum complex composed of functional lighthouse and wharves reflecting maritime business and society from 1670-1937. Library has materials on maritime, US Customs Service, and local and national history. Archives hold materials that document collections, photos, and special collection of custom's service weighing and measuring equipment and documents. Accepts phone inquiries. No fee. Hours: library and study collection by appt; 8:30-5.

Salem State College Library

Alternatives Library, Lafayette St., Salem, MA 01970; (617) 741-6230, ext. 2625. Represents left-wing political and social movements, as well as Third World and feminists through collection of books, pamphlets, periodicals, newspapers, newsletters, ephemera, and recordings. Accepts phone inquiries. Hours: call.

Sandwich Archives and Historical Center

145 Main St., Sandwich, MA 02563; (617) 888-0340. Collects and preserves archival materials from town of Sandwich and its families. Library contains small collections of historical and genealogical materials for Sandwich and Cape Cod.

Archives contain photos, family collections of deeds and papers, and historical maps of Cape Cod region. Restrictions on some items. Accepts phone inquiries. Fee for research. Hours: M-F 8:30-3:30.

Sandwich Historical Society and Glass Museum

P.O. Box 103, 129 Main St., Sandwich, MA 02563; (508) 888-0251. Instructs public in history, products, methods, and people associated with 19th and 20th c glass industry in Sandwich. Museum displays Sandwich glass from 1825-1909, other glass from 19th and 20th c, and other local history artifacts. Library has reference materials on glass and antiques. Archives holds materials relating to 17th-20th c Sandwich, including maps from 18th c, photos of glass factories and town, and genealogical records. Accepts phone inquiries. Fee. Hours: Apr-Oct, 9:30-4:30; Nov-Dec, Feb-Mar, 9:30-4.

Schlesinger Library on History of Women in America

Radcliffe College, 3 James St., Cambridge, MA 02138. Library focuses on women's history and accomplishments. Holds collection of correspondence to and from Amelia Earhart (largely from mother, sister, and husband); papers on or from female physicians Elizabeth and Emily Blackwell, Martha May Eliot, Alice Hamilton, Edith Banfield Jackson, Mary Jacobi, and medical missionary Ida Sophia Scudder; records on New England Hosp for Women and Children and oral history interviews on Family Planning org; interviews from Women in Fed Govt Oral History Project; and collections on Beecher-Stowe family, Betty Freidan, Emma Goldman, NOW, Natl Abortion Rights Action League, and Women's Action Equity League.

Sheffield Historical Society

Main St., Sheffield, MA 01257; (413) 229-2694. Preserves materials on Sheffield history. Museum consists of restored 1744 period furnishings. Library has small collection on history, art, and literature; 19th c map reproductions; early Sheffield photos; and historic records and artifacts. Accepts phone inquiries. No fee. Hours: winter, F 1:30-4; summer, F-Sa 1:30-4.

Society for the Preservation of New England Antiquities

141 Cambridge St., Boston, MA 02114; (617) 227-3956. Regional preservation org maintains 23 house museums in 5 New England states. Archives contain 500 thousand images pertaining to New England domestic life. Accepts phone inquiries. No fee. Hours: by appt, M-F.

Sophia Smith Collection—Women's History Archive

Smith College, Alumnae Gymnasium, Levels A and B, Northampton, MA 01063; (413) 584-2700, ext. 2970. Documents women's history through collection of materials on women's status, role, and achievements. Materials non-circulating. Accepts phone inquiries. No fee. Hours: call.

Springfield Armory National Historic Site

1 Armory Square, Springfield, MA 01105; (413) 734-6477. Preserves history of Springfield Armory and regional heritage. Museum (open spring 1989) houses artifacts from Armory, including military weapons, machines, and related memorabilia. Library provides research materials on museum collection. Archives contains architectural and engineering drawings from Armory, photos, films/videotapes, and oral history interviews with former Armory employees. Accepts phone inquiries. No fee. Hours: library by appt, 8:30-4:30.

Springfield City Library

Documents Collections, 220 State St., Springfield, MA 01103; (413) 739-3871. Collects, preserves, and provides documentation and info on history of Springfield area. Library has large collection of materials on Springfield history. Archives contain records from businesses, civic orgs, and individuals; historic maps; many photos of Springfield, including some from Mass Mutual Insurance Co.; large collection of genealogical records; archives of Springfield insurance companies, including records of Monarch and Springfield Fire & Marine; and Ames Sword Company Collection. Accepts phone inquiries. No fee. Hours: M-Tu, Th-Sa 10:30-5, W 1-9, Su 1-5.

State Library of Massachusetts

341 State House, Boston, MA 02133; (617) 727-2590. Research library for state govt officials and employees and general public. Concentration on public law and affairs, MA history and govt, and local history. Manuscript collection includes papers of MA legislative and special commissions, 19th and 20th c maps and atlases, some Sanborn fire insurance maps, and photos of MA political figures. Special collections include Revolutionary War broadsides, 18th & 19th c newspapers, architectural plans of State House, scrapbooks and memorabilia of MA political activities, and William Bradford manuscript of Plymoth Plantation. Materials circulate only to state employees. Accepts phone inquiries. No fee. Hours: M-F 9-5.

Tufts University

Documents Dept., Wessell Library, Medford, MA 02155; (617) 628-5000 ext. 5234. Academic research library with large collection of US govt publications from late 1800s. Holdings include large number of 20th c maps. Some materials for in-house use only. Accepts phone inquiries. No fee. Hours: M-Th 8-10, F 8-9, Sa 9-5, Su 1-10.

University of Lowell Library

Special Collections, 1 University Ave., Lowell, MA 01854; (617) 452-5000. Lowell History Collection holds photos and other pictorial materials on New England textile industry mills, immigrants to region, and history. Locks and Canal Collection contains photos from 1875-1947 on company operations. Accepts phone inquiries. No fee. Hours: call.

University of Massachusetts Library

Amherst, MA 01003; (413) 545-2765. Academic research library holds pamphlet collection on slavery, abolitionists, and antislavery societies in US from 1725-1911. Accepts phone inquiries. No fee. Hours: call.

USS Massachusetts

Battleship Cove, Fall River, MA 02721; (617) 678-1100 or 1905. Preserves history and spirit of US Navy torpedo boats. Museum displays squadron, base, and WWII PT boat memorabilia and artifacts. Library has reference materials supporting collections, and some on foreign patrol boats. Special collections include restored Higgins and Elco boats. Accepts phone inquiries. Fee. Hours: 8:30-4:30.

War Records Division

Adjutant General's Office, 100 Cambridge St., Saltonstall Bldg, Room 1011, Boston, MA 02202; (617) 727-2964. Oversees collection of MA military records with concentrations on Mexican, Civil, Spanish-American and World Wars. Accepts phone inquiries. Hours: call.

Waterfront Historic Area League

13 Centre St., New Bedford, MA 02740; (617) 997-1776. Preserves historic bldgs and character of New Bedford and region. Library contains historic preservation materials, and photo documentation of historic bldgs in area. Accepts phone inquiries. No fee. Hours: M-F 9-5.

Welfleet Historical Society—Rider House

P.O. Box 58, Main St., Wellfleet, MA 02667; (617) 349-9215 winter/9157 summer. Preserves history of Welfleet and its maritime activity. Museum holds whaling, oyster trade, and indigenous industry artifacts. Library houses many manuscripts pertaining to Wellfleet and Lower Cape, maps of Barnstable county, and limited oral histories. Accepts phone inquiries. Fee. Hours: late June-Labor Day Tu-Sa 2-5.

Wellesley Historical Society

P.O. Box 142, Wellesley, MA 02181; (617) 235-6690. Collects, preserves, exhibits, and preserves history of Wellesley and residents. Museum and library document town history with town directories, reports, clipping file, and books by local authors. Archives hold local family files and papers; costume and textile collection from 1800-1930; maps and architectural and engineering plans; photos from 1870s; oral history tapes; and works by local artists William Ladd Taylor, William Partridge, and Charles Avery Aiken. Special collections of Civil War books, Alexander Graham Bell materials, and Katherine Lee Bates papers. Materials non-circulating. Accepts phone inquiries. No fee. Hours: M, Sa 2-4:30.

Wenham Historical Association and Museum

132 Main St., Wenham, MA 01984; (617) 468-2377. Acquires, preserves, and interprets collections of historical interest in local history. Museum exhibits large collection of dolls from 1350 B.C., 17th c house with period furnishings, costume collection from 19th c, household instruments and decorations, and Wenham Lake ice cutting tools. Library has materials on early American architecture, biography, and genealogy. Archives hold local history materials from mid-1600s, maps from 1800s, photos, videotapes of local historians discussing local history, and genealogic files on local families. Accepts phone inquiries. Fee. Hours: M-F 11-4, Sa 1-4, Su 2-5.

Westford Historical Society and Museum

P.O. Box 411, 2 Boston Rd., Westford, MA 01886; (617) 692-5550. Studies and preserves Westford history, culture, and artifacts. Museum collection includes items from Revolutionary War through WWII. Other holdings include Westford Academy memorabilia, manuscripts, maps, photos, and films/videotapes. Accepts phone inquiries. No fee. Hours: Su 1-4.

Williams College Library

Sawyer Library, Williamstown, MA 01267; (413) 597-2514. Academic research library with collection of federal documents and maps. On-campus museums include the Williams College Museum of Art, and the Francis and Sterling Clark Museum of Art. Archives preserve college records, photos, genealogical materials, and Chapin rare book collection. Special collections include the Paul Whitman collection of early jazz, the Shaker collection, and Strickland Kneass materials on slavery in the US and the slave trade industry. Accepts phone inquiries. No fee. Hours: M-F 8-5.

Woods Hole Library's Historical Collection

Bradley House Museum, P.O. Box 185, Woods Hole Rd., Woods Hole, MA 02543; (617) 548-7270. Collects and exhibits memorabilia, paintings, photos, and artifacts of local history in museum, library, and archive. Holdings include whaling logs and diaries; drawings of 19th c life, and materials on Coast Guard, transportation, summer visitors, and residents; maps; photos; oral history recordings; and genealogical records. Accepts phone inquiries. Hours: museum, Jun & Sept W-Sa, Jul-Aug Tu-Sa; archives, Tu-W 10-2.

Worcester Art Museum

55 Salisbury St., Worcester, MA 01609; (617) 799-4406. Preserves and exhibits collections of works of art, promotes arts and art education, and provides instruction in fine arts. Holdings include collection of colonial silver; early American portraits; paintings by Copley, Stuart, Inness, Eakins, Cassatt, Homer, Sargent, and Whistler; contemporary works by Franz Kline, Kenneth Noland, Ellsworth Kelly, Louis Nevelson, and David Smith; and large photo and drawing collection. Accepts phone inquiries. Fee. Hours: Tu-F 10-4, Sa 10-5, Su 1-5.

Worcester Historical Museum

30 Elm Street, Worcester, MA 01609; (617) 753-8278. Collects, preserves, and interprets city history. Museum exhibits cover local history. Library holds large collection of manuscripts, maps, photos, and special collection of period clothing. Accepts phone inquiries. Hours: call.

Michigan

Alma College Library

Documents Collection, 614 W. Superior St., Alma, MI 48801; (517) 463-7227. Maintains collection of documents and reference materials relating to college, local, and MI history. Holdings include extensive periodicals and publications collections; college archives from 1886; collections of John Wert Dunning sermons, and Robert D. Swanson papers; USGS maps of MI; US Census of MI records, 1850; collection from Japanese Minister of Foreign Affairs, 1868-1945. Accepts phone inquiries. No fee. Hours: M-Th 8-5, 6:30-9:30; F 8-5; Sa 10-5; Su 6:30-9:30.

Ann Arbor Historic District Commission

312 S. Division, Ann Arbor, MI 48104; (313) 996-3008. Commission creates and administrates historic Ann Arbor, MI districts, and offers general advice on historic preservation practices. Holdings include library with materials on local history, preservation, and museum practice; survey photos and data 1973, 1982; maps relating to local historic buildings. Accepts phone inquiries. No fee. Hours: M-F 9-4.

Archdiocese of Detroit Archives

1234 Washington Blvd., Detroit, MI 48226; (313) 237-5846. Collects and preserves historical documents of Roman Catholic Archdiocese of Detroit. Holdings include reference library; archives with bishops' administrative and personal papers, files of parishes, Archdiocesan Central Offices and Departments, and local Catholic orgs; papers of Fr Gabriel Richard, 1800-1832 and Fr Charles E. Coughlin, 1920s-1945; 18th c parish and city maps; large collection of educational and historical photos, films/videotapes and recordings; church sacramental registers, 1704-1984. Restrictions on use of post-1958 materials. Accepts phone inquiries. No fee. Hours: M-F 8:30-4:30.

Bay County Historial Museum

321 Washington Ave., Bay City, MI 48708; (517) 893-5733. Preserves and researches local history through artifacts and archival holdings. Museum holdings document lumbering, coal mining, shipping, agriculture, business, Salt Wells, and decorative arts. Library has research materials on local history. Archive has extensive materials on residents and business; manuscripts; maps; photos from 1860s; Stover film collection on boat races, water carnivals, and early aviation from 1920-30; commercial and oral history recordings; genealogical records; and Alladin Redi-Cut Homes materials from 1830-1930. Accepts phone inquiries. No fee. Hours: 9-4:30.

Calvin College and Seminary Library

3207 Burton, SE, Grand Rapids, MI 49506; (616) 957-6310. Academic resource center holds archival materials on Christian Reformed Church and Dutch settlements in US and Canada. Holdings include library reference materials, manuscripts, photos, and genealogical materials. Materials non-circulating. Accepts phone inquiries. No fee. Hours: M-Th 8-midnight, F 8-8, Sa 9-8.

Center for Cultural and Natural History

Central Michigan University, 124 Rowe Hall, Mt. Pleasant, MI 48859; (517) 774-3829. Preserves, interprets, and displays natural and cultural history of central MI region, 1880-1940, in form of museum, educational lectures, demonstrations, and tours. Holdings include regional natural history artifacts, reference and slide collections on mammals, birds, insects, reptiles, amphibians, plants, and geology; cultural heritage collections of artifacts from prehistoric MI Indians, pioneers, and 20th c residents. Some restrictions. Accepts phone inquiries. No fee. Hours: Sept-Apr, M-F 8-noon, 1-5; Sa-Su, 1-4.

Central Michigan University Library

Documents Division, Mt. Pleasant, MI 48859; (517) 774-3414. Univ library maintains large collection of US and MI govt documents, and provides access to govt information services. Holdings include demography and population records from 1790; industry and commerce records from 1900; law and jurisprudence documents from 1754; Congressional hearing records from 1958; large collection of USGS, DMA, CIA, Forest Service, and Census Bureau maps from 1958. Accepts phone inquiries. No fee. Hours: M-Th 7:50-midnight, F 7:50-10, Sa 9-10, Su noon-midnight.

Clarke Historical Library

Central Michigan Univeristy, Mt. Pleasant, MI 48859; (517) 774-3352. Library collects and maintains reference materials on history of the univ, MI, and the Great Lakes area. Holdings include publications and manuscripts on regional and African history; archival records of Central Michigan Univ from 1892; maps of MI and Great Lakes region from 17th c, and of Africa from 15th c; photos of MI subjects; collection of 78 rpm jazz recordings; US Census schedules for MI 1790-1910. Accepts phone inquiries. No fee. Hours: M-F 8-5, Sa 9-1.

Commerce Township Area Historical Society

P.O. Box 264, Walled Lake, MI 48088; (313) 363-4396. Society works to preserve history and culture of the Commerce Township, MI area through special events, fund-raisers, travelogues, pioneer oral history collection, and planned museum/cultural center. Accepts phone inquiries. Membership fee. Hours: call.

Coppertown USA

1197 Calumet Ave., Red Jacket Rd., Calumet, MI 49913. Maintains exhibits depicting America's first copper-mining boom and equip used. Museum displays pictures and memorabilia from 1800-1968. Audio/visual materials on mining history, 1913 labor union strike, and underground operations. Fee. Hours: call.

Dearborn Historical Museum

915 Brady St., Dearborn, MI 48124; (313) 565-3000. Collects, preserves, and disseminates historical info on Dearborn and region. Museum, library, and archives contain info from 1928. Holdings include manuscripts from mayor, Henry Dearborn, individual, and orgs; maps from 18th-20th c; photos from Civil War arsenal era; films of city functions from 1940s; oral history interviews; genealogical records; and local newspapers. Accepts phone inquiries. No fee. Hours: M-F 9-5, Sept-June, Sa 1-5.

Detroit Historical Society

5401 Woodward Ave., Detroit, MI 48202; (313) 833-1805. Society maintains four museums (Detroit Historical Museum, Dossin Great Lakes Museum, Historic Fort Wayne, and Moross House) with artifacts relating to history and residents of Detroit, MI region. Accepts phone inquiries about the society and its work (313-833-1664); inquiries about history should be directed to Detroit Public Library's Burton Historical Collection (see entry). Hours: W-Su 9:30-5.

Detroit Public Library

Burton Historical Collection, 5201 Woodward Ave., Detroit, MI 48202; (313) 833-1480. Library maintains collection of materials on history of Detroit, MI, and Old Northwest, and genealogical records relating to most of US. Holdings include large reference collection; Detroit City Archives; manuscripts and photos from Old Northwest, early MI and Detroit; early

US and Canadian maps and atlases; large genealogical record collections; Harwell Sports Collection, and Jones Lincoln Collection. Some restrictions. Accepts phone inquiries. No fee. Hours: M-Tu, Th-Sa 9:30-5:30, W 9-9.

Dossin Great Lakes Museum

100 Strand Drive/Belle Isle, Detroit, MI 48207; (313) 267-6440. Museum documents, preserves, and displays commercial and recreational heritage of the Great Lakes. Holdings include ship models, paintings and other maritime-related artifacts; reference library and archives with vessel records, histories, and relevant materials; Great Lakes navigational charts; films and photos of Great Lakes topics and vessels. Use of library and research collections by appt only. Does not accept phone inquiries. Donations accepted. Hours: W-Su 10-5:30.

East Jordan Portside Art and Historical Museum Society

Rte. 2, M 66 Hwy S., East Jordan, MI 49727; (616) 536-2393. Preserves regional history and artifacts from early 1800s in museum, library, and archives. Holdings include records from early lumber and railroad industries, family histories, war records, historic railroad and hwy maps, photos of lumber industry, oral history interviews, and genealogical records. Accepts phone inquiries. No fee. Hours: Jun-Sept 1-4:30.

Finnish-American Historical Archives

Suomi College, Hancock, MI 49930; (906) 487-7273. Collections emphasize Finnish-American heritage, with other holdings in labor, pioneers, socialism and communism, and temperence movement. Collection contains many manuscripts, photos, oral history recordings, and maps. Accepts phone inquiries. Hours: call.

Flat River Historical Society and Museum

213 N. Franklin St., P.O. Box 188, Greenville, MI 48838; (616) 754-5296. Preserves, collects, and displays history of Montcalm County and portions of Ionia and Kent Counties near the Flat River area of MI in form of museum, library, and archival collections. Holdings cover early settlers, fur traders, farmers, and other residents;

cultural and social artifacts; displays on Flat River lumbering and logging industries; stone wheel from Greenville's first grist mill; library, archives, manuscripts, maps, photos, films/videotapes, recordings, and genealogical records of regional history. Accepts phone inquiries. No fee. Museum Hours: Apr-Oct, Su 2-4 or by appt.

Fort Saint Joseph Historical Association

508 E. Main St., Niles, MI 49120; (616) 683-4702. Preserves and studies history and culture of 18th c fur trading outpost Ft St. Joseph and surrounding Four Flags area. Museum covers local history with collection of ft artifacts, Sioux artwork, and autobiographical pictographs of Sitting Bull and Rain-in-the-Face. Library documents local history from 1660-1800 with collections of manuscripts and photos. Accepts phone inquiries. No fee. Hours: Tu-Sa 10-4, Su 1-4.

Frankenmuth Historical Museum

613 S. Main, Frankenmuth, MI 48734; (517) 652-9701. Preserves and displays history of Frankenmuth, MI area with emphasis on the four German-Lutheran (Chippewa Indian) mission settlements. Holdings include artifacts from 1845; library with Saginaw County histories, and local reference materials from 1830; archives of Frankemuth Historical Assn from 1863; family and business papers from 1840s; local maps and atlases of area, missions and Ansbach (German) district; photos; oral history tapes including recording of reunion of a Mustang fighter plane crew; genealogical records of local (mostly German) families. Accepts phone inquiries. Fee. Hours: museum: M-F varies by season, Sa 10:30-5, Su 12:30-5; office: M-F 9-5.

General Motors Research Laboratories Library

General Motors Technical Center, Warren, MI 48090; (313) 986-3314. Documents automobile development in 20th c through oral history project interviews with friends and co-workers of inventor Charles Kettering. Materials available to serious researchers. Accepts phone inquiries. Hours: call.

Genessee Historical Collections

University of Michigan-Flint Library, Flint, MI

48502; (313) 762-3418. Center collects and preserves materials on the history of univ and Flint and Genesee County, MI. Holdings include county histories and atlases; local and county history volumes; maps and photos; univ archives from 1955; records of Junior League of Flint from 1929; A.G. Bishop Papers, 1879-1972, and Orlo L. Crissey Papers, 1944-75. Accepts phone inquiries. No fee. Hours: M, Tu, F 11-5; W, Th 1-10; Sa 1-4:45.

Gerald R. Ford Museum

303 Pearl St., NW, Grand Rapids, MI 49504; (616) 456-2675. Collects and presents the life and times of U.S. President Gerald R. Ford in form of artifacts, memorabilia, and bicentennial collection. Accepts phone inquiries. Fee. Hours: M-Sa 9-4:45, Su noon-4:45.

Grand Blanc Heritage Association

203 E. Grand Blanc Rd., Grand Blanc, MI 48439; (313) 694-7274. Preserves history of Grand Blanc, MI area and residents in form of museum, small library, and archival collections. Holdings include early artifacts; family histories, photos, scrapbooks, and diaries; business, family and Civil War records; plat maps; oral histories; Genesee County, MI census, 1850-1910; Grand Blanc High School yearbooks. Accepts phone inquiries. Donations accepted. Hours: W 10-2 or by appt.

Grand Pacific House Museum

New Baltimore Historical Society, 51065 Washington, New Baltimore, MI 48047; (313) 725-7987. Preserves and makes available artifacts and archival material related to Anchor Bay area, especially New Baltimore. House museum is under renovation. Library and archives have small collection of materials on MI, including maps, photos, limited oral histories, and genealogical records. Accepts phone inquiries. Donations accepted. Hours: W noon-4, Sa 10-2, and 4th Su of month, noon-4.

Grand Rapids Public Museum

54 Jefferson Ave., SE, Grand Rapids, MI 49503; (616) 456-3971. Preserves, interprets, and displays natural and cultural history of Grand Rapids and western MI area. Holdings include artifacts and large collection of 19th c American-made furniture; archives with records of local events, people, and furniture manufacturing industry; large photo collection. Accepts phone inquiries. Fee. Hours: M-F 10-5, Sa 11-5, Su 1-5.

Grand Valley State University

Document Dept., Zumberge Library, Allendale, MI 49401; (616) 895-3252. Univ library maintains selective collection of govt documents, general and historical materials relevant to needs of school. Holdings include univ archives; USGS topographic maps; regional historical collections with manuscripts and photos. Some restrictions. Accepts phone inquiries. No fee. Hours: M-Th 8-midnight, F 8-6, Sa 12:30-9, Su 1-midnight.

Grosse Ile Historical Society

P.O. Box 131, East River Rd. and Parway, Grosse Ile, MI 48138. Preserves and promotes history of Grosse Ile, MI and residents through museum, archives, preservation efforts, and special events. Holdings include clothing, military relics, tools, farm implements, furniture, and other artifacts; archival records of residents and Island history. Does not accept phone inquiries. Donations accepted. Hours: Apr-Dec, Th 10-noon, Su 1-4.

Hackley Public Library

Documents Division, 316 W. Webster Ave., Muskegon, MI 49440; (616) 722-7276. Public library maintains selective collections of US, state and local govt documents, general and historical materials relevant to community. Holdings include reference materials on Indian life and culture; photos of Muskegon area industry, culture, and residents, late 19th-mid 20th c; Michigan census, 1820-1910; genealogical materials with emphasis on New England area and Midwest. Accepts phone inquiries. No fee. Hours: Tu-Th 8:30-8, F 8:30-6, Sa 9-5; summer hours vary.

Henry Ford Estate—Fair Lane

Evergreen Rd., Dearborn, MI 48128; (313) 593-5590. Restores and maintains final home of Henry and Clara Ford, and educates general public on life of Fords. Museum/home and personal library of Henry Ford I relates history of Ford family. On-site 1915 powerhouse was designed with help of Thomas Edison. Accepts phone inquiries. Fee. Hours: May-Sept, Su 1-4:30.

Heritage Hill Association

126 College, SE, Grand Rapids, MI 49503; (616) 459-8950. Preserves community heritage and records of district structures. Holdings include maps of Heritage Hill historic district and Grand Rapids, and photos of bldgs from 1969. Accepts phone inquiries. No fee. Hours: M-F 9-5.

Historic Fort Wayne

6325 W. Jefferson, Detroit, MI 48209; (313) 297-9360. Preserves and interprets military history of Civil War era ft and Detroit area and residents in form of restored ft and related bldgs, and Great Lakes Indian Museum. Holdings include restored Commanding Officer's House c. 1880s; restored Barracks, 1701-1890s; Tuskegee Airmen collection of black WW II flyers' artifacts and history; artifacts of Woodland Indian culture and lifestyles; small reference library; maps of ft from 1840s; photos of ft from Civil War. Accepts phone inquiries. Fee. Hours: May-Labor Day, W-Su 9:30-5.

Historical Society of Michigan

2117 Washtenaw Ave., Ann Arbor, MI 48104; (313) 769-1828. Org preserves and promotes history of MI and residents through publications, conferences, and travel programs. Accepts phone inquiries. Membership fee. Hours: call.

Historical Society of Saginaw County

County Castle Bldg., 500 Federal Ave., P.O. Box 390, Saginaw, MI 48606; (517) 752-2861. Collects, preserves, and promotes history of Saginaw County, MI and residents through special events, museum, library, and archival collections. Holdings include historical and archaeological artifacts and displays; reference collection on museology, and living and local history; local maps and oral histories; large photo collection. Accepts phone inquiries. Fee. Hours: M-Sa 10-4:30, Su 1-4.

Houghton County Historical Society

Lock Box D, Hwy M-26, Lake Linden, MI 49945; (906) 482-6353. Preserves history of

regional copper mining industry and lifestyle of original settlers. Museum houses exhibits in bridal room, mining room, kitchen, and medical room describing local history. Photo collection on regional copper mining from 1900. Accepts phone inquiries. No fee. Hours: May-Oct 9:30-4:30.

Hoyt Public Library

Document Depository, 505 Janes St., Saginaw, MI 48605; (517) 755-0904. Public library maintains selective collection of govt documents, and general and historical materials. Holdings include selected US govt documents from late 19th c, including Bureau of Ethnology Reports, Congressional Record from 1880, Patent Gazette from 1874, Statistical Abstract from 1894, Public Health Reports from 1900, Census materials from 1870, and Vital Statistics from 1900; genealogical records relating MI families of Germanic, Polish, other Slavic, and Afro-American descent. Accepts phone inquiries. No fee. Hours: M-Th 9-9, F-Sa 9-5, Su (Oct-Apr) 1-5.

Iron County Historical and Museum Society

Museum Rd., Iron River, MI 49935; (906) 265-2617 (winter: 3942). (Winter mailing address: 233 Bernhardt Rd, Iron River, MI 49935; summer mailing address: Box 272, Caspari, MI 49915) Society preserves history of Iron County, MI and residents through museum and archival collections. Holdings include miniature logging camp exhibit and other displays on local logging, mining, and cultural history, 1880-1920; local newspapers, reference materials, logging records, and local historical manuscripts; large collections of mining maps and local photos; genealogical records of residents; Carrie Jacobs-Bond photographs and letters. Accepts phone inquiries. Fee. Hours: May-Oct, M-Sa 9-5, Su; Nov-Apr, by appt.

Isle Royal National Park

87 N. Ripley St., Houghton, MI 49931; (906) 482-0986. National Park on Lake Superior Island preserves natural habitat, and several historic or cultural sites, including lighthouses, shipwrecks, a commercial fishery, and an early mine, most of which were built by Scandinavian immigrants. Holdings include restored Edison

Fishery complex (1900-1940s) with original furnishings and tools; small library with Park Service references, local field guides and history books; archives with manuscripts and other documents; 1847 survey maps and early Park Service master plans for park; photos, oral history tapes, and genealogical records. Some restrictions. Accepts phone inquiries. Fee. Hours: M-F 8:30-5.

Jesse Besser Museum

491 Johnson St., Alpena, MI 49707; (517) 356-2202. Museum of science, art, and history relating to MI and Great Lakes history. Museum exhibits cover early man, lumbering and farming, restored historic bldgs, and fossils from northeast MI. Library reference materials on region. Archives contain photos of Alpena area, manuscripts, maps from 1669-1874, limited films/videotapes, recordings, genealogical records, and local arts and crafts. Accepts phone inquiries. No fee. Hours: M-W, F 10-5, Th 10-9, Sa-Su noon-5.

Kalamazoo Public Museum

315 S. Rose St., Kalamazoo, MI 49007; (616) 345-7092. Preserves and displays world history, culture, and technology, with emphasis on Kalamazoo, MI and residents. Holdings include artifacts and displays with emphasis on Kalamazoo and Egypt from prehistoric times; large collection of manuscripts, records, photos, stereographs, and postcards of Kalamazoo, Kalamazoo County, and Southwest MI; Edna Earle doll collection; Winslow family collection; Native American basket collection; Harrison log cabin artifact collection; Stark pewter collection; A.M. Todd collection. Some restrictions; research facilities closed on weekends. Accepts phone inquiries but prefers written inquiries. Fee. Hours: 9-5.

Kimball House Museum

Historical Society of Battle Creek, 196 Capital Ave., NE, Battle Creek, MI 49017; (616) 965-2613. Preserves local history through exhibits and collections in restored Victorian house museum. Library as small collections from local authors. Archives holds collection of Battle Creek area papers, maps, family pictures, genealogical records, and some land contracts. Restrictions

on use. Accepts phone inquiries. No fee. Hours: Tu, Th 1-4:30.

Labadie Collection

University of Michigan, 711 Hatcher Library, Ann Arbor, MI 48109; (313) 764-9377. Academic research library maintains materials on worldwide left, right, and political alternative groups from 1870s. Holdings cover anarchist and labor history, as well as some gay, lesbian, feminist, and ethnic materials. Collection composed of records, tapes, ephemera, and microforms. Archives of American Committee for Protection of Foreign Born, California Labor School, and Sunrise Cooperative Community also in storage. Accepts phone inquiries. Hours: call.

Labor and Urban Affairs Archives

Wayne State University, Walter P. Reuther Library, Detroit, MI 48202; (313) 577-4024. Collects and preserves reference materials on history of American labor unions, social reform, and urban affairs in form of library, archives, and special file collections. Holdings include large collection of research publications, serials, and vertical files on subject matter; archives with documents and records from 1890s, with emphasis on 1930s and 40s; large collections of photos, films/videotapes, and recordings; inactive files of UAW, AFSCME, AFT, Newspaper Guild, Air Line Pilots, Flight Attendants, United Farm Workers, IWW, and CIO. Use by qualified researchers only. Accepts phone inquiries. No fee. Hours: M-F 9-5.

Lake Michigan Maritime Museum

P.O. Box 534, Dyckman Ave. at Bridge, South Haven, MI 49090; (616) 637-8078. Museum of Great Lakes research, preservation, conservation, and education on maritime trades and regional environment. Museum exhibits show lives of Great Lakes boat builders and sailors. Library holds materials on boatbuilding, navigation, maritime activities, commercial fishing, shipping, and lifesaving. Archives hold logs, letters, papers from lighthousekeeper Capt. James Donahue, maps, photos of maritime trades, films/videotapes on maritime and environment, oral histories from Great Lakes lighthousekeepers, and artifacts from archaeological study of shipwreck. Accepts phone inquiries. Fee. Hours: May-Oct, Tu-Su 10-5; Nov-Apr, Tues-Sa 10-4.

Le Sault de Ste. Marie Historical Sites

P.O. Box 1668, Johnston and Water Streets, Sault Ste. Marie, MI 49783; (906) 635-1114. Preserves, interprets, and promotes history of the St Mary's River Systems and Great Lakes Region. Holdings include museum with artifacts and displays on Great Lakes maritime history and transportation, Native Americans, and local historic homes; archives with photos and documents on local history and the Great Lakes; ships' logs. Accepts phone inquiries (906-635-3658). Fee. Hours: May 15-June, Sept-Oct 15, 10-6; July-Aug 9-9.

Madison Heights Public Library

Document Dept., 240 W. Thirteen Mile Rd., Madison Heights, MI 48071; (313) 588-7763. Public library maintains selected collection of govt documents, and general and historical materials relevant to needs of community. Holdings include Madison Heights Historical Collection. Accepts phone inquiries. No fee. Hours: M, Tu, Th 9-9; W, F, Sa 9-5.

Marine Historical Society of Detroit

29825 Joy Rd., Westland, MI 48185; (313) 421-6130. Society preserves and promotes the history of Great Lakes shipping in form of small library and large photo archives. Some restrictions. Accepts phone inquiries. No fee. Hours: call.

Marquette County Historical Society

213 N. Front St., Marquette, MI 49855; (906) 226-3571. Collects and preserves history of the Upper Peninsula and Marquette County, MI in form of museum, library, and archival collections. Holdings include dioramas and exhibits on regional life from prehistoric Copper Culture; research library with rare books, manuscripts, photos, and biographical files; archives with business, census and other local records; large collection of local industrial and geological maps from 1850s; videotapes and oral history recordings; family histories, city directories and cemetery files; Burt, Kaufman & Bretung, Longyear, and Spear collections. Some restrictions. Accepts

phone inquiries. Fee. Hours: M-F 9-4:30, Sa 11-3.

Mason County Historical Society

1687 S. Lakeshore Dr., Ludington, MI 49431; (616) 843-2001. Collects and preserves history of Mason County and MI in form of Rose Hawley Museum and White Pine Village. Holdings include artifacts and exhibits, library, archives, maps, photos, films/videotapes, recordings, and some genealogical records. Fee for village. Accepts phone inquiries (616-843-4808). Hours: museum: M-F 9:30-4:30; village: Tu-Su, 11-5.

Michigan Archaeological Society

P.O. Box 359, Saginaw, MI 48606. Society preserves, documents, and publishes information on MI archaeological sites. Publications include the quarterly journal "The Michigan Archeologist." Does not accept phone inquiries.

Michigan Historical Collections

Bentley Historical Library, University of Michigan, 1150 Beal Ave., Ann Arbor, MI 48109; (313) 764-3482. Univ library collections preserve history of school and MI in form of reference materials, archives, manuscripts, maps, photos, films/videotapes, recordings, and genealogical records. Subjects documented include politics, public policy, the military, transportation, religion, education, and local and family histories. Collections are non-circulating, and there are some restrictions on use. Accepts phone inquiries. No fee. Hours: M-F 8:30-5, Sa 9-12:30; closed Sa during summer.

Michigan Historical Museum

208 N. Capital, Lansing, MI 48918; (517) 373-3359. New state museum scheduled to open in December of 1988. Exhibits will cover all aspects of MI human history from prehistoric times. May be some restrictions. Accepts phone inquiries. No fee. Hours: M-F 9:30-4:30, Sa noon-4:30.

Michigan State University

Documents Library, East Lansing, MI 48824; (517) 353-8707. Academic library has selective collection of US govt documents, including US Congressional Serial Set from 1789, Foreign

Relations of the US documents from 1888, and Census volumes from 1799. Non-circulating except to college community. Accepts brief phone inquiries. No fee. Hours: 8-5, 7-10.

Michigan State University Archives

University Archives and Historical Collections, Main Library Building, EG-13, East Lansing, MI 48824; (517) 355-2330. Maintains collection of records, documents, and historical materials relevant to the history of the univ, the state, and needs of students and school community. Holdings include univ records from 1850; Samaritan Manuscripts, 1470-1928; Land Grant Research Collection, 1774-1954; oral history collection; historical manuscripts, 18th-20th c; historical photo collection; state, US and intl maps; large collection of scrapbooks and photo albums; and materials from American left and right from 1900, New Left from 1969-70, and alternative lifestyle groups. Some restrictions. Accepts phone inquiries. No fee. Hours: M-F 8-noon, 1-5.

Michigan State University Libraries

Special Collections, East Lansing, MI 48824; (517) 355-3770. Academic research library contains materials from radical political and social orgs, including US Communist Party from 1918-60. Materials also cover Vietnam era, gays, feminists, Native Americans, blacks, and Chicano liberation movement materials. Accepts phone inquiries. Hours: call.

Midland County Historical Society

1801 W. St. Andrews Dr., Midland, MI 48640; (517) 835-7401. Collects and preserve history of Midland County, MI area and residents in form of museum, library, and archival collections. Holdings include restored period rooms and buildings; quilts, coverlets, furniture, clothing, and tools; reference collection; extensive photo and slide archives; local maps from 1897; genealogical records. Research or museum tours by appt. Accepts phone inquiries. Fee for museum tour. Hours: M-F 9-5, Sa-Su 1-5.

Monroe County Library System

Documents Division, 3700 S. Custer Rd., Monroe, MI 48161; (313) 241-5277. Public library preserves Monroe county, MI, OH, and

TN genealogical records, as well as cemetery indexes, county histories, and village archives. Special collection of George Custer materials, including books, pamphlets, newspapers, photos, manuscripts, maps, videos, and memorabilia on Custer and his time. Accepts phone inquiries. Fee for non-resident borrowers. Hours: M-Th 9-9, F 9-5, Sa 10-5; Custer collection by appt.

Muskegon County Museum

430 W. Clay Ave., Muskegon, MI 49440; (616) 728-4119. Collects, preserves, and exhibits area cultural and natural history. Museum exhibits cover Indians and fur trade, medicine, and local history. Library and archives hold manuscripts, maps, photos, films/videotapes, and genealogical materials relating to local history. Special collection on lumbering. Accepts phone inquiries. No fee. Hours: M-F 9:30-4:30, Sa-Su 12:30-4:30.

National Hamiltonian Party Library

3314 Dillon Rd., Flushing, MI 48433. Collects materials on life and works of Alexander Hamilton, and has special Kelly collection of over 10 thousand pieces of American politician memorabilia, presidential materials, materials on presidential hopefuls of major and minor parties, and research collection on women, minorities, and families in politics.

Netherlands Museum

Holland Historical Trust, City Hall, 8 E. 12th St., Holland, MI 49423; (616) 394-1362. Collects, preserves, interprets, and displays Dutch heritage and history of Holland, MI area and residents. Holdings include extensive collection of memorabilia from Old and New World Dutch life; library with related reference works in English and Dutch; archives with clippings, letters, city records; collection of pioneer correspondences and memoirs; photos of local subjects from 1870s; maps and genealogical records; Dutch recordings; collection of postcards with images of town and Netherlands. Accepts phone inquiries (museum: 616-392-9084). Fee. Hours: summer, 9-5; Jan-Mar, Th, F, Sa 1-4.

Northeastern Michigan Genealogical Society

c/o Jesse Besser Museum, 491 Johnson St.,

Alpena, MI 49707; (517) 356-2202. Society preserves art, science, and history of northeastern MI and residents in form of museum, library, and archival collections. Holdings include artifacts and exhibits; library with local and regional historical references; archives, manuscripts, films/videotapes, recordings, and genealogical records; maps of Great Lakes from 1640s and region; photos from 1800s. Collections are noncirculating. Accepts phone inquiries. Donations accepted. Hours: M-W, F 10-5, Th 10-9, Sa-Su noon-5.

Northern Michigan University

Olson Library, Marquette, MI 49855; (906) 227-2112. Academic research library has collection of Early and Colonial American biographies and writings. Holdings cover Ben Franklin, John Adams, John Jay, Thomas Jefferson, and Charles Sumner. Accepts phone inquiries. No fee. Also holds personal library of Moses Coit Tyler. Accepts phone inquiries. No fee. Hours: call.

Northwestern Michigan College

Mark Osterlin Library, 1701 East Front St., Traverse City, MI 49684; (616) 922-1065. Community college library maintains collection of general and historical materials relevant to the needs of the school and community. Holdings include Michigan History and Literature Collection; Governor Milliken Collection (films/videotapes and recordings, 1970-82); genealogical reference materials; area newspapers from 1860; local govt, org, and business records from 1880. Accepts phone inquiries. No fee. Hours: M-Th 8-10, F 8-5, Sa 9-4, Su 1-5.

Oakland County Pioneer and Historical Society

405 Oakland Ave., Pontiac, MI 48058; (313) 338-6732. Preserves and maintains history of county. Museum consists of 1860 house with period outbldgs. Library has materials relating to genealogical, architectural, and historical topics. Holdings include manuscripts, maps, photos, films/videotapes, and recordings. Accepts phone inquiries. Fee. Hours: M-F 9-4.

Oakland University

Kresge Library, Walton and Squirrel Rds., Rochester, MI 48309; (313) 370-2476. Univ library maintains selective collection of govt documents, and general, historical, archival, and special collections relevant to the school and community. Holdings include univ archives from 1957; large collection of univ photos; large collections of films/videotapes and recordings; county and local historical and genealogical materials, including Oakland County Tax Records 1860-1890; Springer Collection on Civil War, underground newspapers of MI and Midwest, and Hicks Collection of materials by and about women. Accepts phone inquiries. No fee. Hours: M-F 8-5.

Olivet College

Burrage Library, Olivet, MI 49076; (616) 749-7608. Preserves collection of arctic and antarctic voyage logs and reports from earliest times to mid-20th c. Accepts phone inquiries. Hours: call.

Plymouth Historical Society

155 S. Main St., Plymouth, MI 48170; (313) 455-8940. Preserves and promotes understanding of the history of Plymouth, MI and residents in form of museum and archival collections. Holdings include artifacts and exhibits, 1825-1925; archives with materials on local history, the 24th Michigan Civil War Regiment, and genealogy; local maps from 1825; newspapers, 1887-1958. Accepts phone inquiries. Fee. Hours: M-F 9-4, Sa-Su 1-4.

Polish Genealogical Society of Michigan

Burton Historical Collection, Detroit Public Library, 5201 Woodward Ave., Detroit, MI 48202. Society preserves research materials and promotes interest in Polish genealogy through meetings, publications, archives collection, and genealogical research assistance. Holdings include archives (part of the Burton Historical Collection) with manuscripts, documents, and records relating to Polish family histories; ancestor surname book and other reference publications. Does not accept phone inquiries. Membership fee.

Pontiac Area Historical and Genealogical Society

P.O. Box 901St., 60 E. Pike (lower level), Pontiac, MI 48058. Preserves and researches family histories through library of historical and genealogical works. No fee. Hours: 2nd Th of each month.

Port Huron Museum of Arts and History

1115 6th St., Port Huron, MI 48060; (313) 982-0891. Museum preserves culture and history of Port Huron and St. Clair County, MI and residents in form of museum, library, and archival collections. Holdings include artifacts and exhibits on local history, Great Lakes marine lore, fine and decorative arts, prehistoric Woodlands Indians; small reference library; archives with manuscripts and documents from mid-19th c-mid-20th c; small collection of oral history films/videotapes; photos; cemetery and tax records; archaeological artifacts from prehistoric Draper Park, historic Ft Gratiot, Thomas Edison homesite. Use of archives by appt only. Accepts phone inquiries. No fee. Hours: M-F 8:30-4:30.

Quincy Mine Hoist Association

P.O. Box 265, Hancock, MI 40993; (906) 482-1001. Assn preserves history of mining industry in form of museum filled with mining equipment and artifacts. Accepts phone inquiries. Fee. Hours: 8:30-noon, 1-3:30.

R.E. Olds Transportation Museum

240 Museum Dr., Lansing, MI 48933; (517) 372-0422. Museum preserves and highlights the region's history and contributions to transportation industry from 1836, with emphasis on Oldsmobile products. Holdings include artifacts and exhibits; archives with business papers, product information, manufacturing, and technology related reference materials; small collection of personal diaries and manuscripts; Lauzen Family collection of Reo photos; Oldsmobile product photos and 1950s training films; films/videotapes; Oldsmobile Collection; Bates & Edmonds Motor Company Collection. Accepts phone inquiries. Fee for non-members. Hours: Tu-F 9:30-5; Sa-Su noon-5.

Royal Oak Public Library

Documents Dept., 222 East 11 Mile Rd., Royal Oak, MI 48067; (313) 541-1470. Public library maintains selected collection of govt documents

and general and historical materials. Holdings include collections of Royal Oak historical materials; local newspaper editions from 1877. Accepts phone inquiries. No fee. Hours: M, Tu, Th 10-9, W, F, Sa 10-6.

Saint Clair County Library

Document Dept., 210 McMorran Boulevard, Port Huron, MI 48060; (313) 987-7323. Public library maintains selective collection of govt documents, general and historical materials relevant to needs of community. Holdings include county and local records and histories; county plat atlases, 1859, 76, 97, and 1916, and state and local 20th c maps; photos; local newspaper archives from 19th c; censuses of numerous MI counties, 1845 and 84; state census of 1894; bicentennial oral history tape recordings; DAR lineage books; MI Civil War records. Some restrictions. Accepts phone inquiries. No fee. Hours: M-F 9-9, Sa 9-5:30.

School of Music Library

University of Michigan, Moore Bldg., Ann Arbor, MI 48109. Holds collection of music by women composers from 1750-1950. Includes work associated with Dame Ethel Smyth and small collection of letters by women musicians.

Teysen's Woodland Indian Museum

P.O. Box 399, 416 S. Huron, Mackinaw City, MI 49701; (616) 436-7011. Preserves and displays history and culture of Great Lakes Woodland Indians, 8000 B.C.-1900 A.D., and history of area logging and marine industries. Holdings include tools, clothing, equipment, weapons, foods and other Indian relics; artifacts relating to logging industry of 1900; Great Lakes shipwreck artifacts; letters and literature of Edgar Conkling (founder of Mackinaw City, MI); original plot map of city, 1857; photos of logging, shipping, and local history; collection of 18th and 19th c muskets; local newspaper copies, 1880-1890s. Accepts phone inquiries. Fee. Hours: May-Sept 9-10.

Thomas Edison Institute Henry Ford Museum

Greenfield Village, P.O. Box 1970, Oakwood Blvd., Dearborn, MI 48121; (313) 271-1620. Preserves and collects materials on automotive industry and Henry Ford. Archives and research library hold automotive literature, McGuffey readers, trade catalogs, manuscripts, maps, and photos. Accepts phone inquiries. No fee. Hours: call.

Tri-Cities Museum

P.O. Box 234, 1 N. Harbor, Grand Haven, MI 49417; (616) 842-0700. Collects, preserves, and displays history of Grand Haven, Spring Lake, and Ferrysburg, MI in form of artifacts, exhibits, library, archives, manuscripts, maps, photos, genealogical records, and special collections. Archival material is non-circulating. Accepts phone inquiries. Donations accepted. Hours: June-Aug, Tu-Su 10-10; May, Sept-Oct, Sa-Su 2-5.

Troy Historical Society and Museum

60 W. Wattles Rd., Troy, MI 48098; (313) 524-3570. Preserves history of early Troy and surrounding area. Museum represents Troy twnshp history from 1820-1900, including town settlement. Archives hold town records, manuscripts, photos, and limited oral histories. Accepts phone inquiries. No fee. Hours: Tu-Sa 9-5:30, Su 1-5.

University of Michigan

William Clements Library, Ann Arbor, MI 48109; (313) 764-2347. Library concentrates on US history from discovery period into late 19th c. Materials cover Revolution, antislavery, discovery and exploration of US, American Indians, Civil War, and War of 1812. Research collections focus on Columbus, Paine, Franklin, Washington, Jefferson, and Federalist papers. Holdings include manuscripts, newspapers, extensive map collection, large sheet music collection, and prints. Other holdings include materials on polar explorer Robert Peary, scholar William Hobbs, and others in form of journals, radio logs, reports, and documents. Hours: M-F 10:30-noon, 1-5.

University of Michigan

Documents Center, Harlan Hatcher Graduate Library, Ann Arbor, MI 48109; (313) 764-0410. Library maintains large research collection of US and MI documents. Holdings include complete Serial Set, extensive US history reference collection, and large map and atlas collection. Mainly for use by univ students and faculty.

Accepts phone inquiries. No fee. Hours: M-F 10-noon, 1-5; Sa noon-4.

Western Michigan University

Archives and Regional History Collections, Kalamazoo, MI 49008; (616) 383-1826. Collects, manages, and preserves historical records of the univ and southwestern MI. Holdings include library; univ archives from 1903; regional historical family, church, and business papers; maps of MI; photos, films/videotapes, and oral history recordings of region and univ; C.C. Adams Papers, Caroline Bartlett Crane Papers, Stanley Barney Smith Collection, and Philo Dibble Family Papers. Does not accept phone inquiries. No fee. Hours: M-F 7:45-5.

Western Michigan University

Documents Dept., Dwight B. Waldo Library, Kalamazoo, MI 49008; (616) 383-1435. Maintains selective collection of US and MI documents from 1963. Holdings include complete run of the Congressional Record and its predecessors; microprint collection of the Serial Set, 1789-1891; large collection of 20th c topography and geology maps. Some restrictions. Accepts phone inquiries. No fee. Hours: M-Th 8-midnight, F 8-6, Sa 10-6, Su noon-midnight.

Minnesota

Alexander Ramsey House

Minnesota Historical Society, 265 S. Exchange St., St. Paul, MN 55102; (612) 296-8760. Promotes understanding of historic site and its place in American, regional, and MN history. House museum was home of Alexander Ramsey, first territorial gov of MN, Gov of MN, and Secty of War under Pres Hayes. House is restored and furnished with original family pieces. Accepts phone inquiries. Fee. Hours: Tu-F 10-4, Sa-Su 1-4:30.

American Swedish Institute

2600 Park Ave., Minneapolis, MN 55407; (612) 871-4907. Preserves, collects, and interprets Swedish-American experience in Upper Midwest. Museum exhibits art, decorative arts, and historic artifacts; the research library collects records, family histories, and all American Swedish Institute newpaper publications; some historic photos; and small film/videotape library on Swedish and Swedish-American subjects. Accepts phone inquiries. Fee. Hours: Tu-Sa 12-4, Su 1-5.

Anoka County Historical Society

1900 3rd Ave., S, Anoka, MN 55303; (612) 421-0600. Gathers, preserves, and disseminates historical info on Anoka county. Museum in restored home with period furnishings, and displays on Anoka blacksmithing, logging, and farming from 1850s; small library on county history, genealogy, and atlases; photo collection covers transportation, rivers, churches, schools, and govt; and oral history interviews on early Anoka life. Restrictions on use. Donations accepted. Hours: Tu-F 12:30-4.

Bakken Library and Museum of Electricity in Life

3537 Zenith Ave., S, Minneapolis, MN 55416; (612) 927-6508. Collects books, instruments, and archival materials to further historical understanding and applications of electromagnetism. Museum houses exhibits of electrotherapeutic equipment, 18th c electrical machines, 19th c physiological devices; library focuses on historical role of electricity and magnetism in medicine and life sciences; small manuscript collection, including Ben Franklin's scientific publications; and trade catalogs of eletrical, medical, and electrotherapeutic devices from 1875-1930. Materials non-circulating. Accepts phone inquiries. Donations accepted. Hours: M-F 9-5.

Becker County Historical Society

Courthouse, 915 Lake Ave., Detroit Lakes, MN 56501; (218) 847-2938. Preserves county history, artifacts, and genealogy records, and sponsors educational projects. Museum holds extensive collections on Ojibwa Indians, pioneer life, and Civil War uniforms and memorabilia; small library; archival govt and civic records; manuscripts on Indian trade and railroads from 1880s; maps and atlases; oral history interviews, genealogical records from 1870s; newspapers from 1870s; and collection of archaeological materials. Accepts phone inquiries. No fee. Hours: M-F 8:30-4:30.

Bemidji State University

Documents Division, Clark Library, 1500 Birchmont Dr., NE, Bemidji, MN 56601; (218) 755-2955. Academic research facility with emphasis on govt documents, univ archives, North Central MN history, federal depository maps, and a special collection of published materials on Ojibwa and Native American Indian tribes. Materials do not circulate outside University community. Accepts phone inquiries (218-755-3342). Hours: M-Th 8-9:45, F 8-3:45, Sa 9-4:45, and Su 1-8:45.

Blue Earth County Historical Society

606 Broad St., Mankato, MN 56001; (507) 345-4154. Collects, preserves, and exhibits materials on county history. Museum displays many material culture exhibits; library holds newspapers, published histories, and directories; collections of maps and photos; some oral history interviews and genealogical records; and films/videotapes. Accepts phone inquiries. No fee. Hours: Tu-F 1-5.

Brown County Historical Society

P.O. Box 116, 2 North Broadway, New Ulm, MN 56073; (507) 354-2016. Collects, preserves, and makes available materials on history of county. Museum displays Native American artifacts and settler's tools and household items. Library has large reference section. Archives contain family and business files from 1850s, materials on Dakota War of 1862, maps, photos, and genealogical materials. Materials non-circulating. Accepts phone inquiries. No fee. Hours: M-Sa 1-5.

Canal Park Marine Museum

US Army Corps of Engineers, Detroit District, Canal Park, Duluth, MN 55802; (218) 727-2497. Preserves history of maritime commerce in Lake Superior region. Museum houses materials on commercial Great Lake navigation from 1812, development of harbors, and Corps of Engineers history; library retains extensive ship file collection, many ship photos and much on port development; navigation and harbor charts; and special collection of shipbuilding tools and artifacts from WW II era. Accepts phone inquiries. No fee. Hours: summer, 10-9; spring & fall, 10-6; winter, F-Su 10-4:30.

Carleton College Library

Documents Dept., One North College St., Northfield, MN 55057; (507) 663-4266. Serves college's academic research needs with collections of govt documents and USGS maps. Materials for in-house use only. Accepts phone inquiries. No fee. Hours: 8-5.

Central Minnesota Historical Center

Saint Cloud State University, Room 14-B, Centennial Hall, Saint Cloud, MN 56301; (612) 255-3254. Collects, organizes, and preserves central MN state history records. Manuscript collections include legislators' papers, civic and governmentt records, and labor union materials from late 19th and early 20th c. Center preserves some survey maps and plat books; photos of political figures and some area scenes; oral history interviews with legislators, church leaders, businessmen, and older residents; and Works Project Administration county biographical sketches and personal papers. Materials for in-house use only. Accepts phone inquiries. No fee. Hours: call.

Chippewa County Historical Society

P.O. Box 303, Jct. Hwy 7 & 59, Montevideo, MN 56222; (612) 269-7636. Preserves, collects, and exhibits materials on Chippewa County history. Museum village furnished with artifacts from 1880-1920; small library documents state and local history; and photo collection on historical subjects. Some restrictions on use. Accepts phone inquiries. Fee. Hours: by appt, M-F 9-5.

Clay County Historical Society

Box 501, 202 First Avenue North, Moorhead, MN 56560; (218) 233-4604. Preserves, collects, and disseminates county history. Museum focuses on individual town histories in county from 1860-1970. Library maintains small collection of local and regional history materials, manuscripts, maps, large colletion of photos from 1879, film from 1917, and genealogical materials. Accepts phone inquiries. Fee. Hours: M-F 8:30-5.

Dakota County Historical Society

130 3rd Ave., N, South St. Paul, MN 55075; (612) 451-6260. Collects, preserves, and exhibits county history through maps, photos, oral histories, genealogies, and govt records. Small library holds some state and regional histories, newspapers, and state and federal census records. Some restrictions on use. No fee. Hours: Tu, W, F 9-5, Th 9-8, Sa 10-3.

Douglas County Historical Society

P.O. Box 805, 1219 South Nokomis, Alexandria, MN 56308; (612) 762-0382. Preserves and exhibits local history through collections of manuscripts, plat books, photos, oral history tapes on Depression and WWII, genealogical records, and indexed newspapers from 1875-1926. Accepts phone inquiries. No fee. Hours: M-F 8-4:30.

Evangelical Lutheran Synod

Department of Archives and History, Bethany Lutheran College, 734 Marsh St., Mankato, MN 56001; (507) 388-5969. Preserves history of Synod, Bethany Lutheran College, and Bethany Lutheran Seminary through 19th c holdings in museum, library, and archives. Museum houses furnishings, pictures, and artifacts; archives hold records of church officers, boards, committees, congregations, and individuals connected with Synod and College; manuscript collection includes official correspondence, essays, sermons, and histories; photo collection of pastors, congregations, and church leaders; and some genealogical records. Materials for use with supervision. Accepts phone inquiries. No fee. Hours: by appt.

Goodridge Area Historical Society

RR 1, Goodridge, MN 56725; (218) 378-4380. Preserves local history with holdings on rural school, church, and resident activities. Collections of maps, photos, and country store memorabilia. Accepts phone inquiries. No fee. Hours: 8-5.

Grand Army of the Republic Hall— Meeker County Museum

308 N. Marshall, Litchfield, MN 55355; (612) 693-8911. Research facility for Meeker County history, family genealogy, and Civil War history. Museum displays describe country history from 1856. Library contains materials on Civil War, local newspaper from 1871-1988, diaries, maps,

photos of county pioneers and Civil War veterans, genealogical records, and uniforms. Accepts phone inquiries. Fee. Hours: summer, M-F 9-5, Sa-Su 1-5; winter M-Th 9-5, F 9-noon, Sa 2-4.

Gustavus Adolphus College Library

Special Collections, Folke Bernadotte Memorial Library, St. Peter, MN 56082; (507) 931-7567. Academic research library has special collection on Swedish-Americans and college history. Museum displays college artifacts. Library contains college archives and Swedish-American books, phonograph records, and artifacts. Other holdings include photos, Swedish films, genealogical records of Swedish-American Lutheran churches, and Gene Basset cartoons, Selma Lagerlof collection, and children's literature. May be some restrictions. Accepts phone inquiries. Fee for genealogical research. Hours: M-Th 8-midnight, F 8-9, Sa 9-9, Su noon-midnight.

Hardanger Fiddle Association of America

Rte. 3, Box 86, Granite Falls, MN 56241; (612) 564-3408. Preserves and promotes Scandinavian folk music and dance with emphasis on Hardanger 8-stringed fiddle music. Library holds many fiddle tune scores, books and stories on fiddles; photos of Hardanger fiddles and fiddlers; recordings; and collection of manuals for self-instructed fiddle playing. Accepts phone inquiries. Fee for membership. Hours: 9-4.

Hennepin County Historical Society Museum

2303 3rd Ave., S, Minneapolis, MN 55404; (612) 870-1329. Preserves and interprets Minneapolis and county history. Museum exhibits county history from 1820 with special collections of costumes, toys, and decorative arts; library and archives hold historic photographs, books, manuscripts, clipping files, Confer Realty photos from 1915-45, Waterpower Company records from 1880-1920, oral history interviews; and genealogical records. Accepts phone inquiries. Fee. Hours: Tu-Sa 10-5, Su noon-5.

Hinckley Fire Museum

P.O. Box 40, 106 Old Highway 61, Hinckley, MN 55037; (612) 384-7338. Museum preserves historical aspect of 1894 fire that destroyed 400 square miles and killed 418 people. Holdings include large diorama of fire, exhibits on history of Hinckley from 1894, Fire Relief records from fire, genealogical records, maps, photos, and films/videotapes. Accepts phone inquiries. Fee. Hours: May-mid-Oct 10-5.

Immigration History Research Center

University of Minnesota, 826 Berry St., St. Paul, MN 55114; (612) 627-4208. Documents and promotes study into 24 American ethnic groups with origins in Southern and Eastern Europe and Near East. Large research library; extensive manuscript collections on all facets of immigrant groups; extensive photo collection; and oral history interviews documenting family social histories, with emphasis on Finnish. Accepts phone inquiries. No fee. Hours: M-F 8:30-4:30.

Immigration History Society

Minnesota Historical Society, c/o Professor Carlton C. Qualey, 690 Cedar St., St. Paul, MN 55101; (612) 296-5662. Professional organization devoted to preserving historical experiences of European, African, Oriental, Latin American, and Middle Eastern immigrants to North America. Offers publications, organizes sessions for joint sponsorships, and encourages scholarships in field. Accepts phone inquiries. Hours: call.

Iron Range Research Center

P.O. Box 392, Hwy. 169 West, Chisholm, MN 55719; (218) 254-3321. Collects, preserves, and disseminates history and cultural heritage of Iron Range. Library has reference materials on local, ethnic, and MN mining history. Archives hold govt and school records, maps of surrounding counties and cities, large collection of photos, newspapers, films on local mining and lumbering, oral history recordings, genealogical records, and mining company records and papers. Accepts phone inquiries. No fee. Hours: winter, Tu-Sa 9-4; summer, M-Sa 10-7.

Kanabec County Historical Society and Museum

P.O. Box 113, West Forest Ave., Mora, MN 55051; (612) 679-1665. Discovers, collects, and preserves Kanabec County artifacts and displays them for public. Library contains small collection on state and county histories; manuscripts from churches, civic orgs, and families; complete set of county plat maps; photos of historic agriculture, education, and business activites; oral history tapes; and genealogical and census records. Materials for in-house use only. Accepts phone inquiries. Fee. Hours: M-Sa 10-4:30; Su 12:30-4:30.

Kandiyohi County Historical Society

610 Hwy. 71, NE, Willmar, MN 56201; (612) 235-1881. Discovers, preserves, and disseminates historical info on county and its residents. Museum emphasizes railroad and other regional history. Library provides research materials on MN and Kandiyohi history. Records of civic groups, state and county maps, photos, oral history recordings, newspaper indexes, and county naturalization records found in archives. Accepts phone inquiries. No fee. Hours: museum, Memorial Day-Labor Day, M-F 9-5, Sa-Su 1-5; winter, Su-F 2-5; library, by appt M-F.

Koochiching County Historical Society

P.O. Box 1147, 214 6th Ave., International Falls, MN 56649; (218) 283-4316. Collects, preserves, interprets, and disseminates county and northern MN history. Museum collects Indian and homesteader artifacts and logging, farming, and transportation materials from 1800s-1940. Library and archive keep resident, government, and civic org records. Some forestry maps; many photos on early paper mill and logging industries; limited films/videotapes on Koochiching County, Ojibwa Indians, and immigrants; oral history collection; genealogical records; and Melheim wood-carving collection. Permission required for use of the library, manuscripts, and photos. Accepts phone inquiries. Fee. Hours: May-Sept, M-Sa 10-4; Sept-May, M-Tu 8:30-4.

La Societe Canadienne Francaise du Minnesota

P.O. Box 10913, Minneapolis, MN 55458. Shares and preserves French-Canadian heritage and traditions. Archives hold society's publications as well as French-Canadian articles from MN and regional states, some photos, and various genealogical records.

Lake County Historical Society and Railroad Museum

Depot Building, Two Harbors, MN 55616; (218) 834-4898. Preserves and disseminates history of Lake County. Former depot bldg houses artifacts from early 1800s, with displays covering logging, railroad, Great Lakes shipping, and regional history. Archive has maps, manuscripts, and photos of logging, railroad, and shipping. Accepts phone inquiries. Fee. Hours: May-Oct 9-5.

Lake Superior Museum of Transportation

Minnesota Historical Society, 506 W. Michigan St., Duluth, MN 55802; (218) 727-0687. Interprets history of MN railroading from 1860s through museum displays of R.R. rolling stock. Accepts phone inquiries. Fee. Hours: M-Sa 10-5, Su 1-5.

Landmark Center

75 W. 5th St., Room 404, St. Paul, MN 55102; (612) 292-3225. Restored federal court building acting as a forum for community and private events. Museum houses Schubert Club Keyboard Instrument Collection, which includes mechanical instruments, a harpsichord, and authentic musical manuscripts from composers Beethoven, Haydn, Schumann, and Wagner. Some materials on bldg's restoration. Materials for in-house use only. Accepts phone inquiries. No fee. Hours: M-W, F 8-5, Th 8-8, Sa 10-5, Su 1-5.

Laura Ingalls Wilder Museum

P.O. Box 248, Walnut Grove, MN 56180; (507) 859-2358. Preserves history of Ingalls Wilder family, as well as local community. Museum holds maps and photos from late 19th and early 20th c. Accepts phone inquiries. No fee. June-Labor Day, 10-7; May, Sept, Oct, noon-4, or by appt. Hours: call.

Lindbergh Historic Site

Lindbergh State Park, Route 3, Box 245, Lindbergh Drive., Little Falls, MN 56345; (612) 632-3154. Interprets history of three generations of the Charles Lindbergh family. Accepts phone inquiries. No fee. Hours: May-Labor Day, Tu-Su 10-5; Labor Day-Apr, Sa 10-4, Su

Old Central Minneapolis Public Library in 1889, from the Minneapolis Collection of the Minneapolis Public Library.

noon-4; other times by appointment.

Minneapolis Collection

Minneapolis Public Library and Information Center, 300 Nicollet Mall, Minneapolis, MN 55401; (612) 372-6537 or 6648. Public library with special collection of materials on Minneapolis history. Archives include papers of many individuals and orgs, maps, large photo collection, oral histories, and card index to "Minneapolis Journal" from 1899-1914. Hours: call.

Minneapolis Public Library and Information Center

Special Collections, 300 Nicollet Mall, Minnea-

polis, MN 55401; (612) 372-6648. Serves researchers, scholars, and general public by preserving collections on Minneapolis, WWII, and abolition. Minneapolis holdings include business archives, WPA manuscripts on theater and civic events, maps from 1830, many photos, and oral histories of Depression. Kittleson World War II collection covers military and naval operations, anti-semitism, personal narratives, scrapbooks, posters, strategic maps, records of Minnesotans killed, wounded, or missing in action. Huttner Anti-Slavery Collection has library, archives, manuscripts, and photos. Materials for in-house use only. Accepts phone inquiries. No fee. Hours: M-F 9-5:30; Sa 10-5:30.

Minnesota Finnish-American Historical Society

Rte. 1, Box 17, Garfield, MN 56332; (612) 834-2872. Preserves Finnish-American history in MN through holdings in library and archives. Photos and recordings are held by chapters throughout state. Accepts phone inquiries. No fee. Hours: 6-7.

Minnesota Genealogical Society

P.O. Box 16069, 678 Fort Rd., St. Paul, MN 55116; (612) 222-6929. Promotes interest in genealogical research. Holdings include materials on American, Canadian, Irish, English, Danish, German, and Scandinavian genealogical research. Other holdings include missionary, Native American, Canadian, and MN records. Special collection of county histories and directories. Some videotapes available. Accepts phone inquiries. No fee. Hours: Tu, Th 6:30-9:30, W, F, Sa 10-4.

Minnesota Historical Society

690 Cedar St., St. Paul, MN 55101; (612) 296-6126. Preserves materials and records relating to MN and MN residents. Museum displays cover regional archaeology, history, and material culture from 1820, including native cultures and Munsingwear. Library has many pamphlets, periodicals, and newspapers on MN topics. Archives holds state and local govt materials; papers of MN individuals, including Hubert Humphrey and Eugene MacCarthy; business, labor, and women's history materials, including Great Northern and Northern Pacific railroad records; many maps; large photo collection; films/videotapes from 1930; many oral histories; and genealogical records. Accepts phone inquiries. No fee. Hours: M-Sa 8:30-5, Su 1-4.

Minnesota Pioneer Park

Rte. 2, Box 322, State Hwy 55 East, Annandale, MN 55302; (612) 274-8489. Collects pioneer artifacts and promotes appreciation of nature and environment. Museum consists of historic restored building complex housing artifacts from 1850s-1940. Collects some photos of area and 19th c school activities. Accepts phone inquiries. Fee. Hours: Memorial Day-Labor Day, M-F 10-4:30, Sa-Su 1-5.

Minnesota Transportation Museum

P.O. Box 1796, Pioneer Station, St. Paul, MN 55101; (612) 228-0263. Acquires, restores, maintains, and operates examples of historic land transportation. Museum maintains 4 lines: Como-Harriet Street Car Line and Minnehaha Depot in Minneapolis, Jackson Street Roundhouse in St. Paul, and Stillwater & St. Paul Railroad in Stillwater. Holdings consist of 77 cars, including steam, gas, and diesel electric locomotives; passenger cars; freight cars; caboose, heater car, and tower car; and inner-urban street and "L" cars. Accepts phone inquiries. Hours: call.

Moorhead State University

Documents Dept., Livingston Lord Library, Moorhead, MN 56560; (218) 236-2349. Academic research library with special collection of materials from Northwest MN Historical Center, and collection of manuscripts on history and culture of region. Contains some genealogical materials. Depository document collection contains papers of congressional hearings from 1960s, American state papers from 1789-1838, Dept of State diplomatic dispatches and consular instructions, and territorial papers. Accepts phone inquiries. No fee. Hours: 7:30am-11pm.

Nicollet County Historical Society and Museum

P.O. Box 153, St. Peter, MN 56082; (507) 931-2160. Preserves county history through holdings in museum, library, and archives. Collections on Traverse des Sioux and treaty, plat maps from 19th and 20th c, photos, newspaper collection, and genealogical records. Accepts phone inquiries. No fee. Hours: Tu-Th, 2nd Sa of each month 1-4.

Northeast Minnesota Historical Center

University of Minnesota, Library 375, Duluth, MN 55812; (218) 726-8526. Archives for regional history of Duluth and surrounding four-county area. Holdings from 1853 cover mining, logging, shipping, transportation, and social welfare in area; govt records; rather large map collection; extensive photo collection; films/videotapes on local businesses and historic preservation; and records of War Commission, Old

Settlers Association, GAR, and Duluth Civilian Defense Council. Some restrictions. Accepts phone inquiries. No fee. Hours: M-F 8-noon, 1-4:30.

Northwest Territory French and Canadian Heritage Center

P.O. Box 26372, St. Louis Park, MN 55426; (612) 929-9429 or 224-7988. Preserves history and genealogy through collection of map, photos, films/videotapes, genealogical records of French-Canadians and Metis (French & Indian), and hundreds of Quebec marriage records, histories, and Indian records from Chippewa and Ojibwa. Library collection housed in MN Genealogical Society Library in St. Paul. Accepts phone inquiries. Fee for membership. Hours: 11-8.

Norwegian-American Historical Association

St. Olaf College Library, Northfield, MN 55057; (507) 663-3221. National center for collecting, preserving, and publishing materials on Norwegian-American experience. Archives consist of diaries, personal papers, manuscripts, Rowverg obituary file, emigration records, and church histories; some manuscripts and photos. Materials for in-house use only. Accepts phone inquiries. No fee. Hours: M-F 8-noon; other times by appt.

Olmsted County Historical Society

P.O. Box 6411, Co. Rd. 122 SW, Rochester, MN 55901; (507) 286-9447. Collects, preserves, and interprets area history. History center houses exhibits on Mayowood; library holds books, manuscripts, photos, business and genealogical records. Accepts phone inquiries. Fee. Hours: M-F 9-5, Sa-Su noon-4.

Otter Tail County Historical Society

1110 Lincoln Ave., W., Fergus Falls, MN 56537; (218) 736-6038. Preserves, interprets, and disseminates info on county history. Museum exhibits Native American artifacts from 1870s-1930. Library holds personal, business, and ephemeral collections; archives contains county newspapers and regional and county research resources; map collection; large photo archive; many oral history tapes; and genealogical rec-

ords. Fee. Hours: M-F 9-5, Sa-Su 1-4.

Red River Valley Heritage Society

P.O. Box 733, 202 First Ave. N, Moorhead, MN 56560; (218) 236-9140. Attempts to unify Red River Valley historical regions in MN, ND, and Manitoba. Holds no collections, but sponsors Clay County Historical Society library, archives, photo collections, and genealogical records. Accepts phone inquiries. Hours: M-F 8-5.

Saint John's University

Documents Division, Alcuin Library, Collegeville, MN 56321; (612) 363-2127. Provides resources and services to stimulate intellectual curiousity and research in University. Archival materials on University and St. John's Abbey from 1857; large collection of medieval manuscripts in Hill Monastic Manuscript Library; collection of USGS maps; and special collections on Benedictine Monasticism, theology, and central MN history. Accepts phone inquiries. No fee. Hours: M-F 9-4:30, Su 6-9.

Saint Louis County Historical Society

506 W. Michigan St., Duluth, MN 55802; (218) 722-8011. Gathers, interprets, and preserves county and state history. Museum, library, and archival holdings at other locations; special Eastman Johnson collection on-site. Accepts phone inquiries. Fee for collections held at other locations. Hours: M-F 9-5.

Saint Paul Public Library

Social Sciences and Literature/Reference Dept., 90 W. 4th St., St. Paul, MN 55102; (612) 292-6307. Public library serves St. Paul area with general holdings on US and MN history, with special collection on St. Paul local history. Holdings include city documents, newspapers, clipping files since 1910, and city directories. Special collection materials non-circulating. Accepts phone inquiries. No fee. Hours: M 9-9, T 9-5:30, Th 9-9, F 9-5:30, Sa 9-5:30.

Sinclair Lewis Foundation

P.O. Box 141, Hwy. 71 and 194 South, Sauk Centre, MN 56378; (612) 352-5201. Preserves memory of Nobel prize-winning author through holdings in museum and archives. Collection include clipping files, manuscripts, Lewis family photos, and videotapes of Lewis's life. Site is Lewis's boyhood home with some original furnishings. Fee for boyhood home. Hours: winter, 8-1; summer 8-4:30.

Sons of Norway

1455 W. Lake St., Minneapolis, MN 55408; (612) 827-3611. Fraternal benefit society preserves and promotes Norwegian heritage and culture. Holds reference materials, Norwegian-American literature, and maps in library. Accepts phone inquiries. No fee. Hours: 8-4:30.

Southern Minnesota Historical Center

Mankato State University, Memorial Library, Mankato, MN 56001; (507) 389-1029. Collects, preserves, and makes available unpublished historical materials relating to southern MN. Archives hold University records, manuscripts on southern MN business history and civic orgs, photos, and necrology file from 1880-1932. Accepts phone inquiries. No fee. Hours: call.

Stearns County Historical Society

P.O. Box 702, 235 S. 32nd Ave., St. Cloud, MN 56302; (612) 253-8424. Promotes appreciation of Stearns County and MN history. Museum displays cover local granite and dairy industries, as well has agriculture and natural history. Library has research materials, county newspapers, genealogical materials, manuscripts, maps, photos, films from 1930s-80s, large collection of oral histories, and extensive family dairy farm history artifacts. Accepts phone inquiries. Fee. Hours: Tu-Sa 10-5, Su noon-5; June-Aug, add M 10-5.

United Methodist Church Minnesota Annual Conference

Commission on Archives and History, 122 W. Franklin Ave., Room 400, Minneapolis, MN 55404; (612) 870-3657. Maintains records of MN United Methodism, including local church records, ministerial files, and conference agency records. Some restrictions. Accepts phone inquiries. Hours: M-F 8-4:30.

Vermillion Interpretive Center

1900 E. Camp, Ely, MN 55731; (218) 365-3226. Interprets, collects, and researches history of area. Museum exhibits include prospecting, lumbering, mining, and Indian history; local manuscripts, maps, and photos; oral history recordings; and some films/videotapes of local and national interest. Accepts phone inquiries. Fee. Hours: May-Sept, 10-4; Oct-Apr, W-Sa 1-4.

Waseca County Historical Society

P.O. Box 314, 2nd Ave & 4th St., NE, Waseca, MN 56093; (507) 835-7700. Collects, preserves, and interprets local history from settlement in 1850s. Museum, library, and archives hold info on area church, civic, and educational institutions. Manuscript collections include diaries, wills, memoirs, autobiographies, family histories, and research reports; some maps and photos of community; oral history interviews; genealogical records; films/videotapes from 1960-87; and newspapers and census records collection from 1860. Accepts phone inquiries. Donations accepted. Hours: Tu-F 1-5, or by appt.

Western Minnesota Steam Threshers Reunion

P.O. Box 632, Hawley, MN 56549; (218) 937-5316. Promotes local heritage with emphasis on steam power. Accepts phone inquiries. Fee. Hours: summer months only, 8-6.

Winona County Historical Society

160 Johnson, Winona, MN 55987; (507) 454-2723. Collects, preserves, and interprets human history of county. Museum contains records, library, and official documents of Armory. Library has reference materials on county and state. Archive holds photos of steamboats, manuscripts, maps, drawings, films/videotapes, recordings, and genealogical records. Large collection of vaudeville materials. Accepts phone inquiries. No fee. Hours: M-F 10-5, Sa-Su 1-5.

Wright County Historical Society

101 Lake Blvd., NW, Buffalo, MN 55313; (612) 682-3900. Collects and disseminates info on Wright County history. Library has reference materials on MN and MN county histories. Archives hold files on Wright County, manuscripts, maps, photos, films/videotapes of Historical Society events, oral history recordings,

and genealogical materials. Accepts phone inquiries. No fee. Hours: M-F 8-4:30.

Yellow Medicine County Museum

1193 Sixth St., Granite Falls, MN 56241; (612) 564-4479. Preserves history of county pioneers and Native Americans. Museum displays Indian artifacts, pioneer church and log cabin, and examples of pioneer lifestyle. Library has reference materials on Native Americans, plat books and maps dating to 1872, photos, oral history interviews, genealogical materials, license plates of MN, and toys of yesteryear. Accepts phone inquiries. Donations accepted. Hours: Mid-Apr-mid-May and mid-Oct-mid-Dec, Tu-F 1-5; mid-May-mid-Oct, Tu-S 1-5.

YMCA of the USA Archives

University of Minnesota Library, 2642 University Ave., St. Paul, MN 55114; (612) 627-4632. Documents history of YMCA. Museum displays memorabilia from WWI era, scrolls, quills, etc. Library contains extensive collection of YMCA publications and materials from YMCA affiliates. Archives holds YMCA historical records from 1851, substantial collections of personal papers, maps, large collection of photos, films, oral history recordings from YMCA founders, records on those who served with YMCA during WWI, Jacob Bowne collection of publications from young men's religious societies from early 17th c, and records from YMCA international division. Opens in late fall, 1988. Accepts phone inquiries. No fee. Hours: 8:30-5.

Mississippi

American Society for Legal History

American Council for Learned Societies, University of Mississippi, History Dept., University, MS 38677; (601) 7105. Professional assn promoting study and publication in studies of history of law and legal institutions. Publishes journal twice yearly. No permanent headquarters. Accepts phone inquiries. Fee for membership. Hours: M-F 8-noon, 1-5.

Beauvoir—Jefferson Davis Shrine

P.O. Box 200, W. Beach Blvd., Biloxi, MS 39531; (601) 388-1313. Preserves, collects, and interprets historic materials and memorabilia relating to Jefferson Davis and his family, and Confederate soldiers in museum and library. Museum housed in retirement residence of Davis family. Holdings include some letters, personal materials, and family photographs of Davis family and records of Confederate Soldiers Home. Materials for in-house use only. Fee. Hours: 9-5.

Cottonlandia Museum

P.O. Box 1635, Greenwood, MS 38930; (601) 453-0925. Relates history of MS Delta and its dependence on cotton through holdings in museum and library. Special collections in Indian pottery, beads, and artifacts. Accepts phone inquiries. Fee. Hours: call.

Davis Family Association

P.O. Box 814, Rosemont Plantation, Hwy 24 E, Woodville, MS 39669. Maintains genealogy of Jefferson Davis family, including approx 2500 members. Accepts mail inquiries only.

Delta Blues Museum

Carnegie Public Library, P.O. Box 280, Clarksdale, MS 38614; (601) 627-7341. Collects, preserves, and makes available info, programs, and materials on significance of blues music, and its relationship to jazz, rock, pop, country, and other forms of music. Museum exhibits musical instruments and displays on blues artists. Library collection focuses on blues artists, but also covers slavery, reconstruction period, and early 20th c black history. Other holdings include photos, historical documentaries, footage of festivals and interviews with artists, and records of various artists. Most recent contributions from Billy Gibbons of ZZ Top. Some restrictions. Accepts phone inquiries. No fee. Hours: M 9-8, Tu 9-5:30, F 9-5, Sa 10-2.

Grand Gulf Military Monument Commission

Rte. 2, Box 389, Port Gibson, MS 39150; (601) 437-5911. Preserves historic Civil War battlefield on site of former MS river town. Museum holds Civil War artifacts, Indian arrowhead, period furnishings, 1854 map of US, and photos of Gen Albert Johnston, and cotton fields. Accepts phone inquiries. Fee. Hours: M-F 8-noon, 1-5.

Grand Village of the Natchez Indians

400 Jefferson Davis Blvd., Natchez, MS 39120; (601) 446-6502. Interprets history and archaeology of Natchez history to 1730 through museum exhibits. Educational programs available. Accepts phone inquiries. No fee. Hours: M-Sa 9-5, Su 1:30-5.

J.B. Cain Archives of Mississippi Methodism

Millsaps-Wilson Library, Millsaps College, Jackson, MS 39210; (601) 354-5201. Maintains records and history of United Methodist Church in MS. Archives hold church records and histories; manuscript collections retain manuscripts from some 19th and 20th c Methodist clergy. Accepts phone inquiries. No fee. Hours: M-F 8:30-12:30.

Jackson Civil War Roundtable

809 N. State, Apt. 816, Jackson, MS 39202; (601) 355-4796. Historical group dedicated to preservation of American history with special interest in Civil War period. Individual members retain personal libraries, manuscripts, and maps. Accepts phone inquiries. Membership fee. Hours: call.

John Clayton Fant Memorial Library

Mississippi University for Women, John Clayton Fant Memorial Library, Columbus, MS 39701; (601) 329-7340. Academic research library with museum, library, archives, and genealogical collection preserving MS state history. Holdings include census records from 1790-1840, books on MS authors, Works Project Administration historical source material from 1930, records of debates from 1789-1837, Confederate Congres journal, and extensive literature on MS state history. Accepts phone inquiries. No fee. Hours: 8-4:30.

Manship House

420 E. Fortification St., Jackson, MS 39202; (601) 961-4724. Interprets family life and decorative arts in MS during 19th c. Museum in restored home of Jackson mayor and painter Charles Henry Manship is furnished with period Civil War furnishings. Small library holds materials on decorative arts and Manship family.

Accepts phone inquiries. No fee. Hours: Tu-F 9-4, Sa-Su 1-4.

Mississippi Baptist Historical Commission

Mississippi College Library, P.O. Box 51, College St., Clinton, MS 39056; (601) 925-3434. Preserves history of MS Baptists, and MS Baptist Convention churches, institutions, and personnel. Library holds reference materials. Archives hold vertical files on churches and individuals; albums, scrapbooks, and newsletters; maps and photos; oral history interviews; and archive of weekly Baptist newspaper from 1877. Materials non-circulating. Accepts phone inquiries. No fee. Hours: M-F 8:30-noon, 1-4:30.

Mississippi Historical and Genealogical Association

618 Avalon Rd., Jackson, MS 39206; (601) 362-3079. Gathers, compiles, publishes, and preserves historical and genealogical records of MS and other areas. Operates assn library, and publishes quarterly. Accepts phone inquiries. Fee for membership, and fee for genealogical queries. Hours: 8-5.

Mississippi Military Museum

P.O. Box 627, 120 North State-War Memorial Bldg., Jackson, MS 39205; (601) 354-7555. Presents US military history from Spanish American War through end of Vietnam conflict with emphasis on contributions of MS residents. Holdings include weapons, complete uniforms, WWII patriotic posters, and WWII German and Japanese artifacts. Accepts phone inquiries. No fee. Hours: 8-4.

Mississippi State University

Mitchell Memorial Library, Box 5408, Mississippi State, MS 39762; (601) 325-3060. Preserves social and political history of MS, southern states, and MS authors. Materials include Protestant Church records, and materials on Faulkner, Williams, Carter, Welty, and Young. Special John C. Stennis collection of books, papers, and photos; US Rep David Bowen collection of materials from 1973-1983; and US Rep G.V. Montgomery papers; Hodding Carter II papers; papers of NY Times editor Turner Catledge; Norman Bradley of "Chattanooga Post" and "Chattanooga Times"; and Wilson Minor's papers from days as editor of Jackson's Capitol Reporter. Accepts phone inquiries. Hours: call.

Mississippi University for Women Archives and Museum

P.O. Box W-369, Columbus, MS 39701. Nation's first state-supported institution of higher education for women supports museum and archival collections on university history. Museum features artifacts from University's past. Archival collections include correspondence and papers of past presidents and founders. Special Tennessee-Tombigbee Waterway collection documents the regional Waterway Development Authority activities.

National Agricultural and Aviation Museum

P.O. Box 1609, 1150 Lakeland Drive, Jackson, MS 39516; (601) 354-6113. Preserves, exhibits, and interprets heritage of MS rural regions with focus on agriculture and forestry, with some emphasis on the use of aviation in both fields. Aviation museum displays Boeing Stearman airliner, Piper Pawnee, 49 D Bell Model Helicopter, and Ag-Cat prototype. Agriculture museum preserves exhibits on lumbering, logging, farming, as well as blacksmithing. Library in formative stages, but currently holds limited manuscripts and agricultural and aviation photos. Accepts phone inquiries. Fee. Hours: Tu-Sa 9-5, Su 1-5.

Seafood Industry Museum of Biloxi

P.O. Box 1907, Biloxi, MS 39533; (601) 435-6320. Preserves history of people, products, and technology involved in local seafood history. Museum exhibits artifacts, photos, and implements relating to seafood industry along MS Gulf Coast, fishing vessels, and Biloxi region. Accepts phone inquiries. Fee. Hours: Tu-Sa 9-5, Su noon-5.

Sons of Confederate Veterans

Southern Station, P.O. Box 5164, Hattiesburg, MS 39406; (601) 268-6100. Association commemorates male descendants of those soldiers who served in the Confederate States of America Armed Forces. Accepts phone inquiries. Fee for membership. Hours: M-F 8-noon.

University of Mississippi

Documents Division, 106 Old Gym, Federal Documents Library, University, MS 38677; (601) 232-5857. Depository for federal and regional publications. Also holds special collection on Blues music and history. Accepts phone inquiries. No fee. Hours: M 8-8, Tu-F 8-4:30, Sa 9-noon.

University of Southern Mississippi

William David McCain Graduate Library, Box 5148, Southern Station, Hattiesburg, MS 39406; (601) 266-4345. Academic research library holds materials on WWII US postwar economic policy, history of Confederate states, and Mexican War. Postwar collection consists of Rep William Colmer's papers from Congressional committee. Sec of State Alexander Melvorne Jackson's papers detail his involvement in Mexican and Civil Wars. Accepts phone inquiries. No fee. Hours: call.

Vicksburg Foundation for Historic Preservation

P.O. Box 254, 1107 Washington St., Vicksburg, MS 39180; (601) 636-5010. Preserves architectural heritage of Vicksburg and maintains Museum of Coca-Cola. Museum is first Coca-Cola bottling plant in world, and holds equipment and memorabilia from 1890. Library holds newspaper archives, and vertical files on Vicksburg's architectural environment. Accepts phone inquiries. Fee for museum. Hours: M-Sa 9-5, Su 1:30-4:30.

Vicksburg National Military Park

3201 Clay St., Vicksburg, MS 39180; (601) 636-0583. Memoralizes campaign and seige of Vicksburg through holdings in museum, library, and archives. Museum displays artifacts documenting naval history during Civil War, with focus on ironclad gunboat USS Cairo; library holds official records of Army and Navy, regimental histories, unit rosters, biographies, and general Civil War histories; archives contain Vicksburg campaign letters, diaries, maps, and firsthand accounts; large photo collection on military park dating to early 20th c; some recordings of Civil War period music; and films/videotapes on Vicksburg and Cairo sinking. Accepts phone inquiries. Fee. Hours: 8-5.

Missouri

American Family Records Association

311 East 12th St., Kansas City, MO 64106; (816) 373-6570. Collects genealogical and local history materials, as well as some videotapes. Most materials available ILL. Accepts phone inquiries. No fee. Hours: 9-5.

Battle of Lexington Historic Site

Missouri Dept of Natural Resources, P.O. Box 6, North 13th St., Lexington, MO 64067; (816) 259-2112. Preserves and interprets Battle of Lexington in MO and history of Anderson House. House furnished in period Victorian, with clothing and artifacts dating from Civil War. Some diaries and letters from same period are also in collection. Accepts phone inquiries. Fee. Hours: 9-4.

Bollinger Mill State Historic Site

P.O. Box 248, Burfordville, MO 63739; (314) 243-4591. Preserves and interprets 19th c grist mill and historic info. Also genealogical materials on George Frederick Bollinger. Accepts phone inquiries. Fee. Hours: M-Sa 10-4, Su noon-4.

Church of Jesus Christ of Latter Day Saints

Library and Archives, P.O. Box 1059, Independence, MO 64051; (816) 833-1000. Preserves and makes available church and movement history, with some general religion holdings. Museum holdings on movement leaders and historical events; library of church publications, unpublished works, and newspapers from 1860; church records; manuscripts on development of Mormon movement, its dispersion after 1844, and reorganization; photos of church members and activities; some membership and branch records. Restrictions on use. Accepts phone inquiries. Hours: M-F 8-12, 1-5, Sa 9-1.

Concordia Historical Institute

801 De Mun Ave., St. Louis, MO 63105; (314) 721-5934. Preserves and promotes history of Lutheranism in North America. Museum collects 19th c church artifacts, materials on Dr. C.F.W. Walther, and Lutheran memorabilia.

Library contains materials written or published by Lutherans in US. Archives holds materials of Lutheran Church-MO Synod from 1847; manuscripts from Walther and others; maps; photos of Lutherans; "This is the Life" TV films and other materials on mission work; genealogical resources; and records of Dr. Walter Maier and many Lutheran pastors. Accepts phone inquiries. No fee. Hours: M-F 8:30-4:30.

Confederate Memorial State Historic Site

RR 1, Box 221-A, Higginsville, MO 64037; (816) 584-2853. Memorial to MO state residents who fought for the Confederacy in building that housed dependent Civil War veterans and their families. Museum and archives hold exhibits, documents, and maps of Home; some sketchy genealogical materials on residents; and photos of Home buildings, ground, and residents. Accepts phone inquiries. No fee. Hours: M-Sa 10-4, Su 12-5.

Daniel Boone Home

1836 Hwy F, Defiance, MO 63341; (314) 987-2221. Preserves history of Daniel Boone through preservation of his home and its original furnishings. Some documentation of Boone's life and descendants, manuscripts, maps, and photos in collection. Accepts phone inquiries. Fee. Hours: summer 8:30-8, winter 9-4:30.

Dorothea B. Hoover Museum

P.O. Box 555, Joplin, MO 64802; (417) 623-1180. Preserves history of Joplin area through holdings in museum, library, and archives. Museum diplays history, development and growth of Joplin during Victorian period. Library and archives contain limited collections of manuscripts and photos. Other holdings include Indian artifacts and Merle Evans miniature circus. Accepts phone inquiries. No fee. Hours: W-Su 1-4, or by appt.

First Missouri State Capitol

P.O. Box 721, St. Charles, MO 63301; (314) 946-9282. Presents development of frontier MO govt development and early statehood from 1820s. Other buildings restored in Capitol Complex include House of Representatives, Senate, Governor's office, general dry goods store, and federal-style row building. Guests must be accompanied by guide. Accepts phone inquiries. Fee. Hours: M-Sa 8-5, Su 10-5.

Fort Leonard Wood Museum

ATZT-PTS-OM, Nebraska & S. Dakota Sts., Fort Leonard Wood, MO 65473; (314) 368-4249. Interprets and preserves Army history at Ft with concentration on WWII and Army engineering. Museum consists of 13 restored WWII company buildings with period exhibits; archival photos and maps of ft; Army training films and video of German POW's at ft during 1940s; Army music and oral history tapes; and special collections on army engineering. Accepts phone inquiries. No fee. Hours: M-Sa 10-4.

Fort Osage Historic Site and Museum

Rte. 1, Box 122, Sibley, MO 64088; (816) 249-5737. Preserves govt factory and military post of 1812, and displays materials from Osage and Hopewell archaeological digs. Accepts phone inquiries. Fee. Hours: 9-5.

General John J. Pershing Boyhood Home State Historic Site

P.O. Box 35, 1000 Pershing Dr., Laclede, MO 64651; (816) 963-2525. Interprets history of life and boyhood home of John Pershing. Small museum, archives, and manuscript collection document Pershing's life in Laclede; some maps, photos, and family genealogical records supplement holdings. Accepts phone inquiries (800-334-6946). Fee. Hours: M-Sa 8-4:30, Su noon-5.

Grundy County Historical Society

140 E. 5th St., 1100 Mable, Trenton, MO 64683; (816) 359-6393. Museum and archives of artifacts from county citizens. Mostly local emphasis, with some maps, photos, and recordings. Special collections on coal mining and railroad activity. Accepts phone inquiries. Fee. Hours: Sa, Su, holidays 1-4; other times by appt.

Harry S Truman Birthplace

1109 Truman Ave., Lamar, MO 64759; (417) 682-2279. Preserves and commemorates restored birthplace of Truman with collection of Truman memorabilia, photos, and local history info.

Accepts phone inquiries. No fee. Hours: 9-4.

Historical Missouri Manuscripts

University of Missouri, 5100 Rockhill Rd., Kansas City, MO 64110; (816). Preserves materials on growth and development of MO and Kansas City. Holdings include papers of from business, civic, political, and cultural activities; architectural designs for many bldgs and records of Hoit, Price and Barnes architectural firm; oral histories of Kansas City jazz figures; records of Kansas City Board of Trade; and collections on Charles Wheeler, Charles Kimball, Arthur Mag, Oscar Nelson, Lou Holland, J.C. Nichols, Perry Cookingham, Blevins Davis, and Daniel Macmorris. Hours: call.

Hunter-Dawon Home State Historic Site

Rte. 1, Box 4-A, New Madrid, MO 63869; (314) 748-5340. Preserves and protects culture and history of MO. Library and archives hold photos and genealogical materials, as well as Mitchell & Rammelsberg furniture collection. Research requires prior approval. Accepts phone inquiries. Fee. Hours: M-Sa 10-4, Su noon-5.

Independence Heritage Commission

111 E. Maple, Independence, MO 64050; (816) 836-8300. Preserves city archives, architecture, and archaeological resources. Maintains 3 house museums dating from 19th c, archives of Jackson county history and historical society, manuscripts, maps, video presentations on Harry Truman, and genealogical records. May be restrictions on use. Accepts phone inquiries. Fee. Hours: M-F 8-5.

Jefferson National Expansion Memorial

11 N. 4th St., St. Louis, MO 63102; (314) 425-6012. Memorial to US territorial expansion and men responsible, Jefferson and aides Livingston and Monroe. Museum includes documents, exhibits, and artifacts on Westward expansion and St. Louis history; Jefferson's writings, materials on Gold Rush, Civil War, Indian Wars, sodbusters, ranchers, and MO, CA, and OR history; business ledgers and research reports on St. Louis history; maps on St. Louis, Santa Fe and

Oregon overland trails; photo collections on St. Louis, demolition for and construction of Arch; special collections on fur trade and waterfront and levee history. Materials non-circulating. Accepts phone inquiries. No fee. Hours: M-F 8-4:30.

Jesse James Bank Museum

103 North Water St., Liberty, MO 64068; (816) 781-4458. Restored bank was first to be robbed in daylight in United States. Museum and archives contain materials on Jesse and Frank James and family, including photos of bank and Jesse James gang. Also collection of Friends of James Farm history. Accepts phone inquiries. Fee. Hours: 9-4.

Jesse James Farm and Birthplace

Rte. 2, Box 236, Kearney, MO 64060; (816) 635-6065. Promotes history of Clay county and interprets life of Jesse James. Museum has limited exhibits on James farm, including original photos. Accepts phone inquiries. Fee. Hours: summer, 9-4; winter, M-F 9-4, Sa-Su noon-4.

Jesse James Home
and Patee House Museum

P.O. Box 1022, 12th & Penn, St. Joseph, MO 64502; (816) 232-8206. Preserves history of Pony Express, Jesse James, and early St. Joseph. Two museums, one housing Pony Express communication and transportation history; the other housing James memorabilia. Library strong in local history, with collection of early area newspapers; maps of St. Joseph and Pony Express routes; photos of historic St. Joseph. Accepts phone inquiries. Fee. Hours: Mar, Apr, Nov, Sa-Su; May-Oct, M-Sa 10-5, Su 1-5.

John Olin Library

Washington University, Lindell & Skinker Blvds., Campus Box 1061, St. Louis, MO 63130; (314) 889-5475. Provides govt info services to University community and members of Congressional district. Holds govt documents from 1905 and UN documents from 1946; extensive urban studies collection from 1968-1980. Accepts phone inquiries. No fee. Hours: M-F 9-5.

Kansas City Museum

3218 Gladstone Blvd., Kansas City, MO 64123;

(816) 483-8300. Collects artifacts, records, photos, and films/videotapes that reflect history of Kansas City region. Museum strong in 19th and 20th c clothing, textiles, and American Indian memorabilia; archival business and organizational records; family papers and cultural ephemera from 20th c; extensive collection of Kansas City photos; and some films/videotapes from early 20th c. Accepts phone inquiries. No fee. Hours: by appt, Tu-F 8-5:30.

Landmarks Commission
of Kansas City

26th Floor, City Hall, 414 E. 12th St., Kansas City, MO 64106; (816) 274-2555. Promotes preservation of Kansas City's historic, architectural, and cultural resources. Library contains books on Kansas City art, history, and architecture. Archives holds historical info on many Kansas City properties, National Register nominations and local designations, and bldg permits from 1907-70s; maps from 1886, 1891, and 1907; photos of historic bldgs, and some images from 1941 real estate assessment; and info on Kansas City builders and architects. Most materials for in-house use only. Accepts phone inquiries. No fee. Hours: M-F 8-5.

Laura Ingalls Wilder-Rose Wilder
Lane Home Association

Rocky Ridge Farm, Box 496, Mansfield, MO 65704; (417) 924-3626. Preserves home, writings, and memory of Laura and Rose. Library consists of Wilder's reading collection; 5 original Little House manuscripts on display; maps of Laura's travel from SD to MO; some recordings and genealogical records. Accepts phone inquiries. Fee. Hours: 9-4:30.

Liberty Memorial Museum

100 W. 26th St., Kansas City, MO 64108; (816) 221-1918. Military museum specializing in WWI history from 1914-18. Museum houses uniforms, weapons, vehicles, and other items from nations involved in war; US and British unit histories and artillery reference materials; archives of Liberty Memorial Association, Women's Overseas Service League, and US 89th Division; soldier correspondence and documents; many maps from all theaters of WWI, with emphasis on Western front; large photo collection; small

collection of Signal Corps films; some oral history recordings; and numerous WWI posters and sheet music from various nations around the world. Serious researchers welcome by appointment. Accepts donations. Hours: Tu-Su 9:30-4:30.

Lincoln University
Page Library, 820 Chestnut St., Jefferson City, MO 65775; (314) 751-2325. Academic research library has materials on slavery, black experience, and early black writings. Holdings include books, films, and oral history tapes. Hours: call.

Lone Jack Civil War Museum
Bynum Rd., Lone Jack, MO 64078; (816) 566-2272. Interprets Jackson County Civil War history through displays, reenactments, and special exhibits. Accepts phone inquiries. Fee. Hours: Apr-Nov, W-Su 9-5.

Mark Twain Birthplace State Historic Site
Mark Twain State Park, Rte. 1, Box 54, Stoutsville, MO 65283; (314) 565-3449. Preserves and interprets birthplace, life, and authorship of Twain through museum, library, and photo collections. Library composed of books by and about Twain in several languages and manuscript of "The Adventures of Tom Sawyer" for British publication; collection of photos of Twain and his family members; and assorted other Twain memorabilia. Materials for in-house use only. Accepts phone inquiries. Fee. Hours: M-Sa 10-4, Su noon-5.

Mark Twain Home Board
208 Hill St., Hannibal, MO 63401; (314) 221-9010. Preserves and perpetuates memory of Twain and his ties to Hannibal. Museum consists of Mark Twain Boyhood Home, Mark Twain Museum, J.M. Clemens Law Office, and Pilaster House/Grant's Drug Store. Boyhood home completely furnished with authentic Clemens family artifacts. Twain Museum houses collection of Twain artifacts, first editions of Twain books, personal letters and notes, collection of Twain clothing and personal items, and extensive collection of photos and paintings related to Twain. Accepts phone inquiries. Donations accepted. Hours: vary; winter 10-4, summer 8-6.

Missouri Cultural Heritage Center
University of Missouri, Conley House, Graduate School and Office of Research, Columbia, MO 65211; (314) 882-6296. Promotes research projects and curriculum development in cultural heritage studies and state and regional historic preservation. Collections consist of museum and archives with photo and recording holdings. Restrictions on use. Accepts phone inquiries. No fee. Hours: M-F 8-5.

Missouri Heritage Trust
P.O. Box 895, 1024 East McCarty St., Jefferson City, MO 65102; (314) 635-6877. Promotes and educates public history preservation through publications and meetings. Collections include small library and few maps and photos. Accepts phone inquiries. No fee. Hours: by appt, M-F.

Missouri Historical Society Library
Jefferson Memorial Library, St. Louis, MO 63112; (314) 361-1424. Preserves regional history and collection of materials on prominent St. Louis women, and women who played significant roles in US politics and social reform. Covers Patience Worth, Carry Nation, Fannie Hurst, Susan B. Anthony, Sacajawea, and many others. Accepts phone inquiries. Hours: call.

Missouri State Museum
Jefferson Landing State Historic Site, Capitol Bldg., Rm. B-2, Capitol Ave., Jefferson City, MO 65101; (314) 751-2854. Preserves and interprets heritage, culture, and natural resources of MO. Museum houses displays Civil War, pioneer, WWI, Spanish American, and industrial era exhibits; archives hold materials on state capitol, Jefferson Landing historic site, and Lohman's Landing; some maps of MO and other border states from 1820-70; photos of local agriculture, industry, and structures; oral history projects; and Frank Scwarzer's zither factory and collection memorabilia. Materials for in-house use only. Accepts phone inquiries. No fee. Hours: 8-5.

Missouri Valley Room
Kansas City Public Library, 311 E. 12th St., Kansas City, MO 64106; (816) 221-2698. Preserves Kansas City and MO history. Library

contains newspaper clipping files, photos, maps, county histories, passenger lists, census indexes, manuscripts, maps of streets and railroads, photos of Kansas City outlaws and prominent citizens, and videotapes of local history programming. Special Joe Sanders Music collection and memorabilia, Charlie Parker Jazz Musician collection, and Virgil Thompson archives. Materials for in-house use only. Accepts phone inquiries. No fee. Hours: M-Th 9-9, F-Sa 9-5, Su 1-5.

Montgomery County Historical Society

112 W. 2nd St., Montgomery City, MO 63361; (314) 564-2370. Preserves county artifacts, memorabilia, genealogies, and historical records. Society maintains museum exhibits of living room, kitchen, and restored telephone office; library holds county atlases, cemetery records, family histories, and obituaries; photo collection of county residents. Materials for in-house use only. Accepts phone inquiries. No fee. Hours: by appt.

Museum of Anthropology

University of Missouri, 100 Swallow Hall, Columbia, MO 65211; (314) 882-3764. Provides research materials on North American Indian, MO, and world anthropological studies. Archive of material from 18th c fieldwork in Guatemala; Eichenberger cast collection of North American artifacts. Accepts phone inquiries. No fee. Hours: Tu-F 9:30-3.

Museum of Ozarks' History

603 E. Calhoun, Springfield, MO 65802; (417) 869-1976. Preserves and exhibits all aspects of Ozark region history through holdings in museum, archives, and special collections. Museum exhibits include artifacts and costumes; archives relate local history from 1800; map and photo collections from early 19th c; film/videotape collection from 1920; and special collections of artifacts, costumes, and textiles from 1790. Accepts phone inquiries. Fee. Hours: June-Aug Tu-Sa 9:30-2:30; Sept-May Tu-Sa 11:30-4:30, Su 1-4.

National Archives— Kansas City Branch

2312 E. Bannister Rd., Kansas City, MO 64131; (816) 926-6272. Preserves and makes available

regional history records created by federal govt agencies. Library has reference materials on MO, KS, IA, and NE. Archive holds maps of MO, ND, SD, and KS Indian reservations and upper MI and lower MO River basins from 1880s; photos from federal courts, Bureau of Indian Affairs, and Army Corps of Engineers; films from 1916-72, covering WWI, WWII, and Vietnam, and including copies of Depression and WWII era films; recordings from WWII era on rationing, labor, military and foreign policy, and some Martin Luther King Jr. speeches; and census, military, and IRS records. Accepts phone inquiries. No fee. Hours: M-F 8-4; call for others.

National Personnel Records Center

9700 Page Blvd., St. Louis, MO 63132; (314) 263-3901. Referral agency provides public access to personnel records from over 100 govt agencies, with most extensive holdings in Army records. Individuals may access their own records; court order necessary to access other records. Accepts phone inquiries. Hours: call.

Northwest Missouri State University

Documents Division, B.D. Owens Library, Maryville, MO 64468; (816) 562-1629. Academic support library with holdings on US and MO history. Special collection of Gov A.P. Morehouse's papers from 1878-88. Accepts phone inquiries. No fee. Hours: M-F 8:30-4:30.

Old Trails Historical Society

P.O. Box 852, Manchester, MO 63011; (314) 227-6246. Maintains historic log cabin museum and preserves history of West St. Louis County with a collection of household items from 1830-1910, and limited photos. Accepts phone inquiries. No fee. Hours: by appt, 9-5.

Oregon-California Trails Association

P.O. Box 1019, Independence, MO 64051; (816) 252-2276. Publishes materials on all aspects of westward overland emigration experience and history. Accepts phone inquiries. Hours: M-F 8:30-12:30.

Powers Museum

P.O. Box 593, 1617 W. Oak St., Carthage, MO 64836; (417) 358-2667. Devoted to preserving history of Powers family, local community, and arts. Museum focuses on decorative arts and female fashion accessories; library holds sources on fashion and textiles, MO and local history, and music from 1870s-1930s; archives of quarry business; Dr. Everett Powers medical archives from early 20th c, and diaries, scrapbooks, and personal belongings of family; maps of Carthage and Jasper counties; small photo collection of MO, fashion, and Powers, Wright, and Winchester families; early 20th c opera recordings; and greeting card and sheet music collection. Some restrictions on use. Accepts phone inquiries. No fee. Hours: call.

Randolph County Historical Society

P.O. Box 116, 109 N. 4th St., Moberly, MO 65270; (816) 263-7576. Promotes preservation of country history and genealogical data. Museum exhibits railroad materials from 1870s. Archive contains historical and genealogical materials from 1830, photos, and newspapers. Materials non-circulating. Accepts phone inquiries. No fee. Hours: M 10-noon, Th 1-3.

Saint Joseph State Hospital Psychiatric Museum

P.O. Box 263, St. Joseph, MO 64506; (816) 232-8431. Depicts history of psychiatry and mental health services, and preserves and depicts history of St. Joseph State Hospital. Museum exhibits show treatment equipment from 17th, 18th, and 19th c. Photos show staff and equipment used at hospital from 1874. Special collection includes artwork completed by psychiatric patients. Accepts phone inquiries. Donations accepted. Hours: M-F 8:30-4.

Saint Louis Public Library

Gardener Rare Book Room, 1301 Olive St., St. Louis, MO 63103; (314) 241-2288. Preserves materials on travels from and in St. Louis and MO, including river pilots' handbooks and maps and St. Louis business directories. Accepts phone inquiries. No fee. Hours: call.

Saint Louis University

Documents Division, Pius XII Memorial Library, 3650 Lindell Blvd., St. Louis, MO 63108; (314) 658-3105. Provides support material for univ academic programs. Holdings include depository collection of federal documents,

congressional publications, and reports from Depts of Interior, Commerce, and Labor. Also collection of USGS topographic maps from early 20th c. Accepts phone inquiries. No fee. Hours: M-Th 8:30-10, F 8:30-5:45, Sa noon-5:45.

Soldiers' Memorial Military Museum

1315 Chestnut St., St. Louis, MO 63103; (314) 622-4550. Memorial Bldg houses two-room museum of military artifacts depicting St. Louis's patriotic and active military involvement from 1800. Exhibits include firearms, banners, posters, medals, uniforms, and photos. Accepts phone inquiries. No fee. Hours: 9-4:30.

State Historical Society of Missouri

1020 Lowry St., Columbia, MO 65201; (314) 882-7083. Collects, preserves, and publishes materials on MO and American West. Reference library includes books, pamphlets, magazines and official publications from early 1800s; MO newspaper library from 1808; 19th c census reports; state archives, personal letters, diaries, posters, business records; early river, trails, road, railroad, topography maps; photos of area residents from 1800s; genealogical records; special collections on Middle Western Americana rare books, Mark Twain, Eugene Field, Methodism, child & youth literature, and MO artists Benton, Bodmer, and Bingham. Materials non-circulating. Accepts phone inquiries. No fee. Hours: M-F 8-4:30, Sa 9-4:30.

Still National Osteopathic Museum

311 S. 4th St., Kirksville, MO 63501; (816) 626-2359. Preserves heritage of osteopathic medicine. Museum exhibits artifacts and memorabilia of founder of osteopathy, A.T. Still; materials on his successors and family; and first school of osteopathy. Library has materials focusing on osteopathy history and present college of medicine. Archives contain letters and documents from Still, photos, film/videotape on history of osteopathy and museum, genealogical records, and special William Sutherland Cranial collection. Accepts phone inquiries. Donations accepted. Hours: M-F 8-3.

Thomas Hart Benton Home and Studio

Missouri Dept of Natural Resources, 3616

Belleview, Kansas City, MO 64111; (816) 931-5722. Interprets Benton's life, primarily between 1939-1975. House contains many original Benton furnishings, and studio preserves working and creative environment. Accepts phone inquiries. Fee. Hours: M-Sa 10-4; winter, Su 11-4; summer, Su 12-5.

University of Missouri Archives

University of Missouri, 726 Lewis Hall, Columbia, MO 65211; (314) 882-4602. Collects materials and records on univ history, with emphasis on manuscripts, maps, photos, films/videotapes, and University of Missouri Press books. Some restrictions on use. Accepts phone inquiries (314-882-7567). No fee. Hours: M-F 8-5.

University of Missouri at Columbia

Research Park Library, 131 Dalton Research Center, Columbia, MO 65211; (314) 882-7018. Maintains almost complete collection of research and development reports from US atomic energy departments, as well as foreign organizations they worked with. Holdings include research and development reports from AEC, ERDA, and DOE from 1948. Accepts phone inquiries. Hours: call.

University of Missouri at Kansas City

Documents Division, Leon Bloch Law Library, 5100 Rockhill Rd., Kansas City, MO 64110; (816) 276-1650. Law school library and selective depository for federal, MO, and KS documents. Materials for in-house use; ILL available. Accepts phone inquiries (816-276-2435). No fee. Hours: M-F 9-5.

University of Missouri at Rolla

Documents Division, Curtis Laws Wilson Library, Rolla, MO 65401; (314) 341-4007. Academic support library with holdings in University, scientific, and MO history. Museum houses mineral and scientific equipment collections; library emphasizes science and engineering; manuscripts of state and Western historical societies; some USGS maps; historic campus photo collection; and MO county genealogy histories. Accepts phone inquiries. No fee. Hours: M-Th 8-midnight, F 8am-10:30pm, Sa 8-5, Su

2-midnight.

Watkins Woolen Mill State Historic Site

Rte. 2, Box 270-M, Lawson, MO 64062. Preserves, maintains, and interprets this only fully equipped 19th c textile mill in US. Holdings in museum, library, and archive include Watkins family letters, memorabilia, documents, and genealogical records; 19th c agriculture, milling, and decorative arts materials; photos of Watkins family and home from 1870. Accepts phone inquiries. Fee. Hours: archives by appt; Apr-Oct M-Sa 10-4, Su noon-6; Nov-Mar M-Sa 10-4, Su 11-4.

Western Historical Manuscript Collection

Thomas Jefferson Library, 8001 Natural Bridge, St. Louis, MO 63121; (314) 553-5143. Encourages interest in St. Louis and MO history with collections on women, blacks, labor movements, politics, and social work in 20th c. Large photo collection covers 1896 tornado, Depression, labor unrest, air shows, LA Purchase Exposition, and Arch construction; small videotape collection of local political campaign ad spots, WPA construction in St. Louis, and 1930s May Day; oral history interviews with area immigrants, suffragists, black leaders, riverboat jazzmen, rock musicians, labor leaders, and striking teachers of 1973; genealogical records from 3 local churches. Materials non-circulating. Accepts phone inquiries. No fee. Hours: M-F 8-5, Tu 8-9.

Western Historical Manuscript Collection

University of Missouri, Columbia & State Historical Society, University of Missouri, 23 Ellis Library, Columbia, MO 65201; (314) 882-6028. Collects and preserves MO and Midwest history, with emphasis on folklore and folk music. Archives hold official University records and archives of civic organizations; manuscripts, maps, and photos of military, political, civil, religious, educational, and professional personnel from 19th c.; films/videotapes on MO ethnic groups, and folk musicians; other films/videos donated by US Congressmen; oral history interviews and recordings of folk musicians, storytellers, and authors; genealogical materials; Peter Tamony collection of etymological research files and letters. Some restrictions. Accepts phone inquiries. No fee. Hours: M-F 8-4:45.

Wilson's Creek National Battlefield

Drawer C, Republic, MO 65738; (417) 732-2662. Interprets Battle of Wilson's Creek, its participants, and Civil War effort in MO. Museum houses explanatory exhibits; Hulston Civil War library available for research purposes; small photo collection on park and its development. Library materials for in-house use only. Accepts phone inquiries. Fee. Hours: winter, 8-5; summer, 8-8.

Montana

Big Horn County Historical Society

Rte.1, Box 1206-A, Hardin, MT 59034; (406) 665-1671. Preserves, exhibits, and interprets history of Big Horn County and surrounding area. Maintains cultural exhibits in restored early 20th c bldgs. Archives specializes in development and homesteading of Big Horn county; photo collection depicts Northern Cheyenne and Crow cultures from 1880; oral histories of residents; and genealogical records on births, deaths, marriages, and land acquisitions from 1908-17. Accepts phone inquiries. No fee. Hours: June-Aug, M-Sa 8-8, Su 8-6; Sept, 9-5; Oct-May, Tu-Sa 9-5.

Butte Historical Society

P.O. Box 3913, 17 W. Quartz, Butte, MT 59702; (406) 723-8262. Preserves and interprets Butte's history by preserving public archives, sponsoring scholarly conferences, and issuing publications. Archive holdings cover local govt, newpapers, Butte-Anaconda & Pacific Railroad collection, Anaconda Copper Mining Company papers, mining, and western history; maps on railroad, geology, and mining in Butte; photos; two films; genealogical records; and labor history collection. Materials for in-house use only. Accepts phone inquiries. Fee for membership. Hours: M-Tu noon-6, Th noon-4.

Butte-Silver Bow Public Archives

P.O. Box 81, 17 W. Quartz St., Butte, MT

59703; (406) 723-8262. Collects, preserves, and exhibits material record of Butte and Silver Bow County history. Small library; archival records of city, county, lodges, unions, Butte Anaconda & Pacific Railway; railway and Sanborn insurance maps; small photo collection; oral history interviews; genealogical records; and some films and videotapes. Accepts phone inquiries. No fee. Hours: summer, M, Tu noon-6, Th noon-4; winter, M, Tu 11-5, Th 12-4.

Charles M. Russell Museum Complex

400 13th St., North, Great Falls, MT 59401; (406) 727-8787. Commemorates art of Charles Russell and his contemporaries, while encouraging new art. Museum exhibits works by Russell from 1864-1926, J.H. Sharp, E.S. Curtis, E.E. Heikka, E.I. Couse, C.A. Beil, O.L. Seltzer, and Winold Reiss, as well as Browning Firearms collection. Archives hold Joe deYoung's correspondence and notes in Flood collection; photos related to Russell, Sharp, and Curtis; recordings of art lectures, interview with Sharp, and cowboy music; and genealogical materials on Russell. Accepts phone inquiries. Fee. Hours: reference library by appt; summer, M-Sa 9-6, Su 1-5; winter, Tu-Sa 10-5, Su 1-5.

Eastern Montana College Library

1500 N. 30th St., Billings, MT 59101; (406) 657-1664. Academic research library has General George Custer collection, including his personal and military papers, his widow's papers, records of 7th Calvary, and materials on Battle of Little Bighorn. Also maintains collection of Western History materials on Pacific Northwest and MT. Accepts phone inquiries. No fee. Hours: call.

Fort Benton Museum

c/o Joel F. Overholser, P.O. Box 69, 1212 Front St., Fort Benton, MT 59442; (406) 622-3311. Preserves and expands upon area history through holdings in museum, library, and archives. Museum holds historical files on MO River and steamboating into MT, Ft Benton as trading and supply center from 1831, and area agricultural history; census data from 1870, 1880, and 1900; and photos and genealogical records. Accepts phone inquiries. No fee. Hours: M-F 9-3:30.

Gallatin County Historical Society and Pioneer Museum

317 W. Main, Bozeman, MT 59741; (406) 586-0805. Preserves county's artifacts and written and oral history with holdings in museum and library. Holdings include maps, photos from 1920s, oral history interviews with area pioneers, records of veterans and local families since 1889, and books and pamphlets pertaining to local and MT history. Reference materials for in-house use only. Accepts phone inquiries. Donations accepted. Hours: summer, Tu-F 2-7; winter Tu-Th 2-4.

Grant-Kohrs Ranch National Historic Site

P.O. Box 790, 316 Main, Deer Lodge, MT 59722; (406) 846-2070. Commemorates frontier cattle era with museum complex of historic structures dating from 1860-1940. Museum preserves original furnishings, ranch equipment, vehicles, and tack. Library holds small number of books and documents concentrating on range cattle era, Victoriana, and natural history. Archives hold some manuscripts, photos, and oral histories relating to site. Materials for in-house use only. No fee. Hours: M-F 7:30-11:30, 12:30-4:30.

H. Earl Clack Memorial Museum

P.O. Box 1675 or 1484, Hill Country Fairgrounds, Havre, MT 59501; (406) 265-9913. Preserves history of area from prehistoric times to present. Museum displays artifacts from Wahkpa Chu'gn archaeological dig site, photos from homesteading era, and audiovisual materials on regional bison kill. Accepts phone inquiries. No fee. Hours: 9-9.

Historical Museum at Fort Missoula

Bldg. 322, Fort Missoula, Missoula, MT 59801; (406) 728-3476. Collects, preserves, and interprets history of Missoula county, Ft Missoula, as well as history of forest management and timber production in western MT. Museum on Ft Missoula grounds; holds large collection of artifacts. Library has small reference collection on museum holdings and MT history. Special collection of 640 vintage WWII-era propaganda films on display. Accepts phone inquiries. Dona-

tions accepted. Hours: Labor Day-Memorial Day, Tu-Sa noon-5; Memorial Day-Labor Day, Tu-Sa 10-5, Su noon-5.

Huntley Project Museum of Irrigated Agriculture

P.O. Box 86, Ballantine, MT 59006; (406) 967-3464. Preserves and depicts evolution of agricultural industry in West, and its machinery, technology, crops, and customs. Museum displays explain first federally funded irrigation project in nation, and provide background information on people who participated in program. Library contains collection of pictures, stories, and booklets, maps, photos, recordings, genealogical records, and limited films/videotapes. Accepts phone inquiries. Donations accepted. Hours: 9-4:30.

Montana Historical Society

225 N. Roberts, Helena, MT 59601; (406) 444-2694. Collects, preserves, and documents MT and regional history. Library of state documents and MT newspapers; archives of state agency records; mining business records, including Anaconda Copper Mining Company; many maps, mainly MT from 1865; photos of Northern Pacific Railroad, Yellowstone National Park, and National Cattle Industry from 1870s; large oral history collection; genealogy research materials from original 13 states; and Mason Band Music score collection, 1915-40. Materials do not circulate. Accepts phone inquiries (406-444-2681). No fee. Hours: museum, June-Aug, M-Su 8-5, Sept-May, M-F 8-5, Sa 9-5; library, M-F 8-5, Sa 9-4:30.

Montana State University

Special Collections/Archive Dept., The Libraries, Bozeman, MT 59717; (406) 994-4242. Academic research library with archival collections covering University history from 1893, Yellowstone National Park materials from 1881-1968, agricultural materials, MT and Northwest history, and Abraham Lincoln's life. Holdings include photos, brochures, books, and archives of Yellowstone Park; M.L Wilson's manuscripts and photos on agriculture; WPA files for MT including Federal Writers Project and Historical Records Survey; Architectural Drawing collection of MT bldgs; and Lincoln collection of books and pamphlets. Materials for in-house use only. Accepts phone inquiries. No fee. Hours: archives, M-F 8-noon; special collections, M-F 8-noon, 1-5.

Montana Women's History Project

2626 Garland, Missoula, MT 59803; (406) 251-5951. Educational and research institution on history of women in MT. Library holds papers and archival materials on MT women; small photo collection on MT women from 1880-1920s; oral histories covering homesteading and settling experience; and special collections on illegal abortion and women as community builders. Accepts phone inquiries. No fee. Hours: 8-5.

Northern Montana College

Documents Division, Vande Bogart Library, Havre, MT 59501; (406) 265-3706. Academic research library with collection of govt documents, some maps of western US, extensive photo collection on High Plains area; and limited films/videotapes. May be some restrictions. No fee. Hours: M-F 8-5, with ltd evening hours.

Old Montana Prison

1106 Main St., Deer Lodge, MT 59722; (406) 846-3111. Preserves, protects, and interprets heritage of Powell county and state of MT. Museum housed in prison buildings and grounds. Archives contains prisoners' records from 1871-1960s. Hours: call.

Powell County Museum

1106 Main St., Deer Lodge, MT 59722; (406) 846-3111. Preserves, protects, and interprets heritage of Powell county. Museum covers Native American history, and local history from 1850. Archives holds all records of Milwaukee Railroad Rocky Mountain Division, Sanborn maps of Deer Lodge from 1884-1929, large collection of photos, genealogical records, and extensive collection of clothing from 1870s. Accepts phone inquiries. Donations accepted. Hours: June-Aug noon-6.

Sod Buster Museum

Judith Basin, Rte. 3, Stanford, MT 59479; (406) 423-5358. Preserves artifacts from sod buster and homesteading era with holdings in museum

and library. Photo collection from 1890-1920. Accepts phone inquiries. No fee. Hours: June-Labor Day, 8-5; or by appt.

Towe Antique Ford Museum

1106 Main St., Deer Lodge, MT 59722; (406) 846-3111. Educates and informs public on early American travel, and preserves and protects antique cars. Museum displays antique Ford cars from 1903-50s, including Henry Ford's personal Lincoln Camper. Library contains historical reference materials on mostly Fords, some other cars from early 1900s. Accepts phone inquiries. Fee. Hours: June-Aug, 8-9; Apr-May & Sept-Oct 8:30-5:30; Nov-Mar 9-4, Sa-Su 10-5.

Tri-County Historical Society

P.O. Box 33, E. Commercial & Cedar, Anaconda, MT 59711; (406) 563-8421. Collects, preserves, and makes available records and artifacts relating to local history. Holdings include some personal, business, and org materials; large collection of state and county land maps, mining claims, water rights, and company plans; many historical photos; early films/videotapes; oral history recordings; local genealogical records; special Anaconda Mining Company, Morrisite Church, and copper industry collections. Some restrictions on use. Accepts phone inquiries. Fee for research services. Hours: M-F 1-5.

University of Montana

Maurene & Mike Mansfield Library, Missoula, MT 59812; (406) 243-6700. Academic support library acting as regional US document depository. Library holds special collections on economic and natural history, as well as lumber industry and MT history; archival University records from 1895; MT, West, USGS, and National Forest Service maps; photos of MT residents, towns, and events; films/videotapes on US, MT, West, and Indian history; some recordings of oral histories and folk, patriotic, and ethnic music; and MT census records from 1870-1910. Accepts phone inquiries (406-243-6860). No fee. Hours: during academic yr, M-Th 8-11, F 8-6, Sa 1-6, Su 1-11.

Western Heritage Center

29th and Montana Ave., Billings, MT 59741;

(406) 256-6809. Preserves and presents Yellowstone River region history through museum and library collections. Museum exhibits regional settlement and development, as well as large collection of related artifacts. Library holds small collection on regional history. Accepts phone inquiries. No fee. Hours: Tu-Sa 10-5, Su 1-5.

World Museum of Mining

P.O. Box 3000, Butte, MT 59702. Museum complex consists of complete historic town including mine, print shop, school, bank, general store, jail, blacksmith shop, fire and city hall, and ranger station. Other holdings include uncataloged and unorganized photos, maps, and local history materials. Limited access to archival materials. No fee. Hours: Mar-Nov 9-9.

Yesterday's Playthings

Powell County Museum and Arts Foundation, 1106 Main St., Deer Lodge, MT 59722; (406) 846-3111. Preserves, protects, and interprets history of dolls and toys. Collection of dolls and toys span a century, and include Madame Alexander dolls, artist dolls, ethnic dolls, advertising dolls, Indian dolls, dollhouses, and other toys. Accepts phone inquiries. Fee. Hours: May-Sept 10-7.

Nebraska

American Historical Society of Germans from Russia

631 D St., Lincoln, NE 68502; (402) 474-3363. Preserves heritage of regional German-Russians with genealogical files, historic material preservation, research documents, and informational publications. Museum is collection of buildings furnished for period; library houses some family history and church records; archives preserve correspondance, documents, and ship lists; maps depict German colonies in Russia, immigration routes, settlements in Russia, US, Canada, and South America; some films from 1930s Russia; dialect studies recordings; and genealogical records. Genealogy files for use of members only. Accepts phone inquiries. No fee. Hours: M-F 9-3:30, Sa 9-1; research M-F 9-4, Sa 9-2.

Buffalo Bill's Ranch State Historic Park

Rte. 1, Box 229, North Platte, NE 69101; (308) 532-4795. Interprets and displays this famous showman and scout's home. Accepts phone inquiries. Fee. Hours: 8-5.

Fort Robinson Museum

P.O. Box 304, Crawford, NE 69339; (308) 665-2852. Interprets history of Fort from 1874-1948. Museum houses exhibits on fort activities, and Red Cloud Indian Agency from 1873-77; fort records, local newspapers, regional maps, and photos; and oral history interviews dating from WWII period. Accepts phone inquiries. Fee. Hours: Apr-Nov M-Sa 8-5, Su 1:30-5; winter M-F 8-5.

Hitchcock County Historical Society

P.O. Box 174, 313 First East St., Trenton, NE 69044; (308) 334-5556. Preserves Hitchcock county history with emphasis on Indian presence, pioneer experience, and work of local poet William DeBolt. Museum houses pioneer and Indian history artifacts; library holds work of DeBolt; some local newspapers, writings, maps, and photos; genealogical records; and special collection on 1873 Massacre Canyon Battle between Indian tribes. Accepts phone inquiries. No fee. Hours: Memorial Day-Labor Day, Su 2-5; tours by appt.

Illinois State Genealogical Society

P.O. Box 157, Lincoln, NE 62656; (217) 732-3988. Seeks to promote interest in preservation of IL genealogical history and data. Purchases records for addition to Illinois State Archives and Illinois State Historical Library. Accepts phone inquiries. Hours: call.

Kearney State College

Calvin Ryan Library, Kearney, NE 68849; (308) 234-8542. Academic support library with strengths in colonial, early American, and military history. Holdings include NE topographical maps and historical atlases; NE census records; NE town and city histories; materials on War of Rebellion; FBI report on J.F. Kennedy assassination; materials on Pony Express, Union Pacific, Indians of NE, and cattle industry; and some regional newspaper and genealogy collections.

Some materials do not circulate. Accepts phone inquiries. No fee. Hours: M-F 7:30-5.

Museum Association of American Frontier and Fur Trade

HC-74, Box 18, Chadron, NE 69337; (308) 432-3843. Preserves materials and history of fur trade in North America with museum, library, and archival collections. Holdings include limited manuscripts, maps from 18th and 19th c, some photos of western Indians, and some genealogical records on fur traders. Materials used by permission. Accepts phone inquiries. Fee for non-members. Hours: June-Labor Day, 8-6; rest of year by appt.

Museum of Missouri River History

P.O. Box 124, Brownville, NE 68321; (402) 825-3341. Museum holds some maps and photos. Accepts phone inquiries. Fee. Hours: Apr-Oct 10-6.

National Museum of Roller Skating

7700 A St., Lincoln, NE 68510; (402) 489-8811. Preserves and promotes history of roller skating and its industry origins from early 18th c. Museum collects skates, competition and show costumes, and other memorabilia from 1820s; large number of skating programs; archives of Roller Skating Rink Operators Association from 1937, US Amateur Confederation of Roller Skating record copies; personal papers of skaters and rink operators from 1930s-60s; large photo collection; extensive film/videotape footage of competitions from 1942; skating rink music from 1930s; and Van Roekel patent models and application files for roller skates from 1860s-90s. Accepts phone inquiries. Fee. Hours: 8:30-5.

Nebraska Library Commission

Documents Division, 1420 P St., Lincoln, NE 68508; (402) 471-2045. State library agency and selective federal depository with special collection of NE materials. Accepts phone inquiries. No fee. Hours: M-F 8-5.

Nebraska State Historical Society

P.O. Box 82554, Lincoln, NE 68501; (402) 471-4751. Collects, preserves, researches, and promotes history of NE and Great Plains, as well as history of Greenback party and silver/money

question of late 19th c. Museum holds state records, state govt files, newspapers, materials on N American Indians, agricultural papers, manuscripts, artifacts, maps, photos, genealogical materials, films/videotapes, and recordings. May be some restrictions. No fee. Hours: M-F 10-5, Sa 8-5.

Omaha History Museum

Western Heritage Museum, 801 S. 10th St., Omaha, NE 68108; (402) 444-5072. Preserves artifacts and documents of city's past through extensive collection of photos, restored art deco railway station and streetcar, and collection of coins and paper money. Extensive photo archives consist of Bostwick collection on early 20th c images of Omaha people and places; John Savage photojournalist collection of regional events, news happenings, and visiting dignitaries and celebrities; and F.A. Rinehart-Marsden collection of commercial Omahans portraits from 1898. Byron Reed collections of coins, paper money, signatures, and manuscripts, will open in fall of 1988. Accepts phone inquiries. Fee. Hours: Tu-Sa 10-5, Su 1-5.

Plainsman Museum

Hamilton County Historical Society, 210 16th St., Aurora, NE 68818; (402) 694-6531. Preserves local and regional history with collection of murals, mosaics, and exhibits tracing region's history from pre-historic times to Coronado Expedition. Museum shows period log, sod, and Victorian homes; dolls, toys, agricultural implements, firearms, and early autos from pioneers; photos of Hamilton County; maps of county and landowner divisions; oral history interviews; genealogical records; and large collections of memorabilia from plains settlers. Accepts phone inquiries. Fee. Hours: Apr-Oct, M-Sa 9-5, Su 1-5; Nov-Mar 1-5.

Railroad Station Historical Society

430 Ivy Ave., Crete, NE 68333; (402) 826-3356. Preserves research and history of railroad station depots and other railway buildings through materials in library and photo archives. Accepts phone inquiries. Hours: 9-9.

Scotts Bluff National Monument

P.O. Box 427, Gering, NE 69341; (308) 436-

4340. Preserves history of Oregon/California Trail and interprets westward expansion period of history. Museum houses exhibits on Mormons, fur traders, pioneers, and paintings of William Jackson; library holds info on westward expansion; copies of pioneer diaries; maps; papers and records of James Cook of Agate Springs Ranch; collection of Sioux Indian artifacts; and some photos of park and historic sites. Materials for in-house use only. Accepts phone inquiries. No fee. Hours: M-F 8-4:30.

Union Pacific Museum

1416 Dodge, Omaha, NE 68179; (402) 271-3964. Preserves and promotes history of Union Pacific, its subsidiaries, and branches from 1862. Holdings in library, museum, and archives include maps, photos, and films/videotapes. Accepts phone inquiries. No fee. Hours: M-F 9-5.

United Church of Christ
Department of History and Archives

Nebraska Conference, 2055 E St., Lincoln, NE 68510; (402) 488-0682. Promotes research on history of NE congregationalism since 1854, and United Church of Christ since 1958. Library has records of state and district orgs and some local churches. Archives contain minutes of district and state orgs, some materials on youth work from 1920s, and manuscripts. Accepts phone inquiries. No fee. Hours: M-F 8-4.

United Methodist Church

Nebraska Conference Historical Center, Nebraska Wesleyan University, 50th and St. Paul, Lincoln, NE 68504; (402) 465-2175. Preserves historical materials of United Methodist Church and previous denominations in NE. Museum exhibits pictures and artifacts from local churches, ministers and missionaries, including pulpits, pews, organs, and church commemorative plates. Library collections include Bible collection from 1850s, hymnals from 1960s, Conference minutes of Methodists from 1856 and Evangelical United Brethren from 1873, and histories and biographies. Archives hold records of Methodist ministers and churches and photos of local churches, ministers, bishops, and congregations. Some restrictions. Accepts phone inquiries. Donations accepted. Hours: M 10-noon, Tu-F 9-noon.

University of Nebraska Library

60 & Dodge Sts., Omaha, NE 68132; (402) 554-2361. Special Omaha history collection holds WPA-sponsored manuscripts, radio scripts, newspaper clippings, and other papers on Omaha history. Accepts phone inquiries. No fee. Hours: call.

University of Nebraska—Lincoln

Special Collections, Don Love Library, Lincoln, NE 68588; (402) 472-2848. Academic research library holds materials on author Mari Sandoz, WWII artist Charles Russell, and psychological warfare. Sandoz collection includes letters from 1925, author's personal library, and published and unpublished works. There is also resource collection of reading notes, clippings, and related materials. WWII collection contains propaganda from US and Japan, US newspapers published in Philippines, and other materials on war in Pacific. Russell collection contains large number of reference materials, periodicals, drawings, and family scrapbooks from 1889. Accepts phone inquiries. No fee. Hours: call.

Wayne State College

Documents Division, U.S. Conn Library, 200 East 10th, Wayne, NE 68787; (402) 375-2200. Academic research library with collections of federal and NE documents, and descriptive and topographical maps. Accepts phone inquiries. No fee for college community. Hours: M-F 9-5.

Wilber Czech Museum

P.O. Box 652, 102 W. 3rd St., Wilber, NE 68465; (402) 821-2183. Preserves and displays artifacts of Czech pioneers in US. Museum exhibits period miniature rooms and settings. Archives and library at Dvoracek Memorial Library include manuscripts, photos, and genealogical records. Materials used by approval of board. Accepts phone inquiries. No fee. Hours: 1-4.

Nevada

Alternatives in Contemporary
Issues Collection

Clark County Community College, Learning

Resource Center, 3200 E. Cheyenne, North Las Vegas, NV 89030; (702) 643-6060. Academic research library has collection of US, Canadian, Mexican, and Cuban materials on social movements and alternative lifestyles from 1918. Holdings represent political extremism from Left and Right, as well as non-traditional religions and special interests. Accepts phone inquiries. Hours: call.

Central Nevada Historical Society and Museum

P.O. Box 326, Logan Field Rd., Tonopah, NV 89049; (702) 482-9676. Preserves and displays history of central NV, chiefly Nye County and Esmeralda County areas. Holdings include mining history collection from 1800s, library, archives, maps, oral history library; slide collection of Tonopah and Goldfield, NV and residents. Restrictions for use of some materials. Accepts phone inquiries. No fee. Hours: May-Sept, 11-5; Oct-Apr, noon-5.

Fort Churchill Historic State Park

Silver Springs, NV 89429; (702) 577-2345. Park preserves history of 1860s US Army Ft Churchill in form of small museum with diorama, military artifacts from original Ft; walking trail around Ft. ruins. Accepts phone inquiries. No fee. Hours: Memorial Day-Labor Day, 8-4:30; winter hours vary.

National Judicial College

Law Library, Judicial College Bldg., University of Nevada, Reno, NV 89557; (702) 784-6039. Serves college's mission to improve proficiency, performance, and productivity of judges. Library focuses on courts and judiciary, with some collections of benchbooks and jury instructions. Accepts phone inquiries. No fee. Hours: M-F 7:30-5.

Nevada State Division of Archives and Records

Capital Complex, 101 S. Fall St., Carson City, NV 89710; (702) 885-5210. Govt archives preserve records of NV state and territory from mid-19th c. Holdings include changing museum exhibits of historical documents and photos; archives of NV govt and history, 1851-1984; small collection of maps and surveys, 1863-

1986; tape recordings of NV legislature's floor proceedings, 1965-1981. Accepts phone inquiries. No fee; charges for research undertaken by staff. Hours: M-F 8-5.

Nevada State Library and Archives

Capitol Complex, 401 North Carson St., Carson City, NV 89710; (702) 885-5160. Research agency to NV state govt maintains reference collection and selective depository materials from federal and state govt offices; archives of historic state govt and agency materials; USGS maps; genealogical records, and resource materials. Accepts phone inquiries. No fee. Hours: M-F 8-5.

Nevada State Museum and Historical Society

700 Twin Lakes Dr., Las Vegas, NV 89107; (702) 486-5205. Collects, preserves, and displays history of NV and American West in form of artifacts, documents, and research materials. Holdings include natural history and fine art collections; library, small manuscript collection; archives of Clark County records 1909-1960; photos of Las Vegas and southern NV 1905-1970; local TV-station videotapes 1969-1978. Accepts phone inquiries. Museum fee for non-members. Hours: M-Tu, 11:30-4:30; W-F, 8:30-4:30; Sa-Su (museum only) 8:30-4:30.

Nevada State Railroad Museum

Capital Complex, Carson City, NV 89710; (702) 885-4810. Collects and preserves railroad equipment, artifacts, and memorabilia relating to NV and the American West. Holdings include four steam locomotives and several pieces of rolling stock; history exhibits and photo displays; small library and archives; large collection of historic NV railroad slides and photos. Archives closed to public. Accepts phone inquiries. Fee for train ride. Hours: (museum) summer, F-Su 8:30-4:30; (office) M-F 8-5; (library and photo collections) by appt only.

Nevada Supreme Court Library

Supreme Court Bldg., Capitol Complex, 100 N Carson St, Carson City, NV 89710; (702) 885-5140. Legal research library maintains collection of American and British law documents, original statutes, and reports from Colonial times to current rulings. Some restrictions on rare materials. Accepts phone inquiries. No fee. Hours: M-F 8-5.

University of Nevada

Oral History Program, Reno, NV 89557; (702) 784-6932. Program produces primary source oral histories for use as documentation of history and culture of NV and the Great Basin. Holdings include library of all oral histories produced by program from 1965; videotapes, oral history recordings. Accepts phone inquiries. Fees for purchase of oral history volumes, cassette recordings, and videotapes. Hours: 8-noon, 1-5.

University of Nevada at Las Vegas

Special Collections, James Dickinson Library, 4505 Maryland Parkway, Las Vegas, NV 89154; (702) 739-3252. Academic research library is special repository of info on history of southern NV and gambling. Holdings include manuscripts, maps from 19th c, large photo collection, and videotapes. Special collections include papers of Sen Howard Cannon, collection of menus from 19th c, and Nuclear Regulatory Commission materials for Yucca mountain studies. Restrictions on use of materials. Accepts phone inquiries. No fee. Hours: M-F 8-5, Su 1-5.

University of Nevada Library

Special Collections, Reno, NV 89557; (702) 784-6528. Academic library has Women in West collection focusing on women's 19th and 20th c experiences in West and materials on NV architects and architecture. Women in West holds first-hand accounts, diaries, letters, autobiographies, and major biographies of significant women. Special Women in the West collection has materials on major women in 19th and 20th c. Architecture collection holds plans and papers of 3 major NV architects, DeLongchamps, Parsons, and Wells, as well as NV architecture. Accepts phone inquiries. No fee. Hours: call.

Western History Association

University of Nevada, Reno, Department of History, Reno, NV 89557; (702) 784-6852. Assn promotes the study and preservation of history of US West through conferences, publications, newsletter, and special events. Accepts phone inquiries. Membership fee. Hours: call.

New Hampshire

Dartmouth College

Special Collections, Baker Library, Hanover, NH 03755; (603) 646-2037. Academic research facility with library and resource materials on American literature, Arctic and Antarctic regions, NH White Mountains, northern New England railroads, Daniel Webster, NH political leaders, and writers, artisans, and businesses. Large collection of printed materials on Dartmouth, and surrounding town of Hanover. Holdings include manuscripts, maps, photos, recordings, and genealogical materials. Some NH imprints available. Some restrictions. Accepts phone inquiries. No fee. Hours: M-F 8-4:30.

Manchester Historic Association

129 Amherst Street, Manchester, NH 03104; (603) 627-7531. Collects, interprets, and makes available local history. Museum displays materials on Native Americans, Colonial and Victorian periods, textile mills, and fire fighting. Library documents local history with records of city government and textile manufacturing. Archives holds local business and civic org records, family manuscripts, maps, photos, oral histories, genealogical materials, and textile sample books. Accepts phone inquiries. No fee. Hours: Tu-Sa 9-4.

Nashua Public Library

Documents Division, 2 Court St., Nashua, NH 03060; (603) 883-4141. Provides public with New England, MA, and Nashua history materials. Hunt Room has collection of local history and genealogy. Small collection of maps, and historical Nashua photos available. Genealogical sources for NH, and local history pamphlet file maintained. Some materials non-circulating. Accepts phone inquiries. No fee. Hours: M-F 8:30-9, Sa 8:30-5:30, and Sept-Apr, Su 1-4.

New England Historical Research Associates

Box 453, South Rd., Fremont, NH 03044; (603) 895-4032. Promotes and encourages interest in local New England history and genealogy. Library has materials on NH and New England history from 1607. Archives hold documents from 1700-1880, diaries and journals, maps of NH towns and counties, photos and postcards, and genealogical records. Special collections include historical info on southern NH communities. Materials for in-house use only. Accepts phone inquiries. Fees for lectures, seminars, and research. Hours: M-F 8-5, Sa 8-noon.

New England Ski Museum

P.O. Box 267, Franconia Notch, Pkwy Exit 2, Franconia, NH 03580; (603) 823-7177. Preserves collection of trophies, ski equip from 1890-1950, clothing from 1930s, posters, and memorabilia. Library has reference materials from 1890. Archives contain records of early skiing clubs, meets, and instruction; maps of early Northeast ski areas and trail; large collection of photos from 1890s; and large collection of oral history tapes from ski pioneers. Accepts phone inquiries. Fee. Hours: winter, 10-4; summer 10-5.

New Hampshire Antiquarian Society

RD #3, Box 132, Main St., Hopkinton, NH 03229; (603) 746-3825. Collects and preserves local and genealogy history. Museum exhibits Hopkinton artifacts from 1765. Library has business and personal records from local residents, manuscripts, maps, photos from 1875, videotapes, oral history recordings, and genealogical records. Special collections of early musical instruments, looms, early fire pump, and Indian artifacts. Accepts phone inquiries. No fee. Hours: M-F 1-5, W 9-11, 1-5.

New Hampshire Division of Records Management and Archives

71 S. Fruit St., Concord, NH 03301; (603) 271-2236. Collects and maintains original records of NH. Archival state manuscripts date to mid-17th c. Holdings include records from land transactions, probate, and military. Accepts phone inquiries. No fee. Hours: M-F 8-4:30.

New Hampshire Farm Museum

P.O. Box 644, Rte. 16, Plummer's Ridge, Milton, NH 03851; (603) 652-7840. Dedicated to preserving and carrying on NH agricultural heritage. Museum consists of restored farm struc-

tures. Library contains photos of early farming life, oral histories, genealogies, and special room on historical items and papers of Milton residents. Accepts phone inquiries. Fee. Hours: museum, June-Oct, F-Su 10-4.

New Hampshire Historical Society

30 Park St., Concord, NH 03301; (603) 225-3381. Museum and library preserve NH history from 1650. Holdings include manuscripts from 1700-1950, including papers of Mary Baker Eddy, Josiah Bartlett, John Langdon, Charles Sanger Mellen, Nathaniel Peabody, Mason Weare Tappan, Austin Pike, Charles Marseilles, Jacob Gallinger, George Moses, and many other NH residents; maps from 1700-1950; photos from 1850-1950; records of Dover manufacturing co; military records and orderly books relating to NH military during French & Indian War through Civil War; oral history recordings from 1960, and genealogical records from 1750. Accepts phone inquiries. Fee. Hours: M-F 9-4:30, Sa noon-4:30.

New Hampshire State Library

20 Park St., Concord, NH 03301; (603) 271-2394. Serves NH residents by providing materials on state history, Lincoln, early sermons, and some 18th and 19th c religious tracts and periodicals. Library collects manuscripts, maps, photos, and genealogical records. Some materials do not circulate. Accepts phone inquiries. No fee. Hours: M-F 8:30-4:30.

Old Fort Number Four Associates

P.O. Box 336, Springfield Rd., Rte. 11, Charlestown, NH 03603; (603) 826-5700. Provides for curation of Fort at No. 4 living history museum. Reconstructs life on eastern frontier in 1740s-50s in this fortified settlement. Library is accumulating materials on original Fort families and French and Indian War period, including journals, letters, and town histories. May be some restrictions. Accepts phone inquiries. Fee. Hours: Memorial Day-Labor Day, W-M 10-4.

Plymouth State College Department of History

Rounds Hall, Plymouth, NH 03264; (603) 536-5000. Library collection documents logging and paper making in Berlin, NH from 1900-65.

Holdings include photos and archival materials, and are kept in college library. Accepts phone inquiries. No fee. Hours: M-F 8-4:30.

Portsmouth Athenaeum

P.O. Box 848, Portsmouth, NH 03801; (603) 431-2538. Preserves printed materials on NH and maritime topics. Museum displays objects of historical Portsmouth interest. Holdings include paintings by Smibert, lift models, and images of Portsmouth-built vessels. Library houses 18th and 19th c literature from Europe and America, materials on American ethnology and Indians, maritime, foreign and North American travel, exploration, and NH serials. Archives hold records from NH Fire and Marine Insurance Co, personal manuscripts, and moderately-sized collection of 19th c Portsmouth photos. Some restrictions on use. Accepts phone inquiries. No fee. Hours: Tu-Th 1-4, Sa 10-4, or by appt.

Saint Anselm College

Documents Division, Geisel Library, St. Anselm Dr., Manchester, NH 03102; (603) 669-1030. Academic research library with collection of NH topographical maps, CIA world maps, and atlas collection. Special collections on American civilization, American history, church history, and New England history. Materials for in-house use only. Accepts phone inquiries. No fee. Hours: M-F 8-4:30; call for hours on weekends and eves.

Saint-Gaudens National Historic Site

RR 2, Box 73, Cornish, NH 03745; (603) 675-2175. Preserves gallery, home, and sculpture of Augustus Saint-Gaudens. Exhibits include plaster casts of coin designs and portrait bas-reliefs; original family furnishings and sculpture; historic photos relating to Saint-Gaudens family, their home, Cornish Art Colony members, and related art; and film/video documentaries on Saint-Gaudens. Accepts phone inquiries. Hours: end of May-Oct, 8:30-4:40.

Scouting Museum

Camp Carpenter, P.O. Box 1121, RFD #6, Bodwell Rd., Manchester, NH 03105; (603) 669-8919. Preserves and collects memorabilia of Boy Scouts. Holdings include badges, buttons, kerchiefs, caps, and covers from "Boy's Life."

Library contains reference materials, yearbooks, handbooks, and periodicals. Accepts phone inquiries. No fee. Hours: Sept-June, Sa 10-4; Jul-Aug, 10-4.

Shaker Village

Shaker Rd., Canterbury, NH 03224; (603) 783-9511. Preserves and interprets important Canterbury Shaker collection artifacts. Museum consists of church, dwelling, infirmary, laundry, and school. Library contains reference info. Archives have manuscripts from 19 Shaker communities, including covenants, gift songs, correspondence, religious tracts, financial records, maps, photos of late 19th-20th c Shakers, film footage of Shakers, audio tapes of Eldress Bertha Lindsay's memoirs, and biographical records of all individuals who lived in village. Prior approval for research is available by writing to curator. Accepts phone inquiries. Museum fee; no fee for library. Hours: mid-May-mid-Oct Tu-Sa 10-5.

Strawbery Banke

P.O. Box 300, 454 Court St., Portsmouth, NH 03801; (603) 433-1100. Preserves cultural heritage of Portsmouth and Piscataqua River Basin through collection of artifacts, books, and documents. Museum exhibits cover commercial and domestic artifacts and fine arts of 18th-20th c. Library materials cover regional history, decorative arts, architecture, archaeology, and crafts. Other holdings include personal records, business documents, org and public documents, 19th c Portsmouth-area maps, extensive photo collection from 19th and 20th c, and published and unpublished genealogical records. Accepts phone inquiries. Fee. Hours: 10-5.

Sugar Hill Historical Museum

Village Green, Sugar Hill, NH 03585; (603) 823-8142. Collects, preserves, and exhibits heritage of Sugar Hill and surrounding towns in New Hampshire's White Mountains. Museum documents region history from 1782 through late 19th c and early skiing from 1930s. Library retains town civic and govt records, maps of counties and state, photos of town, and oral history interviews. Other holdings include 19th c carriage collection, materials on early 19th c Franconian Iron Industry, and 19th and early 20th c. Hours: call.

Thalberg Collection

Dartmouth College, Baker Library, Hanover, NH 03755; (603) 646-2037. Contains special Thalberg collection of approx 2500 scripts from 1930s-40s from Warner Bros, MGM, and Twentieth Century Fox movies. Materials non-circulating, and cannot be photocopied. Accepts phone inquiries. No fee. Hours: M-F 8-4:30.

New Jersey

American Labor Museum

Botto House National Landmark, 83 Norwood St., Haledon, NJ 07508; (201) 595-7953. Preserves the heritage of American workers, their unions, workplaces, ethnicity, and culture. Botto House is Italian-American immigrant home designated as landmark. Museum houses materials on 1913 Paterson silk strike and other period artifacts. Library and archives contain resource materials, including atlases from 1800; photos of strike, Botto family, Haledon, and Paterson history; labor films; and oral history collection. Accepts phone inquiries. Fee. Hours: W-Su 1-4.

Archaeological Society of New Jersey

Seton Hall University, South Orange, NJ 07079; (201) 761-9543. Promotes understanding of Lenape Indians and NJ prehistory. Museum displays artifacts from NJ and indigenous Native Americans, as well as mid-Altantic region. Library holds small reference collection on Eastern Woodlands Indians, USGS and NJ Geological Survey maps, and slides of archaeological excavations and artifacts. Accepts phone inquiries. No fee. Hours: M-Sa 9-6.

Army Chaplain Museum

USACHCS-ATSC-SEC-M, Watters Hall, Bldg. 1207, Ft Monmouth, NJ 07703; (201) 532-5809 or 3487. Presents history of Army chaplaincy from early roots to present day. Museum artifacts from colonial period. Library has Bibles and military pamphlets from colonial period. Archives has personal papers, sermons, tracts, and photos from WWII of chaplains and their activities. Accepts phone inquiries. Hours: call.

Atlantic County Historical Society

P.O. Box 301, 907 Shore Rd., Somers Point, NJ 08244; (609) 927-5218. Collects, preserves, and displays Atlantic country, south Jersey, and state history. Museum exhibits Victorian furniture, china, glass, and costumes. Library retains county and state histories and genealogies. Archives holds family, town, and business records, maps, photos, and oral histories. Accepts phone inquiries. No fee for museum; research fee for non-members. Hours: W-Sa 10-4.

Aviation Hall of Fame of New Jersey

Teterboro Airport, Teterboro, NJ 07608; (201) 288-6344. Preserves NJ aeronautical heritage and honors men and women who contributed to development of aviation. Museum exhibits include Curtiss-Wright engines and Arthur Godfrey's aeronautical collection. Library holds large collection of aviation books and manuals. Archives retain largest collection of NJ aviation pioneer biographies available, as well as photos, manuscripts, and films/videotapes on NJ aeronautical industries. Accepts phone inquiries. Fee. Hours: 10-4.

Battleship New Jersey Historical Museum Society

P.O. Box BB-62, Middletown, NJ 07748; (201) 774-0726. Society houses materials on battleship USS New Jersey, and works toward establishing it as museum when it is eventually retired. Society archives retain newspaper articles, small collection of photos, and films/videotapes on ship's history. Also publishes monthly newsletter. Accepts phone inquiries. No fee. Hours: call.

Bayonne Firefighters' Museum

10 W. 47th St., Bayonne, NJ 07002; (201) 858-6005. Collects, preserves, and displays firefighting memorabilia. Museum displays art, artifacts, equipment, badges, helmets, and photos from 1840. Library houses journals from NY city volunteers and Bayonne volunteers from late 1800s, materials on history of Bayonne, Sanborn maps from early 1900s, old training films on fire preventaion in America, original artwork from volunteer fire dept in NY city, and oldest horse carriage in NJ. Some restrictions. Accepts phone inquiries. No fee. Hours: call.

Bayonne Free Public Library

Documents Division, 697 Avenue C, Bayonne, NJ 07002; (201) 858-6970. Academic research library has materials on local history, photo collection, and collection of US govt documents. Accepts phone inquiries. No fee. Hours: M-F 9-9, Sa 9-5.

Bergen County Office of Cultural and Historic Affairs

327 Ridgewood Ave., Room 212, Paramus, NJ 07652; (201) 599-6151. Promotes historic preservation, protection of county historical records, and growth of cultural and historical orgs in Bergen county. Owns eight historic sites: Gethsemane Cemetery, burial site for black residents until Negro Burial Bill passage; 18th Dutch Garretson Forge & Farm; WWI Camp Merritt Memorial Monument; Revolutionary War Baylor Massacre site; restored Campbell-Christie House; Washington Spring Garden; Wortendyke Barn; and Easton Tower. Library and archives have materials on historic preservation and local history, maps, photos, and Surveys of County Historic Sites and Early Stone Houses. Accepts phone inquiries. No fee. Hours: by appt, M-F 9-4.

Burlington County Historical Society

457 High St., Burlington, NJ 08016; (609) 386-4773. Encourages historical study and research, and collects and preserves history of Burlington county. Museum displays lighting equipment, tools, furniture, and dolls. Library holds historical and genealogical materials from 1670s. Archives have collection of manuscripts, old newspapers, maps of Burlington area, photos, and genealogical materials. Lewis Jones collection contains 8mm film footage of Florence/Roebling area from 1933-76. Special collection includes materials on James Fenimore Cooper. Accepts phone inquiries. Fee. Hours: Su 2-4, M-Th 1-4.

Camden County Historical Society

Park Blvd. and Euclid Ave., Camden, NJ 08103; (609) 964-3333. Preserves history of Camden county, southern NJ, and Delaware Valley. Museum exhibits include early American tools, crafts, glass, lighting devices, fire-fighting equipment, toys, and 18th-19th c military and indus-

trial artifacts. Library documents history of Camden county, NJ, and PA. Archives holds manuscripts, large collection of maps, photos, records of Victor Talking Machine Co., genealogical records, and papers of Charles Boyer, Samuel Mickel, Philip Mackey, and Cooper family. Accepts phone inquiries. Fee for tours. Hours: M-Th 12:30-4:30, Su 2-4:30.

Cape May County Historical and Genealogical Society

DN-707, Rte. 9, Cape May Court House, NJ 08210; (609) 465-5458. Preserves objects, artifacts, and documents significant to Cape May county's history and culture. Museum in John Holmes House contains decorative arts from late 17th-early 20th c; medical room documents changes in surgical instruments and techniques from Revolutionary War period to Spanish-American War; military collection has guns, swords, uniforms, and other memorabilia from Revolution to Vietnam War, including Merrimac flag. Other holdings on mining, whaling, and maritime activities. County photos, slide tape presentations, and genealogical materials available. Accepts phone inquiries. Fee. Hours: museum, Tu-Sa 10-4; genealogy library by appt only, Tu, W, F, 10-4.

Cranford Historical Society

124 Union Ave., N., Cranford, NJ 07016; (201) 276-0082. Collects, preserves, protects, and exhibits local oral history materials. Museum exhibits emphasize Victorian period. Archives hold local govt records, maps, photos, oral history recordings, and collections of early household and agricultural implements. Accepts phone inquiries. No fee. Hours: Th 9-noon, 2-4.

Daily Register Library

1 Register Plaza, Shrewsbury, NJ 07701; (201) 542-4000. Library collects thousands of newspaper stories. Accepts phone inquiries. No fee. Hours: M-F 9-5.

Edison National Historic Site

Main St. and Lakeside Ave., West Orange, NJ 07052; (201) 736-0550. Preserves Thomas Edison's West Orange laboratory, artifacts, and documents. Museum exhibits large collection of Edison inventions, materials on general technology and industry, and Victorian home furnishings. Library has materials from Edison, his colleagues, and family, on science, patents, technology, and general literature. Archives contain many Edison papers; company and laboratory records; maps; large photo collection; newsreels and promotional films; copies of early Kinetoscopes; and extensive collection of released and unreleased Edison sound recordings. Accepts phone inquiries. Fee for tours. Hours: tours, W-Su 9-5; archives by appt only, M-F 9-4:30.

Firefighters Museum of Southern New Jersey

E. Ryon Ave., Pleasantville, NJ 08232; (609) 641-9300. Preserves fire apparatus and related items from 1780. Library holds materials on fire-related issues. Archives has small collection of materials on local fire depts, including manuscripts, maps, photos, and other special collections. Materials for in-house use only. Accepts phone inquiries. No fee. Hours: by appt only.

George J. Woodruff Indian Museum

Bridgeton Free Public Library, 150 E. Commerce St., Bridgeton, NJ 08302; (609) 451-2620. Collects artifacts used by Indians in Bridgeton region. Library contains small collection on Indian history, genealogical records from local region, and some New Jersey archival materials. Accepts phone inquiries. No fee. Hours: M-Sa 1-4 and June-Aug, Sa 9-1.

Glassboro State College

Special Collections, Savitz Learning Center, Glassboro, NJ 08028; (609) 863-6317. Academic research library holds materials on Colonial America, including biographies of Franklin and Washington, materials on Loyalists, and details on Revolutionary figures in NJ campaign. Other materials include copies of European archival materials on America from 1773-1783. Accepts phone inquiries. No fee. Hours: call.

Gloucester County Historical Society

P.O. Box 409, 17 Hunter St., Woodbury, NJ 08096; (609) 845-4771. Resource center for south Jersey history and genealogy. Museum displays 18th-20th c artifacts, furnishings, and memorabilia at 58 N. Broad St., Woodbury.

Library specializes in history and genealogy of south Jersey and Delaware Valley region. Archives holds large collection of county papers from 1686-1900, covering election returns, tavern petitions, Revolutionary War, slave records, Civil War, and railroads; maps of NJ, PA, and US; photos; genealogical materials; and special collections of Howell family memorabilia, and Richard Somers' late 19th c Navy and family history. Accepts phone inquiries. No fee. Hours: M-F 1-4, F 7-9:30, and last Su of month 2-5.

Grover Cleveland Birthplace

207 Bloomfield Ave., Caldwell, NJ 07006; (201) 226-1810. Preserves and displays historic personal items and memorabilia from life of Grover Cleveland. Museum and library hold collection of manuscripts, photos, and limited genealogical records. Accepts phone inquiries. No fee. Hours: W-F 9-noon, 1-5; Sa noon-5, 1-6; Su 1-6.

Hardyston Heritage Society

Old Monroe Schoolhouse Museum, RD 1, Box 599, Star Route 49, Monroe, Hamburg, NJ 07419; (201) 827-4459. Provides facility for developing interest in historic preservation. Museum housed in Old Monroe Schoolhouse. Library focuses on materials of educational interest. Archives holds school records and papers from 1900-26, class pictures, and NJ maps. Accepts phone inquiries. Fee. Hours: 1st Su of month, 1-4.

Hermitage

335 North Franklin Turnpike, Ho-Ho-Kus, NJ 07423; (201) 445-8311. Preserves Hermitage historic site, and historic materials on Rosencrantz family. Museums include 2 Victorian houses, clothing collection spanning 3 centuries, exhibits, and programs. Library materials concentrate on clothing and museum collections. Archives contains personal papers and memorabilia of Rosencrantz family from 1800-1970, including manuscripts, maps, photos, genealogical records. Accepts phone inquiries. Donations accepted. Hours: M-F 9-4.

Hightstown East Windsor Historical Society

164 N. Main St., Hightstown, NJ 08520; (609)

448-3332. Preserves history of Hightstown-East Windsor region. Greek Revival home houses museum collection of period antiques. Library has local history reference collection. Archives retain materials from 1680s, including manuscripts, maps, photos, films/videotapes, recordings, genealogical records, and special collections of newspapers, and 19th c legal materials. Restrictions on use. Accepts phone inquiries. No fee. Hours: by appt only.

Historical Society of the Reformed Church in America

21 Seminary Place, New Brunswick, NJ 08901; (201) 246-1779. Preserves archival materials of Reformed Church in America and its institutions and agencies. Holdings include records of denomination's congregations and missions abroad since 1633; records of clergy and missionaries from 1800; large collection of photos; oral histories from church leaders and missionaries; and genealogical records of Dutch Reformed churches from 1700. Accepts phone inquiries. Fee. Hours: by appt only, M-F, 9-4.

Jazz Studies at Rutgers Institute

Bradley Hall, Newark, NJ 07102; (201) 648-5595, 5180. Maintains collections on jazz and related musical subjects. Holdings include Marshall Stearns and George Hoefer collections of records, books, and clippings; Charles Smith collection of records and books; John Owne collection of records; and McVitty collection of records, books, and clippings. Accepts phone inquiries. No fee. Hours: by appt only, M-F 9-5:30.

John Cotton Dana Library

Rutgers University, 185 University Ave., Newark, NJ 07102; (201)648-5901. Academic research library holds special collection of Robert Frost first editions, and some art. Accepts phone inquiries. No fee. Hours: M-Th 8-11, F 8-9, Sa 10-6, Su noon-6.

Johnson Free Public Library

Documents Dept., 275 Moore St., Hackensack, NJ 07601; (201) 343-4169. Public library with materials on NJ, Bergen county, and local history. Serves as depository for US and NJ documents; collects historical maps of Bergen county, including atlases, road maps, and geological survey maps. Houses Bergen County Historical Society collection. Accepts phone inquiries. No fee. Hours: M-Th 9-9, F-Sa 9-5.

Kean College of New Jersey

Nancy Thompson Library, P.O. Box 411, Morris Ave., Union, NJ 07083; (201) 527-2112. Academic research library with special collection on NJ history, and collection of US Congressman Florence Dwyer papers. Accepts phone inquiries. No fee. Hours: 8-10.

Madison Township Historical Society

Thomas Warne Historical Museum and Library, RD 1, Box 150, Morristown Rd., Rte. 516, Old Bridgetown Township, Matawan, NJ 07747; (201) 566-0348. Preserves local history through holdings in museum, library, and archives. Museum exhibits fossils, Indian artifacts, local farm tools, costumes, textiles, and pottery. Library has resource materials on NJ history, religion, and science. Archives contain music collection, including sheet music and records. Other holdings include maps, local photos, and genealogical materials. Accepts phone inquiries. No fee. Hours: W and 1st Su of month, 9:30-noon, or by appt.

Medical History Society of New Jersey

Academy of Medicine of New Jersey, 2 Princess Rd., Lawrenceville, NJ 08648; (609) 896-1717. Provides continuing education programs on history of medicine in NJ. Accepts phone inquiries. Fee for membership. Hours: M-F 8:30-4:30.

Monmouth County Historical Association

70 Court St., Freehold, NJ 07728; (201) 462-1466. Protects, preserves, and interprets history and culture of Monmouth county. Museum housed in four 18th c museums with many exhibits on local history and American decorative arts. Library has materials on Monmouth and Ocean counties, as well as NY, NJ, and New England. Archives retain manuscript collections from North American Phalanx Utopian Community, Freehold Young Ladies' Seminary, Philip Freneau, Allaire Family Papers, and Tinton Falls

Iron Works; maps; photos; and genealogical materials. Materials non-circulating. Accepts phone inquiries. Hours: call.

Monroe Township Historical Society
P.O. Box 474, Williamstown, NJ 08094; (609) 629-4767. Preserves memorabilia and artifacts of Monroe Twshp. Museum exhibits clothing, furnishings, photos, and documents. Other holdings include oral history interviews and some genealogical materials. Accepts phone inquiries. Fee for membership. Hours: Th 2-4, or by appt.

Motor Bus Society
P.O. Box 7058, West Trenton, NJ 08628. Preserves historical and educational materials on motor bus transporation in North America with special collection on Greyhound. Museum collects model buses. Library houses books, magazines, histories, photos, many maps on bus transportation from 1913-87. Archives hold govt records on bus transportation, extensive photo collection on old buses. Visits by appt only through mail inquiries. No fee.

Museums Council of New Jersey
William Paterson College, Ben Shahn Center, Wayne, NJ 07470; (201) 595-2676. Collects and promotes info on historical society museums in NJ, and serves administrative function. Accepts phone inquiries. Hours: M-F 9:30-4.

National Archives and Records Administration
New York Branch, Building 22, Military Ocean Terminal, Bayonne, NJ 07002; (201) 823-7252. Serves as repository for permanent records of field offices of federal agencies in NY, NJ, Puerto Rico, and Virgin Islands. Records cover US Food Administration from 1917-19; US District Courts from 1685; Bureau of Naval Personnel from 1941-46; US Coast Guard from 1942-82; US Customs Service from late 19th c; IRS from NY and NJ; Immigration and Naturalization Service in NY from 1792-1906; case files of Chinese who applied for reentry permits; FAA from 1963-74; USIA from 1948-54; American Revolution Bicentennial from 1974-76; US Attorneys and Marshals from 1821-83; and 1970-71 Puerto Rico Presidential Vote. Accepts phone inquiries. No fee. Hours: M-F 8-4:30.

New Jersey Historical Commission
113 West State Street, CN 305, Trenton, NJ 08625; (609) 292-6062. Commission promotes preservation of New Jersey history and the advancement of public knowledge through scholarly research and publications, public events, grants, Afro-American history and ethnic history preservation, information clearinghouse activities, and consultation services to historical organizations. Commission cooperates with various state agencies. Accepts phone inquiries. Hours: M-F 9-5.

New Jersey Historical Society
230 Broadway, Newark, NJ 07104; (201) 483-3939. Collects, preserves, and disseminates info and materials related to NJ heritage. Museum exhibits material culture of NJ from 1650 with displays of furniture, paintings, prints, textiles, ceramics, metalwares, and utilitarian wares. Library has large collection on state history from early settlement. Archives has NJ Historical Society records from 1845, manuscripts from 1664, large map collection from 1659, NJ photos from 1850, small collection of films/videotapes on various aspects of NJ history, genealogical materials, broadsides, newspapers, periodicals, and pamphlets. Materials non-circulating. Accepts phone inquiries. Fee. Hours: Tu-Sa 10-4, Su noon-4.

New Jersey Museum of Transportation
P.O. Box 622, Allaire State Park, Route 524, Wall, Farmingdale, NJ 07727; (201) 938-5524. Preserves, restores, and operates railway equipment, with special emphasis on industrial railroading. Museum exhibits display Pine Creek Railroad, with working demonstration of steam- and diesel-powered locomotives, freight and passenger cars, and assorted railway structures. Special collection of Plymouth Locomotive Works products from 1917-74, and collection of railroad tools, hardware, signs, lanterns, and headlamps. Accepts phone inquiries. Fee. Hours: 10-4.

New Jersey Postal History Society
28 Briar Lane, Barking Ridge, NJ 07920. Studies postal communications and usages in NJ. Membership fee.

New Jersey Society of the Sons of the American Revolution

P.O. Box 168., 126 Morris Ave., Springfield, NJ 07081; (201) 467-1771. Preserves Revolutionary War research materials and genealogies in museum, library, and archives. Collections include maps and photos. Restrictions on use. Accepts phone inquiries. No fee. Hours: Tu, Th 9-4.

Newark Museum

49 Washington St., Newark, NJ 07101; (201) 596-6550. Art, history, and science museum. Library contains photos and films/videotapes. Accepts phone inquiries. No fee. Hours: Tu-Su noon-5.

Newark Public Library

New Jersey Reference Division, Box 630, 5 Washington St., 3rd floor, Newark, NJ 07101; (201) 733-7775 and 7776. Preserves history of NJ, Newark, and Essex county, including urban affairs and biography. Special collections include Stephen Crane collection, NJ and Newark photos, and clipping and photo archives of "Newark Evening News" from 1912-72. Accepts phone inquiries. No fee. Hours: M-W, Th 9-9, F 9-6, Sa 9-5.

North Jersey Electric Railway Historical Society

Box 1770, Rahway, NJ 07065; (201) 388-0369. Preserves, restores, displays, and operates electric railway rolling stock and other historic transportation vehicles. Collection has cars from Public Service Railway, Erie Lackawanna, Erie Railroad, and CNJ "Blue Comet" Combine. Accepts phone inquiries. No fee. Hours: 9-9.

Ocean City Historical Museum

409 Wesley Ave., Ocean City, NJ 08226; (609) 399-1801. Preserves and displays Ocean City history and historical artifacts. Museum displays Victorian rooms and memorabilia from Ocean City from 1880-1900. Library holds reference materials, limited maps, and photos from 1880s-1930s. Hours: Apr-Dec 10-4.

Old Barracks Association and Museum

Barrack St., Trenton, NJ 08608; (609) 396-1776. Preserves historic Old Barracks bldg and interprets American culture and history of colonial and revolutionary NJ. Museum exhibits restored "squad room" that recreates barracks interior during British occupancy; and period rooms of 18th and 19th c furniture, ceramics, textiles, and decorative arts. Accepts phone inquiries. Fee. Hours: M-Sa 10-5, Su 1-5.

Outdoor Advertising Association of America Archive

Farleigh Dickenson University, Friendship Library, 285 Madison Ave., Madison, NJ 07940; (201) 593-8531. Academic research library is official depository for Outdoor Advertising Industry Association of America. Large collection include manuscripts, photos, slides, and original billboards. Hours: by appt, M-F 8:30-4:30.

Passaic County Historical Society

Lambert Castle, Garret Mt. Reservation, Valley Rd., Paterson, NJ 07503; (201) 881-2761. Preserves county history through restored 1892 museum home of Paterson silk manufacturer and local history materials in library and archives. Holdings include pamphlet collection from local orgs/towns, papers relating to developer of submarine John Holland, materials of industrial magnates active in manufacture of locomotives and Colt revolvers, manuscripts from Society for Establishment of Useful Manufacturers, local history maps, large collection of historical photos, and genealogical records. Special Bertha Schaefer Koempel Spoon Collection. Accepts phone inquiries. Fee. Hours: W-Su 1-4.

Passaic Public Library

195 Gregory Ave., Passaic, NJ 07055; (201) 779-0474. Public library preserves materials on history of NJ and Passaic. Holdings include books; Benjamin Turner collection of Passaic photos from 1920s-30s, William Swartz collection of Passaic photos from 1890-1910, Grace Speer photos from 1850-1930; and Herbert Fisher collection of sketches of Revolutionary War era Dutch homes in county. Accepts phone inquiries. No fee. Hours: M-F 9-9, Sa 9-5.

Plainfield Public Library

Eighth St. at Park Ave., Plainfield, NJ 07060;

(201) 757-1111. Public library with collection of NJ and US depository materials, USGS topographical maps of NJ and national forest, photos of Plainfield, DAR genealogical records, collections of NY State Genealogical and Biographical Society, and Plainfield and NJ history. Accepts phone inquiries. No fee. Hours: M-Th 9-9, F-Sa 9-5.

Preservation New Jersey
180 Township Line Rd., Belle Mead, NJ 08502; (201) 359-4557. Statewide org provides info, education, and advocacy assistance on historic preservation issues. Sponsors conferences and workshops, publishes newsletter on preservation activities, and promotes preservation of NJ's architectural and cultural heritage. Accepts phone inquiries. Fee for membership. Hours: M-F 10-4.

Princeton University Library
Manuscript Collection, Princeton, NJ 08544; (609) 452-3701. Academic research library has records of Committee to Defend America by Aiding the Allies from 1940-42; Blair-Lee family papers dealing with American political and naval history from 1733-1916; Adlai Stevenson collection of personal papers; James Madison collection of materials, including Dolley Madison. Accepts phone inquiries. No fee. Hours: call.

Railroadiana of America
18 Okner Parkway, Livingston, NJ 07039; (201) 956-8273. Maintains collection of materials on history of railroading in library. Holdings include maps and photos. Also publishes on topics concerning historic railroad stations. Materials circulate to members only. Accepts phone inquiries. Fee for membership. Hours: M-Tu 9-3.

Ringwood Manor House
Ringwood State Park, P.O. Box 1304, Sloatsburg Rd., Ringwood, NJ 07456; (201) 962-7031. 19th c house museum preserves period lifestyle, and archival materials on iron industry. Museum displays living conditions of Ryerson, Cooper, and Hewitt families. Archives contains 18th-19th c iron industry records and maps. Special collections include Louis P. West, Sr collection and Anna Parmee collection. Historical Society library can be contacted at (201) 962-

6548. May be some restrictions. Accepts phone inquiries. Fee. Hours: May-Oct, Tu-F 10-4, Sa-Su 10-4:30.

Roebling Historical Society
140 3rd Ave., Roebling, NJ 08554; (609) 499-2415. Preserves history of John A. Roebling Steel Co. and company town. Museum exhibits artifacts from Steel Co. and town, including maps, photos from 1905-80, and work records. Films/videos and slide presentation available. Accepts phone inquiries. No fee. Hours: call.

Rutgers University
Alexander Library, College Ave. & Huntington St., New Brunswick, NJ 08903; (201) 932-7526. Collects and preserves manuscripts of Morris family from 1677-1948; Neilson family from 1680-1930, William Paterson from 1745-1806, Sen Joseph Frelinghuysen from 1869-1948, Gibbons family from 1767-1897, Philip Freneau from 1752-1832, Samuel Smith from 1721-1776, George Cook from 1818-1889, Samuel B. Howe from 1790-1868, Sen Clifford Case from 1904, and Walt Whitman from 1819-1892. Also has materials from corporate bodies, societies, and municipalities; some NJ maps from 16th c; and over 100 19th-20th c lithographic city views. Accepts phone inquiries. Hours: call.

Seton Hall University Museum
Seton Hall University, South Orange, NJ 07079; (201) 761-9543. Promotes understanding of Indian peoples who inhabited NJ and Northeast region. Museum, library, and archival holdings relate to North American Indians, and include journals, manuscripts, maps, photos, and limited recordings. Slide show available on Indians of Lenapehoking. Research facilities restricted. Accepts phone inquiries. No fee. Hours: 9-4:30.

Society of Colonial Wars
in the State of New Jersey
P.O. Box 168, 126 Morris Ave., Springfield, NJ 07081; (201) 467-1771. Preserves Colonial (1607-1775) materials and genealogies in museum and library. Restrictions on use. Accepts phone inquiries. No fee. Hours: Tu, Th 9-4.

Stevens Institute of Technology
Samuel Williams Library, Castle Point Station,

Hoboken, NJ 07030; (201) 420-5198. Library has special collection of original design drawings of US Ironclad Monitor. Accepts phone inquiries. Hours: call.

Stockton State College Library

Pomona, NJ 08240; (609) 652-4343. Academic research library with special collections on Pine Barrens, black studies, women's studies, and Jewish studies. Holdings include maps, films/videotapes, and recordings. Holocaust Center in development stage; will have recordings of local survivors. Accepts phone inquiries. No fee. Hours: M-Th 8-10, F 8-5, Sa-Su 9-10.

Submarine Memorial Association

P.O. Box 395, Hackensack, NJ 07601; (201) 342-3268. Naval museum and park displaying WWII submarine USS Ling. Museum displays naval memorabilia, pictures, and models. Some naval history films/videotapes available. Accepts phone inquiries. Fee. Hours: Feb-Nov 10-4:30; Dec-Jan, W-Su 10-4:30.

Trenton Historical Society

P.O. Box 1112, Trenton, NJ 08606; (609) 883-8260. Promotes and preserves Trenton history. Accepts phone inquiries. Hours: call.

United Methodist Church Commission on Archives and History

P.O. Box 127, 36 Madison Ave., Madison, NJ 07940; (201) 822-2787. Collects, preserves, and disseminates info on history of United Methodist Church. Museum, library, and archival collections consist of manuscripts, large photo collection, 16mm films, videotapes, recordings, and genealogical records. Materials non-circulating. Accepts phone inquiries. No fee. Hours: M-F 9-5.

United States Golf Association Museum and Library

Route 512, Golf House, Far Hills, NJ 07931; (201) 234-2300. Traces history of golf through displays of artwork by Harry Rountree, Dwight Eisenhower, and Vanity Fair; clubs and scorecards of famous individuals, including John F. Kennedy, Alan Shepard, and USGA champions; and trick clubs and golf-related paraphernalia from trophies to ice cream molds. Accepts phone

inquiries. Hours: M-F 9-5, Sa-Su 10-4.

Vineland Historical and Antiquarian Society

P.O. Box 35, Vineland, NJ 08360; (609) 691-1111. Promotes and collects info and material on history and genealogy of south Jersey. Museum exhibits Civil War and Indian artifacts, Victorian furnishings, local glass art, and other household items. Library contains extensive materials on genealogy, and Civil War records. Archives retains rare books, photos, manuscripts, and maps. Materials for in-house use only. Accepts phone inquiries. Donations accepted. Hours: Tu-Sa 1-4.

Wallace House— Old Dutch Parsonage

38 Washington Place, Somerville, NJ 08876; (201) 725-1015. Preserves and presents to public the history of two 18th c families and their homes. Homes are furnished with 18th c decorative arts, and have exhibits on Revolutionary War and New World Dutch Culture. Accepts phone inquiries. No fee. Hours: W-Sa 10-noon, 1-5; Su 1-5.

Walt Whitman Association

328 Mickle Blvd., Camden, NJ 08103; (609) 541-8280. Promotes interest in works and times of Walt Whitman. Museum in Whitman house contains his possessions and artifacts. Library has extensive collection of materials on and by Whitman. Materials non-circulating. Accepts phone inquiries. No fee. Hours: by appt only.

Westfield Historical Society

P.O. Box 613, 614 Mountain Ave., Westfield, NJ 07091; (201) 232-1776. Preserves, interprets, and encourages community interest in history generally and history of Westfield in particular. Museum presents living history program. Library and archives hold maps, photos, household artifacts, assorted cosmetics, newspapers, WWI posters, Victorian clothing, flags, Civil Defense artifacts, and furniture. Restrictions on use. Accepts phone inquiries. Fee. Hours: Sept-Jun, Su 2-5, and by appt.

Wheaton Village

Glasstown Rd., Millville, NJ 08332; (609) 825-

6800. Preserves history of American glass, regional history, and crafts. Museum and library document all periods of American glass, with emphasis on local history. Other holdings include insurance maps, photos of glassmaking, films/videotapes of glassmaking, and oral history interviews. Materials for in-house use only. Accepts phone inquiries. No fee for library; fee for galleries and exhibits. Hours: library by appt only, M-F 10-5.

New Mexico

Albuquerque Museum of Art, History, and Science

P.O. Box 1239, 200 Mountain Rd. NW, Albuquerque, NM 87103; (505) 243-7255. Collects, preserves, and displays art, technology, and history of Middle Rio Grande Valley from 1540 in form of exhibits, library, and archival collections. Holdings include artifacts related to Spanish Colonial, Mexican, and US eras of Albuquerque and the Middle Rio Grande Valley; small library with historical and cultural resource materials; extensive photo archives of Albuquerque area, 1868-1970s; small collection of 16th-20th c maps of Albuquerque and Spanish Southwest. Some restrictions. Accepts phone inquiries. Fee. Hours: Tu-F 10-5, Sa-Su 1-5.

Albuquerque Public Library

Special Collections, 423 Central, NE, Albuquerque, NM 87102; (505) 848-1376. Provides genealogical and local history materials for researchers interested in Albuquerque and NM history. Library holds some census and state history materials, videotapes, Albuquerque oral histories, materials on Navajo, Hopi, Pueblos, and Apaches, and extensive genealogy materials. Materials non-circulating. Accepts phone inquiries. No fee. Hours: T, Th 12:30-8; W, F, Sa 9-5:30.

Aztec Museum Association

125 N. Main, Aztec, NM 87410; (505) 334-9829. Preserves history of Aztec, NM region in form of maps, manuscripts, pioneer artifacts; mineral, fossil and seashell collections; Navajo Indian rugs and silver; Anasazi Indian artifacts

from Aztec Ruins Natl Monument; antique oil, mining and farming equipment; 1900 barber shop. Extensive archives, photos, genealogical records of area and residents. Accepts phone inquiries. No fee. Hours: M-Sa 10-4.

Billy the Kid Museum

Rte. 1, Box 36, 1601 E. Sumner Ave., Fort Sumner, NM 88119; (505) 355-2380. Museum collects, preserves Western American history, 1850-1950 with "Wild West" relics, artifacts of Billy the Kid, and antique farm machinery. Accepts phone inquiries. Fee. Hours: 8:30-5.

Center for Anthropological Studies

P.O. Box 14576, 540 Chama, NE, Albuquerque, NM 87191; (505) 296-4836. Preserves and promotes understanding of human prehistory, ethnohistory, and ethnography in greater Southwest. Museum in planning stages; library houses materials on archaeology, ethnology, and history, including photos. Also holds special collection of Richard and Marietta Wetherill family records. Publishes materials on Southwest cultures. Accepts phone inquiries. No fee. Hours: by appt only, 8-5.

Chaves County Historical Museum

200 N. Lea Ave., Roswell, NM 88201; (505) 622-8333. Preserves and displays historical items related to county, Pecos Valley, NM, and Southwest. Historic house from 1910 era holds museum collecions. Archives collect maps, photos, and oral history recordings from local individuals, businesses, and organizations. Restrictions on use. Accepts phone inquiries. Fee. Hours: F-Su 1-4.

Ernie Pyle Public Library

Albuquerque Public Library System, 900 Girard, SE, Albuquerque, NM 87106; (505) 256-2065. Public library with special collection preserving materials on the life and work of war correspondent Ernie Pyle. Holdings include personal photos, clippings and memorabilia. Pyle collection is non-circulating. Accepts phone inquiries. No fee. Hours: Tu-Th 9-8; W, F, Sa 9-5:30.

Fort Selden State Monument

Box 58, Radium Springs, NM 88054; (505)

526-8911. Remains of ft commemorate military era of 1880s. Museum exhibits uniforms, life at ft, and artifacts from site. Library has limited materials on frontier ft life and photos. Accepts phone inquiries. Fee. Hours: 9-noon, 1-4:30.

Fort Union National Monument

c/o Superintendent, Fort Union National Monument, State Rte. 477, Watrous, NM 87753; (505) 425-8025. Preserves and interprets site of 19th c military post and its relation to the Santa Fe Trail. Holdings include museum with interpretive exhibits and artifacts relating to frontier military life and the Santa Fe Trail; library with publications and other resource materials relating to the US Army during the Indian Wars period, the Santa Fe Trail, and Westward Expansion within the NM Territory; small collections of maps and photos of ft and trail; small collection of oral histories relating to ft, trail, and Northeast NM; genealogical materials on those connected with ft. Materials non-circulating. Accepts phone inquiries. Fee in summer. Hours: 8-4:30.

Ghost Ranch Living Museum

Rte. 84, Abiquiu, NM 87510; (505) 685-4312. Museum promotes environmental education through interpretation and display of local flora and fauna. Holdings include geologic, natural history exhibits; live wild animals native to area; artifacts of early human inhabitants of region; rare books library; videotapes. Accepts phone inquiries. Donations accepted. Hours: Oct-Mar, 8-4:30; Apr-Sept, 8-6.

Historic Preservation Division

New Mexico Office of Cultural Affairs, 228 E. Palace Ave., Santa Fe, NM 87503; (505) 827-8320. Office locates and nominates significant historic properties to the State and National Registers for funding and preservation. Maintains archives of nominations, including photos and other documents pertinent to these records. Accepts phone inquiries. No fee. Hours: 8-5.

Historic Santa Fe Foundation

P.O. Box 2535, Santa Fe, NM 87501; (505) 983-2567. Preserves and maintains historic landmarks and structures of Santa Fe. Library has collection of materials on preservation books.

Archives has files on historic Santa Fe bldgs, photos, and collection of Santa Fe historic publications. Accepts phone inquiries. No fee. Hours: 9-3.

Historical Society of New Mexico

P.O. Box 5819, Santa Fe, NM 87502; (505) 983-2646. Encourages preservation of NM history and heritage through educational programs; special conferences, activities and events; fundraising; publications; and work with local NM historical societies. Accepts phone inquiries. No fee. Hours: 9-5.

Indian Pueblo Cultural Center

2401 12th St., NW, Albuquerque, NM 87102; (505) 843-7270. Collects and preserves artifacts and culture of Pueblo and Southwestern Indians. Holdings include museum with historical materials on Indian myth and culture, and exhibits of the arts and crafts of the Indian Pueblos; library with materials on Pueblos life, culture, and Southwest Indian archeological findings; archives with US Dept of Interior, NM state govt records, and other materials relating to Pueblos; BIA and other govt maps; photos; oral history videotapes; recordings of Pueblo songs and dances. Some restrictions. Accepts phone inquiries. Fee for museum. Hours: Museum: M-Sa 9-5; library and archives: W 8-noon or by appt.

Institute of American Indian Arts Museum

1369 Cerrillos Rd., Santa Fe, NM 87501; (505) 988-6281. (Mailing address: c/o CSF Campus, St. Michaels Dr., Santa Fe, NM 87501) Museum preserves and displays contemporary arts and crafts of over 150 American Indian Tribes. Holdings include baskets, beadwork, ethnic materials, jewelry, paintings, pottery, quillwork, rugs, sculptures, textiles; the Native American Videotape Archives; library, archives, oral histories, photos and slides. Accepts phone inquiries. No fee. Hours: M-F 8-5, Sa-Su 10-5.

Las Vegas Rough Rider and City Museum

P.O. Box 179, Las Vegas, NM 87701; (505) 425-8726. Preserves and displays history and culture of Las Vegas, and life and times of Teddy Roosevelt's Rough Riders in form of exhibits, library, and archival collections. Holdings include Rough Rider memorabilia; Native American, frontier American, and pre-columbian historical artifacts; library with materials relating to Spanish-American War action in Cuba and the Philippines; historic local and state map reproductions; photos of Roosevelt, the Rough Riders, the Cowboys Reunion Rodeo, and 19th and 20th c frontier images. Accepts phone inquiries. Donations accepted. Hours: M-Sa 9-noon, 1-4.

Lea County Cowboy Hall of Fame and Western Heritage Center

New Mexico Junior College, 5317 Lovington Hwy, Hobbs, NM 88240; (505) 392-4510, ext. 371. Preserves Western heritage and history of Lea County in form of publications, educational programs, museum and hall of fame. Holdings include exhibits on early Indian and pioneer living; rodeo artifacts; memorabilia and audio-visual presentations of hall of fame inductees; library, archives, and small photo collection; family albums of local residents. Accepts phone inquiries. No fee. Hours: M-Th 8-5, F 8-3.

Los Alamos County Historical Museum

P.O. Box 43, Los Alamos, NM 87544; (505) 662-6272. Collects, preserves, and promotes history of Los Alamos County, NM and residents in form of exhibits, library, and archival collections. Holdings include artifacts dating back to 12th c, including materials relating to the building and testing of first atomic bomb; small library with materials on local ethnography, archeology, botany, zoology, and history; archives with local historical mansucripts, maps, and photos; local historical films/videotapes, including special collection of films taken at Los Alamos Ranch School, 1918-1942. Some restrictions. Accepts phone inquiries. No fee. Hours: M-Sa 10-4, Su 1-4.

Maxwell Museum Photo Archive

University of New Mexico, Albuquerque, NM 87131; (505) 277-6630 or 4404. Preserves and curates photos with Southwest themes. Archive contains over 50 thousand photos, some from archaeological excavations, and ethnological images from world. Some films/videos available. Accepts phone inquiries. No fee. Hours: call.

Menaul Historical Library of the Southwest

301 Menaul Boulevar., Northeast, Albuquerque, NM 87107; (505) 345-7727 ext. 25. Collects and preserves historical materials on the Menaul School, and on Presbyterianism in the Southwest US. Holdings include 19th c artifacts, bibles and books; library collections of publications, slides, photos, and other resource materials on Southwest Presbyterian history, missions, and churchs; archival collections of General Assembly (PCUSA) Minutes, and Synod and Presbytery Records; small collection of early Southwest mission maps; oral history tapes and transcripts; correspondence of Sheldon Jackson, 1856-1908. Some restrictions. Accepts phone inquiries. No fee. Hours: M-F 8-4, during academic year.

Millicent Rogers Museum

P.O. Box A, Taos, NM 87571; (505) 758-2462. Collects, preserves, and displays prehistoric Southwestern and Plains Native American art and material culture; religious and secular arts of Hispanic New Mexico; and Maria Martinez Family Collection. Accepts phone inquiries. Fee. Hours: May-Oct, 9-5; Nov-April, W-Su 10-4.

Museum of New Mexico

P.O. Box 2087, Palace of the Governors on the Plaza, Santa Fe, NM 87503; (505) 827-6474. Museum complex preserves history, art, and culture of New Mexico. Museum of Fine Arts holdings include paintings, sculpture, arts and crafts of region; The Palace of Governors houses New Mexico history museum, archives, maps, library, and photo archives. Library is non-circulating. Accepts phone inquiries. Fee. Hours: museum, 10-5; archives and research library hours vary.

National Atomic Museum

P.O. Box 5400, Bldg. 20358, S. Wyoming Blvd.; Kirtland AFB, Albuquerque, NM 87115; (505) 844-4225. Preserves and displays history of American nuclear weapons in form of artifacts and records from 1945. Holdings include bomb casings, atomic cannon shells, rocket bodies, solar energy items; library; archives of nuclear weapons historic correspondences; manuscripts, photos, public information recordings on nuclear power. Accepts phone inquiries. No fee. Hours: 9-5.

New Mexico Association of Museums

P.O. Box 5746, Santa Fe, NM 87502; (505) 827-6478. Professional assn of NM museums and museum personnel promotes preservation of state history through publications, conferences, workshops, and seminars. Accepts phone inquiries. No fee. Hours: call.

New Mexico Genealogical Society

P.O. Box 8283, Albuquerque, NM 87198. Org encourages genealogical research by members and researchers for publication. Society plans lectures, workshops, and seminars for genealogists; holds records of NM wills, births, marriages, cemeteries, and mortuaries; and publishes quarterly magazine.

New Mexico Highlands University

Donnelly Library, National Ave., Las Vegas, NM 87701; (505) 425-7511, ext. 332. Academic research library has archives of Ft Union, NM Territorial Archives, and historical photos of Las Vegas. Special collections include Westphall collection of US history materials, Schambery collection on black history, William Gray Reading collection on materials published between 1884-1976, and Arrott collection on local NM and Southwest history. Materials for in-house use only. Accepts phone inquiries. No fee. Hours: 8-noon, 1-5.

New Mexico Medical History Program

University of New Mexico, Medical Center Library, Albuquerque, NM 87131; (505) 277-0656. Documents history of public health and medical care in NM and southwest US, including health professions, Native American and Hispanic healing traditions, and medicine men of Southwest. Library and archive materials are mostly 20th c, including photos and oral history interviews. Materials for in-house use only. Accepts phone inquiries. No fee. Hours: M-F 8-5.

New Mexico State Records Center and Archives

404 Montezuma St., Santa Fe, NM 87503; (505) 827-8860. Preserves and maintains collection of NM state govt public records, and resource materials relating to NM culture and history. Holdings include reading library with materials on NM history from 1540; archives of occupying governments, including the Spanish, 1861-1821, Mexican, 1821-1846, Territorial US, 1846-1912, and Statehood from 1912; manuscripts and maps; extensive collection of photos from 1850; extensive collection of early 20th c films on NM and Southwest; small collection of oral history recordings; NM church records from 18th c; collections of materials from county govts, and from WPA. Some restrictions. Accepts phone inquiries. No fee. Hours: M-F 9-5.

Pecos National Monument

P.O. Drawer 11, Pecos, NM 87552; (505) 757-6414. National monument preserves ruins of 15th c Pecos pueblo and two associated 17th and 18th c Spanish missions. Holdings include exhibits on Pecos Valley area, from Paleo-Indian to 1888; library; photos from 1880; Kidder Collection of excavation artifacts, 1915-1927. Library for on-site users and park staff only. Accepts phone inquiries. Fee May-Oct. Hours: Labor Day-Memorial Day, 8-5; Memorial Day-Labor Day, 8-6.

Rio Grande Historical Collections

New Mexico State University Library, P.O. Box 30006, Branson Hall, Frenger St., Las Cruces, NM 88003; (505) 646-4727. Academic research library holds personal papers and archives of orgs related to NM from 1800, maps, large collection of photos from 1870, and oral history interviews. May be some restrictions. Accepts phone inquiries. No fee. Hours: M-F 8-noon, 1-5.

Roosevelt County Museum

Eastern New Mexico University, Station No. 30 ENMU, Portales, NM 88130; (505) 562-2592. Preserves and displays history of Roosevelt County area and residents through lecture series and seminars; exhibits of artifacts and art; maps; photos 1900-1920. Accepts phone inquiries. No fee. Hours: 9-5.

Roswell Museum and Art Center

100 West 11th, Roswell, NM 88201; (502) 624-

6744. Preserves art and cultural history of Spanish-Colonial, Native American and Anglo-European occupancy of American Southwest. Holdings include 19th c Plains Indians weaponry, clothing, and artifacts; 19th c Anglo-European cattle culture artifacts; 16th and 17th c Spanish arms and armor; Robert H. Goddard rocket research material and archives of 1930s. Accepts phone inquiries. No fee. Hours: M-Sa 9-5, Su and holidays 1-5.

San Juan County Archaeological Research Center and Library

975 U.S. Hwy 64, Farmington, NM 87401; (505) 632-2013. Preserves and exhibits Four Corners prehistoric and historic remains. Museum houses artifacts from Chacoan Pueblo ruin. Library concentrates on historical and archaeological findings from Four Corners area of NM. Archives holds materials and photos from 1877, and field notes and analysis from Salmon Ruin excavation. Collection of unpublished local history manuscripts. Map and photo collections. Genealogical materials on regional pioneer families. Materials for in-house use only. Accepts phone inquiries. No fee. Hours: 9-5.

Silver City Museum

312 W. Broadway, Silver City, NM 88061; (505) 538-5921. Preserves, interprets, and displays history of Silver City, NM and residents through exhibits and outreach programs. Holdings include artifacts from "Frontier Victoriana" period of late 19th c; pre-Columbian Indian pottery, Mimbres and Casas Grandes cultures; small library, newspaper archives; large photo collection 1870-1940. Accepts phone inquiries. No fee. Hours: Tu-F 9-4:30, Sa 10-4, Su 1-4.

Southwest Room

New Mexico State Library, 325 Don Gaspar Ave., Santa Fe, NM 87503; (505) 827-3823. Library provides resources and services to state and federal govt agencies, public libraries, and NM citizens. Holdings include collection of state and federal documents, census materials, USGS maps, assorted films/videotapes on NM history and culture, NM newspapers, and Southwest collection of reference materials. Materials circulate to cardholders only. Accepts phone inquiries. No fee. Hours: M-F 8-5.

Southwestern Oral History Institute

P.O. Box 3411, 3151 W. Main, Farmington, NM 87499; (505) 325-8219. Institute collects and preserves oral histories of NM residents in form of films/videotapes from 1918, and recordings from 1906. Accepts phone inquiries. No fee. Hours: M-F 8-5.

Spanish History Museum

Colonial Infantry of Albuquerque, 2221 Lead Southeast, Albuquerque, NM 87106; (505) 268-9981. (Mailing address: P.O. Box 25531, Albuquerque, NM 87125-0531) Preserves and interprets history and current impact of Spanish influence in America through lectures, changing museum exhibits, and tours. Holdings include genealogical reports on pioneer families. Accepts phone inquiries (505-268-7805). Fee. Hours: 7-5.

Telephone Pioneers of America

1209 Mountain Rd., NE, Albuquerque, NM 87110; (505) 256-2105. Assn of employees and retirees of Mountain Bell and AT&T companies maintains museum collection of historic telephones, switchboards, teletypes, insulators, tools, and other telecommunications items from 1876. Accepts phone inquiries. No fee. Hours: Tu-F 8:30-4:30.

Tucumcari Historical Research Institute

416 S. Adams, Tucumcari, NM 88401; (505) 461-4201. Collects and preserves items relating to history of region. Museum houses Indian artifacts, western gems and minerals, musical instruments, cowboy memorabilia, gun collection, saddle collection, and furnishings and instruments from 1920s-30s hospital. Accepts phone inquiries. No fee. Hours: winter, Tu-Sa 9-5, Su 1-5; summer, M-Sa 9-6, Su 1-6.

University Museum

New Mexico State University, P.O. Box 3564, Las Cruces, NM 88003; (505) 646-3739. Preserves, interprets, and displays history and culture of southern NM, northern Mexico, and southwestern US and regional Native Americans. Holdings include artifacts and small library with publications on Native Americans. Authorization from Director required for use of some materials. Accepts phone inquiries. No fee. Hours: summer, M-Sa 10-5; winter, M-F 10-4.

University of New Mexico

Fine Arts Library, Fine Art Bldg., Albuquerque, NM 87131; (505) 277-5441. Maintains collection of Southwestern music, including extensive Native American, Hispanic, and cowboy music. Accepts phone inquiries. Hours: call.

University of New Mexico

Special Collections, General Library, Albuquerque, NM 87131; (505) 277-4241. Academic research library with special collections focusing on Southwest. Large library concentrates on western America and NM; archives contains univ's records, publications, and photos; manuscript collections include original NM land grant papers, political papers, and literary materials; maps and photos of NM, Southwest, and Latin America; some films/videotapes on NM history; large oral history collection on NM Pueblo Indians; genealogical records of Santa Fe Archdiocese; Southwest collection of architectural plans and drawings; and govt depository documents from 1869. Some restrictions. Accepts phone inquiries. No fee. Hours: M-F 8-4:30.

Western New Mexico University

Documents Division, Miller Library, Silver City, NM 88061; (505) 538-6359. Univ library maintains selective collection of US govt documents and reference materials relevant to needs of students and community. Holdings include publications on NM history, and USGS topographic maps of region. Accepts phone inquiries. No fee. Hours: M-Th 8-10. F 8-5, Sa 9-1, Su 3-10.

Wheelwright Museum of the American Indian

P.O. Box 5153, 704 Camino Lejo, Santa Fe, NM 87502; (505) 982-4636. Preserves and displays history and culture of American Indians, and Navajos in particular, in form of museum exhibits, library, archives and manuscripts, photos, and recordings. Collection is non-circulating; appointment necessary. Accepts phone inquiries. Donations accepted. Hours: M-Sa 10-5, Su 1-5.

New York

1890 House

37 Tompkins St., Cortland, NY 13045; (607) 756-7551. Restored house preserves history of the property and building in form of museum, library, and archives with original manuscripts and photos. Accepts phone inquiries. Fee. Hours: Tu-Su 1-4.

92nd St. Young Men's & Young Women's Hebrew Association

1395 Lexington Ave., New York, NY 10128; (212) 427-6000. This oldest Jewish Community Center in continuous existence contains records of Young Men's Hebrew Assn from 1874-1945; Young Women's Hebrew Assn from 1902-45; combines records from 1945; and Clara de Hirsch for Working Girls from 1897-1962. Holdings include printed and written materials, photos, films, audiotapes, videotapes, and memorabilia. Accepts phone inquiries. No fee. Hours: by appt, Su-F.

Abigail Adams Smith Museum

421 East 61st Street, New York, NY 10021; (212) 838-6878. Preserved 18th c coach house, located on estate of Abigail Adams Smith (daughter of US President John Adams). Museum displays collection of decorative arts from the Federal Period, and houses a reference library with materials on architectural history, the decorative arts, and New York City history. Permission in writing is required for use of library. Accepts phone inquiries. Fee. Hours: Sept-July, M-F 10-4.

Adelphi University

Documents Division, Swirbul Library, South Ave., Garden City, NY 11530; (516) 663-1036. Academic library maintains selective collection of govt documents, general, reference and historical materials relevant to needs of the school and students. Holdings include univ archives and photos; special collections relating to antislavery movement, pre-Civil War New York City, Long Island, William Cobbett, Americana, William Blake, Cuala Press, expatriate literature of the 1920s and 30s, origin and development of the English novel, Spanish Civil War papers, and

Gerhart Hauptman. Does not accept phone inquiries. No fee. Hours: summer, M-Th 8-9, F 8-5, Sa noon-4, Su 1-5; winter, M-Th 8-11, F 8-9, Sa 9-9, Su 1-11.

Adirondack Center Museum

Court St., Elizabethtown, NY 12932; (518) 873-6466. Studies, collects, preserves and promotes history of Essex County, NY and residents in form of museum with artifacts of early pioneer life, culture, and industry; library; archives, manuscripts, maps, photos, films/videotapes, recordings, and genealogical records. Accepts phone inquiries. Fee. Hours: Library and archival collections: Tu, Th 9-3; museum: mid-May-mid-Oct, M-Sa 9-5, Su 1-5; mid-Oct-mid-May, by appt.

Adirondack Museum/Adirondack Historical Association

Rt. 28N and 30, Blue Mountain Lake, NY 12812; (518) 352-7311. Museum preserves heritage of Adirondack region with materials on history, people, furniture, industry, logging, economics, and sites in Adirondacks. Holdings include art, maps, photos, manuscripts, and vertical file material. Hours: May 28-Oct 16, 9:30-5:30.

Akwesasne Museum

Rt. 37, Hogansburg, NY 13655; (518) 358-2240. Preserves and promotes study of Native American culture and history in form of museum, craft classes, library, and archival collections. Holdings include displays of artifacts and photos; library; pamphlets and papers; maps of reserve; educational films and filmstrips; Native American musical recordings. Accepts phone inquiries. Fee for museum. Hours: M-Th 8-9, F 8-4.

Albany County Hall of Records

250 S. Pearl St., Albany, NY 12202; (518) 447-4500. Maintains collections of archival materials on Albany, NY region to support preservation of area's historical resources. Holdings include archives with public, church and genealogical records of City and County of Albany from 1650; maps from 1750; photos of city, Public Works, and streetscapes, 1900-1950; research materials, including oral and video histories, of

New Scotland Ave neighborhood; oral histories of homefront during WWII, and Jewish experience in Albany, 1900-1945; urban renewal project records, 1969-1981. Some restrictions. Accepts phone inquiries. Search fee. Hours: M-F 9-4.

Albany Institute of History and Art

125 Washington Ave., Albany, NY 12210; (518) 463-4478. Dedicated to history, art, and culture of Upper Hudson Valley Region. Museum exhibits paintings, sculpture, and decorative arts from Hudson River School, and Albany silver and 18th c limner paintings. Library has research materials in form of maps, photos, manuscripts, and genealogical records. Accepts phone inquiries. Donations accepted. Hours: Tu-F 10-5, Th 10-8, Sa-Su noon-5.

Almond Historical Society

11 N. Main St., Almond, NY 14804; (607) 276-6166 or 5565. Preserves local history in 19th c house museum. Library has genealogical materials, business records, local maps, local photos, and examples of material culture of region. Accepts phone inquiries. Donations accepted. Hours: call.

American Baptist—Samuel Colgate Historical Library

1106 S. Goodman St., Rochester, NY 14620; (716) 473-1740. Preserves history of Baptist theology, mission work, and church members. Museum displays mission artifacts from US and abroad. Library holds large collection of materials on Baptist history and theology from 17th-20th c, including pamphlets, and periodicals. Archives hold records of American Bible Union and Danish-Norwegian Baptist Conference of America, manuscripts from many Baptists, photos from 19th and 20th c, films/videotapes, recordings, and special collection of Rauschenbusch family papers. Materials non-circulating. Accepts phone inquiries. No fee. Hours: M-F 8:30-4.

American Civil Liberties Union Library

132 West 43, New York, NY 10036; (212) 944-9800. Library retains materials on US civil liberties and social sciences. Holdings include ACLU

publications, annual reports from 1920, and Board and Committee papers. Accepts phone inquiries. No fee. Hours: by appt only.

American Craft Council Library

44 W. 53rd St., New York, NY 10036; (212) 869-9422. Preserves materials and collections of contemporary American crafts. Holdings include biographical portfolio files on over 2000 American craftspeople, archival materials, displays on crafts processes and exhibitions, and catalogs. Accepts phone inquiries. No fee. Hours: Tu-W, F noon-5.

American Foundation for the Blind

M.C. Migel Memorial Library and Info. Center, 15 W. 16th St., New York, NY 10011; (212) 620-2159. Holds collection of Helen Keller papers, correspondence, literary manuscripts, legal and genealogical materials, photos, sound recordings, and one film. Accepts phone inquiries. Hours: call.

American Heritage Picture Collection

Forbes Building, 60 Fifth Ave., New York, NY 10011; (212) 206-5573. Extensive collection of images with emphasis on American history from Colonial period to present. Some strengths include discovery and exploration, decorative arts, and transportation. Most images appeared in magazine. Accepts phone inquiries. No fee. Hours: call.

American Institute of Physics

Neils Bohr Library, Center for History of Physics, 335 E 45 St., New York, NY 10017; (202) 661-9404. Preserves extensive collection of materials on modern physics and physicists, astronomy, and scientists. Archives contain letters, notebooks, and papers of physicists; materials of American physics societies and institutions; autobiographies; oral history interviews; tape recordings; and unpublished film footage. Accepts phone inquiries. Hours: call.

American Irish Historical Society Library

991 Fifth Ave., New York, NY 10028; (212) 288-2263. Maintains collection of materials on American Irish assns and interests. Holdings include documents of Friends of Irish Freedom,

Land League, Catholic Club, Guild of Catholic Lawyers, and papers of NU State Supreme Court Justice Daniel Cohalan. Some biographical materials, Irish-American literature, and Irish newspapers from 1811. Accepts phone inquiries. Hours: call.

American Italian Historical Association

209 Flagg Place, Staten Island, NY 10304; (718) 667-6628. Membership org collects, preserves, studies, and popularizes materials on American-Italian experience in US and Canada. Publishes quarterly newsletters, sponsors conferences and programs, sponsors resource depostories, and maintains info network. Accepts phone inquiries. Membership fee. Hours: call.

American Life Foundation and Study Institute

Box 349, Watkins Glen, NY 14891; (607) 535-4737. Promotes study and preservation of American cultural and architectural history through sale of publication reprints and preservation projects. Accepts phone inquiries. Hours: call.

American Merchant Marine Museum

U.S. Merchant Marine Academy, King's Point, Great Neck, NY 11024; (516) 773-5515. Promotes interest in, and preserves history of, the merchant marine and its role in US development. Holdings include art, artifacts, exhibits, and models of post WWI merchants ships; Blue Ribbon of the Atlantic (Hales Trophy); small library; archives with drawings of WWII merchant marine vessels, passenger lists of several companies of the Intl Mercantile Marine Co; US Lines archival materials; documents, films, seals and other items from the Moore McCormack Lines, Grace Line, and Delta Lin; small collections of photos, and ship line events tapes. Accepts phone inquiries. No fee. Hours: Tu-W 11-3, Sa-Su 1-4:30, or by appt.

American Museum of Fire Fighting

Harry Howard Ave., Hudson, NY 12534; (518) 828-7695. Preserves history, equip, and artifacts of fire fighting in region. Exhibits include 1870 silver-plated carriage wagon, hand- and horse-pulled wagons, 1840 bucket machine, fire extinguishers, firemen's hats, medals, and uniforms. Accepts phone inquiries. Hours: Apr-Oct, Tu-Su 9-4:30.

American Museum of Natural History

Department of Library Services, Central Park West at 79th Street, New York, NY 10024; (212) 769-5400. World's largest natural history museum promotes study of, and research on anthropologic, mineralogic and zoologic sciences through exhibits, educational programs, library, and archival collections. Holdings include extensive collection of natural history exhibits and specimens from around the world; extensive research library; rare book and manuscript collection; archives of museum materials from 1876, including papers of Henry Fairfield Osborn, George Frederick Kuns, and other associated with museum; extensive photo and film collections; Art and Realia Collection. ILL available; some restrictions. Accepts phone inquiries. Fee. Hours: M-F 11-4 (W until 8:30); Sa (winter) 10-3.

American Music Center Library

250 W. 57th St., Rm. 626, New York, NY 10019; (212) 247-3121. Maintains collection of materials on contemporary American music, both published and unpublished. Accepts phone inquiries. No fee. Hours: M-F 9:30-5:30.

American Numismatic Society Museum

Broadway at 155th St., New York, NY 10032; (212) 234-3130. Preserves history of coinage from ancient, medieval, and modern periods. Displays explain life and times of those who used these coins, from the first coins used in China to present. Accepts phone inquiries. Hours: appt suggested; Tu-Sa 9-4:30, Su 1-4.

Anthology Film Archives

32-34 Second Ave., New York, NY 10003; (212) 505-5181. Maintains collections of films and materials on history of motion pictures, with emphasis on independent/avant garde film and video. Holdings include library, with publications, ephemera, and photos of independent/avant garde films from 1920; archive of independent/avant garde films, videos and news

from 1920; dissertations and film scripts; recordings of lectures and symposia on independent video and film; genealogical records of film makers; collections relating to the Film-Makers Cooperative, and to Joseph Cornell, Maya Deren, Jerome Hill, Carl Linder, and others. Use of collections by appt. Accepts phone inquiries. No fee. Hours: 10-5.

Anthropology Museum of New York

Queens College, Dept. of Anthropology, PH234, Flushing, NY 11367; (718) 428-5650. Promotes principles of anthropology and fosters understanding of differences among ethnic groups in city. Museum exhibits cover physical anthropology, cultural anthropology, archaeology, and linguistics, as well as hominoid and early man fossils. Sponsors lectures. Accepts phone inquiries. Fee. Hours: by appt.

Anti-Defamation League of B'nai B'rith

Jacob Alson Memorial Library, 823 United Nation's Plaza, New York, NY 10017; (212) 490-2525. Collects materials on civil rights, Middle East, domestic and foreign anti-Semitism, and discrimination. Accepts phone inquiries. No fee. Hours: by appt only, M-F 9-5.

Antique Phonograph and Record Society

502 E. 17th St., Brooklyn, NY 11226; (718) 941-6835. Preserves materials on history of recorded sound, development of phonograph, and history of patents. Accepts phone inquiries. Hours: call.

Archaeology Society Staten Island

Wagner College, 631 Howard Ave., Staten Island, NY 10301; (718) 981-0973. Membership org promotes study, exploration, and research in fields of archaeology, anthropology, and related areas. Accepts phone inquiries. Fee for membership and lectures. Hours: 10-8.

Art Information Center

189 Lexington Ave., New York, NY 10016; (212) 725-0335. Clearinghouse for info on living artists and their work. Collection composed of files on artists, their work, and their exhibits in

US and abroad. Accepts phone inquiries. No fee. Hours: by appt only, M-F 10-5:30.

Arthur Sulzberger Journalism Collection

Columbia University, 304 Journalism, 116th and Broadway, New York, NY 10027; (212) 280-3860. Reference collection for journalists contains extensive library, periodical, morgue, quotation books, style manuals, and newspaper collections since 1953. Also contains every Pulitzer Prize-winning publication. Accepts phone inquiries. No fee. Hours: M-Th 9-10, F 9-7, Sa 10-5, Su noon-8.

Associated Press News Library

50 Rockefeller Plaza, New York, NY 10020; (212) 621-1580. News and info library retains national and international wire copy, sports wire copy, and New York City wire copy. Restricted to staff and AP members by appt. Hours: 7-5:30.

Aurora Historical Society

5 S. Grove St., East Aurora, NY 14052; (716) 652-8854. Records and preserves history relating to village of East Aurora and town of Aurora. Manages 3 museums, Aurora Town Museum, Millard Fillmore House, and Scheidemantel House. Library and archives contain materials on Hubbard and Roycroft, town history, and Millard Fillmore. Maps, photos, and genealogical materials available. Accepts phone inquiries. Donations accepted. Hours: 9-4.

Avery Architectural and Fine Arts Library

Columbia University, Avery Hall, 117th St. off Amsterdam Ave., New York, NY 10027; (212) 280-3501. Collects and preserves materials for architectural, historical, and archaeological academic study. Holdings include American collection of drawings, photos, letters, and manuscripts relating to architecture and architects; New York City architectural materials; trade catalogs from building products manufacturers from 1840-1950; city view books from 1870-1930; archives of Richard Upjohn, Greene & Greene, Warren & Wetmore, and others; Louis Sullivan sketches and drawings; and Frank Lloyd Wright collection. Accepts phone inquiries. No fee. Hours: call.

Baker-Cederberg Archives of the Rochester General Hospital

1425 Portland Avenue, Rochester, NY 14621; (716) 338-400, ext 3521. Preserves and exhibits medical history of Rochester County, NY and Rochester General Hospitals in form of museum and archival collections. Holdings include exhibits of artifacts relating to the hospital and medical history; archives of the hospital's records from 1847; manuscripts and documents relating to doctors at the hospital; large collection of hospital and local historical photos from 1872; oral history films/videotapes; RGH School of Nursing Alumni Collection; Base Hospital 19 (WWI) Collection, 1917-19; 19th General Hospital (WWII) Collection, 1942-45. Some restrictions. Accepts phone inquiries. No fee. Hours: By appt.

Barnard and Morris Young Library of Early American Music

270 Riverside Dr., New York, NY 10025. Maintains collection of American popular music spanning 1790-1910. Holdings include books, serials, sheet music, broadsides, anthologies, air checks, and broadcasting and music business artifacts.

Bennington Battlefield State Historic Site

RD 2, Box 11W, Hoosick Falls, NY 12090; (516) 686-7109. Historic site of the Battle of Bennington preserves American history, and maintains relief map and picture murals of battle. Accepts phone inquiries. No fee. Hours: Apr-Nov, 10-dusk.

Bronx County Historical Society

3309 Bainbridge Ave., Bronx, NY 10467; (212) 881-8900. Major research and resource center collects, preserves, documents, and exhibits material culture of Bronx area. Museum exhibits over 10 thousand artifacts of Bronx origin. Library documents growth of Bronx from 17th c, with large collection of clippings, directories, periodicals, and local newspapers. Archives holds records of Chamber of Commerce and Board of Trade from 1878-1930s, papers of Congressman Jonathan Bingham from 1962-82, manuscripts, maps, photos, postcards, and tape recordings. Materials for in-house use only. Accepts phone inquiries. Fee. Hours: 9-5.

Brooklyn Collection

Brooklyn Public Library, Grand Army Plaza, Flatbush Ave. & Eastern Pkwy., Brooklyn, NY 11238; (718) 780-7746. Preserves Brooklyn history through collections of out-of-print and defunct Brooklyn dailies. Holdings include morgue of 1841-1955 "Brooklyn Daily Eagle," maps from Army Map Service and USGS, and large photo collection covering Brooklyn residents and scenes from 1870. Special collections include materials on Civil War. Accepts phone inquiries. No fee. Hours: M-Th 9-8, F-Sa 10-6, Su 1-5.

Brooklyn College Library

Bedford Ave. & Ave. H, Brooklyn, NY 11210; (718) 780-5346. Academic research facility collects materials on history of College, community, and those associated with institution. Library holds Brooklyn Borough history collection and rare 18th and 19th c literary works. Archives hold college administration, faculty, and alumni records from 1926; manuscripts from Irwin Shaw, Oscar Handlin, and Norman Rosten; small map collections; photos from 1930s; films of college events and speeches; and large audio collection from alumnus Sam Levenson from 1940s-65. Accepts phone inquiries. No fee. Hours: M-F 9-5.

Brooklyn Historic Railway Association

599 E. 7th St., Brooklyn, NY 11218; (718) 941-3160. Promotes restoration of historic Atlantic Ave tunnel, world's oldest subway, and preservation of downtown Brooklyn light rail system. Museum exhibits cover Brooklyn rail transportation and trollerys from 1832-1914. Holdings include manuscripts, maps, photos, and films/videotapes. Materials non-circulating. Accepts phone inquiries. Hours: M-F 9-5.

Brooklyn Public Library

Languages, Literature, Fiction Division, Grand Army Plaza, Brooklyn, NY 11238; (718) 780-7734. Collection of materials on history of literature, literary criticism, languages, and language education. Special collections include materials on Brooklyn authors, Walt Whitman, and Henry

Miller. Accepts phone inquiries. No fee. Hours: M-Th 9-8, F-Sa 10-6, Su 1-5.

Broome County Historical Society

30 Front St., Binghamton, NY 13905; (607) 772-0660. Collects, preserves and promotes history of Broome County, NY and residents in form of historic house museum, library, and archival collections. Holdings include restored Roberson Mansion and local history gallery; research library with extensive collections on local and state history and genealogy; extensive collection of manuscripts, account books, and diaries from late 1700s; extensive photo collection. Library collections are non-circulating. Accepts phone inquiries. No fee. Hours: Tu-F 10-5.

Buffalo and Erie County Historical Society

25 Nottingham Court, Buffalo, NY 14216; (716) 873-9644. Collects and preserves Buffalo and western NY historical materials. Library documents Niagara Frontier history, including clipping and vertical files, census records, 19th c Buffalo newspapers, and atlases and maps of Western NY state. Manuscripts from 18th c include papers of Joseph Ellicott, Peter Porter, Cary family, Conger Goodyear, and President Millard Fillmore; Fronczak papers on 20th c American-Polish work in medicine and military; and trial transcripts of Leon Czolgosz, assassin of Pres. McKinley. Photo collection covers 19th c Buffalo views, bldgs, Indians, residents, and Pan-American Expo. Accepts phone inquiries. Fee. Hours: W-F 10-5, Sa noon-5.

Buffalo and Erie County Public Library

Lafayette Square, Buffalo, NY 14203; (716) 846-8900. Public library maintains selective collection of govt documents and regional general and historical materials. Holdings include US Patent materials; archives with materials of and on Western NY composers; large collection of topographic maps; photos, films/videotapes, recordings, and genealogical records; the Gluck Collection of Manuscripts and Autographs; collection of American sheet music from 1796; collection of manuscript/early editions of Huck Finn; Complete Elephant Folio of Audubon's

Birds of America; prints of Niagara Falls. Rare book rm has large WWI & WWII posters. Accepts phone inquiries. No fee. Hours: M, Tu, W, F, Sa 8:30-6, Th 8:30-9.

Butler Library
Manuscript Collections

Columbia University, 535 W. 114th St., 6th Floor, New York, NY 10027; (212) 280-3528. Extensive collection of manuscript materials from U.S. authors, businessmen, journalists and publishers, orgs, political leaders, sociologists, and others. Some significant collections include writings by D.H. Lawrence, Steinbeck, Allen Ginsberg, Hart and Stephen Crane, Tennessee Williams, Joseph Pulitzer, Bella Abzug, Alexander Hamilton, and John Jay. Materials on Frederick Douglass, Lincoln, Booker Washington, Harper & Row, Random House, Carnegie Endowment for International Peace, League of Women Voters from NYC and NY state also available. Accepts phone inquiries. No fee. Hours: M-F 9-4:45.

Butler Library
Oral History Collection

Columbia University, 535 W. 114th St., 6th Floor, New York, NY 10027; (212) 280-2273. Collection contains extensive number of interviews and transcriptions from 1948. Some holdings include recordings of Frances Perkins, US Sec of Labor; Millicent Fenwick; Lee Strasberg; Nikola Franges on assassination at Sarajevo; and many others. Accepts phone inquiries. No fee. Hours: M-F 9-5.

Butler Library Rare Book
and Manuscript Collection

Columbia University, 535 W. 114th St., 6th Floor, New York, NY 10027; (212) 280-3528. Academic research library contains extensive collection of American literature and historical writings. Holdings cover classical authors, history of children's literature, photographic history, history of printing, and New York City politics. Holdings include Benjamin collection of Knickerbocker literature; books arts collection; dramatic museum and library; Engel collection of first editions from Poe, Whitman, Frank Baum, and others; historical children's literature; archival Holland Society materials; Kilroe

collection of Tammany Hall materials; and writings from Beat movement and polar exploration. Accepts phone inquiries. No fee. Hours: call.

Butterick Archives and Library

161 Ave. of the Americas, New York, NY 10013; (212) 620-2562. Archives contain extensive materials on costume history, graphic arts, fashion, and advertisements and posters of historic fashions from 1863. Accepts mail inquiries. No fee. Hours: by appt only, M-F 8:45-4:30.

C.W. Post Center
of Long Island University

Special Collections, Schwart Memorial Library, Greenvale, NY 11548; (516) 299-2842. Academic research library has special collection on Theodore Roosevelt, including his writings and naval history; Lindeberg collection on architecture; Underhill collection on Quaker history; and Eugene & Carlotta O'Neill personal library collection. Accepts phone inquiries. Hours: M-Th 8-11, F-Sa 8-5, Su 1-10.

Canal Society of New York State

311 Montgomery St., Syracuse, NY 13202; (315) 428-1862. Collects, preserves and promotes history of the waterways of NY in form of archives with publications, photos, and documents. Accepts phone inquiries. Membership fee. Hours: 9-5.

Carousel Society of
the Niagara Frontier

P.O. Box 672, 180 Thompson St., North Tonawanda, NY 14120; (716) 694-2859. Preserves history and artifacts of American carousel and band organ industries, expeically those on Nieagara Frontier. Museum exhibits historic carousel productsion processes and products from 1883-1950. Library holds reference materials. Archives has records of Herschell Carousel Co, small collection of photos, and band organ music recordings. Materials for in-house use only. Accepts phone inquiries. Fee. Hours: Memorial Day-Labor Day, M, W, F-Su noon-8.

Castle Clinton National Monument

Battery Park, 26 Wall St., New York, NY 10005; (212) 344-7220. National monument preserves local, US and military history in form of exhibits, and museum with collections on the War of 1812, Victorian entertainment 1855-1890, and US immigration. Accepts phone inquiries. No fee. Hours: 9-5.

Catskill Regional Folklife Program

Catskill Cultural Center, Inc., Rt. 28, Arkville, NY 12406; (914) 586-3326. Preserves and promotes history and culture of Catskill mountain region through special programs, archives with oral histories and photos documenting nregional folklife and history, and films/videotapes of Catskill Folk Festival and Catskill and Adirondack Forest Preserves. Some restrictions. Accepts phone inquiries. No fee. Hours: M-F 10-4.

Cayuga County Agricultural Museum

Emerson Park, Rt 38A, Auburn, NY 13021; (315) 252-7644. Preserves and displays artifacts from farming life, 1860-1930, in form of agricultural and dairy exhibits and photos, and recreated blacksmith shop, general store, and farm kitchen. Accepts phone inquiries. No fee. Hours: summer, W-Su 1-5, Sept, Sa-Su 1-5.

CBS News Archives

524 W. 57th St., New York, NY 10019; (212) 975-8275. Catalogs, stores, researches, and retrieves all film/videotape material generated by CBS News from early 1950s to present, including such series as "See it Now," "Person to Person," "Airpower," "CBS Reports," and "The Twentieth Century," as well as regular news broadcasts and specials, and unedited material shot in the field. Archives is primarily for in-house use, but materials are available for outside sales. Does not accept phone inquiries. Hours: 9-5.

Cedar Swamp Historical Society

Cedar Swamp, Long Island, NY 11545; (516) 671-6156. Collects, preserves and promotes 17th c history of Cedar Swamp and residents in form of library and archival collections. Holdings include archives, manuscripts, recordings, and genealogical records; small collection of pre-1830 local maps; collection of flags that flew in Cedar Swamp, 1609-1812. Accepts phone inquiries. Membership fee. Hours: M-F 9-5.

Center for Study of the Presidency

208 E. 75th St., New York, NY 10021; (212) 249-1200. Org specializes in study of US presidency, policymaking, and relationship between executive and Congress. Holds reference materials and distributes publications. Accepts phone inquiries. Hours: call.

Chapman Historical Museum of Glens Falls

Queensbury Historical Association, Inc., 348 Glen St., Glens Falls, NY 12801; (518) 793-2826. Collects, preserves and promotes history of the Southern Adirondacks in form of museum, library, and archival collections. Holdings include furnished period rooms, 1865-1910; changing exhibits on local and regional history from 1700; collections of decorative arts, tools and equipment, dolls, costumes and textiles, and other local artifacts; library and archives with reference materials, local maps, prints, genealogical records, personal and business records from 1700; large photo library with collection of Seneca Bay Stoddard photos, and equipment. Use by appt. only. Accepts phone inquiries. Fee. Hours: Tu-Sa noon-5.

Chemung County Historical Society

415 E. Water St., Elmira, NY 14901; (607) 734-4167. Collects, preserves and promotes history of Chemung County, NY, and residents in form of museum, library, archives, manuscripts, maps, photos, films/videotapes, genealogical, and special collections. Holdings include extensive materials on Mark Twain, and Arctic Explorer Ross Marvin. Accepts phone inquiries. Research fee. Hours: M-F 9-5.

City College of New York Library

Convent Avenue at 135th Street, New York, NY 10031; (212) 690-4292. Academic research library preserves special collections on costumes, Russell Sage Library on Social Welfare, materials on NY State Air Pollution, and US, UN, and NY state depository materials. Accepts phone inquiries. No fee. Hours: M-Th 9-8, F 10-5, Sa noon-6.

City Island Historical Society and Museum

190 Fordham St., P.O. Box 33, City Island, NY

10464. Collects, preserves and promotes history of City Island, NY and residents in form of museum, research library, archives, maps, photos, recordings, and genealogical records. Use of archives, recordings and genealogical collections by appt. Does not accept phone inquiries. Donations accepted.

City University of New York Archives
307 Cohen Library, Convent Ave. & 135th St., New York, NY 10031; (212) 690-5367. Maintains collection of Nazi propaganda of 1930s-40s, WB Yeats materials, Newcomb collection of early scientific treatises, and late 19th and 20th c English literature. Accepts phone inquiries. No fee. Hours: M-F 9-5.

Clearinghouse on Women's Studies
311 E 94th St., New York, NY 10128; (212) 360-5790. Collects materials on women's history, education, vocations, and general women's studies. Accepts phone inquiries. Hours: call.

Clermont State Historic Site
RR 1, Box 215, Woods Rd. off Rte. 9-G, Germantown, NY 12526; (518) 537-4240. Preserves Clermont estate and interprets lives of 7 generations of Livington family. Estate composed of 44-room main house, formal gardens, historic landscape and carriage roads, and architectural ruins, 1728-1930. Small research library on Livingtons, Hudson Valley, and NY state from 1686-1962. Archives contains passenger ticket receipt books from steamboat partnership of Livingston/Fulton; Livingston family papers from 1730-1987; historical maps; photos from 1850-1950; small collection of video histories; recordings from 1920; genealogical materials; and garden collections. Accepts phone inquiries. No fee. Hours: library by appt; museum, May-Oct W-Su.

Columbia County Historical Society
P.O. Box 341, Kinderhook, NY 12106; (518) 758-9265. Preserves and promotes county history. Research museum exhibits paintings and exhibits. Society also curates 1737 Dutch farmhouse museum and 1820 federal town house museum. Library has reference materials on county, NY and US history. Holdings include account books, diaries, correspondence, and old newspapers from Columbia County; maps from 18th and 19th c; photos from 1850; small collection of oral history tapes from residents; and genealogical records. Materials non-circulating. Accepts phone inquiries. Donations accepted. Hours: May-Oct, M-F 10-4, and end of May-Oct, Sa 1-5.

Columbia University Teachers College Library
525 W. 120th St., New York, NY 10027; (212) 678-3045. Academic research library has special collections on New York City Board of Education, NY Juvenile Asylum from 1850-1920, Nursing Archives, and other collections related to juvenile education. Materials for use by those in college community; others for fee. Accepts phone inquiries. Hours: M-Th 10-9:30, F 10-6, Sa 10-6, Su 1-5.

Conde Nast Publications Library
350 Madison Ave., New York, NY 10017; (212) 880-8244. Maintains collection of magazine materials on fashion, architecture, interior and landscape design, personalities, models, and photographers. Holdings include copies of "Vogue" from 1892, "Glamour" from 1950, "Mademoiselle" from 1935, "Self" from 1979, "Gentlemen's Quarterly" from 1943, "Vanity Fair" from 1913-36, "Brides" from 1959, and all art work from Conde Nast magazines. Accepts phone inquiries. Hours: M-F 1-4.

Cooper Union for Advancement of Science and Arts Archives
41 Cooper Square, New York, NY 10003; (212) 254-6300. College library maintains archives relating to history of school, and materials of and about school, Peter Cooper and family, and Abe Hewitt and family. Holdings include manuscripts, clippings, photos, documents, and records. Some restrictions. Accepts brief phone inquiries (ext 186). No fee. Hours: 9-5.

Cooper-Hewitt Museum
Smithsonian Institution National Museum of Design, 2 E. 91st St., New York, NY 10128; (212) 860-6883 or 6887. Provides resources for study of history of decorative arts and design, with emphasis on Western Europe and some US from 18th-20th c. Museum exhibits drawings

and prints, textiles, and decorative arts. Library documents history of furniture, ceramics, glass, textiles, floor coverings, wall coverings, graphic arts, architectural details, paper and paper mache, clocks, toys, and metalwork. Archives contains Henry Dreyfuss materials on symbols, George Kubler collection of 18th-19th c line engravings, Therese Bonney photos, Catharine Lynn materials on wallpaper, rare books, and other collections. Materials non-circulating. No fee. Hours: by appt, M-F 10-5:30.

Cornell University

Dept. of Manuscripts and University Archives, Collection of Regional History, Olin Library, Ithaca, NY 14853; (607) 255-4144. Academic research library holds non-current materials and historical documents from National Grange from 1867. Also holds papers from National Master of Grange, Louis Taber, 1923-41. Accepts phone inquiries. Hours: call.

Corning Community College

Arthur Houghton Jr. Library, Corning, NY 14830; (607) 962-9251. Academic library maintains selective collection of govt documents, general, reference and historical materials relevant to needs of the school and students. Holdings include materials on Native American history and culture; school archives; regional history collection. Accepts phone inquiries. No fee. Hours: M-Th 8-5, F 8-4.

Cortland County Historical Society

25 Homer Ave., Cortland, NY 13045; (607) 756-6071. Collects, preserves and promotes history of Cortland County, NY and residents in form of museum, library, and archival collections. Holdings include local historical exhibits and artifacts, late 19th-early 20th c; extensive collection of costumes; library with materials on local and state history; archives with personal, business, and institutional records; extensive manuscript collection local research works; local maps from 1830s; local photos collections, including negatives of Brockway Motor Truck Co; genealogical, census and church records. Accepts phone inquiries. Fee. Hours: Tu-Sa 1-5.

Costume Collection

Metropolitan Museum of Art, Fifth Ave. and 82nd St., New York, NY 10028; (212) 879-0421. Maintains collection of costumes from Americas, Europe, Asia, and Africa from 16th c. Holdings cover urban, folk, adult, and children's styles. Qualified researchers may study original materials. Accepts phone inquiries. Hours: call.

Crouse Library for Publishing Arts

City University of New York, 33 W. 42nd St., New York, NY 10036; (212) 642-2874. Maintains large collection of materials for researching paperback publishing field. Most materials relate to 20th c technical, financial, and historical aspects of publishing, covering histories of individual publishing houses, economics of authorship, marketing, and distribution. Only open to qualified researchers. Accepts phone inquiries. Hours: call.

Culver Pictures Archives

660 First Ave., New York, NY 10016; (212) 645-1672. Retains collection of photos, old prints, advertisements, memorabilia, and movie stills. Accepts phone inquiries. Fee. Hours: by appt only.

Dance Collection

New York Public Library Performing Arts Research Center, 111 Amsterdam Ave., New York, NY 10023. Public library offers materials documenting American dance history. Collection includes papers from Isadora Duncan, Ruth St. Denis, Agnes De Mille, American Ballet Theatre, Maria Bonfanti, Edward Gordon Craig, Ted Shawn, Jose Limon, Louis Horst, dance historian Lillian Moore, critic Walter Terry, and others. Other holdings include Clair Holt collection on Indonesian dance from 1920s-30s; letters of German Expressionist and modern dancer Mary Wigman, and Gabriel Astruc papers relating to early activities of Sergei Diaghilev from 1904-25.

Dance Theatre of Harlem Library and Archives

466 West 152nd St., New York, NY 10031; (212) 690-2800. Preserves history of Dance Theatre of Harlem, and reference materials on dance history and music. Library has books and records on dance and music. Archives maintains print and audio/vidual records of all aspects of

org history, and small collection on Arthur Mitchell. Photos of company, school, and special events abailable, as well as audio recordings of Theater's repertoire and radio interviews. Accepts phone inquiries. No fee. Hours: M-F 10:30-5:30.

Delaware and Hudson Canal Historical Society Museum

P.O. Box 23, Mohonk Road, High Falls, NY 12440; (914) 255-1538. Preserves historical materials and promotes education on Delaware & Hudson canal. Museum exhibits models, maps, and artifacts. Library contains reference materials, manuscripts, photos, films, and slides. Accepts phone inquiries. Donations accepted. Hours: call.

Dell Publishing Company Library

666 Fifth Avenue, New York, NY 10167; (212) 605-3000. Library has materials on amusement industry, comic books, films, and film making, with special Dell comics archives. Accepts phone inquiries. Hours: M-F 9-5.

DeWitt Historical Society of Tompkins County

Clinton House, 116 N. Cayuga St., Ithaca, NY 14850; (607) 273-8284. Collects, preserves and promotes history of Tompkins County, NY and residents in form of museum, library, and archival collections. Holdings include displays of artifacts from 1800; research library; archives, manuscripts, maps, films/videotapes; photos, including Verne Morton (Groton, NY photographer) Collection, 1896-1945; oral history and local musicians recordings; collection of Edison cylinders; large collection of local genealogical records. Some restrictions. Accepts brief phone inquiries. Some fees for research services. Hours: Tu-F 12:30-5, Sa 10-3.

Dutch Settlers Society of Albany

6 DeLucia Terrace, Albany, NY 12211; (518) 456-7807. Perpetuates memory of Dutch settlers in region through genealogical records dating to 1624-64 period. Materials for use of members and potential members. Accepts phone inquiries. Fee for membership. Hours: eves after 5.

East Hampton Free Library

159 Main St., East Hampton, NY 11937; (516) 324-0222. Academic research library has special collections on Long Island, including 85 years of "East Hampton Star," and biographical art collection from American artist Thomas Moran. Accepts phone inquiries. No fee. Hours: M-F 10-7, Sa 10-5.

East Hampton Historical Society

101 Main St., East Hampton, NY 11937; (516) 324-6850. Collects, preserves, and interprets objects relevant to East Hampton history. Museum displays decorative arts, tools, costumes, boats, vehicles, historic structures, and paintings. Other holdings include photos from 1850 and oral history recordings on history of East Hampton as summer community from 1890, and maritime folklife study. Accepts phone inquiries. Hours: call.

East Hampton Town Marine Museum

Box 858, Bluff Rd., Amagansett, NY 11930; (516) 267-6544. Collects, preserves and promotes maritime history and traditions of Eastern Long Island in form of museum, library, and archival collections. Holdings include exhibits on the area's commercial and sport fishing, water recreation, underwater archeology, and shore whaling; small research library; archives with materials from Long Island Fisherman's Project, including taped interviews and photos; small collection of 19th c navigational charts; extensive collection of early 20th c photos of East Hampton fisheries and related subjects. Accepts phone inquiries. Fee for non-members. Hours: July, Aug, Tu-Su 10:30-5; June, Sept, Sa-Su 10:30-5; other times by appt.

Eastchester Historical Society

P.O. Box 37, Eastchester, NY 10709; (914) 793-1900. Preserves history of town through collections in museum, library, and archives. Library has reference materials. Archive contains children's books of 19th c, costume collection, maps, photos, and genealogical records. Accepts phone inquiries. Fee. Hours: by appt.

Eleanor Roosevelt Center at Val-Kill

Rt. 9G, P.O. Box 255, Hyde Park, NY 12538; (914) 229-5302. Historic Val-Kill home of Eleanor Roosevelt houses center devoted to perpetuating her interests and beliefs through research, educational programs, and conferences. Holdings include slide shows and videotapes relating to Mrs. Roosevelt and the residence. Accepts phone inquiries. Charges for use of facilities by outside groups. Hours: M, W, Th 10:30-3:30.

Electric Railroaders Association

Frank Sprague Memorial Library, 89 E. 42nd St., New York, NY 10018; (212) 986-4482. Collects and preserves materials relating history of electric railroad equip. Collection covers street railways, subways, elevated lines, high-speed interurbans, suburban commuter lines, and others. Accepts phone inquiries. Hours: call.

Electronic Communications Museum

Antique Wireless Association, Main St., Village Green, East Bloomfield, Holcomb, NY 14469. Documents and preserves history of radio communication through holdings in museum, library, and archives. Holdings include photos, films/videotapes, and recordings of early radio pioneers and early broadcasts. Restrictions on use. Accepts phone inquiries. No fee.

Elmira College

Gannett-Tripp Learning Center, Elmira, NY 14901; (607) 734-3911, ext. 287. Academic research library holds materials on Mark Twain, women's education, and history of college. Twain archives contain all of Twain's works, first editions, original letters, autographs, photos, and memorabilia. Women's education materials include college records and audio recordings. College history documented through archival holdings, recordings, and photos. Accepts phone inquiries. Borrowing privileges extended outside College community for fee. Hours: M-F 8:30-5; call for evening and weekend hours.

Erie Canal Museum

318 Erie Blvd. E., Syracuse, NY 13202; (315) 471-0593. Documents history of New York State Canal System from 1833-1930 with collection of engineering and construction records; materials on maintenance of NY canals and construction of Barge Canal System; maps and surveys of canals and property along canals; plans of canal structure, bridges, aqueducts, locks,

water weirs, culverts, etc. Library holds Erie Canal related fiction and non-fiction, with materials on canals around the world, including Panama; photos from 1830s-1950; films/videotapes; and Canal passenger and worker records. Accepts phone inquiries. Fee. Hours: Tu-Su 10-5.

Explorers Club Library

46 East 70th St., New York, NY 10021; (212) 628-8383. Library covers exploration, travel, ethnology, and oceanography of polar regions, and holds special collection of Peary arctic library. For serious researchers only. Accepts phone inquiries. Hours: by appt only.

Farmers Museum

New York State Historical Assn, P.O. Box 800, Lake Rd., Cooperstown, NY 13326; (607) 547-2593. Studies, preserves and interprets history and culture of farming and rural life in upstate NY, in form of artifacts, displays, and archival collection. Holdings include indoor exhibits of agricultural development, and technology in the home; outdoor and craft exhibits, including demonstrations of textile manufacturing, blacksmithing, printing, woodworking, and farming; collection of personal and business letters, diaries, and records relating to local agricultural history. Accepts phone inquiries. Fee. Hours: Apr, Oct, Tu-Su 10-4, May-Sept, 9-6.

Fashion Institute of Technology

Shirley Goodman Resource Center, 227 27th St., New York, NY 10001; (212) 760-7695. Academic research library focuses on fashion, textile, and apparel manufacturing, as well as interior design. Special collections include Meyer collection of original Paris fashion sketches of 1920s; Millinery Trade Review from 1879-32; Frederick Miltion collection of original sketches from 1940-52; Du Berry Fashion Studio Sketchbooks; Bergdorf Goodman Sketchbooks; Sidney Wragge Collection; Haft-Swansdown Collection; and oral history interviews from fashion industry. Accepts phone inquiries. No fee. Hours: M-F 9-10, Sa noon-5, Su noon-8.

Federal Hall National Memorial

26 Wall St., New York, NY 10005; (212) 264-8711. Preserved historic site and museum maintains collections, artifacts and records relating to

President George Washington's inauguration, the Bill of Rights and other related documents. Holdings include the Messmore Kendall Collection of Washingtoniana. Some restrictions. Accepts phone inquiries. No fee. Hours: M-F 9-5.

Fenimore House

New York State Historical Association, P.O. Box 800, Lake Rd. (Route 80), Cooperstown, NY 13326; (607) 547-2455. Museum collects and preserves extensive collection of American folk art. Holdings include over 150 folk portraits, Browere life masks of famous early Americans, 19th c American landscape paintings, sculptures, store signs and advertisements, weather vanes, decoys, and quilts. Museum also displays memorabilia of James Fenimore Cooper family. Library has extensive research materials on art and architecture, folk art and folklife, American theatre, crime, medicine, genealogical materials, and social and economic life of NY residents. Accepts phone inquiries. Fee. Hours: museum, May-Oct 9-6; Nov-Dec, Tu-Su 10-4; library, M-Th 9-10, F 9-5, Sa 10-5.

Fenton Historical Society

67 Washington St., Jamestown, NY 14701; (716) 483-7521. Collects, preserves and promotes history of Jamestown and southern Chautauqua County and residents in form of museum, library, and archival collections. Holdings include Victorian period rooms; Civil War artifacts; exhibits on Chatauqua Lakes, and Swedish settlers; local history and genealogical reference library; archives with records, manuscripts, maps, photos, and genealogical materials from 1810. Does not accept phone inquiries. Fee. Hours: M-Sa 10-4.

Fiorello H. La Guardia Archives

La Guardia Community College, 31-10 Thomson Ave., Long Island City, NY 11101; (718) 482-5065. Collects and preserves materials relating to social history of 20th c New York City, with emphasis on archival collections relating to Fiorello LaGuardia. Holdings include library; archives with records and photos of New York City Housing Authority, the factory records of Steinway & Sons Piano Co., local history collections, and the personal and professional papers of Fiorello H. LaGuardia; city maps, films/vide-

otapes; LaGuardia recordings collection. Some restrictions. Accepts phone inquiries. No fee. Hours: M-F 10-4:30.

Flatbush Historical Society

2255 Church Ave., Brooklyn, NY 11226; (718) 856-3700. Preserves, collects, acquires, and restores historical materials for public use. Collections under storage during relocation. Accepts phone inquiries. Hours: M-F 9-5.

Fordham University Library

Library Annex, Keating Hall, Bronx, NY 10458; (212) 579-2414. Academic research library holds special collection materials on French Revolution, US Revolution and early federal US, and McGarry collection on criminology. Accepts phone inquiries. No fee. Hours: M-F 8:30-11, Sa 9-5, Su 2-11.

Fort Edward Historical Association

P.O. Box 106, 22 & 29 Lower Broadway, Fort Edward, NY 12828; (518) 747-9600. Regional museum of local history pertaining to Ft Edward-Hudson Falls and its environs. Museum composed of 7-bldg complex covering 18th-20th c. Library has large collection of published regional histories, maps from 1730, large photo collection from 1850, limited films/videotapes and recordings, local genealogical records, and special collection of archaeological pottery and artifacts from Ft Edward. Donations accepted. Hours: call.

Fort Ontario State Historic Site

P.O. Box 102, Oswego, NY 13126; (315) 343-4711. Preserves and interprets extant 18th-20th c military post in Oswego. Museum exhibits bldgs, earthworks, casemates, restored rooms, and military objects. Library has secondary sources on military history and local records. Archives contains reproductions of records pertaining to side, including maps, manuscripts, 19th-20th c photos, videotapes regarding WWII refugees at site, radio programs and oral histories, listings of 18th-19th c military units, and Canadian archival materials pertinent to site. Accepts phone inquiries. Fee. Hours: May-Sept, 10-5.

Fort Plain Museum

P.O. Box 324, Upper Canal St., Fort Plain, NY

13339; (518) 993-2527. Preserves site and history of Revolutionary War Fort Plain in form of museum, library, and archival collections. Holdings include historic 1848 limestone Greek Revival home and barn, housing exhibits and artifacts of Fort and area history, and relics of local Mohawk Indians; small reference library; archives; small collection of local family records; local maps and photos. Archives for staff use only. Accepts phone inquiries. Donations accepted. Hours: May-Sept, Tu-F 10-4, Sa-Su 1-4.

Fort Stanwix National Monument

112 E. Park St., Rome, NY 13440; (315) 336-2090. Historic site preserves an interprets 18th c Revolutionary War outpost in form of museum with archeological artifacts from site, and reconstructed, furnished 18th c fort with living history interpretations of fort life and black powder demonstrations. Accepts phone inquiries. Fee. Hours: Apr-Dec, 9-5.

Franklin D. Roosevelt Library and Museum

National Archives and Record Service, 259 Albany Post Rd., Hyde Park, NY 12538; (914) 229-8114. Preserves and promotes history of life and career of US President Franklin D. Roosevelt in form of museum, library, and archival collections. Holdings include exhibits and artifacts relating to Franklin and Eleanor Roosevelt, including documents and personal items; extensive library, including research materials, the President's personal library, and books on naval and local history; archives with oral history and Federal records relating to the Roosevelts; collections of manuscripts and personal papers of Roosevelts and associates; maps, photos, films/videotapes, and genealogical records. Accepts phone inquiries. Fee for museum. Hours: M-F 9-4:45.

Fraunces Tavern Museum

54 Pearl St., New York, NY 10004; (212) 425-1778. Museum preserves and displays early American history and culture, with emphasis on American Revolution, George Washington, and New York City. Holdings include period rooms and furnishings, paintings, prints, textiles, decorative arts, artifacts, and memorabilia; small research library with materials on American history

and genealogy; small collection of manuscripts relating to Revolutionary War and the signers of the Declaration of Independence; maps and photos; small collection of genealogical records. Use of library and genealogical materials by appt only. Does not accept phone inquiries. Fee. Hours: M-F 10-4, Su (Oct-May) noon-5.

Fred L. Emerson Gallery

Hamilton College, Clinton, NY 13323; (315) 859-4396. Gallery preserves and exhibits 19th and 20th c American paintings, prints and drawings, and presents changing exhibits relating to American art and history. Accepts phone inquiries. No fee. Hours: M-F 9-5, Sa-Su 1-5.

Frederic Remington Art Museum

303 Washington St., Ogdensburg, NY 13669; (315) 393-2425. Promotes and displays the artistic works of Frederic Remington in form of exhibits and archival collections. Holdings include Remington oil paintings, watercolors, sketches, and bronze statues; archives with tearsheets, letters, invoices, diaries, and journals belonging to Remington; photos of Remington and wife; Sharp Collection of cut glass; collections on local history of St. Lawrence County. Accepts phone inquiries. Fee. Hours: Nov-Apr, Tu-Sa 10-5; May-Oct M-Sa 10-5, Su 1-5.

Genealogical and Biographical Society Library of New York

122 East 58th St., 4th Floor, New York, NY 10022; (212) 755-8532. Membership org preserves and collects materials on regional genealogy, history, and biography. Accepts phone inquiries. Public access limited. Hours: Oct-May, M-F 9:30-5.

General Society of Mechanics and Tradesmen Library

20 West 44th St., New York, NY 10036; (212) 921-1767. Collection is mostly historic and biographic in nature. Special collections include materials from Gilbert & Sullivan Society of NY. Accepts phone inquiries. Hours: M-Th 9-7, F 9-5.

Genesee Country Museum

Box 1819, Flint Hill Rd., Mumford, Rochester, NY 14603; (716) 538-6822. Recreates NY village and displays advancement of architecture, crafts, and furnishings from 1775-1870. Living history site composed of 57 19th c buildings furnished with period antiques. Special collection of sporting art, collection of over 40 horse-drawn vehicles, and collection of wildlife and animal art. Accepts phone inquiries. Fee. Hours: mid-May-mid-Oct Sa-Su 10-5; Jun-Jul, holidays and M-F 10-5; spring and fall, M-F 10-4.

Geneva Historical Society and Museum

543 S. Main St., Geneva, NY 14456; (315) 789-5151. Collects, preserves, and exhibits knowledge on Geneva history. Museum has 19th c period rooms with exhibits on local history, art, furniture, and costume. Library has materials on architecture, antiques, furniture, art, genealogy, local and NY history, Iroquois tribe, and transportation. Archives contains 19th c local newspapers, Civil War letters, Sanborn insurance maps, oral history interviews, and genealogical records. Materials non-circulating. Accepts phone inquiries. No fee. Hours: M-F 9-5, Sa 1:30-4:30, Tu eve 7-9; archives M-Sa afternoons.

Girl Scouts of USA Library and Archives

830 Third Ave., New York, NY 10022; (212) 940-7881. Library documents history of Girl Scout organization through collection of publications and historical records. For use of staff, members, and public by permission. Hours: M-F 8:30-4:30.

Glenn H. Curtiss Museum

P.O. Box 585, 41 Lake St., Hammondsport, NY 14840; (607) 569-2160. Collects and preserves any and all memorabilia of importance to Curtiss aviation and local history. Museum displays artifacts on early aviation and Hammondsport heritage. Library has small collection on early aviation from 1908-20. Archives contains limited scrapbooks on early aviation, photos documenting Curtiss flight experiements, and videotapes. Special Harry Benner glass slide collection. Restrictions on use. Accepts phone inquiries. Fee. Hours: M-Sa 9-5.

Gowanda Area Historical Society

P.O. Box 372, Gowanda, NY 14070. Collects, preserves and promotes history of Gowanda, NY area and residents in form of museum, library, archives, maps, photos, and genealogical records. Does not accept phone inquiries. No fee. Hours: 2nd and 3rd Th each month, 1-4, 1st Su of each month, 2-4, or by appt.

Granger Collection

1841 Broadway, New York, NY 10023; (212) 586-0971. Maintains large collection of photos and transparencies with emphasis on American history. Subjects covered include movie stills, Civil War, military, historic personalities, and art. Accepts phone inquiries. Fee.

Grant Cottage State Historic Site

P.O. Box 2253, Wilton, NY 12866; (518) 587-8277. Site preserves and interprets history of Ulysses S. Grant short residence (June 16-July 23, 1885) and death at the cottage. Holdings include original cottage and furnishings; ephemera and artifacts; small library with references on Grant and the Civil War; archives with materials on Gen Grant's residence at the cottage, death, and funeral, and preservation of the site; manuscripts of first caretaker's reminiscences; photos of Grant as General and President, and reprints of images from 1885 newspapers and periodicals. Accepts phone inquiries. Fee. Hours: April-Oct, W-Su 10-4, or by appt.

Guild Hall

158 Main St., East Hampton, NY 11937; (516) 324-0806. Cultural center maintains museum, library, and archival collections related to the artists of region and their work. Holdings include exhibitions artworks by Eastern Long Island artists; Alice Baber Memorial Art Library, with materials on 19th and 20th c American art; archives with institutional scrapbooks from 1930, and files on regional artists; extensive collection of photos; films/videotapes and slides of regional artist and their work; taped interviews with artists, and recordings of panels, lecture, and symposia. Use of library and archives by appt. Accepts phone inquiries. Donations accepted. Hours: summer, noon-6; winter, Th-Sa 11-5, Su 1-5.

Hamilton Grange National Memorial

287 Convent Ave., New York, NY 10031; (212)

283-5154. Historic home of Alexander Hamilton preserves the history of his life, and of the Colonial/Revolutionary War period in which he lived, in form of period furnishings, artifacts and exhibits relating to Hamilton's life and times; library and photo collections. Accepts phone inquiries. No fee. Hours: W-Su 9-5.

Hampden-Booth Theatre Collection and Library

16 Gramercy Park South, New York, NY 10003; (212) 228-7610. Library focuses on theatre and drama, magic, burlesque, television, and films. Special collections include materials on Edwin Booth, magician Mulholland, Walter Hampden, Maurice Evans and Franklin Heller materials on theatre and films, Callahan materials on burlesque, Henderson collection of 18th-19th c playbills, Union Square Theatre, The Players, and La Mama Experimental Theatre Club. Accepts phone inquiries. Hours: by appt only, M-F 10-5.

Hanford Mills Museum

P.O. Box 99, East Meredith, NY 13757; (607) 278-5744. Museum collects and interprets this old mill site's rural industrial and commercial history, early 1800s-mid 1900s, with emphasis on examining regional and national themes relating to the role of a mill in community life. Holdings include operating historic mill with working sawmill, gristmill, and waterpowered machinery; library with materials on local history, milling, waterpower, and early industry; archives with personal and business papers of the mill's owners, 1860-1966 and other local documents; local and county maps; photos. Some restrictions. Accepts phone inquiries. Fee. Hours: Museum: May-Oct 10-5; archives: M-F 9-5.

Harbor Defense Museum of New York City

Fort Hamilton, Brooklyn, NY 11252; (718) 630-4349. Museum collects, preserves and displays New York City military history, with emphasis on New York City coastal defense installations. Holdings include artifacts and exhibits relating to New York City harbor defense, 1800-1950; collection of reference publications; maps (mostly reproductions) relating to region; small photo collection. Accepts phone inquiries. No

fee. Hours: early Jan-late Dec, M, Th, F 1-4, Sa 10-5, Su 1-5.

Hastings Historical Society

41 Washington Ave., Hastings-on-Hudson, NY 10706; (914) 478-2935. Collects, preserves and promotes history of Hastings-on-Hudson and residents in form of library and archival collections. Holdings include historical publications about the village, or written by villagers, from mid-19th c; archives from 1609, with biographical and materials, manuscripts and family papers; maps from late 17th c; photos from 1870; small collection of films/videotapes from 1939; small collection of genealogical records from 1830s; oral history and other recordings; Langmuir photo collection, 1928-35; collections of pamphlets, ephemera, clothing, and other historical artifacts. Accepts phone inquiries. No fee. Hours: Th 10-2, or by appt.

Herkimer County Historical Society

400 N. Main St., Herkimer, NY 13350; (315) 866-6413. Discovers, collects, preserves, and publishes materials on history of Herkimer county. Museum holdings documents town from early settlement period to present. Library collects census holdings, obituaries, genealogical records, personal papers from various judges, records of Ft Dayton Steamer Co., Bellinger papers, church records, maps, photos, and special collection on Fairfield Academy from 1802-1950. Fee. Hours: M-F 10-4.

Historic Albany Foundation

44 Central Ave., Albany, NY 12206; (518) 463-0622. Promotes appreciation and preservation of local history built environments through preservation projects and plaque program; funding efforts; educational programs and special events; publications. Accepts phone inquiries. No fee. Hours: M-F 9-5.

Historic Palmyra

P.O. Box 96, 132 Market St., Palmyra, NY 14522; (315) 597-6981. Collects, preserves, and interprets history of Palmyra. Three museums, Phelps General Store, Alling Coverlet Museum, and Palmyra Historical Museum, exhibit local history. Holdings include large collection of American tapestries, period furnishings, toys, printing press equipment, agricultural implements, and artifacts from industrial community. Library and archives hold manuscripts and photos on local history subjects. Materials for in-house use only. Accepts phone inquiries. No fee. Hours: M-F 9-5.

Historical Museum of the Darwin R. Barker Library

7 Day St., Fredonia, NY 14063; (716) 672-2114. Collects, preserves and promotes history of Fredonia area and residents in form of museum (location: 20 E. Main St.) library, archival and special collections. Holdings include 19th c artifacts, re-created 1880s parlor, and changing exhibits; local history and reference materials from 17th c; archives has govt and school records; maps from 19th c; photos from 19th c; films/videotapes; oral history tapes; US Grange Number 1 archives; materials on Cushing, Lafayette, and Twain. Accepts phone inquiries. Donations accepted. Hours: T, Th, F, Sa 2:30-4:30 (also Th 7pm-9pm).

Historical Society of Early American Decoration Museum

19 Dove St., Albany, NY 12210; (518) 462-1676. Society's museum preserves and displays historical examples of American and English decorative arts of late 18th and early 19th c. Holdings include collections of ornamented tinware, papier mache, and wood; library with publications and historical materials relating to early American decoration. Accepts phone inquiries. No fee. Hours: M-F 9:30-4, Sa noon-3.

Historical Society of Greater Port Jefferson

P.O. Box 586, 115 Prospect St., Port Jefferson, NY 11777; (516) 473-2665. Displays and provides access to local history through collections in museum and library. Exhibits displayed in 1840s restored homes and surroundings and shipbuilding artifacts. Library holds books on local and county history, maps, small collection of photos, and genealogical records. Accepts phone inquiries. Fee. Hours: May-Sept, Sa-Su 1-4; Jul-Aug, W, F 1-4.

Historical Society of the Tarrytowns

Library, 1 Grove St., Tarrytown, NY 10591; (914) 631-8374. Collections include documentation of 1780 capture of Major Andre in Tarrytown, his captors, and limited material on Benedict Arnold. Accepts phone inquiries. No fee. Hours: call.

Historical Society of the Tonawandas

113 Main St., Tonawanda, NY 14150; (716) 694-7406. Collects, preserves, and exhibits histories of Tonawanda and North Tonawanda. Museum housed in NY Central railroad station, and has exhibits on Iroquois Indians, lumber industry, Erie canal, local businesses, military, and railroads. Library covers state history, Civil War, WWI, WWII, town records, manuscripts, maps of western NY railroads, Sanborn maps, many photos, Edison's "Great Train Robbery" and movies of local activities, early Edison and Victor records, oral histories, and genealogical and census records. Materials for in-house use only. Accepts phone inquiries. No fee. Hours: W-F 10-5.

Holland Society of New York

122 E. 58th St., New York, NY 10022; (212) 758-1675. Preserves and promotes study of the Dutch Colonial period of American history in form of library, archives, manuscripts, maps, genealogical and church records. Accepts brief phone inquiries. Donations accepted. Library and archives hours: F 11-4, or by appt.

Homeville Museum

49 Clinton St., Homer, NY 13077; (607) 749-3105. Private museum, housed in owner's home, maintains assortment of collections relating to US military and railroad history. Holdings include displays, artifacts and exhibits of military paraphernalia, including uniforms, weapons, flags, and war-related items; extensive collections of toy and model trains, and railroad memorabilia; library and photo collection of military and railroad subjects. Accepts phone inquiries. Donations accepted. Hours: Th 7-9, 2nd and 4th Su each month, 1-4.

Hoosick Township Historical Society-Louis Miller Museum

P.O. Box 366, 166 Main St., Hoosick Falls, NY 12090; (518) 686-4682. Preserves and researches local history. Museum home displays local history exhibits on regional businesses, people, and Victorian period. Library holds books, records, photos, newspapers, news clippings, archival materials, maps, photos, limited films/videotapes, recordings, and limited genealogical records. Donations accepted. Hours: Tu 1-4, or by appt.

Hudson River Maritime Center

One Rondout Landing, Kingston, NY 12401; (914) 338-0071. Preserves history of Hudson River and its Valley. Museum has small collection on regional history pertaining to 19th and 20th c industry and Hudson River navigation. Archives contains manuscripts, maps, photos of steamships and industries on Hudson, films/videotapes on iceboating and sailing, oral histories on shad industry and ferrytenders, genealogical records, and Cornell Steamboat Co. collection. Accepts phone inquiries. Fee. Hours: May-Oct, Tu-Su noon-5.

Huguenot Historical Society

P.O. Box 339, New Paltz, NY 12561; (914) 255-1660. Preserves genealogy, NY state history, and Huguenot materials in museum and library. Holdings include manuscripts, photos, and genealogical records. Accepts phone inquiries. Fee for membership. Hours: W-Sa 9-4.

Huntington Free Library and Reading Room

Museum of the American Indian, 9 Westchester Square, Bronx, NY 10461; (212) 829-7770. Museum library collects and maintains materials on the history and culture of Native Americans of South, Central and and North America. Holdings include publications and reference materials on archeology, ethnology, history, and languages relating to Native Americans; Native American newspaper collection; manuscripts, maps, and small collections of recordings and genealogical records. Collections are non-circulating; use by appt only. Accepts phone inquiries. No fee. Hours: M-F, 1st and 3rd Sa each month, 10-4:30.

Huntington Historical Society

209 Main St., Huntington, NY 11743; (516) 427-7045. Collects, preserves and promotes history and material culture the Town of Hunt-ington and Central Long Island in form of local historic house museums, library, and archival collections. Holdings include Kissam House, c 1795, Conklin House, c 1750, and the Trade School, c 1905; library; society archives from 1903; manuscripts from 17th c; maps and atlases; photos and glass plate negatives from 1845; oral history tapes from 1950s; genealogical records and papers; Nellie R. Scudder genealogical collection; W. Wilton Wood papers; Crossman Brickyard records. Some restrictions. Accepts phone inquiries. Fee. Hours: museum Tu-F, Su 1-4; library Tu-Sa 10-4.

International Center of Photography

1130 Fifth Ave., New York, NY 10128; (212) 860-1777. Center promotes study, use and history of photography through exhibits, educational courses and events, library, archival and special collections. Holdings include New York Museum of Photography with changing exhibits; large reference library with periodicals and publications on and featuring photography; archives with papers relating to lives and work of great photographers; large collection of photos, mainly from 20th c; lecture recordings; Jacob Deschin Collection; Photography in the Fine Arts Collection, 1959-1968. Accepts phone inquiries. Fee. Hours: Tu noon-8, W-F noon-5, Sa-Su 11-6.

International Museum of Photography

George Eastman House, 900 East Ave., Rochester, NY 14607; (716) 271-3361. Museum documents history of photography and cameras through large display of 19th c photos, antique cameras, and antique photographic jewelry. Exhibits include replica of traveling photographer's horse-drawn studio, detective cameras, and many novelty items. Accepts phone inquiries. Hours: Tu-Su 10-4:30.

Jefferson County Historical Society

228 Washington St., Watertown, NY 13601; (315) 782-3491. Discovers, collects, and preserves county and NY state history. Museum consists of Paddock mansion, barn complex, ice house, caretaker's house, and Victorian garden. Library and archives hold maps and photos. Costume collection, Kinne collection of water

turbines, and Tyler coverlets also available. Library materials for in-house use only. Accepts phone inquiries. No fee. Hours: Tu-Sa 10-5.

Jervis Public Library

613 N. Washington St., Rome, NY 13440; (315) 336-4570. Public library has materials on Croton aqueduct, construction of Erie Canal, slavery and apprenticing, and early American statesmen. Holdings include correspondence, documents, deeds, and papers on slavery and apprenticing; letters from signers of Declaration of Independence; and letters from George Washington. Accepts phone inquiries. No fee. Hours: call.

John Brown Farm
State Historic Site

John Brown Rd., Lake Placid, NY 12946; (518) 523-3900. Site of preserves history of abolitionist John Brown's life in form of his last home, furnished with items from the 1850s; his gravesite; library with materials relating to Brown and the anti-slavery movement. Accepts phone inquiries. No fee. Hours: Late May-early Oct, W-Sa 10-5, Su 1-5.

John Howard Payne
Boyhood Home

Home Sweet Home Museum, 14 James Lane, East Hampton, NY 11937; (516) 324-0713. Preserves history of life and work of John Howard Payne in form of boyhood home, and maintains special collections of historical and local household furnishings, artifacts, and archival materials. Holdings include 17th c house furnished with the Gustav Buek collection of furniture, early 19th c English ceramics, East Hampton, NY memorabilia, and artifacts of Payne's boyhood and life; small reference library; archives, with materials relating to the collection, East Hampton history, and John Howard Payne; special collections of pictures, plays and scrapbooks. Collection is non-circulating. Accepts phone inquiries. Fee. Hours: M-Sa 10-4, Su 1-4.

John Jay College
of Criminal Justice Library

445 West 59th St., New York, NY 10019; (212) 489-5168. Library concentration on criminal justice, public administration, forensic science, and fire science. Holdings include NYC criminal court trial transcripts, Police Dept reports, videotapes of dramas by prison inmates (Theatre of the Forgotten), and related manuscripts. Accepts phone inquiries. No fee. Hours: M-Th 9-9, F 9-5, Sa 10-3.

Kent-Delord House Museum

17 Cumberland Ave., Plattsburgh, NY 12901; (518) 561-1035. Museum consists of 9 period rooms covering regional material culture from 1811-1913. Holdings include American portraiture by John Singleton Copley, Robert Fulton, and Henry Ihman; family documents; personal items; textiles; medical equipment; and photos. Accepts phone inquiries. Fee. Hours: Tu-Sa 9-5.

Landmark Society of
Western New York

130 Spring St., Rochester, NY 14608; (716) 546-7029. Preserves, protects and restores sites and buildings of historic, natural, or architectural importance to Western New York and residents. Holdings include three historic home museums (located throughout region); library with general and historical reference publications, maps, paintings, drawings, and photos; archives of newspaper clippings related to regional history, genealogy, and preservation work; plat and insurance maps of Rochester, 1875-1937; architectural and historical surveys of Rochester, NY, and northeastern US. Library materials non-circulating. Accepts phone inquiries. No fee. Hours: M-F 9-5.

Lesbian Herstory Archives

Lesbian Herstory Educational Foundation, Inc., P.O. Box 1258, New York, NY 10116; (212) 874-7232. Gathers, preserves, and makes available materials on all aspects of lesbian history and culture. Library contains reference collection on lesbianism through history, with extensive periodical collection. Archives hold org and personal collections from 1950; published and unpublished manuscripts, diaries, journals, and letters; and biographical photos, films/videotapes, and recordings reflecting lesbian lifestyles in 20th c. Library materials non-circulating; some collections are restricted. Accepts phone inquiries. No fee. Hours: by appt only.

Letchworth State Park Museum

Indian and Pioneer Museum, 1 Letchworth State Park, Castile, NY 14427; (716) 493-2611. Preserves the memory and archival materials of William P. Letchworth and park area in form of museum with local and Letchworth artifacts (circa 1850s), and the Letchworth Collection, which encompasses a library, archives, manuscripts, maps, and photos. Collection is non-circulating. Accepts phone inquiries. No fee. Hours: M-F 9-4.

Life Magazine Picture Service

Time & Life Building, Rockefeller Center, Room 2858, New York, NY 10020; (212) 522-4800. Extensive photo library contains collection of illustrations from Life magazine issues. Catalogued by subject, personality, and photographer's name. Accepts phone inquiries. Fee. Hours: by appt only.

Lincoln Center
Performing Arts Archive

Lincoln Center, 140 West 65th Street, New York, NY 10023; (212) 877-1800. Preserves and manages historical records from the Lincoln Center for Performing Arts, the nation's first performing arts complex. Holdings date from 1950s, and include photos, manuscripts, publications, film, and ephemera. Some materials restricted. Accepts phone inquiries. No fee. Hours: 10-3.

Long Island Historical Society

128 Pierrepont St. at Clinton St., Brooklyn, NY 11201; (718) 624-0890. Collects and preserves materials relating Long Island history, including books, pamphlets, newspapers, periodicals, photos, manuscript collections, run of "Long Island Star" from 1809-63, and "Williamsburg Gazette" from 1835-53. Accepts phone inquiries. Hours: call.

Long Island Studies Institute
at Hofstra University

Hofstra University Library, Hempstead, NY 11550; (516) 560-5097. Research center maintains collection of reference and archival materials on history Nassau County, Long Island and NY. Holdings include Nassau County Museum Reference Library, focussing on Nassau County

and Long Island history; Hoffstra Univ's James N. Maclean American Legion Memorial Library, with materials on Long Island and NY history; manuscripts and documents relating to Nassau County history and culture; large collection of regional maps from 17th c; photos, films/videotapes, and genealogical records; microfilms of newspapers from 18th c. Some restrictions. Accepts phone inquiries. No fee. Hours: M-F 9-5 (Tu 9-8 during spring and fall).

Lorenzo State Historic Site

Ledyard Ave., Cazenovia, NY 13035; (315) 655-3200. Historic site preserves home of Holland Land Co agent John Lincklaen and descendants. Holdings include preserved 1807 mansion with original furnishings, 1807-1967; interpretive museum with local artifacts; library; family archives; letters, account books, legal documents and other historic items related to Lincklaen-Ledyard family, and Holland Land Co; local maps, 1793-1981; photos of local subjects from 1850s; genealogical records of the Ledyard, Seymour, Fitzhugh, and associated families; special collections on the Holland Land Co, and 3rd Great Western Tpke. Research by appt. Accepts phone inquiries. No fee. Hours: May-Oct, W-Sa 10-5, Sa 1-5.

Lower Hudson Conference:
Historical Agencies and Museums

2199 Saw Mill River Rd., Elmsford, NY 10523; (914) 592-6726. Non-profit org serves museums and historical societies of lower Hudson, NY region, through workshops, technical assistance consultations, publications, and referral services. Holdings include technical museum and archive library with books and audio-visual materials relating to administration, exhibition, and collection management. Services restricted to membership. Accepts phone inquiries. Membership fee. Hours: M-F 8:30-4:30.

Madison County Historical Society

P.O. Box 415, 435 Main St., Oneida, NY 13421; (315) 363-4136. Collects, preserves and promotes history of Madison County, NY and residents in form of historic home museum, library, and archival collections. Holdings include 1849 home, housing furnishings, textiles and costumes, and quilts; library with historical research materials on region York, Civil War, Revolutionary War; archives with local historical manuscripts, records, maps, and photos; genealogical records of county families; George W. Walters collection; Traditional Crafts Archives, with research materials, films/videotapes and recordings. Some restrictions. Accepts phone inquiries. Fee. Hours: June-Aug, 9-5; Sept-May, M-F 9-5.

Manhattan College
Cardinal Hayes Library

4513 Manhattan College Pkwy, Bronx, NY 10471; (212) 920-0166. Academic research library holds special collection on Sontag, Fales, and Peace Studies. Accepts phone inquiries. No fee. Hours: M-Th 8:30-11, F 8:30-9, Sa 10-5, Su 2-9.

Martin P. Catherwood Library

Cornell University School of Industrial & Labor Relations, Ives Hall, Ithaca, NY 14853; (607) 255-3100. Academic research library specializes in labor union history, with materials from arbitrators, scholars, and labor journals and manuscripts. Holds records of United Transportation Union, Western Railway, NY and PA Railway, and American Shortline Railroad Assn. Accepts phone inquiries. No fee. Hours: call.

Martin Van Buren
National Historic Site

P.O. Box 545, Kinderhook, NY 12106; (518) 758-9689. Historic site serves as a memorial to US President Martin Van Buren through the preservation and restoration of Lindenwald, the home to which he retired when he left office. Holdings include Lindenwald mansion, with furnishings and artifacts associated with Van Buren; library with materials on Van Buren and 19th c American history and politics; archives with Van Buren's letters and newspapers of his era; maps and drawings used for home's restoration; photos of mansion and its occupants from 19th c; oral history tapes of former owners and occupants; Van Buren family genealogical records. Some restrictions. Some restrictions. Fee. Hours: M-F 9-5.

Masonic Library and Museum

71 W. 23rd St., New York, NY 10010; (212) 741-4505. Preserves history of Freemasonry and voluntary assns in New York City and state through exhibits, and reference and archival collections. Holdings include collection of portraits from 1781; sculpture, pottery, furniture, coins, banners, clothing and other artifacts; library with publications, manuscripts, and other materials; archives of NY masonic societies from late 18th c; maps, photos, films/videotapes, recordings, and genealogical records; Abraham Felt Collection of New York City History; and the Charles Looney Collection of Masonic Memorabilia. Some restrictions. Does not accept phone inquiries. No fee. Hours: M-F 10-4.

Metropolitan Opera Archives

Lincoln Center, 140 W. 65th St., New York, NY 10023; (212) 877-1800. Preserves collection of photos, architectural drawings, clippings, and tearsheets of opera singers, set and stage design, and programs. Hours: by appt only.

Military Academy Library

West Point, NY 10996; (914) 938-2230 or 4841. Library focuses on US Army history, West Point history, and military arts and sciences. Special collections include Faulkner materials, Von Steuben manuals, Omar Bradley papers, military engineering materials, and USMA and Thayer collection. Accepts phone inquiries. Hours: M-Th 8-10:45, F 8-10, Sa 8-9, Su 1-10:45.

Millard Fillmore House

281 Parkdale Ave., East Aurora, NY 14052; (716) 652-1203. Historic home houses artifacts, library, and archival collections relating to the life and residence of US President Millard Fillmore. Holdings include period furnishings and artifacts, 1825-1830; library with materials on Fillmore and other US Presidents; early local maps and atlas; photos of Fillmore and family. Use of library and archival materials restricted to non-members. Town Clerk's office accepts related phone inquiries (716-652-3280). Donations accepted. Hours: June-Oct 15, W, Sa, Su 2-4.

Montgomery County Department
of History and Archives

Old Courthouse, Fonda, NY 12068; (518) 853-3431, ext. 293. Collects, preserves and promotes history of Montgomery County, NY and residents in form of small museum; research library; archives, maps, photos, films/videotapes, and genealogical records; special collections of Fonda, Van Antwerp, Rose, and Gunsolus. Accepts phone inquiries. No fee. Hours: Sept-June, M-F 9-5; July-Aug, M-F 9-4.

Mount Pleasant Public Library

350 Bedford Rd., Pleasantville, NY 10570; (914) 769-0548. Academic research library holds collection of materials on early 20th c American and English plays and Frost Collection of Restoration drama. Accepts phone inquiries. No fee. Hours: M-Th 10-9, F 10-6, Sa 9-4, Su 1-4.

Mount Vernon Public Library

Documents Division, Reference Dept., 28 South First Ave., Mount Vernon, NY 10550; (914) 668-1840 ext. 332. Public library with collection of materials on local history. Museum documents history of Eastchester and Mt Vernon, NY. Archives contains Westchester room; Civil War diary; rough drafts of charters and proclamations; articles of indenture; maps; photos; oral history recordings; genealogical records; rare books and postcards; house, street, and area histories; and celebrity lists. Reference materials non-circulating. Accepts phone inquiries. No fee. Hours: winter, M 11-9, Tu-Th 9-9, F 9-6, Sa 9-5, Su 1-4; summer, same but no Sa-Su hours.

Movie Star News

134 W. 18th St., New York, NY 10011; (212) 620-8160. Commercial org has large collection of movie star photos, posters, and pressbooks. Accepts phone inquiries. No fee. Hours: call.

Munson-Williams-Proctor Institute Museum of Art

Fountain Elms, 310 Genesee St., Utica, NY 13502; (315) 797-0000. Insitution's art museum and historic Victorian home, Fountain Elms, preserve and maintain cultural and social history of school and region. Holdings include large collection of American and European paintings, sculpture, prints, and decorative arts from 19th and 20th c; restored Victorian period rooms and artifacts in Fountain Elms; art reference library with publications and slides; institution's archives from 1935; large collection of Williams

and Proctor family photos, 1850-1920; music library with historic recordings. Accepts phone inquiries (ext 59). No fee. Hours: Tu-Sa 10-5, Su 1-5.

Museum of Broadcasting

1 East 53rd St., New York, NY 10022; (212) 752-4690. Collects, preserves, interprets, and exhibits radio and TV programs. Radio collection has 1920 FDR campaign speech; accounts of Hindenburg disaster; Murrow's "This is...London;" news, sports, and entertainment of WWII era; Fred Allen, Jack Benny, and Ed Wynn; FDR fireside chats; reports of Hiroshima bombing; and highlights of McCarthy hearings. TV collection covers 1939 NBC broadcast; 1944 NBC Symphony with Toscanini; Golden Age dramas; Sullivan, Lucie, Kovacs, Caesar, and Berle shows; moon shots; political ads; and Watergate highlights. Library features thorough program lists. Accepts phone inquiries. Donations accepted. Hours: Tu noon-8, W-Sa noon-5.

Museum of Cartoon Art

Comly Ave., Rye Brook, NY 10573; (914) 939-0234. Museum, housed in historic Ward's Castle, collects, preserves, exhibits and promotes study of cartoon art. Holdings include large collection of original works of caricature, cartoon art, and comic art from 1850; large research library; archives with cartooning memorabilia; large collection of animated films/videotapes and interviews with artists; Historic Comic Collection; Cartoon Art Hall of Fame. Accepts phone inquiries. Fee. Hours: Tu-F 10-4, Su 1-5.

Museum of Migrating People

750 Baychester Ave., Bronx, NY 10475; (212) 320-2300. Preserves and promotes the migration history of ethnic and racial groups in New York City through exhibits of photos, documents, and memorabilia related to the migration experience; library and archives with publications and audiovisual materials; photos, recordings, and genealogical records. Research by appt only. Accepts phone inquiries. Donations accepted. Hours: M-F 10:30-2, during school year.

Museum of Modern Art

Department of Film, 11 West 53rd St., New York, NY 10019; (212) 708-9613. Preserves and makes available museum's film collection and related documentation, with emphasis on avant garde film, Biograph films from 1909-16, British and US documentaries from 1930s-40s, and Fox Studio films. Holdings include films; large collection of screenplays and dialogue continuities; files of contemporary reviews; newspaper and magazine articles; publicity and other materials on films and film personalities; collection of posters, pressbooks, and many stills. Special collection of letters from DW Griffith, Billy Bitzer, and Biograph Company. Materials for in-house use only. Accepts phone inquiries. Service fees. Hours: M-F 1-5.

Museum of the American Indian

Broadway at 155th St., New York, NY 10032; (212) 283-2420. Collects, preserves, studies, and exhibits all things connected with aboriginal people of North, Central, and South America. Exhibits include large collection of Native American artifacts, books, and photos from prehistoric times to present and many folk arts and ceremonies. Accepts phone inquiries. Hours: Tu-Sa 10-5, Su 1-5.

Museum of the City of New York

1220 Fifth Ave., New York, NY 10029; (212) 534-1672. Collects, preserves and promotes history of New York City and residents in form of exhibits and archival collections. Holdings include historical artifacts from 16th c; extensive theater archive collection with posters, clippings, costumes, correspondences, and ephemera; manuscripts of prominent citizens, and ephemera relating to city culture and society; extensive collection of city maps; photos and prints; special collections of Yiddish theater memorabilia, costumes and clothing, paintings and sculpture, decorative arts, portraits, and toys. Research by appt, M-F 9-5. Accepts phone inquiries. Donations accepted. Hours: Tu-Sa 10-5, Su 1-5.

Museum Village in Orange County

Museum Village Rd., Monroe, NY 10950; (914) 782-8247. Museum Village complex presents the 19th c material culture of rural community through historic buildings with artifact exhibits and demonstrations of craft, trade, agricultural,

and domestic life; research library and extensive archives with relevant documents. Research by appt only. Accepts phone inquiries. Fee. Hours: museum: May-Dec, W-Su; office: M-F 9-5.

Museums at Stony Brook

1208 Rte. 25A, Stony Brook, NY 11790; (516) 751-0066. Preserves history through collections of 19th c Long Island and American art and history, and heritage of horse-drawn transportation. Library has Carriage reference library with rare books, trade catalogs, periodicals, and carriage-related art, drawings, and advertising from late 19th and early 20th c. Art collection and archives contains paintings, drawings, personal papers of painter William Sidney Mount, and other assorted historic photos and papers. Approx 250 horse-drawn vehicles on display, as well as costumes, textiles, toys, and decoys. Accepts phone inquiries. Fee. Hours: museum, W-Sa 10-5, Su noon-5; archives & library, researchers and scholars by appt.

Music Division, New York Public Library

111 Amsterdam Ave., New York, NY 10023. Public library holds materials on wide range of musical subjects, representing range of musical styles and histories. Special strengths in folk songs, Americana, American music, full scores of operas, and historical editions. Holdings include programs, record catalogs, manuscripts, sheet music, clippings, broadsides, and large picture collection.

Musical Museum

Route 12-B, Deansboro, NY 13328; (315) 841-8774. Collects restored music boxes, juke boxes, player pianos, band organs, grind organs, Mississippi Steamboat organ, sewing machine organs, mechanized snuff boxes, clavichord, calliope, tel-ektra player, phonographs, pipe organs, harmoniums, melodeons, pump organs, and an assortment of unusual musical instruments. Library and archive have literature and recordings, paper music rolls, manuscripts, recordings, and collection of local history items. Accepts phone and mail inquiries. Fee. Hours: 10-4.

Nassau County Museum

1864 Muttontown Rd., Syosset, NY 11791;

(516) 364-1050. Preserves and promotes history of Nassau County, NY and residents in form of living history village restoration, museum, library, archival and special collections. Facilities include Old Bethpage village restoration, depicting NY colonial life, 1710-1870; Sands Point Museum and Preserve, with early 20th c artifacts and exhibits; reference library (at The Long Island Studies Insitute) with early publications, photo collections, maps, records, genealogical and historical materials relating to region. Accepts phone inquiries. Fees vary by facility. Hours: office: M-F 9-4:45; facilities: vary by site.

Nassau County Museum Historical Library and Archives

Eisenhower Park, East Meadow, NY 11554; (516) 542-4516. Preserves records pertaining to history of county and Long Island. Some genealogies and archival newspapers. Accepts phone inquiries. No fee. Hours: M-F 9-4:45.

National Association of Broadcasters

Television Information Office, 745 Fifth Ave., 17th Fl, New York, NY 10022; (212) 759-6800. Library has collection of materials on social and cultural aspects of TV programming. Accepts phone inquiries. Hours: by appt; M-F 9:30-5.

National Baseball Hall of Fame and Museum

P.O. Box 590, Main St, Cooperstown, NY 13326; (607) 547-9988. Hall of Fame library collects and preserves documents and artifacts related to baseball. Holdings include research library; archives with August Hermann papers, George Weiss Collection, and William Branham Collection; correspondence collection; extensive photo collection; film rental library; films/videotapes of World Series and All Star Game highlights; audio recordings of games, game music, and oral histories; biographical data and clipping file on players and personnel; extensive collections of autographs, scorecards, schedules, cartoons, and poetry. Accepts phone inquiries. Fee for museum. Hours: M-F 9-5.

National Jewish Archives of Broadcasting

The Jewish Museum, 1109 Fifth Ave., New York, NY 10128; (212) 860-1886. Archives collects, catalogues and preserves television programs relating to Jewish experience and topics. Holdings include US and international news reports and documentaries, religious programs, and dramatic and comic entertainment programs. Use of collection limited to scholars and researchers, by appt only. Accepts phone inquiries. No fee. Hours: M-F 9-5.

National Museum of Racing

Union Ave., Saratoga Springs, NY 12866; (518) 584-0400. Preserves and exhibits materials associated with origin, history, and development of horseracing and breeding of thoroughbred horses. Museum traces history of racing from its start in America through exhibits of paintings, sculpture, memorabilia, and audiovisual aids. Small reference library available. Special collections include Kelso's five jockey club Gold cups, coin collection, and thoroughbred racing's Hall of Fame. Accepts phone inquiries. Call for fee. Hours: call.

National Soaring Museum

Harris Hill, RD 3, Elmira, NY 14903; (607) 734-3128. Preserves and promotes history of motorless flight and related aeronautics in America through exhibits, library, and archival collections. Holdings include large collection of classic and contemporary sailplanes and gliders and related artifacts and memorabilia; reference library; archives with plans and drawings of historic gliders and sailplanes; manuscripts and correspondences of gliding and soaring pioneers pilots and designers; photos of planes, instruments, sites, and personalities. Library and archives non-circulating. Accepts phone inquiries. Fee. Hours: 10-5.

National Soccer Hall of Fame

5-11 Ford Ave., Oneonta, NY 13820; (607) 432-3351. Collects and preserves history of the sport of soccer in America. Holdings include museum/Hall of Fame exhibits, artifacts and memorabilia; historical and instructional soccer publications; archives with records and materials on soccer in America from the 1850s, including some intl items; manuscripts from the early 20th c; large photo collection of natl and intl soccer subjects from 1800s; films and videotapes from

A 1933 Bowlus-DuPont Albatross sailplane, from the National Soaring Museum.

1930s; Film and Document Collection of the North American Soccer League; color films of photographer/ filmmaker John Albok, 1937-42. Accepts phone inquiries. Fee. Hours: summer, M-Sa 9-7:30, Su noon-7:30; winter, M-F 9-5, Sa 10-5, Su noon-5.

National Warplane Museum

P.O. Box 159, Big Tree Ln, Geneseo, NY 14454; (716) 243-0690. Preserves and promotes history of military aviation, 1935-55, with emphasis on WWII and Korean conflict aircraft. Holdings include collection of flying-condition aircraft, including B-17G, PT-17, PT-19, PT-26, BT-13, C-45, AT-6, PBY-6A, L-2, L-3, L-21; WWII memorabilia and flight artifacts; library with materials and publications relating to WWII and Korean conflict; small archives; photos of military aircraft; small collection videotapes of oral histories of Western New York AAF veterans. Accepts phone inquiries. Fee. Hours: M-F 9-5, Sa-Su 10-5.

Native New Yorkers Historical Association

503 W. 22nd St., New York, NY 10011; (718) 847-9869. Promotes history of New York City and residents by working to erect plaques at unmarked New York City Historical Sites, conducting walking tours, and maintaining archival collections on native residents. Holdings include photos of graves and gravestones of, and files on, prominent people buried in city's cemeteries; files of Jacob Riis, champion of the homeless; files of President Chester Arthur and the US Civil Service; files on city Christmas traditions and celebrations. Accepts phone inquiries. Hours: call.

New York Academy of Medicine Library

2 East 103rd St., New York, NY 10029; (212) 876-8200. Maintains strong collection on history of medicine, and large library of classic medical works. Accepts phone inquiries. Hours: call.

New York City Fire Museum

278 Spring St., New York, NY 10013; (212) 691-1303. Museum memorializes firefighters and work of the New York City Fire Dept, and preserves the history of the Home Insurance Co., in form of exhibits, library, and archival collections. Holdings include extensive collection of memorabilia and historical artifacts of the NYCFD, and the Home Insurance Co; library, with source materials on firemen's lore, firefighting history and apparatus; archives with insurance indentures and policies, firehouse journals, orders, and other documents; limited company and action photos. Accepts phone inquiries. Donations accepted. Hours: M-F 10-4.

New York City Police Academy Museum

235 E. 20th St., New York, NY 10003; (212) 477-9753. Preserves and presents New York City Police history in form of museum exhibits, artifacts and memorabilia; photos; and historical police personnel records. Displays include weapons from criminals used as trial evidence, uniforms, newspaper clippings, posters, materials on development of fingerprinting, nightsticks, and first NY Police Commissioner Teddy Roosevelt memorabilia. Accepts phone inquiries. No fee. Hours: M-F 9-3.

New York City Technical College of CUNY

300 Jay St., Brooklyn, NY 11201; (212) 643-5323. Academic research library concentrates on hotel & restaurant management and Afro-American studies. Special collections include menu collection and picture collection. Accepts phone inquiries. No fee. Hours: M-Th 9-9, F 9-5, Sa 10-2.

New York Historical Society

170 Central Park West, New York, NY 10024; (212) 873-3400. Collects, preserves and promotes history of New York City and State and residents in form of museum, library, and archival and special collections. Holdings include collections of American historical and cultural artifacts, uniforms, memorabilia, folk arts, decorative arts, paintings and other art; large library with early imprints and newspapers; society archives from 1804; large manuscript collection; many New York and eastern seaboard maps, 1600-1950; large collection of local photos from mid-19th c. Accepts phone inquiries. Donations accepted. Hours: Tu-Sa 10-5, Su 1-6.

New York Law School Library

57 Worth St., New York, NY 10013; (212) 431-2150. Provides legal reference services to students, faculty, legal community, and general public. Holdings include federal and state cases and laws with general collection covering legal, economic, and historical materials on mainly US topics. Materials for in-house use only. Accepts phone inquiries. No fee. Hours: M-Th 8:30-11, F 8:30-10, Sa-Su 10-10.

New York Municipal Archives

Department of Records and Information Service, 31 Chambers St., New York, NY 10007; (212) 566-5292. Retains New York City archives and materials on history of NYC, engineering and architecture, and govt and politics. Holdings include papers of NYC mayors, papers of NY Common Council from 1670-1897, drawings of Brooklyn Bridge, and vital records from 1847-1919. Accepts phone inquiries. No fee. Hours: M-F 9-4:30.

New York Museum of Transportation

P.O. Box 136, 6393 East River Road, West Henrietta, NY 14586; (716) 533-1113. Preserves and displays transportation artifacts relating to upstate and western NY state. Museum exhibits rail vehicles, trolleys, Interurbaner, steam locomotive, railroad artifacts, antique autos, and road building equip from 1890-1950. Library holds books and periodicals on transportation, with emphasis on railroads. Archives contains records of Rochester and Eastern railway, Rochester subway, and Rochester streetcar system; NY state rail maps from 1905; and photos from NY railway. Special collection of trolley signs from different lines. Materials for in-house use only. Accepts phone inquiries. Fee. Hours: Su 11-5.

New York Post

Library, 210 South St., New York, NY 10002; (212) 815-8000. Newspaper has newspaper clipping and photo library from all NY City newspapers dating to before turn of century. Materials arranged biographically and by subject. Accepts phone inquiries. No fee. Hours: 8-8.

New York Public Library

Astor, Lenox, and Tilden Foundations, 5th Ave.

& 42nd St., New York, NY 10018; (212) 930-0830. Public library system maintains extensive collections of research and archival materials on US, NY and New York City history and culture. Holdings (at various locations around city) include major collections on American history, local history, and genealogy; Billy Rose Theater Collection; Jewish Division; Miriam & Ira D. Wallach Division of Art, Prints, and Photographs; Oriental Division; Rogers & Hammerstein Archives of Recorded Sound; Slavonic Division; Schomburg Center for Research in Black Culture. Some restrictions. Accepts phone inquiries. No fee. Hours: vary by location.

New York Public Library
Map Division

Fifth Ave. & 42nd St., Room 117, New York, NY 10018; (212) 930-0587. Division documents history of cartography, and maintains large collection of maps. Holdings include Civil War Maps, 17th & 18th c atlases, Butterfield collection of manuscripts, and real estate atlases. Accepts phone inquiries. No fee. Hours: M, W, F, Sa 10-6, Tu 10-9.

New York Public Library
Newspaper Collection

521 W. 43rd St., between 10th and 11th St., New York, NY 10036; (212) 714-8520. Collects most New York City newspapers and many English and foreign papers. Accepts phone inquiries. No fee. Hours: M-Sa 9-5.

New York Society Library

53 East 79th St., New York, NY 10021; (212) 287-6900. Library collection covers Americana, New York City, history, and biography. Special collections include John Winthrop collection, Goodhue papers, and Hammond collection of early fiction. Limited access to those outside membership. Accepts phone inquiries. Hours: M-Sa 9-5.

New York State
Archaeological Association

Box 1480, 657 East Ave., Rochester, NY 14603; (716) 271-4320, ext. 440. Professional and amateur archaeologist org publishes journal of technical papers on archaeological and anthropological concerns in NY. Accepts phone inquiries. Fee for membership. Hours: M-F 9-5.

New York State Archives

Cultural Education Center, Empire State Plaza, Albany, NY 12230; (518) 474-1195. State repository holds censorship records of NY Motion Picture Div from 1921-65, including large number of scripts. Accepts phone inquiries. Hours: call.

New York State Department of Labor Research Library

One Main St., 1950, Brooklyn, NY 11201; (718) 797-7718. Library has collection of materials on unions, economic and business conditions, industrial relations, wages, women, and unemployment insurance. Special collections include archives of Women's Trade Union League, releases from state labor depts., and NY state labor laws. Restrictions on public access. Accepts phone inquiries. Hours: by appt only, M-F 9-4:30.

New York State Division of Human Rights

Reference Library, Two World Trade Center, Rm. 5356, New York, NY 10047; (212) 870-8400. State office preserves materials on civil rights and liberties, minorities, ethnic groups, human rights, and housing and urban renewal. Holds collection of publications from NYS Division of Human Rights. Accepts phone inquiries. Hours: M-F 9-5:15.

New York State Historical Association Library

P.O. Box 800, Lake Rd., Cooperstown, NY 13326; (607) 547-2533. Collects, preserves, and displays materials relating to history of NY state, American farms, and rural communities from 17th c. Library holds family papers, church and business records, maps, photos, local NY state histories, biographical reviews, DAR patriot index and lineage books from 1890-1939, NY and New England genealogical records from 19th c, L.C. Jones NY State Folklore Archives and Harold Thompson Folklore Archives, murder pamphlet collection, Ward collection of printed and photo materials on Cooperstown history, and assorted broadsides, agriculture ads, and trade catalogs. Accepts phone inquiries. Fee.

Hours: M-Th 9-10, F 9-5, Sa 10-5.

New York State Library

Cultural Education Center, Empire State Plaza, Albany, NY 12230; (518) 474-7646. Collects and preserves materials and resources relating to NY and US history and culture in form of extensive research and archival collections. Holdings include extensive materials on arts/sciences, education, American, and NY history; manuscripts, letters, diaries, and business records relating to NY and US history, including Jacob Javits papers from 1957-78; extensive collection of historical and modern maps and atlases; NY photos; extensive genealogical records; special collections on NY and Eastern US history. Some restrictions. Accepts phone inquiries (mss/special collections: 518-474-4461; history: 474-5161). No fee. Hours: M-F 9-5.

Newburgh Free Library

Genealogical Collections, 124 Grand St., Newburgh, NY 12550; (914) 561-1881. Public library maintains selective collection of govt documents, general and historical materials relevant to genealogy of community. Holdings include NYGBR; NEHGR; lineage books; American Genealogy and Biography Indexes; Census Indexes to 1850; Census Records of Orange, Ulster, Sullivan, Rockland, Dutchess, and Putnam Counties, NY. Accepts phone inquiries. No fee. Hours: M-Th 9-9, F-Sa 9-5.

Niagara Falls Historical Society

c/o President, Public Library, 1425 Main St., Niagara Falls, NY 14305; (716) 278-8229. Collects, preserves and promotes history of Niagara Falls, NY area and residents in form of library, archives, manuscripts, maps, photos, newspapers, and special collections. Some restrictions. Accepts phone inquiries. No fee. Hours: M-F 9-1, 2-5.

Niagara Falls Public Library

Local History Collection, 1425 Main St., Niagara Falls, NY 14305; (716) 278-8229. Public library maintains collection historical materials relevant to the needs of the community. Holdings include collection of artifacts, ephemera, and research materials related to Niagara River, Niagara Falls and area, including photos, stereographs, postcards; local govt records and documents; local newspapers from mid-19th c; atlases and maps of area; small collection of films/videotapes; recordings of local music. Staff assistance required for use of Niagara collections. Accepts phone inquiries. No fee. Hours: 9-1, 2-5.

Northern New York American-Canadian Genealogical Society

P.O. Box 1256, Plattsburgh, NY 12901. Society promotes study of American-Canadian ancestry in form of genealogical repertoires on Quebec and northern NY, and collection of Clinton County records up to 1880. Some restrictions for non-members. Does not accept phone inquiries.

Northport Historical Society and Museum

P.O. Box 545, Northport, NY 11768; (516) 757-9859. Preserves local history of region through holdings in museum, library, and archives, including shipbuilding tools, costumes collection, local artifacts and memorabilia, photos, manuscripts, maps, oral history recordings, and limited genealogical records. Accepts phone inquiries. Donations accepted. Hours: Tu-F 1-4:30.

Office of the State Historian

New York State Museum Division, Research Collections, 3099 Cultural Center, Empire State Plaza, Albany, NY 12230; (518) 473-1299. Collects, preserves and interprets history of NY in form of museum, library, archives, manuscripts, maps, photos, films/videotapes, and recordings. Accepts phone inquiries. No fee. Hours: 8:30-5.

Olana State Historic Site

R.D. 2, Rt. 9-G, Hudson, NY 12534; (518) 828-0135. Historic site preserves and presents the art and life of Hudson River Valley School artist Frederic Edwin Church. Holdings include Olana, the Moorish-style home designed and lived in by Church; the artist's library; archives with Church's correspondences, 1847-1900, and bills, reciepts and other records relating to the artist; diaries of Church and his family; catalog texts; maps of Olana; 19th c American, Euro-

pean and Middle Eastern photos, taken by Church; Church family genealogy; collections of Church's archictectural drawings for the home, and his paintings. Reservations suggested. Accepts phone inquiries. Fee. Hours: May-Oct, W-Sa 10-4, Su 1-4.

Old Fort Niagara Association

Old Fort Niagara, Box 169, Youngstown, NY 14174; (716) 745-7611. Preserves and interprets history of site of Fort Niagara, 1697-1963, in form of museum, library, and archival collections. Holdings include military, archeological and site related artifacts and displays; library; archives with small collection of site-related documents; copies of maps and plans relating to site; large collection of photos of Fort and area. Public use of library limited. Accepts phone inquiries. Fee. Hours: 9-5:30.

Old Rhinebeck Aerodrome

R.D.1, Box 89, Rhinebeck, NY 12572; (914) 758-8610. Historic aerodrome museum preserves history of early aviation through displays, demonstrations, and air shows of original aircraft, and exhibits cultural and aeronautic artifacts, 1900-1937. Accepts phone inquiries. Fee.. Hours: 10-5.

Old Stone House Museum

P.O. Box 306, Windsor, NY 13865; (607) 655-1491. Preserves local and military history with emphasis on Civil War period. Museum artifacts date from Civil War through WWI. Library has small collection of Civil War books, regimental histories, and federal and state records. Archives holds local records and photos. Accepts phone inquiries. Donations accepted. Hours: 9-4:30.

Old Village Hall Museum

P.O. Box 296, 215 S. Wellwood Ave., Lindenhurst, NY 11757; (516) 957-4385. Collects, preserves and displays history of Lindenhurst, NY and residents in form of artifacts and archival collections. Holdings include local historical items from the 17th c; archives with local records and research materials; maps from 18th c; photos; slides of local architecture, banks, fire dept and ponds; oral history recordings of residents; small collection of genealogical records; Dittman Collection; Emil Heger Collection; Frohsian

Singing Society material. Accepts phone inquiries. No fee. Hours: June-Sept, M, W, F 2-4; Oct-May, W, F, Sa, and 1st Su of month, 2-4.

Onondaga County Museums and Historic Sites

P.O. Box 146, Liverpool, NY 13088; (315) 451-7275. Collects, preserves and promotes history of Onondaga County, NY life, residents and industry in form of museums, library, archival and special collections. Holdings include Salt Museum, which preserves and interprets local salt industry history, 1788-1926; Ste. Marie de Gannentaha, a recreated 17th c Jesuit mission with practising craftsmen; library and archives; local, state and Colonial American maps; Wolcott Photograph Collection, with early 20th c photos of the Onondaga (Native American) reservation; Shuelke Photograph Collection of local subjects. Some restrictions. Accepts phone inquiries. No fee. Hours: 8:30-4:30.

Onondaga County Public Library

Local History/Special Collections Dept., Galleries of Syracuse, 451 S. Salina St., Syracuse, NY 13202; (315) 473-2702. Public library maintains selective collection of govt documents, historical, archival and special collections relevant to needs of community. Holdings include US history materials, with emphasis on NY, NJ, PA, and New England; local, county and state maps of northeastern US from 18th c; photos of local subjects from 19th c; Syracuse/Onondaga Collection of genealogical publications, manuscripts and records; selected US and northeastern US govt documents, including census records, 1790-1910, Revolutionary War Pension records; records and materials on Iroquois. Some restrictions. Accepts phone inquiries (315-473-2701). No fee. Hours: M, T, W, F 9-6; Th 9-9, Sa, Su 9-5.

Onondaga Historical Association

311 Montgomery St., Syracuse, NY 13202; (315) 428-1862. Collects, preserves and promotes history of Syracuse and Onondaga County, NY and residents in form of museum exhibits, library, and archival collections. Holdings include historical artifacts and displays; reference library; large archival holdings; large collections of manuscripts, maps, and photos; films/videotapes,

and genealogical records. Accepts phone inquiries. Some research fees. Hours: M-Sa 9:30-noon, 1-4:30.

Ontario County Historical Society

55 N. Main St., Canandaigua, NY 14424; (716) 394-4975. Collects, preserves and promotes history of Ontario County, NY and residents in form of exhibits, library, and archival collections. Holdings include displays relating to county history from 1700-1960; Discovery Room, with archives and artifacts for children; library with materials on local and regional history; archives with regional 19th c ephemera, education materials, industrial and agricultural records; regional family papers,, including Oliver Phelpe papers, Nathaniel Gorham papers, and Granger family papers; photos and genealogical records from county and surrounding region. Library and archives available for society members only. Accepts phone inquiries. No fee. Hours: Tu-Sa 10-5.

Oriskany Battlefield State Historic Site

State Route 69, Oriskany, NY 13424; (315) 768-7224. Preserves history and site of American Revolutionary War Battle of Oriskany through tours and audiovisual presentations. Accepts phone inquiries. No fee. Hours: mid-May-mid-Oct, W-Sa 9-5, Su 1-5.

Ossining Historical Society and Museum

196 Croton Ave., Ossining, NY 10562; (914) 941-0001. Collects, preserves and promotes history of Ossining, NY and residents in form of museum, library, and archival and special collections. Holdings include Victorian period parlor, Native American and early settler artifacts; Sing Sing Prison memorabilia; Map Room and War Exhibit Showcase with early maps, atlases and military artifacts; research library; extensive archives, and collections of manuscripts, photos, oral history recordings, and genealogical records; small collection of films/videotapes; special collections of costumes, flags, and hat boxes. Some restrictions. Accepts phone inquiries. Donations accepted. Hours: museum: Su, M, W 2-4; office: 1-4.

Owen B. Young Library

St. Lawrence University, Canton, NY 13617; (315) 379-5477. Academic library maintains selective collection of govt documents, general, reference and historical materials, and archival and special collections revelant to needs of the school and students. Holdings include local history items; archives with Owen B. Young Papers, and the papers of David Parish and his family from the 19th c; materials on War of 1812 and concurrent social and cultural conditions; St. Lawrence Seaway Collection; Adirondack Collection; and Frederick Remington Collection. Accepts phone inquiries. No fee. Hours: Academic year: Su-Th 6:30-9:30; other times: M-F 8:30-5.

Oyster Bay Historical Society

P.O. Box 297, 20 Summit St., Oyster Bay, NY 11771; (516) 922-5032. Collects, preserves, and disseminates info and materials relating to history of Oyster Bay. Colonial house museum furnished in early 19th c and colonial pieces. Library has small collection of materials on Oyster Bay and Long Island history, deeds and documents relating to local history from 1600s-1930s, small collection of maps, photos, and genealogical records. Materials for in-house use only. Accepts phone inquiries. Donations accepted. Hours: Sa 10-1.

Oysterponds Historical Society

P.O. Box 844, Village Lane, Orient, NY 11957; (516) 323-2480. Studies, collects, and preserves the history of Long Island, with emphasis on the Orient, East Marion area. Holdings include historic buildings with furnishings and exhibits; reference library with publications and materials relating to area history; archives of the society, and local businesses and families; ships' logs, diaries, meeting minutes, wills, and other local historical documents; regional maps and photos; tapes of oral history, and of Roy Latham (naturalist and archeologist of Indian artifacts); local genealogical records; William Steeple Davis collection; early American Indian artifacts. Accepts phone inquiries. Fee. Hours: June-Sept, W-Th, Sa-Su.

Parma Meetinghouse Museum

1300 Hilton, Parma Rd., Hilton, NY 14468; (716) 392-4720. Preserves history of town of Parma from 1796 with exhibits on church, school, women, business, and military activity. Library has materials on NY and local history, maps from 19th and 20th c, photos, genealogical records of regional pioneers, and special collection of school texts from 1830s. Accepts phone inquiries. No fee. Hours: by appt.

Peter Whitmer Sr. Home and Visitors Center

1451 Aunkst Rd., Waterloo, NY 13165; (315) 539-2552. Historic log home and farm preserves history of site of organization of the Mormon church, by Joseph Smith, in 1830. Holdings include period furnishings; colonial chapel; maps, photos, and films/videotapes. Accepts phone inquiries. No fee. Hours: 8-7.

Pierpont Morgan Library

29 E. 36th St., New York, NY 10016; (212) 685-0008. Library maintains and preserves reference, special collections, and exhibits on art, music, literature and Morgan family/bank history. Holdings include changing exhbitions, and Pierpont Morgan's preserved study, with personal artifacts and art objects; collections of rare manuscripts, books and letters, 11th c-20th c; bookbindings, 9th c-20th c; Rembrandt and other rare etchings and prints; Morgan archives; Gilbert and Sullivan Archives. Reading room open only by appt to qualifying scholars, and researchers who have filled out proper application. Accepts phone inquiries. Fee for exhibitions. Hours: Exhibitions: Tu-Sa 10:30-5, Su 1-5; others vary.

Planned Parenthood Federation of America

Katharine Dexter McCormick Library, 810 Seventh Ave., New York, NY 10019; (212) 603-4637. Library holds wealth of materials on birth control, teenagers, contraception and contraceptive research, family plannings, religion, and birth control. Accepts phone inquiries. No fee. Hours: by appt only; M-F 9:15-4:30.

Poetry Society of America

Van Voorhis Library, 15 Gramercy Park, New York, NY 10003; (212) 254-9628. Library preserves materials on poetry, poets, history, criticism, and essays. Special collections on individual poets. Accepts phone inquiries. Hours: by appt; M-F 9:30-5:30.

Preservation League of New York State

307 Hamilton St., Albany, NY 12210; (518) 462-5658. League promotes sensible preservation techniques, planning, and policy, and public involvement through educational programs, advocacy activities, and technical and legal assistance services. Holdings include rental library of films and audiovisual programs on historic preservation topics. Accepts phone inquiries. Hours: M-F 9-5.

Putnam County Historical Society

63 Chestnut St., Cold Spring, NY 10516; (914) 265-4010. Collects, preserves and promotes history of Putnam County and residents in form of museum, library, and archival collections. Holdings include the Foundry School Museum, with local historical artifacts, furnishings, ship models, and art works; library and archives with materials on local, county, and Hudson Valley history. Accepts phone inquiries. No fee. Hours: March-Dec, W 9:30-4, Su 2-5.

Queens Borough Public Library

Long Island Division, 89-11 Merrick Blvd., Jamaica, NY 11432; (718) 990-0769. Public library holds materials on Long Island history with concentration on Queens Borough. Holdings include large collection of photos, maps, manuscripts, genealogical materials from 19th c, clipping files, and broadsides from 1795. Accepts phone inquiries. No fee. Hours: M-F 10-9, Sa 10-5:30, Su noon-5.

Queens College

Alan Copland School of Music, c/o Rufus Hallmark, Dir., Flushing, NY 11367; (718) 520-7340. Academic research library holds collection of Louis Armstrong materials. Holdings under organization; will be open for specific inquiries in 1988. Collection will open for hands-on research in 1989. No fee. Hours: call.

Queens Museum

Flushing Meadow, Corona Park, Flushing, NY 11368; (718) 592-5555. Museum collects, pre-serves and displays contemporary art and design and cultural work, with emphasis on New York City area and NY World's Fairs of 1939 and 1964. Holdings include collections on 20th c American art, with emphasis on New York City artists and material life; reference library with materials on art, architecture, and craft work; photos of local and NY World's Fairs; 9000 sq ft panoramic model of New York City area; films/videotapes; collection of NY World's Fair memorabilia, souvenirs and documents. Accepts phone inquiries. Fee. Hours: Tu-F 10-5 (June-Aug, W 10-8), Sa-Su noon-5:30.

Racquet and Tennis Club Library

370 Park Ave., New York, NY 10022; (212) 753-9700. Library concentrates on early American sports, court tennis, and lawn tennis. Materials circulate to members only. Accepts phone inquiries. Hours: by appt only, M-F 9-5.

Raynham Hall Museum

20 W. Main St., Oyster Bay, NY 11771; (516) 922-6808. Collects, preserves, and interprets artifacts housed in former Townsend family home from 1740-1880, and educates public on Oyster Bay history. Museum consists of historic house with Colonial and Victorian period furnished rooms. Small library of reference materials available. Archives consists of Townsend and Weekes family documents from 1725-1900, maps of Oyster Bay, photos, genealogical records, and survey of Oyster Bay historic structures. Accepts phone inquiries. Fee. Hours: Tu-Su 1-5.

Remington Gun Museum

Catharine St., Ilion, NY 13357; (315) 894-9961. Preserves and displays significant collection of Remington-made handguns, rifles, and shotguns. Museum exhibits date to 1816, and include 1865 double Deringer, Annie Oakley's Remington 22 rifle, Remington typewriter, Parker shotgun, and other Remington-produced items. No fee. Hours: M-Sa 9-4:30.

Rensselaer County Historical Society

59 2nd St., Troy, NY 12180; (518) 272-7232. Society collects and preserves history of Rensselaer County, NY in form of museum, library, and archival collections. Holdings include historic house, and gallery with changing exhibits; local

history resource library with publications, manuscripts, maps, genealogical materials, and large photo collection; archives with local holdings, including the Tibbits and Cluett collections; Fox Hollow Folk Festival recordings archives. Library is non-circulating. Accepts phone inquiries. Donations accepted. Hours: Museum and library: Tu-Sa 10-4; office: M-F 9-5.

Roberson Center of the Arts and Sciences

30 Front St., Binghamton, NY 13905; (607) 772-0660. Preserves artistic and cultural heritage of Southern Tier of NY. Museum exhibits include fine and decorative arts, historical collections from Broome county, folk arts, archaeological materials, and ethnographic collection. Library has materials on Broome county history, personal and business records, maps of Binghamton and Broome county, photos on regional history, early aviation, underwater technology, and archaeology. Special collection of pocket watches and cut and decorative glass. Accepts phone inquiries. Fee. Hours: Tu-Th 10-6, F 10-9, Sa 10-6, Su noon-5.

Rochester Public Library

115 South Ave., Rochester, NY 14604; (716) 428-7323. Public library maintains selective collection of govt documents, general and historical materials relevant to needs of community. Holdings include extensive collection of local historical material. Some restrictions. Accepts phone inquiries. No fee. Hours: M-Th 9-9, F 9-6, Sa 10-9.

Rockefeller Archive Center

Rockefeller University, Pocantico Hills, North Tarrytown, NY 10591; (914) 631-4505. Maintains special collection of materials on Rockefeller family, businesses, foundations, and people related to them. Accepts phone inquiries. No fee. Hours: call.

Rockwell Museum

Cedar St. at Denison Parkway, Corning, NY 14830; (607) 937-5386. Museum preserves and maintains extensive collections of Western American art and artifacts, Carder glass, and turn-of-the-century toys. Holdings include art and relics of the American West, 1840-1980,

including bronzes, Navajo weavings, Native American artifacts, and antique firearms; Steuben and studio glass; toys; library with materials on Western American art, and Carder glass; Pacific Railroad Survey maps, 1857-63, and maps relating to Western US exploration; collection of film Western's by John Ford; videotapes of museum symposiums. Accepts phone inquiries. Fee. Hours: Sept-June, M-Sa 9-5, Su noon-5; July-Aug, M-F 9-7, Sa 9-5, Su noon-5.

Rod Serling Archives

Ithaca College Communications School, Ithaca, NY 14850; (607) 274-3895. Serves as a resource for scholars interested in Rod Serling and his work. Archive holds copies of films/videotapes and scripts of all "Twilight Zone" and "Night Gallery" programs; copies of "Twilight Zone Magazine" since 1981; original Serling screenplays; audio recordings of WICB 1967 Serling press conference; videotapes of Serling interviews with Mike Wallace, lectures, and "Twilight Zone" producer Buck Houghton; and small library on TV/radio writing and art. Some photos of Serling and "Twilight Zone" stills available. Restrictions. No fee. Hours: by appt.

Rye Historical Society

1 Purchase St., Rye, NY 10580; (914) 967-7588. Collects, preserves and promotes history of Rye, NY area and residents in form of restored tavern, library, and archival collections. Holdings include restoration of 18th c Boston Post Rd Tavern; library with references, archives, letters, documents, manuscripts, genealogical records, scrapbooks, and historical materials on area from 1660; local maps from 1850; photos of Old Rye subjects; oral history recordings; collection of Slater papers, account books and documents, 1683-1871. Collection is non-circulating. Accepts phone inquiries. No fee. Hours: Museum: Tu-F, Su 2:30-4:30; office: M-F 9-5.

Sackets Harbor Battlefield State Historic Site

P.O. Box 27, 505 W. Washington St., Sackets Harbor, NY 13685; (315) 646-3634. Site preserves and interprets history of 1814 battlefield and 1812-61 US Navy Yard in form of exhibits, library, and archival collections. Holdings include historic Union Hotel, 1817, with exhibits, and preserved Navy Yard and buildings; small library collection with materials on the War of 1812; archives with microfilm holdings on War of 1812 and US Navy, 1844-68; maps of area and site, 1813; list of men who served at Sackets Harbor during War of 1812. Accepts phone inquiries. No fee. Hours: late May-late Sept, W-Sa 10-5, Su 1-5.

Sag Harbor Whaling and Historical Museum

P.O. Box 1327, Sag Harbor, NY 11963. Collects, preserves and promotes history of Sag Harbor, NY and whaling heritage during 18th and 19th c, in form of exhibits, library, and archival and special collections. Holdings include scrimshaw, ship models, nautical instruments, and other whaling artifacts; furniture and household wares, paintings, musical instruments, coins, shells, clothing and other local historical artifacts; reference library with materials on whaling, fishing, shipping, and Long Island history; archives of ships' log books; letters, records and other local papers; wall maps of area, 1854-1902. Research by appt. Accepts phone inquiries. Fee. Hours: M-Sa 10-5, Su 1-5.

Sagamore Hill National Historic Site

20 Sagamore Hill Rd., Oyster Bay, NY 11771; (512) 922-4447. Preserves history of life and influence of US President Theodore Roosevelt in form of his home, library, and archival collections. Holdings include Theodore Roosevelt Home and original furnishings, the Old Orchard Home exhibition area, and historic outbuildings and grounds; Roosevelt's library (on display in home); archives with historic materials and photos of Roosevelt, family and friends; small map collection; genealogical records, including Roosevelt Family Tree; collection of E. Custis photos of the North American Indian; collection of Roosevelt related political cartoons. Accepts phone inquiries. Fee. Hours: 9:30-5:30.

Saint Francis College Archives

James Kelly Institute for Local Historical Studies, 180 Remsen St., Brooklyn, NY 11201; (718) 522-2300 ext. 202. Documents Brooklyn history from 1643-1898, including papers of prominent Brooklyn figures, maps, photos, vertical file materials, and theses on Brooklyn history. Ac-

cepts phone inquiries. No fee. Hours: call.

Saint John's University

Special Collections Dept., Grand Central & Utopia Pkwys., Jamaica, NY 11439; (718) 990-6161. Preserves O'Dwyer collection of materials on US/Ireland relationship and history; Fischer lawn tennis collection; Baxter collection on American history; and James Buckley Senatorial papers. O'Dwyer holdings include correspondence, speeches, and press releases, as well as materials from American Friends of Irish Neutrality. Accepts phone inquiries. No fee. Hours: M-Th 8-10, F 8-6, Sa 8:30-4:30, Su 1-6.

Saint Lawrence County Historical Association

P.O. Box 8, 3 E. Main St., Canton, NY 13617; (315) 386-8133. Collects, preserves and promotes history of St. Lawrence County, NY and residents in form of historic home and museum exhibits, library, and archival collections. Holdings include 1840 Greek Revival Home with furnished period rooms; local historical exhibits and artifacts; library and archives with publications, letters, diaries, instruments, business records, local maps, photos and other materials on local history form late 18th c; genealogical, cemetery, census, and church records; papers of Silas Wright; J. Henry Rushton collection. Accepts phone inquiries. Donations accepted. Hours: museum: M-F 9-5, library and archives: M-Sa noon-4.

Salvation Army Archives and Research Center

145 W. 15th St., New York, NY 10011; (212) 337-7428. Preserves and promotes history and causes of the Salvation Army in form of library and archival collections. Holdings include reference materials on Salvation Army history and social services from 1860s; archives with manuscripts, records and documents relating to Salvation Army from 1880s; large collections of photos from 1880s, films/videotapes from 1910, and recordings from 1950s; genealogical records of officers from 1880s. Some restrictions. Accepts phone inquiries. No fee. Hours: M-F 8:30-4.

Sarah Lawrence College

Esther Raushenbush Library, One Meadway,

Bronxville, NY 10708; (914) 337-0700. Academic research library emphasizes women's history and related issues. Special collections include materials from Emily Dickinson and Sarah Lawrence faculty. Accepts phone inquiries. No fee. Hours: M-Th 8:30-10, F 8:30-7, Sa 11-7, Su 11-10.

Saratoga National Historical Park

R.D. 2, Box 33, Stillwater, NY 12170; (518) 669-9821. Park preserves and interprets historic site of Revolutionary War Battle of Saratoga in 1777 through audiovisual presentation, exhibits, and small reference library. Library primarily for staff use; others by appt. Accepts phone inquiries. Fee. Hours: 9-5.

Saratoga Springs Museum Historical Society

Box 216, The Casino, Congress Park, Saratoga Springs, NY 12866; (518) 584-6420. Museum preserves local history with emphasis on 19th c. Archives contain manuscripts, maps, and photos on 19th c Saratoga Springs, 19th c resort life, hydrotherapy, history of Reuben Hyde Walworth family, materials on NY State Chancery, and founding of DAR. Special Frank Sullivan collection. Accepts phone inquiries. Fee for archives. Hours: Jul-Aug 9:30-4:30; Jun, Sept, Oct, M-Sa 10-4, Su 1-4; Nov-May, W-Su 1-4.

Saratoga Springs Preservation Foundation

P.O. Box 442, 6 Lake Ave., Saratoga Springs, NY 12866; (318) 587-5030. Preserves architecture and landscape heritage of Saratoga Springs through museum and library holdings of maps and photos. Library open to members only. Accepts phone inquiries. No fee. Hours: M-F 9-5.

Schoharie County Historical Society

Old Stone Fort Museum Complex, P.O. Box 69, Schoharie, NY 12157; (518) 295-8553. Preserves culture and heritage of Iroquois Indians, with emphasis on contributions made by living Iroquois. Holdings include exhibits of contemporary Indian art objects and crafts, historic artifacts from turn-of-the-century, and local archeological artifacts, 8000 BC-1780s; refer-

ence library with materials on the Iroquois; archives with extensive collections on Iroquois communities and art forms; extensive collection of color slides and B/W photos. Materials non-circulating, and used by appt. Accepts phone inquiries. Fee. Hours: May, June, Sept, Oct, Tu-W, F-Sa 10-5, Su noon-5; July, Aug. F-W (closed Th), 10-5; Nov-Apr M-F 10-5 with appt.

Schomburg Center for Research in Black Culture

New York Public Library, 515 Lenox Ave., New York, NY 10037; (212) 862-4000. Collects, promotes, and preserves materials relating to black experience worldwide, in form of educational programs, publications, exhibits and archival collections. Holdings include exhibition hall with changing displays; Rare Books, Manuscripts, and Archives collections, with the original manuscript of Richard Wright's "Native Son," abolitionist documents, and records of black orgs; Art and Artifacts collection; Photographs and Prints collection, with images from mid-18th c; Moving Images and Recorded Sound collection. Some restrictions. Accepts phone inquiries. No fee. Hours: Sept-May, M-W noon-6, Th-Su 10-6; June-Aug, Tu, Th, F 10-6.

Seaman's Church Institute of New York

Joseph Conrad Library, 15 State St., New York, NY 10004; (212) 269-2710. Preserves merchant marine maritime history through collection of ship registers from 1764-1865, photos, and scrapbooks. Accepts phone inquiries. Hours: call.

Seneca Falls Historical Society

55 Cayuga St., Seneca Falls, NY 13148; (315) 568-8412. Studies and preserves materials of local history interest. Library holds books on Victorian life. Archives has county newspapers from 1833-1976; Amelia Bloomer records; records of churches and civic orgs; maps; photos and slides; films/videotapes; and genealogical records. Special collections on Gould pumps, Sylvania, and quilts. Materials for in-house use only. Fee. Hours: M-F 9-5.

Seneca-Iroquois National Museum

Allegany Indian Reservation, Broad St. Extension, P.O. Box 442, Salamanca, NY 14779; (716) 945-1738. Museum preserves and promotes history, present, and future of the Seneca and the Iroquois in form of museum with artifacts and exhibits; research library, maps, photos, films/videotapes, and recordings; small collections of manuscripts and genealogical records. Use of collections by appt. Accepts phone inquiries. No fee. Hours: M-F 9-5.

Seward House

33 South St., Auburn, NY 13021; (315) 252-1283. Historical 19th c house museum with original furnishings and decorations of owner, Sec. of State William Seward. Library contains materials on Civil War, Lincoln, NY, and US history; some letters; photos; genealogical materials; paintings and prints; original prints; and early AK artifacts. Accepts phone inquiries. Fee. Hours: Apr-Dec, Tu-Sa 1-4.

Seymour Library Association

176 Genesee St., Auburn, NY 13021; (315) 252-2571. Public library holds considerable collection of genealogical files and reference works in History room. Special collections on life of Harriet Tubman, files on Auburn State Prison, and imprints of Auburn open to public, with restrictions. Accepts phone inquiries. No fee. Hours: M-W 10-9, Th-Sa 10-6.

Shaker Heritage Society

Shaker Meeting House, Albany Shaker Rd., Albany, NY 12211; (518) 456-7890. Preserves and promotes history of the Shakers in NY, and the site of their first settlement in America in form of exhibit of artifacts and photos, and genealogical research. Some restrictions. Accepts phone inquiries. Donations accepted. Hours: Tu-Th 9-3; appt needed for tour.

Shaker Museum

Shaker Museum Rd., Old Chatham, NY 12136; (518) 794-9100. Collects, preserves, and interprets Shaker history in form of museum exhibits, library, and archival collections. Holdings include exhibits and displays of Shaker tools, agricultural equipment, furniture, domestic items, pre-1840 woodworking machinery, vehicles, and items related to medicinal herb industry; library/archives with extensive collections of reference

materials, publications, manuscripts, diaries, records, paper clothing patterns, ephemera, and other items related to Shaker history; extensive collection of photos and slides; recordings of Shaker music. Accepts phone inquiries. Fee. Hours: library: M-F 9-5; museum: May-Oct, 10-5.

Six Nations Indian Museum

Onchiota, NY 12968; (518) 891-0769. Preserves rich culture of Iroquois confederacy through displays of Pre-Columbian artifacts, clothing, tools, crafts, record belt, pottery, and written materials on Iroquois history and culture. Archives, manuscripts, maps, and photos available. Accepts phone inquiries. Fee. Hours: July-Labor Day 9:30-6:30; May-June and Sept-Oct, by appt.

Sleepy Hollow Restorations Library

Box 245, 150 White Plains Rd., Tarrytown, NY 10591; (914) 631-8200. Preserves history of Hudson River Valley region, Westchester county, and NY from 17th-19th c. Special manuscript collections from Washington Irving, Philipse family, and Van Cortlandt family. Restricted to members and qualified researchers. Accepts phone inquiries. Hours: by appt, M-F 9-5.

Smithtown Historical Society

North Country Rd., P.O. Box 69, Smithtown, NY 11787; (516) 265-6768. Collects, preserves and promotes history of Smithtown and residents in form of educational and preservation projects, library, and archival collections. Historic sites include Caleb Smith House, Epenetus Smith Tavern, Judge J. Lawrence Smith Homestead, and Franklin Arthur Farm. Holdings include reference library; archives with manuscripts, records of Smithtown and Long Island history; local and regional maps from 1837; photos from 1900; Town historian videotapes; recordings; genealogical records of Smith (Richard) and local families; decorative and textile arts collections. Accepts phone inquiries. Donations accepted. Hours: M-F 9-4.

Society of Illustrators Museum of American Illustration

128 E. 63rd St., New York, NY 10021; (212)

Charles Dana Gibson's "At the Recital," from the Society of Illustrators Museum of American Illustration.

838-2560. Preserves and promotes interest in past, present and future of the art of illustration through exhibits, library, and archival collections. Holdings include exhibition hall of original illustrations; reference library with materials on American illustrators and their art; archives with clippings, biographies, photos, and samples of work of American illustrators; small collection of rare, unpublished monographs; large collection of photo portraits of American illustrators; films/videotapes. Use of research collections by appt only. Accepts phone inquiries. No fee. Hours: Exhibition hall: Sept-July, M, W-F 10-5, Tu 10-8; library and archives: M-F 10-noon, 2-5.

Sojourner Truth Library

State University College at New Paltz, New Paltz, NY 12561; (914) 257-2212. Academic library has collection of local history materials and special collection on Sojourner Truth. Accepts phone inquiries. No fee. Hours: 8:30-11.

Sons of the Revolution in the State of New York

Fraunces Tavern Museum Library, 54 Pearl St., New York, NY 10004; (212) 425-1778. Preserves history of downtown New York to 1830, Revolutionary War activities, genealogy, and Fraunces Tavern buildings. Hours: by appt.

South Street Seaport Museum

207 Front St., 213 Water St., New York, NY 10038; (212) 669-9438. Preserves and displays maritime history of New York City in form of exhibits, library, and archival collections. Holdings include preserved historic ships from 19th and 20th c; historical artifacts and exhibits; reference library with materials on maritime and general history of New York City; archives with papers, journals, logbooks, and ship plans relating to New York City shipping and waterfront businesses; maps of city waterfront from 19th c, and world navigational charts; photos from 19th c; small collection of sea chanties; W. & A.

Fletcher steamboat and steam engine plans, 1853-1928. Accepts phone inquiries. No fee. Hours: M-F 10-6.

Southold Indian Museum

P.O. Box 268, Main Bayview Rd., Southold, NY 11971; (516) 765-5577. Collects, preserves and promotes history of Long Island Indians in form of local artifacts, exhibits from Western and South American areas, pottery, and library. Library for use by qualified scholars only. Accepts phone inquiries. Donations accepted. Hours: Su 1:30-4:40 (call for additional summer hours).

State University of New York

Special Collections, Benjamin F. Feinberg Library, Plattsburgh, NY 12901; (518) 564-5206. Academic library maintains govt documents, historical materials, and special collections relevant to needs of the school and students. Holdings include selective collections of Federal documents from 1968, Canadian documents from 1977, and NY documents from 1950; publications on state and North Country history and life; univ archives; manuscripts and genealogical records relating to Clinton County, NY from 1770s; local and state maps; photos of North Country area from 1880; Marjorie Lansing Porter Collection on Folklore and Folk Music of the North Country. Some restrictions. Accepts phone inquiries. No fee. Hour: M-F 9-noon, 1-4, Sa 1-5.

State University of New York
at Albany

Special Collections, University Library, 1400 Washington Ave., Albany, NY 12222; (518) 442-3547. Academic research library has special collection of materials on German resistance to Hitler during WWII in German Exile Collection. Accepts phone inquiries. No fee. Hours: call.

State University of New York
at Binghamton

Glenn Bartle Library, Vestal Parkway East, Binghamton, NY 13901; (607) 798-2368. Academic research library collects and preserves extensive collection of materials on Austrian-born theatre producer, director, and innovator Max Reinhardt. Holdings include his personal library,

letters, photos, and playbills. Hours: call.

State University of New York
at Buffalo

Poetry and Rare Books Collection, 420 Capen Hall, Buffalo, NY 14260; (716) 636-2917. Curates collection devoted to poetry of 20th c in English and translation. Collection contains first and variant editions, records and tapes of poetry readings by authors, magazines, letters, notebooks, portraits, sculpture, and photos. Emphasis on works of James Joyce, Dylan Thomas, William Carlos Williams, Robert Graves, Martin Seymour Smith, and Robert Kelley. Hours: call.

State University of New York
at Oswego

Penfield Library, Oswego, NY 13126; (315) 341-4267. Academic research library holds large collection of letters by and about Millard Fillmore, including about 80 from Dorothea Dix. Accepts phone inquiries. No fee. Hours: call.

State University of New York
at Purchase

Library, Lincoln Ave., Purchase, NY 10577; (914) 253-5096. Academic research library holds McDonald collection of motion picture industry memorabilia. Holdings include books, stills of actresses, actors, and directors, slides, bottle caps, and playing cards. Hours: call.

State University of New York
at Stony Brook

Special Collections, Melville Library, Stony Brook, NY 11794; (516) 632-7110. Academic research library holds printed and manuscript materials related to local and regional Long Island history. Covers regional women's history, environmental history, social welfare, and politics, including political papers of US Rep. Jacob Javits from 1948-54 and 1956-81. Accepts phone inquiries. No fee. Hours: M-Th 8:30-midnight, F 8:30-8, Sa 10-6, Su noon-midnight.

State University of New York
Maritime College

Stephen B. Luce Library, Fort Schuyler, Bronx, NY 10465; (212) 409-7231. Academic library maintains collection of general, reference, maritime and historical materials relevant to needs of the school and students. Holdings include extensive collection of American maritime history reference materials; archives of SUNY Maritime College from 1874, Marine Society of the City of New York, 1769-1967, Sailor's Snug Harbor, 1797-1972, and Sandy Hook Pilots Assn, 1845-1904; photos of college and students from 1874, and of Fort Schuyler from 1865; films/videotapes on maritime history. Some restrictions. Accepts phone inquiries. No fee. Hours: M-F 8:30-noon, 1-4:30.

Staten Island Historical Society

441 Clarke Ave., Staten Island, NY 10301; (718) 351-1617. Collects, preserves, and presents history and culture of Staten Island and region. Outdoor museum consists of 17th-20th c bldgs, emphasizing architecture, furnishings, costumes, tools and equip, folk and popular art, transportation, and military. Library has materials on history, economy, social life, material culture, and industrial technology. Archives holds manuscripts, maps, personal and business records, local history research files, many photos with strengths in women's studies and urban life, films/videotapes, oral history interviews, and genealogical records. Accepts phone inquiries. Fee. Hours: library, by appt M-F; museum, W-F 10-5, Sa-M 1-5.

Staten Island Institute of Arts and Sciences

75 Stuyvesant Place, Staten Island, NY 10301; (718) 727-1135. Collects, preserves, and exhibits objects of artistic, scientific, and historical interest to Staten Island. Museum exhibits paintings, prints, and decorative arts from 19th-20th c. Library holds materials on Island local history, travel, and descriptive materials on NYC and NJ from 19th-20th c; papers of Staten Island naturalists and deeds from 1670-1960; large collection of maps and atlases from 1700-1960; extensive collection of photos from 1850; films/videotapes from 1935-70; oral histories from black community in Staten Island; and genealogical records. Materials non-circulating. Accepts phone inquiries. Fee. Hours: Tu-F 9-5.

Statue of Liberty American Museum of Immigration

Liberty Island, New York, NY 10004; (212) 363-3200. Preserves history of the Statue of Liberty, Ellis Island, and immigration into US, in form of museum, library, and archival collections. Holdings include American Museum of Immigration, with artifacts and displays relating to history of Ellis Island, Statue of Liberty, and American immigration from 1600; research library with archival papers, manuscripts, films/videotapes, photos, oral histories of immigrants; map and blue print collection relating to Island and Statue; Augustus F. Sherman Collection of Ellis Island photos. Some restrictions. Ferry fee; donations accepted for museum. Hours: Sept-May, 9:15-5; June-Aug, 8:30-7.

Steamship Historical Society of America

414 Pelton Ave., Staten Island, NY 10310; (718) 727-9583. Society preserves and promotes US and Canadian history of steam-powered shipping through educational programs, publications, and library/archival collection (location: Univ of Baltimore Library, Baltimore, MD 21201; 301-655-3134). Library holdings include research and reference materials; steamship schedules, cruise brochures and other ephemera; pre-1948 corporate files of the Hudson River Day Line; marine charts, films/videotapes; photos, including collections of R. Loren Graham, Everett Viez, Henry Uhle, and others. Prefers written queries. No fee. Hours: 8:30-4.

Stony Point Battlefield State Historic Site

Box 182, Park Rd. off Rt. 9W, Stony Point, NY 10980; (914) 786-2521. Interprets American Revolutionary War Battle of Stony Point, and preserves oldest lighthouse on Hudson River. Museum exhibits explain history of Battle and its aftermath. Library has reference materials on 18th c life, military history, maps, photos, and limited genealogical materials on Battle soldiers. Accepts phone inquiries. No fee. Hours: 9-4:30.

Strong Museum

One Manhattan Square, Rochester, NY 14607; (716) 263-2700. Museum collects, preserves, and interprets the Margaret Woodbury Strong of material cultural objects from the northeastern US, 1820-1940. Holdings include household furnishings, clothing, dolls and toys, paper ephemera and advertising artifacts; library; archives with manuscripts and Margaret Woodbury Strong papers; Davenport Furniture Company Archives; Aeoloian Piano Factory Archives; local maps; large collection of photos and stereographs; special collections of fore-edge paintings, miniature books, and flow blue china. Collection is non-circulating. Accepts phone inquiries. Fee. Hours: M-F 10-5.

Suffolk County Archaeological Association

P.O. Drawer AR, Stony Brook, NY 11790; (516) 929-8725. Collects, preserves and promotes history of Suffolk County, Long Island, NY and residents in form of archaeological explorations, educational programs, publications, museum, and archival collections. Holdings include museum with exhibits on prehistoric Indian and Colonial American life and technology; archives, manuscripts, maps, and photos; archaeology reports and inventories. Research by appt. Accepts phone inquiries. Fee for membership and educational programs. Museum hours: 10-2.

Suffolk County Historical Society

300 W. Main St., Riverhead, NY 11901; (516) 727-2881. Collects materials and preserves history of Suffolk county, Long Island, from 17th c. Museum displays textiles, decorative arts, agricultural implements, and trade tools. Library holds reference materials on county history and genealogy. Archives retain Dennison papers, Josiah Smith papers, L.I. Railroad collection, papers of Hawking, Mapes, and Prince families, whaling logbooks, DAR applications, Terry manuscript, Frederick Kinsman Smith notebooks, maps, L.I. photos from 1895-1910, genealogical records, and Talmage Weaving collection. Accepts phone inquiries. Donations accepted. Hours: M-Sa 12:30-4:30.

Suffolk Maritime Museum

P.O. Box 144, West Sayville, NY 11796; (516) 567-1733. Preserves maritime history of Great South Bay off Long Island through educational tours, preservation of historic buildings and vessels, exhibits, library, archives, maps, and photos. Research by appt. Accepts phone inquiries. Donations accepted. Hours: W-Sa 10-3.

Susan B. Anthony Memorial

17 Madison St., 52 Kimbark Rd., Rochester, NY 14610; (716) 381-6202 or 235-6124. Preserves home of Susan B. Anthony, and original personal items and furniture. Many photos available of American and foreign suffragettes. Accepts phone inquiries. Fee. Hours: W-Sa 1-4, or by appt.

Tamiment Library

New York University, Elmer Bobst Library, 70 Washington Square, New York, NY 10012; (212) 998-2630. Academic research library holds materials on social and trade union movements until 1956. American socialism and labor movements documented through materials of Socialist Labor Party, League for Industrial Democracy, Socialist Party, Communist Party of USA, and Democratic Socialist Organizing Committee. Rand School archives contain minutes from 19th and 20th c socialist and labor orgs, personal papers of Eugene Debs and other labor leaders. Accepts phone inquiries. No fee. Hours: M, Th 10-9, Tu-W, F 10-5:45, Sa 10-5.

Telephone Pioneers of America

22 Cortland St., Rm. 30-C2569, New York, NY 10007; (212) 393-2512. Community service organization with focus on history of telecommunications industry development. Sponsors museum, library, and archive of materials from 1910. Holdings include photos and films/videotapes. Some restrictions. Accepts phone inquiries. No fee. Hours: 8:30-4:30.

The Turtle

Native American Center for Living Arts, 25 Rainbow Mall, Niagara Falls, NY 14303; (716) 284-2427. Preserves Native American subject matter of historical and contemporary interest in museum, library, and contemporary arts gallery. Museum displays date from pre-Columbian period to date, and include North American and limited Central American baskets, pottery, beadwork, leatherwork, silverwork, rugs, and arrowheads. Library has books, pamphlets, and other materials on Native American art, history, law, health, and education; photos of art and center activities; raw film ftg of interviews and dance and theatre performances. Materials for in-house use only. Accepts phone inquiries. Fee. Hours: summer, 9-6; winter, Tu-F 9-5, Sa-Su noon-5.

Theme Prints Limited

P.O. Box 123, Bayside, NY 11361; (718) 225-4067, or 0446. Mail order company has large collection of documents, autographs, artworks, photos, engravings, and soldier letters from Civil War, Spanish American War, and colonial period. Confederate money, maps, and variety of military orders available. Accepts phone inquiries and orders. Catalogs available. Hours: call.

Theodore Roosevelt Inaugural National Historic Site

Buffalo, NY 14202; (716) 884-0095. Memorializes Roosevelt's inauguration, relates history of site and house, and gives insight into mood of era. Museum preserves 3 Victorian rooms, including room Roosevelt was inaugurated in. Library holds materials on Roosevelt, William McKinley, Pan-American Exposition, architecture, and Victorian lifestyles; photos; films/videotapes; and costumes and accessories from 1850-1970. Accepts phone inquiries. Fee. Hours: library and costume resource center by appt; M-F 9-5, Sa-Su noon-5.

Thousand Island Shipyard Museum

750 Mary St., Clayton, NY 13624; (315) 686-4104. Collects and preserves maritime history of St. Lawrence River and northern NY state. Museum exhibits 150 boats, outboard motors, inboard engines, and nautical artifacts. Library materials focus on nautical history and local history of St. Lawrence region. Archives has patents, logs, and postcards from St. Lawrence River area; historic maps; photos; and oral histories. Special collections of Sparkman and Stevens Yacht brokerage archives and Evinrude archives. Accepts phone inquiries. Fee. Hours: 10-4.

Thousand Islands Craft School and Textile Museum

314 John St., Clayton, NY 13624; (315) 686-4123. Collects and preserves handwoven textile exhibits, artifacts, and study collections of North American articles from 20th c. Accepts phone inquiries. Donations accepted. Hours: Apr-Dec, M-Sa 10-3.

Thrall Library

Documents Division, 22 Orchard St., Middle-town, NY 10940; (914) 342-5877. Public library maintains selective collection of govt documents, general and historical materials relevant to needs of community. Holdings include genealogical materials on some Middletown, NY families; special collection of materials on local history of Orange County, NY. Accepts phone inquiries. No fee. Hours: M-F 10-9, F 10-6, Sa (winter only) 10-5, Su (winter only) 1-5.

Ticonderoga Historical Society

Hancock House, Moses Circle, Ticonderoga, NY 12883; (518) 585-7868. Museum housed in 18th c Georgian mansion. Library has materials on general US and Champlain Valley history. Archives holds newspapers, Justice records, manuscripts, NY state maps, photos, and genealogical materials. Accepts phone inquiries. No fee. Hours: July-Aug, 10-4; Sept-Jun, W-Sa 10-4.

Tobacco Merchants Association

Howard S. Cullman Library, 1220 Broadway, Suite 705, New York, NY 10001; (212) 239-4435. Library collection focuses on all aspects of tobacco industry, including trademark and brand files of products and smokers' articles. Accepts phone inquiries. Hours: by appt only, M-F 9-5.

Town of Yorktown Museum

1974 Commerce St., Yorktown Heights, NY 10598; (914) 962-2970. Conserves, studies, interprets, and exhibits history of area and Yorktown. Museum has exhibits on Mohegan Indians, Colonial era life, agriculture, railroad, and doll houses. Library has materials on local and county history, antiques, and govt. Archives holds church and civic records, business records, letters and diaries, Revolutionary War maps, photos, oral history interviews, and genealogical records. Accepts phone inquiries. Donations accepted. Hours: Tu-F 9:30-4:30, Su 1:30-4:30.

Trans World Airlines Corporate Library

605 Third Ave., 40th Floor, New York, NY 10158; (212) 557-6055. Holds materials on air transportation, aircraft industry, Civil Aeronautics Board, and TWA history. Accepts phone inquiries. Hours: by appt only, M-F 8:30-5.

Trinity Museum of the Parish of Trinity Church

74 Trinity Place, New York, NY 10008; (212) 602-0848. Preserves church, New York City, and US history through holdings in museum, library, and archives. Records date from 17th-20th c, and include registers of baptisms, confirmations, marriages, burials, architectural renderings and drawings, maps from 17th-20th c, diaries, correspondence, photos of Manhattan, ledger, meeting minutes, recordings of church music, films/videotapes of church services as well as history of Parish, and genealogical records from 18th-20th c. Accepts phone inquiries. No fee. Hours: archives, M-F, by appt, 9:30-noon, 2-3:30.

Trotting Horse Museum

240 Main St., Goshen, NY 10924; (914) 294-6330. Promotes, conserves, and protects history of American standardbred horse and US sport of harness racing. Museum has exhibits in two arts galleries, including Currier and Ives collection. Library has small collection harness racing journals from 1860s and magazines from 1900 focusing on racing, horses, and people involved; original book manuscripts on harness racing; photos; and films and videotapes on racing and races. Accepts phone inquiries. Fee. Hours: M-Sa 10-5, Su noon-5.

Troy Public Library

100 Second St., Troy, NY 12180; (518) 274-7071. Public library maintains selective collection of govt documents, general, historical and special collections and materials relevant to needs of community. Holdings include US govt documents from 1869, with emphasis on Census records, military history, Library of Congress, Smithsonian, Agriculture Yearbook, and Congressional Directories; local govt of Troy and Rensselaer County from 19th c; Troy Collection of local genealogical and historical records and artifacts. Some restrictions. Accepts phone inquiries. No fee. Hours: M, Tu, Th 9-9; W, F, Sa 9-5.

U.S. History, Local History, and Genealogy Division

New York Public Library, Fifth Ave. & 42nd St.,

Room 315N, New York, NY 10018; (212) 930-0828. Maintains collection of materials documenting US and local history, as well as British and Irish genealogy, heraldry, and name origins. Special collections include Hine collection of photos on NY social conditions from 1905-35, and extensive post card collection. Accepts phone inquiries. No fee. Hours: M, W, F, Sa 10-6, Tu 10-9.

Ukrainian Museum

203 Second Ave., New York, NY 10003; (212) 228-10003. Museum exhibits Ukrainian heritage and history, including immigration to US, artwork, and festive costumes. Accepts phone inquiries. Hours: W-Su 1-5.

University Club Library

One W. 54th St., New York, NY 10019; (212) 247-2100. Private library holds Southern Society collection of materials on South, Civil War, and Reconstruction; collection of 19th c materials on Harvard, Princeton, and Yale; Tinker and Darrow collections on printing and printing history, and Bickelhaupt library of sporting books. Materials for use of members and their guest; scholars may submit written requests to Library Director. Hours: M-F 10-7; open Sa Oct 15-Apr.

University of Rochester

Dept. of Rare Books and Special Collections, Rush Rhees Library, Rochester, NY 14627; (716) 275-4484. Academic research library has collection of manuscripts related to US, NY, and Rochester history. Holds records of women's suffrage orgs from 1880-1920, including pamphlets, broadsides, and suffrage movement broadsides; large collection of papers by US Sec of State under Lincoln, William Seward, documenting political, social, and diplomatic climate during 19th c; and collection of materials from Vietnam War veterans, including letters to and from families, friends, and dissenters. Accepts phone inquiries. No fee. Hours: call.

Vanderbilt Mansion, Marine Museum, Planetarium and Park

180 Little Neck Rd., P.O. Box F, Centerport, NY 11721; (516) 261-5656. Historic mansion

and museum/planetarium complex maintains collections and exhibits on social and natural history of region and residents. Holdings include preserved 1920s Spanish Revival Style mansion, furnishings, and grounds (now Suffolk County Park), that was once the home of millionaire William Kissan Vanderbilt II (1878-1944); collections of fine and decorative arts and models; marine museum with Vanderbilt's fish collection; modern planetarium; library; Vanderbilt family archives and memorabilia 1880s-1930s; special collection of materials on NY Central Railroad. Accepts phone inquiries. Fee. Hours: Tu-Sa 10-4, Su and Holidays noon-5.

Vassar College Library

Raymond Ave., Poughkeepsie, NY 12601; (914) 452-7000. Academic library maintains selective collection of govt documents, general, reference and historical materials relevant to needs of the school and students. Holdings include materials on demography and populations, education, intl relations, labor, political science, and women. Manuscript collection holds materials related to women's rights, suffrage, and ERA, including papers of Elizabeth Cady Stanton, Paulina Wright Davis, Maria Mitchell, and Alma Lutz. Accepts phone inquiries (ext. 2131). No fee. Hours: call.

Vietnamese Immigration Collection

State University of New York, Buffalo Archives, 420 Capen Hall, Buffalo, NY 14260; (716) 636-2916. Special collection of oral histories, interviews, orientation materials, and refugee camp newspapers relating to Vietnamese immigration to US. Accepts phone inquiries. No fee. Hours: call.

Visual Studies Workshop Research Center

31 Prince St., Rochester, NY 14607; (716) 442-8676. Maintains research collection on history of photography and photographic arts in many subject areas. Some emphasis on early photo processes, and works by selected photographers. Accepts phone inquiries. Hours: M-F 9-5.

Walter Elwood Museum

300 Guy Park Ave., Amsterdam, NY 12010; (518) 843-3180, ext. 445. Preserves history of Amsterdam and Mohawk Valley. Museum has exhibits on Iroquois and Eskimo Indians, Teepees, Blacksmith shop, Amsterdam history, and Thomas Edison. Library has old and rare books, old records and cylinders, Bibles and tracts, maps of US and NY, photos, and recordings. Accepts phone inquiries. Donations accepted. Hours: Sept-June, M-F 8:30-4; July-Aug, M-F 8:30-1.

Washington's Headquarters State Historic Site

P.O. Box 1783, 84 Liberty St., Newburgh, NY 12550; (914) 562-1195. Preserves and interprets the 1782-83 headquarters of General George Washington in form of historic site, museum, library, and archival collections. Holdings include Colonial/Revolutionary War period artifacts, and memorabilia relating to Washington and his family; library with materials on Washington and Revolutionary War; archives with prints of 18th and 19th c people involved in Revolutionary War and the site's development; manuscripts relating to local and military history; genealogical records of Jonathon Hasbrouck descendants. Use of research materials must be staff supervised. Accepts phone inquiries. No fee. Hours: Apr-Dec, W-Sa 10-5, Su 1-5; or by appt.

Washington's Headquarters Elijah Miller Farmhouse

Virginia Rd. # 140, North White Plains, NY 10803; (914) 949-1236. Interprets the history and life of the Miller family in 1770s, with emphasis on how they were affected by General George Washington's presence. Holdings include 18th c Rhode Island style farm house with period furnishings and artifacts; local history collection; collection of textile manufacturing artifacts. Accepts phone inquiries. No fee. Hours: W-Sa 10-4.

Watervliet Arsenal Museum

Watervliet Arsenal, SMCWV-1NM, Watervliet, NY 12189; (518) 266-5805. Preserves and exhibits historic development of the cannon and Watervliet Arsenal, which has served as US Army's gun factory for past century. Holdings include Cast Iron Storehouse with displays and artifacts; small library and collection of Arsenal records; collection of historic Arsenal photos. Accepts phone inquiries. No fee. Hours: Tu-Sa 10-3.

Aviatrix Amelia Earhart, from the Women's Hall of Fame.

West Point Museum

United States Military Academy, West Point, NY 10996; (914) 938-2203. Military museum preserves history of warfare, US Army, and US Military Academy. Museum exhibits 18th-20th c military weapons, uniforms, accoutrements, flags, paintings, and prints and photos. Special collection of Alexander McCook Craighead military art. Accepts phone inquiries. No fee. Hours: M-F 8-4.

Whitney Museum of American Art

945 Madison Ave., New York, NY 10021; (212) 570-3633. Houses permanent collection of 20th c American art from artists Lee Krasner, Elie Nadelman, Andy Warhol, George Bellows, Alexander Calder, Stuart Davis, Philip Guston, Marsden Hartley, Edward Hopper, Jasper Johns, Roy Lichtenstein, Alice Neel, Georgia O'Keeffe, Jackson Pollock, Mark Rothko, David Smith, Frank Stella, Willem de Kooning, and others. Changing exhibits on films, videos, and work of many 20th c artists. New American Filmmakers series supports independent non-commercial American filmmakers. Accepts phone inquiries. Fee. Hours: Tu 1-8, W-Sa 11-5, Su noon-6.

Women's Hall of Fame

P.O. Box 335, 76 Fall St., Seneca Falls, NY 13148; (315) 568-8060. Honors and memorializes women who have made major contributions to the advancement of arts, athletics, business, education, govt, the humanities, philanthropy, and science, through exhibits, library, and special collections. Holdings include Hall of Fame displays and travelling exhibits about women leaders and their achievements; library with materials on and by the women honored in the Hall;

collection of Amelia Earhart's personal items. Accepts phone inquiries (315-568-2936). Fee. Hours: M-Sa 10-4, Su (May-Oct) 1-4.

Women's Independent Film Exchange

50 W. 96th St., New York, NY 10025; (212) 749-1250. Collects info on women filmmakers and directors in US from 1910-70. Accepts phone inquiries. No fee. Hours: call.

Women's Rights Historical Park

P.O. Box 70, 116 Fall Street, Seneca Falls, NY 13148; (315) 568-2441. Park preserves and interprets history of the first women's rights convention, held in Seneca Falls, NY, in 1848. Holdings include Visitor's Center with exhibits on the convention; four separate historical sites, including restored home of Elizabeth Cady Stanton; small library with publications on 19th c and local history, women's roles, and abolition; archives with artifacts from archaeological digs made in park; 19th c maps of area; photos of Seneca Falls, and Elizabeth Cady Stanton. Use of collections by appointment only. Accepts phone inquiries. No fee. Hours: May-Oct, 9-5; Nov-Apr, M-F 9-5.

Yates County Genealogical and Historical Society

200 Main St., Penn Yan, NY 14527; (315) 536-7318. Collects, preserves and promotes history of Yates County area and residents in form of exhibits, library, and archival collections. Holdings include Victorian period rooms and medical office; library with local historical publications; archives with letters, diaries, meeting minutes, and other local records, 1790-1900; local history manuscript written by resident, 1900; 19th c maps of Yates County and Penn Yan; large collection of photos from 1890; genealogical records; special collections of agricultural artifacts, and items relating to the Publick Universal Friend. Accepts phone inquiries. Donations accepted. Hours: M-F 10-5, or by appt.

Yeshiva University Museum

2520 Amsterdam Ave., New York, NY 10033; (202) 960-5390. Preserves, enriches, and interprets Jewish life as reflected in art, architecture, anthropology, history, literature, music, and science. Museum covers many areas of Judaica, including costumes and accessories, ethnographic material, decorative and fine arts, Myer Myers silver, and photos. Archives contain manuscripts, including letter from Jefferson to Mordecai Noah; and oral histories of German Jewish settlers in Washington Heights. Accepts phone inquiries. Fee. Hours: permission and appt necessary for research; Tu-Th 10:30-5, Su noon-6.

Yonkers Public Library

Documents Division, Getty Square Branch, 7 Main St., Yonkers, NY 10701; (914) 337-1500. Public library maintains selective collection of govt documents, general and historical materials relevant to needs of community. Holdings include collections on local history; Yonkers property atlases, 1876-1930. Accepts phone inquiries. No fee. Hours: M-Th 9-9, F-Sa 9-5.

Young-Morse Historic Site

P.O. Box 103, 370 South Bend Rd, Poughkeepsie, NY 12601; (914) 454-4500. Historic home of Samuel F.B. Morse preserves history of his life and works in form of furnished house, designed by Alexander J. Davis with Morse artifacts and Young Family's decorative arts collection; reference library; archives with Morse letters, Innis Dye Work journals, and family diaries, 1895-1970; maps of 1770s Livingston Homested; photos of family and local subjects, 1895-1940; genealogical records of Young, Innis, and Hasbrouk families; Morse/Davis architectural drawings for house. Accepts phone inquiries. Hours: House tour: summer, W-Su 10-4; office, M-F 8-4:30.

North Carolina

82nd Airborne Division War Memorial Museum

War Memorial Museum, Reference Library, Gela & Ardennes St., Fort Bragg, NC 28307; (919) 432-5307. Collection documents activities in development of airborne warfare, with focus on historical perspective of those in 82nd Division. Accepts phone inquiries. No fee. Hours: Tu-Sa 10-4:30, Su 11:30-4.

Alamance   Battleground

Rte. 1, Box 108, Burlington, NC 27215; (919) 227-4785. Interprets battle of Alamance and its significance in 1771 and 18th c life. Museum exhibits deal with War of Regulation and battle of Almance. Library contains colonial reference materials. Archives contain materials on Regulators, Royal Gov William Tryon, Battle of Almance, maps, photos, and genealogical records. Special collection on John Allen House, a local Quaker. Some restrictions. Accepts phone inquiries. No fee. Hours: summer, M-Sa 9-5, Su 1-5; winter, Tu-Sa 10-4, Su 1-4.

Appalachian   Consortium

Appalachian State University, University Hall, Boone, NC 28608; (704) 262-2064. Refferal org for preservation of cultural and natural resources of Appalachia. Archives of Appalachia identifies manuscripts, films/videotapes, recordings, and special collections in region. Accepts phone inquiries. No fee. Hours: M-F 8-5.

Archives of Moravian Church in America, Southern Province

4 East Bank St., Winston-Salem, NC 27101; (919) 722-1742. Preserves official records of Moravian Church in America in library and archives. Manuscripts include personal papers of Moravians from 18th-20th c, maps from 1756, photos, genealogical materials on Moravians in Southeast US, special collection of papers on Moravian mission to GA Cherokee Indians, and some biographical and autobiographical sketches. May be some restrictions. Accepts phone inquiries. No fee. Hours: M-F 9-noon, 1-5.

Bennett Place Historic Site

4409 Bennett Memorial Rd, Durham, NC 27705; (919) 383-4345. Interprets surrender of Gen Joseph Johnston to Gen Sherman at close of Civil War, and interprets life of NC farmer, 1850s-60s. Museum covers antebellum period, NC contributions to war, Johnston/Sherman surrender, and Bennett family history. Accepts phone inquiries. No fee. Hours: Nov-Mar, Tu-Sa 10-4, Su 1-4; Apr-Oct, M-Sa 9-5, Su 1-5.

Bentonville   Battleground State Historic Site

P.O. Box 27, Rte. 1, Four Oaks, Newton Grove, NC 28366; (919) 594-0789. Interprets last major Confederate offensive of Civil War and largest land battle fought in NC. Museum exhibits artifacts from battlefield, restored Harper House used as Union field hospital. Library has maps of troop movements, NC troop register, and some materials on local history. Accepts phone inquiries. No fee. Hours: M-Sa 9-5, Su 1-4.

Brunswick Town State Historic Site

Rte. 1, Box 55, Winnabow, NC 28479; (919) 371-6613. Interprets 18th c region of Brunswick as well as 19th c Confederate fortification of Ft Anderson. Museum exhibits artifacts recovered from both. Library contains some reference materials and maps. Accepts phone inquiries. No fee. Hours: Nov-Mar, Tu-Sa 10-4, Su 1-4; Apr-Oct, M-Sa 9-5, Su 1-5.

Cape Hatteras National Seashore

Reference Library, Box 675, Rte. 1, Manteo, NC 27954; (919) 928-4531. Maintains collection of US lifesaving materials, records, and annual reports. Accepts phone inquiries. No fee. Hours: call.

Carl Sandburg Home National Historic Site

1928 Little River Rd., Flat Rock, NC 28731; (704) 693-4178. Tells story of Carl Sandburg and his work through museum exhibits and limited archival holdings. Accepts phone inquiries. No fee. Hours: 9-5.

Carolina   Room

Public Library of Charlotte and Mecklenburg County, 310 N. Tryon St., Charlotte, NC 28202; (704) 336-2980. Collects local, state, and regional historical and genealogical materials. Library has books and microforms on Charlotte, Mecklenburg county, NC, and Southeast. Other holdings include war records, Southern history with emphasis on NC and SC, census records, WPA cemetery records for NC and SC, selections from Draper manuscripts, current and historical maps, Sanborn maps, extensive vertical files, photos, and Charlotte music archives. Special collection of Harry Golden materials. Accepts phone inquiries. No fee. Hours: M-F 9-9, Sa 9-6, and Sept-May, Su 2-6.

Catawba College Library

Documents Dept., 2300 W. Innes St., Salisbury, NC 28144; (704) 637-4448. Academic research facility with special collection of Southern Chapter of Historical Society of Evangelical and Reformed Church archives. Holdings include manuscripts and photos. Library also collects maps and govt documents. Materials circulate to college community. Accepts phone inquiries. No fee. Hours: call.

Catawba County Historical Association

P.O. Box 73, 1716 S. College Dr., US #321, Newton, NC 28658; (704) 465-0383. Collects and disseminates history of Catawba Valley through holdings in museum and archives. Museum displays cover furniture and textile industries, and agricultural and general history from 1747-1970; library concentrates on local history. Archives hold diaries, journals, photos, maps, films/videotapes, recordings, and genealogical records. Accepts phone inquiries. No fee. Hours: Tu-F 8:30-4:30, Sa-Su 1-4:30.

Cherokee County Historical Museum

205 Peachtree St., Murphy, NC 28906; (704) 837-6792. Preserves history of Cherokee County through museum exhibits on Cherokee Indians and nation, their resettlement and travel along Trail of Tears, and early white settlers in county. Library holds maps, photos, oral histories, and some genealogical records. Accepts phone inquiries. No fee. Hours: M-F 9-5.

Cleveland County Historical Association and Museum

P.O. Box 1335, Court Square, Shelby, NC 28150; (704) 482-8186. Collects, preserves, and exhibits history and heritage of county. Museum exhibits cover agriculture, home and family life, medicine, communications, sports, military, manufacturing, and religion. Library contains research materials. Archives hold personal papers and documents, Sanborn insurance maps, photos, some early films, genealogical records, and clothing collection. Accepts phone inquiries. No fee. Hours: M-F 9-4, Su 2-5.

Department of Cultural Resources

Division of State Library, 109 East Jones St., Raleigh, NC 27611; (919) 733-3683. Provides library and info services to state govt employees. Library concentrates on public policiy issues and NC history. Genealogical, US census, and census index records also available. Materials circulate only to state employees. Accepts phone inquiries (919-733-3270). No fee. Hours: M-F 8-5:30.

Duke Homestead State Historic Site and Tobacco Museum

2828 Duke Homestead Rd., Durham, NC 27705; (919) 477-5498. Preserves original farm and home of Washington Duke and regional history of tobacco farming. Museum displays artifacts dealing with Duke family and tobacco manufacturing and advertising. Library focuses on tobacco history. Other holdings include photos, videotapes of early cigarette commercials, oral history interviews, and recordings of early radio cigarette commercials. Accepts phone inquiries. No fee. Hours: Apr-Oct, M-Sa 9-5, Su 1-5. Nov-Mar, Tu-Sa 10-4, Su 1-4.

East Carolina University

Archives and Manuscript Dept., J.Y. Joyner Library, Greenville, NC 27834; (919) 757-6671. Academic research facility with collection of govt documents and special collection of materials on NC life and history. Manuscript collection has materials on military and tobacco industry history, manuscripts pertaining to NC, large map collection, photos, and genealogical records. Archives hold University records from 1907. May be some restrictions. Accepts phone inquiries. No fee. Hours: M-F 8-5, Sa 9-1.

Elizabeth II State Historic Site

P.O. Box 155, Hwy 400, Manteo, NC 27954; (919) 473-1144. Promotes, educates, and represents first English attempt to colonize New World, with concentration on Roanoke Voyages. Museum exhibits drawings, etchings, and lithographs illustrating English, Spanish, Native American and Elizabethan lifestyles, as well as 16th c navigation and sailing techniques. Accepts phone inquiries. No fee. Hours: summer, M-Su 10-6; winter, Tu-Su 10-4.

Elon College

Iris Holt McEwen Library, P.O. Box 187, Williamson Ave., Elon City, NC 27244; (919) 584-

2338. Academic research library with special collections on history of Southern Conference of United Church of Christ, Elon College, and local area. Archives contain publications of College and Church of Christ, manuscripts, and genealogical materials for NC, VA, SC, and MD. Materials circulate only to members. Accepts phone inquiries. Fee for membership. Hours: M-Th 8-11, F 8-5, Sa 10-6, Su 2-11.

Estes-Winn Antique Automobile Museum

P.O. Box 6854, Asheville, NC 28806; (704) 253-7651. Twelve acres of antique autos on display, some dating from 1905. Accepts phone inquiries. No fee. Hours: Apr-Oct, M-Sa 9-4:30; Nov-Mar, M-F 9-4.

Folk Art Center

P.O. Box 9545, Milepost 382, Blue Ridge Pkwy., Asheville, NC 28815; (704) 298-7928. Nine-state membership org brings together craftsmen of Southern Highlands for benefit of shared resources, education, marketing, and conservation. Library has collection of materials on folk art, history of Southern Highlands, mountain crafts, and craftsmen. Archives hold data on members of Handicraft Guild. Materials circulate to members only. Accepts phone inquiries. Donations accepted. Hours: M-Su 9-5.

Forest History Society

701 Vickers Ave., Durham, NC 27701; (919) 682-9319. Preserves history of forestry and conservation in North America through holdings in library and archives. Accepts phone inquiries. No fee. Hours: M-F 8-5.

Fort Dobbs State Historic Site

Rte. 9, Box A-415, Statesville, NC 28677; (704) 873-5866. Site of French and Indian War Fort from 1756-63 displays artifacts of archaeological investigations. Accepts phone inquiries. No fee. Hours: Apr-Oct, M-Sa 9-5, Su 1-5; Nov & Mar, Tu-Sa 10-4, Su 1-4; Dec-Feb, Tu-F 10-4.

Fort Fisher State Historic Site

Box 68, Kure Beach, NC 28449; (919) 458-5538. Promotes, interprets, and preserves Ft Fisher history with museum collection of Civil War artifacts and sunken vessels. Library pro-vides reference materials, limited maps, photos from 1865, rosters of NC troops, and limited resources on Union troops. Accepts phone inquiries. No fee. Hours: Apr-Oct, M-Sa 9-5, Su 1-5; Nov-Mar, Tu-Sa 10-4, Su 1-4.

Fort Macon State Park

P.O. Box 127, Atlantic Beach, NC 28512; (919) 726-3775. Protects, preserves, and portrays historic areas of statewide importance. Museum holds artifacts detailing Ft history with emphasis on Civil War period. Accepts phone inquiries. No fee. Hours: 9-5:30.

Fort Raleigh National Historic Site

Rte. 1, Box 675, Manteo, NC 27954; (919) 473-5772. Preserves and interprets site of Sir Walter Raleigh's 16th c Roanoke colonies. Museum exhibits cover 16th c Roanoke colonies, Algonquin Indians, and John White's watercolors. Accepts phone inquiries. No fee. Hours: 9-5.

Greensboro Historical Museum

130 Summit Ave., Greensboro, NC 27401; (919) 373-2043. Preserves NC and local history with museum collections covering prehistoric Indian settlements, Dolley Madison, O. Henry, military history, and decorative arts. Archives contain manuscripts, photos, maps, books relating to major collections, and O. Henry materials. Accepts phone inquiries. No fee. Hours: Tu-Sa 10-5, Su 2-5.

High Point Historical Society

1805 E. Lexington Ave., High Point, NC 27262; (919) 885-6859. Collects, preserves, interprets, and exhibits artifacts from historic High Point. Museum emphasizes region's late colonial/early national period in 3 period structures. Collections cover military history, textiles, costumes, toys, and business/industrial materials. Archives contain small collection of manuscripts, photos, and printed materials on High Point history. Accepts phone inquiries. No fee. Hours: Tu-Sa 10-4:30, Su 1-4:30.

Historic Edenton

P.O. Box 474, S. Broad St., Edenton, NC 27932; (919) 482-2637. Composed of orgs involved in preservation and restoration of 1782 Barker

House, 1767 Chowan county courthouse, 1773 James Iredell House, 1736 St. Paul's Episcopal Church, and 1725 Cupola House. Accepts phone inquiries. Fee. Hours: Nov-May, M-Sa 10-4:30; Su 2-5.

Historic Preservation Foundation of North Carolina

P.O. Box 27644, Raleigh, NC 27611; (919) 832-3652. Preserves and restores endangered historic bldgs. Library has small collection of architectural surveys, as well as photos and slides of restored homes and bldgs. Accepts phone inquiries. Hours: M-F 8:30-5.

Indian Museum of the Carolinas

P.O. Box 666, 607 Turnpike Rd., Laurinburg, NC 28352; (919) 276-5880. Preserves info on Southeast Indian archaeology and ethnography. Museum displays cover local Indian prehistory, some materials from other regions, and art: library holds published materials on archaeology. Manuscript file on archaeological site reports. Accepts phone inquiries. No fee. Hours: W-Th 10-noon, 1-4, Su 1-4.

J. Walter Thompson Archives

Duke University, William Perkins Library, Durham, NC 27706; (919) 684-3372. Preserves historic materials on J. Walter Thompson Co. and 19th c American social history. Thompson archives has historical collection of ad materials and proofs. Manuscript holdings cover Civil War and Reconstruction, Methodism, textile and tobacco industries, Socialist Party, labor unions, American writers, 20th c economists, 19th c British military and diplomatic history, American folklore, and 19th and 20th c American politics and foreign relations. Other holdings are photos; film/videotape interviews with Griffis, McNamara, Harriman, Fulbright and others; and oral histories on civil rights and folk music. Accepts phone inquiries. No fee. Hours: M-F 8-5, Sa 9-12:30.

James K. Polk Memorial

P.O. Box 475, Pineville, NC 28134; (704) 889-7145. Preserves birthplace of this 11th President of US and complex of log buildings furnished in late 18th and early 19th c artifacts. Museum exhibits illustrate Polk's life and times. Accepts phone inquiries. No fee. Hours: Apr-Oct, M-Sa 9-5, Su 1-5; Nov-Mar, Tu-Sa 10-4, Su 1-4.

John F. Kennedy Special Warfare Museum

Cmdr, USAJFKSWCS, ATSU-SE-MUS, Bldg. D-2502 Corner Marion & Ardennes Sts., Fort Bragg, NC 28307; (919) 432-4272 or 1533. Illustrates history of unconventional warfare, exp as concerns US Army Special Forces, Rangers, Psychological Operations, Civil Affairs, and aviation. Accepts phone inquiries. No fee. Hours: Tu-Su 11:30-4.

Kings Mountain National Military Park

P.O. Box 40, Kings Mountain, NC 28086; (803) 936-7921. (Street address: Rte. 3, Blacksburg, SC 29702.) Commemorates Revolutionary War battle of October 7, 1780. Museum and library hold documentary materials, including film on battle of Kings Mountain. Materials non-circulating. Accepts phone inquiries. No fee. Hours: M-F 9-5.

Lower Cape Fear Historical Society

P.O. Box 813, Wilmington, NC 28402; (919) 762-0492. Investigates and studies history of area. House museum holds manuscripts, maps, photos, and genealogical collections in its library and archives. Accepts phone inquiries. Fee. Hours: Tu-Sa 10-5.

Mountain Heritage Center

Western Carolina University, University Dr., Cullowhee, NC 28723; (704) 227-7129. Promotes public awareness of southern Appalachian cultural and natural history through museum collections and programs. Accepts phone inquiries. No fee. Hours: M-F 8-5.

Museum of Anthropology

Wake Forest University, P.O. Box 7267, Winston-Salem, NC 27109; (919) 761-5282. Presents cross-cultural perspective of people of the world. Collections cover many people, including NC Indians, Southwest Indians, and Eskimos. Library holds materials on textiles, traditions of Middle America, photos on NC archaeology, and films/videotapes. Accepts phone inquiries. No fee. Hours: Tu-F 10-4:30, Sa-Su 2-4:30.

Native American Resource Center

Pembroke State University, College Rd., Pembroke, NC 28372; (919) 521-4214. Commemorates American Indian art, artifacts, and culture. Museum, library, and archives hold documentation of Lumbee and Tuscarora Indian communities in NC; research papers and theses on American Indian topics; maps of Indian tribe placements and language families; photos of Indians with emphasis on NC Native Americans; films/videotapes; oral history recordings of traditional Indian music, folktales, and some speeches. Accepts phone inquiries. No fee. Hours: M-F 8-5.

New Hanover County Museum of the Lower Cape Fear

814 Market St., Wilmington, NC 28401; (919) 341-4350. Preserves and interprets social and natural history of Wilmington and southeastern NC. Museum exhibits cover beach life in New Hanover and biographical sketches and belongings of local luminaries including Michael Jordan and David Brinkley. Library supports museum holdings with large local history photo archive, limited maps, and oral histories. Special collections of costumes and accessories, building furnishings, tools and equipment, and military artifacts. Accepts phone inquiries. No fee. Hours: Tu-Sa 9-5, Su 2-5.

North Carolina Baptist Historical Collection

P.O. Box 77777, Reynolds Station, Winston-Salem, NC 27109; (919) 761-5472. Collects original materials of interest to NC Baptists, their churches, and pastors past and present. Large library contains materials on assns, conventions, newspapers, and periodicals connected to NC Baptists, manuscripts from churches from 1771, many personal collections from Baptist ministers, missionaries, and Wake Forest College alumni, some maps, photos, recordings of state convention, and genealogical materials. Accepts phone inquiries. No fee. Hours: M-F 9-5.

North Carolina Collection

Park Memorial Public Library, 67 Hay Wood St., Asheville, NC 28801; (704) 252-8701. Documents NC history and culture through collection of early NC manuscripts, Civil War letters, Thomas Wolfe materials, materials on contemporary NC authors, NC censuses from 1790-1910, early maps, Cherokee Indian histories, and general Appalachian materials. Accepts phone inquiries. Hours: call.

North Carolina Collection

University of North Carolina, Wilson Library, Chapel Hill, NC 27514; (919) 962-1172. Collection of published works by NC authors regardless of subject or language, and about NC and residents regardless of author or subject. North Caroliniana gallery open in 1989. Library has 144-year-old collection of a quarter million NC items. Manuscript collection includes Thomas Wolfe collection, and materials on Southern history. Other holdings include maps, photos, films/videotapes, and recordings. Special collection on Sir Walter Raleigh's exploration in NC in Elizabethan period, and Bruce Cotten Collection of fine editions of rare North Caroliniana. Materials for in-house use only. Accepts phone inquiries. No fee. Hours: M-F 8-5, Sa 9-1, Su 2-6.

North Carolina Division of Archives and History

109 E. Jones St., Raleigh, NC 27611; (919) 733-3952. Preserves official state, county, and municipal records of historic significance. Materials date to colonial era, and manuscripts, state and county maps from age of exploration, large photo collection, many films/videotapes on NC topics from WWI, collection of Eugene McCarthy campaign materials, recordings of folk music and political speeches from 1920s-70s, genealogical materials, original posters and military collections pertaining to NC's role in American wars. Materials non-circulating. Fee for out-of-state mail inquiries; otherwise free. Hours: Tu-F 8-5:30, Sa 9-5.

North Carolina Division of Archives and History

Western Office, 13 Veterans Dr., Asheville, NC 28805; (704) 298-5024. Field office cooperates with museums, historic sites, archival institutions, preservation societies, and other historical agencies in NC to preserve historic materials. Retains small collection of historic photos and negatives from western NC. Hours: call.

North Carolina Genealogical Society

P.O. Box 1492, Raleigh, NC 27602. Promotes genealogical publications and educational programs in NC. Answers queries and holds meetings. Fee for membership.

North Carolina Homespun Museum

P.O. Box 6854, Grovewood Rd., Asheville, NC 28806; (704) 253-7651. Depicts history of Biltmore Handwoven Homespun Museum and a variety of recently-made NC crafts, including Cherokee Indian handwork and Appalachian folk art. Accepts phone inquiries. No fee. Hours: 9-4:30.

North Carolina Literary and Historical Association

North Carolina Division of Archives and History, 109 E. Jones St., Raleigh, NC 27611; (919) 733-7442. Fosters interest in literature and history of NC, encourages literary activity, and promotes local history. Accepts phone inquiries. Fee for membership. Hours: M-F 8:30-5:30.

North Carolina Maritime Museum

315 Front St., Beaufort, NC 28516; (919) 728-7317. Researches, collects, exhibits, and preserves NC maritime and coastal natural history. Museum displays small craft, maritime artifacts, textiles, and art work from NC. Library provides reference materials on maritime subjects. Archives hold business records of local maritime activities. Collection also includes navigational charts from 1850s, large collection of maritime-related photos from 1890s, limited films/videotapes, and oral history interviews. Accepts phone inquiries. No fee. Hours: M-F 9-5, Sa 10-5, Su 2-5.

North Carolina State University

D.H. Hill Library, P.O. Box 7111, Hillsboro St., Raleigh, NC 27695; (919) 737-2935. Academic research library with materials on NC history, history of transportation and sciences, and University history. Materials for in-house use only. Accepts phone inquiries. No fee. Hours: M-F 7:30-1, Sa 7:30-5, Su 1-1.

Old Salem

Drawer F, 600 S. Main St., Winston-Salem, Salem Station, NC 27108; (919) 723-3688. Restored Moravian congregation town preserves lifestyle of late 18th and early 19th c through living history. Library and archives contain Moravian church records, manuscripts, maps, photos, films/videotapes, recordings, and genealogical records. Accepts phone inquiries. Fee. Hours: M-Sa 9:30-4:30, Su 1:30-4:30.

PGA World Golf Hall of Fame

P.O. Box 1908, PGA Blvd., Pinehurst, NC 28374; (919) 295-4444. Preserves golf artifacts in museum exhibits dating from 1350. Holdings trace game's evolution. Library to be completed in 1989. Holds photos of players and championships and early films and videos on game. Accepts phone inquiries. Fee. Hours: 9-5.

Raleigh Historic Properties Commission

1 Mimosa St., Raleigh, NC 27604; (919) 832-7238. Preserves Raleigh's historic bldgs, landscapes, and neighborhoods. Maintains library on preservation techniques, architectural styles, and historic color schemes. Holdings include maps of historic districts, photos of Raleigh historic properties, and reference videos on historic architecture. Accepts phone inquiries. No fee. Hours: 9-5.

Reed Gold Mine

Rte. 2, Box 101, Stanfield, NC 28163; (704) 786-8348. Site of first authenticated gold find in US with large museum on gold mining history. Holdings include artifacts, manuscripts, maps, photos, films/videotapes, and genealogical records. No fee. Hours: Apr-Oct, M-Sa 9-5, Su 1-5; Nov-Mar Tu-Sa 10-4.

Roanake Island Historical Association

P.O. Box 40, Manteo, NC 27954; (919) 473-2127. Commemorates Roanoke Voyages of 1584-87 and Paul Green's Lost Colony. Has some historical photos, 1922 film on Lost Colony, and items of interest in production of film. Accepts phone inquiries. Fee. Hours: M-F 9-5.

Saint John's Museum of Art

114 Orange St., Wilmington, NC 28401; (919) 763-0281. Displays, promotes, and provides a

stimulating climate for visual arts in southeastern NC. Museum exhibits 200 years of NC artists' work, American sculpture, paintings, and works on paper. Accepts phone inquiries. No fee. Hours: Tu-Sa 10-5.

Smith-McDowell Museum of Western North Carolina History

283 Victoria Rd., Asheville, NC 28801; (704) 253-9231. House museum reflects history of Buncombe County and Victorian era decoration. Library has small research collection and photos on McDowell family and history of house. Accepts phone inquiries. Fee. Hours: May-Oct Tu-Su 10-4, Nov-Apr Tu-F 10-2.

Society for the History of Technology

Duke University, Department of History, Durham, NC 27706; (919) 689-2758. Encourages study of technological development and its relation to society and culture. Publishes journal and newsletter, and holds annual meetings. Accepts phone inquiries. No fee. Hours: 9-5.

Society of Mayflower Descendants in North Carolina

1108 Ferndale Blvd., High Point, NC 27260; (919) 882-6241. Perpetuates posterity of Pilgrim ancestors through genealogical contributions of members. Membership limited to those who can prove Mayflower heritage. Accepts phone inquiries. Fee for membership. Hours: call.

Society of North Carolina Archivists

P.O. Box 20448, Raleigh, NC 27608; (919) 733-3952. Professional state-wide org discusses and promotes concerns of archivists and manuscript curators. Accepts phone inquiries. Fee for membership. Hours: call.

Southern Appalachian Historical Association

P.O. Box 295, Boone, NC 28607; (704) 264-2120. Preserves cultural heritage of southern Appalachian region. Museum preserves late 18th c homesite and promotes living history program. Small library holds materials on general and local history, genealogy. Archives of association records. Accepts phone inquiries. Fee. Hours: M-F 9-5.

Thomas Wolfe Memorial

P.O. Box 7143, 48 Spruce St., Asheville, NC 28807; (704) 253-8304. Preserves house immortalized in novel, Look Homeward Angel. Library concentrates on Wolfe's works and family's books from early 1900s. Holdings include Wolfe family correspondence, photos, recordings of remaining family members, genealogical records of Wolfes and Westalls. House furnished in original period manner, depicting middle class 20th c life. Accepts phone inquiries. Fee. Hours: Apr-Oct, M-Sa 9-5; Nov-Mar, Tu-Sa 10-4, Su 1-4.

Town Creek Indian Mound State Historic Site

North Carolina Dept of Cultural Resources, Route 3, Box 50, Mount Gilead, NC 27306; (919) 439-6802. Commemorates culture of Creek Indians over 300 years ago through tours of major temple, priests' dwelling, and ceremonial ground. Museum features displays on culture and artifacts as interpreted from excavation site. Accepts phone inquiries. No fee. Hours: Apr-Oct, M-Sa 9-5, Su 1-5; Nov-Mar Tu-Sa 10-4, Su 1-4.

Tryon Place Restoration Complex

P.O. Box 1007, 610 Pollock St., New Bern, NC 28560; (919) 638-1560. Serves community resource and reference needs. Museum consists of reconstructed NC capitol, John Wright Stanly House, and Dixon-Stevenson House. Library emphasizes NC history and English and American decorative arts. Archives contain papers of Tryon Palace Commission, and operating papers of complex. Accepts phone inquiries. No fee. Hours: by appt.

University of North Carolina at Asheville

Documents Division, Ramsey Library, One University Heights, Asheville, NC 28804; (704) 251-6434. Supports needs of University and community. Archive has University records, literary magazines, and school catalogs. Special collections of local history, Thomas Wolfe first editions, and WWI. Circulation limited to University community. Accepts phone inquiries. No fee. Hours: M-Th 8-midnight, F 8-9, Sa 8-6, Su 1-midnight.

University of North Carolina at Chapel Hill

Manuscript Dept. and Southern Historical Collection, Wilson Library 024-A, Chapel Hill, NC 27514; (919) 962-1345. Preserves and makes available historical documents of region. Collections emphasize Southern history and folklife, NC history collection of published materials, rare books, and maps. Archives hold univ records from 1789; manuscripts from all southern states emphasizing 18th-20th c; large photo collection on southern subjects; maps; extensive Southern folklife oral history recordings and films; and small genealogical collection. May be some restrictions. Accepts phone inquiries. No fee. Hours: M-F 8-5, Sa 9-1.

University of North Carolina at Charlotte

Documents Dept., Atkins Library, Charlotte, NC 28223; (704) 547-2140. Collections include first editions of 18th and 20th c American women novelists, family papers from NC and SC, papers of novelist and short story writer Marian Sims, materials from Charlotte DAR and AAUW, and files of first president of Charlotte College and Univ of NC Chancellor, Bonnie Ethel Cone. Also holds materials from radical 1960s-70s groups, mostly from Midwest; papers of Charlotte 3 member T.J. Reddy; materials on Wilmington 10; and prison reform materials. Accepts phone inquiries. Hours: call.

University of North Carolina at Greensboro

Documents Division, Walter Clinton Jackson Library, 1000 Spring Garden Street, Greensboro, NC 27412; (919) 379-5251. Preserves materials from state and regional groups and orgs, as well as women who have made significant contributions in region. NC and other authors of 19th c include Mary Wollenstonecraft, Aphra Behn, and Mary Astell. Records of NC Council on Women's Orgs, Southern Assn of Physical Education for College Women, Harriet Wisemen Elliot, and Ellen Black Winston also available. Accepts phone inquiries. No fee. Hours: call.

World Methodist Museum

P.O. Box 518, Lake Junaluska, NC 28745; (704) 456-9432. Preserves early Methodism from 18th c England with collection of books, manuscripts, prints, portraits, and artifacts. Museum displays Wesley's travelling pulpit and other Wesley memorabilia. Other holdings include original Wesley, Francis Asbury, and Thomas Coke letters; scrapbooks of Methodist bishops and presidents photos, from 1784; portraits of early Methodist founders; and videotapes of conferences and celebrations. Accepts phone inquiries. No fee. Hours: M-F 10-5.

Wright Brothers National Memorial

Rte. 1, Box 675, Milepost 8.5, Kill Devil Hills, Manteo, NC 27954; (919) 441-7430. Commemorates first successful power-driven flight in world history. Museum maintains exhibits on theories of flight, and Wright brothers' experiments from 1899-1903. Library holds Wright brother reference materials and books on aviation, papers of Wilbur and Orville Wright from 1899-1948, maps, photos of Wrights and their flying machines, and films/videotapes on theories of flight and Wrights. Accepts phone inquiries. Fee. Hours: 9-5.

Zebulon B. Vance Birthplace

911 Reems Creek Rd., Weaverville, NC 28787; (704) 645-6706. Reconstructs 1830s mountain home birthplace of NC Civil War Gov. Museum exhibits illustrate Vance's life from 1830-94. Other museum bldgs include reconstructed log homes and outbuildings typical of Southern Appalachians. Accepts phone inquiries. No fee. Hours: Apr-Oct, M-Sa 9-5, Su 1-5; Nov-Mar, Tu-Sa, 10-4, Su 1-4.

North Dakota

Fort Union Trading Post National Historic Site

Buford Rte., Williston, ND 58801; (701) 572-9083. Preserves history of Ft Union and American Fur Company in upper MO country through museum exhibits and library holdings. Manuscripts document area history; photos and maps of regional fur trade, military activity, and Indian history; and small film/videotape collection on American fur trade. Accepts phone inquiries. No fee. Hours: summer 8-8, winter 9-5:30.

Geographical Center Historical Society

RR 4, Box 12A, Rugby, ND 58368; (701) 776-6414. Preserves historical artifacts and documents and exhibits some for public. Museum holdings include Indian and Eskimo artifacts, farm machinery, and pioneer town buildings and furnishings. Some restrictions. Accepts phone inquiries. Fee. Hours: May-Oct 8-7.

Germans from Russia Heritage Society

1008 E. Central, Bismarck, ND 58501; (701) 223-6167. Collects and catalogs materials and personal documents on European migration to US and Canada, and pioneer life on plains. Museum houses small number of articles; library holds family histories, passenger lists, pedigree charts, and many books of German ethnic value; map collection of starting points for German and Russian migration in 1800s; and some oral history collections. Accepts phone inquiries. No fee. Hours: M-F 10-4.

Hatton-Eielson Museum and Historical Association

411 8th St., Hatton, ND 58240; (701) 543-3726. Preserves materials on aviator Eielson and history of region. Museum houses original furnishings from 1920-30; library holds books from 1920s, immigration photos, Civil War diary, Eielson's flight maps, films on Eielson's life and family from 1930s, and some genealogical records. Accepts phone inquiries. Fee. Hours: summer, Su 1-4:30; other times by appointment.

Knife River Indian Villages National Historic Site

RR 1, Box 168, Stanton, ND 58571; (701) 745-3309. Preserves cultural resources related to Mandan and Hidatsa Indian villages on Upper MO River. Museum exhibits explain occupation of Knife River Indian Village by Mandan and Hidatsa Indians. Library has small collections on archaeological excavation in region, Lewis & Clark, Catlin, Bodmer, and fur traders. Materials non-circulating. Accepts phone inquiries. No fee. Hours: 8-4:30.

Makoti Threshers Museum

P.O. Box 94, Makoti, ND 58756; (701) 726-5622. Preserves and shows operation of antique farm machinery. Museum houses 6 large bldgs of machinery, including over 300 stationary gas engines. Accepts phone inquiries. No fee. Hours: by appt.

North Dakota Institute for Regional Studies

North Dakota State University Library, S.U. Station, P.O. Box 5599, Fargo, ND 58105; (701) 237-8914. Collects, preserves, and makes available materials on ND. Library houses substantial historical collection on ND, including county, community and church records; literary works by ND residents; many maps of ND; large photo collection emphasizing pioneer period to WWI; small collection of films/videotapes; recordings of ND artists, German-Russians, and limited oral history interviews; genealogical records including large ND biography index to extensive published biographical sketches; and special collection on major ethnic groups in state. Accepts phone inquiries. No fee. Hours: M-F 8-5.

North Dakota State University Library

Fargo, ND 58105; (701) 237-8886. North Dakota Institute for Regional Studies collects archival materials on ND state history, Red River Valley, Bonanza style farming, pioneer life, regional agricultural history, literary figures, and political collections. Accepts phone inquiries. Hours: call.

North Dakota Supreme Court Law Library

Judicial Wing, Capitol Bldg., Bismarck, ND 58505; (701) 224-2229. Supports research of legal community and general public. Materials circulate to attorneys. Accepts phone inquiries. No fee. Hours: M-F 8-5.

Pioneer Museum

416 N.E. Third, 104 Park Ave. West, Watford City, ND 58845; (701) 842-2990. Acquaints visitors with region's history through exhibits of household and school furnishings from 1900; library of English, German and Norwegian Bibles;

ND maps, area photos, limited genealogical records, and special Bannon collection. Accepts phone inquiries. Fee. Hours: Tu-Su, 1-5.

Plains Architecture

Box 5412, State University Station, 717 3rd Ave. North, Fargo, ND 58105; (701) 293-0815. Researches regional architecture, preserves records, and issues publications. Archives focuses on research materials on architecture in ND, SD, MT, MN, adjacent states, and Canadian provinces. Small collection of architecural drawings and photographs. Fee. Hours: by appt.

Red River and North Plains Regional Museum

P.O. Box 719, 1351 W. Main, West Fargo, ND 58078; (701) 282-2822. Preserves regional history with emphasis on agricultural development since Bonanza Farm era. Pioneer village complex houses exhibits on pioneers, Plains Indians, military, toys, cameras and musical instruments; library holds regional histories and small genealogical collection; archives contains Col M.F. Steele military papers; map collection of county plat atlases; photo archive; film/videotape collection includes reproduction of "Great Train Robbery"; and agricultural machinery collection with displays and manuals. Materials non-circulating. Accepts phone inquiries. Fee. Hours: summer, M-F 9-5, Sa-Su 1-5; winter, Tu-F 9:30-4.

State Historical Society of North Dakota

State Archives & Historical Research Library, North Dakota Heritage Center, Bismarck, ND 58505; (701) 224-2666. Preserves, collects, and exhibits materials on history of state. Museum exhibits materials relating to local area and upper midwest generally. Library and archives contain state and Dakotah territory manuscripts, maps, photos, films/videotapes, recordings, and genealogical records. Accepts phone inquiries (701-224-2091). No fee. Hours: M-F 8-5.

University of North Dakota

Special Collections, Chester Fritz Library, University Station, Grand Forks, ND 58202; (701) 777-4629. Academic research library holds Aandahl collection of western history on ND and northern Great Plains, with emphasis on agriculture, politics, pioneering, and Germans from Russia. Orin G. Libby manuscripts also available. Hours: call.

Valley City State College Library

Allen Memorial Library, College St., Valley City, ND 58072; (701) 845-7275. Academic research library with special collection of materials on ND history, and personal papers of Larry Wolwode and family. Accepts phone inquiries. No fee. Hours: M-Th 7:45-9, F 7:45-4, Sa 1-5, Su 4-9; summer, M-F 8-5.

Ohio

103rd Ohio Volunteer Infantry Memorial Foundation

5501 E. Lake Rd., Sheffield Lake, OH 44054; (216) 233-7610. Preserves artifacts and history of Civil War 103rd regiment of OH Volunteer Infantry. Museum displays artifacts from Civil War era, 1862-65. Library has small collection of materials on period. Archives holds letters, memorabilia, and books from 103rd regiment; news articles and scholarly works on regiment; battle maps; photos of veterans and their families; and genealogical records. Accepts phone inquiries. Donations accepted. Hours: by appt only.

Alden Library

Ohio University, Archives and Special Collections, Athens, OH 45701; (614) 594-6063. Academic research library holds special collection of materials on early county settlers, the Brown and Van Voorhis families. Holdings include letters and Civil War era records of OH 36th and WV 45th Regiments and KY campaigns. Cornelius Ryan WWII Collection holds large collection of papers from individuals in Normandy invasion, Battle of Berlin, and Market-Garden operation. Holdings include recordings of interviews with Eisenhower, Montgomery, Prince Bernhard of Netherlands, and others. Accepts phone inquiries. No fee. Hours: call.

All Southern Ohio Preservation Society

178 Church St., Chillicothe, OH 45601; (614)

774-3510. Works to preserve, save, and restore historic sites and natural environment of southern OH. Holdings include small archives, map and photo collections relating to cultural and natural history of the region. Accepts phone inquiries. Use of collections for society members only. Hours: call.

Allen County Historical Society and Museum

620 W. Market St., Lima, OH 45801; (419) 222-9426. Museum, library, and archives contain collection of manuscripts, maps, photos and genealogical records on railroad and labor history. Materials non-circulating. No fee. Hours: Tu-Su 1:30-5.

American Watchmakers Institute Educational Library

3700 Harrison Ave., Cincinnati, OH 45211; (513) 661-3838. Preserves and promotes education about history of clock making in America. Holdings include a collection of rare and unusual timepieces, and a reference library with horology periodicals, catalogs, and books from 1920s. Use of collections by appt only. Does not accept phone inquiries. No fee. Hours: by appt only.

Ashland County Historical Society

P.O. Box 484, 414 Center St., Ashland, OH 44805; (419) 289-3111. Preserves county history in museum and library. Holdings include archives, manuscripts, maps, photos, recordings, and genealogical records. Accepts phone inquiries. Fee for membership. Hours: W, F, Su 1-4.

Bedford Museum

P.O. Box 46282, 30 S. Park St., Bedford, OH 44146; (216) 232-0796. Preserves US and OH history through holdings in museum, library, and archives. Holdings include antiques, materials on Lincoln and Civil War, 1876 Centennial artifacts, railroad and school memorabilia, archives of town records from 1840, Civil War letters, maps from 1850, photos, and oral history tapes. Special Siegel Railroad collection. Accepts phone inquiries. No fee. Hours: M and W 7:30-10, Th 10-4, and 2nd Su of the month 2-5.

Bexley Historical Society

2242 E. Main St., Bexley, OH 43209; (614) 235-8694, ext 52. Preserves history of Bexley, OH and residents in form of museum, library, archives, and oral histories. Holdings include artifacts, furniture, clothing, scrapbooks, drawings, old farm and home implements; city documents, directories and school yearbooks; histories of Franklin County, OH; local maps and photos from 19th c; several videotapes and a large collection of oral history recordings of area residents; small collection of Bexley family genealogies. Accepts phone inquiries. No fee. Hours: M, W 10-3.

Bowling Green State University

Center for Archival Studies, Jerome Library, Bowling Green, OH 43403; (419) 372-2411. Women's Studies Archives documents experience of women in northwest OH through the records of literary clubs, professional and educational assns, and federated clubs from 1880s. Other holdings include diaries and letters from women involved in farming, education, and politics from 1840s-1970s. Accepts phone inquiries. No fee. Hours: call.

Butler County Historical Society

327 N. 2nd St., Hamilton, OH 45011; (513) 893-7111. Preserves historical materials and disseminates historical info. Museum in Victorian house with collections of Indian artifacts, dolls, textiles, and glass. Library holds OH and Butler county histories, including McGuffey readers. Archives holds marriage records of Butler county from 1803-47, family histories, maps, photos of 1913 flood, letters of John Woods, and old newspapers. Accepts phone inquiries. Fee. Hours: Tu-Su 1-4.

Butler Institute of American Art

524 Wick Ave., Youngstown, OH 44502; (216) 743-1711. Preserves American art and history of American artists. Collection spans over 200 years with works by Peale family, Copley, Stuart, Sully, Bierstadt, Homer, Eakins, Ryder, Harnett, Cassatt, Sargent, Whistler, the Eight, Impressionists, Bellows, Benton, Curry, Wood, Hopper, Burchfield, Marsh, Hartley, Kuhn, Sheeler, Shahn, and Calder. Other collections include works by Sharp, Berninghaus, Remington and others on American Indians; Marine collection composed of images from ships to whaling to

South St, NY. Other collections are miniature portraits of US Presidents, and Homer prints from Harpers. Accepts phone inquiries. No fee. Hours: Tu-Sa 11-4, Su 1-4.

Carillon Historical Park
2001 S. Patterson Blvd., Dayton, OH 45409; (513) 293-2841. Complex of historic sites, buildings and exhibits preserves and interprets development of Miami Valley, OH region. Holdings include 17 historic bldgs, 7 rail cars, 1 covered bridge, 1 iron bridge; replicas of 1930s bldgs housing historic transportation and locally built automobile collections; archival materials relating to Park exhibits; Wright Brothers flight artifacts and photos; small film/videotape and recording collections. Accepts phone inquiries. No fee. Hours: May-Oct, Tu-Sa 10-6, Su 1-6.

Case Western Reserve University
Documents Division, Freiberger Library, 11161 East Blvd., Cleveland, OH 44106; (216) 368-6512. Academic research library with collection of govt documents covering US history, Congressional publications, census records, geological surveys, and topographical maps. Accepts phone inquiries. No fee. Hours: M-F 8:30-5.

Centerville Historical Society
89 W. Franklin St., Centerville, OH 45459; (513) 433-0123. Collects and preserves history of Centerville, OH and residents in form of museum with rotating exhibits, library, and archival materials. Holdings include period furnishings, clothing and American pressed glass; research materials and rare books; archives; maps; large genealogical and photo collections of and by area residents; oral history videotapes. Accepts phone inquiries. No fee. Museum hours: Th 1-5.

Cincinnati Fire Museum
315 W. Court St., Cincinnati, OH 45202; (513) 621-5553. Collects, preserves, interprets, and displays history, role, and influence of fire fighting in Cincinnatti, OH. Holdings include fire service artifacts and historical materials from 1788; library with modern reference works and periodicals on fire fighting, fire engineering, and fire prevention; archives with documents and artifacts on manufacture and local use of steam fire engines; large B/W photo collection from 1880. Research for use by staff-supervised, qualified researchers only (must apply for research time with outline of purpose and needs.) Accepts limited phone inquiries. Fee. Hours: Tu-F 10-4.

Cincinnati Historical Society
Eden Park, Cincinnati, OH 45202; (513) 241-4622. Collects, preserves, and disseminates info relating to Old Northwest Territory and metropolitan Cincinnati from 1780. Holdings include manuscripts, maps, photos, films/videotapes, and genealogical records. Special James Green collection on William Henry Harrison, and Peter Thompson collection on OH and Cincinnati. Accepts phone inquiries. No fee. Hours: Tu-Sa 9-4:30.

Cleveland Landmarks Commission
City Hall, 601 Lakeside Ave., Room 519, Cleveland, OH 44114; (216) 664-2531. Commission is devoted to preservation and protection of significant historic sites and landmarks in Cleveland area. Holdings include archives with files on designated historic sites and studies, and historic inventory forms; manuscripts, photos, maps, films/videotapes and recordings related to historic districts and eras. Some restrictions. Accepts phone inquiries. No fee. Hours: 8-5.

Cleveland Public Library
Literature Dept., 325 Superior Ave., Cleveland, OH 44114; (216) 623-2870. Preserves collection of materials on state political and commercial history, and reviews from "Plain Dealer" film critic W. Ward Marsh. State history materials cover canals and waterworks, business and industry, OH General Assembly records and bills since 1937, and photos and maps of historic OH. Film reviewer collection has production stills, files on actors and actresses, clipping files, press packets, and materials from "Variety" and "Box Office," as well as Marsh's reviews. Accepts phone inquiries. Hours: call.

Cleveland State University
University Libraries, 1860 East 22nd St., Cleveland, OH 44115; (216) 687-2490. Academic support library with holdings on regional personalities, railroad, topography, OH Slavic music, and newspaper clipping file. Archives hold Uni-

versity records, as well as materials from predecessor, Fenn College; papers and memorabilia of local musician Herbert Elwell; Cleveland Union Terminal construction records; Cleveland Composer Guild archives; recordings of South Slavic music from northeast OH; and Cleveland Press clippings, 1932-80. Accepts phone inquiries (216-687-2486). No fee. Hours: M-Th 7:30-10:30, F 7:30-5, Sa 10-5, Su 1-5.

College Football Hall of Fame

National Football Foundation, King's Island Drive, King's Island, OH 45034; (513) 398-5410. Preserves and displays history of college football in form of museum, hall of fame, library, and archival collections. Holdings include "Time Tunnel" of college football evolution; Gold Medal display of college football greats, including some US Presidents (Eisenhower, Hoover, Kennedy, Nixon, Ford, and Reagan); library with reference materials on historic games, teams, and players; photos of famous players and coaches; large collection of game films. Library closed to public. Accepts phone inquiries. Fee. Hours: summer, 9-6; winter, 10-5.

Conneaut Railroad Museum

P.O. Box 643, Conneaut, OH 44030; (216) 599-7878. Explains various aspects of railroading and equipment and employees. Museum exhibits old timetables, lanterns, passes, tools, locomotives and cabooses, signal equip, and fire fighting equip. Library has locomotive instruction manuals from mid-19th c, data from various railroads, and collection of railroad literature. Other holdings include maps, large collection of photos, films/videotapes, and several railroad records and tapes. Accepts phone inquiries. Donations accepted. Hours: Memorial Day-Labor Day, noon-5.

Denison University

Documents Division, William Doane Library, Granville, OH 43023; (614) 587-0810. Library maintains a selective collection of documents relevant to univ curriculum, including univ from 1831 and some local, state and US govt materials. Current reference materials and Congressional materials prior to 72nd Congress are noncirculating. Accepts phone inquiries (ext 682). No fee. Hours: M-Th 9-9:30.

Dover Historical Society

J.E. Reeves Home and Museum, 325 E. Iron Ave., Dover, OH 44622; (216) 343-7040. Preserves and displays history of Dover and the Reeves family through museum, library and archival collections. Holdings include metal products, racing sulkies, grocery store display, furniture, and other local artifacts; library containing J.E. Reeves personal book collection and reference volumes; archives of local records and items, late 1800s-early 1900s; maps of Dover and Tuscarawas County area and residents, 1800s-1920; photos of local subjects from 1870s; Reeves family genealogical records. Some restrictions. Accepts phone inquiries. Fee. Hours: museum: summer, Tu-Su 10:30-3:30; winter, by appt.; office: M-F 9-3.

Enon Community Historical Society

P.O. Box 442, Enon, OH 45323; (513) 864-7756. Collects and preserves history of Enon/Mud River region. Museum collections preserve local artifacts and some Woodland Indian stone tools. Library preserves genealogical and local history materials, maps, photos, oral history recordings, and local school histories. Site of Adena mound, second largest conical mound in OH. Accepts written requests. No fee. Hours: by appt only.

Fairport Marine Museum

129 Second St., Fairport Harbor, OH 44077; (216) 354-4825. Museum preserves and displays local history of Fairport, OH area and residents and Great Lakes merchant mariners in form of artifacts and exhibits, small library, local maps, and maritime and local photos. Accepts phone inquiries. Fee. Hours: summer, Sa-Su and holidays 1-6.

Findlay College

Documents Dept., Shafer Library, 1000 North Main St., Findlay, OH 45840; (419) 424-4627. College library maintains selective collection of govt documents, general and historical materials, and special collections. Holdings include USGS topographic and National Park Service maps; Congressional papers of Jackson Betts and Tennyson Guyer; Hancock County Historical Preservation Guild collection of books and periodicals. Use of Congressional papers by appt only. Accepts phone inquiries. No fee. Hours: academic year: 8-11; other times: M-F 9-4.

Firelands Historical Society Museum
4 Case Ave., Norwalk, OH 44857; (419) 668-6038. Society perpetuates memory of OH pioneers through museum holdings of Indian artifacts, antique guns, early clothing, and paintings. Library has materials on history and genealogy of area, maps, and photos. Accepts phone inquiries. Fee. Hours: Apr & Nov, Sa-Su noon-5; May, June, Sept, Oct, M-Su noon-5; July-Aug, M-Su 10-5.

Fort Laurens State Memorial and Museum
Rte. 1, Box 442, County Rd. 102, Bolivar, OH 44612; (216) 874-2059. Site of OH's only Revolutionary War fort, occupied from Nov 1778-Aug 1779. Museum displays archaeological artifacts found on site, uniforms, weapons, and accoutrements. Slide show available on history of Revolution and Ft. Accepts phone inquiries. Fee. Hours: Memorial Day-Labor Day, W-Sa 9:30-5, Su noon-5; Sept-Oct, Sa 9:30-5, Su noon-5.

Fort Meigs State Memorial
P.O. Box 3, Perrysburg, OH 43551; (419) 874-4121. Memorial preserves history of Ft Meigs and War of 1812 in form of museum with military artifacts and restoration of original log fortification. Accepts phone inquiries. Fee. Hours: Apr-Oct, W-Sa 9:30-5; Su noon-5.

Fort Stephenson Museum
Birchard Public Library, 423 Croghan St., Fremont, OH 43420; (419) 334-7101. Highlights role of Ft in War of 1812. Museum will open March 1989, and will contain displays on Battle of Ft Stephenson. Library has local history collection, materials on northwest OH, and OH. Library will be temporarily relocated to 1005 Everett Rd. Accepts phone inquiries. No fee. Hours: M-Th 9-8:30, F-Sa 9-5:30; in summer, Sa 9-3.

Garst Museum
205 N. Broadway, Greenville, OH 45331; (513) 548-5250. Preserves heritage of Darke County,

OH through holdings in museum, library, and archives. Collections include Lowell Thomas collection of photos and memorabilia; Annie Oakley collection of guns, clothing, touring trunks, and wigs; Treaty of Greenville memorabilia; Buffalo Bill photos, books, and cars; Lohmann Telescopes and related materials; and large collection of assorted memorabilia on local and US history. Birthplace of Thomas is located on Museum grounds and is undergoing renovation. Accepts phone inquiries. No fee. Hours: Feb-Dec, Tu-Su 1-4:30.

Geauga County Public Library
Documents Dept., 110 East Park St., Chardon, OH 44024; (216) 285-7601. Public library maintains selective collection of govt documents, general and historical materials relevant to needs of the community. Holdings include county birth, death, and tax records; wills, photos and other family documents; necrology file; and newspaper microfilms. Some restrictions. Accepts phone inquiries. No fee. Hours: M-Th 9-9, F-Sa 9-5.

Goodyear World of Rubber Museum
1201 E. Market St., Akron, OH 44316; (216) 796-2044. Preserves and displays history of rubber industry, with emphasis on the Goodyear Tire & Rubber Co., from 1898, in form of museum exhibits and library with Goodyear historical records, photos and books. Accepts phone inquiries. No fee. Hours: M-F 8:30-4:30.

Granville Life-Style Museum
H.D. Robinson House, 121 S. Main St., P.O. Box 134, Granville, OH 43023; (614) 587-0373. Preserved Victorian home houses historical collection on life and times of H.D. Robinson family from 1840. Holdings include original family furnishings and belongings; large collection of original daguerreotypes; large lace collection from 1827; large collection of hats from 1820s; women's undergarment collection from 1890s. Accepts phone inquiries. Fee. Hours: mid-Apr-mid-Oct, Su 1-4:30, or by appt.

Great Lakes Historical Society Museum
P.O. Box 435, 480 Main St., Vermillion, OH 44089; (216) 967-3467. Preserves and displays

history of the Great Lakes in form of museum, library, and archival collections. Holdings include artifacts, ship models, paintings, and maritime equipment; Clarence Metcalf library; ships' log books; maritime maps and charts; large photo collection of Great Lakes ships, lighthouses, and region; historical materials on Vermillion, MI (known as the home of lake captains); Dana Bowen collection. Accepts phone inquiries. Fee. Hours: Apr-Dec, 10-5; Jan-Mar, Sa-Su only, 10-5.

Harding Home and Museum
380 Mt. Vernon Ave., Marion, OH 43302; (614) 387-9630. Preserves, interprets, and displays life and times of President Warren G. Harding and his wife, 1865-1923, in form of family home, furnishings, belongings, and artifacts. Accepts phone inquiries. Fee. Hours: museum: summer, W-Sa 9:30-4:30, Su noon-4:30; Apr-May, Sept-Oct, by appt; office: 10-4.

Hebrew Union College— Jewish Institute of Religion
Klan Library, 3101 Clifton Ave., Cincinnati, OH 45220; (513) 221-1881. Preserves American Jewish periodicals and newspapers up to 1925, and holds selective issues from then on. Accepts phone inquiries. Hours: call.

Hickories Museum
Lorain County Historical Society, 509 Washington Ave., Elyria, OH 44035; (216) 322-3341. Preserves Lorain County cultural heritage and history. Museum housed in turn of the century mansion depicting American Work Ethic. Library contains info on local history and genealogy, including maps, manuscripts, photos, and genealogical records. Accepts phone inquiries. Fee. Hours: Mar-Dec M-F 8-4, Su 1-4.

Hiram College
Documents Dept., Teachout-Price Memorial Library, Hiram, OH 44234; (216) 569-5358. College library maintains selective collection of govt documents, general and historical materials, and special collections. Holdings include college archives from 1850; personal papers of prominent personalities from college, including James A. Garfield, Burke A. Hinsdale, Nicholas Vachel, John S. Kenyon, and Edmund Wakefield; Fox collection of regional, historical maps, 1540-1800s; photos of college and local historical subjects; Regional Studies Collection (Western Reserve of Ohio); Disciples of Christ historical collection; Hiram authors and local history collections. Accepts phone inquiries (216-569-5357). No fee. Hours: M-F 8-11, Sa-Su 9-11.

Hoover Historical Center
2225 Easton St., NW, North Canton, OH 44720; (216) 499-0287. Repository of info, objects, pictures, and other collectables related to growth and manufacture of vacuum cleaner industry with emphasis on Hoover Company. Other concentrations include Victorian lifestyle, clothing, and Industrial Revolution. Museum and library have info on tanning, Industrial Revolution, and Victoriana. Archives contain Hoover ads, letters, manuscripts, photos, company songs, and films/videotapes on consumerism and marketing. Permanent collection of antique vacuum cleaners and Victorian clothing from 1840s. Accepts phone inquiries. No fee. Hours: Tu-Su 1-5.

Howard Dittrick Museum of Historical Medicine
11000 Euclid Ave., Cleveland, OH 44106; (216) 368-3648. Museum preserves and displays medical history in form of artifacts and exhibits, library, archives, manuscripts, maps, photos, recordings, and special collections. Accepts phone inquiries. No fee. Hours: M-F 10-5, Sa noon-5.

Hudson Library and Historical Society
22 Aurora St., Hudson, OH 44236; (216) 653-6658. Collects and preserves history of Hudson, OH and residents in form of 1835 period room, library, archives, and special collections. Holdings include period furnishings; local historical and genealogical archives; local maps; photos, including 19th c subjects and slides from early glass negatives; collection of letters relating to John Brown (abolitionist leader) 1800-59; Grace Goulder Izant (Ohio writer) collection. Accepts phone inquiries. No fee. Hours: M, Tu, Th 10-9, Fri-Sat 10-5, Su 1-5.

Indian Museum of Lake County
391 W. Washington, Painesville, OH 44077;

(216) 352-3361, ext. 203. Preserves prehistoric and contemporary artifacts of North American history and antiquities of Lake county and OH. Museum exhibits date from from BC to 1650, and include materials and art of all regions and culture of North America. Library has reference materials. Special collections include Reeve's Village Site, OH and Grantham-Fairport Burial Site. Library materials for in-house use only. Accepts phone inquiries. No fee. Hours: M-Th 10-4, Sa-Su 1-4.

Kent State University Archives
University Library, Kent, OH 44242; (216) 672-2411. Preserves history of University and related events and individuals. Holdings include papers of abolitionist, educator, and women's rights advocate Betsy Mix Cowles; materials on 1850 Women's Rights Convention at Salem, OH; and extensive collection of materials on Kent State anti-Vietnam War rallies and May 4, 1970 shootings of 4 students. Accepts phone inquiries. No fee. Hours: appt suggested for specialized research; M-F 8-noon, 1-5, Sa-Su 1-5.

Lakewood Historical Society
14710 Lake Ave., Lakewood, OH 44107; (216) 221-7343. Collects and preserves history of Lakewood, OH and residents in form of museum, library, and archival collections. Holdings include 1839 stone farmhouse with authentic furnishings, 1838-1870; quilt and coverlet collections; reference materials on antiques, and history of Lakewood, Cuyahoga County, and Western Reserve; record and document archives; large photo collection of local subjects from 1880; Alfred Hall diaries, 1881-1929. Research by appt. Accepts phone inquiries. No fee. Hours: M-F 9-1, or by appt.

Lawnfield
8095 Mentor Ave., Mentor, OH 44060; (216) 255-8722. Historic home of President James Garfield. Preserves story of his life and times with original furnishings and family belongings. Some restrictions. Accepts phone inquiries. Fee. Hours: Tu-Sa 10-5, Su noon-5.

Malong College
Document Dept., Everett L. Cattell Library,

515 25th St., N.W., Canton, OH 44709; (216) 489-0800. College library maintains selective collection of govt documents, general and historical materials relevant to needs of college, with emphasis on Christianity in general and the Evangelical Friends Church in particular. Holdings include archives of the Evangelical Friends Church—Eastern Region, 1809-early 1900s; archives of India and China missions; genealogical records related to the church. Some restrictions. Accepts phone inquiries (216-489-7393). Fee for non-students. Hours: M-Th 8-10, F 8-5, Sa 10-5, Su 3-10.

Marion Public Library
445 E. Church Rd., Marion, OH 43302; (614) 387-0992. Public library maintains extensive collection of materials relating to history of Marion County, OH and residents. Holdings include local newspaper archives from 1877; county census records 1830-1910; county birth and death records 1867-1908 and county marriage records 1824-1964; histories of Marion and other Ohio counties; historical materials on President Warren G. Harding. Accepts phone inquiries. No fee. Hours: M-F 9-9, Sa 9-5:30.

Massillon Museum
212 Lincoln Way, E., Massillon, OH 44646; (216) 833-4061. Collects and exhibits local history and OH art for purpose of educational and cultural purposes. Museum and archives document local and women's history with collection of manuscripts, maps, oral histories, genealogical records, Pease ethnological collection, and photos from Belle Johnson, William Bennett, Nell Dorr, Aaron Siskind "Harlem" collection, and Henry Clay Fleming "Ravenswood" collection. Accepts phone inquiries. No fee. Hours: Tu-Sa 9:30-5, Su 2-5.

Maumee Valley Historical Society
1031 River Rd., Maumee, OH 43537; (419) 893-9602. Society preserves and promotes history of Maumee Valley region and residents through publications, the Wolcott Museum Complex, and historic preservation projects. Museum complex consists of restored Federal-style buildings (1830s), log home, 1840s salt box farmhouse, 1880s railroad cars and depot, Monclova U.B. Church, and 1840 Greek Re-

vival-style home. Accepts phone inquiries. Fee for museum complex. Hours: museum complex: W-Su 1-4; office: M-F 9-5.

McKinley Museum of History, Science, and Industry

P.O. Box 483, 800 McKinley Monument Dr., NW, Canton, OH 44701; (216) 455-7043. Preserves and enhances memory of President McKinley and history of Stark county. Museum and library document McKinley's life. Archives covers years 1805-1950s through collections of manuscripts, maps, photos, recordings, and genealogical records. Accepts phone inquiries. Fee. Hours: summer M-Sa 9-7; winter M-Sa 9-5, Su noon-5.

Medina Community Design Committee

141 S. Prospect St., Medina, OH 44256; (216) 725-7516. Specializes in historic preservation and restoration of Medina's Victorian heritage, and provides resource and library materials on local history. Library features history of county and state, with concentration on preservation and restoration. Archives contain maps from 19th c, large collection of photos from Medina historic district, film/videotapes of city, and small collection of oral histories. Accepts phone inquiries. No fee. Hours: Tu, W, Th 10-5, or by appt.

Mennonite Historical Library

Bluffton College, Musselman Library, 280 W. College Ave., Bluffton, OH 45817; (419) 358-8015, ext 272. College library maintains selective collection of govt documents, and general and historical materials, with emphasis on Mennonite history. Holdings include Mennonite Historical Library; college and Mennonite archives, with manuscripts, and photos; genealogical records relating to Mennonites, Amish, and Church of the Brethren families. Some restrictions. Accepts phone inquiries. No fee. Hours: M-F 8-5, Sa 1-5, Su (except summer) 2-10.

Mercer County Historical Society

130 E. Market, Celina, OH 45822; (419) 586-6065. Preserves heritage of Mercer county residents. Museum displays history of agriculture, homes, business, and Indians of area. Library has

reference materials on region. Other holdings include manuscripts, maps of towns and railroad, photos, recordings, genealogical records, and special Capt James Riley collection on Northwest Territory. Accepts phone inquiries. No fee. Hours: winter, W-F 8:30-4, Su 1-4; summer, closed Su.

Monroe County Historical Society

P.O. Box 538, 217 Eastern Ave., Woodsfield, OH 43793; (614) 472-1933. Promotes and preserves history of Monroe County, OH industries, life, and residents in form of three museums and archival collections. Holdings include restored Victorian house museum with period rooms; Parry Museum collection of antique quilts and Indian artifacts; Dairy Museum authentic home cheese-making plant; old stone school house; archives (at Parry Museum) with manuscripts, records, documents, maps, photos, films/videotapes relating to local history and residents. Accepts phone inquiries. Fee. Hours: museums: June-Sept, Su and holidays, 2-4; office: M, W, F 11:30-3.

Montgomery County Historical Society

7 N. Main St., Dayton, OH 45402; (513) 228-6271. Collects, preserves, and interprets history of Dayton, OH area and residents in form of museum, library, and archival collections. Holdings include 1850 Greek Revival Court House with architectural exhibits, Wright Brothers Collection, and John H. Patterson (founder of NCR) Collection; reference library with historical research materials; archives, maps, genealogical records; collections of Frigidaire, and Lowe Paint Co papers. Research facilities open by appt only. Accepts phone inquiries M-F 8:30-4:30. Donations accepted. Hours: Tu-F 10-4, Sa noon-4.

Mound City Group National Monument

16062 SR 104, Chillicothe, OH 45601; (614) 774-1125. National monument preserves prehistoric Indian burial site. Holdings include museum with prehistoric grave goods excavated from burial mounds on site, Hopewell 200 BC-500 AD; library with research materials on archeology, Native American culture, and the National Park Service. Restricted access to library. Accepts phone inquiries. Fee. Hours: 8-5, with extended summer hours.

Muskingum College Library

Document Dept., New Concord, OH 43762; (614) 826-8152. College library maintains selective collection of govt documents, general and historical materials relevant to needs of the school, with emphasis on Presbyterian Church. Holdings include archives of college and local church; photo collection of college and local subjects; index to the 1850 OH census; local townships census for 1820, 50, and 1960. Some restrictions. Accepts phone inquiries. No fee. Hours: M-Th 8-11, F 8-5, Sa 10-5, Su 1-11.

National Afro-American Museum and Cultural Center

P.O. Box 578, 1350 Brush Row Road, Wilberforce, OH 45384; (513) 376-4944. Documents, preserves, and interprets Afro-American history and culture. Museum exhibits cover Afro-American life from end of WWII to passage of Voting Rights Act in 1965. Library focuses on Afro-American life and culture, with works by and on Afro-Americans. Manuscript collection includes papers of W.E.B. DuBois, Booker T. Washington, and others. Photo collection includes images from across US. Recordings of numerous Afro-American musicians available, as well as works of art by Robert Duncanson, James Washington, and Jacob Lawrence. Accepts phone inquiries. Fee. Hours: M-Sa 9-5, Su 1-5.

National McKinley Birthplace Memorial Association Museum

40 N. Main St., Niles, OH 44446; (216) 652-1704. Museum commemorates birthplace of William McKinley through small collection of materials on his life, OH history, and local ethnic groups. Museum designed by McKim, Mead, and White. Accepts phone inquiries. No fee. Hours: M-Th 8:30-8, F-Sa 8:30-5.

Neil Armstrong Air and Space Museum

P.O. Box 1978, I-75 and Bellefontaine St., Wapakoneta, OH 45895; (419) 738-8811. Museum collects, preserves, and displays history of aeronautics and space exploration from 1850

in form of exhibits and artifacts. Accepts phone inquiries. Fee. Hours: Mar-Nov, M-Sa 9:30-5, Su noon-5.

Oberlin College

Oberlin College Library, Oberlin, OH 44074; (216) 775-8285. College library maintains general, historical, and special collections relevant to needs of school. Holdings include Evans Early American Imprints collection 1639-1800; runs of 19th c periodicals, and monograph, periodical and archival sources on black history; materials on history of American Protestant Evangelism and missionary activities abroad; women's history collection; college archives and records of town from 1833; Anti-Slavery, Oberlin graduates, Spanish Drama, History of the Book, and Dime Novels Special Collections; Violin Society of America/Goodkind Collection. Some restrictions. Accepts phone inquiries. Hours: vary by section.

Ohio Association of Historical Societies and Museums

Local History Department, Ohio Historical Society, 1985 Velma Ave., Columbus, OH 43211; (614) 297-2340. Network of OH historical societies assists and promotes local historical preservation and education efforts through publications, reference collection, regional meetings, and awards. Holdings include library with museum studies and information files on OH historical societies and history reference collections. Accepts phone inquiries. Membership fee. Hours: M-F 8-5.

Ohio Camera Collector's Society

P.O. Box 282, Columbus, OH 43216; (614) 885-3224. Group is dedicated to collecting and preserving photographic materials. Holdings primarily consist of individual's private collections, manuscripts, photos, and reference materials. Society has annual camera show sale and auction, and can supply some reference regarding collections of special interest. Accepts phone inquiries. Fee for membership. Hours: 6-10.

Ohio Genealogical Society

P.O. Box 2625, Mansfield, OH 44906; (419) 522-9077. Society preserves and promotes research on historical records of OH pioneers in

OUT·OF·JAIL!

THE RESCUERS

Are coming TO-NIGHT!

At a public Meeting at the Mayor's Office it was voted that the citizens, en masse, turn out to meet them at the CARS, and escort them to the Church for Public Reception. The undersigned were appointed a Committee of Arrangements:
H. L. HENRY,   A. N. BEECHER,   W. P. HARRIS.
J. M. ELLIS,   E. R. STILES.

The committee appointed Father Keep for President of the Meeting at the church, and Prof. J. M. Ellis, Marshall. All the citizens are invited to meet the Rescuers at the Depot at half-past seven. The procession will form after the Band in the following order:

The Mayor and Council; The Fire Department in Uniform; The Rescuers; The Citizens.

Let there be a grand gathering!
Oberlin, July 6.   By order of Committee of Arrangements.

Announcement for meeting of Ohio anti-slavery organization, The Rescuers, from the Oberlin College Archives.

form of library and archival collections. Holdings include reference works on records files on OH and PA history and residents; small collection of manuscripts on central OH; county maps; Centennial (1876) photos of Richland County pioneers; genealogical, census, military, and bible records; state tax list of 1812; collection of First Families of Ohio (pre-1820) applications. Accepts phone inquiries. No fee. Hours: Tu-Sa 9-5.

Ohio Historical Society
1985 Velma Ave., Columbus, OH 43211; (614) 297-2300. Collects and preserves history of OH and residents in form of Warren G. Harding Home (Marion, OH), library, and museum and archival collections. Holdings include artifacts and exhibits on OH archeology, natural and cultural history; reference library with rare books, newspapers, trade catalogs, and sheet music; archives of state and local govt records; large collections of maps, manuscripts, photos, and oral history recordings; films/videotapes; genealogical records, city directories, county and local histories; Central Ohio architectural records. Some restrictions. Accepts phone inquiries (614-297-5000). No fee. Hours: library: Tu-Sa 9-5; office: 8-5.

Ohio Northern University
Jay P. Taggart Law Library, Ada, OH 45810; (419) 772-2254. Univ law library maintains

selective collection of govt and legal documents and materials relevant to needs of the school. Holdings include selected US govt documents from 1965; papers of Congressman William M. McCullock (R-Ohio, 4th District, 1948-72.) Accepts phone inquiries (419-772-2250). No fee. Hours: academic year: M-F 8am-midnight, Sa 9-10, Su 1pm-midnight; other times, M-F 8-4:30.

Ohio State University Libraries

Info. Services Dept./Documents Division, 1858 Neil Ave. Mall, Columbus, OH 43210; (614) 292-6175. Academic research library with collection of US govt documents, 19th c printed documents, strong holdings in American fiction, and substantial microform holdings. Also depository for USGS maps. Accepts phone inquiries. No fee. Hours: M-Sa 8am-midnight, Su 11am-midnight.

Ohio University Library

Archives and Special Collections Dept., Park Place, Athens, OH 45701; (614) 593-2710. Univ archives preserves selected records and documents of school, region, and state. Holdings include univ archives from 1804; local govt records for 18 southeastern OH counties; Cornelius Ryan WWII research Collection, including interviews with Eisenhower; labor history collections for region; Congressional papers of Wayne Hays and William Harsha; recordings from University oral history project; genealogical reference works on southeastern OH families; Morgan Collection on the History of Chemistry; and Osteopathic Medicine Collection. Accepts phone inquiries. Fees for genealogical inquiries. Hours: M-F 8-5; also Sa noon-4 during academic year.

Ohioana Library

65 S. Front St., Room 1105, Columbus, OH 43266; (614) 466-3831. Library maintains collection of books and references on Ohio subjects and/or by Ohioans. Holdings include books by James Thurber and Sherwood Anderson; archives with manuscripts, atlases, county histories, and other documents relating to state; genealogical records; Louis Bromfield collection. Library is non-circulating. Accepts phone inquiries. No fee. Hours: M-F 8:30-4:30.

Parma Area Historical Society

P.O. Box 29002, 6975 Ridge Rd., Parma, OH 44129. Preserves local history in 1920 home furnished with pieces from 18th-20th c. Some aerial and plat maps available. Accepts phone inquiries. No fee. Hours: May 14-Oct 30, Sa-Su noon-5.

Perry's Victory and International Peace Memorial

P.O. Box 549, Put-In-Bay, OH 43456; (419) 285-2184. Commemorates life and career of Oliver Hazard Perry and Battle of Lake Erie. Museum depicts War of 1812 in old Northwest, international peace, and construction of the Perry memorial. Library provides reference collection and photos. Special collection of papers of Perry's Victory Centennial Commission available. Accepts phone inquiries. Fee. Hours: Apr-Oct 9-6.

Plain Dealer Library

1801 Superior Ave., Cleveland, OH 44114; (216) 344-4195. Serves info needs of paper's editorial and other depts. Library holds paper's clippings from 1920s; international, national, OH, and Cleveland photos; and special collection on OH and Cleveland history from late 19th c. Permission to use library granted by managing editor. No fee. Hours: 8-2.

Preble County Historical Society

7693 Swartzel Rd., Eaton, OH 45320; (513) 787-4256. Preserves and promotes history of Preble County, OH and residents through museum, restored home and farm, and archival collections. Holdings include collections of period furnishings and artifacts in restored home; agricultural tools and machinery in farm barns; maps of area from 1858; photos of historic homes; genealogical and other records for Preble, Darke, Butler, and Montgomery Counties, OH, Wayne County, IN, and PA, MD, NJ, TN, KY, and VA; area newspapers from 1850. Collections are non-circulating. Does not accept phone inquiries. No fee. Hours: Sept-May, M-F 9-8, Sa 9-5, Su 1-5.

Public Library of Cincinnati and Hamilton County

Dept. of Rare Books and Special Collections,

800 Vine St., Cincinnati, OH 45202; (513) 369-6900. Inland River Collection contains logbooks, business records, letters, diaries, and large photo collection pertaining to river traffic, workers, and vessels. Hours: call.

Public Library of Columbus and Franklin County

Documents Division, 96 S. Grant Ave., Columbus, OH 43215; (614) 222-7180. Public library maintains selective collection of govt documents, general and historical materials relevant to needs of community. Holdings include annual reports, trustee records, and card holder registers from 1873; large collection of local, state, US and intl maps; large photo collection; local and state historical references. Accepts phone inquiries. No fee. Hours: M-Th 9-9, F-Sa 9-6, Su 2-5 (summer hours vary).

Public Library of Youngstown and Mahoning County

Documents Division, Reference Department, 305 Wick Avenue, Youngstown, OH 44503; (216) 744-8636. Serves community research needs with library, archival and manuscript collections. Library holds materials on US history. Archives collects publications from local govt and orgs. Manuscript collection includes materials on family histories. Other holdings include topographical maps of area, photos of landmarks and citizens, vital county records and histories from Ohio and western Pennsylvania region, and special Youngstown biography index. Accepts phone inquiries. No fee. Hours: winter, M-Tu 9-8:30, W-Sa 9-5:30; summer, M-Tu 9-8:30, W-F 9-5:30.

Putnam County Historical Society

P.O. Box 264, 201 E. Main St, Kalida, OH 45853; (419) 532-3008. Society collects and preserves history of Putnam County, OH and residents through special events, museum, library, and archival collections. Holdings include artifacts and exhibits on local history housed in original 1902 Kalida church building; reference library with family genealogies and local histories; county and township maps; manuscripts and photos. Accepts phone inquiries (419-532-3041 or 3314). No fee. Hours: May-Oct, W 9-noon, Su 1-4.

Robbins Hunter Museum

221 E. Broadway, P.O. Box 183, Granville, OH 43023; (614) 587-0430. Historic 19th c Hunter family home houses collection of OH furnishings, art, and family artifacts and documents. Holdings include 19th c furniture, portraits, and decorative pieces; art history reference library; papers of Judge S.M. Hunter and family; manuscript of "The Judge Rode a Sorrell Horse" by Robbins Hunter; collection of Hunter family photos, 1860-1950; 1937 recordings of interviews with Denison Univ students in Kappa Sigma fraternity; Kappa Sigma and Phi Gamma Delta fraternity papers from 1905; genealogical records of Avery, Robbins, and Hunter families. Some restrictions. Does not accept phone inquiries. Fee. Hours: M-F 9-5.

Roscoe Village Foundation

381 Hill St., Coshocton, OH 43812; (614) 622-9310 and 2222. Restores and preserves heritage of 4th largest shipping port on Ohio & Erie Canal. Museum, library, and archives hold canal-related materials, including manuscripts, maps, photos of canal, films/videotapes, recordings, and genealogical records of early Roscoe and Coshocton residents. Some restrictions on use of archival materials. Accepts phone inquiries. Fee. Hours: 9-5.

Ross County Historical Society

45 W. 5th St., Chillicothe, OH 45601; (614) 772-1936. Collects and preserves history of Ross county and early OH. Museum exhibits cover prehistoric period to mid-20th c. Library has manuscripts from early OH and Northwest territory development, including OH govt records, and maps. Accepts phone inquiries. Fee. Hours: Apr-Sept, 1-5.

Rutherford B. Hayes Presidential Center

Speigel Grove, Fremont, OH 43420; (419) 332-2081. Preserves history and educates on subjects of Pres Hayes and years between Civil War and WWI (Gilded Age). Museum exhibits devoted to Hayes's career, Indian artifacts, and Gilded Age. Library has large collection of pamphlets, maps, periodicals, and ephemera. Archives has local history archives; papers of Mark Twain, William Evarts, Edward Stoughton, John and

William Sherman, and Benson Lossing; OH and old Northwest maps; many Hayes family photos, Gilded Age, Lake Erie, and Sandusky county photos; and genealogical records. Materials non-circulating. Accepts phone inquiries. No fee for research; fee for museum. Hours: Su-M 1:30-5, Tu-Sa 9-5; no research on

Saint Mary's Ethnic Museum

3256 Warren Rd., Cleveland, OH 44111; (216) 941-5550. Preserves ethnic heritage through museum collection of costumes, artifacts, and embroideries. Library has materials on Rumania. Special collection of paintings by Rumanian artists and icons on wood and glass. Accepts phone inquiries. No fee. Hours: 8:30-4:30, and by appt after hours and on weekends.

Salem Historical Society and Museum

208 S. Broadway, Salem, OH 44460; (216) 332-4959. Preserves, promotes, and displays history of Salem, OH and residents through museum, preservation projects, library, and archival collections. Holdings include artifacts of local history, 1803-1960s, including displays on early factories, Civil War, abolitionism, women's rights, toys, clothing, and household goods; small library; archives with manuscripts, photos, maps, military and genealogical records, materials on US and European burial sites of famous people; oral histories, films/videotapes, recordings; and collections of Charles Burchfield and W.H. Mullins. Accepts phone inquiries. Fee. Hours: F 6:30-8, Su 2-4.

Scioto Society

P.O. Box 73, 215 W. 2nd St., Chillicothe, OH 45601; (615) 775-0700. Society preserves history of the life and death of the Shawnee Indian leader Tecumseh in form of museum with exhibits on his life and times and other local Indian history, and presentation of an outdoor drama about his life. Accepts phone inquiries after March 1. Fee for performance. Hours: early June-early Sept, M-Sa (museum: 3-8; performances nightly).

Shaker Historical Society and Museum

16740 S. Park Blvd., Shaker Heights, OH 44120;

(216) 921-1201. Preserves and promotes history of the North Union Shakers, Shaker Heights, and Warrensville township through special programs, museum, library, and archival collections. Holdings include exhibits on local history featuring furniture, clocks, cradles, boxes, sewing, spinning and other artifacts; library with reference materials on the Shakers and their settlements; small collections of maps and photos; small collection of recorded Shaker choir music and songs; small collection of genealogical records of North Union Shakers and Warrensville families. Some restrictions. Accepts phone inquiries. Fees for group tours. Hours: Tu-F 2-4, Su 2-5.

Sons of the American Revolution

Richard Montgomery Chapter, 540 Monteray Ave., Dayton, OH 45419; (513) 293-2539. Preserves records of application for membership from 1912 to 1988, most of meeting, and Brownell and Kuhns collections. Other holdings include photos, videotapes of SAR story, and recordings from National Congresses. Accepts phone inquiries. No fee. Hours: call.

South Euclid Historical Museum

4500 Anderson Rd., South Euclid, OH 44121; (216) 381-0879. Promotes interest in history of town through holdings in museum, library, and archives. Collections include fan collection, musical instruments, and furniture from 1840-1910, clothing from 1850s-1920s, maps, photos, tapes, and genealogical records. Accepts phone inquiries. No fee. Hours: Sa 1-4, or by appt.

Southern Ohio Museum and Cultural Center

825 Gallia St., P.O. Box 990, Portsmouth, OH 45662; (614) 354-5629. Preserves arts, history, and science materials. Museum displays 18th-20th c art, anthropology, and artifacts from prehistoric Indians. Library provides collection of visual arts resources. Staff member must accompany library users. Accepts phone inquiries. Fee. Hours: Tu-F 10-5.

Thomas Edison Birthplace Museum

9 Edison Dr., Milan, OH 44846; (419) 499-2135. Historic home museum preserves and

interprets history of life and work of Thomas Alva Edison through guided tours of his birthplace. Accepts phone inquiries. Fee. Hours: Jun-Labor Day, Tu-Sa 10-5, Su 1-5; Feb-May, Labor Day-Nov, Tu-Su 1-5 (last tour: 4:30).

Ukrainian Museum Archives

1202 Kenilworth Ave., Cleveland, OH 44113; (216) 781-4329. Preserves and chronicles history and culture of the Ukraine, and Ukrainian-American experience. Holdings include cultural artifacts and exhibits; large library; archives with documents, manuscripts, records and photos of Ukrainian and Ukrainian-American history from 1850; maps of the Ukraine; large collection of genealogical records and family memoirs; complete collection of historical materials on Ukrainian community in Greater Cleveland, OH are from 1900; large library and archives devoted to Taras Shevchenko. Collections are non-circulating. Accepts phone inquiries. Donations accepted. Hours: M-F 9-noon, or by appt.

United Methodist Archives Center

Ohio Wesleyan University, Beeghly Library, 43 University St., Delaware, OH 43015; (614) 369-4431. Preserves, interprets, and organizes historical foundation of Methodist church, especially in western OH area. Museum houses artifacts dealing with history of Methodism from 19th c. Library holds reference materials, hymnals, mission histories, biographies, and relative history from 1780s. Archives holds Conference materials and missionary reports; papers of Francis Asbury, William Abernathy, James Bradley Finley, George Washington Maley, Thomas Asbury Morris, and Edward Thomson; collection on John Wesley; photos; scrapbooks; sermons; and genealogical records of OH Methodist ministers. Accepts phone inquiries. Fee. Hours: Tu-Th 9-5.

University of Cincinnati

Archives and Rare Books, Carl Blegen Library, 8th Fl., Cincinnati, OH 45221; (513) 475-6459. Collects, preserves, and makes available unique and valuable collections. Collections include books on North American Indians, early travel and exploration; German-American heritage materials; University Archives; Urban Studies collection relating to 20th c Cincinnati poli-

tics, planning, housing, and labor history; OH Network collection of govt records from 8 southwestern counties; History of Design collection on history of fashion, graphics, industrial and interior design in 20th c Cincinnati and OH; and archives of medical history, including papers of polio doctor Sabin and regional hospitals. Accepts phone inquiries. No fee. Hours: M-F 8-5.

University of Dayton

Document Dept., Roesch Library, 300 College Park Ave., Dayton, OH 45469; (513) 229-4221. Univ library maintains selective collection of govt documents, and general, historical, archival and special collections. Holdings include Marian Library collection of material on the Blessed Virgin Mary (world's largest); interviews about Wright brothers and Charles Kettering; photos; Congressional papers of Charles W. Whalen, 1966-78; Catholic Council for Civil Liberties Papers, 1958-66; Assn for Creative Change Papers; Science Fiction Writers of America Depository Collection; Dime Novel Club Reprints. Some restrictions. Accepts phone inquiries (513-229-4270). No fee. Hours: 8-midnight (holiday hours vary).

Ward M. Canaday Center

University of Toledo, Toledo, OH 43606; (419) 537-4480. Special collections division of univ library maintains records, manuscripts, and archival materials relevant to univ history and needs. Holdings include library with references on history of Toledo and northwestern OH, and Toledo imprints; univ archives; manuscripts of local historical interest, including mayoral papers, glass industry records, and social historical matters; local maps; photos of univ and Toledo subjects; special collection on women's social history, 1840-1920, focusing on birth control, etiquette, home manuals, other relevant subjects. Collections are non-circulating. Accepts phone inquiries. No fee. Hours: M-F 8-5.

Warder Public Library

P.O. Box 1080, 137 East High St., Springfield, OH 45501; (513) 323-8616.. Library serves needs of Springfield and Clark counties. Collections include strong WWII collection and local history materials. Accepts phone inquiries. No fee. Hours: M-F 9-9, Sa 9-6, Su 1-5.

Warren County Historical Society

P.O. Box 223, 105 S. Broadway, Lebanon, OH 45036; (513) 932-1817. Collects, preserves, and promotes history of Warren County, OH and residents from Ice Age to present time in form of museum, library, and archival collections. Holdings include furniture, vehicles, tools, and other artifacts of southwestern OH; reference library; archives with family, cemetery, bible, tax and census records; large collection of manuscripts, letters, and biographies; township, village, county and cemetery maps from 1800; large photo collection; special collection on Shaker history and culture, including journals, tracts, research publications. Some restrictions. Accepts phone inquiries. Fee. Hours: Tu-Sa 9-4, Su noon-4.

Western Reserve Architectural Historians

2249 Delaware Dr., Cleveland Heights, OH 44112; (216) 229-2427. Membership org meets for lectures on architectural history. Accepts phone inquiries. Hours: call.

Western Reserve Historical Society

10825 East Boulevard, Cleveland, OH 44106; (216) 721-5722. Collects and preserves history of Cleveland and state of Ohio, the Old Northwest Territory, and United States in form of museum, library, and archival collections. Holdings include American furniture from 1770 to 1920, decorative arts collections, costumes, dolls, historical artifacts; extensive library; large collectins of manuscripts, maps, photos, films/videotapes, and genealogical materials; Wallace Hugh Cathcart Collection of Shaker Literature and Manuscripts; William Pendleton Palmer Civil War Collection; Charles Candee Baldwin map collection; Charles King Collection of literature on Costumes; and Lewis and Clark Collection. Accepts phone inquiries. Fee. Hours: Tu-Sa 9-5.

William E. and Ophia D. Smith Library of Regional History

15 S. College Ave., Oxford, OH 45056; (513) 523-3035. Preserves and maintains collection of historical publications and materials on history of southwestern OH from 19th c. Holdings include local, county, and state govt, social and church org records; John Hough James (1800-1881) papers; typescripts of books by William E. and Ophelia D. Smith; photos; census, cemetery, and other genealogical records; personal libraries of Dr. W. E. Smith and Dr. James Rodabaugh; local newspaper archives from 1946. Collection is non-circulating. Accepts phone inquiries. No fee. Hours: M-F 10-noon, 2-5.

William Howard Taft National Historic Site

2038 Auburn Ave., Cincinnati, OH 45219; (513) 684-3267. National Park Service site preserves and presents history and life of President William Howard Taft in form of restored birthplace memorial and museum with artifacts and exhibits. Some restrictions. Accepts phone inquiries. No fee. Hours: call.

Wilmington College

S. A. Watson Library, Pyle Center - Box 1227, Wilmington, OH 45177; (513) 382-6661. College library maintains general, archival, and special collections, with emphasis on study of Quaker religion, and the peace movement. Holdings include records of the Society of Friends (Quakers) in southwest OH from earliest white settlements; college archives from 1870s; family papers; Quaker Collection covering history, faith and practice, testimonies, and concerns; Peace Resources Center, with materials on nuclear war and disarmament, peace activism, Hiroshima and Nagasaki. Accepts phone inquiries. No fee. Hours: academic year: M-Th 8-10, F 8-5, Sa 9-noon, Su 5:30-10; other times: M-F 8-5 (shorter hours for special collections).

Worthington Public Library

Documents Division, 805 Hartford St., Worthington, OH 43085; (614) 885-3185. Public library maintains selective collections of govt documents, general and historical materials relevant to needs of community. Holdings include special collection on Worthington, OH history. Some restrictions. Accepts phone inquiries (614-885-3138). No fee. Hours: M-Th 9-9, F-Sa 9-6.

Wright State University

Archives and Special Collections, University Library, Dayton, OH 45435; (513) 873-2092.

Univ archives preserves and maintains documents and collections relevent to school and community needs. Holdings include local govt records; univ archives; manuscripts on local aviation and regional history; genealogical materials; Special Collection of late 19th and early 20th c children's literature illustrated by Arthur Rackham. Collections are non-circulating. Accepts phone inquiries. No fee. Hours: M-F 8:30-5, Tu, W eves 7-10, Su 2-5.

Youngstown State University

Special Collections, Maag Library, 410 Wick Ave., Youngstown, OH 44555; (216) 742-3126. Academic research library with special collection of Senator Kirwin's papers, composed of correspondence with constitutents. Materials non-circulating. No fee. Hours: M-Th 7:30-11, F 7:30-5, Sa 9-7, Su 1-10.

Zane Grey Museum/National Road

8850 E. Pike, Norwich, OH 43767; (614) 872-3143. Promotes history of OH with special emphasis on history of National Road and Zane Grey. Library contains limited reference collection and some genealogical materials on Zane and Grey families. Accepts phone inquiries. Fee. Hours: Mar-Apr, Oct-Nov, W-Sa 9:30-5, Sun noon-5; May-Sept, M-Sa 9:30-5, Su noon-5.

Oklahoma

45th Infantry Division Museum

2145 NE 36th St., Oklahoma City, OK 73111; (405) 424-5313. Interest in preservation of Oklahoma military history. Holdings include library, manuscripts, maps, photos, films, and extensive genealogical records. No fee. Hours: Tu-F 9-5; Sa 10-5; Su 1-5.

Army Field Artillery School Library

Morris Swett Library, Morris Hall, Fort Sill, OK 73503; (405) 351-5123. Library holds materials on military history and Southwest exploration and settlement. Holdings cover field artillery, artillery, weapons systems, ammunition, Field Artillery unit histories, Indian Territory, OK history, and materials on Indians of Southwest. Accepts phone inquiries. No fee. Hours: call.

Black Kettle Museum

P.O. Box 252, Cheyenne, OK 73628; (405) 497-3929. Museum commemorates Battle of Washita in which Custer attacked Indians. Collection of Indian artifacts on display. Accepts phone inquiries. No fee. Hours: spring-summer, Tu-Sa 9-5, Su 1-5; fall-winter, W-Sa 9-5, Su 1-5.

Caddo Indian Territory Museum and Library

P.O. Box 274, Caddo, OK 74729; (405) 367-2580. Displays historic Caddo artifacts in museum, library, and archives. Holdings include manuscripts, maps, photos, and films/videotapes. Accepts phone inquiries. No fee. Hours: M, W, F, Sa 8-noon, 12:30-3; Tu, Th 8-noon; Su all day.

Center of the American Indian

Kirkpatrick Center Museum Complex, 2100 Northeast 52nd, Oklahoma City, OK 73111; (405) 427-5228. Promotes, preserves, and exhibits art and culture of Native Americans. Museum displays Native American paintings from 1950, Deupree collection of cradleboards from nearly every cultural area in US, and general ethnographic collections. Library has books and periodicals, as well as collection of videotapes of Native American singing and dancing. Accepts phone inquiries. Fee. Hours: M-F 9-5, Sa 9-6, Su noon-6.

Central State University Library

Political and Social Issues Library, 100 North University Drive, Edmund, OK 73034; (405) 341-2980. Library collects and preserves materials from left- and right-wing political and social movements from 1960s-70s. Holdings cover Native peoples orgs, anti-nuclear groups, and alternative lifestyle advocates. Accepts phone inquiries. Hours: call.

Cherokee National Historical Society

P.O. Box 515, Willis Rd., Tahlequah, OK 74465; (918) 456-6007. Collects and preserves Cherokee history. Museum exhibits prehistoric artifacts. Library has research materials. Archives holds modern Cherokee nation records, manuscripts, maps of Cherokee area and allotments, photos from 1850, films/videotapes related to Cherokees, oral histories, genealogical materials, and recordings of dance and gospel music. Special collections include materials of W.W. Keeler (prin Chief from 1949-75), and Earl Boyd Pierce (General Counsel to Cherokee Nation). Accepts phone inquiries. Fee. Hours: museum, M-Sa 10-5; Su 1-5; extended summer hours.

Chickasaw Council House Historic Site

Courthouse Square, P.O. Box 717, Tishomingo, OK 73460; (405) 371-3351. Emphasizes high culture of Chickasaw from 1540. Holdings include small library and collection of maps. Includes personal items of Chickasaw Governor Douglas H. Johnston and OK Governor William H. (Alfalfa Bill) Murray. Accepts phone inquiries. No fee. Hours: Tu-F 9-5; Sa-Su 2-5.

East Central Oklahoma State University

Linscheid Library, Ada, OK 74820; (405) 332-8000, ext. 371. Academic research library with strengths in Indian and OK history. Other holdings include Martin Hauan collection of political advertising, Judge Johnson Tal Crawford Nuremberg Trial papers, maps, genealogical materials, and materials on War of the Rebellion and early explorations. Materials non-circulating. Accepts phone inquiries. No fee. Hours: M-Th 8-10, F 8-5, Su 2-10.

Five Civilized Tribes Museum

Agency Hill, Honor Heights Dr., Muskogee, OK 74401; (918) 683-1701. Preserves history and culture of Cherokee, Creek, Chickasaw, Choctaw, and Seminole. Museum exhibits artifacts of five tribes. Collections of maps, photos, and genealogical records are available. Accepts phone inquiries. Fee. Hours: M-Sa 10-5, Su 1-5,

Fort Washita

Star Rte. 213, Durant, OK 74701; 405-924-6502. Interest in frontier and military history, 1842-65. Holdings include museum, library, archives, and genealogical records. Answers phone inquiries. No fee. Hours: M-F 9-5; Sa-Su 2-5.

Healdton Oil Museum

Oklahoma Historical Society, 315 E. Main St.,

Healdton, OK 73438; 405-229-0317. Interest in early oil discovery and growth of industry. Museum documents artifacts of OK and northern TX oil fields during boom of early 20th c. Accepts phone inquiries. No fee. Hours: Tu-F 9-5; Sa-Su 2-5.

International Photography Hall of Fame

Kirkpatrick Center Museum Complex, 2100 Northeast 52nd, Oklahoma City, OK 73111; (405) 424-4055. Commemorates past and helps shape future of photography through holdings in museum and library. Collections include magazines and books from 1900; photo portraits, ads, commercials, landscapes, and journalism from 1860; videotapes; and collections from several famous photographers. Accepts phone inquiries. Fee. Hours: M-Sa 9-6, Su noon-6.

Jim Thorpe Home

706 E. Boston, Yale, OK 74085; (918) 387-2815. Interprets life of Jim Thorpe and preserves OK history. Museum housed in Thorpe's home from 1917-23. Archives contain clippings on Thorpe's achievements and life from newspapers and magazines. Some cover his Indian school background. Other holdings include photos and 27 medals Thorpe won while at Carlisle Indian School. Some restrictions. Accepts phone inquiries. No fee. Hours: F 9-5, Sa-Su 2-5.

Lutie Coal Miner's Museum

P.O. Box 393, Rte. 2, Wilburton, OK 74578; (918) 465-2216. Preserves regional mining heritage through museum exhibits on Hailey OK Coal Co. from 1901. Holdings include manuscripts, maps, and photos. Accepts phone inquiries. No fee. Hours: 9-noon.

Museum of Higher Education in Oklahoma

Oklahoma State University, Old Central at University & Knoblock, Stillwater, OK 74078; (405) 624-3220. Museum in development; seeks to represent all higher education in OK from 1880. Library has some texts and materials of Univ from 1901. Photo collection covers univ and Bacone College, earliest college in Indian Territory. Accepts phone inquiries. Donations accepted. Hours: Tu-F 9-5, Sa-Su 2-5.

Museum of the Cherokee Strip

507 S. 4th St., Enid, OK 73701; (405) 237-1907. Interest in local history from 1830, especially related to Land Run of 1893. Holdings include small reference library on Oklahoma history, Western history, and American Indians; maps, photos, films, and videotapes; genealogical records; and special collection of Skylab astronaut Owen K. Garriott. Answers phone inquiries. No fee. Hours: Tu-F 9-5; Sa-Su 2-5.

Museum of the Great Plains

Institute of Great Plains, P.O. Box 68, 601 Ferris, Lawton, OK 73502; (405) 353-5675. Researches and exhibits prehistory, history, and natural history of North American Great Plains. Museum exhibits artifacts from numerous excavations from 1960, dealing with regional settlement. Library has large reference collection on Great Plains and Midwest, including hardware and agriculture catalogs from 1880-1930. Archives hold documents on settlements of southwestern OK and north TX. Collections also include maps; photos of Plains Indians, settlers, and OK and TX; and original Comanche County newspapers and records from 1901-70. Hours: call.

National Cowboy Hall of Fame and Western Heritage Center

1700 NE 63rd St., Oklahoma City, OK 73111; (405) 478-2250. Preserves history, heritage, and culture of American West with emphasis on cowboys. Museum, library, and archives hold photos of rodeos, and films/videotapes with western themes. Materials non-circulating. Accepts phone inquiries; prefers mail inquiries. Fee. Hours: summer, 8:30-6; Sept-May 9-5.

National Hall of Fame for Famous American Indians

P.O. Box 548, Anadarko, OK 73005; (405) 247-3331. Provides info and displays to help education about Indians. Museum houses busts, picture, and sculptures of Indians. Accepts phone inquiries. No fee. Hours: M-Sa 9-5, Su 1-5.

National Softball Hall of Fame and Museum

2801 N.E. 50th St., Oklahoma City, OK 73111; (405) 424-5266. Chronicles history of softball.

Includes museum and library. Answers phone inquiries. Admission fee. Hours: M-F 9-4:30; Sa 10-4; Su 1-4.

National Wrestling Hall of Fame

405 W. Hall of Fame Ave., Stillwater, OK 74075; (405) 377-5242. Preserves history of amateur wrestling. Includes library, museum, photos, and film/videotape collection. Large collection of plaques from national and international wrestling champions. Accepts phone inquiries. No fee. Hours: M-F 9-4.

Ninety-Nines Library

P.O. Box 59964, Will Rogers Airport, Oklahoma City, OK 73159. Women's aviation resource center holds materials from first female aviatrix, Harriet Quinley, and Matilda Morant through aviation history. Extensive library materials, periodicals, and catalogs available.

No Man's Land Historical Society and Museum

P.O. Box 278, Sewell St., Goodwell, OK 73939; (405) 349-2670. Collects, preserves, classifies, and exhibits materials on OK Panhandle and surrounding region with emphasis on Dust Bowl. Museum documents history, anthropology, art, geology, and art of No Man's Land. Library and archives hold materials on Dust Bowl. Collections include manuscripts, maps, photos, oral histories, and genealogical materials. Special collections include William Baker Archaeological Collection. Materials for in-house use only. Accepts phone inquiries. No fee. Hours: Tu-F 9-5, Sa-Su 1-5.

Northwestern Oklahoma State University

Documents Division, J.W. Martin Library, Alva, OK 73717; (405) 327-1700. Academic research library holds federal and state documents in depository collection, as well as maps. Accepts phone inquiries. No fee. Hours: M-Th 7:55-10, F 7:55-5, Su 6-10.

Oklahoma Baptist University Library

500 W. University, Shawnee, OK 74801; (405) 275-2850. Academic research library materials concentrate on history of OK Baptists and Baptist denomination. Special collections include

manuscripts from Baptist leader Hobbes, Stover Routh collection, and Baptist Resource Center materials. Accepts phone inquiries. No fee. Hours: M-Th 8-11, F 8-9, Sa 10-9, Su 2-5 and 8-11.

Oklahoma Department of Libraries

Documents Division, 200 NE 18th St., Oklahoma City, OK 73105; (405) 521-2502. Serves needs of OK state govt and public libraries. Depository collects US documents and American State papers from 1893. Materials circulate to state employees only. Accepts phone inquiries. No fee. Hours: M-F 8-5.

Oklahoma State Museum

2100 N. Lincoln, Historical Bldg., Oklahoma City, OK 73105; (405) 521-2491. Collects, preserves, and exhibits history of OK and Southwest. Museum exhibits artifacts relative to OK history from prehistoric period. Library provides reference materials on collections. Archives concentrate on OK Indians and settlers from 1820, with collections of manuscripts, maps of Indian territory, photos from 1880s, films/videotapes, oral histories, genealogical records from Colonial period, and archives of Five Civilized Tribes (Chickasaw, Cherokee, Choctaw, Creek, and Seminole). Materials for in-house use only. Accepts phone inquiries. No fee. Hours: M-Sa 8-5.

Oklahoma Territorial Museum

402 East Oklahoma Ave., Guthrie, OK 73044; (405) 282-1889. Relates history of OK Territory from 1890-1907, and early period of statehood. Exhibits cover OK people, transportation, occupations, law and order, culture, education, and home life, and Carnegie library operation from 1903-70. Archives hold documentary materials, fire insurance maps, photos, films on Plains Indians and early settlement, and genealogical records. Accepts phone inquiries. No fee. Hours: Tu-F 9-5, Sa-Su 2-5.

Osage County Historical Museum

Osage County Historical Society, 700 N. Lynn Ave., Pawhuska, OK 74056; (918) 287-9924. Preserves and displays artifacts and memorabilia of regional interest, and collection of materials from first Boy Scout troop in US. Museum exhibits cover oil industry, Indians, and pioneers in OK. Special collection on first Boy Scout troop of 1909 includes records, papers, and pictures. Other photos available. No fee. Hours: 9-5.

Phillips University

Zollars Memorial Library, University Station, Enid, OK 73701; (405) 237-4444. Preserves regional and Native American history through oral history collection. Interviews cover 1893 Cherokee Outlet Land Run, early OK statehood, and Depression. Accepts phone inquiries. No fee. Hours: call.

Pioneer Woman Museum

701 Monument, Ponca City, OK 74604; (405) 765-6108. Perpetuates history of women in OK through museum exhibits of artifacts from pioneer homes from 1893-1920. Other holdings include maps and WKY-TV ftg of 101 Ranch and Marland area. Accepts phone inquiries. Donations accepted. Hours: Nov-Apr, W-Sa 9-5, Su 1-5; May-Oct, Tu-Sa 9-5, Su 1-5.

Plains Indians and Pioneer Historical Foundation

P.O. Box 1167, 2009 Williams Ave. (S. Hwy 270), Woodward, OK 73802; (405) 256-6136. Preserves heritage of region through museum exhibits of Plains Indian artifacts, pioneer and farm items, prehistoric artifacts, and materials from everyday Woodward life. Other holdings include extensive photos and textile collection composed of quilts and fashions from 1870-1970. Some restrictions on use. Accepts phone inquiries. No fee. Hours: Tu-Sa 10-5, Su 1-4.

Political Commercial Archive

University of Oklahoma, Political Communications Center, Department of Communications, Norman, OK 73019; (405) 325-3111. Preserves and studies political TV and radio advertising, candidates, and issues. Archives hold over 12,000 radio commercials from 1936, and over 33,000 TV commercials from 1950. Accepts phone inquiries. May be restrictions. Fee depends on use. Hours: 9-4:50.

Public Library of Enid and Garfield Counties

P.O. Box 8002, 120 W. Maine, Enid, OK 73702;

(405) 234-6313. Public library with concentration on local history. Holdings include Marquis James first drafts of "The Raven" and "Cherokee Strip," maps, photos of early Enid, films/videotapes, recordings, genealogical records, John Wilkes Booth legend, Marquis James boyhood diary, and Laura Crews doll collection. Reference materials non-circulating. Accepts phone inquiries. No fee. Hours: M-Th 9-9, F-Sa 9-6.

Seminole Nation Museum

Box 1532, 524 S. Wewoke, Wewoka, OK 74884; (405) 257-5580. Preserves history of Seminole Indians and their art. Museum exhibits cover Seminoles from FL to OK dating to pioneer era. Library holds documentation of Seminole history. Map collection of Seminole Indian allotments. Photos of Indian games, homes, churches, and individuals. Accepts phone inquiries. No fee. Hours: Tu-Su 1-5.

Sequoyah Home Site

Rte. 1, Box 141, Sallisaw, OK 74955; (918) 775-2413. Preserves historic home built by Sequoyah, inventor of Cherokee Syllabary, and interprets history, culture, and political life of Cherokees. Period covers their settlement in East through resettlement in Indian Nation. Holdings include maps, photos, tools, basketry, pottery, and projectiles of Cherokees. Accepts phone inquiries. No fee. Hours: Tu-F 9-5, Sa-Su 2-5.

Southern Nazarene University

Special Collections, Williams Learning Center, 4115 North College, Bethany, OK 73008; (405) 491-6350. Academic research library with collections on local history, church activities, and authors and composers. Archives hold church records. Manuscript collection houses John E. Moore collection of works by authors and composers, limited maps, and Ross E. Hagslip Bible collection. Materials circulate to community on limited basis. Accepts phone inquiries. Fee for community patrons. Hours: M-Th 8:30-11, F 8:30-4, Sa 10-8.

Thomas Gilcrease Institute of American History and Art

1400 Gilcrease Museum Rd., Tulsa, OK 74127; (918) 582-3122. Develops awareness and interest in cultural history of Americas. Museum exhibits American art from 18th c through mid-20th c, including artifacts of Indian cultures. Library holds books, documents, photos, maps, and manuscripts documenting exploration of Americas, and westward expansion. Special strenth in Indian genealogical records. Materials non-circulating. Donations accepted. Hours: M-F 9-noon, 1-5, or by appt.

Tulsa County Historical Society

P.O. Box 27303, 2501 West Newton Ave., Tulsa, OK 74127; (918) 585-5520. Preserves and interprets materials pertaining to Tulsa culture. Museum exhibits period rooms and decorative arts from 1907-21. Library has small collection on Tulsa history and books by Tulsa authors. Archives hold records of social and cultural orgs and petroleum industry, photos, 16mm film footage from mid-1950s-70s from local TV news, oral histories, and special collections from syndicated cartoonist Clarence Allen and syndicated columnist Glen Condon. Accepts phone inquiries. No fee. Hours: archives by appt only, Tu-Sa 11-4, Su 1-4.

University of Oklahoma

Health Sciences Center, Library, P.O. Box 26901, 1000 Stanton L. Young Blvd., Oklahoma City, OK 73190; (405) 271-4000. Maintains small collection of materials on health and well-being of American Indians historically and currently. Accepts phone inquiries. Hours: call.

Western Trail Museum

2229 Gary Freeway, Clinton, OK 73601; (405) 323-1020. Preserves history and culture of OK, with emphasis on prehistory and territorial settlement period. Museum exhibits cover local history, and include photos of early residents and area, dolls, Indian artifacts, medical equipment, household furniture, farming equipment, and flags of OK Territory. Accepts phone inquiries. Donations accepted. Hours: Apr-Oct, Tu-Sa 9-5, Su 1-5; Nov-Mar W-Sa 9-5, Su 1-5.

Will Rogers Memorial

Will Rogers Blvd., P.O. Box 157, Claremore, OK 74018; (918) 341-0719. Sustains and perpetuates name and spirit of Will Rogers. Museum exhibits Rogers's personal memorabilia and recordings. Library holds books by and on Rogers, his contemporaries, and OK and Cherokee history from 1800-1935. Archives retain many personal scrapbooks, postcard collection, magazine articles by and on Rogers from 1912, theatre programs and contracts, legal and business correspondence, large collection of photos of Rogers and contemporaries, collection of films featuring Rogers, home movies and outtakes, radio broadcasts and speeches, and small genealogical collection. Accepts phone inquiries. No fee. Hours: serious researchers by appt only, 8-5.

Woolaroc Museum

Rte. 3, State Hwy 123, Bartlesville, OK 74003; (918) 336-0307. Library has reference materials on Western art, ethnology, history, and anthropology. Special permission required for library use. Accepts phone inquiries. Fee. Hours: Tu-Su 10-5.

Oregon

American Advertising Museum

9 NW Second, Portland, OR 97209; (503) 226-0000. Collects, preserves, interprets, and displays history of American advertising industry in form of museum exhibits, library, and archival collections. Holdings include advertising artifacts, including historic examples of print, radio, and television ads, and original advertising art; interpretive exhibits on historical and social impact and development of advertising; small library with research materials on advertising history; archives of early print advertising; collection of specialty advertising items. Library and archives for primarily for staff use. Accepts phone inquiries. Fee. Hours: W-F 11-5, Sa-Su noon-5.

Aurora Colony Ox Barn Museum

P.O. Box 202, Aurora, OR 97002; (503) 678-5754. Collects, preserves, and displays history of Aurora Colony in form of museum complex, library, and research collections. Holdings include artifacts, exhibits, and audiovisual presentation on Aurora Colony life and history; library with letters, manuscripts and papers of colony members; photos of colony and members; col-

ony family files. Visitation by guided tour only. Accepts phone inquiries. Fee for tour. Hours: W-Sa 10-4:30, Su 1-4:30.

Blue Mountain Community College Library

Documents Division, 2411 NW Carden, Pendleton, OR 97801; (503) 276-1260. Provides research and educational support to college and local residents by collecting Oregon state documents. No fee. Hours: M-Th 7:30-10, F 7:30-5, Su 2-6.

Burrows House and Log Cabin Museum

Oregon Historical Society, 545 SW Ninth St., Newport, OR 97365; (503) 265-7509. Collects and preserves Lincoln County historic artifacts, including exhibits demonstrating maritime, logging, and farming from 1870s-1930s. Pioneer and Indian life also documented through photo and manuscript collections. Some maps from early exploration. Accepts phone inquiries. No fee. Hours: June-Sept 10-5, Oct-May 11-4.

Central Oregon Community College Library

2600 Northwest College Way, Bend, OR 97701; (503) 385-5512. Small selective govt document depository. Special collection on Oregon history, particularly in region east of Cascades. Materials circulate to district residents; in-house use for others. Accepts phone inquiries. No fee. Hours: M-Th 8-9, F 8-4, Su 3-9.

City of Portland Records Division

9360 N. Columbia Blvd., Portland, OR 97202; (503) 248-4631. Houses and preserves the official records of Portland from 1851; maps of Portland area from 1865; and photos taken for city management functions from late 19th c. Accepts phone inquiries. No fee. Hours: M-F 8-5.

Columbia River Maritime Museum

1792 Marine Dr., Astoria, OR 97103; (503) 325-2323. Collects, preserves, and exhibits maritime heritage of Pacific Northwest in museum, library, and archive. Holdings on exploration, discovery, and development of Columbia River and coastal region. Large photo collection available. Library, archives, and photos available by appt only. Accept phone inquiries. Fee. Hours: 9:30-5.

Deschutes County Historical Society

P.O. Box 5252, 129 NW Idaho, Bend, OR 97708; (503) 389-1813. Preserves and documents history of county and supporting timber industry. Museum, library, and archives hold maps of homesteads, railroads and timber claims; oral history recordings; genealogical records; and exhibitions on local logging operations. Accepts phone inquiries. No fee. Hours: W-Sa 1-4:30.

Douglas County Museum of History and Natural History

P.O. Box 1550, 1299 SW Medford, Roseburg, OR 97470; (503) 440-4507. Collects, preserves, and exhibits Douglas County history through museum and library collections. Holdings range from manuscripts, maps, and cataloged photo collection to oral history interviews and genealogical records. Accepts phone inquiries. No fee. Hours: library Tu-F 10-4; museum Tu-Sa 10-4, Su 12-4.

Favell Museum of Western Art and Indian Artifacts

P.O. Box 165, 125 West Main, Klamath Falls, OR 97601; (503) 882-9996. Preserves art and artifacts of Native Americans. Holdings span 12,000 years, and extend to contemporary western art and miniature gun collection. Accepts phone inquiries. Fee. Hours: M-Sa 9:30-5:30.

Finnish-American Historical Society of the West

P.O. Box 5522, Portland, OR 97208. Preserves and publicizes Finnish-American ethnicity and history in western US through curation of museum and small library in Finnish room of Portland State University. Also small collection of Finnish-American 1900-1940 artifacts.

Fort Clatsop National Memorial

National Park Service, Rte. 3, Box 604-FC, Astoria, OR 97103; (503) 861-2471. Winter encampment for Lewis & Clark expedition 1805-06. Limited exhibits and replications. Accepts phone inquiries. Fee in summer; no fee in fall and winter. Hours: summer 8-6; winter 8-5.

Historic Preservation League of Oregon

P.O. Box 40053, 26 NW Second St., Portland, OR 97240; (503) 243-1923. Promotes, preserves, and protects OR cultural heritage of Portland and county history materials. Limited archival materials; photos and slides of OR architecture; and videotapes on Oregon heritage. Accepts phone inquiries. No fee. Hours: 9-5.

Jewish Historical Society of Oregon

6651 SW Capitol Hwy, Portland, OR 97219; (503) 246-9844. Maintains records and archives of Jewish community of Portland and OR. Collections include some records of communal institutions, small collections of photos, and oral history tapes and transcripts. Accepts phone inquiries. No fee. Hours: by appt only.

Lewis and Clark College

Aubrey Watzek Library, 615 SW Palatine Hill Road, Portland, OR 97219; (503) 293-2764. Small academic library maintains general, reference, and historical materials relevant to needs of the school and students. Holdings include Chunard Collection of Lewis and Clark Expedition. Accepts phone inquiries. No fee. Hours: academic year: M-Th 9-5, 7-9:30, F 9-5; summer, M-F 1-5, 7-9:30.

Multnomah County Library

801 SW 10th Ave., Portland, OR 97205; (503) 223-7201. Public library houses OR collection of historical, political, and literary materials on Northwest; John Wilson room of rare books; Rose collection; Lois Steers photo collection of musical performers; and collections of 19th c maps, recreational and informational films, recordings, and genealogical materials. Some materials for in-house use only. Accepts phone inquiries. No fee. Hours: M-Th 10-9, F-Sa 10-5:30, Su 1-5.

Oregon Historical Society

1230 SW Park Ave., Portland, OR 97205; (503) 222-1741. Collects Oregon county history. Library emphasizes maritime exploration and trade, N Pacific and Siberia, Westward expansion, and Indian history; vertical files on state and local topics; manuscripts on pioneer migration, architectural drawings, fur trade, labor movements, arts, and ethnic group activities; mine, railroad, Sanborn Fire Insurance map, and land claim maps from 1879-1965; Land Claims and Indian Affairs records; Pacific NW commercial, industrial, and agricultural photos; and oral histories from WWII female shipyard workers, politicians, Mennonites, others. Film footage of OR news and AK oil exploration. Accepts phone inquiries. No fee. Hours: M-Sa 10-5.

Oregon Lewis and Clark Heritage Foundation

2915 NE 35 Place, Portland, OR 97212; (503) 281-3516. Preserves, studies, and interprets the history and impact of the Lewis and Clark explorations in Oregon area. Accepts phone inquiries (503-222-1741). Hours: call.

Oregon Military Museum

Camp Withycombe, Clackamas, OR 97015; (503) 657-6806. Preserves and displays OR military history through 20th c military memorabilia, vehicles, and artillery, with emphasis on Pacific and Japanese Militaria; library with extensive War Dept publications; archives and photo collection; special collection of research materials on OR Fighter Aces. Accepts phone inquiries. No fee. Hours: M-F 8-4:30, and by appt.

Oregon State Library

State Library Bldg., Salem, OR 97310; (503) 378-4276. Serves state govt and agencies by preserving US and govt documents; WPA manuscripts for OR counties; OR's Bush family papers; historic, topographic, and geographic maps; photos from late 19th c; genealogical collections; and OR vertical file and letter file. Materials non-circulating. Accepts phone inquiries. Fee for research assistance. Hours: M-F 8-5.

Oregon State University Library

Special Collections, Corvallis, OR 97331; (503) 754-2075. Holds large collection of Nobel prize-winning scientist, Linus Pauling, papers and archival material. Holdings include nuclear disarmament petition given to UN, original research notebooks, manuscripts, letters, and film on Pauling. Accepts phone inquiries. No fee. Hours: 8:30-4:30.

Portland State University

Millar Library, 934 SW Harrison, P.O. Box 1151, Portland, OR 97207; (503) 464-3673. Serves student and faculty research needs with collection of regional documents from 1972 and federal documents from 1963, and USGS maps. Materials circulate only to University community. No fee. Hours: M-F 8-10, Sa 10-6, Su 11-6.

Reed College Library

3203 SE Woodstock, Portland, OR 97202; (503) 771-1112. Academic library maintains selective collection of govt documents, general, reference and historical materials relevant to needs of the school and students. Holdings include collection of local historical items; Edward Chambreau and Simeon Reed Papers (early OR pioneers). Accepts phone inquiries. No fee. Hours: M-Th 8 am-2:30 am; F 8 am-midnight; Sa 10 am-midnight; Su 10am-2:30am.

Schminck Memorial Museum

Daughters of the American Revolution, Oregon, 128 S. E. St., Lakeview, OR 97630; (503) 947-3134. Preserves and displays pioneer historical artifacts pertaining to regional culture. Large collection of period costumes, dolls, toys, furniture, tools, quilts, and saddles; library of early 20th c history, poetry, and fiction found in homes; local history photo collection; collection of "Ladies Home Journal" from 1897-1957; some genealogical and obituary records. Materials for in-house use only. Accepts phone inquiries. Fee. Hours: Feb-Nov, Tu-Sa 1-5.

Shaw Historical Library

Oregon Institute of Technology Library, 3201 Campus Drive, Klamath Falls, OR 97601; (503) 882-1276. Preserves history of High Desert Area Land of Lakes. Archives holds Modoc War materials, diaries, emigrant trail papers, and photos. Accepts phone inquiries. No fee. Hours: M-Th 7:30-10, F 7:30-5, Sa 1-5, Su 1-10.

Sherman County Historical Society

2nd and Dewey Sts., Moro, OR 97039; (503) 565-3232. Collects and preserves historic Sherman County artifacts, memorabilia, and records. Museum houses period household items and furnishings; archives of historic records; some diaries and original manuscripts; photos of regional families, towns, and farming practices; genealogical files on early settlers; collection of Sherman County cattle brands; and military museum exhibits. Accepts phone inquiries. No fee. Hours: May-Oct, Tu-Su 10-5.

Southern Oregon Library Archives Department

Southern Oregon Historical Society, P.O. Box 480, 206 N. 5th St., Jacksonville, OR 97530; (503) 899-1847. Preserves history of Jackson County, S Oregon, regional Native American and Chinese communities. Jacksonville Museum exhibits costume, industry, decorative arts, mining, and railroading; Chappell-Swedenburg House Museum holds research materials documenting pioneer life; Society's research library and archive supports study of Pacific Northwest with manuscript, map, document, and oral history collections; and large Peter Britt photo collection capture pioneer experience. Accepts phone inquiries. Fee for staff research. Hours: Tu-F 1-5, Sa 10-5; archive M-F 1-5.

Springfield Historical Commission

225 N. 5th St., Springfield, OR 97477; (503) 726-3775. Preserves historic structures and sites of Springfield with small collections of photos and ephemera from 1880s. Holds current photos for Washburne historic district. Accepts phone inquiries. No fee. Hours: M-F 8-5.

Tillamook County Pioneer Museum

2106 2nd St., Tillamook, OR 97141; (503) 842-4553. Collects and preserves Oregon and Tillamook County history. Museum exhibits detail artifacts and industry of region; library and archives house manuscripts, maps, and photos. Some genealogy materials. Special collections on US Naval Lighter-than-Air Station, and Tillamook Indians. Accepts phone inquiries. Fee. Hours: Oct-May, M-Sa 8:30-5, Su 12-5.

University of Oregon Library

Special Collections, Eugene, OR 97403; (503) 686-3070. Academic research library emphasizes political, social, economic, and literary history of 20th c US. Literature collection emphasizes children's literature authors and illustrators; materials of political conservatives and lib-

ertarians; authors of popular Western fiction; and papers of missionaries to Far East. Other holdings include materials from OR political figures, architects, and business; photos; and popular sheet music. Hours: call.

Pennsylvania

Allegheny County Law Library

921 City/County Bldg., Pittsburgh, PA 15219; (412) 355-5353. Public legal library maintains selective collection of govt documents, legal publications and collections relevant to needs of Allegheny County, PA community. Holdings include Anglo-American Law Collection, including legal historical materials from 1500s; road docket petitions of Allegheny County, 1788-1954; collection of papers, maps, and other documents related to the Alaska Boundary Dispute, 1893. Accepts phone inquiries. No fee. Hours: Sept-June, M-F 8:30-5; July-Aug, M-F 8:30-4:30.

Allegheny Portage Railroad National Historic Site

Rt. 22, P.O. Box 247, Cresson, PA 16630; (814) 886-8176. Preserves and interprets history and influence of the Allegheny Portage Railroad, through museum exhibits and research library. Holdings include locomotive models, exhibits, and artifacts relating to the Allegheny Portage Railroad and PA Maineline Canal, 1820-1860; library with historical materials, including National Park Service research and historical reports from 1964; maps, blueprints, and photos relating to railroad, canal, and site. Materials noncirculating. Accepts phone inquiries. No fee. Hours: 8:30-5.

Altoona Area Public Library

1600 Fifth Ave., Altoona, PA 16602; (814) 946-0417. Public library has large collection of photos from PA Railroad Test Plant files from 1885-1968. Subjects include locomotives, cars, and equip. Accepts phone inquiries. No fee. Hours: M-Tu, Th 8:30-9, W, F 8:30-5, Sa 9-5, Su 1-4.

American Canal Sociey

809 Rathton Rd., York, PA 17403; (717) 843-

4035. Promotes use of historic canal resources for research, preservation, restoration, recreation, and parks, and serves as natl clearinghouse of canal info. Has several English canal movies and audio/visual programs and publishes quarterly. Accepts phone inquiries. Hours: call.

American Swedish Historical Museum

1900 Pattison Ave., Philadelphia, PA 19145; (215) 389-1776. Preserves and promotes history of Swedish-Americans through educational programs, museum, library, and archival collections. Holdings include exhibits and artifacts from 1683; research library with materials on Swedish, Scandinavian and early American history; archives with Colonial period materials, and letters and designs of John Ericcson (designer of the USS Monitor); manuscripts, including those of Dr. Amadus Johnson; genealogical records and references, including ship passenger lists and other immigration materials; special collections on Swedish-American art, science, and culture. Accepts phone inquiries. Fee. Hours: Tu-F 10-4, Sa noon-4.

Army Military History Institute

Carlisle Barracks, PA 17013; (717) 245-3611. Institute collects, preserves, and maintains source materials and references on US military history. Holdings include the Hessian Powder Magazine Museum, which preserves the history of Carlisle Barracks; the Omar Bradley Museum on the life of the General; large collection of American unit patches and insignia; US military library collection of WWI personal papers; institutional archives of the US Army War College from 1906; archives of various military and veterans groups; extensive collections of manuscripts, maps, photos, films/videotapes, recordings, and oral histories. Some restrictions. Accepts phone inquiries. No fee. Hours: M-F 8-4:30.

Ashland Athracite Museum

17th and Dine Sts., Ashland, PA 17911; (717) 636-2070. Preserves and displays history of local Anthracite (hard coal) mining industry in form of exhibit and artifacts, including tools, machinery, and photos, depicting miners and mine work. Does not accept phone inquiries. Fee. Hours: M-Sa 9-5, Su noon-5.

Athenaeum of Philadelphia

219 S. 6th St., East Washington Square, Philadelphia, PA 19106; (215) 925-2688. Preserves and maintains research collections relating to the cultural, architectural, and artistic history of Philadelphia and residents. Holdings include museum with 19th c Philadelphia furnishings and decorative arts; library with materials on city's 19th c social, cultural, architectural, and artistic history; archives with materials on architecture and the decorative arts in Philadelphia, late 19th-early 20th c; photos of Philadelphia architecture, late 19th-early 20th c; Ruff Transportation Collection; Sherlockian Collection; Reeve Fox Hunting Collection. Accepts phone inquiries. No fee. Hours: by appt only, M-F 9-5.

Atwater Kent Museum

15 S. 7th St., Philadelphia, PA 19106; (215) 686-3630. Preserves, displays and promotes history of Philadelphia and residents in form of special collections, exhibits, and public programs. Holdings include collections of prints, paintings, ephemera, and other artifacts from 1692; small reference library; small archives relating to history of the museum and its collections; small collections of manuscripts, and maps; large collection of photos of local subjects documenting urban history; Friends Historical Association Collection of artifacts, textiles, documents, and photos of Philadelphia-area Quakers. Accepts phone inquiries. No fee. Hours: Tu-Sa 9:30-4:45.

Automobile Reference Collection

Philadelphia Free Library, Logan Square, Philadelphia, PA 19103; (215) 686-5427. Special collection documents all aspects of automobile heritage and industry. Holdings include shop manuals, instruction books, industry statistics, and materials on environmental dangers and safety. Holdings include many photos and microfilm. Accepts phone inquiries. Hours: call.

Bailey Library

Slippery Rock University, 35 E. Central Loop, Slippery Rock, PA 16057; (412) 794-7243. Academic library maintains selective collection of govt documents and general, reference and historical materials relevant to needs of the school and students. Collections include records from the Pennsylvania Archives, Revolutionary and Civil Wars; materials on Colonial US history; photos; census records, ship lists, biographies, and other genealogical materials; special collection of materials on Japan. Accepts phone inquiries. No fee. Hours: M-F 8-4.

Balch Institute for Ethnic Studies

18 S. Seventh St., Philadelphia, PA 19106; (215) 925-8090. Institute documents and interprets American immigration history and ethnic life in form of educational programs, museum, library, and archival collections. Holdings include immigration artifacts and exhibits; library with materials on ethnic groups from 1789, and immigration history; archives with personal papers of immigrants, research work, and local and national ethnic org records; large collection of photos on ethnic family life; Philadelphia Jewish Archives Center (see that entry); and Scotch-Irish Foundation Library and Archives. Some restrictions. Accepts phone inquiries. No fee. Hours: museum: M-Sa 10-4; library: M-Sa 9-5.

Bob Hoffman Weightlifting Hall of Fame

Box 1707, York, PA 17405; (717) 767-6481. Preserves history of weightlifting and sports-related events and awards. Exhibits include trophies and memorabilia of "Iron Games"; statues and busts of some weightlifting heroes; materials on history of PA amateur softball; and film on weightlifting. Accepts phone inquiries. Hours: M-Sa 10-4.

Boyertown Museum of Historic Vehicles

28 Warwick St., Boyertown, PA 19512; (215) 367-2090. Collects, preserves, studies, and displays historic vehicles built in southeastern PA. Holdings include exhibits of horsedrawn work and pleasure vehicles, bicycles, gasoline, steam and electric cars, and trucks; tools and other vehicular artifacts; small library with materials on museum vehicles; archives with product information, records, and photos of a local vehicle manufacturer. Accepts phone inquiries. Fee. Hours: Tu-F 8-4, Sa-Su 10-2.

Brandywine Battlefield Park

P.O. Box 202, Chadds Ford, PA 19317; (215)

459-3342. Preserves and interprets history of the Revolutionary War Battle of Brandywine in form of museum with military artifacts; historic, furnished houses that served as Washington's Headquarters and Lafayette's Heaquarters; and historic maps of the site and state during the war. Accepts phone inquiries. Fee. Hours: Tu-Sa 9-5, Su noon-5.

Brandywine River Museum

P.O. Box 141, Route 1 at Route 100, Chadds Ford, PA 19317; (215) 388-7601. Collects, preserves, exhibits, and interprets significant artistic and historic objects from region. Restored grist mill museum houses largest collection of Andrew Wyeth, N.C. Wyeth, and Jamie Wyeth paintings. Library has reference materials on American art, exhibition catalogs, and archival materials, as well as photos of collections. Accepts phone inquiries. Fee. Hours: 9:30-4:30.

Bucks County Community College Library

Documents Division, Swamp Rd., Newtown, PA 18940; (215) 968-8013. Academic library maintains selective collection of govt documents, general, reference and historical materials relevant to needs of the school and students. Holdings include Bucks County, PA historical publications, late 17th c-early 20th c; school archives; Tyler Family Collection of WWI posters (located in school's Fine Arts Dept). Accepts phone inquiries. No fee. Hours: academic year: M-Th 8:30-9:30, F-Sa 8:30-8:30, Su 1-6; other times: M-F 8:30-4:30.

Bushy Run Battlefield

Bushy Run Rd., Jeanette, PA 15644; (412) 527-5584. Site preserved as a memorial to location of 1763 battle between Native Americans and British which ended siege of Fort Pitt. Holdings include museum and visitors center with exhibits on Pontiac's War and the Battle of Bushy Run; artifacts from the battle, and from the French and Indian War. Accepts phone inquiries. No fee. Hours: Tu-Sa 9-5, Su noon-5.

Carnegie Library of Pittsburgh

4400 Forbes Ave., Pittsburgh, PA 15213; (412) 622-3175. Library maintains selective collection of govt documents, general and historical materials relevant to needs of community. Holdings include materials on the American fur trade in the Far West, 1832-1842; biographies of mountainmen, and materials on North American Indians; musical history collections; Cruikshank Collection of Americana; Worthington Memorial Library collection of Western Americana; Andrew Carnegie Collection; Isaac Craig Collection; John Neville Papers; George Morgan Papers; Pittsburgh Photographic Library, with B/W photos of local subjects. Accepts phone inquiries. No fee. Hours: M-W, F 9-9, Th, Sa 9-5:30; Su (winter only) 1-5.

Central Council of Polish Organizations of W. Pennsylvania

Hillman Library of University of Pittsburgh, 4291 Stanton Ave., Pittsburgh, PA 15201; (412) 782-2166. Compiles regional Polish historical references, and gathers and researches historical data pertaining to Polish immigrants. Library has materials on immigrants in Pittsburgh area, manuscripts on Pittsburgh's role in Polish Army formation, materials on Polish pioneers Anthony Sadowski, Marie Sklodowski Curie, and Ignacy Jan Paderewski, photos, and some films and videotapes. Accepts phone inquiries. No fee. Hours: 5-7.

Chester County Historical Society

225 N. High St., West Chester, PA 19380; (215) 692-4800. Collects, preserves, and interprets history of region. Museum has large collection of southeast PA decorative, fine, and industrial arts from 1670, including furniture, paintings, samplers, costumes, ceramics, and tools. Library has materials on local history and genealogy of county and surrounding area. Archives has county civil, criminal, and govt records from 1861-mid-1900s. Other holdings include photos and genealogical records. Special collections of historic American bldgs and site surveys and records of early taverns & inns. Accepts phone inquiries. Fee. Hours: museum/library, Tu 10-4, W 1-8, Th-Sa 10-4; museum only, Su noon-4; archives, M-F 9-4.

Christian C. Sanderson Museum

P.O. Box 153, Rt. 100, Chadds Ford, PA 19317; (215) 388-6545. Preserves eclectic collections of Americana, art and artifacts gathered by Christian C. Sanderson. Holdings include artifacts from the Civil and World Wars, family items, commemorative plates, bottles, china, oddities, numerous early Wyeth paintings and drawings, and photos taken by Sanderson, 1905-1965. Accepts phone inquiries. Donations accepted. Hours: call.

Cigna Museum and Art Collection

1600 Arch St., Philadelphia, PA 19103; (215) 523-4894. Preserves and interprets historical artifact related to CIGNA Corp, firefighting, maritime history, and American fine arts. Library holds secondary materials on museum holdings listed above, manuscripts from 19th c volunteer firefighting in Phila, 17th-19th c maps, oral history recordings. Accepts phone inquiries. No fee. Hours: research by appt only, M-F 9-5.

Civil War Library and Museum

1805 Pine St., Philadelphia, PA 19103; (215) 735-8196. Museum and library preserves and promotes study of Civil War history in form of military memorabilia, reference library, manuscripts, photos, and genealogical records. Collections are non-circulating. Accepts phone inquiries. Fee. Hours: M-F 10-4.

Clearfield County Historical Society

104 E. Pine St., Clearfield, PA 16830; (814) 765-6125. Preserves history of county through holdings in museum, library, and archives. Collections include maps, photos, genealogical records, and original manuscripts of composer George Rosencrans. Accepts phone inquiries. No fee. Hours: May-Oct, Th-Su 1:30-4:30.

Colonial Philadelphia Historical Society

292 St. James Place, Philadelphia, PA 19106. Society preserves and promotes Philadelphia's Colonial heritage through preservation projects and awards programs. Does not accept phone inquiries.

Conservation Center for Art and Historic Artifacts

264 S. 23rd St., Philadelphia, PA 19103; (215) 545-0613. Non-profit corporation provides conservation and preservation services to institutions and individuals. Accepts phone inquiries.

Fee for services. Hours: M-F 9-5.

Contemporary Culture Collection

Temple University, Samuel Paley Library, Philadelphia, PA 19122; (215) 787-8260. Collection consists of alternative and underground press materials from 1960, including social and political criticism and small press publications. Holdings include archives of Committee of Small Magazine Editors and Publishers, Liberation News Service materials, feminist papers, military and high school papers, and Third World and gay papers. Groups range from anti-communist to white supremicist and from libertarian and anti-racist. Some recordings, poster, broadsides, manuscripts, and pamphlets available. Accepts phone inquiries. No fee. Hours: call.

Crawford Historical Society

848 N. Main St., Meadville, PA 16335; (814) 724-6080. Collects, preserves, and promotes history of Crawford County, PA and residents in form of historic house museum, library, and archival collections. Holdings include Baldwin-Reynolds House Museum, 1844, built by Henry Baldwin, congressman and US Supreme Court associate justice; library with publications and materials relating to local history, with emphasis on 19th c; archives with manuscripts, records, photos,and maps; small collection of video and audio tapes; extensive collection of genealogical records, with emphasis on Trapani and Pratt families. Some restrictions. Accepts phone inquiries. No fee. Hours: M, W-F 1-5, Tu 4-8, Sa 10-2.

Cumberland County Historical Society

Hamilton County Library Association, 21 N. Pitt St., P.O. Bix 626, Carlisle, PA 17013; (717) 249-7610. Collects, preserves, and promotes history of Cumberland County, PA and residents in form of museum, library, and archival collections. Holdings include displays of decorative arts, domestic artifacts, tools and equipment, folk art, military relics, and other local historical items; artifacts and photos of Carlisle Indian School; library with historical and genealogical materials; archives with historical references and materials; manuscripts from 18th c; maps; large collection of 19th glass-plate negatives; Schim-

mel Collection. Archives non-circulating. Accepts phone inquiries. No fee. Hours: M 7-9, Tu-F 1-4.

Daniel Boone Homestead

R.D. 2, Box 162, Birdsboro, PA 19508; (215) 582-4900. Historic site interprets Boone family and early settlement of Berks County from 1730-1808. Museum consists of seven 18th c structures with collections of rural furniture from 18th c PA, tools, blacksmithing tools, and domestic objects. Library has secondary reference mateials on PA history and decorative arts, Boone family genealogies and biographies. Accepts phone inquiries. Fee. Hours: Tu-Sa 9-5, Su noon-5.

Dauphin County Historical Society

219 S. Front St., Harrisburg, PA 17104; (717) 233-3462. Collects, preserves, and promotes history of Dauphin County and residents through museum, library, and archival collections. Holdings include exhibits of Dauphin County decorative arts and artifacts; library with genealogical and local historical materials; archives with materials on Dauphin County, and emphasis on Harrisburg, PA; manuscripts of early settlers; local historical maps, photos, films/videotapes, oral history tapes, and genealogical records. Accepts phone inquiries. Fee. Hours: museum: M-F noon-4; library: M-Th 1-4; office: M-F 9-5.

Dickinson College Archives

Boyd Lee Spahr Library, Carlisle, PA 17013; (717) 245-1399. Academic research library holds non-current records of college and special manuscript collections. Library has materials on travel, missionaries, and missionary histories. Archives contains records of Dickinson College and Evangelical United Brethren Church. Manuscript collection has papers of James Buchanan, Justic Roger Taney, Marianne Moore, John Drinkwater, and Robert Bridges. Accepts phone inquiries. No fee. Hours: M-F 8-4.

Drake Well Museum

RD 3, Titusville, PA 16354; (814) 827-2797. Explains history of petroleum industry in PA by collecting objects, documentary material, and photos related to industry in Titusville area and elsewhere. Museum exhibits working well models, tools and artifacts of early oil industry, lamps, tank cars, and standard rig. Library has reference materials on oil companies and oil history; manuscript collections from oil companies and individuals related to business, and large photo collection on people and areas involved in oil industry. Accepts phone inquiries. Fee. Hours: M-Sa 9-5, Su noon-5.

Dwight D. Eisenhower National Historic Site

Gettysburg, PA 17325; (717) 334-1124. Interprets life and work of Dwight Eisenhower by preserving his presidential and retirement home and exhibits on his life during that period. Holdings include maps, photos from 1950-79, oral histories with family and associates relating to Eisenhowers at Gettysburg. Some restrictions. Accepts phone inquiries. Fee. Hours: by appt only, M-F 9-5.

East Stroudsburg University

Documents Division, Kemp Library, Smith & Normal Sts., East Stroudsburg, PA 18301; (717) 424-3150. Academic library maintains selective collection of govt documents, and general, reference and historical materials relevant to needs of the school and students. Holdings include US govt documents from 1966; Parliamentary Papers, 1820-1900. Some restrictions. Accepts phone inquiries. No fee. Hours: academic year only, M-Th 8-11, F 8-5, Sa 9-4, Su 2-10.

Edgar Allan Poe National Historic Site

532 N. 7th St., Philadelphia, PA 19123; (215) 597-8780. Historic site preserves house, and history of life and works of Edgar Allen Poe. Small library and reading room contain photos and present slide show. Poe manuscripts held in manuscript division of Philadelphia Free Library. Accepts phone inquiries. No fee. Hours: 9-5.

Erie County Historical Society

417 State St., Erie, PA 16501; (814) 454-1813. Promotes interest in county history. Museum exhibits county tools and equip, architecture, 1840-80 decorative arts, and changes in shore of Lake Erie. Library covers history of west PA, Lake Erie region, genealogy, and historic preser-

vation. Archives hold records of county history, Nagle Steam Engine & Boiler Works, Erie Academy, PA Population Co., Judah Colt land patents, WPA transcripts, Irving Literary Institute, Josiah Kellogg papers, composer Harry Burleigh, Reed collection on railroad and canals, Koehler/Erie Brewing Co., and others. Many maps, photos, films/videotapes, and genealogy records available. Accepts phone inquiries. Fee. Hours: Tu-F 9-4, Sa 1-4.

Erie Historical Museum and Planetarium

356 W. 6th St., Erie, PA 16507; (814) 453-5811. Collects, preserves, and promotes history of Erie, PA and residents in form of decorative Victorian arts mansion housing exhibits and archival collections. Holdings include local industrial, military, social, and historical artifacts and furnishings; archives with letters, documents, deeds and ledgers relating to local history; maps of Presque Isle and Erie County; photos; collection of Moses Billings, local painter; Marx Toys (local business) collection. Accepts phone inquiries. Fee. Hours: Sept-May, Tu-Su 1-5; June-Aug, Tu-F 10-5, Sa-Su 1-5.

Federalism Study Center

Temple University, Gladfelter Hall, 10th Floor, Philadelphia, PA 19122; (215) 787-1480. Promotes research of American federalism and intergovernmental relations, comparative federal systems, and political culture. Maintains archives of American and Comparative Federalism, which contains research collections, public documents, survey data, interviews, historical data, and national, state, and local files. Org publishes regularly, and holds seminars and conferences. Accepts phone inquiries. No fee. Hours: call.

Fort Hunter Mansion and Park

5300 N. Front St., Harrisburg, PA 17110; (717) 599-5751. Historic country house museum preserves and interprets 19th c life and culture through period furnishings, artifacts, and archival collections. Holdings include artifacts of the Reily Family; archives of personal and business papers of local figures; extensive collection of toys, 1860-1900; collection of women's costumes and clothing articles, 1860s-1930s. Accepts phone inquiries. Fee. Hours: May-Nov,

Edgar Allan Poe, from the Edgar Allan Poe National Historic Site.

Tu-Sa 10-4:30, Su noon-4:30; Dec, Tu-Su noon-7.

Fort Ligonier Association

S. Market St., Ligonier, PA 15658; (412) 238-9701. Interprets history of Ft Ligonier and French and Indian War. Museum exhibits Ft Ligonier archaeology, and 18th c fine arts, graphics, and film. Library contains reference materials on museum holdings. Accepts phone inquiries. Fee. Hours: Apr-Oct, 9-5.

Fort Necessity National Battlefield

National Pike, RD 2, Box 528, Farmington, PA 15437; (412) 329-5512. Park commemorates history of the events surrounding the start of the French and Indian War in 1754. Holdings include Visitor Center with displays on the Battle of Ft Necessity; Mount Washington Tavern, a restored 19th c establishment that served travellers on the National Road, 1820s-1850s; library with materials on the French and Indian War and the early Western expansion; films/videotapes relating to the French and Indian War and George Washington. Accepts phone inquiries. Fee. Hours: park: daylight hours; visitor center: 10:30-5.

Friends Historical Library of Swarthmore College

Swarthmore College, Swarthmore, PA 19081; (215) 328-8496. Academic research library has large collection on history and philosophy of Society of Friends. Collection covers Quaker contributions to literature, science, business, education, govt, peace movement, Indian rights, women's rights, and abolition of slavery. Holdings include largest collection of Quaker meeting archives, papers of Quaker leaders, and minutes of meeting in New England, NY, NC, IN, and UK. Most materials non-circulating. Accepts phone inquiries. No fee. Hours: Sept-July, M-F 8:30-4:30, Sa 9-noon when classes in session.

German Society of Pennsylvania

611 Spring Garden St., Philadelphia, PA 19123; (215) 339-5376. Promotes understanding of German history and contemporary culture abroad and in US. Library covers German classic literature, history, politics, travel books, cooking, and art. Archives has special collection of German-Americana; maps from late 19th and early 20th c; recordings of museum, and early passenger lists from 18th c. Materials for in-house use only. Accepts phone inquiries. No fee. Hours: W-Th 10-5, Sa 10-4.

Germantown Historical Society

5214 Germantown Ave., Philadelphia, PA 19144; (215) 844-0514. Collects, preserves, and promotes history of Germantown, PA and residents in form of museum, library, and archival collections. Holdings include local historical artifacts and exhibits dating from Colonial times; library with materials and publications on Germantown and Philadelphia, PA history; archives with records of local businesses and institutions; collection of personal papers, letters, deeds, and other local historical documents; local plat maps; large collection of photos and glass negatives; genealogical records; collection of Sower & Billinger press imprints. Accepts phone inquiries. Fee. Hours: Tu-Th 10-4, Su 1-5.

Gettysburg National Military Park

Gettysburg, PA 17325; (717) 334-1124. Preserves and promotes history of Civil War Battle of Gettysburg in form of historic battleground site, museum, library, and archival collections. Holdings include exhibits and artifacts relating to the Civil War; library with materials and publications on the battle; archives with materials on battle, and history of the park; maps relating to the battle from 1863; large collection of photos of Gettysburg and battlefield from 1860s. Materials are non-circulating. Accepts phone inquiries. No fee. Hours: M, W, F 9-5.

Greene County Historical Society

Box 127, Old Rte. 21, Waynesburg, PA 15370; (412) 627-3204. Collects and preserves books, papers, records, writings, and relics related to history of Greene County and its region. Museum exhibits rooms furnished in Victorian era. Library has genealogical and local history materials, maps, and photos. Special collections of Indian artifacts, pottery, spinning wheels, W&W Narrow Gauge steam locomotive, and early hand and farming tools. Materials for in-house use only. Accepts phone inquiries. Fee. Hours: 12:30-4:30.

Harmonist Historic and Memorial Association

P.O. Box 524, Main & Mercer Streets, Harmony, PA 16037; (412) 452-7341. Preserves and promotes history Harmony Society's founding, and later Mennonite period, in form of museum, library, and archival collections. Holdings include exhibits and artifacts of local and Harmonist history, 1804-1900; resource library with local historical materials and genealogical records of Harmonist Society, Mennonites; special collection of Harmonist furniture. Accepts phone inquiries. Fee. Hours: June-Sept, Tu-Su; other times by appt.

Haverford College Library

Special Collections and Archives, , Haverford, PA 19041; (215) 896-1161. Academic library maintains special and archival collections on school history, the Quakers, and other areas of interest to the academic community. Holdings include Haverfordiana collection and archive, with artifacts and records on college history; Quaker Collection of rare books and manuscripts; Philips Collection of rare books from Renaissance-era Europe; Lockwood Collection of works by and about Italian Humanists; Christopher Morley Alcove; Maxfield Parrish Alcove; C.C. Morris Cricket collection with historical materials and artifacts from the sport. Some restrictions on use. Accepts phone inquiries. No fee. Hours: M-F 9-12:30, 1:30-4:30 (closes at 4 in summer)

Hershey Museum of American Life

Hershey Park Arena, P.O. Box 170, Hershey, PA 17033; (717) 534-3439. Museum preserves and promotes history of American life and culture through educational programs, exhibits, and artifacts. Holdings include displays and exhibits focussing on 19th c American life, including PA German "house without walls," furniture and other items; Native American galleries; collections of pewter, china, glass, fire equipment, and clocks. Accepts phone inquiries. Fee. Hours: summer, 10-6; winter, 10-5.

Historic Bethlehem

459 Old York Rd., Bethlehem, PA 18018; (215) 691-5300. Restores, interprets, and preserves bldgs and artifacts related to history of Bethlehem. Museum exhibits early Bethlehem trade and industry. Library holds materials on early American trade and history and photos. Accepts phone inquiries. Fee. Hours: call.

Historic Fallsington

4 Yardley Ave., Fallsington, PA 19054; (215) 295-6567. Preserves history of Fallsington and surrounding region through museum, library, and archival collection of manuscripts, maps, and photos from 18th-19th c. Restrictions on use. Accepts phone inquiries. Fee for membership. Hours: by appt.

Historic Gettysburg/Adams County

12 Lincoln Square, Gettysburg, PA 17325; (717) 334-8188. Preserves and promotes historic sites and buildings in Gettysburg and Adams County, PA. Holdings include furnished, original room where Abraham Lincoln wrote the Gettysburg Address; library with materials on Adams County history, and historic preservation and restoration; Adams County archives, including service medals, Civil War items, books, diaries, school records and other items donated by residents; local maps and photos; recorded reminiscences of people who attended Lincoln's delivery of the Gettysburg Address; survey of Adams County historic homes. Accepts phone inquiries. Membership fee. Hours: 9-5.

Historic Pithole City

RD #1, Pleasantville, Titusville, PA 16354; (814) 589-2797. Site preserves history of Pithole City, famed boom town of the early petroleum industry, in form of original buildings and exhibits. Holdings include Visitors Center with model of Pithole city, artifacts, and tools used by early oil well drillers. Accepts phone inquiries. Fee. Hours: summer, M-F 9-5, Su noon-5.

Historical Society of Pennsylvania

1300 Locust St., Philadelphia, PA 19107; (215) 732-6201. Collects, preserves, and interprets all phases and periods of American history by documenting political, commercial, and social history of 18th c US; mid-Atlantic and Southern states prior to Civil War; and Philadelphia from early colonial period. Exhibits include paintings, silver, furniture, costumes, and flags. Archives contain papers of William Penn and his secretary;

first proof of Declaration of Independence; handwritten drafts of Constitution; Washington's papers; large collection of PA maps from 1683; extensive photo collection; genealogical records; and newspapers. Accepts phone inquiries. Fee for non-members. Hours: Tu, Th-F 9-5, W 1-9.

Historical Society of Western Pennsylvania

4338 Bigelow Blvd., Pittsburgh, PA 15213; (412) 681-5533. Collects, preserves, and promotes history of Western PA region and residents in form of museum, library, and archival collections. Holdings include exhibits of regional art, artifacts, glass, furniture, and costumes; library with holdings on regional history and genealogy; archives with records of regional businesses and orgs, family and personal papers, city and county records, newspapers, and photos; extensive collection of maps of Western PA and Eastern North America from 17th c; local photos; taped oral histories of regional ethnic women; holdings of the Western PA Genealogical Society. Accepts phone inquiries. Fee for non-members. Hours: Tu-Sa 9:30-4:30.

History and Heritage Commission

Pittsburgh Section, American Society of Civil Engineers, 221 Fawcett Church Rd., Bridgeville, PA 15017; (412) 355-6645. Documents and recognizes historic civil engineering landmarks in Pittsburgh section. Holdings include small library and small collection of recorded interviews with local engineers Levi Bird Duff and John Laboon. Accepts phone inquiries. No fee. Hours: 9-4:30.

Independence National Historical Park

313 Walnut St., 143 South Third St., Philadelphia, PA 19106; (215) 597-8047. Preserves American history from 1750-1830; Philadelphia and PA history and decorative arts of 18th c. Museum and library holdings include Judge Edwin Lewis papers, insurance survey files from 18th c, Philadelphia directories, Henry Knox papers, Jonathan Trumbull Jr. papers, papers of Continental Congress, Annals of Congress, English Pattern Books, Landreth Seed catalogues, and Elfreth's Alley Assn Records from 1932-36. Collections include large collection of photos,

pamphlets, tapes, records, audiovisual cassettes, and research notecard file. Accepts phone inquiries. No fee. Hours: 8-4:30.

Indiana University of Pennsylvania

Special Collections, University Library, Indiana, PA 15705; (412) 357-3039. Academic library maintains special collections relating to local, school, and Western PA history. Holdings include the Rare Book Collection, including collections of works by Washington Irving, John Greenleaf Whittier, and Norman Mailer; Univ archives with school records from 1875; manuscripts relating to regional history, with emphasis on the bituminous coal industry, and the United Mine Workers of America. Some restrictions. Accepts phone inquiries. No fee. Hours: M-F 9-4:30, Sa-Su 1-4.

James Buchanan Foundation for the Preservation of Wheatland

1120 Marietta Ave., Lancaster, PA 17603; (717) 392-8721. Preserves Wheatland and interprets life of James Buchanan and his family during mid-19th c. Historic museum furnished with artifacts from 1820-60, some belonging to Buchanans. Holdings include American Empire and Victorian furniture, silver, porcelain, paintings, and prints. Accepts phone inquiries. Fee. Hours: 10-4:15.

John Wanamaker Memorial Museum

John Wanamaker Department Store, P.O. Box 7497, Thirteenth and Market St., 8th floor, Philadelphia, PA 19101; (215) 422-2737. Preserves memory of this dept. store entrepreneur through ads, newspaper clippings, personal Wanamaker artifacts, awards and assorted memorabilia. Some notable holdings include chair William Howard Taft seated in during store dedication, hat-fitting mechanism, and Wanamaker's office. Accepts phone inquiries. No fee. Hours: noon-3.

Johnstown Flood Museum Association

304 Washington St., Johnstown, PA 15901; (814) 539-1889. Preserves and portrays history of greater Johnstown area. Museum documents 1889 flood. Library covers successive floods, Cambria Iron Works and steel, and general steel,

The Johnstown Flood's path of destruction, from the Johnstown Flood National Memorial.

iron, and coal industries. Archives contain local corporate and govt records, maps, photos of floods and steel and coal industries, films/video tapes of floods, oral history interviews, flood songs, genealogical records of city founders and early settlers, and special collection on Johnstown area transportation. Accepts phone inquiries. Fee. Hours: Tu-Sa 10:30-4:30, Su 12:30-4:30.

Johnstown Flood National Memorial

P.O. Box 247, Cresson, PA 16630; (814) 886-8176. Memorial preserves history of 1889 Johnstown Flood caused by South Fork Dam collapse. Museum holds flood artifacts and exhibits; reference library; maps of flood area; before and after photos. Accepts phone inquiries (814-495-5718). No fee. Hours: 8:30-5.

Lackawanna Historical Society

232 Monroe Ave., Scranton, PA 18510; (717) 344-3841. Collects, preserves, and promotes history of Lackawanna County area and residents in form of historic house museum, library, and archival collections. Holdings include historic furnished home 1912 Tudor home housing memorabilia, clothing, Catlin Indian prints, and John Willard Raugh breaker paintings; library with materials on local history and genealogy; archives, with Delware Lackawanna and Western Railroad Coal Co record books, letters of George and Joseph Scranton, ephemera, maps, deeds and other documents; photos of local subjects, orgs and industry; Lackawanna Iron and Coal Co records. Accepts phone inquiries. Fee for library. Hours: Tu-F 10-5.

Lake Shore Railway Museum

P.O. Box 571, 31 Wall St., North East, PA 16428; (814) 825-2724. Collects, preserves, and displays historic railway equipment and structures in form of exhibits, library, and archival collections. Holdings include historic locomotive and railway cars; George M. Pullman Collection of Pullman Cars and railroadiana; library with railway publications from 1875; archives with artifacts from 19th c; railroad maps and photos from 1850; General Electric Co Locomotive & Car Equipment Dept promotional films, 1930-60, and photos, 1939-50; Heislar Locomotive Works photos of Cleveland Union Station construction, 1925-30. Non-circulating. Accepts phone inquiries. Donations accepted. Hours: June-Aug, W-Su 1-5, Sept, Sa-Su 1-5.

Lancaster Mennonite Conference Historical Society Library

2215 Millstream Rd., Lancaster, PA 17602; (717) 393-9745. Maintains large collection of Mennonite and Amish books, along with current Mennonite titles, periodicals, and newspapers. Accepts phone inquiries. Hours: call.

Lehigh County Historical Society

Old Courthouse, Hamilton at 5th St., Allentown, PA 18101; (215) 435-4664. (Mailing address: P.O. Box 1548, Allentown, PA 18105) Preserves, and promotes history of Lehigh County, PA and residents. Holdings include social, cultural, and historical artifacts from 18th and 19th c; library with reference materials and ephemera; portion of County of Lehigh Archives; local maps from 18th c; large photo collection; genealogical records from 18th c; oral history recordings; archives and 3-D collections of US Army Ambulance Corps (WWI); Stahl pottery collection; collection of 20th c PA impressionist paintings. Some restrictions. Accepts phone inquiries. Fee for library use by non-members. Hours: office: M-F 9-5; library: M-F 10-noon, 1-4, Sa 1-4.

Liberty Bell Shrine of Allentown

Zion United Church of Christ, 622 Hamilton Mall, Allentown, PA 18101; (215) 435-4232. Shrine memorializes site where the original Liberty Bell and other Philadelphia bells were hidden during the American Revolution. Holdings include museum with 1976 Liberty Bell of Pennsylvania, period uniforms, furniture, clothing and other artifacts; historical mural depicting story of Liberty Bell's preservation. Accepts phone

inquiries. No fee. Hours: noon-4 or by appt.

Library Company of Philadelphia

1314 Locust St., Philadelphia, PA 19107; (215) 546-2465. Historic library, founded in 1731 by Benjamin Franklin and friends, maintains collections of rare books, prints, and artifacts from 18th c. Holdings changing exhibits; materials on American cultural history, 18th c-Civil War era; special collections on American cultural, social, political, and ethnological, and scientific; Philadelphia history collection; archives of library records from 1731; manuscripts and papers of Benjamin Franklin, James Rush, Pierre Eugene Du Simitiere, and Anne Hampton Brewster; local and state maps, 1680-1930s; photos of local subjects, 1840s-1950s. Some restrictions. Accepts phone inquiries. No fee. Hours: M-F 9-4:45.

Lititz Historical Foundation

P.O. Box 65, 137 E. Main St., Lititz, PA 17543; (717) 626-7958. Collects, preserves, and promotes history of Lititz and surrounding Warwick Township and residents in form of historic house and archival collections. Holdings include home of Johannes Mueller, late 18th c local craftsman; collection of local newspapers, manuscripts, and textbooks used in Moravian Church and Beck School for Boys, circa 1830; maps, photos, genealogical records, and local history artifacts. Accepts phone inquiries. Fee. Hours: summer, M-Sa 10-4.

Little League Baseball Museum

P.O. Box 3485, Route 15, South Williamsport, PA 17701; (717) 326-3607. Collects, preserves, and displays history of Little League Baseball in form of museum, library, and archival collections. Holdings include theme rooms with memorabilia, artifacts, and interactive exhibits; pitching and batting areas with TV replays; small reference collection; archives with Little League team rosters, articles and ephemera; extensive collection of photos; Little League World Series footage, and training films; collection of baseballs signed by championship teams; collection of vintage magazines featuring youth and baseball theme on cover. Accepts phone inquiries. Fee. Hours: summer, M-Sa 10-8, Su 1-5; winter, M-Sa 8-5, Su 1-5.

Lycoming County Historical Museum

858 W. 4th St., Williamsport, PA 17701; (717) 326-3326. Preserves history of north central PA through holdings in museum and archives. Exhibits cover lumber, industry, Indians, and pioneers of region. Holdings include early records of county, maps of county and Williamsport, photos from 1910-40, genealogical records, and toy train collection. Accepts phone inquiries. Fee. Hours: Tu-Sa 9:30-4, Su 1:30-4.

Medical College of Pennsylvania

Florence Moore Library of Medicine, 3300 Henry Ave., Philadelphia, PA 19129; (215) 842-6910. Special collection on Women in Medicine offers one of most comprehensive collection of historical materials. Holdings include personal papers of women physicians; oral history interviews from Oral History Project on Women Physicians; American Medical Women's Assn historical collection; American Women's Hospitals Service collection; Kate Campbell Hurd-Mead collection; and large photo collection relating to female physicians. Accepts phone inquiries. Hours: call.

Mennonite Historians of Eastern Pennsylvania

24 Main Street, Soudertown, PA 18964; (215) 723-1700. Preserves and promotes the Anabaptist-Mennonite heritage in southeastern PA in form of museum, library, and archival collections. Holdings include Mennonite artifacts from early 18th-mid-20th c,; library with genealogical materials, 16th-19th c German books, Bibles, historical reference materials; archives with materials from local churches, and organizations from 1900; extensive collection of local, family, and church records and documents; local maps from 1825; photos, films/videotapes; recordings of church services from 1948; Jacob B. Mensch Collection; J.C. Clemmons Collection. Accepts phone inquiries. No fee. Hours: W-Sa 10-4, Su 2-4.

Mercer Museum of Bucks County Historical Society

Pine St., Doylestown, PA 18901; (215) 345-0120. Preserves and displays collection of pre-Industrial American cultural artifacts, with emphasis on tools and craft work. Holdings include extensive collection of early American artifacts and ephmera, particularly items from southeastern PA area; library with materials on local history and genealogy of Bucks County residents, technology, trades and crafts; Bucks County archives of tax and court records, 1683-1950; manuscripts, family and business papers, records of local orgs, and large collection of craftsmen's account books; local maps, photos and genealogical records. Accepts phone inquiries. Fee. Hours: March-Dec, M-Sa 10-5, Su 1-5.

Millersville University

Ganser Library, , Millersville, PA 17551; (717) 872-3624. Academic support library holds special collections on Lancaster County and PA history, Amish and Mennonites, PA dialects, Afro-American arts and letters, Leo Ascher Center for Operetta music, and Richard Gehman papers. Accepts phone inquiries. No fee. Hours: M-Th 8:30-midnight; call for Sa-Su hours.

Moravian Museums and Tours

Gemein Haus, 66 W. Church St., Bethlehem, PA 18018; (215) 867-0173. Preserves and demonstrates history, culture, and industry of Moravian Church society in Bethlehem, PA. Holdings include historic building museum with furnishings, decorative arts, and church objects from 1741; artifacts from mission fields around the world; small collection of 19th c manuscripts relating to Bethlehem Female Seminary; 19th c local maps; photos of local subjects former 19th c. Accepts phone inquiries. Fee. Hours: museum: Tu-Sa 1-4; tours: M-Sa 9-4, by appt.; office: 9-1.

Moravian Pottery and Tile Works

130 Swamp Rd., Doylestown, PA 18901; (215) 345-6722. Preserves, collects, and interprets structure, equip, and ceramics of Moravian Pottery and Tile Works. Museum exhibits working early 20th c arts and crafts tile factory, with displays of manufacturing tools and equip. Accepts phone inquiries. Fee. Hours: 10-5.

Morton Homestead

100 Lincoln Ave., Prospect Park, PA 19076; (215) 583-7221. Preserved 17th c log home houses local historical artifacts and collections

relating to the New Sweden colonial experience and 17th c PA. Holdings include period rooms, furnishings and artifacts; photos of Morris Homestead neighborhood; genealogical records of Morton Mortenson, New Sweden colonist, and his great grandson, John Morton, signer of the Declaration of Independence. Accepts phone inquiries. Fee. Hours: June-Aug W-Sa 10-4, Su noon-4; March-May, Sept-Dec, Sa 10-4, Su noon-4.

National Archives— Philadelphia Branch

9th and Market St., Philadelphia, PA 19107; (215) 597-3000. Branch of the Natl Archives and Records Administration preserves and promotes US history and archival research through a collection of federal and eastern US-related documents and records, and educational programs. Holdings include records from federal agencies (mainly legal and military) in PA, DE, MD, VA, and WV; Census records, 1790-1910; Civil War records, 1861-1865; Revolutionary War records, 1775-1783; passenger list indexes for vessels which arrived in Ports of Philadelphia, 1800-1948, and Baltimore, 1820-1952; naturalization petitions, 1795-1968. Some restrictions apply. Accepts phone inquiries. No fee. Hours: M-F 8-5, 1st and 3rd Sa of month, 9-1.

National Jewish American History Museum

55 N. 5th St., Independence Mall East, Philadelphia, PA 19106; (215) 923-3811. Collects, preserves, interprets and exhibits history of Jewish settlement and contributions in America, in form of art, artifacts, library, and archival collections. Holdings include permanent and changing exhibitions of relics and material relating to Jewish American history from 18th c; library with reference materials on Jewish history, religion, and people's archives, manuscripts, maps, films/videotapes, genealogical records, and special collections; large photo collection; tapes of historical lectures, and recorded oral histories of Vineland, NJ Jewish citizenry. Use of research collections by appt. Accepts phone inquiries. Fee. Hours: M-Th 10-5, Su noon-5.

New Berlin Heritage Association

Box 223, Market and Vine St., New Berlin, PA

17855; (717) 966-0065. Preserves Berlin history through collection of books, maps, photos, genealogical records and locally-produced crafts. Accepts phone inquiries. Hours: call.

New Year's Shooters and Mummers Museum

2nd St. at Washington Ave., Philadelphia, PA 19147; (215) 336-3050. Collects, preserves, and displays artifacts from the Philadelphia Mummers Parade. Holdings include museum with costumes, paraphernalia, photos, and interactive exhibits; resource library with publications and audiovisual materials; archives and manuscripts; vintage home movies; complete television coverages from 1976 and other videos; recordings of music used in the parade; taped interviews with Mummers; McGlinchy Collection of circa 1900 costumes; Bulletin Collection of circa 1960 photos; Gill Photo Collection, 1960-70. Library for use by members only; collections are non-circulating. Accepts phone inquiries. Fee. Hours: Tu-Sa 9:30-5, Su noon-5.

North American Society for Sport History

Penn State University, 101 White Bldg., University Park, PA 16802; (814) 865-2416. Society promotes study and research of the history of sport. Holdings include society archives with official records and correspondences from 1972. Accepts phone inquiries. No fee. Hours: 8-5.

Old Bedford Village

P.O. Box 1976, Old Rt. 220, Bedford, PA 15522; (814) 623-1156. Re-created Colonial village serves as living history enviromnemt to preserve the heritage and craft skills of early America in form of preserved buildings with period furnishings and artifacts, craft demonstrations, Native American artifacts, and the Major Simon M. Lutz Collection. Some restrictions. Accepts phone inquiries. Fee. Hours: Apr-Oct, 9-5; Nov, Dec: special events and tours.

Old Economy Village

14th & Church Sts., Ambridge, PA 15003; (412) 266-4500. Preserves and interprets the social, religious, and economic history of the Harmony Society, a German pietist group, 1825-1905. Holdings include museum with Harmonist and local historical artifacts, including tools, household furnishings, and musical instruments; library with volumes (many owned by Harmony Society) on religion, science, and the arts from 18th c; archives with manuscripts, genealogical records, daybooks, and legal documents of the Harmony Society; Harmonist photos, late 19th-early 20th c; collection of music written by Harmonists; collection of 19th c natural history specimens. Accepts phone inquiries. Fee. Hours: Tu-Sa 9-5, Su noon-5.

Pennsbury Manor

400 Pennsbury Memorial Rd., Morrisville, PA 19067; (215) 946-0400. Reconstructed historic site preserves and interprets life and works of William Penn in form of museum, library, and archives. Holdings include Colonial Revival reconstruction of William Penn's 17th c country estate; library with materials on 17th c social and political history, museum management, William Penn, Quakers, and related topics; archives with microfilms of Penn's papers, extensive collection of records, films, blueprints and photos of Pennsbury construction; recordings of lectures held at Pennsbury. Some restrictions. Accepts phone inquiries. Fee. Hours: museum: M-Sa 9-5, Su noon-5; library/archives: Tu-F 9-5.

Pennsylvania Dutch Folk Culture Society

Lenhartsville, PA 19534; (215) 562-4803. Preserves customs, homelife, and dialect of people of southeastern PA in form of museum, library, and archival collections. Holdings include exhibits and artifacts from the Colonial fireplace era, and turn of the century woodstove era; Bauer Memorial Library with publications, research materials, archives, manuscripts, maps, photos, films/videotapes, recordings, and genealogical relating to local history and folklore, with emphasis on Berks County area. Accepts phone inquiries. Fee. Hours: summer, M-F 10-5, Su 1-5; winter, by appt only.

Pennsylvania Farm Museum of Landis Valley

2451 Kissell Hill Rd., Lancaster, PA 17601; (717) 569-0401. Preserves and displays history of PA farm life through historic farm bldgs and artifacts, 1750-1900, library, and collection of

PA decorative arts. Library by appt. Accepts phone inquiries. Fee. Hours: Tu-Sa 9-5, Su noon-5.

Pennsylvania Lumber Museum

P.O. Box K, Galeton, PA 16922; (814) 435-2652. Documents, preserves, and interprets PA lumber history through holdings in reconstructed logging camp/sawmill visitor center and library. Holdings include logging artifacts and objects, logging locomotive, and photos and some films available for loan. Accepts phone inquiries. Fee. Hours: Mar-Nov, M-Sa 9-4:30, Su 1-4:30; Dec-Feb, M-F 9-4:30.

Pennsylvania Military Museum, 28th Division Shrine

P.O. Box 148, Boalsburg, PA 16827; (814) 466-6263. Displays and exhibits military history of PA and citizens from French and Indian War through Vietnam, and memorializes PA soldiers through holdings in museum, library, and archives. Holdings include maps of WWI and WWII, photos, and genealogical records from Civil War and WWI. Accepts phone inquiries. Fee. Hours: Tu-Sa 9-5, Su noon-5.

Pennsylvania Postal History Society

Paupack, PA 14851. Society gathers and disseminates info on PA postal history though publications and meetings. Membership fee.

Pennsylvania State Archives

Box 1026, Third & Forster Sts., Harrisburg, PA 17108; (717) 787-2701. Acquires, preserves, and makes available valuable PA public records, with attention on records of state govt from 17th c. Holdings include maps; large photo collection; posters; motion pictures created by state agencies; genealogical records; military records from 1775-1945; Penn Charter; Constitution of 1776; Indian deeds; minutes of Constitutional Convention of 1776; papers of PA govs; forest preservation records; records of early iron and coal industries; transportation files on highways, railroads, canals, and railroads; oral histories of PA miners and industrial workers; and social welfare records. No fee. Hours: Tu-F 8:30-4:45.

Pennsylvania State University

Special Collections, Fred Lewis Pattee Library,

University Park, PA 16802; (814) 865-6481. Preserves materials on PA history, covering PA Gov James Beaver, county histories, regimental Civil War histories, and canals, railroad, and civil law. Holds special collection of United Steel Workers of America records and oral history interviews. Accepts phone inquiries. No fee. Hours: call.

Perelman Antique Toy Museum

270 South Second St., Philadelphia, PA 19106; (215) 922-1070. Museum preserves extensive collection of antique toys, ranging from toy banks, dolls, cars, horses, circus wagons, boats, etc. Holdings date to 1887. Accepts phone inquiries. Hours: 9:30-5.

Perry Historians

P.O. Box 73, Newport, PA 17074; (717) 556-0990. Collects, preserves, and promotes history of Perry County, PA and residents in form of museum, library, and archival collections. Holdings include exhibits of local historical artifacts, and the Taufschein collection, 1800-1950; library with local historical materials; topographic atlas of Perry, Juniata, and Mifflin Counties, 1863, 1877; large collection of Perry County land drafts from 1700; photos of local subjects; church records, tombstone transcriptions, surname files and other genealogical records, with emphasis on eastern PA. Some restrictions. Accepts phone inquiries after 5. No fee. Hours: Apr-Nov, three days/month (call), or by appt.

Peter Wentz Farmstead

P.O. Box 240, Schultz and Shearer Rds., Worcester, PA 19490; (215) 584-5104. Exhibits 18th c rural life in Montgomery County. Museum consists of 1777 working farm once used by Gen. Washington as headquarters. Library has reference materials on 18th c crafts, social customs, and local history; photos of farm restoration; and genealogical records of Wentz family. Accepts phone inquiries. No fee. Hours: Tu-Sa 10-4, Su 1-4.

Phi Alpha Theta International Honor Society in History

233 Liberty St., Allentown, PA 18104; (215) 433-4140. Society recognizes academic excellence and encourages study of history, and history of historical study. Accepts phone inquiries. Hours: 8-5.

Philadelphia Jewish Archives Center

Balch Institute for Ethnic Studies, 18 S. Seventh St., Philadelphia, PA 19106; (215) 925-8090. Collects and preserves historical records of the Greater Philadelphia Jewish community Holdings include library with publications and reference materials; archives of the Federation of Jewish Americans and its constituent agencies from 1822; records of Hebrew Immigrant Aid Society, 1884-1971; passenger lists, naturalization records and other immigration-related documents; manuscripts for local Zionist orgs and groups; immigrants' memoirs and autobiographies; synagogue records; photos; small collections of films/videotapes and recordings. Some restrictions. Accepts phone inquiries (ext. 23). No fee. Hours: M-F 9-5.

Philadelphia Maritime Museum

321 Chestnut St., Philadelphia, PA 19106; (215) 925-5439. Preserves and exhibits history and influence of port of Philadelphia. Exhibits include models of sailing ships from 1683, early navigational instruments, shipbuilding tools, marine art, and ship figurehead believed to have been carved by William Rush. Accepts phone inquiries. Hours: M-Sa 10-5, Su 1-5.

Photojournalism Collection

Temple University, Rare Books and Manuscript Collection, Philadelphia, PA 19122; (215) 787-8230. Academic research library collections and curates collection of Philadelphia news materials. Collection includes newsfilm from WPVI-TV from 1947-present and WKYW-TV from 1950-60s; photos archive of "Philadelphia Inquirer" from 1937-72; clipping file, photo archive, and library of "Evening Bulletin"; and "Bulletin" archives from 1847-82. Accepts phone inquiries. Hours: call.

Pittsburgh History and Landmarks Foundation

450 Landmarks Bldg., Station Square, Pittsburgh, PA 15219; (412) 471-5808. Foundation promotes historic preservation and historic education in Allegheny County, PA through special

programs and publications, library, and archival collections. Holdings include library with materials on archictectural history of Pittsburgh area, and industrial, social, corporate, and institutional history of region; archives with clippings, photos, architectural and engineering drawings; manuscripts of James D. Van Trump; maps, plat books and Sanborn atlases of Pittsburgh area; photos of regional subjects. Collections primarily for use of members only. Accepts phone inquiries. Membership fee. Hours: M-F 9-5.

Pittsburgh Press Library

Blvd. of the Allies, Pittsburgh, PA 15230; (412) 253-1901. Daily newspaper maintains reference library for in-house use. Not open to public, but reference calls will be taken. No fee. Hours for reference calls: Tu, F 1-2.

Pottsville Free Public Library

Documents and Special Collections, Third & W. Market Sts., Pottsville, PA 17901; (717) 622-8880. Public library maintains selective collection of govt documents and general and historical materials relevant to community. Holdings include Anthracite Collection; Molly Maguire Collection; Schuykill County history collection. Accepts phone inquiries. No fee. Hours: summer, M-Th 8:30-8:30, F 8:30-5, Sa 8:30-noon; winter, M-Th 8:30-8:30, Sa-Su 8:30-5.

Railroad Museum of Pennsylvania

P.O. Box 15, No. 300 Gap Rd., Strasburg, PA 17579; (717) 687-8628. Collects and preserves historical materials relating to the railroads of PA, and, to a degree, US and the world. Holdings include railroad artifacts, exhibits and displays; library with historical materials on state, US and world railways; archives with curatorial and research materials; railway maps; extensive collection of photos and negatives, including those of the Baldwin Locomotive Works; small collection of films and recordings on railroad subjects. Use of library and archival materials by appt only. Accepts phone inquiries. Fee for museum. Hours: 9-4:30.

Railroaders Memorial Museum

1300 9th Ave., Altoona, PA 16602; (814) 946-0834. Museum preserves and exhibits the history and societal contributions of American railroaders from the Industrial Revolution to the present day. Holdings include operating K-4s steam locomotives; displays and artifacts relating to locomotives, rolling stock, local railroad people, landmarks and events; library with rare publications and manuscripts; photo archives, with PRR photos, glass negatives and the Rau Collection; archival collections of film/videotapes, original works, and blueprints; PRR Master Mechanics Library Manuscripts; PRR route maps; Red Arrow wreck artifacts. Accepts phone inquiries. Fee. Hours: Tu-Sa 10-5, Su 12:30-5 (open M in summer).

Reading Public Library

Fifth & Franklin Sts., Reading, PA 19602; (215) 374-4548. Public library maintains selective collection of govt documents and general and historical materials relevant to needs of community. Holdings include Col Wayne Holman Collection of Reading and Berks County History; Pennsylvania German Collection; Haag Collection of clippings of featured performers with the Reading Symphony Orchestra; Reading Collection of local historical materials, including social, cultural, religious, governmental, and genealogical history of area. Some restrictions. Accepts phone inquiries. No fee. Hours: M-W 8:15-9, Th-F 8:15-5:30, Sa 8:45-5.

Resource and Research Center for Beaver County

1301 7th Ave., Beaver Falls, PA 15010; (412) 846-4340, ext. 5. Preserves history of Beaver County and residents in form of historical reference library and archival collections of maps, photos, and genealogical records from 1790. Collections are non-circulating. Accepts phone inquiries. No fee. Hours: M 5-8, Tu-Th 11-5, F 11-4.

Robert Fulton Birthplace

Box 33, Quarryville, PA 17566; (717) 548-2697. Preserves and interprets life and works of Rober Fulton, (steamship builder) in form of historic birthplace museum with furnishings, artifacts and displays. Accepts phone inquiries. Fee. Hours: summer, Sa 11-4, Su 1-5.

Rosenbach Museum and Library

2010 Delancey Place, Philadelphia, PA 19103;

(215) 732-1600. 19th c townhouse museum furnished with English, French, and American furniture and decorative arts. Library holds rare books and materials on American history and literature and English literature from 15th-20th c. Archives hold contents of Rosenbach Company archive from 1903-54 and papers of Marianne Moore, Rush-Biddle, and Maurice Sendak; and 16th-19th c American and English historical manuscripts, including Chaucer, and originals by Joyce and Conrad. Accepts phone inquiries. No fee for research; fee for museum. Hours: Sept-July, M-F 9-5.

Rough and Tumble Engineer's Historical Association
P.O. Box 9, Kinzers, PA 17335; (717) 442-4249. Assn commemorates the lives and work of thresher men in form of museum, with their machinery and related agricultural and industrial equipment. Accepts phone inquiries. Fee. Hours: 10-4.

Saint Joseph's University
Drexel Library, 5600 City Avenue, Philadelphia, PA 19131; (215) 879-7558. Academic library maintains selective collection of govt documents and general, reference and historical materials relevant to needs of school and students. Holdings include publications and historical materials on the Colonial period, slavery the Civil War, and the Roosevelt era; archives with holdings relating to Jesuit, Catholic, and Philadelphia history. Accepts phone inquiries. No fee. Hours: M-Th 8:30-noon, F-Sa 9-5, Su noon-midnight.

Scranton Public Library
Washington at Vine, Scranton, PA 18503; (717) 348-3008. Public library has special collection of materials on Scranton and Lackawanna County history, including census materials and directories from late 19th c. Accepts phone inquiries. No fee. Hours: M-Th 9-9, F-Sa 9-5:30; summer, M, W, F 9-5:30, Tu, Th 9-9.

Society of Architectural Historians
1232 Pine St., Philadelphia, PA 19105; (215) 735-0224. Society preserves and promotes history of architecture and related arts in form of historic preservation projects, publications, special programs, forums and tours, and small

museum. Accepts phone inquiries. No fee (except for membership dues). Hours: 8:30-4:30.

Southern Alleghenies Museum of Art
P.O. Box 8, St. Francis College Mall, Loretto, PA 15940; (814) 472-6400. Preserves American visual arts of regional, state, and national perspective. Most exhibits 19th-20th c paintings and graphics, with emphasis on work of regional and PA artists. Accepts phone inquiries. No fee. Hours: M-F 9-4:30, Sa-Su 1:30-5:30.

State Library of Pennsylvania
Documents Division, Box 1601, Walnut St. & Commonwealth Ave., Harrisburg, PA 17105; (717) 787-3752. Serves state govt and provides resources for public use. Library preserves PA and US documents from earliest times. Accepts phone inquiries. No fee. Hours: M-F 8:30-5.

State Museum of Pennsylvania
P.O. Box 1026, Harrisburg, PA 17108; (717) 787-4978. Collects, preserves, and interprets cultural and natural history of PA in form of extensive collection of artifacts and exhibits from covering PA history from prehistoric times to present; curatorial research library with materials on museology; planetarium. Does not accept phone inquiries. Fee for planetarium showings. Hours: Tu-Sa 9-5, Su noon-5.

Stephen C. Foster Memorial
University of Pittsburgh, Forbes Ave., Pittsburgh, PA 15260; (412) 624-4100. Research center collects and preserves materials relating to music in American life, with emphasis on Stephen Foster and popular music, 1850s-1930s. Holdings include changing exhibits on Foster's life and music; library with publications, sheet music, ephemera, and other materials on American popular music and Foster; Foster Hall (archives) Collection and Fosteriana, from 1930s; Foster's original copybook, 1851-61; holograph manuscripts; Dvorak manuscript parts; city maps, 1850s; films of Foster and performances; antique and modern recordings of Foster's music. Some restrictions. Accepts phone inquiries. No fee. Hours: academic year, M-F 9-4.

Swarthmore College Peace Collection
Swarthmore College, Swarthmore, PA 19081;

(215) 328-8557. Collects, preserves, and re-searches history and nature of peace and peace movements. Holdings include library with pub-lications and materials on the peace movement; archives with records of pacifist orgs, including Strike for Peace, and Women's International League for Peace and Freedom; collections of papers of peace activists, and peace org records; photos of peace movement people and events; small collection of films on peace and non-violence; tapes from SANE Education Fund and other orgs; Jane Addams Papers; collection of pacifism posters from WWI. Some restrictions. Accepts phone inquiries. No fee. Hours: M-F 8:30-4:30, Sa (during school) 9-noon.

Swigart Museum

Box 214, Museum Park, Rt. 22 East, Hunting-don, PA 16652; (814) 643-3000. Preserves and displays history and development of the Ameri-can automobile in form of restored vehicles and memorabilia, library, and archival collections. Holdings include antique autos and related arti-facts; extensive collection of license plates; col-lections of manuscripts, maps, photos, and films/ videotapes. Use of library by appt. Accepts phone inquiries. Hours: 9-5.

Sword and Saber

P.O. Box 400, Gettysburg, PA 17324; (717) 334-0205. Commercial mail order co specilizes in Southern Civil War memorabilia from 1861-65. Holdings include Confederate newspapers, imprints, letters from soldiers to their families, papers from Confederate generals, Confederate stamps, Union sheet music, photos of Booth and Lincoln families, Confederate veterans maga-zines, materials on slavery, Union maps and illustrations, Confederate money and bonds, and Union generals' orders. All materials for sale. Accepts phone inquiries. Fee. Hours: call.

Theater Collection

Philadelphia Free Library, Logan Square, Phila-delphia, PA 19103; (215) 686-5427. Collection of materials from Philadelphia performing arts from 19th c to date. Theater, film, minstrel show, vaudeville, circus, radio, and TV perform-ances represented through books, magazines, playbills, broadsides, poster, photos, autographs, reviews, and newspaper articles. Theater Index

lists major Philadelphia shows since 1855. Mate-rials non-circulating. Accepts phone inquiries. Hours: call.

Thomas Newcomen Library and Museum

412 Newcomen Rd., Exton, PA 19341; (215) 363-6600. Preserves early history and technol-ogy of steam power. Museum displays working steam engine models. Library holds books, trade catalogs, periodicals, and photos on early steam technology. Special collection of Sears and Roebuck catalogs. Accepts phone inquiries. No fee. Hours: M-F 9-4:30.

Thorton Oakley Collection

Philadelphia Free Library, Logan Square, Phila-delphia, PA 19103; (215) 686-5427. Collection made up of over 1,000 works of art by illustrator Howard Pyle and his students, Maxfield Parrish, Frank Schoonover, Jessie Wilcox Smith, and N.C. Wyeth. Collection includes autographs, letters, books, and periodicals. Accepts phone inquiries. No fee. Hours: call.

Tioga County Historical Society

Robinson House, P.O. Box 724, 120 Main St., Wellsboro, PA 16901; (717) 724-6116. Col-lects, preserves, and promotes history of Tioga County, PA and residents in form of museums, library, and archival collections. Holdings in-clude Robinson House Museum, an historic home with Victorian parlor, Cheney Tavern Room, Nessmuk Room, Webster/Whittaker family room, and military, cultural, and millinery artifacts; Farm, Mine, and Lumber Museum at county fairgrounds maintains collections of rec-ords and artifacts relating to local industry; genealogical library (at Robinson House); local historical maps, photos, and newspapers. Ac-cepts phone inquiries. Donations accepted. Hours: Robinson House: Apr-Dec, M-F noon-4; Farm Museum: vary.

Tioga Point Museum

P.O. Box 143, 724 S Main St, Athens, PA 18810; (717) 888-7225. Preserves and displays local history in form of exhibits and artifacts, library, and archival collections. Holdings in-clude displays on Indian lore, local history, mili-tary history, Stephen C. Foster, early canals and steam railroads, arts and sciences; library with rare books and documents relating to local history; archives and manuscript collections; local maps and photos. Materials are non-circulating. Accepts phone inquiries. Donations accepted. Hours: call.

Union County Historical Society

Union County Courthouse, South 2nd St., Lewisburg, PA 17837; (717) 524-8666. Preserves local history, material culture, and genealogy. Library holds family histories and genealogies. Archives retain county newspapers, school records, business records, photos, post cards, collection of films/videotapes on local craft traditions, and oral history interviews. No fee. Hours: W-Th 8:30-1, 2-4; Tu, F most of day.

Union League of Philadelphia Library

140 S. Broad St., Philadelphia, PA 19102; (215) 563-6500. Maintains collection of materials on Civil War and US, PA, and Philadelphia social and political history. Holdings include manuscripts and photos. Hours: call.

United Methodist Church Commission on Archives and History

326 New St., Philadelphia, PA 19106; (215) 925-7788. Archive, library, and museum for eastern PA Conference has much Methodist memorabilia, including Asbury Bible and John Wesley Chalice, library of 18th and 19th c materials, and records from 1785. Photos available. Materials non-circulating. Accepts phone inquiries. No fee. Hours: 10-4.

University of Pittsburgh

Special Collections, Darlington Memorial Library, 601 Cathedral of Learning, Pittsburgh, PA 15260; (412) 624-4491. Darlington collection holds materials on US history, with emphasis on western PA, from French and Indian War, Revolution, and War of 1812. Holdings include Indian treaties, captivity accounts, US and PA travelogues, and collection of early American fiction and prose. Accepts phone inquiries. No fee. Hours: call.

Urban Archives Center

Temple University, 13th & Berks Mall, Philadel-phia, PA 19122; (215) 787-8260. Academic research library concentrates on Philadelphia history from Civil War, student experiences during WWI and WWI; and Afro-American history. Regional holdings include papers of PA Housing Assn from 1909-72; DE Valley Regional Planning Commission from 1965-72; YWCA and YMCA; Health and Welfare Council of Philadelphia from 1922-69; Philadelphia Urban League from 1935-67; Legal Aide Society from 1933-76; and ACLU from 1948-75. Materials available on changing women's role in church; WWI & WWII student letters and accounts of fighting; WWI, II and Vietnam War posters; Afro-American literature, history of slavery, and Carribean history and culture. Hours: call.

Ursinus College

Myrin Library, , Collegeville, PA 19426; (215) 489-4111, ext. 2283. Academic research library holds materials relating to 1860s schism in German Reformed Church and manuscripts from James I Good and J.H.A. Bomberger. Researcher must be accompanied by staff archivist. Accepts phone inquiries. No fee. Hours: Tu-F 8:30-4:30.

Valley Forge Historical Society

P.O. Box 122, Rt 23, Valley Forge, PA 19481; (215) 783-0535. Collects, preserves, and promotes history of Revolutionary War and the Valley Forge Encampment through museum, library, archival collections, and publications. Holdings include military and local historic artifacts; historical and 19th c china collection; American history library; manuscripts relating to Colonial period, Revolutionary War, and George Washington; collection of artifacts belonging to Washington and family. Accepts phone inquiries. No fee. Hours: M-Sa 9:30-4:30, Su 1-4:30.

Washington and Jefferson College Library

Washington, PA 15301; (412) 223-6070. Academic research library has materials on Revolutionary War, 1794 Whiskey Rebellion, American Indians, and western PA history. Accepts phone inquiries. No fee. Hours: call.

Washington Crossing Historic Park

P.O. Box 103, 1112 River Rd., Washington

Crossing, PA 18977; (215) 493-4076. Perpetuates history and significance of Washington's crossing of Delaware River, and regional events in subsequent 50 years. Museum composed of 6 restored and historically furnished buildings and exhibits. Small library on general American Revolution topics. Accepts phone inquiries. Fee. Hours: museum, M-Sa 9-5, Su noon-5; library by appt.

Watch and Clock Collectors Association Museum

514 Poplar St., Columbia, PA 17512; (717) 684-8261. Preserves, promotes, and displays history of horology in form of museum, library, and archival collections. Holdings include American, European, and Oriental watches, clocks, various timepieces, and tools from 16th c; library with research materials, 19th c trade publications, and US patent copies of timepieces; Hamilton Watch Co records. Accepts phone inquiries. Fee. Hours: Tu-Sa 9-4.

Wayne County Historical Society

P.O. Box 446, 810 Main St., Honesdale, PA 18431; (717) 253-3240. Gathers and exhibits artifacts of Wayne County in museum and library. Holdings include maps from railroad and canal era, photos, newspapers and census records, genealogical records, and first steam locomotive to run on track in America. Accepts phone inquiries. Fee. Hours: call.

Waynesburg College Library

93 Locust Ave., Waynesburg, PA 15370; (412) 627-8191. Academic library maintains collection of general, reference, and historical materials and artifacts relevant to needs of the school and community. Holdings include French Room, with furnishings and objects of vertu from the Louis XVI period; Trans-Appalachian Room, with publications and research materials on southwestern PA history, and genealogical records of Grace County. Accepts phone inquiries (ext 278). No fee. Hours: M-Th 8-10, F 8-5, Sa 10-5, Su 2-10.

Westmoreland County Community College

Documents Division, Learning Resources Center, Armbrust Rd., Youngwood, PA 15697; (412)

925-4101. Academic library maintains selective collection of govt documents, general, reference, and historical materials relevant to needs of the school and students. Holdings include American history collection with research items, maps, photos, films/videotapes, and recordings; John H. Dent Collection of papers and memorabilia. Accepts phone inquiries. No fee. Hours: M-Th 8-9:30, F 8-4:30, Sa 8:30-4:30.

Westmoreland County Historical Society

102 N. Main St., Suite 250, Greensburg, PA 15601; (412) 836-1800. Collects, preserves and promotes history of Westmoreland County, PA, and residents in form of library, archival collections, and historic site. Holdings include Hanna's Town National Historic Site (3 miles north of Greensburg), the first court west of the Allegheny Mountains, 1773-1786, with restored buildings, museum, and artifacts; library; archives with documents, records, and manuscripts relating to local history; local and county maps and atlases; photos; slide-tape local history show; collections of architectural drawings, and fine and decorative arts. Some restrictions. Accepts phone inquiries. Fee for use of library by non-members. Hours: Tu-F 9-5, Sa 10-1.

Wyoming Historical and Geological Society

49 S. Franklin St., Wilkes-Barre, PA 18701; (717) 823-6244. Collects, preserves, and promotes history of Wyoming Valley and Luzerne County, PA, and residents in form of museum, library, archives, manuscripts, maps, and photos. Use of manuscript collection by appt. Accepts phone inquiries. Fee for non-members. Hours: Tu-F noon-4, Sa 10-4.

Rhode Island

Abraham Lincoln Collection

Brown University, John Hay Library, 20 Prospect St., Providence, RI 02192; (401) 683-2148. Collection contains extensive documentation of Lincoln's life and events during his era. Manuscript collection contains substantial number of letters and documents written and signed by Lincoln and materials of Lincoln's family; collection of song sheets, ballots, and political posters; newspapers from 1860-65; prints of most photos taken of Lincoln, caricatures, portraits of Lincoln, and paintings of his death-bed; scrapbook of Thomas Nast's Civil War sketches; and extensive sheet music collection on minstrel songs, funeral marches, memorial songs, and campaign songs related to Lincoln. Accepts phone inquiries. No fee. Hours: call.

Anne Brown Military Collection

Brown University, John Hay Library, 20 Prospect St., Providence, RI 02912; (401) 683-2148. Collection focuses on history of military and naval uniforms of all nations from 17th c, and military and naval history. Holdings include paintings, drawings, and miniature model soldiers; materials on military tactics, wars, campaigns, ceremonies, biography; portraits and caricatures; and materials on slavery and slave trade in "New World" until 1883, with emphasis on British and French abolition movements. Accepts phone and mail inquiries. Hours: by appt only.

Bristol Historical and Preservation Society

48 Court St., Bristol, RI 02809; (401) 253-7223. Promotes interest in historical research and preservation of southern New England and Bristol. Museum exhibits artifacts, memorabilia, and ephemera reflecting 300 years of Bristol history. Library has small collection of materials of local interest, including ship logs, crew lists, wills, church records, maps from 1684, photos and postcards, videotapes of events, genealogical records, ship manifests, and 18th and 19th c correspondence of ship captains. Accepts phone inquiries. Fee. Hours: library, W 1-5, and by appt; museum, summer, W 1-5.

Harris Collection of American Poetry and Plays

Brown University, John Hay Library, Prospect St., Providence, RI 02912; (401) 683-2148. Collection of American and Canadian poetry and plays from 17th c. Holdings include first editions from most American poets and playwrights, including Whitman, Poe, Wallace Stevens, Eugene O'Neill, Edward Albee, Ezra Pound, T.S. Eliot, William Carlos Williams, Phyllis Wheatley, Robert Frost, Allen Ginsberg, Bliss Carman, and Amy Lowell; Stephen Foster sheet music; Cushman collection of plays and prompt copies; MacDougall collection of psalters and hymnals; and Yiddish American literature. Hours: call.

International Tennis Hall of Fame Tennis Museum

194 Bellevue Ave., Newport, RI 02840; (401) 849-3990 or 6378. Preserves history of tennis, and provides landmark for tennis enthusiasts worldwide. Museum exhibits cover tennis and court tennis, major competitions, equip, and trophies. Library has reference materials on sport's history. Archives retain files on tennis history and players, photos of players, and special collection of materials on Newport Casino history. Accepts phone inquiries. Fee. Hours: library by appt only; May-Oct 10-5, Nov-Apr 11-4.

Naval War College Museum

Naval War College, Coasters Harbor Island, Newport, RI 02840; (401) 841-4052 or 1317. Preserves history of naval presence in Narragansett Bay and history of naval warfare. Museum exhibits encompass theories and concepts of sea power, international and maritime law, foreign policy formulation, and naval power and strategic and tactical objectives. Materials on Narragansett Bay date to 1775, and document careers of Oliver and Matthew Perry, Naval Academy's temporary residence in Newport, Naval Torpedo Station, and current development of underwater technology. Holdings include college archives, maps, and photos from 1864. Accepts phone inquiries. No fee. Hours: M-F 10-4, and June-Sept, Sa-Su noon-4.

New England Wireless and Steam Museum

697 Tillinghast Rd., East Greenwich, RI 02818; (401) 884-1710. Preserves technological history through museum, library, and archive holdings of manuscripts and photos. Accepts phone inquiries. Fee. Hours: library by appt only; museum, Su 1-5.

Newport Automobile Museum

One Casino Terrace, Newport, RI 02840; (401)

846-6688. Preserves and collects antique and classic cars such as Woodrow Wilson's 1923 Rolls Silver Ghost, 1941 Alfa-Romeo given to Hitler by Mussolini, 1939 Woody, and 1904 Maxwell. Accepts phone inquiries. Hours: summer, 10-7, winter 10-5.

Newport Historical Society

82 Touro St., Newport, RI 02840; (401) 846-0813. Preserves and displays Newport decorative arts, documents, and history in museum. Library has supporting materials on naval history, state and local history, decorative arts, and biographies. Other holdings include maps from Colonial period, photos, oral histories, and genealogical records. Special collections include Roderick Terry collection of rare books, Aaron Lopez letters and accounts, Touro synagoge, and Society of Friends records from 1658. Accepts phone inquiries. Donations accepted. Hours: Tu-F 9:30-4:30, Sa 9:30-12:30.

Providence Athenaeum

251 Benefit St., Providence, RI 02903; (401) 421-6970. Membership library/cultural institution with interest in local history. Library collects American history materials, including very early and rare artifacts. Holdings have strong RI and Providence focus. Materials circulate only to members. ILL available. Accepts phone inquiries. No fee. Hours: M-F 8:30-5:30, Sa 9:30-5:30.

Providence City Archives

Providence City Hall, Providence, RI 02903; (401) 421-7740, ext. 314 & 315. Repository for city documents from 1636. Materials housed in library and archives include manuscripts, maps, photos, vital statistics, land records, and probate records. Accepts phone inquiries. No fee. Hours: 8:30-4:30.

Providence College

Special Collections, Phillips Memorial Library, River Ave. at Eaton St., Providence, RI 02918; (401) 865-2242. Preserves materials on ethnic and political RI history. Extensive manuscript collections include anti-Communist witness Louis Francis Budenz materials; Rhode Island 1964-60 Constitutional Convention Collection; Urban League of Rhode Island Collection; Nazi Bund Collection; Rhode Island United States Colored Artillery Collection; Irish Literature Collection; Civil War diary of William Walsh; black nfrom 1932-57; Rhode Island Confederate period newspapers; Reunification of Ireland clippings; NAACP Collection; 1657-1905 Rhode Island court records; and WWI newspapers. Some restrictions. Accepts phone inquiries (401-865-2377). No fee. Hours: M-F 9-5.

Providence Public Library

Special Collections, 150 Empire St., Providence, RI 02903; (401) 521-7722. Public library preserves and promotes use of source of study of Civil War and slavery in Harris Collection. Holdings include 18th and 19th c books, rare pamphlets, periodicals on slave trade and slavery, Civil War regimental histories and personal narratives, women's accounts of Civil War, music and broadsides from war, copy of "The Liberator" from 1843, and many editions of "Uncle Tom's Cabin." Materials for in-house use only. Accepts phone inquiries. No fee. Hours: M, Tu, Th 9:30-9, F-Sa 9:30-5.

Rhode Island College

James Adams Library, 600 Mount Pleasant Ave., Providence, RI 02903; (401) 456-8125. Academic research library houses Social and Political Materials Collection on political and social extremism in US. Holdings include materials from New World Liberation Front, Committee of Russian Slavery to Jewish Communism, and others. Most materials date to early 1960s. Accepts phone inquiries. Hours: call.

Rhode Island Committee for the Humanities

463 Broadway, Providence, RI 02909; (401) 273-2250. Makes grants to local non-profit orgs to support humanities projects. Has complete library of RICH-funded media projects. Accepts phone inquiries. Hours: M-F 9-5.

Rhode Island Historical Preservation Commission

150 Benefit St., Providence, RI 02903; (401) 277-2678. Identifies and preserves RI historic resources. Holdings include survey sheets of historic resources and National Register nominations. Accepts phone inquiries. No fee. Hours:

by appt only, M-F 8:30-4:30.

Rhode Island Historical Society

110 Benevolent St., Providence, RI 02906; (401) 331-8575. Collects, preserves, and makes available books, manuscripts, graphic materials, and musuem objects relating to RI history. Library and museum collect manuscripts from 1636, maps, photos, large collection of TV newsfilm and documentaries, collection of RI music, genealogical materials, and superior collections of RI newspapers and imprints. Accepts phone inquiries. No fee for library; fee for museum. Hours: M-F 9-5.

Rhode Island Jewish Historical Association

130 Sessions St., Providence, RI 02906; (401) 331-1360. Collects and preserves memorabilia on history of Jews in RI. Library has materials on RI history, authors, genealogy, and Jewish culture during colonial period. Archives contains documents, photos, clippings, and records from individuals connected with Jewish activities; large collection of photos; oral histories; and genealogies of local families. Materials for in-house use only. Accepts phone inquiries. No fee. Hours: 9:30-1:30, and by appt.

Rhode Island School of Design Museum of Art

224 Benefit St., Providence, RI 02903; (401) 331-3511. Museum houses large collection of artworks spanning centuries and continents. Special American collection in Pendleton House. Holdings include sizeable collection of 19th and 20th c photos. Accepts phone inquiries. Fee. Hours: Tu, W, F, Sa 10:30-5, Th noon-8, Su 2-5.

Rhode Island State Archives

Rm. 43, State House, Smith St., Providence, RI 02903; (401) 277-2353. Serves public with materials on history and genealogy. Museum houses collection of state artifacts and portraits of governors. Library holds legislative records and historical and genealogical materials. Archives retains manuscripts from 1636, original colony records, Revolutionary War records, collection of RI maps, small collection of photos of old streets and towns, and few films/videotapes

on 1986 Constitutional Convention. Some restrictions. Accepts phone inquiries. No fee. Hours: M-F 8:30-4:30.

Slater Hill Historic Site

P.O. Box 727, Roosevelt Ave., Pawtucket, RI 02862; (401) 725-8638. Interprets American Industrial Revolution and its social and economic impact. Museum consists of 3 historic bldgs: Slaren Mill of 1793, Sylvanus Brown House of 1758, and Wilkinson Mill of 1810. Holdings relate process of hand-to-machine textile production. Library has materials on history of textile industry, manuscripts from Wilkinson families, maps of Pawtucket, photos of RI textile industry depicting child labor and history of American Industrial Revolution, oral histories, genealogical records, and Lewis Hine collection of sea photos. Accepts phone inquiries. Fee. Hours: Mar-May and Labor Day-Dec, Sa-Su 1-5; June-Labor Day Tu-Sa 10-5, Su 1-5.

Sloop of War Providence

Seaport 76 Foundation, P.O. Box 76, Newport, RI 02840; (401) 846-1776. Non-profit group preserves history and promotes knowledge of US maritime heritage by maintaining replica of Continental Navy ship. Library holds some reference materials on the Providence, navigational charts, and photos of ship construction. Some restrictions. Accepts phone inquiries. Fee. Hours: call.

Warwick Historical Society

25 Roger Williams Circle, Warwick, RI 02888; (401) 737-8160. Preserves documents materials dealing with history of Warwick and RI. Museum houses artifacts, furniture, prints, and clothing. Library holds small collection of letters, ephemera, deeds, and books. Archives contain photos and postcards, maps, and some genealogical materials. Accepts phone inquiries. No fee. Hours: by appt only, M 9-noon.

Westerly Public Library Granite Collection

Broad St., Westerly, RI 02891; (401) 596-2877. Library collects artifacts and info on granite industry. Museum houses samples, hand tools, and union memorabilia. Library retains published works on granite. Archives retains company records, union records, manuscripts, photos of quarries and workers, company movie from 1927, and company advertising records from 1935. Accepts phone inquiries. No fee. Hours: M-W 8-9, Th-F 8-5, Sa 8-3.

South Carolina

Aiken County Historical Museum

433 Newberry St., SW, Aiken, SC 29801; (803) 642-2015. Collects, researches, preserves, and interprets county history. Museum exhibits cover archaeology, drugstore, school, and log house of 18th-20th c. Library provides research materials. Archives hold maps, legal documents, papers, historic architectural photos, and some Savannah River plant materials. Accepts phone inquiries. No fee. Hours: Tu-F 9:30-4:30; 1st Su each month 2-5.

Camden Archives

1314 Broad St., Camden, SC 29020; (803) 432-3242. City archives, museum, tourist, and research facility for Camden, SC, and Kershaw county. Museum exhibits Indian artifacts and original 1825 town clockworks. Library features materials on SC architecture, biography, Colonial and Revolutionary War period, Civil War, South, and military. Archives retains local govt and civic records, local newspapers, maps of SC and NC from Civil War, land grant maps, small photo collection from 1860-1970, genealogical materials. Special SC Daughters of American Revolution state collection and Colonial Dames 17th c state collection available. Accepts phone inquiries. No fee. Hours: M-F 8-noon, 1-5, Su by appt.

Camden District Heritage Foundation

Historic Camden, P.O. Box 710, S. Broad St., Camden, SC 29020; (803) 432-9841. Preserves nationally significant Revolutionary War historic area. Museum and small library hold manuscripts and maps. Accepts phone inquiries. Fee. Hours: 10-4.

Charles Towne Landing

1500 Old Town Rd., Charleston, SC 29407; (803) 556-4450. Nature and historic park emphasizing period of 1500-1750, with emphasis on education. Museum exhibits trace first hundred years of Carolina history. Library concentrates on SC history. Some films/videotapes. Materials non-circulating. Accepts phone inquiries. Fee. Hours: 9-5.

Charleston Division of Archives and Records

P.O. Box 304, 100 Broad St., Ste. 300, Charleston, SC 29401; (803) 724-7301. Preserves city municipal records for legal, historical, administrative, and financial purposes. Library holds reference materials on Charleston and "Lowcountry." Archives contain newspaper articles, local govt records, correspondence, 20th c house plans and permits, 18th c maps, photos of residents and historic bldgs, limited films/videotapes, genealogical records from Charleston Orphan House, yearbooks, 19th c earthquake relief records, records of Enston Home for old and infirm residents, and City Hospital records. Some materials closed to public. Accepts phone inquiries. No fee. Hours: M-F 9-5.

Charleston Library Society

164 King St., Charleston, SC 29401; (803) 723-9912. Public library holds special collections on agriculture, Confederacy, architecture, horticulture, SC Jews, and 18th-19th c manuscripts. Holdings include maps, photos, and genealogical records, as well as archives of Library Society from 1748. Accepts phone inquiries. Fee. Hours: M-F 9:30-5:30, Sa 9:30-2.

Clemson University Cooper Library

Documents Dept., Clemson, SC 29634; (803) 656-5174. Academic research library with large collection of federal documents emphasizing agriculture, technology, and statistics. Large USGS map collection available. Materials circulate within university community. Accepts phone inquiries. No fee. Hours: M-F 8-1, Sa 8-6, Su 1-11.

College of Charleston Library

Special Collections Dept., Charleston, SC 29401; (803) 792-5530. Academic research library holds materials on slaves and slave trade in region, regional banking records from Civil War period, papers of families and individuals relating Civil War experiences, SC Province Court of Cannon Pleas papers from 1748-60, and other documentation of 19th c slavery in region. Also has special collection of radical left- and right-wing groups in South, including Ku Klux Klan. Holdings include pamphlets, periodicals, newspapers, and some gay org materials from 1960s. Accepts phone inquiries. No fee. Hours: call.

Columbia Museum
1112 Bull St., Columbia, SC 29201; (803) 799-2810. General art museum and planetarium with exhibits of art and decorative art from ancient to contemporary time. Library holds materials relating to collections. Archives collects materials on artists represented in museum. Other holdings include maps, photos, and some films/videotapes. Accepts phone inquiries. Fee. Hours: Tu-F 10-5, Sa-Su 1-5.

Cowpens National Battlefield
P.O. Box 308, Intersection of SC Hwys 110 & 111, Chesnee, SC 29323; (803) 461-2828. Preserves Cowpens Battlefield for public use. Museum displays Revolutionary War artifacts. Library covers SC history, Cowpens Battle, and American Revolution and its southern campaign. Accepts phone inquiries. Fee. Hours: 9-5.

Florence Air and Missile Museum
P.O. Box 1326, Hwy 301 N., Airport Entrance, Florence, SC 29503; (803) 665-5118. Memorial to Air Force and Air Corps pilots who served in WWI, WWII, Korea, and Vietnam. Museum exhibits include 38 aircraft, missiles, and rockets, including jet fighters, bombers, anti-tank missiles, tanks, and ground-to-ground rockets. Other holdings include Gemini capsule, Alan Shepherd's Apollo space unit, Apollo launch computers, and Saturn V components. Room dedicated to Lafayette Escadrille. Library holds reference materials, and photos from 1912. Accepts phone inquiries. Fee. Hours: 9-6.

Florence County Library
Documents Division, 319 S. Irby St., Florence, SC 29501; (803) 662-8424. Provides materials on county and SC history. Library contains old local maps, 8mm films, genealogical records, and SC collection. Some restrictions. Accepts phone

inquiries. No fee. Hours: M-Th 9-8:30, F-Sa 9-5:30, Su 2-5.

Fort Jackson Museum
Bldg. 4442, ATTN: ATZJ-PTMP, Fort Jackson, SC 29207; (803) 751-7355. Preserves history of ft and soldier training procedures. Accepts phone inquiries. No fee. Hours: Tu-Su 1-4.

Fort Sumter National Monument
1214 Middle St., Sullivan's Island, SC 29482; (803) 883-3123. Shows how coastal defense changed over period 1776-1947. Museum concentrates on development of sea coast fortification and weapons. Library provides reference on area history, artifacts, arms, and wildlife. Map collection shows channels leading into Charleston harbor and blueprints of forts and battalions. Photo collection documents Ft Sumter and Ft Moultrie from 1809-1947. Materials for in-house use only. Accepts phone inquiries. No fee. Hours: 9-5.

Ida Jane Dacus Library
Winthrop College, Oakland Ave., Rock Hill, SC 29733; (803) 323-2131. Academic research library holds special collection of materials on women's history in SC, local history, college history, and archives. Accepts phone inquiries. No fee. Hours: M-Th 8-11, F 8-5, Sa 11-5, Su 1-10.

Macaulay Museum of Dental History
Medical University of South Carolina, 171 Ashley Ave., Charleston, SC 29425; (803) 792-2288. Promotes interest in history of dentistry in SC. Museum exhibits dental chairs, cabinets, foot-powered drills, x-rays, dental chests, and antique instruments from mostly 19th and 20th c. Very small library collection. Archives hold SC dentist invention patents. Materials non-circulating. No fee. Hours: M-F 8:30-5.

McKissick Museum
University of South Carolina, Columbia, SC 29208; (803) 777-7251. Provides exhibits and programs in SC art, history, and sciences. Museum holds SC folklife and materials culture exhibits from 1770s. Archives retain univ records from 1801. Holdings include Bernard Baruch

silver collection; Laurence Smith Geology Museum; Museum of Education's textbooks, photos, and artifacts from SC, Broadcasting Communications Archives of 20th c radio and TV materials; and Twentieth Century-Fox Movietone newsreels. Special SC Folk Arts Program sponsors documentation and publication of traditional SC arts, and collects photos, recordings, and films/videotapes. Accepts phone inquiries. No fee. Hours: M-F 9-4, Sa 10-5, Su 1-5.

Museum of African-American Culture

Historic Columbia Foundation, 1403 Richland St., Columbia, SC 29201; (803) 252-1450. Preserves and protects black American culture and heritage. Museum holdings explain life of one of Columbia's first free black women, Celia Mann, and history of her family from 1850s-1978. Accepts phone inquiries. Fee. Hours: Tu-F 10-4, Sa 11-2.

National Society of Colonial Dames of America

Powder Magazine, Cumberland St., Charlestown, SC 29402; (803) 722-3767. Museum, library, and archives. Accepts phone inquiries. Hours: 9-4.

Ninety-Six National Historic Site

P.O. Box 496, Ninety-Six, SC 29666; (803) 543-4068. Commemorates Ninety-Six's role in 18th c English settlemt of SC and southern campaign of American Revolution through holdings in museum and library. Collections include historical maps, slides/photos, films/videotapes, genealogical records, and collection of Revolutionary War artifacts. Accepts phone inquiries. No fee. Hours: 8-5.

Parris Island Museum

MCRD, Parris Island, SC 29905; (803) 525-2951. Preserves history of Parris Island, Marine Corps Recruit training, Marine Corps, Spanish settlement of Santa Elena from 1566-87, and local military operations through museum and library holdings. Archives retain Parris Island records, personal papers, maps, photos, eductional films of Marine Corps, archaeological digs, and recordings of interviews and songs. Accepts phone inquiries. No fee. Hours: 10-4:30.

Patriot's Point Naval and Maritime Museum

P.O. Box 986, Mt. Pleasant, SC 29464; (803) 884-2727. Historical and educational institution preserves WWII naval history. Museum exhibits Navy and maritime materials. Library has research materials on naval history, including manuscripts, WWII Pacific maps, photos, films, recordings, genealogical records, and Beaumont art collection. Accepts phone inquiries. Fee. Hours: Oct-Mar, 9-5; Apr-Sept, 9-6.

Sons of the American Revolution, South Carolina Society

P.O. Box 1273, Beaufort, SC 29901; (803) 524-4712. Acquires and preserves individual service records of Revolutionary War patriots, and promotes fellowship among their descendents. Holdings include records of members past and present, with only records of deceased members open to public. Materials non-circulating. Accepts phone inquiries. No fee. Hours: call.

South Carolina Baptist Historical Society

Furman University Library, Special Collections Department, Greenville, SC 29613; (803) 294-2194. Collects materials on SC Baptists and their interests. Library concentrates on Baptist history; archives hold church minutes, state annuals, and assn records; manuscripts from Basil Manley, Jr, Edmund Botsford, Oliver Hart, Richard Furman, and Raven McDavid, Jr; maps of Baptist sites; photos of Baptist churches and members; and recordings of speakers from pastor's school and Furman University from 1969. Accepts phone inquiries. No fee, Hours: M-F 8:30-4:30.

South Carolina Committee for the Humanities

P.O. Box 6925, 6-C Monckton Blvd., Columbia, SC 29260; (803) 738-1850. Encourages public understanding and appreciation of humanities through collection of books, videotapes, and slide presentations on Afro-American studies, sociology and aging, architecture and historic preservation, art and music, business, education, SC and general history, international relations, law and politics, literature, and women's studies. Accepts phone inquiries. Hours: 9-5.

South Carolina Confederate Relic Room and Museum

World War Memorial Building, 920 Sumter St., Columbia, SC 29201; (803) 734-9813. Collects and displays artifacts from all periods of SC history and maintains war memorial. Library provides reference materials. Special collection of SC Confederate flags, uniforms, and weapons. Materials for in-house use only. Accepts phone inquiries. No fee. Hours: M-F 8:30-5.

South Carolina Criminal Justice Hall of Fame

5400 Broad River Rd., Columbia, SC 29210; (803) 737-8600. Preserves history of SC law enforcement and its historical and contemporary aspects. Accepts phone inquiries. No fee. Hours: M-F 8:30-5.

South Carolina Department of Archives and History

P.O. Box 11669, 1430 Senate St., Columbia, SC 29211; (803) 734-8596. Official respository of non-current public records of SC. Small reference library covers SC history and related topics. Archives hold state and political records from 1671; maps of SC, southeastern US, and SC counties and municipalities from colonial period; microfilm copies of Draper papers, Continental Congress papers, American Missionary Society records, Compiled Service Records of SC Confederate Soldiers, Revolutionary War pension applications, and other materials relevant to SC history. May be some restrictions. Accepts phone inquiries. No fee. Hours: M-F 9-9, Sa 9-6, Su 1-9.

South Carolina Historical Society

Fireproof Bldg., 100 Meeting St., Charleston, SC 29401; (803) 723-3225. Documents all aspects of SC history through library and archives. Holdings include books and pamphlets from 1670s, maps, photos from Civil War, films from 1920s, recordings from 1950s, and genealogical materials from thousands of SC families from 1900s. Fee. Hours: M-F 9-4, Sa 9-2.

South Carolina State Museum

South Carolina Museum Commission, P.O. Box 100107, 301 Gervais St., Columbia, SC 29202;

(803) 737-4921. Collects, preserves, exhibits, and interprets all facets of SC life connected to art, history, natural history, and science and technology. Accepts phone inquiries. Fee. Hours: M-Sa 10-5, Su 1-5.

South Caroliniana Library

University of South Carolina, Columbia, SC 29208; (803) 777-3131. Collects materials on history, literature, and culture of SC from time of settlement to present. Library holds large collection of SC-related books and pamphlets, many private papers, institutional and business records, maps from 16th c, photos, music recorded by SC artists, and genealogical records. Restrictions on some collections. Accepts phone inquiries. No fee. Hours: M, W, F 8:30-5; T, Th 8:30-8; Sa 9-5.

Thurmond Center for Excellence in Government and Public Service

Clemson University Library, 201 Martin St., Clemson, SC 29631; (803) 656-4700. Preserves papers and memorabilia of Sen Strom Thurmond. Accepts phone inquiries. No fee. Hours: call.

University of South Carolina Newsfilm Library

Instructional Services Ctr, Columbia, SC 29208; (803) 777-6841. Academic research and stock footage library. Holdings include part of Movietone News collection, local TV station archives, footage from private collections, and other major collections totaling 20 million feet of film. Accepts phone inquiries. Hours: M-F 8-5.

Waring Historical Library

Medical University of South Carolina, 171 Ashley Ave., Charleston, SC 29425; (803) 792-2288. Promotes interest in SC health science and medical history. Museum exhibits 19th c artifacts. Library concentrates on medical history, dating to 16th c. Archives holds biographical files on SC doctors, manuscripts on medicine, and photos. Materials non-circulating. Accepts phone inquiries. No fee. Hours: M-F 8:30-5.

Williams-Brice Museum and Archives

Sumter County Historical Society, P.O. Box

An example of a South Dakota sod house, from the Agricultural Heritage Museum.

1456, 122 N. Washington St., Sumter, SC 29150; (803) 775-0908. Collects, preserves, and exhibits county and state museum and archival materials. Museum presents period rooms dating from antebellum to 1920s; library holds genealogical references; and photo collection depicts county people and places from 1845. Accepts phone inquiries. No fee. Hours: museum, Tu-Sa

South Dakota

Agricultural Heritage Museum
South Dakota State University, Box 2207C, Brookings, SD 57007; (605) 688-6226. Preserves agricultural and rural history of SD. Museum houses many farm and household items; library holds catalogs, brochures, and current

publications; large collection of photos with focus on 1920-40; many maps of state and Dakota territory; and some films/videotapes from 1930s. Some restrictions on use. Accepts phone inquiries. No fee for admission; fee for material use and research. Hours: M-Sa 10-5, Su 1-5.

American Indian Culture Research Center
Blue Cloud Abbey, P.O. Box 98, Marvin, SD 57251; (605) 432-5528. Supports Indian leaders and educators in rebuilding their community, and educates general public on Indian culture and philosophy. Museum exhibits Dakota/Lakota and Ojibwa artifacts and pottery; archival holdings housed at Center for Western Studies at Augustana College; large photo collection of historic value; and few self-produced films/videotapes on residents. Accepts phone inquiries. No fee. Hours: M-F 8-4:30.

Archives of the North American Baptist Conference

1605 S. Euclid Ave., Sioux Falls, SD 57105; (605) 335-9071. Collects and preserves Baptist mission artifacts from Africa, India, China, Japan, and Brazil. Library holds historical materials from 1563. Archives documents German-speaking churches and their institutions from 1850 through biographical data, official records, and photos. Special collections include Conference records, and some genealogical materials. Fee for research and translation. Hours: by appt, M-F

Big Thunder Gold Mine

P.O. Box 706, Keystone, SD 57751; (605) 666-4847. Educational tourist attraction with gold mine museum dating to 1880s. Some photos of period. Film/videotape on history of gold discovery in Black Hills, regional Keystone gold mine, and General Custer. Accepts phone inquiries. Fee. Hours: May-Oct, 8-8.

Black Hills State College

Leland Case Library for Western Historical Studies, College Station, Box 9511, 1200 University Ave., Spearfish, SD 57783; (605) 642-6361. Academic research library concentrates on study and research of history of West, with emphasis on Black Hills of South Dakota and surrounding area. Museum contains artifacts from Sioux Indians. Library holds archival materials from college, manuscripts from E.Y. Berry's congressional service from 1950-70, large collection of maps from late 1800s, photos, films related to Berry's congressional career, and recordings on Sioux Indians. Materials for in-house use only. No fee. Hours: M-F 9-noon and 1-4 when classes in session.

Center for Musical Instrument Study

414 E. Clark St., Vermillion, SD 57069; (605) 677-5306. Preserves major collection of rare musical instruments and supporting library of music, books, and sound recordings. Museum has over 4,500 American, European, and non-Western instruments dating from 1500. Library has reference materials on instruments and music. Archives hold photos of American bands and bandsmen, manuscripts, correspondence, and many recordings from 1900-40. Hours: call.

Center for Western Studies

Augustana College, P.O. Box 727, 29th and Summit Ave., Sioux Falls, SD 57197; (605) 336-4007. Collects, preserves, and interprets history and cultures of Upper Great Plains. Museum exhibits Sioux Indian artifacts from 1700-1870, Western bronzes from 20th c, wood sculptures by regional artists, and railroadiana from 1890-1950. Library has large collection on American Midwest. Archives contain papers of Episcopal Diocese of SD, United Church of Christ of SD, letters and diaries, maps, photos of SD and Midwest, films/videotapes, recordings, and genealogical records. Special Reuben Goertz Germans from Russia collection, and Herbert Krause collection. Accepts phone inquiries. No fee. Hours: M-F 8-noon, 1-5.

Dacotah Prairie Museum

P.O. Box 395, 21 S. Main St., Aberdeen, SD 57401; (605) 622-7117. Relates history of Dakota Prairie and residents through collecting, preserving, and interpreting artifacts exemplifying early pioneer life and artwork, as well as natural history. Accepts phone inquiries. Donations accepted. Hours: Tu-F 9-5, Sa 1-5.

Dakota Territorial Museum

P.O. Box 1033, Yankton, SD 57078; (605) 665-3898. Collects, preserves, and exhibits history of Yankton county, and acquires documents on pioneers in SD. Displays include 1870 parlor, reconstructed kitchen, horse-drawn vehicles, sculpture, paintings and photos, steamboat history, railway depot, Gunderson rural school house, blacksmith shop, and historic American LaFrance fire engine. Accepts phone inquiries. Donations accepted. Hours: Memorial Day-Labor Day, W-Su 1-5; winter, M, W, Th 1-4.

Friends of the Middle Border Museum

P.O. Box 1071, 1311 S Duff St., Mitchell, SD 57301; (605) 996-2122. Preserves Middle West history as it pertains to cultural, social, political, economic, educational, and religious development of area peoples. Museum consists of restored seven-building complex, with collections of antique cars, farm machinery, art, Indian artifacts, and period furnishings dating from 1870s through 1930s. Large photo collection of early Mitchell. Film/videotape interviews with early settlers. Special collections of Sen Francis Case papers, Dr Leland Case office memorabilia, and other pioneer physician equipment. Accepts phone inquiries. Fee. Hours: May-Sept, M-F 9-5, Sa-Su 1-5; June-Aug, M-Sa 8-6, Su 10-6; Oct-Apr M-F 9-4.

Heritage Center

P.O. Box 100, Red Cloud Indian School, Pine Ridge, SD 57770; (605) 867-5491. Collects materials on local history and American Indian art. Museum houses collection of Indian paintings and tribal arts from 1960; library specializes in Sioux Indians and Native American art; archival materials and photos of Oglala Sioux, and mission and school activities from 1930s. Materials for in-house use only. Accepts phone inquiries. No fee. Hours: 8-noon, 1-5.

House of Roses—
Senator Wilson Home

15 Forest Ave., Deadwood, SD 57732; (605) 578-1879. Victorian home with period furnishings, and exhibiting clothing and glassware. Library and archives hold maps, photos, and mine records tracing history of 19th c West. Accepts phone inquiries. Donations accepted. Hours: noon-6, or by appt.

Indian Museum of North America

Avenue of the Chiefs, Black Hills, Crazy Horse, SD 57730; (605) 673-4681. Preserves and exhibits Native American culture and history, as well as monument to Chief Crazy Horse. Museum houses artifacts of Teton Sioux, and artwork of other US and Canadian Indian tribes from 14th-18th c; displays of heavy equipment and sculpting techniques, stagecoach, and sculpture gallery. Large library collection on Indian art and history. Archives hold documents, photos, historical records, maps, and genealogical records. Answers inquiries, but library and archives closed to public. Accepts phone inquiries. Fee. Hours: 7-7.

Keystone Area Historical Society

P.O. Box 177, Keystone, SD 57751; (605) 666-4447. Preserves and displays area history. Museum housed in oldest SD school. Library and archives contain materials on area mining from

1870s, biographies, maps from 1870s-1920s, photos of area mining and disasters from 1980, and obituaries. Special collections include documents and memorabilia relating to Laura Ingalls Wilder and Charles Ingalls family, Mt Rushmore, and local pioneers. Accepts phone inquiries. No fee. Hours: M-Sa 2:30-5:30.

Minnilusa Pioneer Museum

515 West Blvd., Rapid City, SD 57701; (605) 394-6099. Preserves and promoted historical legacy of Rapid City and Black Hills region. Museum exhibits fur trade history from 1820-30s, military and scientific expeditions, and Indian/settler confrontation over mining, cattle, lumber, and transportation industries. Small research library. Archives hold personal materials of Dr. Valentine McGillycuddy, C. Irwin Leedy, Carl Leedy, and George Mansfield; maps of Black Hills region, including some from 1874 Custer expedition; and hundreds of photos. Accepts phone inquiries. No fee. Hours: June-Sept, M-Sa 9-5, Su 1-5; Oct-Dec & Feb-May, Tu-Sa 10-5, Su 1-5.

Old Fort Meade Museum
and Historic Research Association

P.O. Box 134, Fort Meade, SD 57741; (605) 347-2818. Collects, preserves and displays Ft Meade artifacts from 1878-1944. Museum exhibits holdings on ft history as peace-keeping post on Dakota frontier; library collects old books, pamphlets, and literature; and photo collection covering ft events. Accepts mail inquiries. Fee. Hours: May-Sept 9-8.

Old West Museum

P.O. Box 275, Chamberlain, SD 57325; (605) 734-6157. Collects many artifacts ranging from branding irons to fencing tools, and weapons. Many Indian artifacts as well. Transportation exhibits include early 20th c automobiles, tractors, and gas engines. Accepts phone inquiries. Fee. Hours: 7:30-9:30.

Pioneer Auto Museum
and Antique Town

P.O. Box 76, on I-90, Murdo, SD 57559; (605) 669-2691. Private collection of over 200 antique and classic cars, motorcycles and cycles, antique tractors and farm machinery, and many buildings of exhibits. Accepts phone inquiries. Fee. Hours: Apr-May, 8-6; June-Aug, 7-10.

Rapid City Public Library
610 Quincy St., Rapid City, SD 57701; (605) 394-4171. Public library provides historical info on SD and regional settlers. Archives have SD collection of books on state and books by SD authors, maps from 1884, small collection of historical photos, audiovisual materials of 1972 Rapid City flood, oral history recordings of pioneers, and genealogical materials from Dakota Territory. Accepts phone inquiries. No fee. Hours: M-Th 9-9, F-Sa 9-5:30.

Sioux Empire Medical Museum
Sioux Valley Hospital, School of Nursing, 1000 S. Euclid St., Sioux Falls, SD 57105; (605) 333-6397. Preserves medical history of hospital and area. Museum displays period nurse uniforms; orthopedic, pediatric, dental, and surgical history; 1910 patient room; nursery; iron lung for polio victims; and doctor's office. Libary has medical reference materials. Archives hold hospital and School of Nursing records and photos of medical staff. Library for in-house use only. Accepts phone inquiries. No fee. Hours: Su 1-4, M-F 11-4.

Sioux Falls Public Library
201 N. Main Ave., Sioux Falls, SD 57102; (605) 339-7082. Holds collection of SD census records from 1880-1910. Accepts phone inquiries. No fee. Hours: M-Th 9:30-9, F 9:30-6, Sa 9:30-5; and Sept-May, Sun 1-5.

Siouxland Heritage Museums
200 W. Sixth St., Sioux Falls, SD 57102; (605) 335-4210. Collects, preserves, interprets, and exhibits items on Minnehaha County and Sioux Falls history. Two historic buildings, Minnehaha courthouse and Pettigrew home, hold collections of historic and natl history items. Library holds materials from library of SD Sen Pettigrew's library, including books on politics, history, religion, and ethnology. Archives contain Pettigrew's papers, Northern Baseball League papers, state and county maps from territorial days, large photo collection, and George German archives of tapes, records, videos, and sheet music from SD musicians. Accepts phone inquiries. No fee.

Hours: Su-M 1-5, Tu-Sa 9-5.

South Dakota Hall of Fame
P.O. Box 568, Fort Pierre, SD 57532; (605) 223-2574. Honors outstanding SD residents and preserves their biographies through holdings in library, archives, and genealogical materials. Some video biographies and photos available. Accepts phone inquiries. No fee. Hours: 8-5.

South Dakota Office of History
Soldiers Memorial Bldg., E. Capitol Ave., Pierre, SD 57501. Preserves SD state and territorial historical materials. Holdings include biographical, autobiographical, political, geological, economic, and local history materials, as well as extensive photo collection.

South Dakota State Archives
State Library, Office of History, 800 N. Illinois, Pierre, SD 57501; (605) 773-3458. Collects, preserves, and makes available for research historical SD resources. Large library collection on history of SD and West, and genealogical sources from entire US; archives of SD govt; manuscripts from 1846; US, regional, SD, Sanborn Insurance, and Fire Underwriters Inspection Bureau maps from 1850; enormous photo collection on Dakota territory history from 1860; films/videotapes on local history, Custer's Last Stand, and other topics; large oral history collection; and SD daily and weekly newspapers. Accepts phone inquiries. No fee. Hours: M-F 8-5.

South Dakota State University
H.M. Briggs Library, P.O. Box 2115, Brookings, SD 57007; (605) 688-5106. Academic research library is depository for US documents since 1889, and holds SD documents since 1975. Archives contain materials from SD Agricultureal Experiment Station, Dakotah territorial records, Sanborn Fire Insurance and Fire Underwriters Inspection Bureau maps, and photos. Materials only circulate within university community. Accepts phone inquiries. No fee. Hours: M-Th 7:45-11:30, F 7:45-9, Sa 10-9, Su 1-11:30.

State Historical Preservation Center
P.O. Box 417, Vermillion, SD 57969; (605)

677-5314. Conducts national and state preservation programs for SD. Materials for in-house use only. Accepts phone inquiries. No fee. Hours: M-F 8-5.

W.H. Over State Museum

414 E. Clark, Vermillion, SD 57069; (605) 677-5228. Preserves, collects, and exhibits history and natural history of SD. Special Stanley J. Morrow collection of photos of Dakota Territory from 1869-1883. Accepts phone inquiries. No fee. Hours: M-F 8-5.

Tennessee

Abraham Lincoln Museum

Lincoln Memorial University, U.S. Hwy 25E, Harrogate, TN 37752; (615) 869-3611. Perpetuates principles exemplified by Lincoln through holdings in museum, library, and archives. Museum and library hold manuscripts, maps, photos, films/videotapes, and recordings relating to Lincoln and Civil War era. Special collections on Cassius Marcellus Clay and John L. Worden. Some restrictions. Accepts phone inquiries. Fee. Hours: M-F 9-4, Sa 11-4, Su 1-4.

African-American Cultural Alliance

P.O. Box 22173, Nashville, TN 37202; (615) 254-0970. Holds annual African Festival and Civil War tribute of Battle of Nashville, and houses special collection of materials on Civil War. Holdings include news photos and video footage from past tributes and festivals, and list of Civil War soldiers. Accepts phone inquiries (615-360-5362). No fee. Hours: 11-noon.

American Association for State and Local History

172 Second Ave., North, Suite 102, Nashville, TN 37201; (615) 255-2971. Natl membership org publishes books, newsletters, and pamphlets; conducts school programs and audiovisual presentations, and presents awards for excellence in field of American history. Accepts phone inquiry. No fee. Hours: call.

Beck Cultural Exchange Center

1927 Dandridge Ave., Knoxville, TN 37915; (615) 524-8461. Afro-American museum and archives with emphasis on local black history and culture. Museum holds some memorabilia and paintings, sculptures, and works of art; library concentrates on black history and slavery issues; archival materials include news clippings and personal biographies; photo collection concentrates on local black citizens; small film/videotape library; oral history interviews; and some genealogical records. Accepts phone inquiries. No fee. Hours: Tu-Sa 10-6.

Carson-Newman College Library

Box 1837, Jefferson City, TN 37760; (615) 475-9061. Academic research library with collection of USGS maps, archives of college materials, genealogical records of 14 TN families, and special Baptist history collection. Some restrictions. Accepts phone inquiries. No fee. Hours: M-Th 8-11, F 8-5, Sa 9-5, Su 2-6.

Carter House

P.O. Box 555, 1140 Columbia Ave., Franklin, TN 37064; (615) 791-1861. Commemorates 1864 Civil War Battle of Franklin. Museum holds war artifacts, uniforms, guns, swords, maps, documents, and photos of Civil War soldiers. May be some restrictions. Accepts phone inquiries. Fee. Hours: M-Sa 9-4, Su 2-4.

Casey Jones Village and Railroad Museum

Casey Jones Village, Jackson, TN 38305; (901) 668-1222. Home of Jones at time of his death houses railroad memorabilia, and is furnished with period artifacts. Holdings include photos of Jones and trains, genealogical records, letters and newspaper clippings on Jones, and large collection of railroad items donated by railroad employees and families. Accepts phone inquiries. Fee. Hours: 8-5.

Center for Southern Folklore

Box 40105, 1216 Peabody Ave., Memphis, TN 38104; (901) 726-4205. Non-profit corp dedicated to preservation and dissemination of info on folk and ethnic cultures of South. Library houses small collection of books, periodicals, and newsletters. Archives hold large collection of photos, extensive film footage, large collection of recordings, and special Rev L.O. Taylor collection on Memphis's black community from 1920s-77. Accepts phone inquiries. No fee. Hours: M-F 8:30-5:30.

Chattanooga Regional History Museum

4th & Chestnut Sts., Chattanooga, TN 37402; (615) 265-3247. Collects, researches, and exhibits materials on heritage of greater Chattanooga region and tri-state area. Library collects diaries, manuscripts, some maps, and photos of region. Accepts phone inquiries. Donations accepted. Hours: Tu-F 10-4:30, Sa-Su noon-4:30.

Chattanooga-Hamilton County Bicentennial Library

Local History Dept, 1001 Broad St., Chattanooga, TN 37402; (615) 757-5317. Collects and maintains history of Chattanooga and surrounding area. Library holds large collection of materials on Southeast, NC, Hamilton County, and Chattanooga. Manuscript collection contains archives of orgs, personal papers, govt records, maps from 1700s, large collection of photos dating to Civil War, oral history videotapes, genealogical records, and extensive vertical file on Chattanooga, Hamilton County, and TN. Materials for in-house use only. Accepts phone inquiries. Fee for mail inquiries. Hours: M-Tu 9-9, W-Sa 9-6.

Cleveland State Community College Library

Document Dept., P.O. Box 3570, Shiloh Church Rd., Cleveland, TN 37320; (615) 472-7141. Academic research library with emphasis on local and TN history, with small collection of TN and regional maps, photos, and Clemmer scrapbooks. Materials circulate within college community. Accepts phone inquiries (615-478-6209). No fee. Hours: school in session, M-Th 7:30-10, F 7:30-4:30, Sa 10-2; other times, M-F 7:30-4:30.

Columbia State Community College

Documents Dept., John Finney Memorial Library, Hampshire Pike, Hwy 99 W, Columbia, TN 38401; (615) 388-0120. Academic support library with materials on Columbia and TN history, James Polk family, American Revolution, and Salem witch trials. Map collection includes topographical images of TN and surrounding states. Genealogical materials detail Maury county court, marriage, and census records. Materials do not circulate outside college community. Accepts phone inquiries. No fee. Hours: M-Th 7:45-9, F 7:45-4:15.

Country Music Hall of Fame and Museum

Country Music Foundation, 4 Music Square East, Nashville, TN 37203; (615) 256-1693. Preserves and interprets American country music through holdings in museum, library and archives. Museum covers country music's folk roots through contemporary period, with exhibits on instruments, costumes, and memorabilia. Library and archives have manuscripts, many photos of personalities, large number of films/videotapes, and extensive library of country music recordings. Accepts phone inquiries. Fee for museum; no fee for library/archives. Hours: library/archives by appt only, 9-5.

Cragfront Project Summer County

Rte. 1, P.O. Box 73, Castalian Springs, TN 37031; (615) 452-7070. Historic house museum once owned by Gen James Winchester depicts lifestyle of period 1789-1864. Home decorated with antique furnishings, decorative arts, and textiles; museum houses documents and books. Accepts phone inquiries. Fee. Hours: Apr-Nov, Tu-Sa 10-5, Su 1-5.

David Crockett Cabin

Hwy 45 West, Rutherford, TN 38369. Preserves history of David Crockett and reconstruction of cabin, with some genealogical and local history materials. Fee.

Disciples of Christ Historic Society

1101 19th Ave., South, Nashville, TN 37212; (615) 372-1444. Preserves historic materials of Campbell-Stone movement in Church of Christ. Holdings in museum, library, and archives include manuscripts, photos, recordings, and films/videotapes. Membership required for use of materials. Accepts phone inquiries. Fee. Hours: M-F 8-4:30.

Fort Donelson National Battlefield

P.O. Box 434, U.S. Hwy 79, Dover, TN 37058;

(615) 232-5348. Preserves and interprets battle-field history with library collection of official Civil War records and biographies, and unpublished research materials on ft. Accepts phone inquiries. Fee. Hours: May-Sept, 8-5; Oct-Apr, 8-4:30.

Governor John Sevier Home, Marble Springs

P.O. Box 9204, Knoxville, TN 37940; (615) 573-5508. Restored home of first TN governor, with kitchen, smokehouse, and loomhouse. Accepts phone inquiries. Fee. Hours: M-S 10-noon, 2-5, and Su 2-5.

Grand Guitar Museum

535 New Kingsport Hwy, Bristol, TN 37620; (615) 968-1719. Museum preserves large collection of rare stringed instruments in addition to guitars, with emphasis on folk, country, and mountain music instruments. Other holdings include birthplace map of local country and bluegrass performers, recording studio, and instrument shop. Accepts phone inquiries. No fee. Hours: call.

Great Smoky Mountains National Park

U.S. Hwy 441, Gatlinburg, TN 37738; (615) 436-5615. Preserves natural, cultural, and scenic values of southern Appalachian area. Museum holds exhibits on Cades Cove and Ononaluftee and Cataleochee regions; archives collect land records, park history manuscripts and maps, photos of regional history and people, oral history interviews, and genealogical records. Special collection of park development materials. Materials for on-site use only. Accepts phone inquiries. No fee. Hours: 8-4:30.

Hank Williams Jr. Museum

P.O. Box 24362, 1524 Demonbreun St., Nashville, TN 37202; (615) 242-8313. Exhibits personal effects from lives of country music legends Hank Williams Sr and Jr. Museum displays over 500 items, including manuscripts of original Hank Williams songs; photos on display; films/videotapes; and copies of birth and death certificates. Restrictions on some materials. Accepts phone inquiries. Fee. Hours: May 15-Oct 31, 8-10; Nov-May 14, 8-6.

Hermitage, Home of Andrew Jackson

4580 Rachel's Lane, Hermitage, TN 37076; (615) 889-2941. Preserves, conserves, and interprets historic Hermitage mansion, Tulip Grove mansion, church, outbuildings, and their period furniture. Library contains materials of and on Andrew Jackson family, from 1800-50. Archives holds records of Ladies' Hermitage Assn, letters and documents relating to Jackson and Hermitage, photos, genealogical materials on Jackson and Donelson families, and portraits by Jackson's friend, Ralph E.W. Earl. Research by prior approval only. Accepts phone inquiries. Fee for tour. Hours: 9-5.

Historic Nashville

P.O. Box 2785, Nashville, TN 37201; (615) 244-7835. Org preserves historic environment and promotes public history awareness. Has small slide collection on architectural heritage and neighborhoods of Nashville. Accepts phone inquiries. No fee. Hours: 8:30-5.

Hunter Museum of Art

10 Bluff View, Chattanooga, TN 37403; (615) 267-0968. Collects, preserves, and interprets cultural objects of American heritage. Collection covers American art from colonial times to the present. Library has materials for reference. Archives holds materials on Museum's history. Regional art gallery highlights work of local artists. Photos and films/videotapes are available. Accepts phone inquiries. No fee. Hours: Tu-Sa 10-4:30, Su 1-4:30.

James K. Polk Memorial Association

P.O. Box 741, 301 W. 7th St., Columbia, TN 38402; (615) 388-2354. Preserves amd interprets Polk home and its collections. Museum holdings include possessions of President Polk and his family and artifacts documenting his life and presidency. Photo collection holds photos of Polk, his family and his Cabinet. Genealogical collection holds incomplete family records from late 17th c. Accepts phone inquiries. Fee. Hours: Apr-Oct, M-Sa 9-5, Su 1-5; Nov-Mar, M-Sa 9-4, Su 1-5.

Lambuth College

Documents Dept., Luther Gobbel Library,

Jackson, TN 38305; (901) 425-3290. Academic research library with archival holdings of Lambuth and Memphis Methodist Church Conferences. Holdings include photos and recordings. Materials non-circulating. No fee. Hours: M-F 8-4.

Memphis Pink Palace Museum

3050 Central Ave., Memphis, TN 38111; (901) 454-5607. Interprets and preserves items related to cultural and natural history of mid-South. Museum exhibits 19th and 20th c materials on Memphis and surrounding area. Library holds materials on local history and archaeology. Accepts phone inquiries. Fee. Hours: M-F 9-5.

Memphis State University

Special Collections, Brister Library, Memphis, TN 38152; (901) 454-2206. Academic research library has collection of materials from 1968 Memphis Sanitation Workers strike during which Martin Luther King, Jr, was killed. Holdings include newspaper clippings, TV footage, interviews with strike members, and photos and negatives. Accepts phone inquiries. No fee. Hours: M-F 8-10, Sa-Su 1-6.

Mississippi River Museum

125 N. Front, Memphis, TN 38103; (901) 576-7230. Preserves and interprets natural and cultural history of Lower MI River Valley. Museum diplays region's history over past 10 thousand years; library provides reference materials; collection of maps includes annotated navigational charts; photo collection of river boats documents past 100 years of river transportation; and special collection of showboat performers Tommy and Jeanne Windsor memorabilia. Accepts phone inquiries. Fee. Hours: 10-5.

Mississippi Valley Collection

West Tennessee Historical Society, Memphis State University, Library, Memphis, TN 38152; (901) 454-2211. Promotes wider knowledge of West TN life and history. Library holds archival materials in form of books, periodicals, photos, and maps. Manuscript collections composed of papers from C.B. Adamson, Ella Costillo Bennett, R.C. Donaldson, George Gordon, James Hamner, Robert Johnson, Memphis and Charleston Railroad Depot, and Meriwether family.

Accepts phone inquiries. No fee. Hours: call.

Museum of Appalachia

Box 359, Norris, TN 37828; (615) 494-7680. Preserves pioneer Appalachian life through 28 bldg complex, living history, and large collection of regional memorabilia. Accepts phone inquiries. Fee. Hours: call.

Museum of Tobacco Art and History

800 Harrison St., Nashville, TN 37203; (615) 242-9218. Preserves and displays art objects related to tobacco history from American Indians to major cultures in world. Library holds small reference collection on history and art of tobacco. Reference materials non-circulating. Accepts phone inquiries. No fee. Hours: Tu-Sa 10-4.

Nashville Room

Nashville Public Library, 8th Ave., North and Union, Nashville, TN 37203; (615) 259-6125. Preserves history of Nashville and middle TN in Tennesseana collection, genealogical collection, Nashville authors collection, biography file, Jeter-Smith dance collection, map collection, Naff collection of regional entertainment memorabilia, Nashville and TN history clipping file, photo collection, and TN artists file. Holdings include manuscripts, posters, photos, slides, genealogical materials, and historic Nashville materials. Accepts phone inquiries. No fee. Hours: M-F 9-8, Sa 9-5, and Oct-May, Su 2-5.

P.T. Boat Museum

P.O. Box 109, 663 S. Cooper, Suite 4, Memphis, TN 38101; (901) 272-9980. Preserves history and spirit of US Navy patrol torpedo boats, and men who ran them. Library has limited reference materials. Archives retains documents, squadron histories, and correspondence; maps of Pacific, Alaskan, and European theatres; large collection of photos; and WWII training and propoganda film footage. Accepts phone inquiries. No fee. Hours: M-F 8:30-4:30.

Quillen-Dishner College of Medicine Library

Box 23290 A, East Tennessee State University, Johnson City, TN 37614; (615) 929-6252.

Academic research library features museum on 19th and 20th c Appalachia, archives of College of Medicine, and special History of Medicine Collection on 19th and early 20th c practices. Materials circulate to health professionals only. Accepts phone inquiries. No fee. Hours: call.

Rocky Mount Historical Association

Rte. 2, Box 70, Piney Flats, TN 37686; (615) 538-7396. Museum presents exhibits and living history displays on 1770-1792 period. Restored home was capitol of US Territory south of OH River in 1790, and is decorated with period furnishings. Museum, library, and archives hold limited collections of manuscripts, maps, and photos. Fee. Hours: museum, M-Sa 10-5, Su 2-6; library, M-F 10-5.

Shiloh National Military Park and Cemetery

P.O. Box 67, Hwy 22, Shiloh, TN 38376; (901) 689-5275. Interprets Civil War Battle of Shiloh through collections in museum, library, and archives. Holdings include manuscripts, maps, and photos. Accepts phone inquiries. Fee. Hours: library and study collection by appt only; 8-5.

Society for the Preservation of Old Mills

Old Mill News, c/o Michael LaForest, Editor, 604 Ensley, Rte. 29, Knoxville, TN 37920; (615) 577-7757. Promotes public and private interest in old grain and saw mills. Society archives hold books and news clippings on mills, some from 19th c. Photo collection consists of mills throughout US. Hours: call.

Southern Baptist Historical Library and Archives

Historical Commission, Southern Baptist Convention, 901 Commerce St., Suite 400, Nashville, TN 37203; (615) 244-0344. Records history and work of Southern Baptist Convention with artifacts, records, papers, photos, films/videotapes, and recordings in museum, library, and archives. Holdings cover history of Mission and Sunday School boards, commissions; papers of pastors, teachers, missionaries, and workers; many photos portraying Southern Baptist history and church life; films and videotapes of conventions; and recordings of meetings, sermons, oral histories, and music. Some materials restricted. Accepts phone inquiries. No fee. Hours: M-F 9-4.

Southern Resources Unlimited

5632 Meadowcrest Lane, Nashville, TN 37209; (615) 356-3211. Provides research and editorial services for films and books on TN and Southern history. Extensive library holdings on TN, South and Southern women, Natchez Trace, Cherokee Indians, TN archaeology, and TN General Assembly. Accepts phone inquiries. No admission fee. Hours: 9-5.

Stones River National Battlefield

Rt. 10, Box 495, Old Nashville Hwy, Murfreesboro, TN 37129; (615) 893-9501. Preserves site of Battle of Stones River and provides for its study. Museum and library hold materials on 1862 battles, and campaign for middle TN. Genealogical materials on Union soldiers buried in Stones River Cemetery available. Accepts phone inquiries. Fee. Hours: 8-5.

Tennessee Antiquities Preservation Association

110 Leake Ave., Nashville, TN 37205; (615) 352-8247. Parent organization for maintenance and restoration of historic properties. Accepts phone inquiries. No fee. Hours: M-W 9-4.

Tennessee Historical Commission

701 Broadway, Nashville, TN 37219; (615) 742-6716. State historic preservation office with large collection of photos and survey sheets of TN bldgs and structures. Materials non-circulating. Accepts phone inquiries. No fee. Hours: M-F 8-4:30.

Tennessee Humanities Council

P.O. Box 24767, 1003 18th Ave., S., Nashville, TN 37212; (615) 320-7001. Offers grants to non-profit orgs for production of public education programs in humanities. Accepts phone inquiries. No fee. Hours: M-F 8-5.

Tennessee State Library and Archives

403 7th Ave. North, Nashville, TN 37219; (615) 741-2764. Research collection houses

info on southeast US, and federal and state documents. Library holds materials on history, politics, economics, geography, geology, culture, law, industry, and genealogy of TN; archives collections include TN governors' papers, military service records, and TN newspapers; map collections cover county surveys and highways; photos of TN people and places; recordings of legislative debates from 1955; genealogical materials; broadsides; and Rose sheet music collection. Accepts phone inquiries. No fee. Hours: M-F 8-6, Sa 10-6, Su 1-6.

Tennessee State Museum

James K. Polk Center Office Bldg. and Cultural Ctr., 505 Deaderick St., Nashville, TN 37219. Preserves TN history through holdings in museum and library. Museum displays printed materials, firearms, fashion, textiles, military artifacts, decorative arts, and furniture. Library has small collection on TN history, map of Shiloh drawn by Gen Beauregard, and small collection of TN scene file photos.

Tennessee Valley Historic Collection

Tennessee Valley Association, 238 Natural Resources Bldg., Ridgeway Dr., Norris, TN 37828; (615) 632-1585. Collects artifacts from 7-state TVA region on flood control, river navigation, power generation, economic and community development, agricultural and fertilizer development, national defense projects, and social, cultural, and political activites. Archives contain TVA archival records and materials from oral history history program, as well as manuscripts, maps, photos, films/videotapes/recordings, and genealogical records. Accepts phone inquiries. No fee. Hours: 8-4:45.

Travellers' Rest Historic House

636 Farrell Pkwy., Nashville, TN 37220; (615) 832-2962. Interprets life and history in middle TN through perspective of Judge John Overton family, household, and associates. Museum is restored historic house with exhibits, and furnished in early 19th c pieces. Accepts phone inquiries. Fee. Hours: M-Sa 9-5, Su 1-5.

University of Tennessee at Knoxville

Documents Division, John C. Hodges Library,

015 Volunter Blvd., Knoxville, TN 37996; (615) 974-4171. Academic research library with holdings on TN and Univ of TN history, radiation research, WWII, papers of Robert Hartman, and special Estes Kefauver collection. Also collects maps, photos, motion pictures and documentaries, Galston Busoni archives, WPA records, and US census materials. Materials do not circulate outside college community. Accepts phone inquiries. No fee. Hours: M-Th 7:30-midnight, F 7:30-8, Sa 9-8, Su 10-midnight.

University of Tennessee at Chattanooga

Library, Chattanooga, TN 37401; (615) 755-4501. Academic research facility holds Civil War collection of Southern Americana, with emphasis on Confederacy and Federal point of view. Hours: call.

University of Tennessee at Martin

Document Dept., Paul Meek Library, Martin, TN 38238; (901) 587-7065. Academic research library with collection on Civil War, Native Americans, and Southern history. Holds some maps and genealogical records; holds books based on TN and by TN authors; and keeps special collection of "Time" journalist Holland McComb papers. Materials non-circulating. Accepts phone inquiries. No fee. Hours: M-Th 8-11, F 8-6, Sa 8-5, Su 2-11.

Vanderbilt Television News Archive

Vanderbilt University, Jean & Alexander Heard Library, Nashville, TN 37240; (615) 322-2927. Tapes network news programs and makes them available for research. Archive covers Aug 5, 1968, to present with some selected special news broadcasts. Accepts phone inquiries. Call for fee. Hours: M-F 8-4:30.

World O' Tools Museum

Rte. 1, Box 180, Waverly, TN 37185; (615) 296-3218. Collects and displays variety of tools with emphasis on wood and metalworking, and gives info on their technical history and use. Museum houses over 15 thousand tools. Library holds reference materials dating to mid-19th c, craftsmen's ledgers and account books from late 19th c, and photos of craftsmen at work. Materials non-circulating. Accepts phone inquiries. No fee. Hours: call.

Texas

Abilene Christian University
Margaret and Herman Brown Library, University Station, 1600 Campus Ct., Abilene, TX 79699; (915) 677-1911. Academic research library holds Donner Library of Americanism. Holdings include pamphlets, documents, and periodicals on US far right during and after WWII. Also has some materials on Jews and Freemasonry. Accepts phone inquiries. No fee. Hours: call.

African-American Cultural Heritage Center
Children's Cultural Heritage Center and Museum, 3434 South R.L. Thornton Frwy., Dallas, TX 75224; (214) 375-7530. Children's cultural heritage center focuses on African American cultural heritage. Library and archives have slides, records, filmstrips, books, photos, genealogical records, and other materials focusing on African-American Texans. Primarily for use of Dallas Independent School District. Accepts phone inquiries. No fee. Hours: 9-4.

Age of Steam Railroad Museum
P.O. Box 26369, Dallas, TX 75226; (214) 421-8754. Interest in railroad history. Museum includes extensive artifacts of railroading, and restored train equipment. Answers phone inquiries. Admission fee. Hours: Th-F 9-1, Sa-Su 11-5.

Amarillo Art Center
P.O. Box 447, Amarillo, TX 79178; (806) 371-5050. Museum features 20th c American art and photography, with museum emphasis on Russell Lee and other Farm Security Administration photos. Library contains general art history and criticism materials, and videotapes on Farm Security Administration photography. Accepts phone inquiries. No fee. Hours: Tu-F 10-5, Sa-Su 1-5.

Amarillo Public Library
Southwest Collection, 413 E. Fourth St., Amar-illo, TX 79101; (806) 378-3054. Library collection covers history of TX, LA, NM, AR, MO, KS settlement, overland journeys, biographies, Indian captivities, outlaws, Mexican War, Catholic missionary reports, fur trade, western trails, Indian Wars, cowboys, TX Rangers, and TX history. Holdings include documents, maps, pamphlets, interviews, and photos. Accepts phone inquiries. No fee. Hours: call.

Amon Carter Museum of Western Art
P.O. Box 2365, 3510 Camp Bowie Blvd., Fort Worth, TX 76113; (817) 738-1933. Collection attempts to interpret American history through its art. Holdings include reference materials on 19th and 20th c American artists, with emphasis on Charles Russell and Frederic Remington; materials on American and Canadian West; indexing materials for entire runs of "Harper's Weekly" and "Leslie's Illustrated Newspaper"; and pictorial and artistic materials. Accepts phone inquiries. No fee. Hours: call.

Angelo State University
Documents Division, Porter Henderson Library, 2601 W. Avenue N, San Angelo, TX 76909; (915) 942-2300. Extensive Civil War and local genealogical holdings. Restricted use outside library. Accepts phone inquiries (915-942-2222). No fee. Hours: M-Th 7:45am-11pm, F 7:45-5, Sa 9-5, Su 2-10.

Army Air Defense Artillery Museum
ATZC-DPTM-M, Fort Bliss, TX 79916; (915) 568-5412. Collects, preserves, and interprets history of Air Defense in US Army. Museum exhibits include weapons park. Small library supports research. Archives holds documents, manuscripts, military maps of WWII, photos of aircraft and antiaircraft machinery, films/videotapes on military and cultural subjects, and recordings of several eras of US Army military music. Visits only by 45-day prior written notice. Accepts phone inquiries. No fee. Hours: by appt, 9-4:30.

Austin College
Abell Library Center, Sherman, TX 75090; (214) 892-9101. Academic research library with collection of govt documents, Austin College archives and photos, Texana collection of books,

and local history interviews. Accepts phone inquiries. No fee. Hours: M-Th 8am-10pm, F 8-5, Sa 9-5, Su 2-10.

Austin History Center

Austin Public Library, P.O. Box 2287, Austin, TX 78701; (512) 473-4279. Collects and preserves materials about Austin and Travis county. Library holds monographs, budgets, reports, materials from Austin authors, and directories from 1839. Archives have records and papers of city and country govt, civic orgs, and businesses, manuscripts, maps, large photo collection, films/videotapes, oral history and local music recordings, and architectural archives of local architectural firms. Special collections on O. Henry and TX women's suffrage movement. No fee. Hours: Tu-Th 9-8:45, F-Sa 9-5:45.

Battleship Texas
State Historical Site

Texas Parks and Wildlife Department, 3527 Battleground Rd., La Porte, TX 77571; 713-479-2411. Displays battleship to public. Archives, manuscripts, and photos not available for public use. Admission fee. Accepts phone inquiries. Hours 10-5.

Boom Town Revisited,
Hutchinson County Museum

Texas Association of Museums, 618 N. Main, Borger, TX 79007; 806-273-6121. Local history and art museum collecting history of Hutchinson County, TX. Library includes petroleum artifacts, local history, photo archive, and buffalo hunter artifacts circa 1874. Some materials available for examination only by appt. No admission fee, but hourly curatorial fee for access to some files. Accepts phone inquiries. Hours: M-Sa 11-5, Su 2-5.

Carson County Square
House Museum

Box 276, Fifth & Elsie Sts., Panhandle, TX 79068; (806) 537-3524. Preserves, researches, and displays history of surrounding region. Museum exhibits include Santa Fe Railroad caboose, Eclipse windmill, Indian art, and historic photos and documents. Library has info on TX, and oral histories. Accepts phone inquiries. No fee. Hours: M-Sa 9-5:30, Su 1-5:30.

Catholic Archives of Texas

Roman Catholic Dioceses of Texas, P.O. Box 13327, Capitol Station, 1600 N. Congress, Austin, TX 78711; 512-476-4888. Records and preserves documents related to the Catholic historical heritage in the United States from 1650. Library, archives, photos, and films/videotapes emphasize presence of church in Texas, especially Diocese of Austin. Answers phone inquiries. No fee. Hours: M-F 9-5.

Civil War Round Table of Texas

P.O. Box 7004, Fort Worth, TX 76111; (817) 732-5220. Membership org studies, preserves, and promotes interest in battles of Civil War. Accepts phone inquiries. Fee for membership. Hours: call.

Confederate Research Center
and Gun Museum

P.O. Box 619, Hillsboro, TX 76645; (817) 582-2555. Preserves and displays Confederate military history materials. Museum holds 3 rooms of military art, artifacts, and weapons. Library covers Civil War history with emphasis on Confederacy. Archives retains files, regimental histories, manuscripts, letters, diaries, maps, and photos. Special collection of muster rolls from 30 companies in Hood's TX brigade, and 1860 TX census records. Accepts phone inquiries. No fee. Hours: 8-4:30.

Cowboy Artists
of America Museum

Box 1716, (1550 Bandera Hwy.), Kerrville, TX 78029; 512-896-2553. Interest in fine art of American West. Holdings include museum; extensive library; biographical records on members of Cowboy Artists of America; and extensive collections of photos and negatives. Answers phone inquiries. Admission fee. Hours: Tu-Sa 9-5, Su 1-5; M 9-5 only June-Aug.

Cowboy Country Museum

P.O. Box 1206, 113 Wetherbee, Stamford, TX 79553; (915) 773-2411. Preserves Western art and artifacts, with emphasis on Stamford area. Collection includes art of Tom Ryan and Wain Baize. Archives hold Stamford newspapers, maps, photos. Accepts phone inquiries. No fee. Hours: 8-5.

Crosby County Pioneer Memorial Museum

P.O. Box 386, Crosbyton, TX 79322; (806) 675-2331. Provides facilities for exhibition of Crosby County and Southwest history. Museum documents regional material culture from 1870-1930. Library contains regional Texana materials. Archives retains local manuscripts, maps of county and west TX, large photo collection, and genealogical records of county residents. Research with staff supervision or by staff only. Accepts phone inquiries. No fee. Hours: Tu-Sa 9-noon, 2-5.

Dallas County Heritage Society

Old City Pk, 1717 Gano St., Dallas, TX 75215; (214) 421-5141. Museum of architectural and cultural history with focus on north central TX life from 1840-1910. Museum has commercial, transportation, medical, legal, printing, residential, educational, religous, and rural displays. Library has materials on TX history, decorative arts, architecture, "Harpers Magazine" and "Ladies Home Journal" series, Sears catalogs, and censuses. Archives hold TX currency, business records, Dallas sheet music, architectural drawings, Sanborn maps, photos, TX family records, and textiles and furniture. Requires letter and appt for collection use. Accepts phone inquiries. Fee. Hours: Tu-Sa 10-4, Su 1:30-4:30.

Dallas Historical Society

P.O. Box 26038, Dallas, TX 75226; 214-421-5136. Research facility, collects and preserves history of TX and Dallas, from Spanish exploration. Maintains museum and library, including maps, photos, films/videotapes, recordings, and manuscripts. Does not lend materials. No fee. Accepts phone inquiries. Hours: M-F 9-5.

Dallas Public Library

Documents Division, 1515 Young St., Dallas, TX 75201; (214) 670-1468. Depository for federal and TX documents and US patents from 1790 to present. Most of collection for in-library use only. Accepts phone inquiries. No fee. Hours: M, W 9-9; Tu, Th, Sa 9-6; F 9-5; Su 1-5.

East Texas State University

James Gilliam Gee Library, East Texas Station, Commerce, TX 75428; (214) 886-5726. Academic research library with collections of US geologic atlases, atlas to accompany records of Union and Confederate armies from 1891-95, and genealogical records. Other holdings include TX folklore, WWII posters, and materials on TX printing arts. Accepts phone inquiries. No fee. Hours: M-F 8-6, Su 9-noon.

El Paso Museum of History

12901 Gateway West, El Paso, TX 79927; (915) 858-1928. Collects, preserves, and researches artifacts from El Paso and surrounding area. Exhibits illustrate history from era of Spanish conquistadors, and include blacksmith and saddle-making shops and Victorian room. Accepts phone inquiries. No fee. Hours: Tu-Su 9-5.

Eugene C. Barker Texas History Center

University of Texas at Austin, Sid Richardson Hall 2.101, Austin, TX 78713; 512-471-5961. Collects and preserves information on history and development of Texas, the West, and the South. Holdings include extensive library, including rare reprints from 1556; university archives; extensive photo, map, and record and tape collections; genealogical records; newspaper collections; special collections. Answers phone inquiries. No fee. Hours: M-Sa 8-5.

Fielder Museum

1616 W. Abrams St., Arlington, TX 76013; (817) 460-4001. Cultural, historical learning center covering local history from late 1800s through 1940s. Sponsors public classes. Accepts phone inquiries. Fee. Hours: Tu-F 10-4, Su 1:30-4:30.

First Cavalry Division Museum

P.O. Box 5187, Bldg. 2218, Headquarters Ave., Fort Hood, TX 76545; (817) 287-3626. Collects, preserves, and interprets material culture related to history of 1st Cavalry Division. Museum exhibits trace division development from Indian Wars through Vietnam. Library has reference materials. Archives contains unit histories, after-action reports, and photos from 1880s to Vietnam. Accepts phone inquiries. No fee. Hours: M-F 9-3:30, Sa-Su noon-3:30.

First Ladies of Texas Historic Costumes Collection

DAR Museum, Box 23975, TWU Station, (Campus, Texas at Bell), Denton, TX 76204; 817-898-2683. Preserves Texas history in form of fashion apparel of wives of state governors. Museum collection has garments and related documents; photographs; and special collections. Answers phone inquiries. No fee. Hours: M-Th 8-5:30.

Fort Bliss Historical Holding

ATZC-DPTM-M, Fort Bliss, TX 79916; (915) 568-2804. Researches, preserves, and interprets cultural interaction of Army's garrisons with Mexical civilians in El Paso. Museum and library holdings document period from 1848 and cover local history and culture to military history. Archives retains post publications and papers from early 20th c. Photos of Ft date from Punitive Expeditions. Special Brigadier Gen Terry Allen collection and Brigadier Gen "Blackjack" Pershing collections. No fee. Hours: closed for renovation; normal hours M-F 9-4.

Fort Concho National Historic Landmark

213 East Ave. D, San Angelo, TX 76903; (915) 657-4441. Preserves Ft Concho site and artifacts and illustrates its history. Museum contains military period and San Angelo and west TX pioneers artifacts. Exhibits cover tools and equip, ethnology, natural history, textiles, and communications and transportation. Library has materials on Western frontier history after 1865 and military history. Archives has 19th c documents, maps, photos, and oral history interviews. Special collections include papers of Capt G.G. Huntt, M.C. Ragsdale photos, Oscar Ruffini architectural drawings, and textiles. Materials non-circulating. Accepts phone inquiries. Fee for museum, no fee for library. Hours: M-F 8-noon, 1-5.

Fort Davis National Historic Site

P.O. Box 1456, Fort Davis, TX 79734; 915-426-3224. Interprets role of Ft Davis (1854-91) in western expansion and Indian wars. Library covers western history 1850-90, including women's diaries, history of black soldiers at ft,

and books. Holdings include public and private papers of ft, maps of surrounding area, photos of ft and residents, recordings, genealogical records, and extensive newspaper files; extensive film/videotape collection. On-site use only. Accepts phone inquiries. Admission fee. Hours: summer 8-5; 8-6 Labor Day-Memorial Day.

Fort Lancaster State Historic Site

Texas Parks and Wildlife Department, P.O. Box 306, Sheffield, TX 79781; 915-836-4391. Preserves ruins, educates public about ft (1855-71), natives, soldiers, camel experiment, and archeology. Has small map collection and items excavated from site. Answers phone inquiries. No fee. Hours: Tu-Th 8-5; F-M 8-5, but closed 1 hour for lunch.

Fort McKavett State Historic Site

Ft. McKavett S.H.S., P.O. Box 867, Ft. McKavett, TX 76841; (915) 396-2358. Preserves, restores, and reconstructs role of military and ft during Indian Wars period, 1852-83. Museum has interpretive exhibits in old hospital ward emphasizing military history, community, and historic archaeology. Other holdings include maps and photos. Accepts phone inquiries. No fee. Hours: 8-5.

Fort Sam Houston Museum

(AFZG-PTM-M, Ft. Sam Houston, TX 78234-5000), San Antonio, TX 78234; (512)221-4886. Preserves and depicts history of fort and U.S. Army in San Antonio area from 1845. Holdings include museum, library, archives, maps, and extensive photos. Answers phone inquiries. No fee. Hours: W-Su 10-4.

Fort Worth Museum of Science and History

1501 Montgomery St., Fort Worth, TX 76107; (817) 732-1631. Promotes interest in technoloy that has broadened understanding of self, society, and natural world. Museum covers Ft Worth history, dinosaurs, and objects from all over globe. Small collection of manuscripts, maps, and photos on Ft Worth. Collection of sheet music from '30s-'60s, musicbox disks, wax cylinders, Edison disks, and recordings of Big Band era also available. Accepts phone inquiries. No fee. Hours: M-Sa 9-5, Su 2-5.

French Legation

802 San Marcos St., Austin, TX 78702; (512) 472-8180. Historic museum home built by French charge d'affaires as Legation de France in 1841. Decorated in period furnishings. Accepts phone inquiries. Fee. Hours: Tu-Su 1-5.

Friends of the Governor's Mansion

P.O. Box 13022, (322 Congress Avenue, Suite 202), Austin, TX 76711; (512) 474-9960. Interest in history of Texas governor's mansion. Maintains collection of 19th c antiques. Holdings include photos of the mansion from 1856, films, and historical pieces from past residents. Accepts phone inquiries. No fee. Hours: M-F 8-5.

Gregg County Historical Museum

P.O. Box 3342, 214 N. Fredonia St., Longview, TX 75606; (214) 753-5840. Collects, preserves, studies, and exhibits information on history of Gregg county. Museum displays materials on natural resources, settlement, education, agriculture, manufacturing, and trade and transportation of area from 1850s-1930s. Library has small collection of books on TX. Archives contains legal documents pertaining to Gregg county development, maps, photos, and genealogical records. Special Arthur Northcutt Brown Memorial Military collection has significant number of artifacts from WWI, WWII, Korean, and Vietnam wars. Accepts phone inquiries. Fee. Hours: Tu-Sa 1-4.

Hardin-Simmons University

Richardson Library, 2200 Hickory, Abilene, TX 79601; (915) 677-7281. Academic research library has materials on Western Americana, TX, and Mexico history. Holdings cover part of US once part of Mexico, and ranching, railroads, discovery, and exploration in that region of TX. Accepts phone inquiries. No fee. Hours: call.

Heritage Museum at Falfurrias

P.O. Box 86, North St. Marys St., Falfurrias, TX 78355; (512) 325-2907. Local history museum holds materials on TX Rangers. Library has old textbook collection, TX materials, and Mexican folklore. Archives contains copy of Dodson text, maps, large photo collection, and slide shows on Faith Healer of Los Olmos. Special collection of materials on TX Rangers from Capt McMurrey and Capt Brooks. Accepts phone inquiries. Donations accepted. Hours: Tu-F 11-5.

Hertzberg Circus Collection

210 W. Market St., San Antonio, TX 78205; (512) 229-7810. Preserves and promotes circus history with extensive collection of circus artifacts in museum, reference works and periodicals in library, and letters, documents, programs, clippings, photos, and posters in archives. Accepts phone inquiries. No fee. Hours: M-Sa 9-5:30, and May-Oct, Su 1-5.

Hoblitzelle Theatre Arts Library

University of Texas at Austin, Harry Ransom Center, Austin, TX 78712; (512) 471-9122. Maintains large collection on life and career of Gloria Swanson. Holdings cover 1913-83, and include correspondence with Mary Pickford, William Faulkner, and Kennedy family. Restrictions on holdings. Accepts phone inquiries. Hours: call.

Houston Public Library

Govt Documents Division, 500 McKinney Ave., Houston, TX 77002; (713) 236-1313. Public library with strong collections of Census Bureau, Dept. of Commerce, Dept. of Agriculture, Interior Dept., Dept. of Energy, and NASA materials. Depository collection closed to public; accessible through public service depts. Accepts phone inquiries. No fee. Hours: M-F 9-9, Sa 9-6, Su 2-6.

Jefferson Davis Association

c/o James McIntosh, Editor, Rice University, Houston, TX 77001; (713) 527-4990. Underwrites preparation of complete and scholarly edition of Jefferson Davis's personal and public papers. Accepts phone inquiries. No fee. Hours: call.

John E. Conner Museum

Texas A&M University, P.O. Box 2172 - Station 1, Kingsville, TX 78363; (512) 595-2810. Interest in history of south TX. Holdings include personal, printed, and photographic publications; maps; films/videotapes; oral histories; and local artifacts. Answers phone inquiries. No fee. Hours: M-F 9-5, Su 2:30-5, Sa by appt.

Jose Antonio Navarro
State Historic Site

228 S. Laredo St., San Antonio, TX 78207; (512) 226-4801. Preserves and maintains 1850s home of Jose Antonio Navarro and interprets his life and contributions to Texas history. Holdings include genealogical records of Navarrro family, copies of Navarro correspondance 1819-70, and Navarro personal records. Some restrictions on use. Answers phone inquiries. Admission fee. Hours: Tu-Sa 10-4.

Jourdan Bachman Pioneer Farm

11418 Sprinkle Cut-Off, Austin, TX 78754; (512) 837-1215. Provides living history interpretation of 3 socio-economic levels of rural central TX life from 1880. Museum exhibits are outdoor 19th c buildings with period furnishings and equipment. Library holds small reference collection, and genealogical materials on local families. Accepts phone inquiries. Fee. Hours: M-F 8-5, Su 1-5.

Judge Roy Bean Visitor Center

P.O. Box 160, Langtry, TX 78871; (915) 291-3440. Museum commemorating life of Judge Roy Bean. Answers phone inquiries. No fee. Hours: M-Su 8-5, except Dec 24-25 and Jan 1.

Layland Museum

201 N. Caddo St., Cleburne, TX 76031; (817) 641-3321. Museum preserves Indian, Civil War, and local history. Exhibits include prehistoric fossils; Indian artifacts from Pueblo, Plains, and Northwest Coastal Areas; and Civil War guns and uniforms. Library concentrates on Civil War, with official records of War of Rebellion, TX historical materials, and large collection on local history. Other holdings include maps of old TX and city of Cleburne, photos, and recordings of Civil War songs and Theodore Roosevelt. Some restrictions. Accepts phone inquiries. Donations accepted. Hours: M-F 9-noon, 1-5.

Lyndon B. Johnson
National Historical Park

P.O. Box 329, Johnson City, TX 78636; (512) 868-7128. Site marks region where Johnson was born, had lived, and is buried. Museum park includes Johnson's boyhood home, birthplace, grandfather's ranch headquarters, and ranch.

Library holds books, vertical files, and photos of Johnson. Special collection of oral history interviews on Johnson's life and times. Accepts phone inquiries. No fee. Hours: by appt only, 8-5.

Lyndon B. Johnson Space Center

History Office Documents Collection, Bldg. 420, Houston, TX 77058; (713) 483-3111. Documents history of manned spaceflight and related materials from govt, industry, and other sources. Holdings include Apollo program correspondence from 1957-1972; photos on development of spacecraft; Apollo mission documents from Dec 1964-72; oral history interview transcripts from 200 Apollo program participants; correspondence from 1959 on Space Shuttle development; contractor development proposals for Shuttle; reports, press kits, flight and operating plans from each Shuttle mission; activity reports on progress of Mercury, Gemini, and Apollo from 1962-68; newsclipping files; and congressional hearing files. Accepts phone inquiries. Hours: call.

Lyndon Baines Johnson
Library and Museum

2313 Red River St., Austin, TX 78705; (512) 482-5137. Museum contains materials relevant to life, govt service, and presidency of Johnson. Holdings include records, recordings, photos, and motion pictures from Secret Service and Natl Archives Inaugural Committee. Other holdings include court files of Gen Westmoreland's counsel in his suit against CBS, William Bundy's unpublished manuscript on development of US policy in Vietnam, head-of-state gifts, political cartoons, and campaign memorabilia. Accepts phone inquiries. No fee. Hours: 9-5

Marshall Military History Collection

University of Texas at El Paso, El Paso, TX 79968; (915) 747-5697. Collection contains all personal papers, published works, and personal library materials of journalist and military historian Gen Samuel Lyman Atwood Marshall. Materials cover WWI and WWII, Korean War, and Vietnam War. Hours: call.

Masonic Grand Lodge Library
and Museum of Texas

P.O. Box 446, (715 Columbus), Waco, TX

76703; (817) 753-7395. Encourages study of Masonic history, especially in Texas. Answers phone inquiries. Materials checked out only to Texas Masons, but research open to anyone. No fee. Hours: M-F 8:30-4.

Museum and Archives of the Big Bend

Sul-Ross State University, P.O. Box C-210, Alpine, TX 79832; museum (915) 837-8143/ archive 8127. Collects, preserves, and exhibits public and cultural Big Bend region materials. Museum displays American Indian artifacts, ethnology items, and art objects. Library has rare book collection, Roy Aldrich collection, and materials on Big Bend. Archives holds regional materials; manuscripts on ranching, mining, politics, military, and Indians; collection of TX maps, pioneer ranches, forts, and settlements; extensive photo collection; Wilson collection of local folk music; large collection of genealogical materials; and oral history interviews. Some restrictions. Accepts phone inquiries. No fee. Hours: museum, Tu-Sa 9-5, Su 1-5; archives, M-F 8-noon, 1-5, Th 6-10.

NASA Collection

Rice University, Woodson Research Center, Fondren Library, 6100 S. Main St., Houston, TX 77251; (713) 527-8101. Houses large collection of Johnson Space Center's historical documents. Holdings include chron files and working papers from project Mercury, including audio and videotapes; files on Gemini projects from 1958-71, mission flight plans, oral history interviews and transcripts, tapes of TV interviews from 1963-66, and transcripts of ground-to-air communication; working papers of Apollo project, oral history interviews from 1961-76, tapes of astronaut speeches, and film of Apollo 16 landing; Skylab materials from 1970-79; Apollo-Soyuz press releases, flight transcripts, and oral histories and photos. Accepts phone inquiries. No fee. Hours: M-F 9-5.

National Archives— Fort Worth Branch

P.O. Box 6216, 501 W. Felix St., Bldg. 1, Fort Worth, TX 76115; (815) 334-5525. Preserves and makes available permanently valuable records of federal agencies in AR, LA, OK, NM, and

TX. Holdings include materials for genealogical research; military service records; IRS records; land documents; census materials; and official documents from Bureau of Customs, General Land Office, Bureau of Indian Affairs, Immigration and Naturalization Service, US Attorneys and Marshals from 1895, Office of Quartermaster General, Selective Service System, War Manpower Commission, Federal Aviation Administration, Agricultural Research Service, Federal Highway Administration, Consumer Products Safety Commission, and many others. No fee. Hours: M-F 8-4.

National Cowgirl Hall of Fame and Western Heritage Center

P.O. Box 1742, 515 Ave. B, Hereford, TX 79045; (806) 364-5252. Honors women who contributed to heritage of American West, including Annie Oakley, Willa Cather, Laura Ingalls Wilder, Georgia O'Keefe, and others. Holdings include personal memorabilia, cowgirl artifacts, photos, and artwork. Accepts phone inquiries. Fee. Hours: M-F 9-noon, 1-5.

National Museum of Communications

6305 N. O'Connor Rd., Suite 123, Four Dallas Communications Complex, Irving, TX 75039; (214) 556-1234. Museum preserves communication history from prehistoric period to present high-tech age. Library holds large collection of materials for communications reference, including trade journals, hobby magazines, service manuals, newsfilm, videotapes, radio news tapes, and commercial and consumer motion picture film. Other holdings include antique phonographs, TV sets, telephones, typewriters, radios, TV and radio broadcasting equip, and printing presses. Accepts phone inquiries. Fee. Hours: Tu-Sa 10-4.

Navarro College

Gaston Gooch Library, 3200 W. 7th Ave., Corsicana, TX 75110; (214) 874-6501. Community college library with materials on general American history, and special collection on Stone Age Indian culture in TX, NM, and Mexico. Oral history collection from Corsicana and Navarro country, covering 1920s oil boom and Jewish community. Accepts phone inquiries. No fee.

Hours: library, M-F 8-5; special collections, by appt, M-F 8-5.

O. Henry Museum
409 E. Fifth St., Austin, TX 78701; (512) 472-1903. Interprets life of William Sydney Porter, a.k.a. O. Henry. Museum housed in cottage occupied by Porter and family from 1892-95. Archives hold his letters and papers, as well as photos. Accepts phone inquiries. Donations accepted. Hours: Tu-Sa 11-4:30, Su 2-4:30.

Old Jail Art Center
RR 1, Box 1, 211 S. Second St., Albany, TX 76430; (915) 762-2269. Preserves regional and state historical materials. Library has small reference and Texana library collections. Archives hold pictures from 1867, manuscripts from local historians, Sanborn maps from 1886-1927, newspapers from 1874, obituaries, census records, and pioneer memoirs from 1850s. Some restrictions. Accepts phone inquiries. Fee. Hours: Tu-F 10-5.

Petroleum Museum
1500 Interstate 20 West, Midland, TX 79701; (915) 683-4403. Collects, preserves, and exhibits history of Permian Basin Petroleum Industry. Museum exhibits cover exploration, production, refining, and marketing of oil and gas in west TX and NM, as well as portraits and biographies of petroleum pioneers. Library holds historical materials on oil industry, autobiographies and biographies of oil men, city/county histories, and catalogs of early oil equipment. Archives retain maps, photos, portraits of oil men and women, films from 1927, and oral histories chronicling industry from origins to energy crunch. Genealogical materials available. Accepts phone inquiries. Fee. Hours: M-Sa 9-5, Su 2-5.

Presidential Museum
622 N. Lee, Odessa, TX 79761; (915) 332-7123. Provides info on presidency and American political process. Holdings in museum and library include photos and recordings. Accepts phone inquiries. No fee. Hours: Tu-Sa 10-5.

Railroad and Pioneer Museum
P.O. Box 5126, (710 Jack Baskin St.), Temple, TX 76505. Preserves, exhibits, and interprets railroad and pioneer history. Museum includes extensive artifacts of railroading, farming, ranching, and home life. Holdings include books, letters, certificates, photos, and railroad memorabilia. Answers phone inquiries. Admission fee. Hours: Tu-F 1-4, Sa 10-4.

Rice University
Woodsen Research Center Special Collections, Fondren Library, 6100 S. Main St., Houston, TX 77251; (713) 527-8101. Repository for University's special collections, archives, manuscript collections, and rare books with emphasis on science and space exploration. Library documents history of science, aeronautics, and TX. Archives hold University archives, architectural drawings and plans, and papers of faculty and administrative officers. Manuscript collection holds historical, literary, scientific, political, and economic materials on TX, entrepreneurs, politics, Civil War, British naval history, NASA, and Univ. authors. Special collections on Johnson Space Center history and papers of Julian Huxley. Accepts phone inquiries. No fee. Hours: M-F, 9-5.

Rio Grande Valley Museum of Harlingen
Boxwood St., Industrial Air Park, Harlingen, TX 78550; (512) 423-3979. Preserves history of Rio Grande Valley of TX. Museum display artifacts, furniture, clothing, ranching tools, and office machines. Other holdings include maps from 1900-40s, photos, and oral history tapes. Materials for in-house use only. Accepts phone inquiries. No fee. Hours: M-F 8-noon, 1-5.

Rosenberg Library
2310 Sealy Ave., Galveston, TX 77550; 409-763-8854. Documents history of Galveston and TX. Holdings include museum, extensive library, archives, manuscripts, maps, photos, films/videotapes, sheet music, oral history interviews, and genealogical records. Also collects 19th-20th c architectural drawings, and labor, black, German, and Italian newspapers from 1840. Answers phone inquiries. No fee. Hours: Tu-Sa 10-5.

Sam Houston Memorial Museum
P.O. Box 2057, SHSU, Huntsville, TX 77341.

Preserves, exhibits, and promotes history of Sam Houston, his life, and influential role in 19th c TX history. Accepts limited mail inquiries. Donations accepted. Hours: Tu-Su 9-5.

Sam Rayburn Library

P.O. Box 309, 800 W. Sam Rayburn Dr., Bonham, TX 75418; (214) 583-2455. Documents life and career of Rayburn, Speaker of the House. Holdings include books, papers, and oral histories of and about Rayburn; photos; films; and genealogical records of Fannin County, TX. Answers phone inquiries. No fee. Hours: M-F 10-5; Sa 1-5; Su 2-5.

San Antonio Missions National Historic Park

2202 Roosevelt Ave., San Antonio, TX 78210; (512) 229-5701. Collects resources related to Missions and TX in general. Library has books, periodicals, reports, and pamphlets. Materials non-circulating. No fee. Hours: M-F 8-4:30.

San Antonio Museum Association

3801 Broadway, San Antonio, TX 78299; (512) 226-5544. Collects, preserves, and interprets local history and art in Witte Museum and San Antonio Museum of Art. Witte library covers history, anthropology, textiles, decorative arts, through collection of rare books and photos and slides on decorative arts and anthropology. Art museum covers folk art, art history and photography, and photos of art. Other holdings include transportation collection, maps, and historical documents. Accepts phone inquiries. Fee. Hours: library by appt only; M-Sa 10-5, Su noon-5, Tu noon-9.

San Antonio Public Library

History, Social Science, and General Reference, 203 South Saint Mary's St., San Antonio, TX 78205; (512) 299-7813. Public library with extensive holdings on San Antonio, including genealogies and census population schedules 1790-1880; and for South and Midwest for 1900-1910. Accepts phone inquiries. No fee. Hours: M-F 9-9, Sa 9-6.

Slavonic Benevolent Order for the State of Texas

P.O. Box 100, 520 Main St., Temple, TX 76503;

(817) 773-1575. Fraternal Czech benefit society preserves heritage, culture, and language of its members. Museum displays artifacts brought to TX or used by pioneers from 1850-1935, including kitchen, blacksmith, farming, and doctor's tools. Also selection of costumes and handcrafts. Library has large collection of Czech materials, including almanacs, fiction, maps, photos, recordings, and genealogical records. Accepts phone inquiries. No fee. Hours: M-F 8-noon, 1-5.

Sophienburg Museum

401 W. Coll St., New Braunfels, TX 78130; (512) 629-1572. Depicts local history from founding through museum exhibits, library reference materials, and archival holdings. Archives retain records of German immigration to region; social and civic org materials; maps; photos from 1925-72; many oral history interviews; genealogical materials; and archive of community German language newspaper from 1852-1957. Accepts phone inquiries. Fee. Hours: museum, M-Sa 10-5, Su 1-5; archives, Tu & Th 9-4.

Southwest Aerospace Museum

P.O. Box 5462, Dept. B-36, 300 N. Spur 341, Fort Worth, TX 76108; (817) 735-4143. Preserves those aircraft that have played vital role in aviation development and defense of US. Aircraft displayed include Beech, Boeing, Cessna, Lockheed, McDonnell, and Republic planes; B-52 optical sight, B-58 ejection seats, Falcon and Sidewinder missiles, aircraft engine carburetors, and scale models of WWI space age hardware. Missiles and helicopters also on display. Accepts phone inquiries (817-244-1067). No fee. Hours: Th-Su 10-3.

Southwest Collection

El Paso Public Library, 501 N. Oregon St., El Paso, TX 79901; (915) 541-4880. Library has collection on history of El Paso, TX, NM, AZ, and border area of northern Mexico. Archives holds extensive clipping file on El Paso, including papers of former mayors; architectural plans by Trost & Trost, Percy McGhee, and Frazer & Benner; maps; many photos of El Paso, southern NM, and Mexican Revolution in Chihuahua; and cemetery records. Accepts phone inquiries. No fee. Hours: M-Th 10-8, F-Sa 10-5:30.

Scene from "Souls of Sin," from the Southwest Film/Video Archives Black Film Collection.

Southwest Film/Video Archives

Center for Communication Arts, Southern Methodist University, P.O. Box 4194, 3108 Fondren Dr. #11, Dallas, TX 75275; (214) 373-3665. Locates, restores, and preserves American cinema, with emphasis on Southwest. Museum exhibits film posters, 25 antique film projectors dating to early 20th c, 50 original screenplays, stills from motion pictures, oral history materials, and extensive collection of films including Atlanta Cinema Showcase, Channel 8 (Belo) newsfilm, Benchmarks of Animation Art from 1909, Ingmar Bergman collection, Burke/Jones Filmclip; Comic Film; Contemporary History; Howard/NCET Collection, International Non-Fiction Film; Ginger Rogers Films; War on Poverty collection; Black Film collection; Japanese films; and WWII films. Accepts phone inquiries. Fee. Hours: M-F 9-5.

Southwest Museum

1705 W. Missouri St., Midland, TX 79701; (915) 683-2882. Attempts to broaden understanding and enjoyment of Southwest art and culture. Museum complex includes historic mansion and stables, planetarium, and art galleries. Holdings include art and archaeology of American Southwest. Accepts phone inquiries. No fee. Hours: M-F 9-5, Sa 10-5, Su 2-5.

Star of the Republic Museum

Washington-on-the-Brazos State Historical Park,

P.O. Box 317, Washington, TX 77880; (409) 878-2461. Interprets history of Republic of TX with emphasis on Brazos Valley. Museum housed on site of Texas Declaration of Independence signing. Library holds materials on TX history. Archives retains documents and maps, films/videotapes, genealogical records and photos on TX from 1836-46. Accepts phone inquiries. No fee. Hours: Mar-Aug, 10-5; Sept-Feb, W-Su 10-5.

Stephen F. Austin State University

Special Collections, Steen Library, Box 13055, Nacogdoches, TX 75962; (409) 568-4100. Serves as research center for East TX studies. On-campus Stone Fort Museum exhibits objects from east TX Indian culture. Library holds reference materials on region. Archives retains University records from 1923. Manuscript collection includes papers of east TX residents from 1787, maps from 1818, photos, genealogical materials, R.B. Blake collection, and Forest History collection on local lumber companies. Accepts phone inquiries. No fee. Hours: M-F 8-5, Sa 10-6.

Strecker Museum

Baylor University, S. 4th St, Sid Richardson Science Bldg., Waco, TX 76798; (817) 755-1110. Preserves reference materials on natural and cultural history of region. Museum consists of relocated 19th c TX town and buildings, as well as artifacts related to natural and cultural history. Library holds John Strecker materials, including correspondence, manuscript, and publications. Archives retains early TX photos, materials on museum history, and films/videotapes on relocation of TX town to Baylor campus. Materials for in-house use only. No fee. Hours: M-F 9-4, Sa 10-1, Su 2-5.

Tarrant County Black Historical and Genealogical Society

1020 E. Humbolt, Fort Worth, TX 76104; (817) 332-6049. Researches, records, and distributes genealogical info. Museum exhibits artifacts, documents and photos. Library has reference materials on black history, poetry magazines, genealogies, works of local authors, 19th c Ft Worth and Africa maps, extensive black film library on local TX history, and recordings of black musicians. Other holdings include works by R.A. Ransom, Bertha Collins, and Lillian Horace. Accepts phone inquiries. No fee. Hours: M-F 11-5.

Texarkana Historical Society and Museum

P.O. Box 2343, 219 State Line Ave., Texarkana, TX 75501; (214) 793-4831. Preserves, restores, exhibits, and displays documents, artifacts, and other objects of historical value. Museum exhibits document Caddoan Indian sites, 19th c textiles and costumes, architecture, and domestic and industrial artifacts. Archives holds materials on local black history and culture. Photo collection covers many aspects of city's development. Accepts phone inquiries. Fee. Hours: Tu-F 10-4, Sa-Su noon-3.

Texas A&M University

Special Collections, Evans Library, College Station, TX 77843; (409) 845-2551. Academic research library holds special Western Illustrators Collection of works by Charles Russell, Frederic Remington, and other Western artists. Large collection include books, pamphlets, and unique original drawings by historical and contemporary artists of Southwest and West. Accepts phone inquiries. No fee. Hours: call.

Texas Archives and Records Division

General Land Office, 1700 N. Congress, Austin, TX 78701; (512) 463-5277. Collects and maintains records relating to public lands of Texas. Archives include Spanish Collection (1719-1836) of land titles and related materials; and 250,000+ republic and state land grants; military grants and lists; patents, deeds, colony lists, county maps, and other collections. Answers phone inquiries. No fee. Hours: M-F 7:30-6.

Texas Christian University

Mary Couts Burnett Library, Box 32904, Fort Worth, TX 76129; (817) 921-7669. Academic research library has Marguerite Oswald collection, based on son Lee Harvey Oswald. Holdings include Warren Commission report and personal Marguerite's annotations and comments. Accepts phone inquiries. No fee. Hours: call.

Texas Collection

Baylor University, P.O. Box 6396, S. Fifth St. at Speight Ave., Waco, TX 76706; (817) 755-1268. Provides research resources on all aspects of TX life. Library collects TX state documents, vertical file materials, and Region Historical Resource program materials. Archives contain unofficial records of University, large collection of post-Civil War historical manuscripts, large collection of oral history transcripts, many maps, extensive photo holdings, videotapes of oral history interviews and "Deep in the Heart of TX" TV programs, large collection of audio oral history recordings, genealogy records, and TX newspapers and biographical sketches. Some restrictions on use. Accepts phone inquiries. No fee. Hours: M-Th 9-10, F 9-5, Sa 9-3; summer, M-F 9-5.

Texas Historical Commission

Capitol Station, P.O. Box 12276, Austin, TX 78701; (512) 463-6100. (1511 Colorado, Austin, TX 78701) Preserves state's prehistoric and historic resources. Holdings include county, local, and architectural histories; statewide survey files of historic resources; plans of many historic buildings; 1936 state highway maps by county; photos of buildings, cemetaries, historical markings. Special collections include reports of historic and archeological investigations in Texas, conducted for compliance with federal laws. Accepts phone inquiries. No fees. Hours: M-F 8-5.

Texas Historical Foundation

Center for Historic Resources, College of Architecture and Environmental Design, Texas A&M University, College Station, TX 77843; (409) 845-7886. Funds development of historic preservation. Archives includes special collection on built environment; manscript; maps; collections of historic photos (publishes "Photographic Collections in Texas, A Union Guide"); films/videotapes; selected oral histories; some special collections. Accepts phone inquiries. No fee. Hours: M-F 8-5.

Texas Memorial Museum

University of Texas at Austin, 2400 Trinity, Austin, TX 78705; (512) 471-3551. Focus on local and Texas history, from 1750. Holdings include artifacts of early Texas life, including Native American and Euro-American communities; extensive photo colleciton; special collections. Answers phone inquiries. No fee. Hours: M-F 9-5, Sa-Su 1-5.

Texas Ranger Hall of Fame and Museum

Moody Texas Ranger Memorial Library, P.O. Box 2570, Waco, TX 76702; (817) 754-1433. Portrays Texas Rangers and clarifies their role in Texas and southwestern history. Holdings include library; service records of Rangers 1847-1935 on microfilm; manuscripts; maps of Mexican, colonial, and Republic of Texas; photograph collection; videotapes; and special collections. Answers phone inquiries. Admission fee for museum. Hours: M-F 9-5.

Texas Tech University

Documents Dept., Texas Tech University Library, Lubbock, TX 79409; (806) 742-2268. Academic research library with collection of federal documents from 1935. Also holds USGS maps of western US states. Materials circulate within University community. Accepts phone inquiries. No fee. Hours: M-Th 8-midnight, F 8-6, Sa 9-6, Su 1-midnight.

Texas Woman's University

Special Collections, Bradley Memorial Library, Box 23715, TWU Station, Denton, TX 76204; (817) 898-2602. Academic research library has Hermine Tobolowsky Collection of materials on this TX lawyer who spearheaded Equal Legal Rights Ammendment in TX. Holdings include congressional bills and resolutions, court case records, campaign and platform congressional pledges of support, and correspondence. Accepts phone inquiries. No fee. Hours: call.

Texas-Dallas History and Archives Division

Dallas Public Library, 1515 Young St., Dallas, TX 75201; (214) 670-1435. Provides materials for comprehensive area studies for Dallas and TX with histories and biographies. Archives holds business, performing arts, ethnic and women's, and political and municipal histories. Some collections include Dallas Morning News editorial cartoons, Neiman-Marcus archives, People's

The Texas Rangers, from the Texas-Dallas History Division's Clint People's Collection at the Dallas Public Library.

Collection of TX Ranger files and photos, and personal papers of Congressman Bruce Alger. Vertical files, historical maps, newspapers, Sanborn fire insurance maps of TX, Streeter collection, oral history interviews, and large collection of photos available. Materials non-circulating. Accepts phone inquiries. No fee. Hours: M, W 9-9; Tu, Th 9-6; F 9-5; Sa 9-6; Su 1-5.

Trinity University
Elizabeth Coates Maddux Library, 715 Stadium Dr., San Antonio, TX 78284; (512) 736-7213. Academic research library maintains Paul Campbell Man and Space Collection of primary and secondary materials relating to space exploration. Holdings include press releases and photos.

Accepts phone inquiries. No fee. Hours: call.

University of North Texas Archives
University of North Texas, 5188 NT Station, Denton, TX 76203; (817) 565-2766. Provides information on development of north Texas region. Archives includes records of University of North Texas from 1890; papers of individuals and businesses of region, including interview materials from cosmetics entrepreneur Mary Kay Ash and Bettie Graham of Liquid Paper Corp; maps, photos, and genealogical records. Separate oral history collection has interviews with Pearl Harbor survivors, WWII POWs, Corregidor survivors, Bataan death march survivors, TX legislators, TX Govs, TX administrators em-

ployed by FDR, TX businessmen and business-women, and Mexican-American social activists. Answers phone inquiries. No fee. Hours: M-F 8-5.

University of Texas at Arlington Libraries

Special Collections, P.O. Box 19497, 701 S. Cooper St., Arlington, TX 76019; (817) 273-3391. University library with various collections, including Texana collection from 1555 and Mexican War (1846-48). Special collections include Texas Labor Archives (1866-1975), University Archives (1885-), Texas Writers Collection (1906-86), and Texas Political Collection (1951-82). Holdings include manuscripts, maps, photos, films/videotapes, and oral histories. Answers phone inquiries. No fee. Hours: M-F 8-5, Sa 10-2.

University of Texas at Austin

Documents Division, Edie & Lew Wasserman Public Affairs Library, SRH 3.243 (2313 Red River, Austin, TX 78705), Austin, TX 78712; (512) 471-4486. Holdings include general Texas and Austin history, including local city and county budgets and financial reports. Accepts phone inquiries. No fee. Hours: M-Th 8am-11pm, F 8-5, Sa noon-6, Su 1-11.

University of Texas at El Paso Library

Documents and Map Division, El Paso, TX 79912; (915) 747-5685. Academic and community research facility. Holdings include federal and TX documents; US and TX law materials; and large map collection, including census, geological, historical, road, soil, vegetation, oil, gas, mineral, aerial, Landsat, and National Geographic maps. Materials circulate within local and academic community. Accepts phone inquiries. No fee. Hours: M-Th 8-10, F 8-5, Sa 9-6, Su 1-10.

University of Texas at San Antonio Library

University of Texas, San Antonio, TX 78285; (512) 691-4570. Academic research facility with large collection of federal, state, and local documents; manuscripts on explorers and settlers in Mexico and TX from 1488-1845; maps of to-

pography, geology, and minerals; and special John Peace collection of books and documents from Texas Republic era. Kathryn Stoner O'Connor collection maintains TX and Mexican materials owned by Sons of Texas Republic. Accepts phone inquiries. No fee. Hours: M-Th 8-10, F 8-4:30, Sa 9-4:30, Su 1-9.

University of Texas Libraries

General Libraries, Humanities Research Center, Box 7219, Austin, TX 78712; (512) 471-3840. Academic research library has special collection of John Dulles materials, including materials on three relatives who were Sec of State, John Foster Dulles, Robert Lansing, John Foster; paintings on historical figures from 17th c; and correspondence and speeches. Accepts phone inquiries. No fee. Hours: call.

White Deer Land Museum

P.O. Box 1556, Pampa, TX 79065; (806) 665-5521. Preserves area history through collections in museum, library, and archives. Holdings include manuscripts, maps, photos, and oral history interviews. Accepts phone inquiries. Donations accepted. Hours: M-F 9-5, Sa-Su 1:30-4.

Utah

Anasazi State Park

P.O. Box 393, Boulder, UT 84716; (801) 355-7308. Archeological site preserves artifacts, history, and culture of Anasazi in form of museum with excavated items and interpretive exhibits; videotapes of Anasazi and archeolgic work; excavation site trail. Accepts phone inquiries. Fee. Hours: summer, 8-6; winter, 9-5.

Brigham Young University

Harold Lee Library, Provo, UT 84602; (801) 378-6179. Federal, Canadian, and UT depository library with reference materials and special collections on Mormon and US history. Holdings include USGS, early American, and WWII German maps; photos and archives of American West; Jimmy Stewart manuscript collection; Cecil B. DeMille Collection; worldwide genealogical records. Accepts phone inquiries (801-378-4090). No fee. Hours: M-Sa 7am-midnight.

Church of Jesus Christ of Latter-Day Saints

Historical Dept., 50 E. North Temple St., Salt Lake City, UT 84150; (801) 531-2745. Documents history of LDS Church through holdings in museum, library, and archives. Library holds materials on church doctrine and religious and general reference items. Archival holdings include papers of church members, maps of UT, photos, films/videotapes, and genealogical records. Approved researchers only. Accepts phone inquiries. No fee. Hours: 7:30-4:30.

Daughters of Utah Pioneers

300 N. Main St., Salt Lake City, UT 84103; (801) 538-1050. Preserves history of UT pioneers and their way of life 1847-1869 in form of artifacts, guns, coins, furniture, household items, clothing, and wagons; manuscripts, diaries, videotapes, photos, and genealogical records. Library and archives for use by members only. Accepts phone inquiries. Donations accepted. Hours: M-Sa 9-5.

Eccles Health Sciences Library

University of Utah, Bldg. 89, 10 N. Medical Dr., Salt Lake City, UT 84112; (801) 581-5534. Medical library holding US govt documents relating to health and medical sciences. Archival materials on history of medicine, and extensive media collection in health sciences. Accepts phone inquiries. No fee. Hours: call.

Fort Douglas Military Museum

Potter St., Bldg. 32, Fort Douglas, UT 84113; (801) 524-4154. Preserves and interprets history of US Army influence and activities in UT territory from 1857. Holdings include weapons, uniforms, equipment; photos of Ft Douglas from 1863; military history reference library. Library non-circulating. Accepts phone inquiries. No fee. Hours: Tu-Sa 10-noon, 1-4.

Genealogy Library

Church of Jesus Christ of Latter-Day Saints, 50 E. North Temple St., Salt Lake City, UT 84150; (801) 531-2331. World's largest, most fully staffed repository of genealogical info. Holdings include family group records of over 8 million families all over world, and has index of well over 88 million names. Records on file include microfilmed copies of parish registers, census records, vital and court records, land transactions, deeds, probates, military records, cemetery records, and many other records from deceased people. Not limited to members of church. Accepts mail and phone inquiries that can be answered briefly. Provides assistance in use of library and on research problems. No fee. Hours: M 7:30-6, Tu-F 7:30-10, Sa 7:30-5.

Golden Spike National Historic Site

P.O. Box W, Promontory Summit, Brigham City, UT 84302; (801) 471-2209. Preserves and interprets history of US's first transcontinental railroad and its effect on American West. Holdings include artifacts and documents on building of the railroad 1830-69 and last spike ceremony; library, photos, films/videotapes; oral history collections about Promontory, UT 1890-1930. Non-circulating collection. Accepts phone inquiries. Fee in summer. Hours: summer, 8-6; winter, 8-4:30.

Hill Air Force Base Museum

00-ALC/XPH, Hill Air Force Base, UT 84056; (801) 777-6818 or 8623. Preserves history of Hill Air Force Base and UT. Exhibits include approx 40 aircraft and missiles, as well as historical aeronautical displays. Accepts phone inquiries. No fee. Hours: M-F 9-2:45, Sa 10-4.

Marriott Library

University of Utah, Salt Lake City, UT 84112; (801) 581-6085. Academic research library has materials concerning women in UT history, politics, religion, and orgs. Oral history materials available. Special collection of papers from former NASA director James Fletcher. Some manuscripts and papers from historian/biographer Fawn Brodie, including interviews with Richard Nixon, and research notes and clippings on Thomas Jefferson and Richard Burton. Accepts phone inquiries. No fee. Hours: call.

Mormon History Association

P.O. Box 7010 University Station, Provo, UT 84602. Scholarly org fosters scholarly research and publication in Mormon history and promotes fellowship and communication among all those interested in Mormon past. Publishes articles, quarterly newsletter of Mormon history topics, and holds annual meetings and lectures. Fee for membership.

Pioneer Village

P.O. Box N, Farmington, UT 84025; (801) 451-0101. Recreation of a typical 1900s pioneer town in form of residences, artifacts, tools, guns, clothing, carriages, and furniture. Accepts phone inquiries. Fee. Hours: May-Labor Day, 10-9.

South Box Elder Daughters of Utah Pioneers

566 N. 1st St., East, Brigham City, UT 84302; (801) 723-8144. Org maintains historical collections relating to UT pioneers in form of gallery with artifacts and displays, 1849-1900, library, and genealogical records. Accepts phone inquiries. Hours: call.

State of Utah Law Library

125 State Capitol, Salt Lake City, UT 84114; (801) 538-1045. Law library maintains collection of legal documents and publications relevant to needs of state Supreme Court and other state agencies. Materials for on-site use only. Accepts phone inquiries. No fee. Hours: 9-5.

Utah Heritage Foundation

355 Quince St., Salt Lake City, UT 84103; (801) 533-0858. Promotes preservation and appreciation of historic architecture in UT. Library has limited research materials, and slide programs on UT history. Accepts phone inquiries. No fee. Hours: M-F 9-5.

Utah State Historical Society

300 Rio Grande St., Salt Lake City, UT 84101; (801) 533-5755. Collects and preserves history of UT, the Mormons, the West, and Native Americans through museum exhibits, archives, manuscripts, maps, photos, films/videotapes, and recordings. Accepts phone inquiries (801-533-5808). No fee. Hours: M-F 9-5.

Utah State Library

Suite 16, 2150 S. Third West, Salt Lake City, UT 84115; (801) 466-5888. Provides support and info services to UT libraries and agencies, with holdings that include local and state historical materials. Materials available only through ILL. Accepts phone inquiries. Postal fees. Hours: 8-5.

Utah State University

Special Collections and Archives, Merrill Library & Learning Resources Center, Logan, UT 84322; (801) 750-2682. Academic research library holds collection of Western American folklore and folksongs. Holdings include pictures, slides, field recordings, and materials on cattle grazing from 1540-1936. Accepts phone inquiries. No fee. Hours: call.

Wheeler Historic Farm

6351 South 900 East, Salt Lake City, UT 84121; (801) 264-2241. Collects and exhibits objects and living skills related to Salt Lake county agriculture and settlement. Museum consists of Victorian farmhouse and dairy farm outbuildings, antique furniture, and farming implements. Special collections of spinning looms and dolls. Accepts phone inquiries. Fee. Hours: M-Sa 9-4.

Vermont

Barre Museum

Archives of Barre History, P.O. Box 453, Washington St., Barre, VT 05641; (802) 479-0450. Collects, preserves, and makes available materials relevant to Barre history. Museum has 19th c American portrait collection, tools, and spinning wheels. Library holds materials on Barre, county, and state history; ethnic history; genealogy; and geography. Archives hold records of regional granite industry, civic and business records, and materials on immigration, labor, and radical political history; manuscripts relating to Barre history; maps from 1700s; photos of local political, social events and transportation; oral history interviews; and genealogical records. Restricted. Accepts phone inquiries. No fee. Hours: M 10-8, Th noon-8, F noon-6, Sa 10-4.

Bennington Museum

West Main St., Bennington, VT 05201; (802) 447-1571. Regional museum of history, art, and decorative arts displays Battle of Bennington artifacts; largest collection of Grandma Moses paintings anywhere; Bennington pottery, furniture, sculpture, and clocks. Artists represented include Blackburn, Rembrandt Peale, Jennys, Chase, Field, Hunt, Inman, MacMonnies, and

Fraser. Library has genealogy and local, state, and New England history from earliest settlement, including manuscripts and maps. Special collections include 1925 Wasp touring car and Battle of Bennington flag. Fee. Hours: museum, Mar-Nov, 9-5; genealogy library by appt.

Billings Farm and Museum
P.O. Box 489, Woodstock, VT 05091; (802) 457-2355. Living museum of VT rural history, with emphasis on dairy farming. Library houses agricultural books and periodicals focusing on 19th c agricultural practices. Accepts phone inquiries. Fee. Hours: May-Oct 10-5.

Calvin Coolidge Memorial Foundation
Box 97, Plymouth, VT 05056; (802) 672-3389. Portrays life of President Coolidge and promotes greater understanding of his life, times, and career. Museum located at National Coolidge Historical Site. Library collects titles on Coolidge, his family, and era he lived in, as well as Plymouth and VT history. Archives retain Coolidge photos, newspapers, magazines, campaign items, family films, voice recordings, and genealogical materials. Some Plymouth oral history interviews available. Accepts phone inquiries. No fee. Hours: 8:30-5.

Champlain Maritime Society
P.O. Box 745, 14 So. Williams St., Burlington, VT 05402; (802) 862-8270. Preserves history and artifacts of Lake Champlain Region. Library collects Lake Champlain publications covering all topics and time periods, maritime maps from European contact to present, and limited collection of films/videotapes on underwater archaeological activities. Maps available by request only. Accepts phone inquiries. No fee. Hours: 9-4.

Johnson State College
Special Collections, John Dewey Library, Johnson, VT 05656; (802) 635-2356. Academic research library with slave narrative collection and materials from Federal Writers' Project. Hours: academic yr, M-Th 8-11, F 8-8, Sa 9-9, Su 10-11; summer hours vary.

Martha Canfield Library
Russell Vermontiana Collection, Arlington, VT 05250; (802) 375-6307. Preserves VT local history through collections of letters, diaries, business records, 19th and 20th c maps, and genealogical records for Arlington, Sandgate, and Sunderland, VT. Special Dorothy Canfield Fisher collection. Accepts phone inquiries. No fee. Hours: Tu 9-5, and by appt.

Museum of the Americas
Rte. 14, Brookfield, VT 05036; (802) 276-3386. Museum and library preserve Anglo-American and Hispanic-American art, architecture, and history. Museum exhibits engravings, maps, folk art and paintings from English Americans, Pre-Columbians, and Latin Americans. Library has 18th-19th c American maps, videotapes, and collection of 18th c English literature, 19th c American literature, and Americana. Donations accepted. Hours: by appt only, 9-5.

New England Maple Museum
P.O. Box 1615, Rutland, VT 05701; (802) 483-9414. Preserves history of VT's maple industry from early beginnings to present. Museum houses largest collection of maple sugaring artifacts in existence. History also depicted in paintings on display. Fee. Hours: Mar 15-May 25 and Nov-Dec 23, 10-4; May 26-Oct 31, 8:30-5:30.

Norwich University Library
Documents Dept., S. Main St., Northfield, VT 05663; (802) 485-2170. Academic research library with special collections on university history, military history, mountaineering, and education. Museum exhibits materials on university history and alumni from 1819; manuscripts from Alden Partridge, 1778-1854; I. D. White and Edward Brooks papers on WWII history; topographic maps for New England and NY; historic films of Norwich Univ activities; and special Southard Military Collection and Joel E. Fisher Mountaineering collection. Accepts phone inquiries. No fee. Hours: 8am-midnight.

Plymouth Notch Historic Site
Division for Historic Preservation, Pavilion Bldg., Plymouth Notch, Montpelier, VT 05602; (802) 828-3226. Village preserved as memorial to Pres Calvin Coolidge, who was born, raised, and buried in Plymouth Notch. Museum area consists of 9 historic buildings. Vermont Historical

library holds Coolidge family papers, archives, manuscripts, maps, photos, films/videotapes, recordings, and genealogical records. Other holdings include gifts to President, and family items. Accepts phone inquiries. Fee. Hours: Memorial Day-Columbus Day 9:30-5:30.

President Chester A. Arthur Historic Site

Historical Preservation Pavilion Bldg, Fairfield, Montpelier, VT 05602; (802) 828-3226. Relates the life history of this Fairfield resident. Museum is reconstructed home of Arthur family with mounted displays on Chester Arthur and his life. Accepts phone inquiries. No fee. Hours: Memorial Day-Columbus Day, W-Su 9:30-5:30.

Putney Historical Society

Town Hall, Putney, VT 05346; (802) 387-5862. Preserves documents and artifacts of local significance in museum, library and archives. Holdings include papers on community settlement, maps, photos from 1880, oral history tapes, and genealogical materials. Accepts phone inquiries. No fee. Hours: W, Sa 2-4.

Robert Hull Fleming Museum

University of Vermont, Colchester Ave., Burlington, VT 05405; (802) 656-0750. Preserves works of art and anthropological collections. Museum exhibits American and European fine arts, decorative arts, historical collections, photos, and non-Western art and artifacts. Library holds materials related to collections. Accepts phone inquiries. No fee. Hours: Tu-F 10-5, Sa-Su 1-5.

Rokeby (Ancestral Estate of Rowland Evans Robinson)

U.S. Rte. 7, Ferrisburg, VT 05456; (802) 877-3406. Preserves and interprets Robinson family home and contribution to VT history. Museum consists of farmhouse and outbuildings, with decorative and fine arts, personal and household items, and farm tools. Library has 17th-20th c materials on agriculture, religion, poetry, abolition, and other reform movements; many family letters; photos; and films/videos. Accepts phone inquiries. Fee. Hours: May-Oct, Th-Su 10:30-3.

University of Vermont

Documents Division, Bailey/Howe Library, Burlington, VT 05405; (802) 656-2542. Academic support library with US govt documents since 1776 and maps from 20th c. Accepts phone inquiries. No fee. Hours: M-Th 8:30-10, F 8:30-4:30, Sa 1-5, Su 1-10.

Vermont Archaeological Society

P.O. Box 663, Burlington, VT 05402; (802) 655-2000 M-F/863-4121 Sa-Su. Promotes knowledge of VT prehistory and its artifactual heritage. Society's archives located at Univ of VT, Williams Hall, Dept of Anthropology. Holdings include manuscripts, maps, photos, films/videotapes, and recordings. Special collections includes archaeological artifacts. Accepts phone inquiries. Hours: call.

Vermont Historical Society

109 State St., Montpelier, VT 05602; (802) 828-2291. Collects and displays items pertaining to VT history. Museum exhibits cover all periods. Library has materials on genealogy, business, and residents of VT. Archives retain private papers, maps, broadsides, and photos. Accepts phone inquiries. Donations accepted. Hours: M-F 8-4:30, Sa 9-4.

Vermont State Archives

26 Terrace St., Redstone Bldg., Montpelier, VT 05602; (802) 828-2363. Collects, arranges, and preserves VT's administrative, legislative, and electoral history. Small library hold basic VT reference sources, laws, and General Assembly journals. Archives holds state govt records focusing on executive and legislative branches, materials from office of Sec of State from 1790s, papers from Henry Stevens collection, VT Surveyor General maps, photos from Houston Studio/county camera collection, and films/videotapes from various state agencies. Accepts phone inquiries. No fee. Hours: M-F 7:45-4:30.

Virginia

Abby Aldrich Rockefeller Folk Art Center

Division of Colonial Williamsburg Foundations, P.O. Box C, 307 S. England St., Williamsburg,

VA 23187; (804) 220-7670. Collects, preserves, studies, and interprets American folk art. Museum composed of nine galleries of thousands of examples of folk art. Library maintains reference collection on topic. Core of collection is Rockefeller's folk art collection. Accepts phone inquiries (804-229-1000). Fee. Hours: library by appt; museum, 10-6.

Aerospace Museum and Park
Air Power Museum, 413 W. Mercury Blvd., Hampton, VA 23666; (804) 727-6781. Emphasizes and encourages interest in military aircraft design. Museum displays collection of aircraft dating from Korean conflict to Vietnam War, and satellites and missiles. No fee. Hours: 9-5.

Albemarle County Historical Society
220 Court Square, Charlottesville, VA 22901; (804) 296-1492. (Research library at Jefferson-Madison Regional Library, 201 E. Market St.). Collects materials on Charlottesville/Albemarle region and residents. Museum covers local decorative arts, textiles, military, and paintings from 18th c through 1950s. Library documents local history with vertical files, pamphlets, and genealogical materials. Map collection includes historical and topographical issues. Photo collection details people, places, and events from 1870s. Audio recordings of local history TV programs, oral histories, and videotape on Hatton Ferry available. Materials non-circulating. Accepts phone inquiries. No fee. Hours: M-F 10-4.

Alexandria Library
Lloyd House, 220 N. Washington St., Alexandria, VA 22314; (703) 838-4577. Collects and makes accessible research materials on Alexandria and VA history and genealogy. Museum is furnished 19th c home. Library holds materials on Alexandria and Confederate states history and genealogy from time of settlement and Native American occupation. Archives holds city records from 18th, 19th, and 20th c, manuscripts, early and recent maps of region, photos, and oral history interviews and lectures. Accepts phone inquiries. No fee. Hours: M-Sa 9-5.

American Automobile Association Library
8111 Gatehouse Rd., Room 605, Falls Church,

VA 22047; (703) 222-6466. Holdings include books, reports, vertical files, and map collection covering automobile history, safety, statistics, highway development, legislation, and insurance. Hours: researchers by appt only; M-F 9-4.

American Canal Society
35 Towana Rd., Richmond, VA 23226; (804) 288-1334. Acts as referral agency for historic canal research, preservation, and restoration info. Actual materials held by member societies. Small collection of films/videotapes available for loan to canal societies. Accepts mail or phone inquiries. No fee. Hours: call.

American Work Horse Museum
P.O. Box 88, Paeonian Springs, VA 22129; (703) 338-6290. Commemorates role of work horse and its importance in American history. Museum composed of office and library, implement buildings, blacksmith shop, harness shop, veterinary bldg, and museum of tools. Museum also cares for two Clydesdale horses. Library contains small collection of materials on work horses and many pictures. Accepts phone inquiries. No fee. Hours: 9-5.

Amphibious Museum
U.S. Naval Amphibious Base, Little Creek, Norfolk, VA 23521; (804) 464-8130. Preserves amphibious naval history, including warfare stragegy and technology. Holdings include artifacts, memorabilia, and reference materials. Accepts phone inquiries. Hours: Sa-Su 10-3.

Anne Spencer Memorial Foundation
1306 Pierce St., Lynchburg, VA 24501; (804) 846-0517. Historic landmark marking home of nationally and internationally recognized writer. Home was meeting place of writers and critics, including H.L. Mencken, W.E.B. DuBois, Walter White, and others. Library contains materials on and by writers of 1866-1975 period; manuscripts of Spencer's writings; photos of family members, actors, singers, and visitors; genealogical records; and films/videotapes. Accepts phone inquiries. Fee. Hours: M-F 9-4.

Appomattox Court House National Historical Park
P.O. Box 218, Appomattox, VA 24522; (804)

352-8987. Preserves and interprets site of Lee's surrender to Grant and end of Civil War. Museum composed of historic village furnished with period artifacts. Library concentrates on Civil War in VA and regimental histories. Archives hold materials on history of Appomattox Court House and surrounding structures; business records from regional stores; maps of Appomattox Campaign; photos of Courthouse from 1865; oral history interviews; and 1850-60 census records. Accepts phone inquiries. Fee. Hours: library by appt only; museum 9-5.

Arlington Historical Museum

P.O. Box 402, Arlington, VA 22210; (703) 892-4204. Supports research, preservation, discovery, restoration, and dissemination of Arlington county local history. Museum housed in county's oldest school building, and includes displays of photos and memorabilia on Arlington and VA history. Archives contains papers of prominent citizens and orgs, maps, and photos. Accepts phone inquiries. No fee. Hours: F-Sa 11-3, Su 2-5.

Army Quartermaster Museum

A Ave. and 22nd St., Fort Lee, VA 23801; (804) 734-1854. Collects, preserves, and exhibits US Army Quartermaster Corps historical items. Museum and library hold some photos, artifacts, and articles used by Army. Accepts phone inquiries. No fee. Hours: library by appt; museum, M-F 8-5, Sa-Su 11-5.

Army Transportation Museum

US Army Transportation Center, Building 300, ATZ-PTM, Besson Hall, Fort Eustis, VA 23604; (804) 878-1115. Preserves history of transportation in Army and Transportation Corps from 1914. Museum contains exhibits on army transportation beginning with Continental Army in 1775. Library provides reference materials. Archives hold personal papers. Map collection details Ft Eustis region. Photo collection. Accepts phone inquiries. No fee. Hours: M-Su 9-4:30.

Bedford City/County Museum

201 E. Main St., Bedford, VA 24323; (703) 586-4520. Preserves history and genealogy of Beford area. Museum houses artifacts from Indian era through modern wars, with focus on Civil War and residents in 19th and 20th c. Library holds some local history and genealogical materials. Archives contain some personal papers, maps, photos of local interest, and oral history interviews. Accepts phone inquiries. No fee. Hours: Tu-Sa 10-5.

Blue Ridge Farm Museum

Blue Ridge Institute, Ferrum College, Ferrum, VA 24088; (703) 365-4416. Presents history and culture of early VA settlements in southwestern mountains of state. Museum presents 1800 German farm living-history program. Archival holdings include photos of architecture, regional life, and work; traditional music recordings; and films/videotapes on VA black music and folk art. Accepts phone inquiries. Fee. Hours: May-Aug, Sa 10-5, Su 1-5; or by appt.

Booker T. Washington National Monument

Rte. 3, Box 310, Hardy, VA 24101; (703) 721-2094. Honors memory of Washington. Small library provides reference materials. Free film loan program available for organized groups. Accepts phone inquiries. No fee. Hours: 8:30-5.

Bridgewater College

Documents Dept., Alexander Mack Memorial Library, East College St., Bridgewater, VA 22812; (703) 828-2501. Academic research library with museum, library, and archives. Holdings include Indian artifacts, archives of Bridgewater College and Church of Brethren, papers of VA historian John Wayland, USGS and topographical maps of VA, photos dating from 1880, and genealogical records. Library holds collection of govt documents from 1902, and materials on VA history and Confederacy. Some restrictions on use. Accepts phone inquiries. No fee. Hours: M-Th 8-11, F 8-5, Sa 9-5, Su 3-11.

Casemate Museum

P.O. Box 341, Casemate #20 Bernard Rd., Fort Monroe, VA 23651; (804) 727-3973. Depicts history of Ft Monroe, Old Point Comfort, and US Army Coast Artillery Corps through research and exhibits. Library concentrates on local history, Civil War, artillery, and notable persons from Ft Monroe. Archives hold Coast artillery journals and memoranda, typescripts of books on Chesapeake, maps from 1832, photos, rare Coast Artillery operations footage, taped interviews with veterans and commanders, and Bernard family genealogy records. Special collections from Gen Rollin Tilton, Col Parry Lewis, Irma Ireland, Larrabee family, and Lt Col Edward Dennis. Materials non-circulating. Accepts phone inquiries. No fee. Hours: by appt only, 10:30-5.

Chesapeake Public Library
Civic Center, 300 Cedar Rd., Chesapeake, VA 23320; (804) 547-6591. Provides info and resources for general public in form of US govt and VA state documents; VA topographical maps including Atlantic ecological inventory series and sounding charts for Atlantic coast; and historical collection on Norfolk County. Accepts phone inquiries. No fee. Hours: M-Th 9-9, F 9-5, Sa 9-5, Su 1-5.

College of William and Mary
Earl Gregg Swem Library, Williamsburg, VA 23185; (804) 253-4407 or 4550. Academic research library preserves materials on college, VA, and colonial US history. Library strong in early US and VA history. Archives contain resources on history of William & Mary, people related to College, and founding in 1693; manuscripts relating to VA and residents from 17th c; maps of VA from 17th-19th c; large collection of photos; and genealogical records of some VA families. Special collections of VA historic materials, including private libraries, materials on European military history, and books on history of printing. Materials circulate to college community. Accepts phone inquiries. No fee. Hours: Su 1-midnight, M-F 8-midnight, Sa 9-6.

Collingwood Library and Museum on Americanism
8301 East Blvd. Dr., Alexandria, VA 22308; (703) 765-1652. Fosters appreciation of American heritage through collections in museum and library. Museum displays American Indian artifacts, Paul Revere lantern, and copy of Magna Carta. Library provides reference materials on American history and culture from pre-colonial period, maps of northern VA from Washington's time, images of signers of Declaration of Independence and their grave sites, genealogical records of Mayflower descendents, and lettered display on Washington's rules of civility. Accepts phone inquiries. No fee. Hours: M, W-Sa 10-4, Su 1-4.

Colonial Williamsburg Foundation Library
P.O. Box C, 415 N. Boundary St., Williamsburg, VA 23187; (804) 220-7423. Composed of 9 library research collections supporting Colonial Williamsburg educational programs. Holdings include info on colonial VA, Chesapeake, decorative arts of 18th and 19th c, architecture history, archaeology, and technology. Archives hold foundation materials and research papers on this 18th c capital of VA; manuscripts from VA 17th-19th c residents and papers of W. Blathwayt and John Norton; many maps; extensive photo collection, many documenting restoration; some films/videotapes; genealogical records; and VA Colonial Records Project on 1607-1783. Materials for in-house use only. Accepts mail inquiries. No fee. Hours: M-F 8-5, Sa 9-1.

Confederacy Museum
Eleanor S. Brockenbrough Library, 1201 E. Clay St., Richmond, VA 23219; (804) 649-1861. Collects, interprets, and preserves materials relating to 19th c Southern history and culture, and preserves Confederate Executive Mansion. Museum holdings date from 1861-1920. Library documents Old South, Confederacy, and post-war period. Archives hold records of Confederate Memorial Literary Society, papers of Confederate political and military leaders, north VA Army maps, large collection of wartime photos, Jefferson Davis family papers, Confederate currency and bonds, and materials on Confederate Army and Navy service. Materials non-circulating. No fee for library, fee for museum. Hours: by appt only, M-F 10-noon, 1-5.

Conservation and Historic Resources Association
Division of Landmarks, 221 Governor St., Richmond, VA 23219; (804) 786-3143. Library provides general info on preservation, VA history, and architecture. Archives hold large collection of files on historic sites and bldgs in VA, Mutual Assurance Society fire policies from 1793-

1870, historic Civil War maps, USGS maps for VA, photos of surveyed properties, and special collection of artifacts from excavated archaeological sites in VA. Materials generally only for use of serious researchers. Accepts phone inquiries. No fee. Hours: 8:30-5.

Council on America's Military Past
P.O. Box 1151, Fort Myer, VA 22211; (703) 440-0216. Natl org concentrates on preservation of military history material remains by identifying, locating, and memorializing military installations no longer in service. Issues publications, supports restoration projects, and provides grants. Accepts phone inquiries.

Danville Community College
Documents Division, Learning Resources Center, 1008 S. Main St., Danville, VA 24541; (804) 797-3553. Academic research library serving community needs with museum, library, and archives. Accepts phone inquiries. No fee. Hours: M-Th 8-9:30, F 8-5, Su 1-5.

Danville Museum of Fine Arts and History
975 Main St., Danville, VA 24541; (804) 793-5644. General art and history museum serving Danville and south central VA. Museum exhibits Civil War era fine and decorative arts and historic Danville memorabilia from 19th and early 20th c. Small library houses reference materials on art and history with emphasis on Civil War, topographic 19th c maps, early photos of Danville, and genealogical records of prominent locals. Special collections of artifacts from "Wreck of Old 97," photorealist prints, portraits of area residents, and collection of 16th-19th c textiles. Accepts phone inquiries. No fee. Hours: Tu-F 10-5, Su 2-5.

Edgar Allan Poe Museum
1914-16 E. Main St., Richmond, VA 23223; (804) 648-5523. Preserves and exhibits works of Poe and objects associated with his life. Museum consists of 5 bldgs depicting Richmond in Poe's era. Holdings include Poe memorabilia, and illustrations from "The Raven." Library contains all Poe first editions and periodicals and biographies. Archives in process will contain Poe's letters to Hiram Haines, Thomas White, and oth-

ers. Photos of Ultima Thule, Virginia Clemm, and others available. Accepts phone inquiries. Fee. Hours: Tu-Sa 10-4, Su-M 1:30-4.

Flowerdew Hundred Foundation
1617 Flowerdew Hundred Rd., Hopewell, VA 23860; (804) 541-8897. Studies, preserves, and interprets cultural history of Flowerdew Hundred Plantation and lower Tidewater VA. Museum exhibits archaeological artifacts from prehistory-19th c. Library holds manuscripts, maps, photos, and genealogical materials. Accepts phone inquiries. Fee. Hours: Tu-Su 10-5, or by appt.

Fort Ward Museum and Historic Site
4301 W. Braddock Rd., Alexandria, VA 22304; (703) 838-4848. Interprets Ft history and themes related to local and general Civil War history. Museum patterned after Union headquarters bldg, and contains diverse Civil War collection emphasizing Northern interest. Library and archives hold materials on defense of Washington during Civil War. Small photo collection on Civil War. Accepts phone inquiries. No fee. Hours: library by appt only, Tu-Sa 9-5, Su noon-5.

Frank Lloyd Wright's Pope-Leighey House
P.O. Box 37, 9000 Richmond Hwy., Mount Vernon, VA 22121; (703) 780-3264. Interprets Wright's Usonian architecture. Museum housed in 1941 Usonian home built by Wright. Archives document design and construction of home through correspondence between architect and client. Holdings include copies of architectural renderings, photos, and oral history interviews with second owner of home. Accepts phone inquiries. Fee. Hours: Mar-Dec, M-F 9:30-4:30.

Fredericksburg and Spotsylvania National Military Park
P.O. Box 679, Fredericksburg, VA 22404; (703) 373-4461. Preserves 4 Civil War battlefields and several other sites. Museums include house Stonewall Jackson died in, Chatham historic house, and two modern visitor centers with exhibits and audiovisual programs. Library concentrates on Civil War in central VA, and holds large manuscript collections, many unpublished maps of

Brigadier General Douglas MacArthur at his 1918 Fresnes, France, brigade headquarters, from the General Douglas MacArthur Memorial.

troop movements, and service and pension records for VA Confederate soldiers. Accepts phone inquiries. No fee. Hours: library and archives by appt only; museums 9-5.

Gadsby's Tavern Museum

Box 178, City Hall, 134 N. Royal St., Alexandria, VA 22314; (703) 838-4242. Tells story of Gadsby's Tavern and its relationship to other taverns and Alexandria. Museum exhibits include decorative arts from late 18th to early 19th c. Library holds materials on history of taverns, Alexandria, decorative arts, and American history during colonial and federal periods. Photo collection features early and recent images of tavern. Oral history recordings on changing Alexandria available, as well as research materials on those who ran tavern. Accepts phone inquiries. Fee. Hours: Tu-Sa 10-5, Su 1-5.

General Douglas MacArthur Memorial

MacArthur Square, Norfolk, VA, 23510; (804) 441-2965. Commemorates life and times of General Douglas MacArthur. Museum displays uniforms, photos, gifts, maps, and copies of documents from WWII, Korean War, and occupation of Japan. Library holds books from and on MacArthur. Archives retain his headquarter files from 1935-51; personal papers of MacArthur and associates from 1848-64; maps of WWI, WWII, and Korean War, large collection of photos and transparencies; films from 1939-64 on his career and times; statements, speeches, and interviews from 1944-77; and genealogical records. Some materials classified. Accepts phone inquiries. No fee. Hours: museum, M-Sa 10-5, Su 11-5; library, M-F 8:30-5.

Geological Survey Library

Dept of Interior, USGS National Ctr, Mail Stop 950, 12201 Sunrise Valley Dr., Reston, VA 22092; (703) 860-5514. Provides earth science info to USGS staff and researchers. Library has large collection of natural resource info, maps of all aspects of geological sciences, and photos from 1860s on USGS. Special Kunz collection on gems and minerals also available. Field records notebook collection held in Denver, CO, facility. Materials circulate through ILL. Phone inquiries accepted. No fee. Hours: 7:30-4:15.

George C. Marshall Research Foundation and Library

Virginia Military Institute, P.O. Box 1600, Lexington, VA 24450; (703) 463-7103. Holdings include regimental histories, operation reports, army manuals, govt documents and personal papers from WWI and WWII. Other holdings include large collection of operations maps; photos of military leaders and events, including materials on making of film "Patton;" vertical file materials; US, UK, and French war posters; US Signal Corps photos; official WWII US and British military histories; papers of Generals George Marshall, Lucian Truscott, Frank McCarthy, and others; "Why We Fight" films; Women's Army Corps records; William Freidman cryptography collection; and much on Marshall Plan. Accepts phone inquiries. No fee. Hours: M-Sa 9-5, Su 2-5.

George Mason University

Fenwick Library, 4400 University Dr., Fairfax, VA 22030; (703) 323-2393. Academic research library holds special collections of materials on theater, American symphonies, and early VA maps. Holdings include Federal Theater Project Collection of scripts, posters, production notebooks, and musical scores from people associated with 1935-39 WPA project; Mann collection of early VA maps from 1700; American Symphony Orchestra League Archives of programs and correspondence from symphony orchestras across nation from 1941; and Ollie Atkins Photo Collection. Materials circulate within univ community. Accepts phone inquiries. No fee. Hours: M-Th 7:30-midnight, F 7:30-6, Sa 9-8, Su 1-midnight.

George Mason University Oral History Program

4400 University Dr., Fairfax, VA 22030; (703) 323-2546. Collects northern VA oral histories from 1930s, with concentration on govt sponsored arts projects. Accepts phone inquiries. No fee. Hours: call.

George Washington Masonic National Memorial

101 Callahan Dr., Alexandria, VA 22301; (703) 683-2007. Memorial to Washington preserving

valuable personal and Masonic artifacts. Museum houses items documenting Washington's life as Mason, General, and President, as well as involvement with Mt Vernon and Alexandria. Library concentrates on Masonic lodges, history, philosophy, and biographies. Special collection of Washington personal papers, family Bible, and trowel used to lay Capitol cornerstone. Library use by permission of curator. Accepts phone inquiries. Donations accepted. Hours: 9-5.

George Washington's Birthplace National Monument

RR 1, Box 718, Washington's Birthplace, VA 22575; (804) 224-7895. Educates on country's colonial period, Washington, and founding fathers. Holdings include Washington's journals and papers, maps from VA colonial period, colonial music, genealogical records on Washington, and reproductions of artifacts belonging to Washington. Accepts phone inquiries. No fee. Hours: summer, 9-5; winter, 10-5.

Gunston Hall

Gunston Hall Plantation, Lorton, VA 22079; (703) 550-9220. Preserves historical materials on George Mason, VA, and Americana. Collections include rare books issued between 1493 and late 18th c; Robert Carter of Nomini Collection; Pamela Copeland Collection of genealogy and early Americana; and Mason family papers and records. Other holdings include materials on decorative arts. Hours: by appt only, M-F 9:30-5.

Hampden-Sydney College

Eggleston Library, P.O. Box 7, 12 Via Scara, Hampden-Sydney, VA 23943; (804) 223-4381. Academic research library maintaining small depository of US documents and maps. Small college museum also on campus. Materials non-circulating. Accepts phone inquiries. No fee. Hours: M-Th 8-4:30, F 8-4:30.

Hampton University Archives

Hampton University, Hampton, VA 23668; (804) 727-5374. Academic research library preserves univ history and materials on history and culture of blacks and American Indians. Manuscript collection holds materials on Hampton founder Gen S.C. Armstrong from 1880-

1979; maps from 1868-1970; large collection of photos on University activities from 1878; genealogical records; films and reels on blacks in America; Roscoe Lewis collection of materials on blacks in National Defense Conference; and J. Saunders Redding materials on American Civil Liberties Union. Accepts phone inquiries. No fee. Hours: M-Th 8-9, F 8-5, Sa 9-1.

Hampton University Museum

Hampton University, Hampton, VA 23668; (804) 727-5308. Collects, preserves, and interprets traditional art from African and American Indian cultures, works by Afro-American artists, and objects related to univ history. Collection also includes contributions from Asian and Oceanic cultures. Accepts phone inquiries. No fee. Hours: M-F 8-5, Sa-Su noon-4.

Historic Alexandria—The Lyceum

Box 178, City Hall, 201 S. Washington St., Alexandria, VA 22313; (703) 838-4994. This history museum for Alexandria is dedicated to preservation and interpretations of the city's material culture, history, and traditions. Museum exhibitions relate to regional history. Small collection of photos and transparencies. Accepts phone inquiries. No fee. Hours: 10-5.

Historic Alexandria/Alexandria Archaeology

Box 178, City Hall, 105 N. Union St., Alexandria, VA 22313; (703) 838-4399. Studies and preserves city's archaeological sites and interprets them through exhibitions, publications, seminars, workshops, and tours. Museum exhibits 18th and 19th c artifacts. Library contains reference materials on material culture and sites. Archives holds records of taxes, census, and manufacturers from 1750-1977; archaeological field notes and research manuscripts, insurance, plat, city, and Civil War maps; large photo collection dating from 1860-1940s. Videotape materials on archaeological field work and small collection of oral history interviews also available. Materials non-circulating. Accepts phone inquiries. No fee. Hours: Tu-Sa 9-5.

Historic Crab Orchard Museum and Pioneer Park

P.O. Box 12, Tazewell, VA 24651; (703) 988-

6755. Collects, preserves, and interprets objects and customs of Tazewell county and southwest VA from prehistoric times. Museum, library, and archives hold materials on archaeological and historical research, Civil War period, and local history. May be restrictions. Accepts phone inquiries. Fee. Hours: Tu-Sa 10-5, Su 2-5.

Historic Fredericksburg Foundation

P.O. Box 162, 904 Princess Anne St., Fredericksburg, VA 22401; (703) 371-4505. Preserves and protects historic districts and adjacent region. Library emphasizes architecture and historic preservation of Fredericksburg. Archives hold bldg inventory of historic district, including photos, construction info, and architectural descriptions. Some maps, Mutual Assurance Society Fire Policies for area, and films/videotapes. Materials for in-house use only. Accepts phone inquiries. No fee. Hours: call.

Hollins College

Fishburn Library, Hollins College, VA 24020; (703) 362-6232. Academic research library for one of country's oldest women's college. Holdings include college archives, letters and diaries of students and administrators, and photos pertaining to college history. Special collections on Benjamin Franklin, printing and papermaking, and women's education. Accepts phone inquiries. No fee. Hours: M-F 8-5:30.

Jacob Payton Library

5001 Echols Ave., Alexandria, VA 22311; (703) 820-7200. Preserves Methodist history of northern VA. Museum displays artifacts related to early Methodism in VA. Library has collection of Methodist histories and biographies. Archives have extensive collection of materials on VA and MD conferences, manuscripts, and photos. Materials non-circulating. Accepts phone inquiries. No fee. Hours: M-F 8-3:30.

James Madison Museum

129 Caroline St., Orange, VA 22960; (703) 672-1776. Memorializes this 4th president of US, as well as relating history of Orange county, and regional agriculture. Collections include Madison letters, photos of family and Montpelier home, genealocial records, Orange county land patents, and some local history items. Ac-

cepts phone inquiries. Fee. Hours: Mar-Nov, M-F 10-noon, 1-5, Sa-Su 1-4. Dec-Feb, M-F 10-noon, 1-4.

James Madison University

Document Depository, Carrier Library, Harrisonburg, VA 22807; (703) 568-6929. Academic research library with collection of US govt and regional VA documents. Accepts phone inquiries. No fee. Hours: call.

James Monroe Law Office Museum and Memorial Library

908 Charles St., Fredericksburg, VA 22401; (703) 373-8426. Collects, preserves, and interprets Monroe family artifacts, and emphasize Monroe's years in France and White House. Museum exhibits rooms furnished for period. Memorial library holds large collection of Monroe's books, and books on him. Archives contain documents, maps, photos, and manuscripts. Genealogical records contain materials on Byrd, Carter, Minor, Monroe, Washington, and Overton families. Accepts phone inquiries. Fee. Hours: 9-5.

Jamestown Festival Park/ Yorktown Victory Center

Jamestown-Yorktown Foundation, P.O. Drawer JF, Rte. 31 S., Williamsburg, VA 23187; (804) 253-4938. Depicts earliest beginnings of English colonization attempts in North American, and interprets lifestyle of Native Americans of southeastern VA. Museum consists of indoor and outdoor exhibits on early years of English settlement in VA. Library has small collection of materials on early VA, 16th and 17th c England, archaeological reports, and VA Indians. Archival materials deal with foundation and park; historic manuscripts; southeastern VA maps; 20th c photos; films/videotapes on early Jamestown and sea voyage to VA; and British Colonial Records. Materials non-circulating. Accepts phone inquiries. Fee for museum; no fee for library. Hours: M-F 8:30-noon, 1-5.

Lee Chapel

Washington and Lee University, Lexington, VA 24450; (703) 463-8768. Museum housed in chapel constructed by Robert E. Lee in 1867. Holds Lee archives, family crypt, and office furnishings, as well as Custis-Washington-Lee art collection. Accepts phone inquiries. No fee. Hours: Apr-Nov, M-Sa 9-5; Nov-Mar, M-Sa 9-4, Su 2-5.

Lynchburg Historical Foundation
P.O. Box 248, Lynchburg, VA 24503; (804) 528-5353. Promotes preservation of historically and architecturally significant bldgs in central VA. Accepts phone inquiries. No fee. Hours: M-F 8:30-12:30.

Lynchburg Museum
P.O. Box 60, 901 Court St., Lynchburg, VA 24505; (804) 847-1459. Municipal museum collects and exhibits materials on Lynchburg, its citizens, history, and environment, as well as VA and US history. Holdings include diplays on local history, reference library, manuscripts, maps, and photos of local residents from 1850. Some restrictions on use. Accepts phone inquiries. Fee. Hours: 1-4.

Maier Museum of Art
Randolph-Macon Woman's College, 1 Quinlan St., Lynchburg, VA 24503; (804) 846-7392. Displays permanent collection of 19th and 20th c American paintings and European and American prints. Accepts phone inquiries. No fee. Hours: Sept-May, Tu-Su 1-5; Jun-Aug by appt.

Manassas City Museum
9406 Main St., Manassas, VA 22110; (703) 368-1873. Collects, interprets, and preserves history and material culture of Manassas area. Museum exhibits span prehistory through present, with emphasis on Civil War. Library has small reference collection. Archives hold Civil War materials, copies of state and local maps, and photos. Accepts phone inquiries. Donations accepted. Hours: 10-5.

Manassas National Battlefield Park
P.O. Box 1830, Manassas, VA 22110; (703) 754-7107. Research library for topics specific to battles fought at site. Museum exhibits include uniforms and weapons from battles. Library and archives contain materials relevant to park, including letters, memoirs, manuscripts, maps, photos, and genealogical records. Special collection of Maj Gen James Ricketts papers. Accepts

phone inquiries. Fee. Hours: 8:30-4:30.

Marine Corps Education Center
Documents Division, James Carson Breckinridge Library, Dunlap Hall, Quantico, VA 22134; (703) 640-2248. Library collections support Marine Corps Development and Education Command, and include materials on amphibious operations, Marine Corps, military and naval art and science, and military history. Holdings include manuscripts, maps, periodicals, and books. Materials for in-house use only. Hours: M-F 8-4:30.

Marine Corps Film Depository
Building 2013, Quantico, VA 22134; (703) 640-2844. Collects and preserves over 7 million feet and 700 titles relating to Marine Corps history. Collection has some pre-1927 footage, but most later. Holdings cover WWII, combat, peacetime maneuvers, ceremonies, and Marine personalities. Much stock film available. For viewing at depository. Some restrictions. Accepts phone inquiries. Fee for staff research. Hours: by appt only, M-F 7:30-4.

Mariners' Museum
Museum Dr., Newport News, VA 23606; (804) 595-0368. Preserves materials on culture and heritage of mariners, and their impact on civilization. Museum, library, and archives hold manuscripts, maps, photos, and films/videotapes. Special collection of pleasure boat manufacturer Chris-Craft Corp archives. Accepts phone inquiries. Fee. Hours: M-Sa 9-5, Su noon-5.

Mary Ball Washington Museum and Library
P.O. Box 97, Star Rte. 3 at Court House, Lancaster, VA 22503; (804) 462-7280. Preserves and exhibits articles of historic importance associated with Ball and Washington families. Museum displays textiles, costumes, photos, and quilts. Library provides genealogical, historical, and biographical materials. Archives hold papers of Washington, Ball, Chowning, Chilton, Peirce, and Tapscott families and 19th c photos of people and places. Special collections of Ball-Washington family memorabilia, and Millenbeck archaeological materials. Accepts phone inquiries. No fee. Hours: Tu-F 9-5, Sa 10-3.

Meadow Farm Museum

P.O. Box 27032, Richmond, VA 23273; (804) 672-5100. Farm museum depicts rural life during mid-1850s. Museum details Southern farm history. Library has research material on 19th c life. Archives retain business, household, and medical records; advertising materials; photos; limited maps of Richmond; military and personal photos from late 19th c-early 20th c; and genealogical records of Sheppard, Crump, and related families. Accepts phone inquiries. Fee. Hours: Tu-Sa noon-4.

Monticello, Home of Thomas Jefferson

P.O. Box 316, Route 53, Charlottesville, VA 22902; (804) 295-1832. Preserves, maintains, and interprets life and interests of Thomas Jefferson through exhibits in this statesman's homes. Museum covers Jefferson's design and construction of Monticello, his life there, and his interests in architecture, gardening, slave life, and his family. Library contains research materials on Jefferson, corresponding VA history, period decorative arts, and microfilm of Jefferson's papers. Special Howard Rice collection of materials on 18th c France, Paris, Marquis de Chastellux, and Jefferson's Paris. Some photos of Monticello from 1800s. Accepts phone inquiries. No fee for research. Hours: by appt only, M-F 9-5.

Montpelier, Home of James Madison

Box 67, Montpelier Station, Orange County, VA 22957; (703) 672-2728. Presents life and contributions of James Madison, including political, agricultural, and philosophical interests. Mansion museum was Madison's home, and is currently undergoing restoration. Library has limited materials on Madison and Constitution; photos of Madison, wife Dolley, and Montpelier; and films on Madison. Restrictions on use. Accepts phone inquiries. Fee. Hours: 9-5.

Mount Vernon—Ladies' Association of the Union

Mount Vernon, VA 22121; (703) 780-2000. Preserves and interprets home of George Washington. Museum is restored mansion with extensive collection of original furnishings and memorabilia. Library holds materials on Washington, 18th c American history, plantation life, and historic preservation. Archives hold papers of Ladies' Association. Map collection, extensive photo archives, and films/videotapes document estate. Some genealogical records on Washington, Curtis, and Ball families. Curatorial study collection composed of textiles, china, paintings, and prints. Accepts phone inquiries. Fee. Hours: Mar-Oct 9-5; Nov-Feb 9-4.

NASA Langley Research Center

Historic Documents Collection, Mail Stop 123, Bldg. 1194, Rm. 200, Hampton, VA 23665; (804) 875-3511. Holds large collection of materials on NASA predecessor, National Advisory Committee for Aeronautics (NACA), and is premier collection for aerospace research. Holdings include NACA correspondence and research authorization files; NACA engineer Milton Ames collection on Langley history, including personnel, experiments and developments, records, and project reports; Floyd Thompson space history collection; John Stack collection of correspondence and research on transsonic and supersonic technology; and extensive collection of photos, negatives, and motion picture films. Accepts phone inquiries. Hours: call.

NASA Langley Visitor Center

Langley Research Center, Mail Stop 480, Bldg. 1202, Freeman Rd., Hampton, VA 23665; (804) 865-2855. Informs public of NASA contributions to aeronautics and space exploration through exhibits, educational programs, and films. Museum displays exhibits and quiz games of space themes, satellite maps, and variety of film footage taken on space flights. Accepts phone inquiries. No fee. Hours: M-Sa 8:30-4:30, Su noon-4:30.

National Archives and Record Service Stock Film Library

1411 South Fern St., Arlington, VA 22202; (703) 557-1114. Depository for storage and preservation of stock footage produced by govt. Holding from Dept of Agriculture; Dept of Commerce; Dept of Energy; Atomic Energy Commission; Dept of Health, Education, and Welfare; Administration on Aging; Dept of Interior; the State Dept; Dept of Transportation; Coast Guard; Federal Aviation Administration; Environmental Protection Agency; National

Science Foundation; and Postal Service. Most materials outtakes and trims from completed programs. Some completed NASA productions. Accepts phone inquiries. No fee. Hours: M-F 8-4:30.

National Cartographic Information Center

507 National Center, Reston, VA 22092; (703) 860-6045. Clearinghouse for info on domestically produced maps and charts, mapping materials, aerial and space photos, and satellite imagery. Offers research services on federal, state, local, and privately produced cartographic materials, and houses records of approx 12 million aerial photos. Accepts phone inquiries. No fee. Hours: M-F 7:45-4:15.

National Future Farmers Hall of Achievement

P.O. Box 15160, 5632 Mt. Vernon Memorial Hwy, Alexandria, VA 22309; (703) 360-3600. Promotes excellence in agricultural education and future through thematic exhibits and library. Displays highlight Future Farmers of America themems, including "Pride and Prestige," "A Challenge to Excellence," "The South Forty," "Milestones of Progress," and "The Success Story of American Agriculture;" library with materials on FFA history and programs, and on agriculture in general. Accepts phone inquiries. No fee. Hours: 8:30-4.

National Genealogical Society Library

4527 17th St. North, Arlington, VA 22207; (703) 525-0050. Library specializes in American local history and genealogy. Holdings include large collection of source materials, Bible records, cemetery inscriptions, probate records, vital records, vertical files of unpublished genealogical materials, pamphlets, extensive library, and periodicals. Accepts phone inquiries. Fee. Hours: M, F, Sa 10-4; W 10-9.

National Inventors Hall of Fame Foundation

Crystal Plaza Bldg., 3-1D01, 2021 Jefferson Davis Highway, Arlington, VA 22301; (703) 557-3341. Honors inventors for their significant contributions to science and technology. Mu-

seum holds exhibits on each inductee to National Inventors' Hall of Fame. Accepts phone inquiries. No fee. Hours: M-F 8-5.

National Sporting Library

P.O. Box 1335, Middleburg, VA 22117; (703) 687-6542. Library preserves history of field sports, horses, and related sports. Special collections date from 1550. Accepts phone inquiries. Hours: M-F 9-4:30.

National Tobacco-Textile Museum

P.O. Box 541, 614 Lynn St., Danville, VA 24543; (804) 797-9437. Preserves history of tobacco and textile industries. Museum displays working industrial textile machinery, tobacco agriculture and advertising art. Library has collection of periodicals, newspapers, and manuscripts. Archives retain over 30,000 items from 1830s. Limited videotapes available. Accepts phone inquiries. Fee. Hours: M-F 10-4.

Norfolk Historical Society

P.O. Box 9472, Olney Rd. & Stockley Gardens, Norfolk, VA 23505; (804) 625-1720. Promotes and preserves Norfolk history through holdings in museum, library, and archives. Displays include local artifacts, manuscripts, and photos. Accepts phone inquiries. No fee. Hours: W 9:30-noon.

Office of Judge Advocate General

Document Division, Department of the Navy, Law Library, 200 Stovall St., Alexandria, VA 22332; (202) 325-9565. Supports Judge Advocate General's Corps. Library holds some early court-martial orders, and other dated military, Justice, and Navy materials. Special collections of Judge Advocate General opinions. Accepts phone inquiries. No fee. Hours: by appt only, M-F 8-5.

Old Guard Museum

Building 249, Sheridan Ave., Ft. Myer, VA 22211; (202) 696-6670. Provides materials for education and training on US Army and 3rd US Infantry. Museum houses Infantry uniforms, equipment, and memorabilia. Library concentrates on US Infantry. Archives contain letters, reports, and orders of 3rd US Infantry, including some materials on military district of Washington. Manuscript, photo, and film/video collections from Mexican and Civil War. Accepts phone inquiries. No fee. Hours: M-F 9-4.

Old Stone Jail Museum

Fluvanna County Historical Society, P.O. Box 8, Palmyra, VA 22963; (804) 842-3378. Collects and preserves materials pertaining to Fluvanna county history. Museum exhibits local and regional military, farm, and household artifacts from 1800-1925. Houses special collection of elegant women's clothing from 1920s. Maintains collection of local genealogical records. Accepts phone inquiries. No fee. Hours: June-Sept, Sa noon-4; Su 1-5.

Organ Historical Society

P.O. Box 26811, Richmond, VA 23261; (804) 353-9226. Studies American pipe organs, their builders, music, players, composers, and audiences from 18th-20th c. Library documents American organ building, materials on Westminster Choir, and source materials from organists; photos; and recordings of American organs. Publishes quarterly magazine. Hours: M-F 9-5.

Patrick Henry Community College Library

Learning Resource Center, P.O. Drawer 5311, Rte. 108 North to College Dr., Martinsville, VA 24115; (703) 638-8777. Academic research library with selective collection of US govt documents. Special library collection on Civil War. Accepts phone inquiries. No fee. Hours: M-Th 8-9, F 8-5, Sa 9-midnight.

Patrick Henry Memorial

Red Hill, Rte. 2, Box 27, Brookneal, VA 24528; (804) 376-2044. Restored final home and burial place of Patrick Henry memorializes his life. Museum exhibits cover Henry's entire life from 1736-1799, and houses paintings of Henry. Library has small reference collection on Henry and local history. Archives have Robert Meade collection of research material on Henry's life; Fontaine-Winston papers on Henry family genealogy; Henry's letters and land grants; maps; photos; biographical films and PSAs; and recordings of "Liberty or Death" speech and oral history interviews. Accepts phone inquiries. Fee. Hours: 9-5, and Nov-Mar 9-4.

Petersburg Museums

15 West Bank St., Petersburg, VA 23803; (804) 733-2402. Preserves and interprets history of Petersburg. Museums consist of five sites: Centre Hill Mansion, Trapezium House, Blanford Church, Siege Museum, and Farmer's Bank. Library focuses on Petersburg history, 19th c decorative arts and historic interiors, and Civil War materials, Archives contain materials on Petersburg history from 1860s, maps, and photos. Special collection on microfilm of Spotswood scrapbooks. Materials non-circulating. Fee. Hours: museum, M-Sa 10-4, Su 12:30-4; library M-F 10-4.

Petersburg National Battlefield

Rte. 36, Box 549, Petersburg, VA 23803; (804) 732-3531. Preserves and interprets Civil War battlefield and related sites in the Petersburg and Hopewell, VA region. Museum presents interpretive displays on Seige of Petersburg, Civil War artifacts, and archaeological recoveries. Library concentrates on Civil War and Seige of Petersburg. Archives hold information on establishment and operations of battlefield, maps, historic photos, and some troop rosters and local cemetery listings for battle deaths. Accepts phone inquiries. Fee. Hours: research by appt; museum, mid-Aug-mid-June 8-5, mid-June-mid-Aug 8-7.

Pohick Episcopal Church

Parish of Mt. Vernon and Gunston Hall, 9301 Richmond Highway, Lorton, VA 22079; (301) 550-9449. Former church of George Washington and George Mason, restored for present-day active duty. Archival collection includes copy of church's 1733-1802 vestry, copy of prayer book imported by Washington that became prayer book of colonies, and Washington Bible. Accepts phone inquiries. No fee. Hours: 8:30-4:30.

Point of Honor

P.O. Box 60, 112 Cabell St., Lynchburg, VA 24504; (804) 847-1459. Home of Patrick Henry's physician restored to recreate lifesyle of central VA family. Furnished in period decorative arts and accessories from 1800-30 period. Some restrictions. Accepts phone inquiries. Hours. Hours: 1-4.

Portsmouth Naval Shipyard Museum

P.O. Box 248, 2 High St., Portsmouth, VA 23705; (804) 393-8591. Promotes history of Portsmouth, Norfolk Naval Shipyard, and armed forces serving area. Museum exhibits diplays from 1949. Library provides reference materials. Archives retain some maps, manuscripts, photos, genealogical materials, and naval history. Accepts phone inquiries. Donations accepted. Hours: library by appt, Tu-F 10-4:30; museum, Tu-Sa 10-5, Su 1-5.

Preservation of Historic Winchester

530 Amherst St., Winchester, VA 22601; (703) 667-3577. Monitors and protects Winchester heritage. Library holds materials on historic preservation and conservation, photos and slides of Winchester architecture, and materials from Winchester National Register Historic Survey. Accepts phone inquiries. No fee. Hours: M-F 9-5.

Richmond National Battlefield Park

3215 E. Broad St., Richmond, VA 23223; (804) 226-1981. Preserves, protects, and interprets nationally historic sites in and around Richmond. Museum covers history of Civil War, Seven Days campaign, and Cold Harbor from 1864. Library provides reference materials. Manuscripts collection contains Christian Fleetwood papers, maps, photos, genealogical records, and small collection of films/videotapes on Park Service sites. Accepts phone inquiries. No fee. Hours: library by appt only; museum 9-5.

Roanoke Museum of Fine Arts

1 Market Square, Roanoke, VA 24011; (703) 342-5760. Fine arts museum with emphasis on American and regional art. Exhibits include American printings from 1920s-40s, as well as some ancient Roman, Greek, Egyptian, and Japanese art. Library has collection of local reference materials and photos of 20th c art. Special collection of 20th c works by local artists. Accepts phone inquiries. No fee. Hours: Tu-Sa 10-5.

Robert E. Lee Boyhood Home

607 Oronoco, Alexandria, VA 22314; (703) 548-8454. Museum preserves history, genealogy, artifacts, and stories of interest in life of Robert E. Lee. Home is decorated in period antiques. Library provides reference materials. Some restrictions on use. Accepts phone inquiries. Fee. Hours: Feb-Dec 15, M-Sa 10-4, Su noon-4.

Robert E. Lee Memorial Association

Stratford Hall Plantation, Stratford, VA 22558; (804) 493-8038. Provides educational and historical interpretation of 18th and 19th c Stratford Lees of VA. Museum exhibits artifacts of Stratford Lees and displays on Constitutional Debate. Library covers 18th c Lees, VA history, and Robert E. Lee. Archives hold papers of Robert E. Lee Memorial Association from 1929. Manuscript collection of Lee family correspondence. Early 20th c views of Stratford Hall plantation. Accepts phone inquiries. Fee. Hours: 9-4:30.

Saint John's Episcopal Church

2401 East Broad St., Richmond, VA 23223; (804) 648-5015. Interprets church where Patrick Henry gave his historic speech to 2nd VA Convention. Accepts phone inquiries. Fee. Hours: M-Sa 10-3:30, Su 1-3:30.

Sargeant Memorial Room

Norfolk Public Library, 301 E. City Hall Ave., Norfolk, VA 23510; (804) 441-2503. Maintains collection of local history and genealogical data. Library has census records for VA, NC, MD, WV, DC, SC, and KY from early 1800s; VA newspapers from 1736-80 and 1795-1972; secondary source materials on many phases of VA and early US history; extensive Norfolk picture file from 19th c; postcards; scrapbooks; pamphlet and clipping file from regional papers; and genealogical records. Materials non-circulating. Accepts phone inquiries. No fee. Hours: M-Tu, Th-Sa 9-5; W 9-9.

Scotchtown, Home of Patrick Henry

Rte. 2, Box 168, Beaverdam, VA 23015; (804) 227-3500. Preserves home of Henry, and disseminates info on his life, work, ideas, and relationship to 19th c Hanover, VA. Museum preserves 1719 house and exhibits Henry's letters and furniture. Library holds early biographies of Henry. Maps and photos document area's history from 1770s. Accepts phone inquiries. Fee.

Hours: Apr-Oct, M-Sa 10-4:30; Su 1:30-4:30; or by appt.

Southwest Virginia Museum

Box 742, W. First St. & Wood Ave., Big Stone Gap, VA 24219; (703) 523-1322. Displays and interprets culture and history of early southwest VA. Accepts phone inquiries. Fee. Hours: Memorial Day-Labor Day 9-5; Labor Day-Dec and Mar-Memorial Day, Tu-Su 9-5.

Stonewall Jackson House

8 E. Washington St., Lexington, VA 24450; (703) 463-2552. Commemorates Jackson's life while he lived in Lexington and taught at VA Military Institute pre-Civil War. Museum includes rooms restored to appearance during Jackson's occupancy. Library holds research materials on Jackson, Civil War, historic preservation, and decorative arts. Special T.M. Wade collection. Accepts phone inquiries. No fee. Hours: library by appt only, M-Sa 9-5, Su 1-5.

Thayer Engineer Library

Bldg. 270, Fort Belvoir, VA 22060; (703) 664-1140. Library preserves materials on civil and military engineering and American and military history. Holdings include rare books, large collection of military publications, photos, and tapes. Hours: by prior permission only; M-Tu 9-9, W-Th 9-6, F 9-5.

University of Virginia

Manuscripts Department, Alderman Library, Charlottesville, VA 22901; (804) 924-3021. Academic resource library has materials on Afro-Americans and VA families from 19th c documenting issues of the times. Research collections cover slavery, women's history, US magic and witchcraft, agriculture, and politics, and include manuscripts, maps, and photos. John Hartwell Cocke, Berkeley family, Joseph Carrington Cabell, Watson family, Carter-Smith family, Pocket Plantation, Bruce family, Carter family, Mather family, and Hubard family represented. Afro-American collection contains letters and accounts from slaves, slaveholders, immigrants, desegregation movement during 1960-70, and VA political leaders. Accepts phone inquiries. No fee. Hours: call.

Valentine Museum

1015 E. Clay St., Richmond, VA 23219; (804) 649-0711. Urban history museum collecting, preserving, and interpreting history of Richmond. Museum holds children's gallery, commemorates Wickham-Valentine historic house, and holds Richmond history. Library documents Richmond history from 17th c, with info on decorative arts, textiles, and architecture. Small map collection. Photo archives depict Richmond and residents during Civil War. Small collection of genealogical records. Special collections include Cook, Mary Wingfield Scott, and Colonial Studios collections. Accepts phone inquiries. Fee. Hours: museum, M-Sa 10-5, Su 1-5; reference by appt only, M-F 10-5.

Virginia Association of Museums

301-A North Sheppard St., Richmond, VA 23220; (804) 367-1079. Service org promotes professional museum work in VA museums, historic sites, and galleries. Reference library holds books, periodicals, and resource materials on museum administration. Also collects technical articles relating to museum work. Offers training programs, meetings, and newsletter. Accepts phone inquiries. Membership fee. Hours: M-F 9:30-4:30.

Virginia Canals and Navigation Society

c/o Russ Harding, historian/archivist, Box 80, RFD Route 4, Mineral, VA 23117; (703) 894-5703. Membership organization for canal historians. Materials retained in historian's personal collection are manuscripts, maps, photos, films/videotapes, audio recordings, genealogical materials, and some special collections. Accepts phone inquiries. Fee for membership. Hours: call.

Virginia Historical Society

P.O. Box 7311, 428 N. Blvd., Richmond, VA 23221; (804) 358-4901. Collects, preserves, publishes, and makes available scholarly materials on VA history. Museum contains artifacts and a mural gallery on Civil War. Library holds large collection of VA and colonial history materials, including maps, broadsides, sheet music, and newspapers. Archives contain extensive family papers from 17th c, and unpublished and published works on VA families. Special collections on VA silver, furniture, and sculpture. Accepts phone inquiries. Hours: M-Sa 9-4:45.

Virginia Military Institute Museum

Jackson Memorial Hall, Lexington, VA 24450; (703) 463-6232. Relates history of VA Military Institute, its cadets, and alumni from 1839. Museum exhibits artifacts from alumni such as Stonewall Jackson, Matthew Fontaine Maury, and George Marshall; chronicles history of school with emphasis on Civil War. Library, archives, and manuscript collections kept at VMI library. Accepts phone inquiries. No fee. Hours: M-Sa 9-5, Su 2-5.

Virginia Polytechnic Institute and State University

University Libraries, Blacksburg, VA 24061; (703) 961-6170. Academic research facility with collections of VA agricultural history, history of southwest VA, transportation history, and Western Americana. Collections include many maps, recordings, and films/videos. Materials circulate to University community and state residents. Accepts phone inquiries. No fee. Hours: Su-Th 7:30-midnight, F 7:30-10, Sa 9-10.

Virginia Research Center for Archaeology

College of William and Mary, Wren Kitchen, Williamsburg, VA 23185; (804) 229-0898. Promotes study of archaeology and anthropology, with concentration on prehistoric and historic periods in VA, and promotes conservation and exploration of sites and materials. Materials for members only. Accepts phone inquiries. No fee. Hours: by appt only.

Virginia Room

Fairfax Public Library, 395 Chain Bridge Rd., Fairfax, VA 22030; (703) 246-2123. General library with special collection of VA, local, and govt history. Holdings include manuscripts, maps, large photo collection on Fairfax county, films/videotapes, and genealogical materials. Accepts phone inquiries. No fee. Hours: M-Th 9-9, F 9-6, Sa 9-5, Su noon-8.

Virginia State Library

12th St. & Capitol Square, Richmond, VA 23219; (804) 786-8929. Reference library for state seat and govt contains large collection of reference and archival materials on VA history, Confederacy, local history, tobacco, and wine industries, and Revenue stamps. Other holdings include VA maps, extensive photo collection, and genealogical records. Materials circulate only to VA residents. Accepts phone inquiries. No fee. Hours: M-Sa 8:15-5.

Virginia Trust for Historic Preservation

Lee-Fendall House Museum, 614 Oronoco St., Alexandria, VA 22314; (703) 548-1789. Presents and interprets history of house and lives of occupants over last 200 years. Museum house was home to Lee family until 1903. Exhibits based on 1850s renovation and Lee family possessions. Accepts phone inquiries. Fee. Hours: Tu-F 10-3:45, Sa-Su call for hours.

Virginia Union University

William Clark Library, 1500 N. Lombardy St., Richmond, VA 23220; (804) 257-5820. Academic research facility has special collection on slavery and oral histories from black VA residents, with emphasis on religous context. Accepts phone inquiries. No fee. Hours: call.

War Memorial Museum of Virginia

9285 Warwick Blvd., Huntington Park, Newport News, VA 23607; (804) 247-8523. Studies, preserves, and exhibits US military history from 1775, detailing impact of war upon American history. Museum holds large collection of weapons, uniforms, art, propoganda posters, insignia, vehicles, flags, and artillery documenting war activities from 1700-1985. Library complements museum exhibits, covering 1500-1985. Collections include maps, photos on 20th c military topic, and 500 films/videotapes on 20th c military operations. Special collections include military illustrations of Herbert Morton Stoops, and artifacts and documents of embarkations from Hampton Port. Accepts phone inquiries. Fee. Hours: M-Sa 9-5, Su 1-5.

Warren Rifles Confederate Museum

95 Chester St., Front Royal, VA 22630; (703) 636-6982. Memorializes Confederate soldiers, and promotes history of period 1861-65. Mu-

seum displays uniforms, documents, letters, and artifacts used by soldiers; paroles of soldiers from prison; citizenship records given to Confederates by President Johnson; discharge letters from Confederate hospitals; autographs of Confederate officers; and some genealogical materials. Accepts phone inquiries. Fee. Hours: M-Sa 9-5, and Apr-Oct, Su noon-5.

Winchester-Frederick County Historic Society

401 National Ave., Winchester, VA 22601; (703) 662-6550. Encourages research, publication, and collection of Winchester and regional history. Administers George Washington's office museum, Abram's Delight museum, and Stonewall Jackson's headquarters. Society library associated with Handley library (Braddock and Piccadilly Sts.), which holds most Society materials. Accepts phone inquiries. No fee for use of archives; fee at museums. Hours: 9-4.

Woodlawn Plantation

P.O. Box 37, 900 Richmond Hwy, Mount Vernon, VA 22121; (703) 780-4000. Interprets history of Lewis family and their 19th c affluent lifestyle, as well as federal period of American history. Museum period rooms furnished in Federal and Empire style decorative arts. Library holds materials on local history, George Washington, and American decorative arts. Archives holds correspondence, papers on operation of plantation, materials on Quakers, documents on 20th c owners, maps of Washington, DC, and Mt Vernon, and photos from 1860. Genealogical records of Washington, Custis, Troth, Mason, and Gillingham families. Accepts phone inquiries. Fee. Hours: 9:30-4:30

Woodrow Wilson Birthplace

P.O. Box 24, 20 North Coalter Street., Staunton, VA 24401; (703) 885-0897. Preserves and interprets life of President Wilson and house he was born in. Museum consists of furnished period rooms. Library holds 50 years worth of Wilson papers, manuscripts from senators, governors, and preservation leaders, books on Wilson, and large collection of photographs on Wilson, his family members, and the Paris Peace Conference. Accepts phone inquiries. Fee. Hours: M-F 9-5.

Yorktown Victory Center

P.O. Box 1976, Rt. 238, Yorktown, VA 23690; (804) 887-1776. Collects, preserves, and exhibits objects and materials on Battle of Yorktown, American Revolution, and Revolution's effect on American colonists. Museum has exhibits relating to Revolution. Library contains books, periodicals, and journals relating to 18th c history, American Revolution, VA history, Yorktown, and museum studies. Some films/videotapes availably on Bicentennials of country and Battle of Yorktown, and special collections available on local history publications. Some restrictions. Accepts phone inquiries. Fee. Hours: 8:30-5.

Washington

Bing Crosby Historical Society

P.O. Box 216, Tacoma, WA 98401; (206) 627-2947. Small collection of Bing Crosby memorabilia commemorating his roots in Tacoma and his contributions to entertainment history. Holdings include small library, scripts, photos, films/videotapes, Crosby genealogical records, and considerable collection of Crosby recordings. Museum to become Gallery of Washington State Entertainment in 1989. Hours: call.

Black Diamond Historical Society

P.O. Box 232, 32627 Railroad and Baker, Black Diamond, WA 98010; (602) 886-2327. Collects, preserves, and promotes history of Black Diamond, WA and residents in form of museum, library, and archival collections. Holdings include Black Diamond Depot Museum, with historic railroad and artifacts; library has local historical publications and research materials; archives with local historical artifacts from 19th c; mining maps and charts, 1882-1969; early photos of local subjects; small collections of manuscripts and genealogical records; collection of mining artifacts. Accepts phone inquiries. Donations accepted. Hours: Th 9-3, Sa-Su noon-3.

Black Heritage Society of Washington State

P.O. Box 22565, Seattle, WA 98122; (206) 325-8205. Collects, preserves, and makes available artifacts relating history of blacks in WA. Archives contain letters from 1923 UNIA convention in New York, photos of Seattle residents from 1914, oral history interviews pre-WWII, and small collection of artifacts from WA families from 1891. Accepts phone inquiries. Hours: call.

Center for Wooden Boats

1010 Valley, Seattle, WA 98109; (206) 382-2628. Exhibit and park complex preserves the history and heritage of small-craft building and boating in form of restoration projects, museum, and library. Holdings include collection of historic small craft, some of which may be used by public; library with publications and reference materials on the history, design, construction, and voyages of small craft; small photo collection. Some restrictions. Accepts phone inquiries. Some fees. Hours: winter, M-F noon-6, Sa-Su 10-6; summer, M-F noon-7, Sa-Su 10-8.

Central Washington University Library

Documents Division, Ellensburg, WA 98926; (509) 963-1541. Supports University study and research with collection of US govt documents from 1964. Some materials do not circulate. Phone inquiries accepted. No fee. Hours: M-Th 8-10, F 8-5, Sa 9-5, Su 1-10.

Clark County Historical Museum

Fort Vancouver Historical Society, Inc., P.O. Box 1834, 1511 Main St., Vancouver, WA 98668; (206) 695-4681. Preserves history of Clark County through museum collections on Hudson Bay Co, Vancouver Army Barracks, Indians, and Lewis and Clark. Library collection includes maps and photos. Accepts phone inquiries. No fee. Hours: Tu-Su 1-5.

Coast Artillery Museum at Fort Worden

Puget Sound Coast Artillery Assn, Box 57401, Port Townsend, WA 98368; (206) 937-0592. Illustrates and explains operation of first modern weapons systems of 20th c. Museum exhibits uniforms and regimental flags from 1898-1954; photos of people and munitions of early Puget Sound harbor defenses, and films/videotapes on mortar and disappearing rifle use. Accepts phone inquiries. No fee. Hours: May-Oct, M-F 12-5.

Coast Guard Museum/Northwest

1519 Alaskan Way, S., Seattle, WA 98134; (206) 286-9608. Preserves Coast Guard artifacts, documents, manuscripts, and navigational charts from 1850. Small library on Coast Guard and naval history; large photo collection on Life Saving Service, Coast Guard, and Navy Lighthouse Service from 1875; some films and videotapes. Accepts phone inquiries. No fee. Hours: M, W, F 10-4, Sa-Su 1-5.

Eastern Washington State Historical Society

Cheney Cowles Memorial Museum, W. 2316 1st Ave., Spokane, WA 99204; (509) 456-3931. Preserves the history of eastern WA/northern ID Inland Empire region from 1880s with library and archival collections. Holdings include business and personal papers of residents; early Spokane manuscripts; women's history materials; map collection from 1890s; extensive photo archive from 1870s; and 50 films and 800 reels of newsfilm, 1969-1978. Materials non-circulating. Accepts phone inquiries. Fee. Hours: Tu-Sa 10-5.

Eastern Washington University

Archives and Special Collections, Library, MS-84, John F. Kennedy Memorial Library, Cheney, WA 99004; (509) 359-2475. Academic research library with strong collection of materials on Pacific Northwest, area residents, and science fiction and fantasy. Library holds Herman Deutsch Pacific Northwest clipping and pamphlet file and books pertaining to MT, OR, ID, WA, AK, and British Columbia. Archives collects univ history materials, state and local govt records, some diaries from Civil War, letters of Col Mosby family from 1858-1916, photos, films of univ events, oral history interviews with regional pioneers, genealogical records, and Almeron Perry Science Fiction & Fantasy collection. Some restrictions. Accepts phone inquiries. Fee for staff research. Hours: M-F

Ethnic Heritage Council of the Pacific Northwest

1107 NE 45th St., Suite 315A, Seattle, WA 98105; (206) 633-3239. Referral service supporting ethnic community documentation and preservation. Holds archival information and photos regarding Council's history, programs, services and activities; compiles Puget Sound ethnic group directory. Accepts phone inquiries. Membership fee. Hours: M-F 9-5.

Evergreen State College Library

Evergreen State College, Olympia, WA 98505; (206) 866-6000. Academic library maintains selective collection of govt documents, general, reference and historical materials relevant to needs of the school and students. Holdings include archives and college-related historical materials; USGS, Forest Service, and other maps. Accepts phone inquiries. No fee. Hours (academic year): M-F 8:45-10, Sa-Su 10:30-6:15.

Fire Department Museum

W-44 Riverside, Spokane, WA 99201; (509) 456-2694. Collects and protects fire service equip and materials. Museum displays materials from 1881, including fire engine, steam pumper, and photos. Archives hold old fire books, journals, reports, and newspaper articles. Accepts phone inquiries. No fee. Hours: 9-noon.

Fort Nisqually Historic Site

Point Defiance Park, P.O. Box 11, North 54th & Pearl Sts., Tacoma, WA 98407; (206) 591-5339. Collects and preserves materials on Hudson Bay Co. presence at Ft Nisqually from 1832-1869. Museum and library hold photo collection of 1832-69 Ft occupation and 1933-40 restoration; oral history interviews with WPA and CCC restoration workers; file of period clothing patterns, drawings, and photos. Materials non-circulating. Accepts phone inquiries. No fee. Hours: winter, W-Su 1-4; summer, W-Su 12-6.

Fort Spokane Visitor Center

P.O. Box 37, Coulee Dam, WA 99116; (509) 633-9441. Preserves and promotes history of Ft Spokane through museum displays of military post items; small collection of photos relating to site's use as Indian boarding school, and tuberculosis sanitorium; and living history demonstrations. Accepts phone inquiries (509-725-2715). No fee. Summer hours: 9:30-5:30.

Fort Vancouver National Historic Site

612 E. Reservest, Vancouver, WA 98661; (206) 696-7655. Site preserves history of Ft Vancouver and area in form of Visitor Center with historical exhibits, and small reference library. Accepts phone inquiries. No fee. Hours: Standard Time, 9-4; Daylight Savings Time, 9-5:30.

Fort Walla Walla Museum Complex

Rte. 5, Box 32 B, Myra Rd., Walla Walla, WA 99362; (509) 525-7703. Collects, preserves, and exhibits history of Walla Walla Valley and Pacific Northwest. Complex of 14 buildings and museum photo collection emphasize regional agriculture and military activity. Accepts phone inquiries. Fee. Hours: 1-5.

Highline Community College Library

Documents Division, P.O. Box 98000, 2400 S. 240th St.& Pacific Hwy. South, Des Moines, WA 98198; (206) 878-3710. Provides academic research support for college students and staff. Holdings include federal documents, small map collection, and small genealogical collection. Accepts phone inquiries. No fee. Hours: M-Th 7:45-9:30, F 7:45-4:45, Sa 12-4.

History and Industry Museum

2700 24th Ave. East, Seattle, WA 98112; (206) 324-1125. Preserves photos, records, and artifacts of Pacific Northwest and Alaskan maritime. Holdings include small uncataloged library; extensive photos of large variety of ships from 1865, including sailing, commercial industry, and passenger ships; and small collection of maritime artifacts. Accepts phone inquiries. Fee. Hours: 10-5.

Kingdome Sports Museum

The Kingdome Stadium, 201 S. King St., Seattle, WA 98104; (206) 340-2100. Museum preserves and displays sports memorabilia and photos, and the Royal Brougham Collection. Accepts phone inquiries. No fee. Hours: open during public tours and events.

Klondike Gold Rush National Historical Park

National Park Service, 117 S. Main St., Seattle, WA 98104; (206) 442-7220. Commemorates the Klondike Gold Rush of 1897-98, emphasizing Seattle's participation. Museum exhibits tools and equipment used, diaries and letters of stampeders, and many photos of era's events and people. Accepts phone inquiries. No fee. Hours: 9-5.

Labor History Association of the Pacific Northwest

Northgate Station, P.O. Box 25048, 1018 NE 96, Seattle, WA 98125; (206) 524-0346. Society studies and preserves social, economic, political, and cultural history of working people in Pacific Northwest. Accepts phone inquiries. Membership fee. Hours: call.

Laird Norton Company Archives

801 2nd Ave., 13th Floor, Norton Bldg., Seattle, WA 98104; (206) 464-5090. Business archive serving Laird Norton interests. Holdings include business and family collection of Laird Norton families from late 18th c, with emphasis on lumber industry; maps of lumber lands and railroad routes; photos; genealogical records; and small number of architectural drawings of Winona, MN- and Seattle, WA-based facilities. Researchers must have prior approval from management committee. Accepts phone inquiries. Fee for staff research and copying and handling. Hours: 9-5.

Lewis and Clark Interpretive Center

P.O. Box 488, Fort Canby State Park, Ilwaco, WA 98624; (206) 642-3029. Preserves historical materials on Lewis and Clark, coastal defense, and navigation. Holdings include photos, journals of Lewis and Clark, maps, manuscripts, and films. Restrictions on use. Accepts phone inquiries. No fee. Hours: May 7-Sept, 9-5; Oct-Apr, 8-5.

Longmire Museum

Mt. Rainier National Park, Star Rte.—Takoma Woods, Ashford, WA 98304; (206) 569-2211. Preserves and promotes natural and cultural history of park and region in form of artifacts and exhibits; library with materials on Mount Rainier history and ecology; park archives from 1899; maps of region from 1907; extensive collection of photos; oral history tapes. Library for use by park personnel only. Accepts phone inquiries. Park entrance fee. Hours: 8-4:30.

Lopez Island Historical Society and Museum

P.O. Box 163, Lopez Island, WA 98261; (206) 468-3447. Collects, preserves, and exhibits regional history. Museum exhibits Native American artifacts, maritime items, pioneer materials, farming materials, household artifacts, and regional records. Archives contain records from business, families, ferry, and local newspapers; local diaries; regional maps; photos from 1890s; oral history tapes; and cemetery and census records from 1870. Accepts phone inquiries. No fee. Hours: May-Sept, F-Su noon-4.

National Archives—Seattle Branch

6125 Sand Point Way, Seattle, WA 98115; (206) 526-6507. Collects and preserves archival materials relating history of Pacific Northwest and AK and their govt agencies. Many govt agency records and maps; Sir Henry Wellcome photo collection spanning 1856-1936, and covering Father Duncan controversy and Tsiushian Indian experience; and large federal census microfilm collection. Some materials restricted. Phone inquiries accepted. No fee. Hours: call.

Native American Cultures Museum

E. 200 Cataldo, Spokane, WA 99202; (509) 326-4550. Collects and preserves Indian artifacts, art, and related items. Museum displays artifacts; research library holds old books and manuscripts; photo collection being cataloged and not readily available to public. Accepts phone inquiries. Fee. Hours: Tu-Sa 10-5, Su 11-5.

Nordic Heritage Museum

3014 N.W. 67th St., Seattle, WA 98117; (206) 789-5707. Documents Nordic emigration experience, and contribution to Pacific Northwest development library, museum, and archival materials. Some Danish oral history recordings; fairly large photo collection on Nordic families and life-styles. Accepts phone inquiries. Fee. Hours: Tu-Sa 10-4, Su noon-4.

Northwest Room

Spokane Public Library, West 906 Main Ave., Spokane, WA 99201; (509) 838-3361. Serves community research needs with collection of materials on history of Northwest and North American exploration and settlement. Library emphasizes history of missions, Indians, pioneers, and explorers; Sanborn, Ogle, and Netskers maps of Spokane and Northwest region; many historic photos of Spokane, Northwest, and Native American tribes of Colville, Spokane and Coeur D'Alene; pioneer oral histories; extensive genealogical collection; and special George Fuller collection of printing industry, fine arts, Americana, and religious histories. Materials non-circulating. Accept phone inquiries (509-838-4737). No fee. Hours: W 1-5, Th 10-4, F 1-5, Sa 12-4.

Pacific Northwest Collection
University of Washington, Suzzallo Library, FM-25, Seattle, WA 98195; (206) 543-1937. Collects materials pertaining to Pacific Northwest history and 20th c western WA. Holdings cover history of Seattle Jewish population, urban problems and policies, women's history, environmental politics, ethnic history, race relations, the arts, and oral histories. Also has large photo collection, many original blueprints and plans of Pacific NW architecture from 1880-1940, unpublished journals from expeditions, newspapers from regional Japanese relocation camps from 1942-45, Sanborn fire insurance maps for Seattle, and materials relating to 1980 eruption of Mt. St. Helens. Accepts phone inquiries. Hours: call.

Pacific Northwest Historians Guild
2724 N.E. 45th St., Ste. 730, Seattle, WA 98105; (206) 776-7227. Scholarly organization that promotes study and dissemination of Pacific Northwest history. Accepts phone inquiries. Hours: call.

Puget Sound Maritime Historical Society
2161 E. Hamlin St., Seattle, WA 98112; (206) 324-1125. Operates History & Industry museum, which hold extensive photo documentation of maritime activities. Consult that listing for holdings. Hours: call.

Sacajawea Interpretive Center
Washington State Parks & Recreation Commission, RR 9, Box 2503, Pasco, WA 99301; (509) 545-2361. Interprets culture of southeastern Washington Indians, and preserves history of Lewis & Clark expedition with Sacagawea. Museum, library, and archives hold materials on Indian traditions, Lewis & Clark's expedition, and Northern Pacific Railroad town site of Ainsworth. Accepts phone inquiries. No fee. Hours: Apr-Sept, W-Su 10-6.

Shoreline Historical Museum
P.O. Box 7171, Seattle, WA 98133; (206) 542-7111. Preserves history and heritage of Shoreline area. Museum consists of restored 1930 school room and home room, blacksmith shop, and post office. Holdings include naval materials, vintage radios, and pre-1920 costume display. Library and archives hold books, clipping files, manuscripts, maps, photos, oral histories, and genealogical records. Special collection of Morris Graves's art work. Accepts phone inquiries. Donations accepted. Hours: Th-Su 1-4.

Tacoma Public Library
1102 Tacoma Ave. South, Tacoma, WA 98402; (206) 591-5666. Preserves materials relating to WWI activities. Holdings include propaganda pamphlets and posters. Accepts phone inquiries. No fee. Hours: call.

Thomas Burke Memorial Washington State Museum
University of Washington, DB-10, Seattle, WA 98195; (206) 543-5590. Exhibits extensive collections dealing with Native American culture of Washington State, Pacific Northwest, Alaskan Arctic, and some plateau and plains regions. Fee for special exhibits. Hours: M-F 10-5:30, Sa-Su 9-4:30.

Thomas Handforth Art Gallery
Tacoma Public Library, 1102 Tacoma Ave. So., Tacoma, WA 98402; (206) 591-5622. Public library concentrates on Pacific Northwest Americana, genealogy, and local history. Collection covers history of WA, OR, ID, AK, British Columbia, and West with archival holdings, manuscripts, photos, and files. Archive holds historic Tacoma documents; large manuscript collection covers transportation, local history, and govt official papers; USGS and local history maps; large photo collection; and genealogical records. Special collections of Bing Crosby recordings, WWI, Bashaw folk dance recordings, and WWI

posters. Accepts phone inquiries. Fee for books borrowed by non-residents. Hours: M-Th 9-9, F-Sa 9-6.

Washington National Guard Historical Office

Camp Murray, Tacoma, WA 98430; (206) 581-8498. Preserves and maintains collection of documents relating to the history of the Washington National Guard in form of personnel files, unit histories, and manuscripts. Personnel files restricted. Prefers written correspondences but will accept phone inquiries when necessary. No fee. Hours: 7:30-4.

Washington State Archives

3 Sunset Activity Center, 1809 S. 140th St., Seattle, WA 98168; (206) 764-4276. Provides records management assistance and collects local govt agency archival records within region. Holdings include materials from 1850s from King, Kitsap, Pierce, and Washington counties, and photos of King county buildings from 1937-40. May be some restrictions on use. Accepts phone inquiries. No fee. Hours: by appt only, 8:30-4:30.

Washington State Historical Society

315 N. Stadium Way, Tacoma, WA 98403; (206) 593-2830. Collects and interprets extensive range of material on Washington and Pacific Northwest history in museum, library, and archives. Holdings include manuscripts, maps, photos, films/videotapes, genealogical records; special Asahel Curtis photo collection; microfile of Yale University Western America Collection. Accepts phone inquiries. No fee. Hours: Tu-Sa 9-5, Su 2-5.

Washington State University

Holland Library, Pullman, WA 99164; (509) 335-2691. Academic library maintains historical materials, archival and special collections relevant to needs of the school and students. Holdings include publications on regional and transportation history; univ historical materials from 19th c; archives with extensive collection of historical manuscripts; 20th c US Army maps; Historical Photograph Collection; Northwest Film Collection; oral history recordings; genea-

logical materials, including US census records, 1790-1880; De Smet Papers; Pacific Northwest Agricultural History Archives. Some restrictions. Accepts phone inquiries. No fee. Hours: M-F 7:30-midnight, Sa 9-6, Su 1-midnight.

Washington State University Library

Manuscripts, Archives, and Special Collections, Pullman, WA 99164; (509) 335-3564 (main #). Academic research library has materials on literary Woolf family, American Indians, and Western pioneers. Woolf collection centers on library of Virginia and father Leonard Woolf, including their collection of Hogarth Press publications from 1917-41; works by both Woolfs and Bloomsbury group; and works of Elizabeth Robins, Victoria Sackville-West, and Harold Nicholson, D.H. Lawrence, the Sitwells, Charles Williams, and others. Western collection documents fur trade and trapping, pioneer life, and natural wildlife. Accepts phone inquiries. No fee. Hours: call.

Washington Trust for Historic Preservation

P.O. Box 111763, Tacoma, WA 98411; (206) 591-7172. Provides historic preservation reference assistance to researchers. Accepts phone inquiries. No fee. Hours: call.

Western Washington University

Documents Division, Mable Zoe Wilson Library, 516 High St., Bellingham, WA 98225; (206) 676-3075. Serves as depository for US, Canadian, and Washington State documents. No fee. Hours: M-Th 7:45-11, F 7:45-5, Sa 9-6, Su 1-11.

Weyerhaeuser Company Archives

Tacoma, WA 98477; (206) 924-5051. Company support service that selects, preserves, and makes available records of development of Weyerhaeuser businesses, branches, regions, and subsidiaries. Holdings include business records, correspondence, biographical info, speeches, maps, large photo collection on lumbering, some edited and unedited film footage, memorabilia from mills and wood operations, oral history interviews, and press releases. Most materials date from 19th c. Some restrictions on outside

Weyerhaeuser lumbermen, from the Weyerhaeuser Company Archives.

researchers. Accepts phone inquiries. No fee. Hours: 8-4:45.

Whitman College

Documents Division, Penrose Memorial Library, Walla Walla, WA 99362; (509) 527-5191. Academic research library supporting research needs of College community through archival Pacific Northwest and Whitman College materials, USGS and Pacific Northwest maps, and photos of local, college, and regional history. Materials for in-house use only. Accepts phone inquiries. No fee. Hours: M-F 8-noon, 1-5.

Whitman Mission National Historic Site

National Park Service, Rte. 2, Box 247, Walla Walla, WA 99362; (509) 522-6360. Commemorates missionaries Marcus and Narcissa Whitman and their role in settling Oregon territory. Museum and library preserve history and artifacts of Whitman Mission and Cayuse Indians. Photo collection documents the excavation of Mission site. Accepts phone inquiries. Fee. Hours: winter 8-4:30, summer 8-8.

Wing Luke Asian Museum

Asian and Asian-American Folk Art and Historical Museum, 407 7th Ave. S., Seattle, WA 98104; (206) 623-5124. Preserves and promotes history and culture of Asian-Americans in Seattle and King County, WA area, in form of museum with folk art, pottery, woodcarving, basketry, and textiles from Asian countries; library, archives, manuscripts, maps and photos. Accepts phone inquiries. Fee. Hours: M-F 9:30-4:30, Sa-Su noon-4.

Yakima Valley Museum and Historic Association

2105 Tieton Dr., Yakima, WA 98902; (509) 248-0747. Museum houses materials on Native American culture, central WA region, and textiles. Library and archives hold maps, photos, and few films/videotapes. Special collections include Justice William O. Douglas collection, textile collection, horse-drawn vehicle collection, Martha Wiley missionary correspondence collection, and WA state legislator Marjorie Lynch collection. Accepts phone inquiries. No fee. Hours: W-F 10-5, Sa-Su noon-5.

West Virginia

Americana Museum

401 Auroroa Ave., Terra Alta, WV 26764; (304) 789-2361. Collects early American artifacts. Accepts phone inquiries. Fee. Hours: call.

Chesapeake and Ohio Historical Society

P.O. Box 146, Alderson, WV 24910; (304) 445-7365. Collects, preserves, researches, and makes available info on Chesapeake & Ohio railway and its predecessors. Library and archives hold engineering and mechanical drawings showing railway development from 1860, correspondence and documents, maps, and large photo collection. Also exhibits of passenger cars. Hours: call.

General Adam Stephen Memorial Association

P.O. Box 1496, Martinsburg, WV 25401; (304) 267-4434. Memorializes Gen. Stephen, founder of city of Martinsburg. Museum maintains Stephen house and surrounding outbuildings, archives, manuscript collection, photos, and local history collection. Archives not open to public at present. Accepts phone inquiries. No fee. Hours: May-Oct, Sa-Su 2-5.

Glenville State College

Documents Dept., Robert Kidd Library, Glenville, WV 26351; (304) 462-7361. Academic research library for residents of WV. Holdings include films/videotapes on WV, Greenbank Observatory, and Hare Krishna temple at Moundsville; genealogical and census records; local history materials on 1985 flood, newspapers from 1905, and Glenville's WV folk festival. Some materials non-circulating. Accepts phone inquiries. No fee. Hours: M-Th 8-10, F 8-4:30, Sa 11-4, Su 2-10.

Harpers Ferry Historical Association

Harpers Ferry National Historic Park, P.O. Box 197, High St., Harpers Ferry, WV 25425; (304) 535-6881. Assn sells interpretive materials on National Parks, Civil War, Harpers Ferry, black history, transportation, and 19th c life. Photos, films/videotapes, and books available. Accepts phone inquiries. Hours: 9-5.

Humanities Foundation of West Virginia

P.O. Box 204, 232 Hill Hall, Burron DR., Institute, WV 25122; (304) 768-8869. Promotes and supports educational programs in humanities. Holdings include photos, films/videotapes, exhibits, and publications funded by foundation. Accepts phone inquiries. No fee. Hours: M-F 8-5.

Kanawha County Public Library

Documents Division, 23 Capitol St., Charleston, WV 25301; (304) 343-4646. Serves info needs of county residents with emphasis on WV history. Archives hold collection of historical Charleston-area photographs. Some materials may be non-circulating. Accepts phone inquiries. No fee. Hours: M-F 9-9, Sa 9-5, and Sept-May, Su 1-5.

Mary Weir Public Library

3442 Main St., Weirton, WV 26062; (304) 797-8510. Provides reference materials on variety of local and regional institutions and topics. Concentration on WV panhandle and nearby parts of OH and PA. Small archival collection on history of Weirton, Weirton Steel Corp, and library. Small collection of govt documents. Some materials non-circulating. Accepts phone inquiries. No fee. Hours: M-Th noon-8, F-Sa 10-5; summer, M-F 10-6, Sa 10-5.

National Park Service History Collection

Office of Library and Archival Services, Harpers Ferry Center, Harpers Ferry, WV 25425; (304) 535-6371. Preserves history and culture of Natl Park Service from 1916. Museum contains uniforms, badges, insignia, art exhibits, cameras, and Civilian Conservation Corps equip. Large library provides reference materials. Archives hold records of operations, and Bicentennial and Conservation Corps activities. Manuscripts of employees, history, and personalities available. Map, photo, and film/videotape collections document 1920-1970s. Special collections include Park Service Dir Albright's films from 1920s-30s, and Evison's oral history interviews. Materials for in-house use only. Accepts phone inquiries. No fee. Hours: M-F 8-5.

President's Cottage Museum— Greenbrier

White Sulphur Springs, WV 24983; (304) 536-1110. Relates history of this house where five pre-Civil War presidents stayed and relates history of resort. Library has small collection of reference materials. Archives contain hotel registers, scrapbooks, diaries, journals, maps of resort property, and photos of prominent visitors. Accepts phone inquiries. No fee. Hours: 10-4.

Shepherd College

Documents Dept., Ruth Scarborough Library, Shepherdstown, WV 25443; (304) 876-2511. Academic research library with holdings of maps, films/videotapes, and recordings. Special WV history collection available. Materials circulate within college community. Accepts phone inquiries. No fee. Hours: M-Th 8-10, F 8-4:30, Sa 9-4:30, Su 2-10.

West Virginia and Regional History Collection

West Virginia University Library, Morgantown, WV 26506; (304) 293-0111. Collects manuscripts, broadsides, pictures, photos, and related items pertaining to WV and Appalachian region history. Accepts phone inquiries. No fee. Hours: call.

West Virginia Historical Society

Dept. of Culture and History, Capitol Complex, Charleston, WV 25305; (304) 348-0230. Coordinates and represents many local and county historical societies, and promotes WV history. No fee. Hours: call.

West Virginia State Museum Archives

Capitol Complex-Cultural Center, Charleston, WV 25305; (304) 348-0230. Collects and preserves WV historical materials. Museum portrays WV from prehistoric Indian period to present, and displays fine arts and crafts. Library covers history of US, WV, Civil War, colonial period, and military. Archives contain records of govt agencies, personal and business manuscripts, WV and VA maps, many photos, and genealogical records. WV TV stations' newsfilm and videotape from 1955-82. Oral history interviews with WV artists. Special collections of governors' papers and Boyd Stutler-John Brown materials. Materials non-circulating. Accepts phone inquiries. No fee. Hours: library, M-Th 9-9, F 9-5, Sa 1-5; museum, M-F 9-9, Sa-Su 1-9.

West Virginia Supreme Court Law Library

Room E-404, State Capitol, Charleston, WV 25305; (304) 348-2607. Provides reference service for court and legal reference for public. Library has complete collection of federal and state resources, including early WV and VA codes and court decisions. Materials non-circulating. No fee. Hours: M-F 8:30-9, Sa 9-5.

Wisconsin

American Women Writers Collection

Dept. of Rare Books and Special Collections, University of Wisconsin, 728 State St., Madison, WI 53706; (608) 262-3193. Collection holds primary and secondary materials for major American women writers, including Anne Bradstreet, Louisa May Alcott, Emily Dickinson, Kate Chopin, Mary Williams Freeman, Margaret Fuller, Sarah Orne Jewett, Charlotte Perkins Gilman, Harriet Beecher Stowe, and some lesser-known authors. Holdings include manuscripts, archives, letters, memoirs, diaries, and travel writings. O. Henry (aka William S. Porter) collection features all first editions, contracts, and personal memorabilia. Accepts phone inquiries. Hours: call.

Beloit College

Col. Robert Morse Library, 731 College St., Beloit, WI 53511; (608) 365-3391, ext. 482. Academic research library has special collections ranging from US pacifism to intl affairs to Presidents Lincoln and FDR. Cullister International Center has materials on world affairs, intl orgs, and future world order. Martin Luther King, Jr. collection on nonviolence has books and pamphlets on King, Mahatma Gandhi, Henry David Thoreau, and others connected with pacifism. Irving Kull collection has books by and about Woodrow Wilson. Joseph Rheingold collection has books and magazine articles by and on FDR.

White collection has materials on Lincoln and Civil War. Materials limited to college community. No fee. Hours: M-Th 8:30-midnight, F 8:30-8:

Burnett County Historical Society

P.O. Box 31, Siren, WI 54872; (715) 349-2219. Preserves and disseminates cultural heritage of northeastern WI. Museum exhibits cover geological formation of region, prehistoric inhabitants, Indians, white settlement of region, logging and farming industries. Library and archives contain county, state, and township records; and journals of settlers, travelers, and fur traders; maps of county, regional, state, and Midwestern territory; photos from 1870s; genealogical records; and special fur trade collection. Restrictions on use. Accepts phone inquiries. Fee. Hours: 8-4:30.

Camp Five Museums Foundation

1011 8th St., Wausau, WI 54401; (715) 674-3414-s; 845-5544-w; (summer address: RFD 1, Laona, WI 54541). Preserves history of steam train and logging industry, with emphasis on forest conservation. Museum holds exhibits on logging, railroad, transportation, blacksmithing, and Indian artifacts. Collections include logging, railroad, and gasoline era photos from 1860-1950s; lumberjack and railroad song recordings; special collection of lumber company money. Accepts phone inquiries. Fee. Hours: summer, M-Sa.

Chippewa Valley Museum

P.O. Box 1204, Eau Claire, WI 54702; (715) 834-7871. Encourages collection and preservation of historical resources relative to Eau Claire. Library and archives hold photos, manuscripts, scrapbooks, maps, oral history tapes, and music from area. Photos emphasize regional logging and lumbering. Recordings include lumberjack and Norwegian fiddler songs. Genealogical records and personal family histories also available. Materials for in-house use only. Accepts phone inquiries. Donations accepted. Hours: Tu-Su 1-5.

Circus World Museum

426 Water St., 415 Lynn St., Baraboo, WI 53913; (608) 356-8341. Collects, preserves,

and utilizes references to circus history from 1793. Museum, library, and archives hold numerous photos, programs, lithographs, business files, tickets, contracts, newspapers, and genealogical records on circus people. There are also some films/videotapes. Materials for in-house use only. Accepts phone inquiries. No fee. Hours: M-F 8:30-5.

Experimental Aircraft Museum

Wittman Airfield, Oshkosh, WI 54903; (414) 426-4818. Museum preserves and displays many famous experimental aircraft, including Double Eagle V balloon, gliders, and trick planes. Other exhibits explain theme of aerodynamics. Accepts phone inquiries. Fee. Hours: M-Sa 8:30-5, Su 11-5.

Fond du Lac Public Library

32 Sheboygan St., Fond du Lac, WI 54935; (414) 921-0066. General public library with special collections on American Indian and local history. Archives hold newspapers from 1846 and territorial censuses from 1850-1910. Accepts phone inquiries. No fee. Hours: winter, M-F 9-9, Sa 9-5; summer, M, W, F 9-9, Tu, Th 9-6.

Fort Crawford Medical Museum

P.O. Box 1109, 717 S. Beaumont Rd., Madison, WI 53701; (608) 257-6781. Reconstructed military hospital traces history of WI medicine in 19th c with exhibits on Indian remedies, pharmacological practices, pioneer Dr. William Beaumonts, and surgical advances of period. Accepts phone inquiries. Fee. Hours: May-Oct 10-5.

Green Bay Packers Hall of Fame

P.O. Box 10567, 1901 S. Oneida, Green Bay, WI 54304; (414) 499-4281. Preserves and displays materials relating to football team and its community. Museum exhibits date from 1919. Collections include Vince Lombardi collection of manuscripts; photos of individuals connected to team; and some film and videotape materials from 1923. Accepts phone inquiries. Fee. Hours: 10-5.

Hawks Inn Historical Society

P.O. Box 104, Delafield, WI 53018; (414) 646-2140. Preserves, advances, and disseminates info on history of Delafield and surrounding area. Museum house in restored Stagecoach Inn. Collections include info on early area settlers including Hawks and Cushing families. Accepts phone inquiries. Fee. Hours: call.

Hoard Historical Museum

407 S. Merchants Ave., Fort Atkinson, WI 53538; (414) 563-7769. Collects, preserves, and researches history of Ft Atkinson with museum and library holdings on local history, Black Hawk War, and dairy farming. Some manuscripts in form of pioneer diaries and reminiscences from 1830-1900; maps of Ft and Jefferson County; photos of local residents and history; genealogical records; and large special collection of local archaeological finds. Accepts phone inquiries. No fee. Hours: Tu-Sa 9:30-3:30.

John Michael Kohler Arts Center

P.O. Box 489, Sheboygan, WI 53082; (414) 458-5144. Encourages art education and exposure, with emphasis on WI artists. Library holds collection of regional and national arts publications and exhibition catalogs. Archives contain documentation of 20th c folk artists from WI in slide and photo form and Kuehne collection of prehistoric Indian artifacts from Sheboygan county. Accepts phone inquiries. No fee. Hours: by appt only, noon-5; M add 7 pm-9.

La Crosse Public Library

Archives and Local History Dept., 800 Main St., La Crosse, WI 54601; (608) 784-8623. Preserves materials on La Crosse local history in museum, library, and archives. Holdings include histories of region, works by local authors, clipping files on La Crosse businesses and residents, newspapers and periodicals from 1853, early state and city maps from 1857, genealogy and census materials, Hirschheimer biographical file pre-1900, records of La Crosse fire and police depts from 19th and 20th c, materials of German Society of La Crosse, and Wendell Anderson papers. Accepts phone inquiries. Fee for non-local borrowing card and research. Hours: M-Th 10-9, F-Sa 10-5, Su 1-5.

Marathon County Public Library

400 First St., Wausau, WI 54401; (715) 847-

5530. Public library with collection of local history materials. Holdings include Wausau and Marathon county histories, newspapers, and census materials. Some genealogical materials available. Accepts phone inquiries. No fee. Hours: M-F 10-8:30, Sa-Su 10-5.

Milwaukee County Historical Society

910 N. 3rd St., Milwaukee, WI 53203; (414) 273-8288. Collects, preserves, and exhibits material relating to county history. Museum exhibits on coopers, pharmacists, doctors, painters, and black history; library of genealogical resources, personal and business manuscripts, county govt records; extensive photo collection, maps, naturalization papers from 1836-1941; census and WI Civil War Veteran records; church directories; national defense program registration cards from post-WWII era. Special collection materials from Mayor Hoan, Gen William Mitchell, Jeremiah Curtin, John Cudahy, and Gimbels Department Store. Accepts phone inquiries. Fee for library. Hours: M-F 9:30-noon, 1-4:30.

Milwaukee Public Library

Humanities Division, 814 W. Wisconsin Ave., Milwaukee, WI 53233; (414) 278-3000. Large public library holds materials on local history and Great Lakes maritime activity. Museum holds some Great Lakes artifacts from 1850. Library covers US, state, and local history; history of Great Lakes; genealogy; Civil War; and US Olympic Committee publications. Archives contain Milwaukee city archival materials from 1846; manuscripts from WI, Milwaukee, Great Lakes; Socialist papers; papers of Mayor Frank Zeidler; general US and WI maps; photos of Great Lakes and commercial vessels; and genealogical materials. Accepts phone inquiries. No fee. Hours: M-Th 8:30-9, F-Sa 8:30-5:30; in winter, Su 1-5.

National Railroad Museum

P.O. Box 28171, 2285 S. Broadway, Green Bay, WI 54304; (414) 435-7245. Collects, preserves, and interprets documents, artifacts, and photos relating to American railroad heritage. Museum houses locomotives, passenger cars, freight cars, work cars, and artifacts from 1880s. Library

holds small collection of books on railroading. Archives collect documents, maps and other materials on WI railroads. Special collection on Green Bay railroad employee genealogical records. Accepts phone inquiries. Fee. Hours: museum, May-Oct, 9-5; library and archives, by appt.

Northland Historical Society

Wisconsin State Historical Society, P.O. Box 325, Lake Tomahawk, WI 54539; (715) 277-2629. Promotes interest and study in local history through manuscript, map, and photo collections. No fee. Hours: call.

Old World Wisconsin

S103 W37890 Hwy 67, Eagle, WI 53119; (414) 594-2116. Preserves heritage of rural and ethnic WI from late 19th and early 20th c through living history museum exhibits on Danish, Finnish, German, Norwegian, Irish, and Bohemian culture. Accepts phone inquiries. Fee. Hours: May-Oct, M-F 8-5.

Oshkosh Public Museum

1331 Algoma Blvd., Oshkosh, WI 54901; (414) 236-5150. Presents history, natural history, and archaeology of Oshkosh and WI, as well as work of local artists. Museum holds exhibits ranging from prehistory to present; library collects city, state, and county history materials; maps from 1858; photos of individuals, business, steamboats from area; and genealogical records of local families. Special collections on Frank Finkel, supposed survivor of Custer's last stand, and sculptor Helen Farnsworth Mears. Accepts phone inquiries. No fee. Hours: Tu-Sa 9-5, Su 1-5.

Pharmaceutical Library

University of Wisconsin, School of Pharmacy, 425 N. Charter St., Madison, WI 53706; (608) 262-2894. Academic research library holds historic pharmaceutical materials from 1850 in Kremers Reference files. Holdings include historic drug catalogs, pharmacological literature, lab records, biographical sketches, prescriptions, photos, and pamphlets on drug history. Accepts phone inquiries. Hours: call.

Portage Canal Society

528 W. Cook St., Portage, WI 53901; (608)

742-2889. Preserves history of canal through collection of canal maps, photos of boats, and publication on Portage canal and Fox River. Accepts phone inquiries. Donations accepted. Hours: call.

Racine County Historical Society and Museum

Local History and Genealogy Library, 701 S. Main St., Racine, WI 53403; (414) 637-8585. Collects, compiles, and preserves history and traditions of Racine county. Museum exhibits local artifacts and history of regional industries. Library provides research info on local history, family history, and some genealogy; manuscripts; maps from 1887; photos; and large collection of local history vertical files. Materials non-circulating. Accepts phone inquiries. No fee, except for mail inquiries. Hours: museum, Tu-F 9-5, Sa-Su 1-5; library, Tu-Sa 1-4.

Research Center on Women

Alverno College, 3401 S. 39th St., Milwaukee, WI 53215; (414) 382-6061. Research and resource collection of library materials, periodicals, newsletters, and clipping files on women in region. Accepts phone inquiries. No fee. Hours: M-F 8-10:30, Sa-Su vary.

Ripon College Library

Special Collections, Box 248, 300 Seward St., Ripon, WI 54971; (414) 748-8328. Academic research library with general history materials stressing American social history and African history. Special Pedrick local history collection available. Materials circulate to local residents. Accepts phone inquiries. No fee. Hours: M-Th 7:45-midnight; F 7:45-10; Sa 9-5; Su noon-midnight.

Rock County Historical Society and Archives

P.O. Box 896, Janesville, WI 53547; (608) 756-4509. Preserves, advances, and disseminates info on history of Rock county. Museum has materials on Tallman restoration. Library holds reference materials on decorative arts, historic preservation, and general history. Archives hold archival materials of county manufacturing, business, and court and law records; Tallman family papers on 19th c land speculation in WI and IL; maps of

Rock county, photos, and some genealogical materials. Accepts phone inquiries. Fee. Hours: M-F 1-4.

S.S. Meteor Maritime Museum

Head of Lakes Maritime Society, P.O. Box 775, Superior, WI 54880; (715) 392-5742. Provides info on ships and maritime industry with emphasis on whaleback ships. Museum has models, displays, and ship artifacts from Great Lakes. Other holdings include maps of Lake Superior, ship charts, photos of Edmund Fitzgerald, Titanic, and other whalebacks. Special collections include Christopher Columbus section, Diver collection, and display of flags and Coast Guard equip. Accepts phone inquiries. Fee. Hours: Memorial Day-Jul 10-5, Jul-Aug 10-7, Sept-Oct, Sa-Su 10-5.

Seventh Day Baptist Historical Society

P.O. Box 1678, 3120 Kennedy Rd., Janesville, WI 53547; (608) 752-5055. Provides materials for study of Seventh Day Baptists' life and thought from 1650 to present. Small museum of rotating displays; library of denomination's historical manuscripts and pamphlets; central depository for Seventh Day Baptist Conference, agencies, and societies; photo collection; genealogical records; and special Julius Sachse Ephrata Collection on 18th and 19th c German Seventh Day Baptists in PA. Some materials require librarian's permission for use. Accepts phone inquiries. Hours: M-F 9-5.

Sheboygan County Historical Society

3110 Erie Ave., Sheboygan, WI 53081; (414) 458-1103. Discovers, collects, and preserves info, records, and artifacts on Sheboygan county history. Museum collections in 4 bldg complex with 19th c furnishings. Library and archives hold manuscripts, maps, photos, films/videotapes, recordings, and genealogical records. Accepts phone inquiries. Fee. Hours: Apr-Oct, Tu-Sa 10-5, Su 1-5.

South Milwaukee Historical Society

104 Brookdale Dr., 717 Milwaukee Ave., South Milwaukee, WI 53172; (414) 764-2118. Rec-

ords and exhibits south Milwaukee history with emphasis on Lincoln. Accepts phone inquiries. No fee. Hours: by appt, June-Oct, Su 2-4.

University of Wisconsin Archives and Area Research Center

University of Wisconsin, Parkside, P.O. Box 2000, Wood Rd, Kenosha, WI 53141; (414) 553-2411. Preserves historical University records and encourages historical research in Racine/Kenosha area. Library holds genealogical and local histories from area; manuscripts of area residents, orgs, and businesses; plat and Sanborn maps; state and federal censuses for WI through 1910. Special collections on Irving Wallace, 18th & 19th c British and American plays, and area newspapers. Accepts phone inquiries. No fee. Hours: M-Tu, Th-F 8-noon, W 5-9. Appt suggested.

University of Wisconsin, Eau Claire

Documents Division, William McIntyre Library, Park & Garfield Sts., Eau Claire, WI 54702; (715) 836-3247. Research support facility serving academic and local community. Operates James Newman Clare Bird museum, library including govt documents and publications, and university archives. Map collection includes USGS maps and Army and Canadian Map service issues. Special collections include historical records of surrounding counties. Materials circulate only to card-holders. Accepts phone inquiries (715-836-3859). No fee. Hours: M-Th 7:45-4:30, 6:30-9:30; Sa 9-5, Su 1-9:30.

University of Wisconsin, Green Bay

Library Learning Center, 2420 Nicolet Dr., Green Bay, WI 54311; (414) 465-2303. Academic research library holds govt records for northeast WI, manuscripts, maps of local historical interest, photos, oral history tapes of Belgian-Americans, and genealogical materials of region. Accepts phone inquiries. No fee. Hours: by appt only.

University of Wisconsin, La Crosse

Special Collections, Murphy Library, 1631 Pine St., La Crosse, WI 54601; (608) 785-8511.

Maintains research collectsion for study of local, regional, and inland river history, with emphasis on steamboating. Small libraries on Midwest history, Civil War, and inland river steamboating; archival govt and civic records from western WI region; manuscripts from lumbering, labor, and agriculture from 1850; Upper Midwest, WI, and MI River maps; extensive oral histories relating to La Crosse area; and special collections of WI and Midwest magazines and poetry. Materials for in-house use only. Accepts phone inquiries. No fee. Hours: M-F 9-noon, 1-5.

University of Wisconsin, River Falls

Document Dept., Chalmer Davee Library, River Falls, WI 54022; (715) 425-3874. Academic research library with archival materials focusing on St. Croix Valley in WI. Accepts phone inquiries (715-425-3343). No fee. Hours: M-F 7:45-11, Sa 11-5, Su 2-11.

University of Wisconsin, Superior

Documents Division, Jim Dan Hill Library, Superior, WI 54880; (715) 394-8341. Supports research needs of univ and community. Holdings include univ archives; manuscripts from area research center for Douglas county; immigration records and 1890 and 1900 county census records; and Beecroft collection of Literary Guild founders' papers, and a collection of Guild selections. Reference materials non-circulating. Accepts phone inquiries (715-394-8512). No fee. Hours: browsing, 12:30-4:30; access, M-Th 7:45-10, F 7:45-4:30.

University of Wisconsin, Whitewater

Documents and Research Collections Service, Harold Andersen Library, 800 W. Main St., Whitewater, WI 53190; (414) 472-4671. Houses state, federal, and international documents, as well as historical records and manuscripts relating to Jefferson, Rock, and Walworth counties. Library is partial depository for govt documents, Defense Mapping Agency, Dept of Interior, and Wisconsin Quadrangles. Holds many maps, some photos, and genealogical and naturalization records from 1836. Accepts phone inquiries. No fee. Hours: M-F 8-5.

Waukesha County Historical Museum

101 W. Main St., Waukesha, WI 53186; (414) 548-7186. Collects, preserves, and exhibits articles on history of Waukesha county. Museum exhibits pioneer and Indian memorabilia, Victorian parlor, military history, and children's and toy history. Library has research materials on WI and county. Archives contain primary family, business, and org papers, Civil war records, land records, scrapbooks, photos, maps, oral history recordings, naturalization records from 1847-1955, and census materials. Materials for in-house use only. Accepts phone inquiries. No fee. Hours: museum, M-F 9-4:30, Sa 10-2, Su 1-5; research center, M-F 9-4:30.

Wisconsin Center for Film and Theatre Research

State Historical Society of Wisconsin, 816 State St., Madison, WI 53706; (608) 262-7723 or 0585. Joint collection of Univ of WI and state historical society contains materials from movie theaters, stars, and directors, and large collection of films from Warner Bros and RKO studios. Holdings include large collection of stills, lobby cards, posters, and pressbooks; photos and clippings on film, TV, theater, radio, vaudeville, ballet and opera performers; collection of over 7000 films from 1930s-40s; and special collections on Robert Altman, Paddy Chayefsky, Kirk Douglas, Edith Head, Hal Holbrook, Hollywood Ten, MTM, Norman Jewison, Rod Serling, and others. Accepts phone inquiries. Hours: by appt only.

Wisconsin Electric Railway Historical Society

P.O. Box 17701, Milwaukee, WI 53217; (414) 383-8444. Preserves materials relating to electric railways. Museum has collection of passenger and work cars and other railway equip. Library has reference materials. Archives hold letters, company memos, plans, and other documents from TMER & L and CNS & M Railway Cos; maps of WI and Milwaukee routes, photos, and films from 1920. Hours: call.

Wisconsin Evangelical Lutheran Synod Historical Institute

2929 N. Mayfair Rd., Milwaukee, WI 53222; (414) 771-9357. Promotes interest in Lutheran history, with emphasis on Wisconsin Evangelical Lutheran Synod. Museum and archives hold early Synod manuscripts and photos from 1850; also film/videotape material. Accepts phone inquiries. No fee. Hours: by appt.

Wisconsin Labor History Society

6333 W. Bluemound Rd., Milwaukee, WI 53213; (414) 771-0700. Encourages study of history of WI workers and their labor orgs. Film available on Bay View Massacre of 1886. Accepts phone inquiries. No fee. Hours: call.

Wisconsin State Historical Museum

30 North Carroll St., Madison, WI 53703; (608) 262-3266. Houses collections on WI Indians and history. Accepts phone inquiries. Hours: call.

Wisconsin State Historical Society

816 State St., Madison, WI 53703; (608) 262-3266. Collects, preserves, disseminates, and interprets WI and Old West history. Library has large collections on US, Canadian, and WI history, genealogy, newspapers, and govt. Archive holds movies and TV programs from Warner Bros and RKO; special manuscript collections of Lymand Copeland Draper; mass communications history manuscripts; US Labor history; maps of early American exploration, Great Lakes region, Sanborn maps; huge photo collection including cartoons, TV news films, and portraits emphasizing Midwest from 1880-1920s. Some materials non-circulating. Accepts phone inquiries. No fee. Hours: M-Th 8-9, F-Sa 8-5.

Wisconsin State Old Cemetery Society

WSOCS-SW Region, Carolyn Habelman, Rte. 3, Box 253, Black River Falls, WI 54615; (608) 378-4388. Provides resources for study of Monroe county history through holdings in library and archives. Collections include genealogical records from early Evangelical Lutheran and Catholic churches; maps from 1832; many photos of logging industry; county newspapers; census records from 1910; and land and probate abstracts. Accepts phone inquiries. No fee. Hours: by appt only.

Wisconsin Veterans Historical Museums

State Capitol 419 N., Madison, WI 53702; (608) 266-1680. Official state military and veteran memorial collecting, displaying, and preserving military artifacts and records. Museum collects materials on military and veteran history from Civil War era; library holds materials on Civil War; archives focus on veteran and military records, manuscripts, and letters; some maps, photos, and films/videotapes on Civil War and WWI; and special Civil War battle flag collection and GAR records. Accepts phone inquiries. No fee. Hours: M-F 9-4:30; June-Oct, extended Sa-Su hrs.

Wyoming

Anna Miller Museum

P.O. Box 698, Newcastle, WY 82701; (307) 746-4188. Preserves history of Weston County/Black Hills region from early 1800s. Holdings include Cambria Mining Collection; oral history recordings of pioneers; fire-fighting equipment; horse-drawn transportation. Small library and archives have publications, maps, genealogical records of region and residents. Accepts phone inquiries. No fee. Hours: M-F 9-5.

Archive of Contemporary History

University of Wyoming, Coe Library, Laramie, WY 82071; (307) 766-6385. Holdings cover many women's issues in US and world. Collection of subject files on politics, rape, prostitution, employment, women and law, and black and Third World women. Also holds collection of compositions by Carl Stalling, writer of cartoon music for "Bugs Bunny," "Looney Tunes," "Silly Symphonies," and other Walt Disney and Warner Bros. productions. Accepts phone inquiries. No fee. Hours: call.

Bradford Brinton Memorial Museum and Historic Ranch

Box 460, 239 Brinton Rd., Big Horn, WY 82833; (307) 672-3173. Gentleman's working ranch of the 1930s preserves and displays art and artifacts of late 19th and early 20th c Western

US. Holdings include Western art; Northern Plains Indian artifacts and clothing; Navajo and Rio Grande blankets; European, English, and American furnishings and decorative arts. Accepts phone inquiries. No fee. Hours: May 15-Labor Day, 9:30-5.

Buffalo Bill Historical Center

P.O. Box 1000, 720 Sheridan Ave., Cody, WY 82414; (307) 387-4771. Museum complex devoted to preserving Western American history, artifacts, and art. Buffalo Bill Museum displays items from life and times of Buffalo Bill Cody and his Wild West shows; Whitney Gallery of Western Art has collection of paintings, sculptures by Western artists from 1800; Winchester Arms Museum displays collection of historic American fire arms; Plains Indian Museum preserves ceremonial, artistic and military artifacts of regional tribes. Accepts phone inquiries. Fee. Hours: Jun-Aug, 7-10; May, Sept, Oct 8-5; March, Apr, Nov, Tu-Su 10-3.

Campbell County Public Library

Documents Division, 2101 4-J Rd., Gillette, WY 82716; (307) 687-0115. Public library maintains selective collection of US govt documents, general reference materials, and publications on Campbell County history and residents. Holdings include USGS topographic maps of northern WY, and Campbell County newspaper archives from 1912. Accepts phone inquiries. No fee. Hours: M-Th 9-9, F-Sa 9-5.

F.E. Warren Military Museum

90 SMW/PA, F.E. Warren AFB, Cheyenne, WY 82005; (307) 775-2980. Museum preserves and displays military artifacts 1867-1945 in form of weapons, uniforms, photos; maps late 1800s-early 1900s. Located on closed AF base; non-military visitors require gate pass. Accepts phone inquiries. No fee. Hours: winter, W, Sa, Su 1-5; summer, Tu, Th, Sa, Su 1-5.

Fort Caspar Museum and Historic Site

4001 Ft. Caspar Rd., Caspar, WY 82604; (307) 235-8462. Preserves and interprets social and natural history of Ft Caspar, city of Caspar and WY. Holdings include military relics from Civil War, Indian Wars; pioneer, Indian artifacts; central

WY materials; archives of city; photos from 1865; oral history audiotapes. Accepts phone inquiries. No fee. Hours: May-Sept, M-F 8-6, Sa 8-5, Su noon-5; Oct-Apr M-F 8-5, Su 2-5.

Fort Laramie Historical Association

P.O. Box 218, Fort Laramie, WY 82212; (307) 837-2222. Assn operates visitors' center, museum and library preserving history of Ft. Laramie 1834-1890. Holdings include fur trading artifacts, US Army relics; maps, photos, film/videotapes on Ft, history of Oregon Trail. Accepts phone inquiries. Fee. Hours: 8-4:30.

Grand Encampment Museum

P.O. Box 395, Encampment, WY 82325; (307) 327-5310. Preserves and interprets history of the Grand Encampment area in the form of a replicated early 1900s mining community. Holdings include restored historic buildings; library, archives, and large manuscript collection; local, mining and Forest Service maps; photos and negative file; films/videotapes; genealogical records and recorded interviews with pioneers; local newspaper files. Accepts phone inquiries. No fee. Hours: Memorial Day-Labor Day, 1-5; Sept-Oct, Sa-Su, 1-5.

Hot Springs County Museum and Cultural Center

700 Broadway, Thermopolis, WY 82443; (307) 864-5183. Preserves and displays history of Hot Springs county and northwestern WY from 1870. Holdings include geologic specimens; petroleum, coal mining and agricultural industry artifacts; furniture, tools; early cabin and school house; Indian artifacts; library, manuscripts, maps; large WY archives from 1870s; large photo collection of county and residents 1875-1940. Phone inquiries accepted. No fee. Hours: Sept-May, M-Sa 8-5, Su 1-5; Jun-Aug, M-Sa 8-6, Su 1-5.

Jackson Hole Museum

P.O. Box 1005, 105 N. Glenwood, Jackson, WY 83001; (307) 733-2414. Collects, preserves, and promotes history of Jackson Hole, WY, and residents in form of exhibits and artifacts relating to local prehistory, fur trade, 1810-1840, valley settlement, and natural history; oral history recordings; photos, genealogical records, and maps.

Accepts phone inquiries. Fee. Summer hours: M-Sa 9-6, Su 10-5.

Lander Pioneer Museum

630 Lincoln St., Lander, WY 82520; (307) 332-4137. Restores and preserves artifacts and records of area pioneers 1880s-1940s and local Indian Tribes from 1880. Holdings include clothing, tools and machinery, furnishings, pioneer log cabins, wagons; photos, old dance music recordings; Shot Antelope Hunt memorabilia collection; J.K. Moore (Indian trader) Collection. Library includes local newspaper morgue early-mid 20th c, reference books, manuscripts; archives includes diaries, ledgers, military souvenirs. Accepts phone inquiries. No fee. Hours: M-F 9-5.

Natrona County Public Library

307 East Second St., Casper, WY 82601; (307) 237-4935. Public library has collection of federal and state govt documents, USGS and insurance maps, local history collection including films/videotapes, and genealogical records from 1889. Hours: call.

Sheridan College

Documents Division, Griffith Memorial Library, Sheridan, WY 82801; (307) 674-6446, ext 213. College library maintains a selective collection of US govt documents and reference materials relating to American and local history. Holdings include US Constitution Bicentennial publications, and USGS geologic atlas folios for CO, ID, MT, SD, UT, and WY, 1890s-early 1900s. Accepts phone inquiries. No fee. Hours: M-Th 7:45-10, F 7:45-6, Sa 11-8, Su 11-9.

State Historic Preservation Office

2301 Central, Barrett Bldg., Cheyenne, WY 82002. (Mailing address: c/o Wyoming State Archives and Historical Dept, 604 E. 25th St., Cheyenne, WY 82002) Office identifies, evaluates, and protects historic WY sites, research materials and other items relating to state's cultural heritage. Holdings include collection of cultural resource management project reports and files conducted in WY; maps and records of research projects documenting historic trails; photos of historic structures and sites; environmental documentations, and urban surveys.

Original materials for on-site use only. Accepts phone inquiries. No fee. Hours: M-F 8-5.

Teton County Historical Research Center

P.O. Box 1256, 105 Mercill, Jackson, WY 83001; (307) 733-9605. Collects, preserves, and maintains collection of research materials relating to history of Jackson Hole, WY region in form of library, and archival collections. Holdings include publications and materials on Western history, Americana, and Jackson Hole region; archival collections of photos, manuscripts and other records, oral histories, maps, and genealogical records; W.C. Lawrence family papers; John E. Weida Collection; Shoshone cultural materials. Materials are non-circulating. Accepts phone inquiries. No fee. Hours: M-F 9-1.

Western History Research Center

University of Wyoming, Coe Library, Box 3334, 13th & Ivinson, Laramie, WY 82071; (307) 766-2174. Collections concentrate on development of American West. Materials cover cattle industry history, Western literature, mining and petroleum history, transportation history, conservation history, and related western topics. Hours: call.

Western Wyoming Community College Library

Documents Division, P.O. Box 428, 2500 College Dr., Rock Springs, WY 82902; (307) 382-1701. College library with selective collection of US govt documents and reference materials reflecting needs of students and community. Holdings include topographical maps of WY, and collection of materials on history of Sweetwater County, WY and residents. Accepts phone inquiries (307-382-1700). No fee. Hours: M-F 8-5.

Wyoming State Archives

Museums and Historical Department, Barrett Building, Cheyenne, WY 82002; (307) 777-7022. Collects materials on state and Western history. Holdings include manuscripts, maps, pamphlets, and photos. Hours: call.

Appendixes

Key Dates in American History

1492:   Christopher Columbus sails to North America.

1497:   John Cabot navigates New World coast, traveling as far south as the Chesapeake Bay.

1513:   Ponce de Leon sails to Florida.

1524:   Giovanni da Verrazano sails to New York and Narraganset Bays.

1539:   Hernando de Soto travels in what will become Florida, Georgia, and Alabama, and reaches the Mississippi River.

1540:   Francisco Vasquez de Coronado leads expedition to Southwest; member of expedition discovers Grand Canyon.

1579:   Sir Francis Drake arrives on the coast of California and claims it for England.

1607:   Captain John Smith settles Jamestown, VA.

1609:   Henry Hudson sails in New York harbor.
Spanish settle Santa Fe.

1614:   Native American Princess Pocahontas marries settler John Rolfe.

1619:   Calling of the first General Assembly of Virginia.
First black slaves brought to Virginia.

1620:   Pilgrims arrive in Cape Cod and sign Mayflower Compact, which establishes majority rule.

1625:   Dutch settle on Manhattan Island and rename it New Amsterdam.

1629:   Colony of Massachusetts founded.

1630:   John Winthrop and 1,000 settlers land in New England. Boston is founded and Winthrop designated first governor of Massachusetts.

1634:   Maryland founded as Catholic colony with religious tolerance.

1635:   Connecticut settled.

1636:   Harvard College founded.
              Roger Williams banished from Massachusetts; he had founded Rhode Island
              and proclaimed religious freedom.

1637:   Royal proclamation limits English emigration to America.

1639:   First printing press in North America introduced, in Cambridge, MA.

1649:   Maryland Assembly passes Toleration Act, granting religious freedom.

1654:   First Jews arrive in New Amsterdam.

1664:   British capture New Amsterdam and rename it New York.

1665:   Colony of New Jersey founded.

1669:   South Carolina founded.

1670:   English settlment founded in Charleston, SC.

1678:   First U.S. medical publication is Thomas Thatcher's treatise on smallpox.

1682:   LaSalle claims Mississippi River area for the French and names it Louisiana,
              for Louis XIV.

1692:   Witchcraft hysteria begins in Salem, MA.
              William and Mary College founded in Virginia.

1698:   Paper first manufactured in North America.

1699:   French settlements established in Louisiana.

1701:   Colonists begin fight for England against French in Queen Anne's War.

1704:   "Boston News Letter," first regular newspaper, started by John Campbell,
              postmaster.

1716:   First colonial theater opens in Williamsburg, VA.

1721:   Regular postal service begins between London and New England.
              Rifles introduced to U.S. by Swiss immigrants.

1731:   Benjamin Franklin founds a subscription library in Philadelphia.
              Philadelphia's State House building, later to become Independence Hall,
              designed by Andrew Hamilton.

Norman Price's "Oatfield Near Saratoga, New York," from the Society of Illustrators Museum of American Illustration.

1732: Benjamin Franklin publishes "Poor Richard's Almanac."

1733: Founding of Georgia, last of the thirteen original colonies.

1734: First U.S. horse race run at Charleston Neck, SC.

1735: John Peter Zenger case establishes precedent of freedom of the press. First musical theater in U.S. opens in Charleston, SC.

1740: Captain Vitus Bering, a Dane employed by Russians, reaches Alaska. University of Pennsylvania founded.

1750: First playhouse opens in New York.

1752: Benjamin Franklin proves lightning is electricity.

1754: French and Indian War begins. British tighten colonial administration in North America.

1764: British pass Sugar Act, placing a tax on sugar in colonies.

1765: British pass Stamp Act, placing a tax on letters, newspapers, and other items.

1766: Britain repeals Stamp Act, but passes Declaratory Act maintaining England's right to tax U.S.
Mason-Dixon Line created between Pennsylvania and Maryland by English surveyors.

1767: Townshend Acts place duties on paper, glass, tea, and paint.

1770: Boston Massacre.

1772: Samuel Adams forms Committee of Correspondence for action against Britain.

1773: Boston Tea Party protests tea duty levied by British.

1774: First Continental Congress held in Philadelphia.

1775: First shots fired in Revolutionary War, in Concord and Lexington.
Paul Revere makes midnight ride warning the colonists that British are landing on U.S. shores.
Second Continental Congress appoints George Washington Commander-in-Chief of Armed Forces.

1776: Tom Paine's "Common Sense" published.
Declaration of Independence adopted.
Colonies declare themselves the "Thirteen United States."
Adam Smith writes "An Inquiry into the Nature and Causes of the Wealth of Nations," which supports free trade and mercantilism.

1777: Army wins Battle of Princeton, but spends a harsh winter at Valley Forge.
France recognizes colonies' independence.
Stars and Stripes adopted as Continental Congress flag.

1778: British abandon Philadelphia and retreat in New York.
Congress prohibits importation of slaves into U.S.

1779: John Paul Jones defeats British on the high seas.

1780: Benedict Arnold found to be a traitor.
American Academy of Sciences founded in Boston.

1781: Articles of Confederation ratified.
Gen. Cornwallis surrenders to Colonial Army at Yorktown.

1782: Bank of North America established in Philadelphia.

1783:   British and United States sign peace treaty.

1784:   First successful daily newspaper, "Penn Packet and General Advertiser," published.

1786:   Delegates from five states gather to write Constitution.

1787:   Shays' Rebellion of debt-ridden farmers protests excess taxation.
Northwest Ordinance established, determining government of newly acquired Northwest Territory.
Constitutional Convention opens.
U.S. Constitution adopted.
Dollar currency introduced in U.S.
Inventor John Fitch launches steamboat in Delaware River.

1788:   New Hampshire becomes ninth and final state needed to ratify U.S. Constitution.
New York declared capital of U.S.

1789:   George Washington is chosen president and John Adams vice-president.
First Congress meets.

1790:   Rhode Island becomes 13th state.
Philadelphia voted federal capital of U.S.
First patent law enacted.
Washington, DC founded.
Supreme Court holds first session.

1791:   Vermont becomes 14th state.
Bill of Rights ratified.

1792:   Kentucky becomes 15th state.
Republican Party formed by Thomas Jefferson, and Federalist Party formed under Alexander Hamilton and John Adams.

1793:   Eli Whitney invents cotton gin.
George Washington lays cornerstone for U.S. Capitol.

1794:   Pennsylvania farmers protest tax during Whiskey Rebellion.
Charles Wilson Peale opens first U.S. museum, in Philadelphia.
U.S. Navy established.
Thomas Paine writes "The Age of Reason."

1795:   University of North Carolina becomes first state university.
U.S. Treaty of Lorenzo with Spain gives U.S. right to navigate Mississippi River and establishes Florida boundary.

1796:   Tennessee becomes 16th state.

1797:   John Adams becomes second president.

1799:   George Washington dies.

1800:   Washington, DC, becomes permanent national capital.
            Eli Whitney manufactures muskets with interchangeable parts.

1801:   Thomas Jefferson becomes third president.

1803:   Ohio becomes 17th state.
            U.S. buys Louisiana Territory from France.
            Supreme Court, under Justice John Marshall, establishes right of Court to
            declare an act of Congress unconstitutional.

1804:   Twelfth Amendment ratified.
            Lewis and Clark expedition ordered by Jefferson.
            Alexander Hamilton dies after duel with Aaron Burr.

1806:   Noah Webster publishes dictionary, which helps standardize English lan-
            guage.

1807:   Robert Fulton's steamboat makes first trip between New York City and
            Albany, at 5 mph.

1808:   Slave importation from Africa outlawed.

1809:   James Madison becomes fourth president.

1812:   Congress declares war on Britain, 1812-13.
            Louisiana becomes 18th state.

1814:   British burn Capitol and White House.
            Francis Scott Key writes words to "Star Spangled Banner."

1815:   First steam warship, *USS Fulton*, christened.
            U.S. forces defeat British in Battle of New Orleans.

1816:   Indiana becomes 19th state.

1817:   Mississippi becomes 20th state.
            James Monroe becomes fifth president.
            Construction of Erie Canal begins between Buffalo and Albany.

1818:   Illinois becomes 21st state.

1819:   Alabama becomes 22nd state.
             Spain cedes Florida to U.S.

1820:   Maine becomes 23rd state.
             Congress passes Missouri Compromise.
             Washington Colonization Society establishes Liberia for repatriation of
             blacks from U.S.

1821:   Missouri becomes 24th state.
             James Monroe begins second term as president.

1823:   President Monroe issues Monroe Doctrine, which closes American conti-
             nent to colonial settlements by European powers.

1824:   John Quincy Adams elected president by House of Representatives when no
             candidate wins majority of popular vote.

1825:   Erie Canal opens.

1826:   James Fenimore Cooper writes "The Last of the Mohicans."

1828:   Construction of Baltimore & Ohio passenger railroad begins.

1829:   Andrew Jackson becomes seventh president.
             First U.S. patent for typewriter registered.
             James Smithson bequeathes large sum of money to found Smithsonian
             Institution in Washington, DC.

1830:   Congress authorizes the Indian Removal Act.
             Mormon Church organized by Joseph Smith in Fayette, NY.

1831:   Nat Turner leads slave revolt in Virginia.
             Samuel Francis Smith writes words to "America," one of nation's anthems
             until 1931.
             Chloroform simultaneously invented by American, Samuel Guthrie, and
             German, Justus von Liebig.

1832:   Andrew Jackson reelected as president.
             First horse-drawn trolleys used in New York.

1833:   Oberlin College becomes first in U.S. to adopt coeducation.
             Whig Party formed.
             First successful penny daily newspaper, "The New York Sun," founded.

1834:   Andrew Jackson censured by Senate for withdrawal of deposits from the Bank
             of the United States.

1834:   Abraham Lincoln enters Illinois political arena.
(cont.)   Cyrus McCormick patents reaping machine.

1835:   Phineas Taylor (P. T.) Barnum begins his showman career by hyping a
                  supposed 160-year-old nurse of George Washington.

1836:   Texas, formerly a Mexican territory, declares itself an independent republic.
                  Arkansas becomes 25th state.
                  Davy Crockett killed at the Alamo.
                  Ralph Waldo Emerson publishes "Nature."

1837:   Michigan becomes 26th state.
                  Martin Van Buren becomes eighth president.
                  First U.S. boat race held, at Poughkeepsie, NY.
                  Samuel Morse exhibits electric telegraph at the College of the City of New
                  York.
                  American Presbyterians split into "old" and "new" factions.

1839:   Abner Doubleday conducts first baseball game, in Cooperstown, NY.
                  Charles Goodyear discovers process of vulcanization of rubber.
                  Edgar Allan Poe writes "Fall of the House of Usher."

1841:   William Harrison becomes ninth president, but dies after one month in
                  office.
                  John Tyler becomes first vice-president to become president.
                  Slave ship USS Creole taken over by the slaves it was carrying from Virginia
                  to Louisiana.
                  First university degrees granted to women in U.S.

1842:   New York Philharmonic founded.
                  Georgia physician Crawford Long uses ether as anesthetic.
                  Boston and Albany are connected by railroad.

1843:   Jefferson Davis enters politics and becomes a delegate to the Democratic
                  convention in Alabama.
                  Samuel Morse given appropriation by Congress to build first telegraph line,
                  to run between Washington and Baltimore.

1845:   Florida becomes 27th state.
                  Texas becomes 28th state.
                  James K. Polk becomes 11th president.
                  U.S. Naval Academy opens in Annapolis, MD.

1846:   Mass Irish immigration to United States begins.
                  U.S. treaty with Great Britain sets boundary in Oregon territory at 49th
                  parallel.

1846: Elias Howe invents sewing machine.
(cont.) Iowa becomes 29th state.
Brigham Young leads Mormons from Illinois to Great Salt Lake, UT.
American inventor John Deere constructs plow with steel moldboard.

1848: Gold discovered in California.
First Chinese brought to California to work in gold mines.
Wisconsin becomes 30th state.
U.S. acquires lands from Mexico and northern territory from Great Britain.

1849: Zachary Taylor becomes 12th president.

1850: Henry Clay drafts Compromise of 1850 in attempt to settle slavery disputes.
California becomes 31st state.
Millard Fillmore becomes 13th president.
Levi Strauss begins manufacturing blue jeans.
Chesapeake & Ohio Canal completed.
Hawthorne writes "The Scarlet Letter."

1851: Peak year of Irish immigration.
Harriet Beecher Stowe publishes "Uncle Tom's Cabin."
Herman Melville publishes "Moby Dick."
U.S. wins America's Cup.
"New York Times" first published.
Maine and Illinois begin to enforce liquor prohibition.

1852: Wells Fargo Company founded.

1853: U.S. buys what will become parts of Arizona and New Mexico, for $10 million.
Franklin Pierce becomes 14th president.
Henry Steinway opens a piano manufacturing firm in New York.

1854: Republican Party formed in Jackson, MI.
Henry David Thoreau writes "Walden."

1855: Walt Whitman publishes "Leaves of Grass."

1857: Dred Scott decision invalidates Missouri Compromise.
James Buchanan becomes 15th president.

1858: Minnesota becomes 32nd state..

1859: John Brown raids Harper's Ferry.
First oil well drilled, in Titusville, PA.
Oregon becomes 33rd state.

1861:   Abraham Lincoln becomes 15th president.
Confederacy established, with Jefferson Davis as president.
Civil War begins with Confederate seizure of Fort Sumter, SC.
First Battle of Bull Run fought at Manassas, VA.
Kansas becomes 34th state.

1863:   Lincoln issues Emancipation Proclamation, ending slavery.
Union forces win victory at Gettysburg.
West Virginia becomes 35th state.
Gettysburg Address delivered by Lincoln at dedication of military cemetery.
National Academy of Sciences founded in Washington, DC.

1864:   Nevada becomes 36th state.
Gen. Ulysses S. Grant becomes head of Union armies.
Gen. William Sherman marches Union troops from Chattanooga, TN, to Atlanta, GA, and defeats Confederate troops there.
Lincoln elected to second term as president.
"In God We Trust" first appears on U.S. coins.
First racetrack established in Saratoga, NY.
Cheyenne and Arapahoe Indians massacred at Sand Creek, CO.

1865:   Civil War ends when Gen. Robert E. Lee surrenders at Appomattox Courthouse, VA.
Thirteenth Amendment takes effect, abolishing slavery.
President Lincoln assassinated by John Wilkes Booth.
Andrew Johnson becomes 17th president.
Confederate President Jefferson Davis captured and imprisoned.
Sleeper railroad cars designed by George Pullman first used in U.S.
First train held up, in North Bend, OH.
Massachusetts Institute of Technology founded.

1866:   Ku Klux Klan formed, in Pulaski, TN.

1867:   Nebraska becomes 37th state.
U.S. buys Alaska from Russia for $7.2 million.
President Johnson avoids impeachment by one vote.
Gold discovered in Wyoming.

1868:   Fourteenth Amendment ratified, guaranteeing civil rights, denying office to certain Confederates, and disclaiming responsibility for Confederate debt.
First professional baseball club formed as the Cincinnati Red Stockings.

1869:   First transcontinental railroad completed as tracks of Central Pacific and Union Pacific railroads are joined by golden spike at Promontory, UT.
Ulysses S. Grant becomes 18th president.
U.S. National Prohibition Party formed in Chicago.

Major General William Luther Sibert during the construction of the Panama Canal, from the Gadsden Public Library.

1870:   The last of the Confederate states are readmitted to the Union.
Fifteenth Amendment ratified, guaranteeing voting rights for all men.
Hiram Revels of Mississippi becomes first black elected to U.S. Senate.
Standard Oil Company established by John D. Rockefeller.

1871:   P. T. Barnum introduces his "Greatest Show on Earth," in Brooklyn, NY.
Great Fire rages in Chicago.

1872:   Congress establishes Yellowstone as the first national park.
U.S. General Amnesty Act passed to pardon most Confederates.
Brooklyn Bridge opens.
Thomas Edison perfects the duplex telegraph.

1873:   Remington & Sons begins to produce typewriters.

1874:   First U.S. zoo opens in Philadelphia.

1875:   Mark Twain writes "The Adventures of Tom Sawyer."

1876:   Colorado becomes 38th state.
              Alexander Graham Bell invents the telephone.
              Gen. Custer and his 7th Cavalry massacred in Battle of the Little Big Horn.
              World Exhibition held in Philadelphia, PA.

1877:   Rutherford B. Hayes becomes 19th president.
              Thomas Edison invents the phonograph.

1878:   First bicycles manufactured in U.S.

1879:   Edison invents the electric light bulb.

1880:   New York streets lit with electricity.

1881:   James A. Garfield becomes 20th president, but is assassinated almost as soon
              as he takes office.
              Chester A. Arthur becomes 21st president.
              Clara Barton organizes the American Red Cross Society.

1882:   U.S. bans Chinese immigration for ten years.
              Thomas Edison designs first hydroelectric plant, in Appleton, WI.

1883:   Civil Service Commission organized to make federal jobs competitive.
              Brooklyn Bridge opens to traffic.
              First skyscraper constructed in Chicago.

1884:   Suffragettes form Equal Rights Party.

1885:   Grover Cleveland becomes 22nd President.
              John Fox introduces golf to U.S. in Foxburg, PA.
              Mormons split into polygamous and monogamous factions.

1886:   Statue of Liberty dedicated.

1888:   George Eastman perfects the box camera.
              Nikola Tesla constructs the electric motor for George Westinghouse.

1889:   North Dakota, South Dakota, Montana, and Washington become 39th
              through 42nd states.
              Benjamin Harrison becomes 23rd president.

1890:   Idaho and Wyoming become 43rd and 44th states.
              Wyoming becomes first state where women can vote.
              Battle of Wounded Knee rages in South Dakota.

1891:   U.S. inventor W. L. Judson develops the clothing zipper.
Dr. James Naismith introduces basketball, in Springfield, MA.

1892:   Ellis Island opens to receive immigrants.

1893:   Grover Cleveland becomes 24th president.
World Exhibition opens in Chicago.
Henry Ford builds first car.

1895:   First professional football game played, in Latrobe, PA.
First U.S. Open Golf Championship held.

1896:   Supreme Court decides *Plessy vs. Ferguson*, establishing doctrine of "separate but equal."
Utah becomes 45th state.

1897:   William McKinley becomes 25th president.
Rudolph Dirks creates first U.S. comic strip, "Katzenjammer Kids."
Jell-O, condensed soup, and bottled milk are introduced in U.S.

1898:   U.S. declares war on Spain after destruction of battleship *Maine.*

1900:   U.S. scientist R. A. Fessenden transmits human speech via radio waves.
Frank Baum writes "Wizard of Oz."

1901:   President McKinley assassinated.
Theodore Roosevelt becomes 26th president.
J. P. Morgan organizes U.S. Steel Corporation.
Ragtime jazz takes off in U.S.

1902:   U.S. acquires perpetual control of Panama Canal.

1903:   First successful cross-country automobile trip.
First air flight, by Orville and Wilbur Wright, at Kitty Hawk, NC.
Henry Ford establishes Ford Motor Company.
J. P. Morgan forms International Mercantile Marine Company.
First Teddy bears introduced; named after Theodore Roosevelt.

1904:   U.S. physician W. C. Gorgas eradicates yellow fever epidemic in Panama Canal region.
St. Louis, MO hosts first U.S. Olympics and World Exhibition.

1906:   Earthquake levels most of San Francisco, killing more than 600.
Congress passes Pure Food and Drug Act and Meat Inspection Act.
U.S. troops occupy Cuba.
President Roosevelt visits Panama Canal.

1907: Oklahoma becomes 46th state.
President Roosevelt halts Japanese immigration.
First Ziegfield Follies presented in New York.

1908: General Motors Corp. formed.
First Model T's produced by Ford Motor Company.

1909: Admiral Robert E. Perry reaches North Pole.
National Association for the Advancement of Colored People founded.
William Taft becomes 27th president.
Bakelite, the first plastic, is produced commercially.
Frank Lloyd Wright designs the Robie House in Chicago.

1910: Boy Scouts founded.

1911: First transcontinental airplane flight.
Irving Berlin writes "Alexander's Ragtime Band."

1912: New Mexico and Arizona become 47th and 48th states.
Girl Scouts founded.
F. W. Woolworth Company founded.
Jim Thorpe's Olympic medals revoked when his brief stint as semiprofessional baseball player is discovered.

1913: Sixteenth and Seventeenth Amendments ratified, legalizing federal income tax and electing senators by popular election.
Woodrow Wilson becomes 28th president.
U.S. Federal Reserve System established.
Henry Ford develops assembly line technique for manufacturing cars.
Charlie Chaplin first appears in films.

1914: World War I begins.
Panama Canal completed.
Lincoln Memorial designed by Henry Bacon.
World's first traffic light introduced, in Cleveland, OH.

1915: U.S. Coast Guard established.
First U.S. transcontinental telephone call, between Alexander Graham Bell in New York and Dr. Thomas Watson in San Francisco.
D. W. Griffith releases "Birth of a Nation."

1916: National Park Service formed.
Margaret Sanger opens first birth control clinic.
Prohibition of alcoholic beverages approved by 24 states.
Woodrow Wilson reelected as president.
U.S. purchases Virgin Islands

1917:   U.S. declares war on Germany.

1918:   World War I ends as Germany accepts harsh armistice.
Eugene V. Debs sentenced for violating espionage and sedition law.
Airmail established in U.S., between New York and Washington, DC.
Daylight savings time introduced in U.S.

1919:   Eighteenth Amendment ratified, banning sale of alcoholic beverages.
President Wilson presides over first meeting of League of Nations.
Radio Corporation of America founded.

1920:   Nineteenth Amendment ratified, giving women the right to vote.
Height of Red Scare, as U.S. Attorney General A. Mitchell Palmer orders 2,700 alleged Communists arrested.
Nicola Sacco and Bartolomeo Vanzetti arrested.
U.S. Senate votes against joining League of Nations.
Babe Ruth traded by Boston Red Sox to New York Yankees.
First U.S. broadcasting station opens, in Pittsburgh, PA.
Retired Army officer John Thompson patents the submachine gun.

1921:   Quota law places ceiling on number of immigrants allowed entry each year.
William G. Harding becomes 29th president.
First radio broadcast of a baseball game, from Polo Grounds in New York.
KDKA in Pittsburgh broadcasts first regular radio programs.
Former president Howard Taft named Chief Justice of Supreme Court.
Stock market boom begins in U.S.

1923:   Calvin Coolidge becomes 30th president.
First birth control clinic opens, in New York.
Martial law established to ensure protection of Oklahomans and their property from Ku Klux Klan.
Charles Birdseye introduces concept of quick frozen food.

1924:   Law approved by Congress makes all Native Americans citizens.
J. Edgar Hoover appointed director of Federal Bureau of Investigation.

1925:   Charleston dance becomes popular.
Madison Square Garden opens in New York.
State of Tennessee prohibits sex education in schools.
John Scopes brought to trial for teaching theory of evolution in TN school.
Charlie Chaplin stars in "The Gold Rush."
F. Scott Fitzgerald writes "The Great Gatsby."
"The New Yorker" begins publication.
Chrysler Corporation founded.

1926:   Gene Tunney beats Jack Dempsey for heavyweight boxing championship.

U.S. scientist Robert Goddard launches first liquid-fueled rocket.
Kodak produces first 16mm movie film.
Ernest Hemingway writes "The Sun Also Rises."

1927:   Charles A. Lindbergh completes first solo flight across the Atlantic.
"The Jazz Singer" starring Al Jolson, is first full-length sound motion picture.
Harlem Globetrotters organized by Abe Saperstein.
Sacco and Vanzetti executed.

1928:   Mickey Mouse created by Walt Disney.
D. H. Lawrence writes "Lady Chatterly's Lover."
George Gershwin composes "An American in Paris."
WGY in Schenectady, NY, broadcasts first scheduled TV programs.

1929:   Herbert Hoover becomes 31st president.
Stock market crashes.
Albert Fall, Secretary of Interior, convicted of accepting bribe in Teapot Dome scandal.
Richard Byrd and three others fly over South Pole.
Valentine's Day Massacre claims lives of six Chicago gangsters.
First Mickey Mouse musical film appears.
Ernest Hemingway writes "A Farewell to Arms."
Thomas Wolfe writes "Look Homeward, Angel."
Virginia Woolf writes "A Room of One's Own."

1930:   Clyde Tombaugh discovers Pluto.
Congress creates Veterans Administration.
Federal Bureau of Narcotics created.
Grant Wood paints "American Gothic."
Sliced bread and Twinkies are introduced.

1931:   Empire State Building opens in New York City.
"Star Spangled Banner" made U.S. national anthem.
Senate passes Veterans Compensation Act over Hoover's veto.
Al Capone jailed for income tax evasion.
Hattie Caraway becomes first woman elected to Senate.
U.S. physicist E. O. Lawrence invents cyclotron.
Charlie Chaplin stars in "City Lights."
Boris Karloff stars in "Frankenstein."
Pearl Buck writes "The Good Earth."

1932:   Lindbergh baby kidnapped and later found dead.
Cole Porter writes "The Gay Divorcee."
Johnny Weismuller appears in "Tarzan."
First unemployment insurance enacted, in Wisconsin.

1933:   Franklin Delano Roosevelt becomes 32nd president.
Frances Perkins becomes first woman to be appointed cabinet member.
Supreme Court rules that blacks cannot be excluded from juries.
Twentieth and Twenty-first Amendments ratified, providing line of succession for office of president and repealing Prohibition.
School of American Ballet founded by George Balanchine and Lincoln Kirstein.
U.S. abandons gold standard.
Chicago World's Fair opens.
Works Project Administration created to support U.S. artists.
Gertrude Stein writes "The Autobiography of Alice B. Toklas."

1934:   Treaty ends Cuba's 33-year status as U.S. protectorate.
Cole Porter writes "Anything Goes."
F. Scott Fitzgerald writes "Tender is the Night."
John Dillinger shot by F.B.I.

1935:   Congress passes Wagner Labor Relations Act, granting workers the right to organize unions.
Social Security Act passed.
Huey Long assassinated by Carl Weiss in Louisiana Capitol.
George Gershwin writes "Porgy and Bess."
Clark Gable stars in "Mutiny on the Bounty."
Board game Monopoly introduced.

1936:   Boulder Dam completed.
Franklin Delano Roosevelt reelected.
Jesse Owens wins four gold medals at Olympic Games in Berlin.
Severe flooding hit Johnstown, PA.

1937:   Amelia Earhart is lost during Pacific flight.

1938:   First synthetic fiber, nylon, introduced to commercial market.
House Un-American Activities Committee formed.
FDR appeals to Hitler and Mussolini to end European conflict.
Forty-hour work week established in U.S.
Howard Hughes flies around world.
Orson Welles' fictional radio production, "War of the Worlds," causes panic among many listeners.
Chester Carlson invents photocopying but is unable to sell it.

1939:   Albert Einstein alerts FDR to A-bomb possibility.
"Gone With the Wind," by Margaret Mitchell, released as film.
First baseball game televised in U.S.
John Steinbeck publishes "Grapes of Wrath."
U.S. inventor Edwin Armstrong develops use of FM radio.

1940:   Lend-Lease program begins, providing war supplies to allied forces.
First peacetime draft begins.
FDR reelected for third term.
Successful flight of a helicopter designed by Vought-Sikorsky Corporation.
Film "Fantasia" released by Disney Studios.

1941:   Japan attacks Pearl Harbor.
U.S. declares war on Japan and Italy.
U.S. Savings Bonds are sold.
Joe DiMaggio hits safely in 56 games to set Major League record.
Manhattan Project activity begins on development of atomic bomb.
Orson Welles directs and stars in "Citizen Kane."

1942:   Federal government forcibly moves 110,000 Japanese-Americans from West Coast into detention camps.
First nuclear chain reaction is achieved.
FBI captures eight German saboteurs who landed in Florida and New York.
Rationing of gasoline, coffee, and other items begins.
Animated film "Bambi" released.
Bell Aircraft tests first U.S. jet.
Irving Berlin writes "White Christmas."

1943:   Allied forces invade Italy.
Roosevelt, Churchill, and Stalin meet for a conference.
President Roosevelt freezes wages, prices, and salaries to combat inflation.
"Big Inch" oil pipeline opens from Texas to Pennsylvania.
Rodgers and Hammerstein's "Oklahoma" opens on Broadway.
Supreme Court rules that religious objectors aren't required to salute U.S. flag in schools.

1944:   Allied forces under Gen. Eisenhower land in Normandy, France, to liberate Europe.
The G.I. Bill goes into effect.
Dumbarton Oaks Conference held in Washington, DC, to discuss future of United Nations.
FDR reelected to fourth term.
Tennessee Williams writes "Glass Menagerie."

1945:   Yalta Conference convenes in Crimea, USSR.
Roosevelt, Churchill, and Stalin agree that Soviet Union will enter war against Japan.
Roosevelt dies; Harry Truman becomes 33rd president.
Germany surrenders.
First atomic bombs, produced at Los Alamos, NM, dropped on Hiroshima and Nagasaki, Japan.
Japan surrenders.

1945:
(cont.)
Frank Lloyd Wright designs Guggenheim Museum in New York.
Nuremberg war trials begin.

1946:
U.S. grants Phillippine Islands independence.
United Nations headquarters permanently housed in New York.
President Truman creates Atomic Energy Commission.
U.S. Navy tests atom bomb on Bikini Islands.
Benjamin Spock writes "Baby and Child Care."

1947:
U.S. launches Marshall Plan, extending aid to European countries.
Congress passes Taft-Hartley Act to restrict rights of labor unions.
Flying saucers first sighted in U.S.
Jackie Robinson becomes first black to sign contract with Major League baseball club.
First U.S. airplane flies at supersonic speeds.
Bell Labs invents transistors.
Tennessee Williams writes "Streetcar Named Desire."

1948:
USSR begins land blockade of Berlin.
Organization of American States founded.

1949:
The North Altantic Treaty Organization established.
U.S. forces completely withdraw from South Korea.
Arthur Miller writes "Death of a Salesman."

1950:
Guam becomes U.S. territory.
Truman sends U.S. troops to South Korea after invasion by northern forces.
Sen. Joe McCarthy claims that State Department is filled with Communists.
Alger Hiss sentenced for perjury.
Truman tells Atomic Energy Commission to design H-Bomb.
Two Puerto Rican nationalists attempt to assassinate Truman.

1951:
Twenty-second Amendment ratified, limiting a president to a maximum of two terms.
Julius and Ethel Rosenberg found guilty of conspiracy to commit wartime espionage.
Color television introduced in U.S.
Movie "African Queen" released.

1952:
Jonas Salk develops polio vaccine.
First U.S. H-Bomb detonated in Pacific Ocean.

1953:
Korean War ends.
Dwight D. Eisenhower becomes 34th president.

1954:
Senate reprimands Sen. McCarthy for his conduct in investigating suspected Communists.

1954:　Supreme Court orders desegregation of public schools.
(cont.)　U.S. and Canada agree to construct radar warning stations across Canada.
　　　　Atomic physicist Richard Oppenheimer dismissed from government service after his security clearance is withdrawn.
　　　　Dr. Jonas Salk tests polio vaccine and begins innoculating children in Pittsburgh, PA.

1955:　U.S. agrees to help train South Vietnamese army.
　　　　Rosa Parks refuses to give her bus seat to a white man in Montgomery, AL.
　　　　Bus segregation ordinance declared unconstitutional.
　　　　Major labor unions merge, forming AFL-CIO.
　　　　Disneyland opens in California.
　　　　First McDonald's restaurant opens, in Des Plaines, IL.

1956:　H-bomb tests take place in South Pacific.
　　　　CBS introduces first TV soap opera, "As the World Turns."
　　　　Eisenhower reelected president.
　　　　Oral polio vaccine developed by Dr. Albert Sabin.

1957:　Elvis Presley releases first record, "Heartbreak Hotel."
　　　　"American Bandstand" debuts on national TV, starring Dick Clark.
　　　　Eisenhower sends Army to Little Rock, AR, to forced school desegregation.
　　　　At age 13, Bobby Fischer becomes chess champion.
　　　　Leonard Bernstein's musical "West Side Story" hits Broadway.
　　　　Dr. Seuss writes "The Cat in the Hat."
　　　　Ayn Rand writes "Atlas Shrugged."

1958:　Explorer 1, first earth-orbiting satellite, launched at Cape Canaveral, FL.
　　　　Arkansas Gov. Faubus defies Supreme Court order to desegregate schools.
　　　　U.S. establishes NASA.
　　　　Elizabeth Taylor stars in "Cat on a Hot Tin Roof."

1959:　Alaska and Hawaii become 49th and 50th states.
　　　　Musicians Buddy Holly, Richie Valens, and J. P. Richardson ("Big Bopper") killed in plane crash.

1960:　U.S. launches first weather satellite.
　　　　Almost 1,000 U.S. advisors are in South Vietnam.
　　　　Birth control pill is approved by the FDA.
　　　　U.S. pilot Francis Gary Powers shot down over USSR.
　　　　U.S. scientists develop laser devices.
　　　　Alfred Hitchcock's film "Psycho" opens.

1961:　John F. Kennedy becomes 35th president.
　　　　Bay of Pigs invasion by U.S.-trained Cubans fails to overthrow Fidel Castro.
　　　　Alan Shepard, Jr., becomes first American in space.

1961: Twenty-third Amendment ratified, allowing District of Columbia residents to vote in presidential elections.
Peace Corps created by JFK.
First U.S. combat troops are sent to Vietnam.
Joseph Heller writes "Catch-22."

1962: John Glenn becomes first American to orbit the earth.
Rachel Carson's book "Silent Spring" spurs environmental movement.
Supreme Court bans prayer in public schools.
Actress Marilyn Monroe found dead of apparent suicide.
Ken Kesey writes "One Flew Over the Cuckoo's Nest."

1963: Birmingham, AL, is site of civil rights demonstrations; JFK called out troops to end violence.
"Hot Line" installed between Washington and Moscow.
Martin Luther King, Jr., gives "I Have a Dream" speech at Washington, DC, demonstration.
John Kennedy assassinated in Dallas, TX.
Lyndon Johnson becomes 36th president.
Lee Harvey Oswald is shot and killed by Jack Ruby as America watches on live TV.
U.S. troops in Vietnam total over 15,000.
U.S. Post Office institutes zip codes to speed mail delivery.

1964: Lyndon Johnson reelected president.
National Wilderness Preservation System established.
Twenty-fourth Amendment ratified, banning poll taxes.
Congress approves War on Poverty.
Beatles arrive in U.S. to appear on "The Ed Sullivan Show."
Warren Commission reports that Oswald acted alone in JFK assassination.
Martin Luther King awarded Nobel Peace Prize.
Verranzano-Narrows Bridge, world's longest suspension bridge, opens in New York.
Elizabeth Taylor divorces Eddie Fisher and marries Richard Burton within ten days.

1965: Major force of U.S. troops land at Da Nang, South Vietnam.
President Johnson signs Voting Rights Act.
Blacks riot in Watts section of Los Angeles.
National quota system of immigration established.
First of many large anti-Vietnam War rallies held.
Martin Luther King leads civil rights march from Selma to Montgomery, AL.
President Johnson signs bill enacting Medicare.
Northeastern U.S. and parts of Canada hit with power blackout.
U.S. astronaut Edward White walks in space.

1966:   Bombing of Hanoi begins.
              National Organization of Women founded.
              First sex change operation performed in U.S.
              U.S. spacecraft Surveyor lands on moon and transmits TV images.

1967:   Twenty-fifth Amendment ratified, refining provisions for presidential suc-
              cession.
              Thurgood Marshall becomes the first black Supreme Court justice.
              The first Super Bowl pairs the Green Bay Packers and Kansas City Chiefs.
              U.S. manned spaceflights suspended after three astronauts killed in fire on
              launch pad.

1968:   USS Pueblo seized by North Koreans.
              Tet Offensive by Communist troops inflicts heavy casualty on U.S. forces.
              Paris Peace Talks begin.
              Martin Luther King, Jr., assassinated in Memphis, TN.
              Sen. Robert F. Kennedy assassinated by Sirhan Sirhan.
              Democratic convention in Chicago marked by riots and police brutality.
              Jackie Kennedy marries Aristotle Onassis.
              Films "The Odd Couple," "Funny Girl," and "2001: A Space Odyssey"
              released.
              Jerome Ragni and James Rado write "Hair."

1969:   Richard Nixon becomes 37th president.
              Expanded four-party Vietnam peace talks begin in Paris.
              Number of U.S. soldiers in Vietnam peaks.
              Antiwar demonstrations in U.S. peak as 250,000 people march in Washing-
              ton, DC.
              Neil Armstrong becomes first person to walk on the moon.
              Woodstock Music Festival is held in Bethel, NY.
              Sen. Edward Kennedy drives off a bridge on Chappaquiddick Island, MA,
              killing passenger Mary Jo Kopechne.
              Chicago Eight trial begins for violation of antiriot clause of Civil Right Act.
              Supreme Court Justice Abe Fortas resigns after questionable dealings with
              convicted financier disclosed.
              Charles Manson family murders actress Sharon Tate and four others.
              Kurt Vonnegut writes "Slaughterhouse Five."

1970:   Environmental Protection Agency founded.
              National Guard kills four student war protesters at Kent State University in
              Ohio.

1971:   Twenty-sixth Amendment ratified, granting voting right to 18-year-olds.
              Lt. William L. Calley is convicted of killing Vietnamese women in My Lai
              massacre. His conviction is later overturned.
              Walt Disney World opens in Orlando, FL.

President Johnson and family celebrate 1968 reelection victory, from the National Archives.

1971:	Cigarette ads banned from U.S. television.
(cont.)	Prisoner uprising at Attica prison in New York.
	Mariner 9 orbits Mars.
	Sylvia Plath writes "The Bell Jar."
	"Pentagon Papers" appear in the *New York Times*.
1972:	President Nixon visits China.
	Alabama Governor George C. Wallace shot while campaigning for president.
	Shirley Chisholm is first black woman to run for president.
	Nixon signs landmark strategic arms pact at Moscow summit.
	Break-in at Democratic National Committee headquarters leads to discovery of Watergate coverup.
	U.S. military draft phased out.
1973:	OPEC oil embargo creates gas shortage in U.S.
	Vice-President Spiro T. Agnew resigns and pleads no contest to charges of tax evasion.
	Gerald Ford becomes first appointed vice-president.

1973:   Supreme Court decision strikes down antiabortion laws in U.S.
(cont.)   Wounded Knee, SD, is site of American Indian uprising.

1974:   Impeachment hearings held against President Nixon.
                Nixon resigns.
                Gerald Ford becomes 38th president and immediately pardons Nixon.
                President Ford grants limited immunity to draft evaders and deserters.
                Carl Bernstein and Bob Woodward write "All the President's Men."

1975:   Last U.S. troops leave Vietnam.
                FBI agents capture Patty Hearst, who is indicted for bank robbery.
                Two assassination attempts made on President Ford.
                New York City appeals to federal government for money to avoid default.

1976:   U.S. celebrates bicentennial of Declaration of Independence.
                Viking II lands on Mars.
                Howard Hughes dies.
                Legionnaires' Disease kills 29 people in Pennsylvania.
                Alex Haley publishes "Roots."

1977:   Jimmy Carter becomes 39th president.
                Department of Energy formed.
                President Carter pardons most draft evaders of Vietnam War.
                Elvis Presley dies.

1978:   U.S. Senate votes to turn Panama Canal over to Panama in 1999.
                Allan Bakke wins reverse discrimination suit against University of California medical school.
                Mass suicide by members of the People's Temple in Guyana, headed by Rev. Jim Jones.

1979:   First major nuclear power plant accident occurs, at Three Mile Island, PA.
                Sixty-three Americans taken hostage in Iran.
                Chrysler Corporation given $1.5 billion loan by federal government in order to continue operations.

1980:   Carter announces grain embargo against USSR; U.S. boycotts Olympics.
                Mount St. Helens erupts.
                John Lennon killed by Mark David Chapman.

1981:   Ronald Reagan becomes 40th president.
                American hostages held in Iran released.
                President Reagan shot by John W. Hinckley, Jr.
                Air traffic controllers begin illegal nationwide strike; most are fired by President Reagan.
                Sandra Day O'Connor becomes first female Supreme Court justice.

1982:   AT&T monopoly dismantled.
Equal Rights Amendment defeated.
Space shuttle Columbia completes first flight.
Barney Clark becomes first recipient of an artificial heart.

1983:   National Commission on Excellence in Education issues "Nation at Risk."
Sally Ride becomes first U.S. female in space.
U.S. Marines and Rangers invade island of Grenada.

1984:   Walter Mondale choses Geraldine Ferraro as first female vice-presidential candidate.
Ronald Reagan reelected as president.

1985:   Reagan and Gorbachev of Soviet Union have first U.S.-USSR summit in six years.
Televised 17-hour rock concert, "Live Aid," raises $70 million for famine relief in Africa.

1986:   Space shuttle Challenger explodes on lift-off, killing all seven crew members.
U.S. planes bombed Libya in retaliation for Libyan bombing in Germany.
Acquired Immune Deficiency Syndrome (AIDS) reaches epidemic levels.
Reagan and Gorbachev meet in Iceland for arms talks.

1987:   Reagan and Gorbachev sign Intermediate Nuclear Forces Reduction Treaty.
Iran-Contra arms deal revealed to American public.
Stock market drops 508 points in one day.

An American History Bibliography

A Directory of U.S. Government Depository Libraries. Washington, D.C.: Congressional Joint Committee on Printing, 1987.

A Guide to Manuscripts Relating to America in Great Britain and Ireland. Westport, Conn.: Published for the British Association for American Studies by Meckler Books, 1979.

Albion, Robert G. *Naval and Maritime History: An Annotated Bibliography, 4th edition.* Mystic, Conn.: American Munson Institute of Marine History, 1972.

Allard, Dean C., et al. U.S. *Naval History Sources in the United States.* Washington, D.C.: Department of the Navy, Naval History Division, 1979.

Allen, Jack. *U.S.A.: History With Documents.* New York: American Book Co., 1971.

American Geographical Society of New York. *Index to Maps and Periodicals.* Boston: G.K. Hall, 1968.

American Headlines, Year by Year. Nashville, Tenn.: Nelson Publishers, 1985.

American History Booklist for High Schools. Washington, D.C.: National Council for the Social Studies, 1969.

American Jewish Archives. *Guide to the Holdings of the American Jewish Archives.* Cincinnati: The Archives, 1979.

Anderson, Elizabeth L, editor. *Newspaper Libraries in the United States and Canada, 2nd Edition.* New York: Special Libraries Association, Newspaper Division, 1980.

Ash, Lee, and William G. Miller. *Subjects Collections: A Guide to Special Book Collections and Subject Emphases as Reported by University, College, Public, and Special Libraries and Museums in the United States and Canada, 6th Edition.* New York: R.R. Bowker Co., 1985.

Barnouw, Erik. *A History of Broadcasting in the United States.* New York: Oxford University Press, 1966-70 (3 volumes).

Beach, Mark. *A Bibliographic Guide to American Colleges and Universities: From Colonial Times to the Present.* Westport, Conn.: Greenwood Press, 1975.

Beers, Henry Putney. *Bibliographies in American History, 1942-1978.* Woodbridge, Conn.: Research Publications, 1982.

Bemis, Samuel F. and Grace Gardner Griffin. *Guide to the Diplomatic History of the United States, 1775-1921.* Gloucester, Mass.: Peter Smith, 1975 (reprint).

Bolton, Herbert Eugene. *Guide to Materials for the History of the United States in the Principal Archives of Mexico.* Washington, D.C.: Carnegie Institution of Washington, 1913.

Bonar, James A. *The History of American Civilization by Its Interpreters.* Albany, N.Y.: University of the State of New York, Division of Educational Communications, 1967.

Bradford, Thomas L. *The Bibliographer's Manual of American History, Containing and Account of All State, Territory, Town and County Histories Relating to the United States....* Detroit: Gale Research Co., 1968 (reprint).

Bremer, Ronald *A. Selected American Historical Sources.* Salt Lake City: Gencor, 1974.

Breton, Arthur J. *A Guide to the Manuscript Collections of the New York* Historical Society. Westport, Conn.: Greenwood Press, 1972.

Brunvand, Jan H. *Folklore: A Study and Research Guide.* New York: St. Martin's Press, 1976.

Buenker, John D., and Nicholas Burckel. *Immigration and Ethnicity: A Guide to Information Sources.* Detroit: Gale Research Co., 1977.

Burnette, O. Lawrence, Jr. *Beneath the Footnote: A Guide to the Use and Preservation of American Historical Sources.* Madison, Wisc.: State Historical Society of Wisconsin, 1969.

Burr, Nelson R. *A Critical Bibliography of Religion in America.* Princeton, N.J.: Princeton University Press, 1961.

Carruth, Gorton. *The Encyclopedia of American Facts & Dates.* New York: Harper & Row, 1987.

Carter, Clarence Edwin. *The Territorial Papers of the United States.* Washington, D.C.: U.S. Government Printing Office 1934-.

Catchpole, Brian. *A Map History of the United States.* London, Heinemann Educational, 1972.

Chicago Public Library. Special Collections Division. *One Hundred Important Additions to the Civil War and American History Research Collection.* Chicago: The Division, 1978.

Cole, Donald B. *Handbook of American History.* New York: Harcourt, Brace & World, 1968.

Colket, Meredith B., and Frank E. Bridgers. *Guide to Genealogical Records in the National Archives.* Washington, D.C.: National Archives and Records Service, 1964.

Commager, Henry Steele. *Documents of American History*, 10th Edition, Volumes I and II. New York: Prentice Hall, 1988.

Crouch, Milton, and Hans Raum, editors. *Directory of State and Local History Periodicals*. Chicago: American Library Association, 1977.

Daniells, Lorna M., editor. *Studies in Enterprise: A Selected Bibliography of American and Canadian Company Histories and Biographies of Businessmen*. Boston: Harvard University School of Business Administration, 1957.

Danky, James, and Shore, Elliott. *Alternative Media in Libraries*. Metuchen, N.J.: Scarecrow Press, 1982.

Decker, Peter. *Peter Decker's Catalogues of Americana*. Austin, Tex.: Jenkins Pub. Co.: Frontier America Corp, 1979.

DeNovo, John A. *Selected Readings in American History*. New York: Scribner, 1969.

Directory of Business Archives in the United States and Canada. Chicago: Society of American Archivists, 1975.

Directory of State and Local Archives. Austin, Tex.: Society of American Archivists, 1975.

Emery, Edwin. *The Story of America as Reported by its Newspapers, 1690-1965*. New York: Simon & Schuster, 1965.

Emery, Michael C. *America's Front Page News, 1690-1970*. New York: Doubleday, 1970.

David C. Roller and Robert W. Twyman, editors. *Encyclopedia of Southern History*. Baton Rouge, La.: Louisiana State University Press, 1969.

Eyewitnesses to American Jewish History. New York: Union of American Hebrew Congregations, 1976-1982.

Faust, Albert Bernhardt. *Guide to the Materials for American History in Swiss and Austrian Archives*. Washington, D.C.: Carnegie Institution of Washington, 1916.

Ferguson, Eugene S. *Bibliography of the History of Technology*. Cambridge, Mass.: Society for the History of Technology, 1968.

Filby, P. William. *Passenger and Immigration Lists Bibliography, 1538-1900*. Detroit, Mich.: Gale Research Co., 1984-.

Filler, Louis. *The President Speaks: From William McKinley to Lyndon B. Johnson*. New York: Putnam, 1964.

Fingerhut, Eugene R. *The Fingerhut Guide: Sources in American History.* Santa Barbara, Calif.: American Bibliographical Center — Clio Press, 1973.

Fish, Carl Russell. *Guide to the Materials for American History in Roman and Other Italian Archives.* Washington, D.C.: Carnegie Institution of Washington, 1911.

Fogarty, Robert S. *Dictionary of American Communal and Utopian History.* Westport, Conn.: Greenwood Press, 1980.

Franklin, John Hope. *From Slavery to Freedom: A History of Negro Americans. 5th ed.* New York: Knopf, 1980.

Frazier, Nancy. *Special Museums of the Northeast: A Guide to Uncommon Collections from Maine to Washington, D.C.* Chester, Conn.: The Globe Pequot Press, 1985.

Freidel, Frank Burt. *Harvard Guide to American History.* Cambridge, Mass.: Belknap Press of Harvard University Press, 1975.

Furnas, Joseph C. *The Americans: A Social History of the United States, 1587-1914.* New York: G.P. Putnam's, 1969.

Gaustad, Edwin S. *Historical Atlas of Religion in America.* New York: Harper & Row, 1976.

Gephart, Ronald M. *Periodical Literature on the American Revolution: Historical Research and Changing Interpretations, 1895-1970; A Selective Bibliography.* Washington, D.C.: Library of Congress, 1971.

Gohdes, Clarence. *Literature and Theatre of the States and Regions of the U.S.A.* Durham, N.C.: Duke University Press, 1967.

Golder, Frank Alfred. *Guide to Materials for American History in Russian Archives.* Washington, D.C.: Carnegie Institution of Washington, 1917-37.

Great Events as Reported in The New York Times. Glen Rock, N.J.: Microfilming Corp. of America, 1978.

Greene, Evarts Boutell. *A Guide to the Principal Sources for Early American History (1600-1800) in the City of New York.* New York: Columbia University Press, 1953.

Grele, Ronald J., and Gaile A. *Oral History: An Annotated Bibliography.* Boulder, Colo.: ERIC Clearinghouse for Social Studies/Social Science Education, 1974.

Griffin, Appleton Prentiss Clark. *Bibliography of American Historical Societies (the United States and the Dominion of Canada).* Detroit: Gale Research Co., 1966.

Griffin, Bulkley S. *Offbeat History.* Cleveland: World Pub. Co., 1967.

Guide to the Study of United States History Outside the U.S., 1945-1980. White Plains, N.Y.: Kraus International Publications, 1985.

Hefner, Loretta L. *The WPA Historical Records Survey.* Chicago: Society of American Archivists, 1980.

Henry E. Huntington Library and Art Gallery. *Guide to American Historical Manuscripts in the Huntington Library.* San Marino, Calif.: H. E. Huntington Library and Art Gallery, 1979.

Higham, Robin, ed. *A Guide to the Sources of United States Military History.* Hamden, Conn.: Archon Books, 1975.

Hinding, Andrea, editor. *Women's History Sources: A Guide to Archives and Manuscript Collections in the United States.* New York: R.R. Bowker Co., 1979.

Historic Newspapers, 1559-1865. Worcester, Mass.: Worcester Telegram and Gazette, 1973.

Horn, David. *The Literature of American Music in Books and Folk Music Collections: A Fully Annotated Bibliography.* Metuchen, N.J.: Scarecrow Press, 1977.

Hotchkiss, Jeanette. *American Historical Fiction and Biography for Children and Young People.* Metuchen, N.J.: Scarecrow Press, 1973.

Index to Literature on the American Indian. San Francisco: American Indian Historical Society, 1970.

Inge, M. Thomas. *Handbook of American Popular Culture.* Westport, Conn.: Greenwood Press, 1978-81 (3 volumes).

Jennings, Margaret, editor. *Library and Reference Facilities in the Area of the District of Columbia.* White Plains, N.Y.: Knowledge Industry Publications, 1986.

Jessup, John E., Jr. and Robert W. Coakley, editors. *A Guide to the Study and Use of Military History.* Washington, D.C.: U.S. Army, Center for Military History, 1979.

Jones, H.G. *Local Government Record: An Introduction to Their Management, Preservation, and Use.* Nashville, Tenn.: American Association for State and Local History, 1980.

Karpel, Bernard, editor. *Arts in America: A Bibliography.* Washington, D.C.: Smithsonian Institution Press, 1979-80.

Kirchmar, Albert, et al. *The Women's Rights Movement in the United States, 1848-1970: A Bibliography and Sourcebook.* Metuchen, N.J.: Scarecrow Press, 1972.

Kirkham, E. Kay. *A Handy Guide to Record-Searching in the Larger Cities of the United*

States. Logan, Utah: Everton Publishers, 1974.

Kirkham, E. Kay. *The Handwriting of American Records for a Period of 300 Years.* Logan, Utah: Everton Publishers, 1973.

Krout, John Allen. *United States Since 1865.* New York: Barnes & Noble, 1971.

Krout, John Allen. *United States to 1877.* New York: Barnes & Noble, 1967.

Kull, Irving Stoddard. *A Chronological Encyclopedia of American History.* New York: Popular Library, 1969.

Kull, Irving Stoddard. *A Short Chronology of American History, 1492-1950.* Westport, Conn.: Greenwood Press, 1980.

Lamar, Howard R., editor. *The Reader's Encyclopedia of the American West.* New York: Thomas Y. Crowell, 1978.

Lancour, Harold. *A Bibliography of Ship Passenger Lists, 1538-1825.* New York: New York Public Library: Readex Books, 1978.

Lane, Jack C. *America's Military Past: A Guide to Information Sources.* Detroit: Gale Research Co., 1980.

Larned, Josephus Nelson. *The Literature of American History.* New York: F. Ungar Pub. Co., 1966.

Library of Congress. General Reference and Bibliography Division. *The American Revolution: A Selected Reading List.* Washington, D.C.: Library of Congress; for sale by the Supt. of Docs., U.S. Government Printing Office, 1968.

Library of Congress. *U.S. Local Histories in the Library of Congress: A Bibliography.* Baltimore: Magna Carta Book Co., 1975.

Library of Congress, Rare Book Division. *Catalog of Broadsides in the Rare Book Division.* Boston: G. K. Hall, 1972.

List and Index Society. *Source List of Manuscripts Relating to the U.S.A. and Canada.* London: P. & D. Swift Ltd., 1970.

Livermore, George. *An Historical Research Respecting the Opinions of the Founders of the Republic on Negroes as Slaves, as Citizens, and as Soldiers.* New York: A. M. Kelley, 1970.

Lowenstein, Eleanor. *Bibliography of American Cookery Books, 1742-1860.* Worcester, Mass.: American Antiquarian Society, 1972.

MacDonald, William. *Documentary Sourcebook of American History, 1606-1926.* New York: B. Franklin, 1968.

Massachusetts Historical Society, Boston. *Library Catalog of Manuscripts of the Massachusetts Historical Society/First supplement.* Boston: G. K. Hall, 1980.

McBrearty, James C. *American Labor History and Comparative Labor Movements: A Selected Bibliography.* Tucson, Ariz.: University of Arizona Press, 1973.

McLennan Library. Reference Dept. *United States History.* Montreal: McLennan Library, Reference Dept., McGill University, 1974.

McPherson, James M., et al. *Blacks In America: Bibliographic Essays.* Garden City, N.Y.: Doubleday, 1971.

Mecler, Alan, and Ruth McMullin, editors. *Oral History Collections.* New York: R.R. Bowker, 1975.

Meyer, Mary K., editor. *Directory of Genealogical Societies in the U.S.A. and Canada.* Pasadena, Md.: Libra Publications, 1980.

Milden, James W. *The Family in Past Time: A Guide to the Literature.* New York: Garland Publishing, 1977.

Miller, Marion Mills. *Great Debates in American History.* Metuchen, N.J.: Mini-Print Corp., 1970.

Miller, Wayne C., et al. *A Comprehensive Bibliography for the Study of American Minorities.* New York: New York University Press, 1976.

Minnesota Historical Society. *Guide to the Personal Papers in the Manuscript Collections of the Minnesota Historical Society.* Saint Paul, Minn.: Minnesota Historical Society, 1935.

Minterling, Philip. *U.S. Cultural History: A Guide to Information Sources.* Detroit: Gale Research Co., 1980.

Morris, Richard B., editor. *Encyclopedia of American History.* New York: Harper & Row, 1982.

Morris, Richard B. *Basic Documents in American History.* Huntington, N.Y.: Krieger, 1980.

Morris, Richard Brandon. *Encyclopedia of American History.* New York: Harper & Row, 1976.

Morris, Richard Brandon. *Great Presidential Decisions.* New York: Harper & Row, 1973.

Morris, Richard Brandon. *Significant Documents in United States History*. New York: Van Nostrand Reinhold, 1969.

National Archives and Record Administration. *Guide to the National Archives of the United States*. Washington, D.C.: National Archives and Records Administration, 1987.

National Archives and Record Administration. *Guide to Cartographic Records in the National Archives*. Washington, D.C.: National Archives and Records Administration, 1971.

National Archives and Records Administration. *Microfilm Resources for Research*. Washington, D.C.: National Archives and Records Administration, 1986.

National Archives and Records Administration. Office of Educational Programs. *The Written Word Endures*. Washington, D.C.: Office of Educational Programs, National Archives and Records Service, 1978.

National Museum of American History. *Guide to Manuscript Collections in the National Museum of History and Technology*. Washington, D.C.: Smithsonian Institution Press, 1978.

Neufeld, Maurice J. *A Representative Bibliography of American Labor History*. Ithaca, N.Y.: Cornell University, School of Industrial and Labor Relations, 1964.

New York Historical Society. *Muster and Pay Rolls of the War of the Revolution, 1775-1783*. New York: Printed for the Society, 1916.

Nicholson, Margaret Gale. *Catalogue of pre-1900 Imprints Relating to America in the Royal Library, Brussels*. London, England Millwood, N.Y.: Kraus International Publications, 1983.

Official Museum Directory. New York: American Association of Museums and National Register Publishing Company, 1986.

Okinshevich, Leo. *United States History & Historiography in Postwar Soviet Writings 1945-1970*. Santa Barbara, Calif.: Clio Books, 1976.

Oral History Collection on the Performing Arts. Dallas, Tex.: Southern Methodist University, 1984.

Pamphlets in American History. Sanford, N.C.: Microfilming Corp. of America, 1979.

Parker, David W. *Calendar of Papers in Washington Archives Relating to the Territories of the United States (to 1873)*. Washington, D.C.: Carnegie Institution of Washington, 1911.

Parker, David W. *Guide to the Materials for United States History in Canadian Archives*. Washington, D.C.: Carnegie Institution of Washington, 1913.

Peckham, Howard H. *Historical Americana: Books from Which Our History Is Written.* Ann Arbor, Mich.: University of Michigan Press, 1980.

Peterson, Clarence S. *Consolidated Bibliography of County Histories in Fifty States in 1961.* 2nd edition. Baltimore: Genealogical Publishing Co., 1963.

Poulton, Helen J. *Historian's Handbook: A Descriptive Guide to Reference Works.* Norman, Okla.: University of Oklahoma Press, 1972.

Princeton University Library, Manuscripts Division. *A Descriptive Catalogue of the Papers in the Area of Twentieth Century American Statecraft and Public Policy.* Princeton, N.J.: 1972.

Prucha, Francis P. *A Bibliographical Guide to the History of Indian-White Relations in the United States.* Chicago: University of Chicago Press, 1977.

Rath, Frederick L, Jr., and Merrilyn Rogers O'Connell, editors. *A Bibliography of Historical Organization Practices: Research.* Nashville, Tenn.: American Association for State and Local History, 1984.

Rider, Fremont. *The American Genealogical-Biographical Index to American Genealogical-Biographical and Local History Materials.* Middletown, Conn.: Godfrey Memorial Library, 1952- (116 volumes).

Rothman, David J., and Sheila M., editors. *Sources of the American Social Tradition.* New York: Basic Books, 1975.

Sandeen, Ernest R., and Frederick Hal. *American Religion and Philosophy: A Guide to Information Sources.* Detroit: Gale Research Corp., 1978.

Scammon, Richard M., editor. *America at the Polls: A Handbook of American Presidential Election Statistics, 1920-1964.* Pittsburgh: University of Pittsburgh Press, 1965.

Schapsmeier, Edward L. and Frederick H. *Encyclopedia of American Agricultural History.* Westport, Conn.: Greenwood Press, 1975.

Schlebecker, John T., editor. *Bibliography of Books and Pamphlets on History of Agriculture in the United States, 1607-1967.* Santa Barbara, Calif.: American Bibliographic Center-Clio Press, 1969.

Scott, John Anthony. *Living Documents in American History.* New York: Washington Square Press, 1964-68.

Scotti, Cecelia B., and Fody, Barbara. *Special Libraries Directory of Greater New York, 16th Edition.* New York: Special Libraries Association, 1985.

Selected Readings on Great Issues in American History, 1620-1968. Chicago: Encyclopaedia Britannica Educational Corp, 1969.

Shapiro, Larry. *A Book of Days in American History.* New York: Scribners, 1987.

Shenkman, Richard. *Legends, Lies, and Cherished Myths of American History.* New York: Morrow, 1988.

Shumway, Gary L. *Oral History in the United States: A Directory.* New York: Oral History Association, 1971.

Smith, Betty Pease, editor. *Directory of Historical Agencies in North America, 13th Edition.* Nashville, Tenn.: American Association for State and Local History, 1986.

Smithsonian Institution. *Guide to the Smithsonian Archives.* Washington, D.C.: Smithsonian Institution Press, 1978.

Some Fundamental Documents in the Early History of the United States. New York: J. F. Fleming, 1974.

Special Libraries Association, Geography and Map Division. *Map Collections in the United States and Canada: A Directory.* New York: Special Libraries Association, 1970.

State Historical Society of Wisconsin. Library. *Subject Catalog; of the Library of the State Historical Society of Wisconsin, Madison, Wisc.* Westport, Conn.: Greenwood Pub. Corp., 1971.

Steiner, Dale R. *Historical Journals: A Handbook for Writers and Reviewers.* Santa Barbara, Calif.: American Bibliographic Center-Clio Press, 1981.

Syrett, Harold Coffin. *American Historical Documents.* New York: Barnes & Noble, 1960.

The Almanac of American History. New York: Bramhall House, Distributed by Crown, 1986.

The Book of Great American Documents. Brookeville, Md.: American History Research Associates, 1976.

The Publication of American Historical Manuscripts. Iowa City, Iowa: University of Iowa Libraries; distributed by the University of Iowa Press, 1976.

Thernstrom, Stephan, editor. *Harvard Encyclopedia of American Ethnic Groups.* Cambridge, Mass.: Harvard University Press, 1980.

Thornton, Willis. *Almanac for Americans.* Detroit: Gale Research Co., 1973.

Tingley, Donald Fred. *Social History of the United States.* Detroit: Gale Research Co., 1979.

Wasserman, Paul, and Jean Morgan, editors. *Ethnic Information Sources of the United States: A Guide to Organizations, Agencies, Foundations, Institutions, Media, Commercial and Trade Bodies, Government Programs.* Detroit: Gale Research Co., 1976.

Wiltz, John E. *Books in American History.* Bloomington, Ind.: University Press, 1981.

Wynar, Lubomyr R., and Pat Kleeberger. *Slavic Ethnic Libraries, Museums, and Archives in the United States: A Guide and Directory.* Chicago: Association of College and Research Libraries, 1980.

Photo Credits

page 7: Helen Keller Property Board, Tuscumbia, AL; **page 8:** Tuskegee Institute National Historic Site, Tuskegee Institute, AL; **page 11:** National Park Service; **page 29:** A.K. Smiley Public Library, Redlands, CA; **page 40:** Wrather Port Properties, Ltd., Long Beach, CA; **page 45:** Colorado Ski Museum, Vail, CO; **page 48:** Prorodeo Hall of Champions and Museum of the American Cowboy, Colorado Springs, CO; **page 51:** Bridgeport Public Library Historical Collections, Bridgeport, CT; **page 83:** National Archives; **page 87:** National Archives; **page 117:** Museum of Science & Industry, Chicago, IL; **page 121:** Theatre Historical Society Archives, Chicago, IL; **page 123:** Illinois Historic Preservation Agency's Alfred Mueller Collection, Galena, IL; **page 128:** Indianapolis Motor Speedway, Speedway, IL; **page 134:** Herbert Hoover Presidential Library, West Branch, IA; **page 139:** Emmett Kelly Museum, Sedan, KS; **page 146:** U.S. Army photo courtesy of Patton Museum, Fort Knox, KY; **page 151:** Louisiana State Museum, New Orleans, LA; **page 158:** Allegany Community College Library Appalachian Collection, Cumberland, MD; **page 173:** National Archives; **page 178:** photo by Louie Lamone, courtesy of Norman Rockwell Museum at Stockbridge, MA; **page 198:** Minneapolis Collection at the Minneapolis Public Library, Minneapolis, MN; **page 259:** National Soaring Museum, Elmira, NY; **page 271:** Society of Illustrators Museum of American Illustration, New York, NY; **page 278:** National Women's Hall of Fame, Inc., Seneca Falls, NY; **page 298:** Courtesy Oberlin College Archives, Oberlin, OH; **page 318:** Edgar Allan Poe National Historic Site, Philadelphia, PA; **page 322:** National Park Service; **page 340:** South Dakota Historical Society, State Agricultural Heritage Museum, Brookings, SD; **page 359:** Southwest Film/Video Archives at Southern Methodist University, Dallas, TX; **page 362:** from the Clint Peoples Collection at the Dallas Public Library, Dallas, TX; **page 372:** U.S. Army Signal Corps; **page 389:** Weyerhaeuser Company Archives, Tacoma, WA; **page 405:** Society of Illustrators Museum of American Illustration, New York, NY; **page 413:** Courtesy Gadsden Public Library, Gadsden, AL; **page 425:** National Archives.

Indexes

Organization Index

Courtyard Exhibition Center, Baltimore City Life Museums (MD), 161

Cowboy Artists of America Museum (TX), 351

Cowboy Country Museum (TX), 351

Cowpens National Battlefield (SC), 337

Cragfront Project Summer County (TN), 345

Crane Museum (MA), 171

Cranford Historical Society (NJ), 223

Crawford Historical Society (PA), 316

Crawford W. Long Medical Museum (GA), 99

Criminal Library, Department of Justice (DC), 65

Crosby County Pioneer Memorial Museum (TX), 352

Crouse Library for Publishing Arts, City University of New York (NY), 244

Culbertson Mansion State Historic Site (IN), 125

Cultural Heritage Foundation of Southern California (CA), 24

Culver Pictures Archives (NY), 244

Cumberland County Historical Society, Hamilton County Library Association (PA), 316

Custer Museum (ID), 107

Customs Service Library and Information Center, U.S. Customs Service (DC), 65

Dacotah Prairie Museum (SD), 341

Dade Heritage Trust (FL), 91

Dahlonega Courthouse Gold Museum (GA), 99

Daily Register Library (NJ), 223

Dakota County Historical Society (MN), 195

Dakota Territorial Museum (SD), 341

Dallas County Heritage Society (TX), 352

Dallas Historical Society (TX), 352

Dallas Public Library, Documents Division (TX), 352

Dalton College Library, Documents Department (GA), 99

Dance Collection, New York Public Library Performing Arts Research Center (NY), 244

Dance Theatre of Harlem Library and Archives (NY), 244

Daniel Boone Home (MO), 205

Daniel Boone Homestead (PA), 316

Danville Community College, Documents Division (VA), 371

Danville Museum of Fine Arts and History (VA), 371

Dartmouth College, Special Collections (NH), 219

Daughters of the American Revolution Museum (DC), 65

Daughters of Utah Pioneers (UT), 364

Daughters of Utah Pioneers Relic Hall (ID), 107

Dauphin County Historical Society (PA), 316

Davenport Public Library, Special Collections (IA), 132

David Crockett Cabin (TN), 345

Davis Family Association (MS), 202

Dearborn Historical Museum (MI), 184

Death Valley House, National Park Service (CA), 24

Decatur County Historical Society, Last Indian Raid in Kansas Museum (KS), 138

Decorative and Propoganda Arts, Miami-Dade Community College (FL), 91

Defense Department Still Media Depository (DC), 65

DeKalb Historical Society (GA), 99

Delaware Agricultural Museum (DE), 56

Delaware and Hudson Canal Historical Society Museum (NY), 245

Delaware Bureau of Museums and Historic Sites, Division of History and Cultural Affairs (DE), 56

Delaware Art Museum (DE), 56

Delaware Society for the Preservation of Antiquities (DE), 56

Delaware Technical and Community College Library (DE), 56

Dell Publishing Company Library (NY), 245

Delta Blues Museum, Carnegie Public Library (MS), 202

Democratic National Committee Research/Issues Library (DC), 66

Denison University, Documents Division (OH), 292

Department of Cultural Resources, Division of State Library (NC), 281

Department of Interior Museum, Department of Interior (DC), 66

Department of Justice Main Library (DC), 66

Department of Labor Library (DC), 66

Department of State Diplomatic Reception Rooms (DC), 66

Department of State Library (DC), 66

Department of Transportation Main Library (DC), 66

DePauw University and Indiana United Methodism Archives, Special Collections of DePauw and United Methodist Church (IN), 125

Deschutes County Historical Society (OR), 310

Desert Caballeros Western Museum (AZ), 13

Des Plaines Historical Museum (IL), 111

Detroit Historical Society (MI), 184

Detroit Public Library, Burton Historical Collection (MI), 184

DeWitt Historical Society of Tompkins County (NY), 245

Dickinson College Archives (PA), 316

Dickinson County Historical Museum (KS), 139

Dime Novel Collection, Rare Books and Special Collections Division (DC), 66

Dimock Gallery, George Washington University (DC), 66

Diplomatic Branch, National Archives (DC), 67

Directors Guild of America (CA), 24

Disciples of Christ Historic Society (TN), 345

District of Columbia Housing and Community Development (DC), 67

District of Columbia Preservation League (DC), 67

Lyndon B. Johnson Space Center, History Office Documents Collection (TX), 355

Lyndon Baines Johnson Library and Museum (TX), 355

Lynn Historical Society (MA), 174

Lynn Public Library (MA), 174

Lyon County Historical Society and Museum (KS), 141

Macaulay Museum of Dental History (SC), 337

Machine Readable Branch, National Archives (DC), 76

Madison County Historical Society (IL), 116

Madison County Historical Society (NY), 254

Madison Heights Public Library, Document Department (MI), 189

Madison Township Historical Society, Thomas Warne Historical Museum and Library (NJ), 225

Maier Museum of Art, Randolph-Macon Woman's College (VA), 376

Maine Historical Society (ME), 155

Maine Law and Legislative Reference Library (ME), 155

Maine Maritime Museum (ME), 155

Maine State Archives (ME), 155

Maine State Library (ME), 156

Maine State Museum (ME), 156

Makoti Threshers Museum (ND), 288

Malki Museum (CA), 30

Malong College, Document Department (OH), 295

Mamie Doud Eisenhower Birthplace (IA), 135

Manassas City Museum (VA), 376

Manassas National Battlefield Park (VA), 376

Manatee County Public Library, Eaton Room (FL), 95

Manchester Historic Association (NH), 219

Manhattan College Cardinal Hayes Library (NY), 255

Manship House (MS), 203

Marathon County Public Library (WI), 393

Marblehead Historical Scoeity (MA), 174

March Field Museum (CA), 30

Margart Herrick Library and Film Archive, Academy of Motion Picture Arts and Sciences (CA), 31

Marine Corps Education Center, Documents Division (VA), 376

Marine Corps Film Depository (VA), 376

Marine Corps Historical Center and Museum, Marine Corps Headquarters (DC), 77

Marine Historical Society of Detroit (MI), 189

Mariners' Museum (VA), 376

Marin Museum of the American Indian (CA), 31

Marion Public Library (OH), 295

Mariposa Museum and History Center (CA), 31

Mark Twain Birthplace State Historic Site (MO), 208

Mark Twain Home Board (MO), 208

Mark Twain Memorial (CT), 53

Marquette County Historical Society (MI), 189

Marriott Library, University of Utah (UT), 364

Marshall Gold Discovery State Historic Park (CA), 31

Marshall Military History Collection, University of Texas at El Paso (TX), 355

Martha Canfield Library, Russell Vermontiana Collection (VT), 366

Martin Luther King Center for Nonviolent Social Change, Library and Archives (GA), 102

Martin P. Catherwood Library, Cornell University School of Industrial and Labor Relations (NY), 255

Martin Van Buren National Historic Site (NY), 255

Mary Baker Eddy Museum, Longyear Historical Society (MA), 174

Mary Ball Washington Museum and Library (VA), 376

Maryland Historical Society (MD), 164

Maryland Historical Trust (MD), 164

Maryland State Archives, Hall of Records (MD), 164

Maryland State Law Library (MD), 164

Mary Pickford Collection, Motion Picture, Broadcasting, and Recorded Sound Division (DC), 77

Mary Weir Public Library (WV), 391

Mashpee Wampanoag Indian Tribal Council (MA), 174

Mason County Historical Society (MI), 189

Masonic Grand Lodge Library and Museum of Texas (TX), 355

Masonic Library and Museum (NY), 255

Massachusetts Archaeological Society, Robbins Museum of Archaeology (MA), 174

Massachusetts Historical Commission (MA), 175

Massachusetts Historical Society (MA), 175

Massachusetts Institute of Technology, Special Collections (MA), 175

Massachusetts Society of Mayflower Descendents (MA), 175

Massachusetts State Archives (MA), 175

Massillon Museum (OH), 295

Maumee Valley Historical Society (OH), 295

Max Factor Museum (CA), 31

Maxwell Museum Photo Archive (NM), 232

Mayflower Society Museum (MA), 175

McAllister House Museum (CO), 47

McGeorge School of Law Library, University of the Pacific (CA), 31

McGuffey Reader Collection, Rare Books and Special Collections Division (DC), 77

McKinley Museum of History, Science, and Industry (OH), 296

McKissick Museum (SC), 337

McLean County Historical Society (IL), 116

Meadow Farm Museum (VA), 377

Medical College of Georgia Library (GA), 102

Medical College of Pennsylvania, Florence Moore Library of Medicine (PA), 324

Medical History Society of New Jersey (NJ), 225

Subject Index